FINANCIAL AND ECONOMIC SYSTEMS

Transformations and New Challenges

FINANCIAL AND ECONOMIC SYSTEMS

Transformations and New Challenges

Edited by

Zied Ftiti
EDC Paris Business School, France

Hachmi Ben Ameur
INSEEC School of Business and Economics, France

Waël Louhichi
ESSCA School of Management, France

World Scientific

NEW JERSEY • LONDON • SINGAPORE • BEIJING • SHANGHAI • HONG KONG • TAIPEI • CHENNAI • TOKYO

Published by

World Scientific Publishing Europe Ltd.
57 Shelton Street, Covent Garden, London WC2H 9HE
Head office: 5 Toh Tuck Link, Singapore 596224
USA office: 27 Warren Street, Suite 401-402, Hackensack, NJ 07601

Library of Congress Cataloging-in-Publication Data
Names: Ftiti, Zied, editor. | Ameur, Hachmi Ben, editor. | Louhichi, Waël, editor.
Title: Financial and economic systems : transformations and new challenges / edited by
Zied Ftiti, EDC Paris Business School, France, Hachmi Ben Ameur, INSEEC School of Business and Economics, France, Waël Louhichi, ESSCA School of Management, France.
Description: New Jersey : World Scientific, [2021] | Includes bibliographical references and index.
Identifiers: LCCN 2020038661 (print) | LCCN 2020038662 (ebook) |
ISBN 9781786349491 (hardcover) | ISBN 9781786349507 (ebook) |
ISBN 9781786349514 (ebook other)
Subjects: LCSH: Finance. | Financial institutions.
Classification: LCC HG173 .F4888 2021 (print) | LCC HG173 (ebook) | DDC 332--dc23
LC record available at https://lccn.loc.gov/2020038661
LC ebook record available at https://lccn.loc.gov/2020038662

British Library Cataloguing-in-Publication Data
A catalogue record for this book is available from the British Library.

For any available supplementary material, please visit
https://www.worldscientific.com/worldscibooks/10.1142/Q0279#t=suppl

Desk Editors: Balamurugan Rajendran/Michael Beale/Shi Ying Koe

Typeset by Stallion Press
Email: enquiries@stallionpress.com

https://doi.org/10.1142/9781786349507_fmatter

Preface

Part I: The Changes in the Real Sphere

Chapter 1 (Elias Bengtsson)

Macroprudential policy has, since the global financial crisis, become a firmly established policy area to prevent excessive risk taking in the financial sector and mitigate its effects on the real economy. However, for macroprudential policy to fulfil its role in curbing systemic risk, it needs to manage several challenges relating to its political sensitivity and institutional context. This chapter discusses these challenges and maps the current policy debate on the most appropriate governance arrangements to manage them. Thereafter, it provides an overview of macroprudential policy in the EU, both in terms of EU-wide regulation, and at the national level. The chapter continues by discussing how institutional contexts and governance arrangements appear to have influenced the exertion of macroprudential policy across EU countries in the post crisis period. The chapter ends with a presentation of a number of policy conclusions and contrast them with the current international policy debate on macroprudential policy.

Chapter 2 (Xiaofei Ma)

We develop a two-country model with an explicitly microfounded interbank market and sovereign default risk. Calibrated to the Euro Area, we use the model to qualify the potential effects of alternative austerity measures and fiscal policies on the dynamics of GDP, sovereign default risk, and public indebtedness, in short run and in long run. Our simulation shows that the effects of alternative austerity measures in the Periphery Country can be transmitted to the

Core Country through the interbank market. While the rise in consumption tax and in pay-roll tax are beneficial for both country's long-run growth, the rise in capital-income tax cannot cope with the government's indebtedness and tends to suppress economic growth in the long run.

Chapter 3 (Abir Abid)
This chapter aims at providing a brief insight on how and to what extent the financial markets can be responsive to the Economic Policy Uncertainty (EPU). After briefly discussing how such an observable phenomenon can be measured, we study how the stock markets behave in economic environment less predictable. Furthermore, apart from its domestic impacts, we analyze the extent to which the EPU in a given country might spill to foreign financial markets. In addition, our analysis is extended to study how the EPU can be a driving force of the equity premium movements. Finally, we examine its potential role as a determinant of the interconnections of the international equity system. The idea is to explore the ways in which the EPU can affect the correlation between financial markets.

Chapter 4 (Zaineb Hlioui *et al.*)
The last global crisis provided evidence that corporate unethical behaviors are the main cause of eroding trust and triggering crises. In our chapter, we define ethical business conduct, its main drivers, and its influence on economic stability. Moreover, based on the institutional and legitimacy theories, we investigate the mediating effect of corporate corrupt behaviors on the regulatory characteristics and macroeconomic stability link in the Eastern European Countries. Using the fifth wave of the BEEPs data, we select 6140 companies over 24 countries and confirm the partial mediation association. Furthermore, we prove that ethical behaviors are influenced by the corporate framework and regulatory environment rather than the corporate specificities. Thus, improving regulation is not an option. Nevertheless, in corrupt contexts, unethical practices are common. Therefore, ensuring higher financial returns is more important than having a corporate sound depiction, which leads to law violations and challenges regulatory compliance.

Part II: Financial Markets: Post-crisis Challenges

Chapter 5 (Jean-François Boulier)

Finance theory has helped the fast development of markets and economies around the world. Despite this success, some of the underlying assumptions of the main theories remain questionable. Empirical studies have often contradicted these assumptions and a number of them rely more on credence than facts. This article reviews eight main assumptions and tries to offer some alternatives to them. More realistic hypothesis would bring finance closer to other fields of knowledge and support a more inclusive finance for practitioners.

Chapter 6 (Eric Le Fur)

In this chapter, we present a review of the literature on the relationship between financial markets and collectibles. Just under a hundred articles are analyzed. Most of the academic literature focuses on the returns of investments in collectibles and then on the contagion that may exist with financial markets. Art, wine, and stamps are the most studied collectibles. Many other collectibles are considered as possible investment opportunities such as furniture, cars, diamonds, Lego, books, coins, violins, and whisky.

Chapter 7 (Mazin A. M. Al Janabi)

This chapter examines robust modeling techniques and algorithms for the computation and reporting of market and liquidity risk exposures for multiple-assets portfolios. The computational methods are based on the notion of Liquidity-Adjusted Value at Risk (LVaR) along with the application of robust optimization risk algorithms. Practical optimization case studies are performed with the objective of simulating a practical framework of liquidity trading risk measurement, in addition, to the application of a robust risk optimization process for the computation of maximum permitted LVaR boundary limits. The applied novel methodology and risk assessment algorithms can aid in advancing risk management practices in emerging markets, particularly in the wake of the 2007–2009 global financial crisis. In addition, the proposed computational techniques and risk reporting process can have key uses and applications in machine learning & artificial intelligence, expert systems, smart financial functions, regulatory technology (RegTech), and financial technology (FinTech) in big data environments.

Chapter 8 (Saker Sabkha)

The study of an efficient financial assets' modeling method is still an open hot issue, especially during the recent crises. The aim of this chapter is to assess the predictability performance of multivariate GARCH models with an application to the sovereign CDS markets and the underlying bond markets over a period running from January 2006 to April 2014. Using credit risk data from 33 worldwide countries, this chapter investigates the performance of 9 Dynamic Conditional Correlation models taking into account different properties of financial markets (long memory behavior, asymmetry and/or leverage effects...). This comparative study is based on the results of several multivariate diagnostic tests. Findings show that no model outperforms the others in all situations, though, the straightforward DCCGARCH model seems to provide the most relevant estimator parameters.

Also, the innovations' distribution assumption significantly impacts the statistical fit of the model. Our work is useful for financial markets' participants so as to making decision in terms of arbitrage, hedging, or speculation.

Chapter 9 (Warwick Anderson *et al.*)

This chapter provides an overview of the growth of socially responsible investment (SRI) mutual fund industry over the past thirty years and summarizes the quite extensive research record explaining its characteristics. First we examine the substantial growth of SRI market share relative to that of conventional funds. This growth is predominantly concentrated in developed countries and our findings suggest that capital market and economic development are important factors for the adoption of responsible investing. The second section explores differences in financial performance between SRI and conventional funds. It also addresses the question as to what actually constitutes SRI and how the behaviour of SRI investors differ from investors in conventional mutual funds. Third, we discuss the appearance, over time, of a number of record-keeping bodies that define and track SRI in the US and more widely. Finally, we offer thoughts on factors that might help SRI growth in the future.

Part III: CSR, Sustainability, and Ethical Finance: New Trends

Chapter 10 (Lan-Phuong Nguyen *et al.*)

This study investigates the relationship between corporate social responsibility disclosure and corporate social responsibility performance. The fixed effect models incorporated with the Granger causality approach was applied to examine the nature of the association between CSR disclosure (hereafter, CSRD) and CSR performance (hereafter, CSP), and further whether there is a "virtuous circle" in this link. Our results support the positive association between CSRD and CSP as predictions of economic-based voluntary disclosure theory. Moreover, this relation runs from both sides: CSP $\rightarrow$ CSRD and CSRD $\rightarrow$ CSP; and the CSP $\rightarrow$ CSRD has stronger power than the inverse side. However, this is not a lead-lag relationship, and there is no evidence for the causality relationship between CSRD and CSP.

Chapter 11 (Rania Béji *et al.*)

This chapter aims to critically review the existing literature on the relationship between corporate social responsibility (CSR) and corporate governance features. Drawn on management and corporate governance theories, we develop a theoretical model that makes explicit the links between board diversity, CSR committees' attributes, CSR and financial performance. Particularly, we show that focusing on the cognitive and demographic characteristics of board members could provide more insights on the link between corporate governance and CSR. We also highlight how the functioning and the composition of CSR committees could be valuable to better understand the relationship between corporate governance and CSR.

Chapter 12 (Anissa Naouar)

The study examines the Environmental, Social and Governance (ESG) dimensions of the performance and the evolution of the concept worldwide. It also offers a critical review of the screening methodologies adopted by the main rating agencies to evaluate the ESG performance of financial and non-financials firms. The analysis provides evidence that individual ESG ratings' methodologies have significant shortcomings and disparities and that ESG rating providers would need a common core benchmark reporting that would serve as the basement of a standardized ESG framework.

Chapter 13 (Zyed Achour *et al.*)

This chapter aims to analyze the role played by Corporate Social Responsibility (CSR) in reducing firm risk. We investigate the relationship between Corporate Social Responsibility and global risk using panel data of listed French companies (SBF120) over the period 2008–2017. We applied a fixed effect estimation that allows us to consider the time and firm unobserved heterogeneity using the aggregate environmental, social and governance (ESG) scores as a CSR proxy. Our findings are in line with the signalling theory, stakeholder theory and legitimacy theory suggesting that CSR initiatives would be a mechanism for enhancing corporate reputation and sound depiction, which affects in return firm's global risk.

Chapter 14 (Meriam Attia *et al.*)

This chapter shows how boards' characteristics could influence two aspects of innovation: (1) innovation effort (such as R&D expenditures and R&D team composition) and (2) innovation performance, specifically product, process, organizational, and marketing innovation. First, we focus on individual characteristics of board members and their influence on innovation effort, and performance. Then, we examine how the internal organization of boards, specifically the committees' roles and their composition, to address to what extent they could be meaningful to innovation processes. Specially, we discuss the influence of the committee size, the frequency of meetings, and the presence of independent and female members. Finally, the chapter sheds light on the effectiveness of initiatives and programs introduced to increase diversity such as gender quota laws, and the presence of minorities in top management positions.

Part IV: Transformations, Digitalization, Blockchain, FinTech

Chapter 15 (Assen Slim *et al.*)

New Blockchain-based applications provide an alternative technological tool to ensure the integrity, the traceability, the anti-tampering, and the reduction of costs of digital transactions. The infrastructure and nature of Blockchain makes it a revolutionary solution to reconfigure many industries and to modify the way in which they produce value. In this chapter, we review non-cryptocurrencies applications of Blockchain and we discuss how alternative applications are used in other previously unexplored industries. Our study proposes a typology of business applications based on Blockchain.

Chapter 16 (Teresa Schützeichel)
Technology adoption in Africa is mainly determined by its ability to solve problems. The Kenyan mobile money platform M-PESA has rapidly evolved to allow customers to make payments, save money, get loans and even overdrafts. This chapter analyses M-PESA's disruption of the financial industry in Kenya, portraying its success in raising households' social and economic well-being. However, with increasing technology use arises the question of consumer protection. The information asymmetry that exists between user and service provider has highlighted a gap for regulatory technology (RegTech) to fill. In this regard, this chapter explores the Sandbox concept for FinTech firms, which allows them to market test their products in a controlled environment whilst giving regulators a chance to figure out the necessary regulations. Its success or failure in Kenya is an open question, and this chapter aims to open-up the forum for discussion.

Chapter 17 (Youssra Ben Romdhane Loukil *et al.*)
In recent years, the development of Fintech marked financial transactions. Several studies have focused on the effects of Fintech on economic performance through financial inclusion and crowd funding. But few studies aimed to understand the development factors of such *a driver of* economic growth. To address this literature gap, our empirical research is designed to study such phenomena in ten MENA countries during 2011–2017. We find that digital platform and government effectiveness are supportive environment for the development of Fintech. Also, we interestingly find that social movements accompanied with a great *breakthrough* in the field of *freedom* of opinion and expression do significantly slow down the development of Fintech. In addition, we find empirical support for the reducing effect of corruption. In terms of practical implications, decisions-makers are asked to formulate and implement sound policies and regulations to promote the positive role of Fintech in terms of economic performance.

Chapter 18 (Firas Batnini and Florian Bercaut)
This article underscores the evolution that Fintechs have undergone and the contribution of new technologies, notably Artificial

Intelligence, Machine Learning, and Cloud Technology, to their success. The entire sector has been undergoing profound changes since the 2008 recession and, though banks have fared well, Fintechs are nonetheless growing into their role as important financial players.

There has been much talk about "disruptive innovation" and the challenge to banks that have lagged behind in innovation. Through an analysis of European markets, mainly the French market, we present a much different picture of Fintechs, where development remains highly dependent on assistance from banks, either directly, through partnerships, or indirectly, the latter performing an advisory role.

Chapter 19 (Małgorzata Pawłowska and Aleksandra Staniszewska)

The IT revolution brought new factors that influenced the traditional banking market. Banks were forced to compete not only with other players from the banking sector but also with unregulated Fintech companies. A lack of regulation gave a competitive edge to providers of Fintech services over the banking sector. This paper aimed to investigate the impact of innovative financial technology (Fintech) on the level of competition in the EU banking sector. We attempted to isolate the channels of the impact of new Fintech technologies on the level of competition in the financial market. Our investigation is mainly based on panel analysis for data obtained from payments statistics from the European Central Bank (ECB), Eurostat and the KFTX index. Our results confirmed our hypothesis that despite growing concentration within the European banking market, Fintech factors stimulate the level of competition in the EU banking sector.

https://doi.org/10.1142/9781786349507_fmatter

Author the Editors

Hachmi Ben Ameur is an Associate Professor of Finance and Associate Dean for Research at INSEEC School of Business and Economics. He received his PhD in Management from Cergy-Pontoise University where he worked as Assistant Professor. In 2020, he obtained Habilitation for Supervising Doctoral Research in Finance, from the University of Cergy-Pontoise. His main research areas are operations research, financial markets, portfolio management, structured products, portfolio insurance, behavioral finance, wine and financial econometrics. His research works are published in well-ranked journals: *European Journal of Operational Research*, *The Energy Journal*, *Annals of Operations Research*, *Economic Modelling*, *Macroeconomic Dynamics* and *Applied Economics.* Hachmi Ben Ameur is the co-organizer of the International Symposium of Computational Economics and Finance.

Zied Ftiti is Full Professor of Financial Econometrics and Head of the Research Center (OCRE) and Associate Dean of Research at EDC Paris Business School. After completing his Master's degree in Money, Finance and International Economics (Option of Applied Macroeconomics) at University of Lyon 2, he has obtained his PhD in Economics from the University of Lyon (GATE Laboratory, CNRS-UMR 5824) and a PhD in Business from the University of Tunis, High Institute of Management. In 2013, he obtained Habilitation for Supervising Doctoral Research in Management Sciences, from University of Tunis, and in 2019 he obtained Habilitation for Supervising Doctoral Research in Economics, from University of Cergy-Pontoise. His research area includes Financial Econometrics, Econometrics, Financial Markets, Monetary Economics, and Macroeconomics. Prof. Zied Ftiti has published books and many papers in top-tier journals such as *Journal of Economic Dynamics and Control*, *Econometric Reviews*, *Annals of Operations Research*, *Applied Economics*, *Journal of International Monetary and Finance*, *The Energy Journal*, *Energy Policy*, *Energy Economics*, *Quarterly Review of Economics & Finance*, *Economic Modelling*, *Economic Systems*, *Journal of Economic Integration*, *European Journal of Comparative Economics*, *Emerging Market Review*, *Open Economic Review*, *Applied Economics Letters*, *Finance Research Letters*, *International Review of Financial Analysis*, *Pacific-Basin Finance Journal*, *Bankers, Markets & Investors*, *Energy Studies Review*, etc. Prof. Zied Ftiti is organizer of the Financial Economic Meeting conference.

Waël Louhichi is currently Full Professor and Head of the Finance Research Group at ESSCA School of Management. He obtained a PhD from both Perpignan University (France) and Louvain School of Management (Belgium). He has published several articles in international journals such as *Journal of Financial Markets*, *Economic Modelling*, *Applied Economics*, *Review of Quantitative Finance and Accounting*, *International Review of Financial Analysis*, *Review of Accounting and Finance*, *Management Decision*, *Journal of Applied Accounting Research*, *Macroeconomic Dynamics*, *Econometric Reviews*, among others. He was the invited chairman for the Global Finance Conference (GFC, Paris 2018).

https://doi.org/10.1142/9781786349507_fmatter

About the Contributors

Abir Abid is a final-year PhD candidate in Economics at the University of Orléans (LEO), France, and the Higher Institute of Management of Tunis (MacMA), Tunisia. Her main research interest centers on how financial markets react to domestic and foreign macroeconomic shocks. She takes a multidisciplinary approach that encompasses the fields of finance, macroeconomics, international economics, and econometrics. Her doctoral project particularly investigates the economic policy uncertainty shock transmission to financial markets (stock and foreign exchange markets). Her thesis research resulted in a published paper, working papers, and international conferences presentations. Since 2018, she teaches macroeconomics, financial analysis, accounting and management accounting at ESSCA Business School (Angers, France).

Zyed Achour has a PhD in Management Science and is an Assistant Professor at the National Institute of Labour and Social Studies, University of Carthage. He is member in the Gouvernance d'Entreprise Finance Appliquée et Audit (GEF2A) Laboratory. Among his research interests are social dimensions of strategic management, firm performance, sustainability, and corporate social responsibility.

Mazin A. M. Al Janabi is a Full Research-Professor of Finance and Banking and Financial Engineering at EGADE Business School, Tecnologico de Monterrey, Santa Fe Campus, Mexico City, Mexico. He holds a PhD degree (1991) from the University of London, UK, and has more than 30 years of real-world experience in science and technology think tanks, engineering enterprises, financial markets, and academic institutions, and in many different roles. He has worked for top international financial groups (e.g. ING-Barings and BBVA) where he held several senior management positions, such as Director of Global Market Risk Management, Head of Trading Risk Management, and Head of Derivative Products. Prof. Al Janabi has strong interest in research and development within emerging economies and has several publications in international refereed journals, books, and chapters in books. Furthermore, his research and developments in quantitative finance have been formally classified in the academic literatures as "Al Janabi Model" for Liquidity Risk Management (Liquidity Adjusted Value–at-Risk, LVaR Model). Prof. Al Janabi has published in top-tiered journals such as: *European Journal of Operational Research*, *Journal of Forecasting*, *International Review of Financial Analysis*, *Physica A: Statistical Mechanics and its Applications*, *European Actuarial Journal*, *Annals of Operations Research*, *Applied Economics*, *Economic Modelling*, *Review of Financial Economics*, *Journal of Asset Management*, *Service Industries Journal*, *Studies in Economics and Finance*, *Emerging Markets Finance and Trade*, *Journal of Risk Finance*, *Journal of Banking Regulation*, *Annals of Nuclear Energy*, among others. He received several awards for excellence in teaching and research, and his biography is featured in *Who's Who in the World* (2013–present) and in *Who's Who in Science and Engineering* (2016–present).

Warwick Anderson is a Lecturer in Finance at the University of Canterbury, New Zealand. His research interests are in the area of dividend policy, event study analysis, corporate governance, and now socially responsible investments. In 2009 he won the Peter Brownell Manuscript Award for best paper published that year in the journal, *Accounting and Finance*, awarded by the Accounting and Finance Association of Australia and New Zealand (AFAANZ).

Fernanda Arreola is Associate Dean of Faculty and Research and Professor of Strategy and Entrepreneurship at ISC in Paris. Her research focuses on innovation and entrepreneurship with a specific interest on the governance practices relative to innovation, technology, and entrepreneurial achievement.

Meriam Attia is a PhD student in Finance. She is affiliated to the research unity Montpellier Research in Management (MRM), University of Montpellier (France), and to Gouvernance d'Entreprise,

Finance Appliquée et Audit (GEF2A) Laboratory, High Institute of Management, University of Tunis, (Tunisia). Her research interests include corporate governance, innovation and corporate finance.

Firas Batnini is a Professor of Finance in ESSCA School of Management, graduated from Sorbonne. He is the Head of the Master's Degree in Banking and Financial Engineering, he regularly publishes research papers and books. His work focuses on venture capital and start-up financing.

Rania Béji is a third year PhD student in Finance at University of Montpellier and Institut Supérieur de Gestion de Tunis. She is a member of Montpellier Research in Management Laboratory and GEF2A Laboratory. She is also a research assistant at Montpellier Business School.

Her research aims to examine the relationship between corporate social responsibility (CSR) and corporate governance features. More specifically, she examines how the board's characteristics could be associated with globally corporate social responsibility and specific areas of CSR.

Her current projects include research on CSR strategies and how corporate social responsibility committees could affect the involvement of companies in strategic CSR and the adoption of voluntarily strategies that go beyond regulatory requirements.

Elias Bengtsson has held various positions in financial services including Principal Economist at the European Central Bank, Advisor at the central bank of Sweden, and Senior Economist at the European Fund and Asset Management Association. In these roles, he has been involved in a variety of tasks relating to financial regulation, including the development of Basel III and the European framework for macroprudential policy. Dr Bengtsson received his PhD from Stockholm University and has held visiting positions at Stanford University, London School of Economics, and Banco de España.

Dr Bengtsson's research examines how and why the financial systems differ over time and spatial dimensions. His research aims to link disparate fields of scholarship, including financial economics, institutional theory, and comparative political economy. A key empirical focus is how differences across financial systems are influenced by regulation and innovation. His current projects include research on cryptocurrencies and how policy responses to the great recession have influenced national financial systems across Europe.

Dr Bengtsson's publication record includes a large number of articles in a variety of leading international academic journals. His research is widely cited in policy papers by a variety of public and private bodies, including the Bank for International Settlement, Financial Stability Board, Deutsche Bundesbank, National Bank of Belgium, Banque Central de Luxembourg, and International Organization of Securities Commissions (IOSCO).

Florian Bercaut is co-founder and President of Estimeo, a rating and valuing platform dedicated to startups. Graduated from Sciences Po and HEC Paris, Florian began his career in a green equity crowdfunding platform incubated by ENGIE. This shift to digital and inclusive finance led him to co-develop new methods of company valuation for investors. At the same time, Florian teaches a module on economics and risk management at CY Tech and entrepreneurial finance at ESSCA. Florian is also a member of the Advisory Board of Orange Business Services, Vice-President of the Evaluation Commission of the Société Française des Analystes Financiers (SFAF), member of the European Financial Reporting Advisory Group's (EFRAG) Advisory Committee on Intangibles. He regularly publishes in national and specialized media, notably as a Forbes contributor where he writes a bimonthly column on startups.

Jędrzej Białkowski (FRM, PRM) is Professor of Finance at the University of Canterbury, New Zealand. His international cooperation has resulted in nearly 30 publications in peer-reviewed journals. He has published in top ranked journals such as *Journal of Banking and Finance, Journal of Derivatives, The Journal of Futures Markets* and *Quantitative Finance.* Jędrzej has also had his work accepted by the top finance conferences: American Finance Association (AFA) and European Finance Association (EFA). Jędrzej's research focuses on the derivatives products, financial risk management, algorithm trading, and socially responsible investing. Two of his papers in the area of investments were awarded with Best Paper Award in Investments Category by Institute of Finance Professionals New Zealand (INFINZ). In 2019, he won the prestigious award BLR cup for Best

Overall Paper at the 2019 New Zealand Finance Colloquium. He serves as associate editor of the *Bulletin of Economic Research.*

Sonia Boukattaya obtained her PhD in Finance at Institut Supérieur de Gestion de Tunis, Université de Tunis. She is member of Gouvernance d'Entreprise Finance Appliquée et Audit (GEF2A) Laboratory. Her research interests include corporate governance, corporate social responsibility, sustainability, corporate finance and accounting.

Jean-François Boulier is Chairman of Af2i, the French association representing institutional investors. Prior to that, he was CEO of Aviva Investors France for 10 years. He joined Aviva Investors in 2008 and had several positions: CIO in Paris, then CEO in Europe, and Global CIO for Fixed Income. Between 2002 and 2008 he was Euro FI at Credit Agricole Asset Management. He started his career in finance in 2007 with Credit Commercial de France where he headed the Research and Innovation Department, then the Market Risk Department, and then became CIO of Sinopia asset management and deputy CEO. A polytechnician and holding a doctorate in Fluid Mechanics, he was a Researcher at CNRS in Grenoble. He is Honorary Chairman of AFFI as well of AFGAP. He is the founding and current Editor of *Bankers, Markets and Investors.* He is (co)author of three books.

Zaineb Hlioui is PhD student in financial researches in the Institut Supérieur de Gestion de Tunis (ISG) and member in the Gouvernance d'Entreprise Finance Appliquée et Audit (GEF2A) Laboratory. Her research interests focus on ethical finance and corporate governance.

Souhaila Kammoun holds a PhD in Economics from the University of Social Sciences of Toulouse 1, France. She has taught Economics at the University of Social Sciences of Toulouse and in several university institutions in Tunisia. Her research interests focus on Innovation, Corporate Social Responsibility, and Fintechs. She has published a number of research articles in international journals and collective books. She is currently an active member of the Executive Board of the Association Université Environnement, at the University of Sfax. She was Director of the Master's Degree in Entrepreneurship and International Development (Tempus Project funded by the European Union) and member of the scientific council at IHEC of Sfax. She has held the positions of Head of the Department of Economics, Director of Studies, and Vice-Director. She was also Director of IHEC of Sfax, Tunisia.

Eric Le Fur is Associate Professor at INSEEC Grande Ecole Bordeaux. He holds a PhD in Economics from the University of Bordeaux. His research focuses on the determinants of the prices of real alternative assets (art, classic cars, real estate, wine) as well as on the relationships of these assets with financial markets (cointegration, contagion, transmission of volatility). Eric Le Fur is also Director of the "market trends" division of the INSEEC Wine and Spirits Chair.

Sahar Loukil is a Doctor in Finance from Faculty of Economics and Management of Sfax (Tunisia). She is currently Contract Assistant in the University of Gabes, Tunisia, Department of Accounting and Finance. Her research interests focus on corporate governance, Fintechs, CSR, research and development, and pollution exposure.

Xiaofei Ma is an Assistant Professor at ESSCA School of Managment, France. She obtained her PhD degree in 2017 from Université Lumière Lyon 2 and CREST (Center for Research in Economics and Statistics) in France. Her PhD supervisors are Prof. Stéphane Auray from CREST-Ensai and Prof. Aurélien Eyquem from Université Lumière Lyon 2. Xiaofei held a post-doctoral position at Université d'Evry-Val-d'Essonne. Her post-doc supervisor is Prof. Eleni Iliopulos. Her research interests include macroeconomics, monetary policies, currency union, and structural change.

Éric Magnin is a Professor-Researcher at the University of Paris and a member of the Ladyss laboratory (CNRS), where he is in charge of a research program on transitions. His work focuses on the diversity and transformations of capitalism.

Anissa Naouar is an Assistant Professor and Researcher in Economics at HEC Sfax, Tunisia and also a Faculty Member at Paris-Sorbonne Abu-Dhabi. Previously, she worked as Research Assistant for the Center of European Policy Studies in Brussels and as Project Manager for the French Prudential Supervision and Resolution Authority within the French Central Bank (Banque de France). Dr Anissa Naouar holds a PhD in Economics from the University of Paris X, Nanterre. She is currently working on a number of projects in the Middle East and North African countries. She remains actively engaged in research and has published a wide variety of academic papers and conference proceedings, and has presented topic related to sustainability and economic growth, financial development, risk and governance.

Lan-Phuong Nguyen is a Lecturer of Accounting at Danang University of Economics. Her research topics primarily focus on corporate governance and corporate disclosure (i.e. CSR disclosure, financial reporting) and then on accounting in public sector. She acquired her PhD at IGR-IAE, University of Rennes 1 with three studies on CSR disclosure, the quality of corporate governance and financial reporting, and firm performance.

Abdelwahed Omri is a Full Professor in Financial and Accounting Methods at Institut Supérieur de Gestion de Tunis. He is the Director of GEF2A Laboratory.

Dr Omri has held various positions. He served as Director of the Doctoral School at Institut Supérieur de Gestion de Tunis. He was served for various time as the President of National Committee of Recruitment of Assistant, Associate and Full Professors. He also served as a member of the Technical Evaluation Panel for projects to improve the quality of teaching (World Bank funded project).

Dr Omri's publication record includes a large number of articles in various leading international academic journals. His research field includes the choice of accounting methods and manipulation of financial information, corporate governance, information asymmetry and banking risk, risk analysis, business combinations, mergers and acquisitions, and empirical research on financial information and financial forecasts.

His areas of research are corporate governance, risk and organizational effectiveness. His research has been published in several journals including *Applied Economics*, *Corporate Governance: The International Journal of Business in Society*, *The Australian Economic Review*.

Małgorzata Pawłowska graduated from the University of Warsaw and earned the title MSc in Mathematics. In 2003, she completed her PhD thesis in Economics titled: "Analysis of the technical efficiency, scale efficiency and the productivity change in the Polish banking sector in years 1997–2001 based on the non-parametric approach DEA" at the Warsaw School of Economics. In 2014, she completed habilitation in Finance.

Since 2015, Małgorzata is Associated Professor at the Warsaw School of Economics. Her scientific research deals with issues related to the banking sector and the credit market as well as quantitative methods in finance. She is the author and co-author of scientific papers in the field of economics and banking and finance regarding efficiency and competition of the banking sector. She has presented the results of her research at many foreign conferences. Her current position at Warsaw School of Economics is Head of Traditional Banking Unit, Institute of Risk and Financial Markets in Collegium of Management and Finance. Małgorzata is also employed as an Advisor of the National Bank in Poland.

Youssra Ben Romdhane Loukil is a Doctor on Economic Sciences from Faculty of Economics and Management of Sfax (Tunisia). She is a Researcher at LED Unit Research. She is currently a Contract Teacher at IHEC Sfax. She has taught macroeconomics I and II and microeconomics I. Her research interests focus on the following themes: macroeconomic aggregates, policy uncertainty, and technology. She has published a number of research articles in international journals and collective books.

Saker Sabkha obtained a PhD in Finance from the Institute of Financial and Insurance Sciences (ISFA) of University Lyon 1 in 2018. His research works enabled him to obtain the thesis prize in the annual competition of the National Association of PhDs in Economics and Management (ANDESE). This author has received several other awards and distinctions including the EIFFEL prize for excellence and the IDEXLYON prize. After a postdoctoral position at the University Paris Nanterre, Saker Sabkha joined the South Brittany University in September 2019 as a Lecturer in Market Finance and Head of the Master Program in Banking and Finance. His major works include: *Review of Quantitative Finance and Accounting*, 2018; *Research in International Business and Finance*, 2019; *Managerial Finance*, 2019.

Teresa Schützeichel is a Postdoctoral Researcher in the School of the Economics and Business Sciences at the University of the Witwatersrand (Wits) in Johannesburg, South Africa. She joined the School in May 2020. Teresa completed her PhD at the Technical University of Munich (TU München) in Munich, Germany, in

2019. Prior to that she had completed her undergraduate and masters studies at Strathmore University in Nairobi, Kenya, where she also worked as a Research and Teaching Assistant (2009–2012) and served as the first Faculty Manager of the Strathmore Law School from 2012–2014.

Her research interests are in household finance, focusing on digital finance for financial inclusion, financial literacy, and digital financial technology for financial markets access in Africa. She has recently started research work on inclusive value chains. Teresa lives in Johannesburg, South Africa, with her husband and three children.

Assen Slim is Professor of International Economics and International Trade at the ESSCA School of Management, Paris, France, and at INALCO, Paris, France. He is a Research Staff Member at the CREE (Paris) Laboratory and associate member at the CESSMA (Paris) Laboratory. His research includes using blockchain technology to build and secure noncryptocurrency systems and helps standardize them.

Aleksandra Staniszewska graduated from the Banking Department, Warsaw School of Economics in 2003. In 2008, she defended her PhD thesis on housing finance, in particular refinancing methods of mortgage portfolios. The research for the thesis was conducted during her Fulbright Scholarship at Columbia Business School, NY, in 2007. Since 2004, Aleksandra is employed in Warsaw School of Economics as an Academic Teacher and Researcher. Her range of interest vary from gift and experimental economy to the impact of Fintech solutions on the finance market. She is the co-author of an academic handbook on management of credit portfolio and several scientific papers on altruism and dictator game. She is also managing her own start-up concept in the MedTech area, with a pending patent.

Lionel Touchais is Professor of Accountancy at IGR-IAE Rennes, Rennes 1 University, France. His research topics focus, first, on the quality of financial information (regulated financial information with IFRS and alternative performance measures) and non-financial information (i.e. CSR disclosures), and second, the firms' strategic responses to the implementation of new accounting standards. He has published in several academic and professional accounting journals. He also is the author of a French book explaining and analyzing IFRS.

Jean-Laurent Viviani is Professor of Finance at IGR-IAE Rennes, Rennes 1 University, France, and Associate Professor at GSBA, Meiji University, Tokyo, Japan. He is member of the CREM — UMR 6211 research lab. His research topics are in risk management in banking (liquidity risk, systemic risk, and bank failure), corporate finance (convertible bonds, dividends announcements, capital constraint), ethics and social responsibility (ISR, CSR, impact investing, Islamic finance), and supply chain finance. He has published in several academic journals (*Economic Modelling, The Quarterly Review of Economics and Finance, International Journal of Production Economics, Management International*).

Moritz Wagner is a Lecturer in Finance at the University of Canterbury in New Zealand and serves on the investment committee of a national broker. His research interests are in the area of mutual funds, socially responsible investing, and capital markets. He has published in top ranked journals such as the *Emerging Markets Review,* and the *Journal of Financial Services Research.* Prior to joining academia, he worked in corporate finance and transaction advisory services.

Ouidad Yousfi is an Associate Professor of Finance at Management Research in Montpellier (MRM) in the University of Montpellier (France).

Dr Yousfi has published a large number of articles in various international academic journals. Her research concerns corporate governance, corporate social responsibility, diversity, innovation, and stock market liquidity. Her current projects include studies on corporate social responsibility performance, and CEO power.

https://doi.org/10.1142/9781786349507_fmatter

Contents

Preface v

Author the Editors xiii

About the Contributors xvii

Introduction xxxi

Part I: The Changes in the Real Sphere 1

Chapter 1. Macroprudential Policy in the EU — Policy Reflections on Institutional Contexts and Governance Arrangements 3
Elias Bengtsson

Chapter 2. The Effect of Austerity Measures Under Sovereign Risk and *Financial* Frictions 27
Xiaofei Ma

Chapter 3. How Do Financial Markets Listen to the Economic Policy Uncertainty? 57
Abir Abid

Chapter 4. Regulation, Ethics, and Economic Stability Evidence from Eastern European Countries 87

Zaineb Hlioui, Sonia Boukattaya, and Zyed Achour

Part II: Financial Markets: Post-crisis Challenges 121

Chapter 5. Beyond the Myths: Questions for Post Modern Finance 123

Jean-François Boulier

Chapter 6. Contagion Effect Between Financial Markets and Collectibles Markets: A Review of Empirical Research 135

Eric Le Fur

Chapter 7. Machine Learning, Computational Techniques, and Reporting Processes: Risk Exposure in GCC Markets in the Wake of the 2007–2009 Global Financial Meltdown 161

Mazin A. M. Al Janabi

Chapter 8. On the Performances of Dynamic Conditional Correlation Models in the Sovereign CDS Market and the Corresponding Bond Market 187

Saker Sabkha

Chapter 9. Development of Socially Responsible Investing (SRI) — Evidence from the Mutual Funds Industry 213
Warwick Anderson, Jędrzej Białkowski, and Moritz Wagner

Part III: CSR, Sustainability, and Ethical Finance: New Trends 251

Chapter 10. The Relationship Between CSR Disclosure and CSR Performance: A Western European Sample 253
Lan-Phuong Nguyen, Lionel Touchais, and Jean-Laurent Viviani

Chapter 11. Corporate Social Responsibility and Corporate Governance: A Cognitive Approach 285
Rania Béji, Ouidad Yousfi, and Abdelwahed Omri

Chapter 12. ESG Performance and ESG Rating: A Critical Review of the Screening Methodologies and the Way Forward 327
Anissa Naouar

Chapter 13. Corporate Social Responsibility and Firm Risk: Evidence from France 361
Zyed Achour, Zaineb Hlioui, and Sonia Boukattaya

Chapter 14. Does Board Structure Matter for Innovation? 385
Meriam Attia, Ouidad Yousfi, and Abdelwahed Omri

Part IV: Transformations, Digitalization, Blockchain, FinTech 425

Chapter 15. Blockchain Technology: Beyond Cryptocurrencies 427
Assen Slim, Fernanda Arreola, and Éric Magnin

Chapter 16. FinTech Development, Digital Infrastructure and Institutions in the SSA Zone 451
Teresa Schützeichel

Chapter 17. Fintech Development, Digital Infrastructure and Institutions in the MENA Zone 481
Youssra Ben Romdhane Loukil, Souhaila Kammoun, and Sahar Loukil

Chapter 18. Banks vs FinTech in the French Market 507
Firas Batnini and Florian Bercaut

Chapter 19. Impact of Fintech on the Level of Competition in the EU Banking Sector 537
Małgorzata Pawłowska and Aleksandra Staniszewska

Index 561

https://doi.org/10.1142/9781786349507_fmatter

Introduction

Over the past decades, several periods of turmoil have affected and ultimately shaped the financial and economic system. As a result, regulatory policies have been introduced to overcome further crises and scandals, while the monetary policy has experienced the transition from conventional to unconventional frameworks in most industrialized and emerging economies. Specifically, the substantial increase in uncertainty has affected the economic environment and financial markets. Overall, these changes have influenced governance at both the macro and micro levels. These developments call for more ethical and sustainable standards in finance and economics, which have experienced a growing trend since 2007, especially since the financial industry has undergone significant changes due to digitalization and the development of fintech and blockchain technology.

The objective of this handbook is thus to provide readers insights about the transformation and challenges of both financial and economic systems. We focus on four main areas in the four parts of the handbook. The first part, titled *The Changes in the Real Sphere*, covers issues related to sovereign debt risk, macroprudential policy, and economic uncertainty, among others. In the Chapter 1, titled "Macroprudential Policy in the EU — Policy Reflections on Institutional Contexts and Governance Arrangements", authored by Elias Bengtsson overviews macroprudential policy in terms of the lessons learned from financial crises for preventing excessive risk taking. Specifically, this first chapter maps the European macroprudential policy, both in terms of EU-wide regulation and at the national levels, and highlights the roles of institutional contexts and governance arrangements in the exertion of the macroprudential policy across EU countries in the post-crisis period. In the Chapter 2, titled "The Effect of Austerity Measures Under Sovereign Risk and *Financial* Frictions", authored by Xiaofei Ma focuses on sovereign default risk, identifying the potential effects of alternative austerity measures and fiscal policies on the dynamics of GDP, sovereign default risk, and public indebtedness in the short and long run. In the Chapter 3, titled "How Do Financial Markets Listen to the Economic Policy Uncertainty?", authored by Abir Abid deals with economic policy uncertainty and its impact on financial markets. The author is generally interested in the role of uncertainty in asset prices predictability and particularly in the interconnections of the international equity system. Finally, a new literature trend highlights that corporate unethical behaviors hinder economic stability. In the Chapter 4, titled "Regulation, Ethics, and Economic Stability Evidence from Eastern European Countries", authored by Hlioui, Boukattaya, and Achour investigate the mediating effect of corporate corrupt behaviors on the regulatory characteristics and macroeconomic stability of Eastern European countries.

The second part of the book is titled *Financial Markets: Post-crisis Challenges* and sheds light on the interdependence of financial markets, with particular regard to the impact of financial crises and the positioning of new financial products and instruments. We start the discussion with the main financial fundamentals challenged by the crises of the past two decades. As such, in the Chapter 5, titled "Beyond the Myths: Questions for Post Modern Finance", authored by Jean-François Boulier, uses a practitioner's perspective to critically analyze the fundamental issues related to financial markets, such as liquidity, efficiency, and rationality among market dimensions. Then, in the Chapter 6, titled "Contagion Effect Between Financial Markets and Collectibles Markets: A Review of Empirical Research", authored by Eric Le Fur reviews the studies on collectibles returns and the sensibility of these assets to financial markets over the past 50 years. The Chapter 7, titled "Machine Learning, Computational Techniques, and Reporting Processes: Risk Exposure in GCC Markets in the Wake of the 2007–2009 Global Financial Meltdown", authored by presents Mazin A. M. Al Janabi's robust modeling approach, which can be used in machine learning context for measuring the liquidity risk exposures of emerging markets' equity trading portfolios. In the Chapter 8, titled "On the Performances of Dynamic Conditional Correlation Models in the Sovereign CDS Market and the Corresponding Bond Market", authored by Saker Sabkha considers the interdependence between credit markets in an international context and shows the particularities of each credit market in terms of the use of different multivariate GARCH models. In the Chapter 9, titled "Development of Socially Responsible Investing (SRI) — Evidence from the Mutual Funds Industry", authored by Warwick Anderson, Jędrzej Białkowski, and Moritz Wagner analyze the recent developments of the SRI phenomenon in comparison to conventional funds. Interestingly, the performance of SRI funds tends to be statistically indistinguishable from that of conventional mutual funds, even if the behavior of the two investor types is distinctively different.

The third part of this handbook, titled *CSR, Sustainability, and Ethical Finance: New Trends*, focuses on the current challenges for CSR. The Chapter 10, titled "The Relationship Between CSR Disclosure and CSR Performance: A Western European Sample", authored by Lan-Phuong Nguyen, Lionel Touchais, and Jean-Laurent Viviani, who revisit the relationship between CSR disclosure and CSR performance using a western European sample. They find that the well-known relationship between the two variables is bilateral, with the relationship from CSR performance to CSR disclosure having a higher magnitude. The Chapter 11, titled "Corporate Social Responsibility and Corporate Governance: A Cognitive Approach", authored by Rania Béji, Ouidad Yousfi, and Abdelwahed Omri reviews the relevant literature, highlighting how board features could be a determinant for CSR decision-making processes. It thus improves our understanding of the role of board diversity for CSR performance. The Chapter 12, titled "ESG Performance and ESG Rating: A Critical Review of the Screening Methodologies and the Way Forward", authored by Anissa Naouar. Its goal is twofold. First, it sheds light on the recent developments in sustainable performance and, second, it provides an interesting overview of ESG rating methodologies. The Chapter 13, titled "Corporate Social Responsibility and Firm Risk: Evidence from France", authored by Zyed Achour, Zaineb Hlioui, and Sonia Boukattaya investigates the relationship between CSR and reducing firm risk. Using panel data on listed French companies (SBF120) over 2008–2017, the authors show that CSR can enhance corporate reputation and reduce firm global risk. The Chapter 14, titled "Does Board Structure Matter for Innovation?", authored by Meriam Attia, Ouidad Yousfi, and Abdelwahed Omri, which sheds light on the relationship between board structure and corporate innovation. The authors also show that committee size, frequency of meetings, and presence of independent female members on the board have significant impact on corporate innovation.

The fourth part of this book is titled *Transformations, Digitalization, Blockchain, FinTech* and provides interesting insights into how these new technologies have transformed financial transactions in different parts of the world. In the Chapter 15, titled "Blockchain Technology: Beyond Cryptocurrencies", authored by Assen Slim, Fernanda Arreola, and Éric Magnin present the origins of the Blockchain and its operating principles and highlight the diversity of its applications for both financial and non-financial sectors. In the Chapter 16, titled "FinTech Development, Digital Infrastructure and Institutions in the SSA Zone", authored by Teresa Schützeichel deals with the FinTech evolution and financial regulation in sub-Saharan Africa, identifying the roles to be played by regulators and regulatory institutions in encouraging digital economic development. In the Chapter 17, titled "Fintech Development, Digital Infrastructure and Institutions in the MENA Zone", authored by Youssra Ben Romdhane Loukil, Souhaila Kammoun, and Sahar Loukil identify the factors that influence fintech growth in MENA countries, since these countries are considered greenfield opportunities for the expansion of financial technologies. In the Chapter 18, titled "Banks vs FinTech in the French Market", authored by Firas Batnini and Florian Bercaut analyze the impact of the new innovation wave brought by fintech on the French financial market, focusing on the traditional banking sector. In the Chapter 19, titled "Impact of Fintech on the Level of Competition in the EU Banking Sector", authored by Małgorzata Pawłowska and Aleksandra Staniszewska investigate the impact of innovative financial technology (Fintech) on the level of competition in the EU banking sector.

Part I:

The Changes in the Real Sphere

https://doi.org/10.1142/9781786349507_0001

Chapter 1

Macroprudential Policy in the EU — Policy Reflections on Institutional Contexts and Governance Arrangements

Elias Bengtsson

University of Gothenburg, Department of Economics, Göteborg, Sweden
elias.bengtsson@economics.gu.se

1.1 Introduction: The Ascent of Macroprudential Policy

The global financial crisis offered a stark reminder of how excessive risk taking in combination with weaknesses in the financial system can lead to detrimental consequences for financial stability and the real economy. An important lesson was that prevailing regulatory and supervisory regimes were not properly equipped to identify and curb systemic risk.

In response to this, macroprudential policy has emerged as a key area in economic and financial policy, complementing those of micro-prudential and monetary policy. In essence, macroprudential policy seeks to prevent and mitigate the effects of excessive risk taking in the financial sector. In the broad sense, macroprudential policy includes both the wider institutional frameworks and regulation for policy enactment; the analytical tools and processes to identify and assess system risks; as well as the set and use of macroprudential measures to address them.

This chapter provides an overview of and discusses key macroprudential policy issues relating to institutional contexts and governance arrangements, with a particular focus on the EU. It seeks to highlight differences and commonalities between EU Member States, explain how these relate to international best practice and policy recommendations, and present empirical outcomes of how institutional contexts and governance arrangement appear to influence the effectiveness of macroprudential policy in fulfilling its role in economic policy. The chapter highlights that Member States with single macroprudential authorities with strong transparency requirements generally adopt more intense policy stances. Overall, both accountability and independence arrangements appear to have weaker power to explain policy outcomes. Finally, policy frameworks that are multi-layered and complex and pose conundrums on how to ensure sufficient institutional autonomy and policy capacity among macroprudential authorities. One such example is the Eurozone area, where the ECB has an overlay function in domestic macroprudential policy.

The following section provides an overview of the international policy debate on macroprudential policy, with a particular focus on policy issues relating to institutional factors and governance arrangements ("macroprudential set-up"). Section 1.3 covers macroprudential policy stances in the EU. It begins by providing an overview of the legal foundations of macroprudential policy in the EU, including how European law/Directives has been transposed across the Member States. Thereafter, it presents some stylized facts on macroprudential policy stances across countries and over time. Section 1.4 illustrates — in a non-technical manner — how institutional factors and governance arrangements have influenced macroprudential policy stances across Europe. Section 1.5 concludes by discussing these findings in the light of the international policy debate on macroprudential policy and presents a number of policy conclusions.

1.2 The International Policy Debate on Macroprudential Policy

Macroprudential policy is now firmly integrated in the work programmed of global standard setters and international organizations (Financial Stability Board (FSB), Basel Committee of Banking

Supervision (BCBS), International Organization of Securities Commissions (IOSCO), International Monetary Fund (IMF), Bank for International Settlements (BIS), European Central Bank (ECB), European Systemic Risk Board (ESRB) etc.) and in financial regulation at the regional and national levels.

1.2.1 *Inaction bias and macroprudential policy*

Part of this policy work, and related debates and discussions, are centered on how to address the various difficulties facing macroprudential policymakers in the concrete execution of policy. This includes how to identify and assess systemic risk, the choice and calibration of instruments, domestic and international policy coordination, and policy evaluation (ESRB, 2015; Bengtsson *et al.*, 2018). But there is also important policy work that relates to the incentives of policymakers and related stakeholders that arise as a consequence of institutional and governance structures in the policy context. Within this field of policy work, the discussion and debates tend to revolve around finding solutions to the risk of inertia among responsible authorities and policymakers. Such inaction biases are compounded by a number of interrelated factors — time inconsistencies, distributional effects, and path dependencies and cognitive constraints — and tend to be reinforced by other important stakeholders rather than the policymaker themselves:

- Time inconsistencies are well documented in the literature on monetary policy (Persson *et al.*, 1987), and also in the literature on microprudential regulation (Taylor *et al.*, 2005; Quintyn *et al.*, 2007). They imply that policy measures are likely to have direct impact on the real economy, tending to reduce its (near-term) future growth prospects. The benefits, on the other hand, are in the future and uncertain, and may in any case be difficult to explain to the public. Such time inconsistencies are perhaps even more pronounced in macroprudential policy than in other policy areas; one of its key objectives is to "take the punchbowl away" in the risk accumulation phase, when conditions seemingly appear benign, but vulnerabilities may be growing. For instance, increasing capital requirements for mortgages to fend of future events with a relatively low probability is likely to face opposition from mortgage associations and perhaps also the general public if it increases interest rates on mortgages. For this reason, time inconsistencies can make macroprudential policy prone to criticism and opposition (Baker, 2015; Brunnermeier *et al.*, 2009).

- Distributional effects are also likely to increase the risk of inaction bias. Again, that distributional effects may dampen the appetite of policymakers to take action is well documented in the literature on monetary policy, but some claim that the distributional effects of macroprudential policy are more explicit and conspicuous (Baker, 2015; Haldane, 2013). Although the former has distributional consequence by influencing values of assets and debt, macroprudential policy may introduce measures such as limits and requirements on particular types of transactions, exposures or market actors. This in turn is likely to influence prices and credit flows from particular sectors to others, and may reduce access to credit for particular population cohorts or economic sectors at certain times. Such distributional effects are likely to strengthen inaction biases, even in situations when it may be in the public interest to pursue active and appropriate macroprudential policy stances.
- Path dependencies and cognitive constraints are well documented in the financial governance strand of the literature on political economy. It highlights that path dependencies and cognitive constraints among financial regulators and supervisors are powerful explanatory factors behind inaction bias. A reluctance to adapt to new circumstances and a tendency to continue to follow established routines, interpretative frameworks and cognitive modes are likely to make macroprudential regulators fail to take sufficient action to curb systemic risk (Tarullo, 2008; Buiter, 2012; Bengtsson, 2016). Haldane (2013:7) has described this as the "risk of disaster myopia, of ignoring worrying dots on distant horizons, of being "information-rich-yet-attention-poor", "of forgetting fat tails". Such cognitive constraints are likely to be compounded in contexts where there is shortage of embedded knowledge of the past or little institutional memory (Haldane, 2013). This implies that in cases when a country has not experienced serious financial stress or a significant financial crisis for a long period of time, the preferences among key actors are more likely to favor inaction compared to countries with more recent and/or more substantial financial crises.

1.2.2 *Private interest and macroprudential policy*

Time inconsistencies, distributional effects and cognitive constraints do not merely affect macroprudential policymakers. They are also likely to induce key stakeholders, such as industry associations within and outside financial services, consumer groups and politicians, to voice their concerns to influence policymakers, either directly or by influencing each other and/or the general public to strengthen their message. Facing such opposition, policymakers are more likely to remain inactive in their policy stance.

Such political or private sector captures are often highlighted in the international policy debate due to time inconsistencies and distributional effects of macroprudential policy (Borio, 2011). Political tenures typically range between 3 and 5 years (the time between parliamentary elections), whereas financial cycles tend to have prolonged upturns that typically last a decade or more (Adrian and Shin, 2008). This compounds issues relating to time inconsistencies, since it may tempt politicians or political decision-makers to pursue their own interests (such as re-election or re-appointment) at the expense of society's long-term interests. For instance, a potentially destabilizing financial boom could be allowed to persist in order to harness popularity (Tucker, 2014b). A parallel reasoning is easy to apply on distributional effects, where politicians (or authorities they directly or indirectly control) may wish to avoid distributional consequences that would result from public interest policies. This, in turn, could please particular voter groups and thereby increase their chances of remaining in office.

Naturally, politicians' preference formation is influenced by constituents and key stakeholders. This also implies that private interest — such as industry or consumer groups — may pressure macroprudential policymakers into inaction, both directly and indirectly through the political sphere. Although regulators and politicians may face competing demands from voters and — for instance — banks (Oatley and Nabors, 1998; Mattli and Woods, 2009), this implies that commercial interests and political interest often become intertwined. For instance, both mortgage lenders and homeowners may oppose increasing capital requirements for residential real estate exposures if this is believed to lower profitability and increase mortgage interest rates. Another example is the concept of institutional memory discussed above, which by nature is a shared characteristic among actors within a particular shared context.

In particular, the literature contains ample evidence that the financial industry — and banks in particular — has considerable powers in influencing economic policymaking (Bengtsson, 2013, 2016; Tarullo, 2008). These powers appear to have been compounded by a number of social trends and conditions. One is the larger and more concentrated banking systems that are the results of increasing internationalization and consolidation of banking in recent decades. This, in turn, has reduced collective action problems relating to influencing regulatory outcomes (Verdier, 2013). These structural characteristics — such as the size and/or concentration of a particular banking system — can also make banking more important in providing services, generating tax revenues or contributing to employment and growth (Bengtsson *et al.*, 2013).

But there are also other factors that may strengthen the power of the financial system and banks. One is the presence of institutional arrangements that grant financial sector actors privileged access to regulators. This provides opportunities to informally influence regulatory processes (Pagliari and Young, 2014), which in particular enables the financial industry to provide input in the initial and important agenda-setting phase of policy processes (Verdier, 2013). Privileged access and repeated interactions also tend to reinforce "cognitive alignment". This implies that discourses, concepts and terminologies of both the regulators and the regulated become institutionalized. It also means that these terminologies and concepts become less accessible or understood by the public or other stakeholders, which thereby limits their abilities to have an influence (Mattli and Woods, 2009). Mosley (2009) argues that the interests of politicians and regulators tend to particularly align with those of the domestic financial sector when regulatory issues are highly technical. High levels of technicality are a prominent feature of many macroprudential policies, such as those that impose limits and restrictions based on technical standards (such as risk weights, exposure limits, funding and liquidity ratios, etc.).

1.2.3 *Macroprudential set-up*

The inherent risk of inaction bias in macroprudential policy has spurred an intense international policy debate with many contributions by various policy bodies. As in most policy debates, there are also many disagreements on what constitutes the most appropriate set-up for macroprudential policy. This also relates to the fact that there are many ambiguities on the effects of various institutional and governance arrangements. Unlike other areas of financial policy, research is in its infancy and tends to be largely theoretical (Bengtsson, 2019). Goodhart (2015:281) notes that there is "little assessment of the institutional impact of macroprudential policy [...], despite the strong likelihood that regulated entities will resist tighter regulation and that conflicts over macroprudential policy will be politically mediated".

This said, there are at least tendencies for an emerging consensus on how various institutional and governance arrangements relating to macro-prudential policy should be structured. In other words, it appears that an increasingly shared policy view is underway on issues such as independence, accountability and transparency requirements of macroprudential regulators and on issues relating to which authorities should be involved in policymaking. The various arguments and counterarguments put forward on the design of various key dimensions of macroprudential policy set-up are discussed below. The discussion largely reflects the positions of relevant international bodies such as the IMF and BIS, or central banks. In the subsequent section, Section 3, an account of the choices European Member States have made in terms of their macroprudential set-up is provided.

1.2.3.1 *Institutional set-up*

When deliberating on the most appropriate institutional set-up, the policy debate centers on three broad features: whether particular authorities are better suited for shouldering macroprudential responsibility due to the degree of alignment of objectives; whether particular authorities are better suited due to their availability of resources, and whether a committee structure or a single macroprudential authority is preferable. Unsurprisingly, policy debates typically stress that advantages and disadvantages of specific institutional forms require further analysis (IMF, 2014).

- Alignment of objectives. A lack of alignment between policy objectives may give rise to tensions for the authorities involved in macroprudential policy. For microprudential authorities, increasing capital requirements of banks to strengthen resilience may be warranted in financial stress. However, from a macroprudential perspective, such capital increases may be procyclical and deepen financial stress (IMF, 2011). For central banks, one important transmission channel for monetary policy is the "risk-taking channel". But even though increased risk taking is an intended effect of expansionary monetary policy, it may also lead to unintended and potentially excessive risk taking in particular sectors or market segments. Conversely, activation of macroprudential measures may also affect the business cycle (CGFS, 2010; Blanchard *et al.*, 2010; Galati and Moessner, 2013; Svensson, 2018). This in particular calls for nationally specific macroprudential policy in currency unions (Dehmej and Gambacorta, 2019). These type of policy tensions may lead to policy confusion and potentially inhibit decision-making and timely intervention (Osinski *et al.*, 2013). Whereas political bodies, such as finance ministries/treasuries, benefit from being able to internalize any goal conflicts between fiscal and macroprudential policy, tensions between policy objectives are clearly linked to time inconsistencies and distributional effects. These are likely to cause inaction bias due to the lack of independence from other political preferences and processes. For this reason, the international policy debate often emphasizes the need for politically independent macroprudential policy (see further below).

- Availability of resources for effective macroprudential policy includes capabilities, experiences and information access. They all tend to benefit from synergies with existing tasks of the relevant authorities. Central banks may have advantages from synergies in analysis and data, especially in analyzing business and financial cycles. They also tend to be well informed on financial markets structures and developments through their market operations and payment system monitoring. For microprudential supervisors, synergies may arise through access and experience in analyzing granular firm-level data. In addition, microprudential supervisors are also likely to have direct experience of using the macroprudential measures (albeit for microprudential purposes).

Availability of resources seems be an important reason (the other one being independence — see below) for the apparent consensus that central banks should play a key role in macroprudential policy

(IMF, 2011). Borio, a prominent economist at the BIS, argues that "[...] we should be bold in designing new governance arrangements. Given their expertise, central banks should play a key role" (Borio, 2011:13). Similar, the ESRB Recommendation (2011) advises countries to designate central banks as the national macroprudential authorities, based on their expertise and roles in financial stability monitoring.

- Committee structure or a single macroprudential authority. The discussion on the choice between mandating a single institution to pursue macroprudential policy or opting for a committee structure comprising several relevant authorities also relates to potential tensions between policy objectives and resource availability. The policy debate highlights a number of advantages and challenges relating to joint decision-making in committees. In term of advantages, a committee structure may ensure that information is effectively shared among participating authorities. It also increases the pool of human resources generally, and also broadens the analytical scope by including different types of expertise. This may be required to spot systemic risk with diverse root causes and transmission channels (Sibert, 2010). Potential challenges relate to prolonged processes due to coordination problems, which may slow decision-making, especially when membership is large, and the interests of represented authorities diverge. Committee structures may also lead to motivational losses and dilution of accountability (see further below). Also, information sharing may be difficult in practice. People may feel reluctant to speak freely and question assumptions, since this carries a risk of making a fool of oneself in front of co-members.

The US provides an interesting case on institutional arrangements. The US regulatory system is fragmented across several authorities, and a Financial System Oversight Committee (FSOC) consisting of these agencies and the Treasury was set up in charge of financial stability oversight. This, in turn, has prompted a political and academic debate on whether this is appropriate, given that this leads to particular political, resource-related and accountability implications (Allen, 2015). In policy circles, a neutral stance is often expressed regarding the choice between a single macroprudential authority or a committee structure (IMF, 2011; ESRB, 2011 etc.).

1.2.3.2 *Governance arrangements*

How best to counteract inaction biases through appropriate governance arrangements remains an unresolved issue in the macroprudential policy debate, but there is an emerging consensus developing in the three areas:

- Independence from political or private interest is frequently stressed in the international policy debate (Haldane, 2013; Borio, 2011; IMF, 2014 etc.). Also, the ESRB has recommended countries to ensure both operational and financial independence of macroprudential authorities (2011). The preference for independent authorities is buttressed by significant research within the field of monetary policy (Rogoff, 1985). Similar arguments are made in the field of microprudential supervision, where Masciandaro *et al.* (2008) argue that political and industry capture require independent supervisors. Das and Quintyn (2002), Das *et al.* (2004), Quintyn *et al.* (2007) and others highlight the importance of microprudential supervisors being able to pursue objective without fear of dismissal or other punitive measures, even with dissentient views from politicians or other powerful stakeholders. Central banks typically have greater political independence than other authorities in order to protect monetary policy from political influence; central bank governors are usually appointed over a fixed period extending several years, with very little political accountability and limited possibilities of being ousted. These institutional arrangements generally provide central banks with more independence, which is another reason for the common policy preference for designating central banks as macroprudential authorities.
- Accountability is often advocated to reduce the potential pursuit of private (and self-) interests. Among others, the ESRB (2011) has emphasized the need for appropriate accountability mechanisms (including reporting to the national parliament, board meeting disclosures, etc.). ESRB further specifies that macroprudential authorities should be explicitly entrusted the tasks to identify, monitor and assess risks to reduce inaction bias. However, the literature also flags that independence is a double-edged sword; with more independence, the risks of "self-interest capture" increases (Boot and Thakor, 1993). The literature on the governance of financial supervisors (Quintyn *et al.*, 2007; Masciandaro *et al.*, 2008) argues that governance arrangements need to be more

complex in financial supervision compared to monetary policy, since the former pursues objectives that are many in number and harder to measure. In addition, supervisors often have multiple mandates and face more difficult conflicts between these mandates (Taylor *et al.*, 2005). Furthermore, supervisors have more stakeholders that are particularly affected by supervisory policies or regulation. Research shows that legislators are less willing to grant independence to financial supervisors and regulators than to central banks (Quintyn and Taylor, 2003), which may relate to these conditions.

- Transparency on the underpinnings of macroprudential authorities' policy decisions is another important and widely debated governance feature. Transparency may manage market expectations and allow market actors to adjust to avoid future measures (largely similar to the "forward guidance" function of monetary policy). This may increase the effectiveness of any particular policy stance. But transparency is also linked to accountability in the sense that substantial transparency requirements would require authorities to disclose the motives for taking particular measures or for being inactive (Osinski *et al.*, 2013). Openness and transparency are often argued to minimize political or other influences (Quintyn *et al.*, 2007). For these reasons, several policy bodies also recommend transparency requirements on macroprudential authorities (ESRB, 2011; IMF, 2014 etc.).

1.3 Macroprudential Policy in the EU

This section elaborates on the set-up and concrete exertion of macroprudential policy across the EU Member states. In the EU, macroprudential policy is regulated by the Capital Requirements Directive (CRD) and the Capital Requirements Regulation (CRR). CRD/CRR provides EU Member States with a common legal framework and a set of macroprudential instruments to mitigate systemic risk in the banking sector. Among other things, it requires national legislative bodies to formally designate macroprudential authorities and equip them with various macroprudential instruments.

In fact, EU law (Art. 136 of Directive 2013/36/EU (CRD IV)) requires Member States to appoint one Designated authority which is responsible for setting the countercyclical capital buffer rates.

In addition, the ESRB (ESRB/2011/3) recommends that Member States establish "macroprudential authorities" with, at minimum, the tasks of identifying, monitoring and assessing risks to financial stability and of implementing policies to achieve its objective by preventing and mitigating those risks. This also includes ensuring that the macroprudential authorities have control over appropriate instruments for achieving their objectives. Capital requirements, funding ratios, liquidity buffers, intra-financial sector and large exposure limits and public disclosure requirements all form part of the EU macroprudential toolkit.

Figure 1.1 illustrates the distribution of the institutional set-up of Designated and Macroprudential authorities in the EU. It demonstrates that central banks are the most preferred choice for both the Macroprudential and Designated authority. In fact, for around half of EU Member States, the Designated authority coincides with the Macroprudential authority. When they don't, the macroprudential authority very often takes the form of a cooperative committee structure, while the designated authority is the central bank, the financial supervisory authority or even government agencies (PL; DK). In comparison with (Edge and Liang's, 2019) study on a larger global sample of countries, EU appears to rely on central banks as macroprudential authorities more frequently. Table 1.1 provides

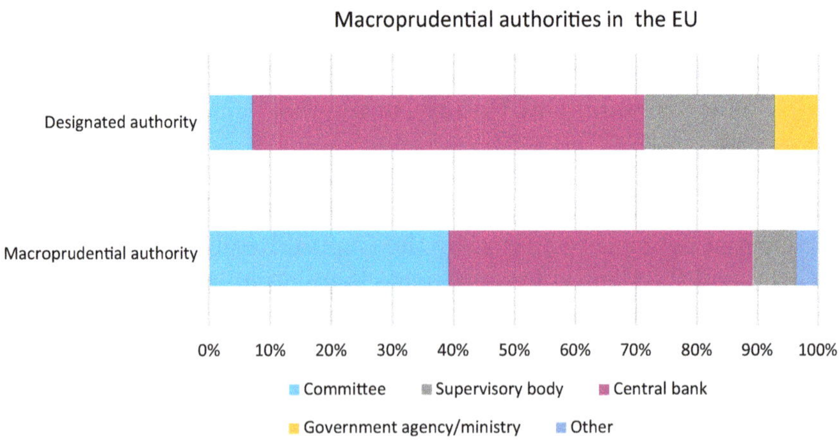

Fig. 1.1. Designated and Macroprudential authorities in the EU.
Source: ESRB (2018).

Table 1.1. Macroprudential and Designated authorities in the EU.

Country	Macroprudential and Designated authority
BE	Nationale Bank van België/Banque Nationale de Belgique
CZ	Ceská národní banka
EE	Eesti Pank
IE	Central Bank of Ireland
IT	Banca d'Italia*
GR	Bank of Greece
FR	Haut Conseil de Stabilité Financière (High Council for Financial Stability)
CY	Central Bank of Cyprus
LT	Lietuvos bankas
HU	Magyar Nemzeti Bank
MT	Central Bank of Malta
PT	Banco de Portugal
RO	Comitetul National pentru Supravegherea Macroprudentială (National Committee for Macroprudential Oversight)
SK	Národná banka Slovenska
FI	Finanssivalvonta (Finnish Financial Supervisory Authority)
SE	Finansinspektionen (Financial Supervisory Authority)
UK	Bank of England/Financial Policy Committee

Country	Macroprudential authority	Designated authority
BG	Financial Stability Advisory Council	Bulgarian National Bank
DK	Det Systemiske Risikoråd (Systemic Risk Council)	Erhvervsministeren (Minister for Industry, Business and Financial Affairs)
DE	Ausschuss für Finanzstabilität (Financial Stability Committee)	Bundesanstalt für Finanzdienstleistungsaufsicht (Financial Supervisory Authority)
ES	Autoridad Macroprudencial Consejo de Estabilidad Financiera	Banco de España
HR	Vijeće za financijsku stabilnost (Financial Stability Council)	Hrvatska narodna banka
LV	Latvijas Banka	Finanšu un kapitāla tirgus komisija (Financial and Capital Market Commission)

(Continued)

Table 1.1. (*Continued*)

Country	Macroprudential authority	Designated authority
LU	Comité du risque systémique (Systemic Risk Committee)	Commission de Surveillance du Secteur Financier (Financial Supervisory Authority)
NL	Financieel Stabiliteitscomité (Financial Stability Committee)	De Nederlandsche Bank
AT	Finanzmarktstabilitätsgremium (Financial Market Stability Board)	Finanzmarktaufsichtsbehörde (Austrian Financial Market Authority)
PL	Komitet Stabilności Finansowej (Financial Stability Committee)	Minister Finansów (Minister of Finance)
SI	Odbor za finančno stabilnost (Financial Stability Board)	Banka Slovenije

Notes: *In Italy the powers granted to set up a macroprudential authority have since expired, leaving the Banca d'Italia responsible for addressing financial stability concerns.

additional details on the Designated and Macroprudential authorities across the EU Member States.

Thus, interinstitutional cooperation structures are much more frequent choice for Macroprudential authorities. In general, such committees merely have soft powers at their disposal, such as issuing recommendations, opinions or warnings. But in some cases, such as FR, they are also able to take binding policy decisions. These committee structures typically include the central bank, supervisory authorities and government agencies/ministries. In some rare cases, other actors are also involved (e.g. of the deposit guarantee agency, resolution agency or accounting body). The central bank often plays a leading role in the committee work, e.g. by either chairing it or providing secretariat and/or analytical functions. In some Member States, the Ministry of Finance representatives are the chairs (AT, DE, LU). In this respect, most Member States share many commonalties with the US in terms of the set-up of macroprudential policy. The US also relies on a committee structure, in this case chaired by the US Treasury. The Federal Reserve is among the committee members, and it also has a separate mandate on macroprudential policy (Mayes *et al.*, 2019).

Another feature of macroprudential policy in the EU is that when using macroprudential measures, national authorities must also comply with particular procedures of coordination with various European bodies. This includes the European Banking Authority (EBA), the ESRB, the European Commission, the EU Council and the European Parliament.

Moreover, since 2013 and the creation of the EU Banking Union, the responsibility for macroprudential policy is shared between the ECB and national authorities in the Euro area. National authorities retain the power to activate macroprudential measures in their Member States (subject to notification and coordination mechanisms), but the ECB can both object to measures as well as top up a number of macroprudential instruments assigned to it through EU legislation.

Turning to macroprudential policy stances in the EU, Fig. 1.2 covers substantial macroprudential measures in EU Member States between 2014 and 2017. One observation is the general increase in the number of measures. This is likely a combined result of increased systemic risk due to low interest rates/increasing asset prices and that macroprudential stances are still in their build-up phase (both from a legal and economic/post-crisis perspective). However, there are also large differences between member states. For some of the

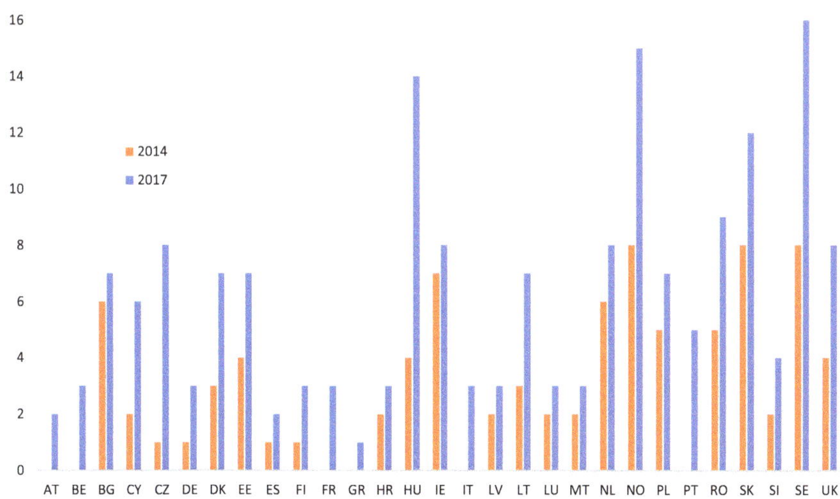

Fig. 1.2. Macroprudential policy stances in the EU 2014 and 2017.

larger EU Member States, and for those that suffered greatly in the global financial and EURO crises, more lax policy stances are visible. For many northern, central and eastern Member States, macroprudential policy stances tend to be more intense.

1.4 Determinants of Macroprudential Policy Stances

Variations in macroprudential policy stances can be due to a range of explanatory factors. Obviously, the degree and nature of systemic risk in a particular country matters, which may also relate to the different phase in the financial cycle the country finds itself in. Other factors may include differing views as regards the role of macroprudential policy, and the related set-up of macroprudential policy in terms of its institutional and governance structure.

Research on these latter issues is very limited. Some exceptions exist but tend to focus on ex ante theoretical reasoning (Tarullo, 2014) rather than empirical policy manifestations. Edge and Liang's study (2019) does not focus on policy stances but empirically investigates the motivational factors behind the macroprudential set-up across 58 countries within and outside the EU. Regression analysis suggests financial stability committees are designed to facilitate information sharing and coordination across agencies rather than making policy stances more effective. Similarly, cross-matching information on governance variables and different institutional structures across EU Member States provides some cues. Figure 1.3 depicts the percentage of Member States with either a single or a committee-type macroprudential authority that achieve the highest rating in terms of independence, accountability and transparency. A larger share of single macroprudential authorities attain the highest rating for all these dimensions.

If single authorities in general are more independent, accountable and transparent, does this reduce their inaction bias and lead to more intense policy stances? Bengtsson (2019) analyzed macroprudential policy stances across EU countries and sought to understand how institutional and governance arrangement of relevant authorities influence macroprudential policy.

Based on data from common reporting requirements in the EU, the analysis tests whether countries with single macroprudential

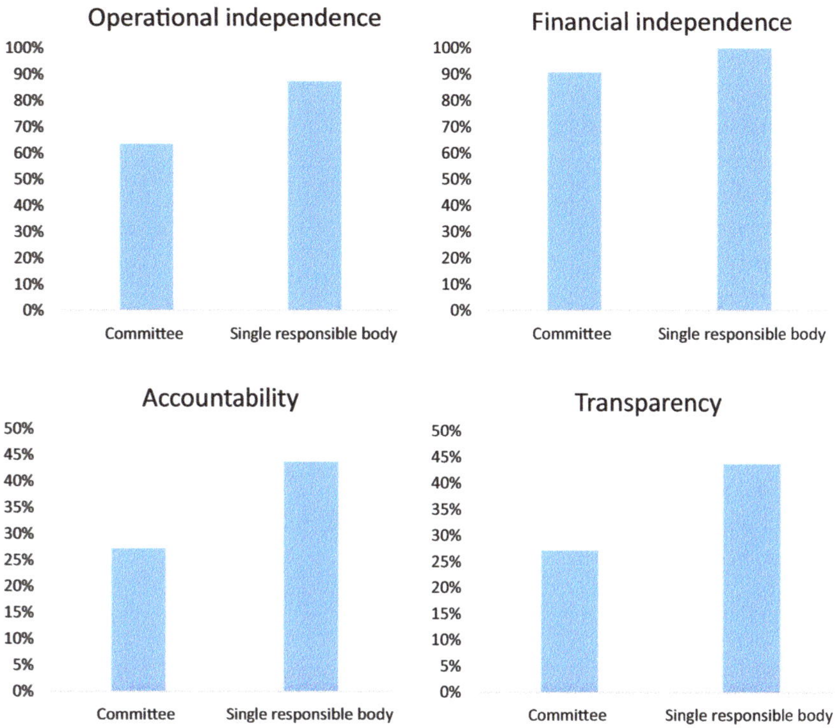

Fig. 1.3. Independence, accountability and transparency by types of macroprudential authorities.
Source: ESRB (2014).

authorities and whether countries with central banks in charge of macroprudential policy adopt more intense policy stances after taking the level of systemic risk into account. Moreover, whether governance arrangements relating to independence, accountability and transparency matter for macroprudential policy stances is also looked into.

Figure 1.4 provides an overview of the institutional and governance dimensions that were found to influence policy stances or not, including whether the influence was statistically significant or not. It also illustrates the direction and magnitude of the influence, where the latter is measured as percentages in relation to the "control group". For instance, the bars that displays the effects of having single macroprudential authorities display policy intensity in relation to

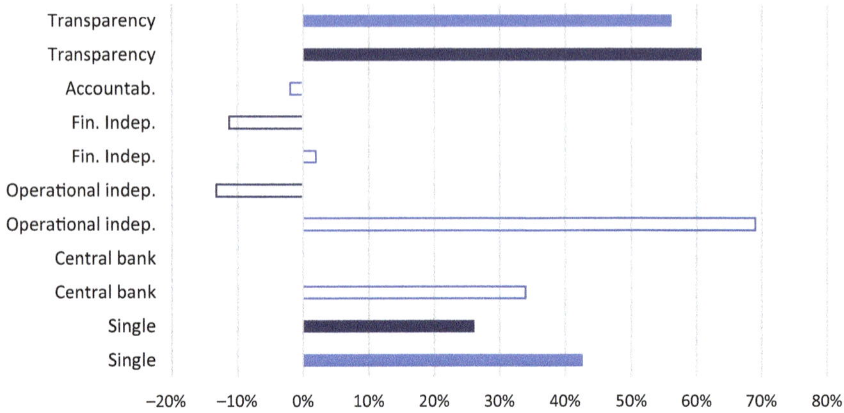

Fig. 1.4. Significance in relationships between macroprudential set-up dimensions and policy stances.

Note: Filled bars indicate statistically significant relationships below 10% level.

Source: Bengtsson (2019).

the group of countries where there is no single authority, etc. A general comment is that many of the results differ depending on whether countries are based in the Eurozone or not. For instance, more intense policy stances are associated with countries where a single macroprudential authority is established. But there is no significant effect when single authorities are appointed in the Eurozone. Appointing a central bank does not significantly influence policy stances in any of the samples. Figure 1.4 also demonstrates that neither formal independence nor accountability arrangements matters, but that there are significant positive effects from transparency arrangements.

1.5 Policy Conclusions and Discussion

A general policy conclusion on macroprudential policy is that appropriate institutional and governance arrangements are needed to safeguard public interest and to counteract inaction biases. Many specific dimensions relating to governance arrangements have been suggested by policy bodies such as the IMF, BIS and the ESRB, although they often provide several suggestions among alternatives and point to their respective benefits and shortcomings. This chapter seeks to venture further and outline a number of policy implications that emerge from discussion and arguments outlined below:

- Macroprudential policymakers' inaction biases appear to be best counteracted by appointing a single macroprudential authority. Single authorities display generally more intense policy stances and are associated with stronger independence and accountability arrangements, as well as stricter transparency requirements. This suggests that the benefits from committee structures (coordination advantages, pooling of resources etc.) appear to be overshadowed by their shortcomings (coordination problems, divergence of interests, contradictory policy objectives etc.).
- There is an international consensus that strong transparency requirements are beneficial for macroprudential policy (ESRB, 2011; IMF, 2014 etc.). Strong governance arrangements on transparency tend to influence policy stances. Transparency matters since openness tends to reduce political or other influence. But transparency is also linked to accountability in the sense that substantial transparency requirements force authorities to disclose the motives for taking particular measures or not.
- However, both accountability and independence arrangements appear to have weak power to explain policy outcomes. This does not suggest they are unimportant but rather that they are difficult to rate due to complexity and that their interaction may matter more than individual effect. However, independence may also lead to unintended consequences, including "self-interest capture" at the expense of public interest.
- Another policy implication is that policy frameworks that are multi-layered and complex pose conundrums on how to ensure sufficient institutional autonomy and policy capacity among macroprudential authorities. The differences found among Eurozone and non-Eurozone countries is a telling example. For instance, the benefits of having a single macroprudential authority is not visible in the Eurozone sample. One potential explanation could be that the ECB has an overlay function in domestic macroprudential policy, which implies a very different institutional setting and overarching governance structure.

A final remark is that there is still no agreement on the most appropriate set-ups of macroprudential policy to counter inaction bias.

Perhaps it will never be known. Systemic risk is complex and varies over time and place, not least due to the dynamism of the financial systems and its innovative capacity. For this reason, it is unlikely that there is panacea to the policy problems surrounding macroprudential policy. This also points to the need for an ongoing and vibrant policy discussion and debate.

The findings also raise important topics to pursue in further research. Since the findings seem to imply that non-bank intermediation influences macroprudential policy, an interesting topic would be to investigate how such influence is accomplished in practice within and across jurisdictions. Another important issue relates to the wider interactions between macroprudential policy and other policy areas, such as monetary, microprudential or fiscal policy, or even the wider political context. This is also relevant on a regional or global scale, where much of the policy debate in macroprudential policy takes place. A particular dimension of the wider social context is also to explain why particular institutional arrangements for macroprudential policy are established, where historical factors and path dependencies may provide important cues. Given the distributional consequences of macroprudential policy, and since it redefines the role of public authority over private interest, gaining a better understanding of its political economy is necessary and urgent.

References

Allen, H. J. (2015). Putting the financial stability in financial stability oversight council. *Ohio State Law Journal*, **76**: 1087.

Baker, A. (2015). The bankers' paradox: The political economy of macroprudential regulation, *SRC Discussion Paper No. 37*, London School of Economics.

Bengtsson, E. (2013). The political economy of banking regulation — Does the Basel 3 accord imply a change? *Credit and Capital Markets*, **3**: 303–329.

Bengtsson, E. (2016). *The Political Economy of Basel III*, Working paper, Stockholm University.

Bengtsson, E., Holmberg, U., and Jönsson, K. (2013). Identifying systemically-important banks in Sweden — What can quantitative indicators show us? *Sveriges Riksbank Economic Review*, **2**: 50–76.

Bengtsson, E., Grothe, M., and Lepers, E. (2018). Home, safe home: Cross-country monitoring framework for vulnerabilities in the residential real estate sector. *Journal of Banking and Finance*, **112**: 105268.

Bengtsson, E. (2019). Macroprudential policy in the EU: A political economy perspective. *Global Finance Journal*, 100490.

Blanchard, O., Dell'Ariccia, G., and Mauro P. (2010). *Rethinking Macroeconomic Policy, SPN/10/03*, IMF Staff Position Note.

Boot, A. W. and Thakor, A. V. (1993). Self-interested bank regulation. *The American Economic Review*, **83**(2): 206–212.

Borio, C. (2011). Implementing a macroprudential framework: Blending boldness and realism. *Capitalism and Society*, **6**(1): 1–2.

Brunnermeier, M. and Pedersen, L. (2009). Market liquidity and funding liquidity. *Review of Financial Studies*, **22**: 2201–2238.

Buiter, W. H. (2012). *The Role of Central Banks in Financial Stability: How Has It Changed?* CEPR Discussion Paper.

Committee on the Global Financial System (2010). Macroprudential instruments and frameworks: A stocktaking of issues and experiences, *CGFS Publications* No. 38.

Dehmej, S. and Gambacorta, L. (2019). Macroprudential policy in a monetary union. *Comparative Economic Studies*, **61**(2): 195–212.

Edge, R. and Liang, N. (2019). New financial stability governance structures and central banks. *Finance and Economics Discussion Series 2019–019*, Board of governors of the federal reserve system (US).

ESRB (2011). *Recommendation of the European systemic risk board of 22 December 2011 on the macro-prudential mandate of national authorities* (ESRB/2011/3) (2012/C 41/01).

ESRB (2014) *Follow-up report — overall assessment: Recommendation on the macro-prudential mandate of national authorities* (ESRB/2011/3).

ESRB (2015). *The ESRB handbook on operationalising macroprudential policy in the banking sector*, European Central Bank, available at: https://publications.europa.eu/en/publication-detail/-/publication/df401d9f-25d0-4587-ad3f-47599f4d29ae/language-en/format-PDF/source-search.

ESRB (2018). *A Review of macroprudential Policy in the EU in 2017.*

Galati, G. and Moessner, R. (2013). Macroprudential policy — A literature review. *Journal of Economic Surveys*, **27**: 846–878.

Goodhart, L. (2015). Brave new world? Macro prudential policy and the new political economy of the Federal Reserve, *SRC Discussion Paper No. 29*, Systemic Risk Centre. The London School of Economics and Political Science, London.

Haldane, A. (2013). *Why institutions matter (more than ever)*, Speech at Centre for Research on Socio-Cultural Change (CRESC) annual conference, School of Oriental and African Studies, London, 4 September.

IMF (2011). *Macroprudential Policy: An Organizing Framework*, Monetary and capital markets department, March 14.

IMF (2014). *Staff Guidance Note on Macroprudential Policy*, 6 November available at: http://www.imf.org/external/np/pp/eng/2014/110614.pdf.

Masciandaro, D., Quintyn, M., and Taylor, M. W. (2008). Inside and outside the central bank: Independence and accountability in financial supervision: Trends and determinants. *European Journal of Political Economy*, **24**(4): 833–848.

Mattli, W. and Woods, N. (Eds.). (2009). *The politics of global regulation*, Princeton University Press.

Mayes, D., Siklos, P., and Sturm, J.-E. (2019). *The Oxford handbook of the economics of central banking*, Oxford University Press.

Mosley, L. (2009). *Private governance for the public good? Exploring private sector participation in global financial regulation*, In Milner, H. V. and Moravcsik, A. (Eds.). Power, interdependence, and nonstate actors in world politics, Princeton University Press.

Osinski, J., Seal, K., and Hoogduin, M. L. (2013). Macroprudential and microprudential policies: Toward cohabitation. *International Monetary Fund WP No. 13–15.*

Pagliari, S. and Young, K. (2014). Leveraged interests: Financial industry power and the role of private sector coalitions. *Review of International Political Economy*, **21**(3): 575–610.

Persson, M., Persson, T., and Svensson, L. E. O. (1987). Time consistency of fiscal and monetary policy. *Econometrica*, **55**(6): 1419–1431.

Quintyn, M., Ramirez, S., and Taylor, M. (2007). *The fear of freedom: Politicians and the independence and accountability of financial sector supervisors (No. 7–25)*. International Monetary Fund.

Rogoff, K. (1985). The optimal degree of commitment to an intermediate monetary target. *The Quarterly Journal of Economics*, **100**(4): 1169–1189.

Sibert, A. (2010). A systemic risk warning system, *VoxEU*, 16 January, available at: http://www.voxeu.org/index.php?q=node/4495.

Svensson, L. E. (2018). Monetary policy and macroprudential policy: Different and separate? *Canadian Journal of Economics/Revue canadienne d'économique*, **51**(3): 802–827.

Tarullo, D. (2008). Banking on basel: The future of international financial regulation. *Peterson Institute for International Economics*, Washington D.C.

Tarullo, D. K. (2014). Macroprudential regulation. *Yale J. on Reg.* **31**, 505.

Taylor, M. M., Quintyn, M. M., and Hüpkes, M. E. H. (2005). *The accountability of financial sector supervisors: Principles and practice (No. 5–51)*, International Monetary Fund.

Verdier, P.-H. (2013). The political economy of international financial regulation. *Indiana Law Journal*, **88**(4): 1405–1475.

https://doi.org/10.1142/9781786349507_0002

Chapter 2

The Effect of Austerity Measures Under Sovereign Risk and *Financial* Frictions

Xiaofei Ma*

ESSCA School of Management, Department of Finance,
55 Quai Alphonse le Gallo, 92513 Boulogne-Billancourt, France
xiaofei.ma@essca.fr

2.1 Introduction

In this chapter, we analyze the interaction between interbank markets and default risk using a two-country dynamic general equilibrium model, with a focus on the transmission of alternative austerity measures proposed by the government. We also study how the austerity measures in one country transmit through the integrated interbank market to the other country. Interbank markets are at the crossroads of financial and real spheres as they match creditor and debtor banks. Their dynamics crucially affects the amount of credit in the economy, with has effects on investment and GDP. As such, they play an important role in the transmission of fiscal policy decisions.

The austerity measures proposed by the government can have two potential effects on the economy. First, the decline of transfer to

---

*The author is grateful for the kind support from her PhD supervisors Prof. Stéphane Auray and Prof. Aurélien Eyquem. The author is responsible for all remaining errors.

households may reduce the demand for consumption, thus resulting in a contraction of loans and credits supplied to the private sector and interbank market. Second, the austerity measures may reinforce the government's balance sheet and reduce the country's indebtedness, thereby reducing the sovereign default risk and the interest rate of government bonds, releasing the financial tensions in the interbank market and credit supply to private sector. In this chapter, we study the dynamics of these two effects on the economy in the short run and in the long run.

Over the last fifteen years, European banks have increasingly owned government bonds of member countries. In particular, banks of the Core European countries such as France and Germany have gradually become major holders of the sovereign debt issued by Periphery countries like Greece, Italy, Portugal, and Spain. As shown by, who used combined data from the Bank for International Settlements and the Bank of France, the ratio of French banks' holdings of Periphery's sovereign debt over their holdings of French government debt was 56% in the last quarter of 2009, up from 19% in the first quarter of 2005 (Guerrieri *et al.*, 2013). As a consequence, European banks were significantly exposed to the sovereign default risk of Periphery countries. This vicious spiral of twin crises between banks and sovereigns imposes potential losses for banks who invested massively in the sovereign market and resulted in the reduced ability and propensity of banks' to extend lending to the market.

The rising interdependence between interbank and sovereign bonds markets was at the heart of the governments' concerns about rising sovereign risk in the Euro Area. It was also partly exploited by the governments' austerity measures, to release the sovereign risk and tensions on both markets at the same time. To capture this interdependence, we developed a two-country model based on (Guerrieri *et al.*, 2013), who study the international propagation of sovereign debt default, and add an interbank market *à* la (Dib, 2010). We quantify the effects of alternative austerity measures and fiscal policies on financial variables (credit, lending rates), real variables (investment, GDP), and fiscal variables (debt-to-GDP ratios, sovereign spreads). We also compute welfare losses/gains from the crisis and from the various policies, distinguishing between different types of agents (banks, households, entrepreneurs) in the short run and in the long run. Concerning the sovereign risk channel, we differ from

(Guerrieri *et al.*, 2013) and follow (Corsetti *et al.*, 2013), assuming that sovereign default risk is increasingly and positively related to a country's debt-to-GDP ratio. As in (Gertler and Kiyotaki, 2010), we restrict attention to a purely real model and focus on fiscal policies only.

For the banking sector, our model incorporates an optimizing banking sector with two types of monopolistically competitive banks in the interbank market "Savings Banks" and "Borrowing Banks", supplying different banking services and transactions in the interbank market as in (Dib, 2010) and (Auray *et al.*, 2018).[1] Savings Banks are financial intermediaries that are net lenders (creditors) in the interbank market, whereas Borrowing Banks are net borrowers (debtors). Banks have monopoly power when setting real deposit and prime lending rates. Savings Banks collect deposits from workers, set real deposit rates, and optimally choose the composition of their portfolio (composed of government bonds and risky interbank lending). Borrowing Banks borrow from Savings Banks in the interbank market and raise bank capital (equity) from bankers (shareholders) in the financial market to satisfy the capital requirement imposed by the regulation.

Further, following (Goodhart *et al.*, 2006) and (Dib, 2010), we assume endogenous strategic default on interbank borrowing. Finally, we introduce alternative austerity measures in the model as in (Auray *et al.*, 2016). The austerity measures include reducing transfer to households, increasing income tax for workers, increasing capital income tax for entrepreneurs and banks, and increasing VAT tax for consumers. We will simulate the effects of the alternative approach on production, consumption, financial tension, interbank dynamics, credit lending to private sector, and social welfare effects in the short run and long run. We also simulate the effects of alternative austerity measures during the period of bank–sovereign twin crisis. Compared to the previous literature, so far as we know, we are the first to study the potential effects of alternative austerity measures in a two-country model with integrated micro-founded interbank market and

[1]The two different banks are necessary to generate heterogeneity, from which different banks can interact in the interbank market (see Dib (2010)).

study the transmission channel through the international interbank market.

The chapter is organized as follows. Section 2.1 is introduction. Section 2.2 describes the model. Section 2.3 presents the calibration. Section 2.4 discusses the results. Section 2.5 concludes.

2.2 Model

The world economy consists of two types of countries, Core and Periphery. In each country there are infinitely-lived households, entrepreneurs (capital good producers), final good producers, and bankers. All agents of a given type are homogeneous. In addition, in each country there is a government that purchases final goods-financing expenditure with debt and lump-sum taxes. There is one Central Bank in this two-country model, representing the ECB. The final good is produced using labor (non-tradable internationally) and capital. Goods markets are competitive. The banking sector consists of two types of heterogeneous monopolistically competitive banks. We call them "savings" and "borrowing" banks, to indicate that they offer different banking services but interact in the interbank market. The Periphery and the Core have symmetric preferences and technology functional forms, and only the calibration will differ. In what follows, we concentrate on the description of the Periphery, and assume that similar relations hold in the Core country. We assume that the size of Periphery Country is 1, while Core Country has a size of n.

Agents' activities are as follows. In each period, households supply labor to entrepreneurs. Households can save by holding deposits in domestic banks. Entrepreneurs receive loans from banks and invest into physical capital, which they rent to final good producers. Final good producers produce the final good using labor and capital. Saving Banks receive deposits, lend to Borrowing Banks in the interbank market, or purchase non-state contingent government bonds issued by both governments. Borrowing Banks make loans to domestic entrepreneurs combining borrowing from the interbank market and bank capital. Bank capital is held in the form of bonds issued by both governments. Bankers are owners of the two types of banks, from which they receive profits. They consume, save in local government bonds, and accumulate bank capital supplied to Borrowing banks. In our model, the deposit D_{t-1}, loan L_{t-1}, bank capital Z_{t-1}, and physical capital stock K_{t-1} are assumed to be predetermined variables.

2.2.1 *Households*

We focus on the Periphery Country and assume behavioral symmetry in the Core country. Households maximize their expected discounted utility

$$\max_{\{C_t^H, N_t, D_t\}} E_0 \sum_{t=0}^{\infty} \beta_H^t \left[\log(C_t^H) - \frac{\chi_N (N_t)^{1+\eta}}{1+\eta} \right] \tag{2.1}$$

subject to

$$(1+\tau_{ct})C_t^H + D_t + AC_t^H = R_{t-1}^D D_{t-1} + (1-\tau_{nt})W_t N_t \tag{2.2}$$

where C_t^H represents households' consumption, N_t is their labor supply, D_t are households' holdings of deposits in domestic banks, $AC_t^H = \frac{\phi_D}{2}\left(\frac{D_t}{D} - 1\right)^2$ denotes quadratic portfolio adjustment costs paid by the household when deviating from the steady-state value of deposit D. In addition, R_{t-1}^D is the gross real interest rate on deposit between period $t-1$ and period t. W_t is the wage rate, τ_{ct} is the consumption tax imposed on households by the government, and τ_{nt} is the pay-roll tax. First-order condition implies that

$$(1+\tau_{ct})\lambda_t^H = \frac{1}{C_t^H} \tag{2.3}$$

$$\lambda_t^H \left[1 + \frac{\phi_D}{D}\left(\frac{D_t}{D} - 1\right) \right] = \beta_H E_t \left[R_{t+1}^D \lambda_{t+1}^H \right] \tag{2.4}$$

$$\chi_N (N_t)^\eta = \lambda_t^H (1-\tau_{nt}) W_t \tag{2.5}$$

2.2.2 *Bankers*

Bankers are the owners of the two types of banks, from which they receive profits. They consume, save in domestic government bonds, and accumulate bank capital supplied to Borrowing Banks. Bankers thus enter the period with Z_{t-1} shares of bank capital. Bank capital pays a contingent real return R_t^Z, also interpreted as dividend.

Bankers maximize their discounted utility function

$$\max_{\{C_t^B, Z_t, B_t^B\}} \sum_{t=0}^{\infty} \beta_B^t \log C_t^B \tag{2.6}$$

subject to

$$\begin{aligned}
&(1+\tau_{ct})C_t^B + B_t^B + Z_t + AC_t^B \\
&\quad = R_{t-1}(1-p_{t-1})B_{t-1}^B + [1+(1-\tau_{kt})(R_t^Z-1)]Z_{t-1} \\
&\qquad + (1-\tau_{kt})\Pi_t^{sb} + (1-\tau_{kt})\Pi_t^{bb}
\end{aligned} \tag{2.7}$$

where

$$AC_t^B = \frac{\phi_Z}{2}\left(\frac{Z_t}{Z}-1\right)^2 + \frac{\phi_B}{2}\left(\frac{B_t^B}{B^B}-1\right)^2$$

and where C_t^B is the consumption of bankers, B_t^B is the amount of local bonds held by bankers paying R_{t-1} with a possibility of default p_{t-1} in period $t-1$. Π_t^{sb} and Π_t^{bb} are the profits of savings banks and borrowing banks, respectively, and τ_{kt}^B is the capital-income tax paid to the government. First-order condition is

$$(1+\tau_{ct})\lambda_t^B = \frac{1}{C_t^B} \tag{2.8}$$

$$1 + \frac{\phi_B}{B^B}\left(\frac{B_t^B}{B^B}-1\right) = \beta_B E_t\left(\frac{\lambda_{t+1}^B}{\lambda_t^B} R_t\left(1-p_t\right)\right) \tag{2.9}$$

$$1 + \frac{\phi_Z}{Z}\left(\frac{Z_t}{Z}-1\right) = \beta_B E_t\left(\frac{\lambda_{t+1}^B}{\lambda_t^B}(1+(1-\tau_{kt+1})(R_{t+1}^Z-1))\right) \tag{2.10}$$

2.2.3 *Banks*

The banking sector of each country consists of two types of heterogeneous profit-maximizing banks: the Savings Banks (SBs) and Borrowing Banks (BBs).

2.2.3.1 *Savings banks*

Savings Banks (SBs) refer to all financial intermediaries that are net creditors (lenders) in the interbank market. There is a continuum of monopolistically competitive, profit-maximizing SBs indexed by $j \in (0,1)$. Each SB j collects fully insured deposits from workers $D_{j,t}$ and pays a deposit interest rate $R^D_{j,t}$, which is optimally set as a markdown over the marginal return of its assets.

The supply of deposits is given by

$$D_{j,t} = \left(\frac{R^D_{j,t} - 1}{R^D_t - 1}\right)^{\upsilon_D} D_{t-1} \tag{2.11}$$

where $\upsilon_D > 1$ is the elasticity of substitution between different types of deposits and D_t is the total amount of deposits. SB j optimally allocates a fraction $s_{j,t}$ of deposits to lending in the domestic and foreign interbank markets that return $R^{IB,C}_t$ and $R^{IB,P}_t$, respectively. SB j also uses the remaining fraction $1 - s_{j,t}$ to purchase government bonds, both domestic and foreign. Lending on the interbank market is subject to a default probability δ^D_t and induces a quadratic monitoring cost

$$\Delta^s_{j,t} = \frac{\chi_s}{2}((s_{j,t} - \bar{s})D_{j,t})^2 \tag{2.12}$$

that depends on deviations of $s_{j,t}$ from a constant target $\bar{s}$. The remaining fraction of deposits is allocated to bonds and split between domestic bonds and foreign bonds. These assets pay $R^P_{t-1}(1-p^P_{t-1})$ for bonds issued in the Periphery and $R^C_{t-1}(1-p^C_{t-1})$ in the Core between period $t-1$ and t, where p^P_{t-1} and p^C_{t-1} are the percentage default rates, that can also be interpreted as *ex ante* default probabilities in both countries.

Changing the composition of bonds portfolio incurs the payment of adjustment cost

$$Ad^B_{j,t} = \frac{\phi_{\delta^B}}{2}\left(\frac{\delta^B_{j,t}}{\delta^B} - 1\right)^2 \tag{2.13}$$

Meanwhile, changing the composition of the portfolio of interbank lending incurs a similar adjustment cost

$$Ad^{IB}_{j,t} = \frac{\phi_{\delta^{IB}}}{2}\left(\frac{\delta^{IB}_{j,t}}{\delta^{IB}} - 1\right)^2 \tag{2.14}$$

Formally, the jth saving bank's optimization problem is

$$\max_{\{s_{j,t},R^D_{j,t},\delta^B_{j,t},\delta^{IB}_{j,t}\}} E_0 \sum_{t=0}^{\infty} \beta^t_B \lambda^B_t \Big\{ [s_{j,t} R^{IB,SB}_t + (1 - s_{j,t}) R^B_t$$
$$- R^D_{j,t}] D_{j,t} - \Delta^s_{j,t} \Big\} \tag{2.15}$$

where

$$R^B_t = \delta^B_t R^P_t (1 - p^P_t) + (1 - \delta^B_t) R^C_t (1 - p^C_t) - Ad^B_{j,t} \tag{2.16}$$

and

$$R^{IB,SB}_t = \delta^{IB}_t R^{IB,P}_t (1 - \delta^{D,P}_t) + (1 - \delta^{IB}_t) R^{IB,C}_t (1 - \delta^{D,C}_t) - Ad^{IB}_{j,t} \tag{2.17}$$

subject to the constraints above.

In the definition of R^B_t, δ^B_t is the fraction of deposits invested in bonds issued in the Periphery, and R^P_t and R^C_t are the gross returns on bonds in the Periphery and Core countries, respectively.

Similarly, in the definition of $R^{IB,SB}_t$, δ^{IB}_t is the fraction of deposits invested in the Periphery interbank market, $R^{IB,P}_t$ and $R^{IB,C}_t$ are the gross returns of interbank lending in the Periphery and Core countries, respectively; $\delta^{D,P}_t$ and $\delta^{D,C}_t$ are the default probabilities on interbank lending in the Periphery and Core countries, respectively.

In the symmetric situation, where $s_{j,t} = s_t$ and $R^D_{j,t} = R^D_t$ for all $t > 0$, the first-order conditions of this optimization problem with respect to s_t, R^D_t, $\delta^B_{j,t}$, and $\delta^{IB}_{j,t}$ are

$$s_t = \bar{s} + \frac{R^{IB,SB}_t - R^B_t}{\chi_s D_{t-1}} \tag{2.18}$$

$$\frac{1 + \upsilon_D}{\upsilon_D}(R^D_t - 1) = [s_t R^{IB,SB}_t + (1 - s_t) R^B_t - 1] - \chi_s (s_t - \bar{s})^2 D_{t-1} \tag{2.19}$$

$$\frac{\delta^B_t}{\delta^B} = 1 + \frac{\delta^B}{\phi_{\delta^B}} [R^P_t (1 - p^P_t) - R^C_t (1 - p^C_t)] \tag{2.20}$$

$$\frac{\delta^{IB}_t}{\delta^{IB}} = 1 + \frac{\delta^{IB}}{\phi_{\delta^{IB}}} [R^{IB,P}_t (1 - \delta^{D,P}_t) - R^{IB,C}_t (1 - \delta^{D,C}_t)] \tag{2.21}$$

2.2.3.2 *Borrowing banks*

Borrowing Banks (BBs) refer to all net debtor (borrower) banks in the interbank market. There is a continuum of monopolistically competitive BBs indexed by $j \in (0,1)$. BBs borrow from SBs in the interbank market and raise bank capital from bankers to satisfy the capital requirement. We assume that the stock of bank capital $Z_{j,t}$ is held by the BBs as government bonds in a portfolio with a fraction δ_t^{BB} invested in government bonds issued by the Periphery.[2]

In addition, BBs can receive money from the Central Bank, which can be interpreted as quantitative easing.[3] To produce loans $L_{j,t}$ supplied to entrepreneurs, each borrowing bank j combines funds received from SBs in the interbank market, $D_{j,t}^{IB}$.

We assume that BBs use the following Leontief technology to produce loans

$$L_{j,t} = \min\{D_{j,t}^{IB};\ \kappa_{j,t}Z_{j,t}\}\Gamma_t \tag{2.22}$$

where $\kappa_{j,t} \leq \overline{\kappa}$ is bank j's leverage ratio and $\overline{\kappa}$ is the maximum leverage ratio imposed by regulators. Γ_t is a shock to the financial intermediation process affecting credit supply. Leontief technology implies perfect complementarity between interbank borrowing and bank capital, and imposes the capital requirement, which attenuates the real effects of different shocks. When lending to entrepreneurs, BB j faces the following demand function for loans

$$L_{j,t} = \left(\frac{R_{j,t}^L - 1}{R_t^L - 1}\right)^{-\upsilon_L} L_{t-1} \tag{2.23}$$

where $\upsilon_L > 1$ is the elasticity of substitution between different types of loans. The BB j optimally sets the prime lending rate, $R_{j,t}^L$, as a markup over the marginal cost of producing loans.

The jth BB's leverage ratio is given by $\kappa_{j,t} = \frac{L_{j,t}}{\Gamma_t Z_{j,t}}$, which is subject to the maximum leverage ratio imposed by the regulators, $\overline{\kappa}$. Whenever BBs have a lower-than-target leverage ratio, they receive

[2] $Z_{j,t} = Z_{t-1}$ in symmetric case.

[3] Nominal money divided by the price index.

convex gains in the form of

$$\Delta^{\kappa}_{j,t} = \frac{\chi_{\kappa}}{2}\left(\left(\frac{\overline{\kappa} - \kappa_{j,t}}{\overline{\kappa}}\right)\right)^2 Z_{j,t} \tag{2.24}$$

Moreover, following (Goodhart *et al.*, 2006) we allow BBs to optimally default on a fraction of their interbank borrowing, $\delta^D_{j,t} > 0$. The default on interbank lending can be strategic or mandatory (when banks cannot afford to repay their debt). Nonetheless, it is costly for banks to default on the interbank borrowing. In this case, banks must pay convex penalties in the next period. The jth bank's penalty is given by

$$\Delta^D_{j,t} = \frac{\chi_{\delta^D}}{2}\left(\delta^D_{j,t-1} D^{IB}_{j,t-1}\right)^2 R^{IB}_{t-1} \tag{2.25}$$

where χ_{δ^D} is a positive parameter determining the steady-state value of $\Delta^D_{j,t}$. Furthermore, we assume that borrowing banks bear the same adjustment cost as SBs when they adjust the holding of domestic and foreign government bonds.

The jth borrowing bank's optimization problem is thus

$$\max_{\{R^L_{j,t},\delta^D_{j,t}\}} E_0 \sum_{t=0}^{\infty} \beta^t_B \lambda^B_t \left\{ \begin{array}{c} R^L_{j,t} L_{j,t} - (1-\delta^D_{j,t}) R^{IB}_t D^{IB}_{j,t} \\ -(R^Z_t - R^B_t) Z_{j,t} \\ -\Delta^D_{j,t} + \Delta^{\kappa}_{j,t} \end{array} \right\} \tag{2.26}$$

subject to the equations listed above. In the symmetric equilibrium, where $R^L_{j,t} = R^L$, $\kappa_{j,t} = \kappa_t$, $\delta^D_{j,t} = \delta^D_t$, for all $t > 0$. The first-order conditions of this optimization problem are

$$\frac{\upsilon_L - 1}{\upsilon_L}(R^L_t - 1) = \Omega_t - 1 \tag{2.27}$$

$$\delta^D_t = E_t\left(\frac{\lambda^B_t}{\beta_B \lambda^B_{t+1}} \frac{1}{\chi_{\delta^D} D^{IB}_t}\right) \tag{2.28}$$

where Ω_t is the marginal production cost of loans

$$\Omega_t = \Gamma^{-1}_t \left[(1-\delta^D_t) R^{IB}_t + E_t \beta_B \chi_{\delta^D} \frac{\lambda^B_{t+1}}{\lambda^B_t} (\delta^D_t)^2 R^{IB}_t D^{IB}_t \right.$$
$$\left. + \frac{\chi_{\kappa}(\overline{\kappa} - \kappa_t)}{\overline{\kappa}^2}\right] \tag{2.29}$$

2.2.4 *Entrepreneurs*

In each country, there is a continuum of identical infinitely-lived entrepreneurs who borrow from local BBs, consume, and accumulate physical capital that depreciates at rate δ. Entrepreneurs maximize their lifetime utility

$$\max_{\{C_t^E, K_t, L_t\}} \sum_{t=0}^{\infty} \beta_E^t \log C_t^E \tag{2.30}$$

subject to the budget constraint

$$\begin{aligned}(1+\tau_{ct})C_t^E + K_t + R_t^L L_{t-1} + AC_t^E \\ = [1+(1-\tau_{kt})(R_{K,t}-\delta)]K_{t-1} + L_t\end{aligned} \tag{2.31}$$

where

$$AC_t^E = \frac{\phi_I^E}{2}\left(\frac{I_t}{I}-1\right)^2 + \frac{\phi_L^E}{2}\left(\frac{L_t}{L_{t-1}}-1\right)^2 \tag{2.32}$$

denotes quadratic portfolio adjustment costs paid by the entrepreneurs to change the investment, and the holdings of loans. The investment I_t is defined as

$$I_t = K_t - (1-\delta)K_{t-1} \tag{2.33}$$

In addition, entrepreneurs are subject to a constraint that limits their leverage to a constant fraction m of their capital holdings

$$L_t = \rho_E L_{t-1} + (1-\rho_E)mK_t \tag{2.34}$$

where the parameter ρ_E captures the elasticity of the loan limit to the current capital choice of the entrepreneur. Therefore, the FOCs of the program are

$$(1+\tau_{ct})\lambda_t = \frac{1}{C_t^E} \tag{2.35}$$

$$\begin{aligned}\lambda_t\left[1+\frac{\phi_I^E}{\delta K}\left(\frac{I_t}{\delta K}-1\right) - \frac{\beta_E\phi_I^E(1-\delta)}{\delta K}\left(\frac{I_{t+1}}{\delta K}-1\right)\right] \\ -m(1-\rho_E)\widetilde{\lambda}_t\end{aligned} \tag{2.36}$$

$$= \beta_E E_t \lambda_{t+1}[1 + (1 - \tau_{kt+1})(R_{K,t+1} - \delta)] \tag{2.37}$$

$$\lambda_t \left[\frac{\phi_L^E}{L_{t-1}}\left(\frac{L_t}{L_{t-1}} - 1\right) - 1\right] + \tilde{\lambda}_t$$
$$= E_t \beta_E \lambda_{t+1}\left[\frac{\phi_L L_{t+1}}{L_t^2}\left(\frac{L_{t+1}}{L_t} - 1\right) - R_{L,t+1}\right] + \beta_E \tilde{\lambda}_{t+1}\rho_E \tag{2.38}$$

where λ_t and $\tilde{\lambda}_t$ are the Lagrange multipliers for constraints (2.31) and (2.34).

2.2.5 *Final good producers*

The representative final good producer operates a Cobb–Douglas production function given by

$$Y_t = A_t(K_{t-1})^{\alpha}(N_t)^{1-\alpha}$$

where Y_t is the output of domestic final good, K_{t-1} is the capital stock rented from entrepreneurs at the rate, $R_{K,t}$, N_t is the labor input, and A_t is a stochastic process for productivity. Producers make zero profits because of perfect competition and constant returns to scale. With competitive factor market and profit maximizing producers, we have

$$W_t = (1 - \alpha)\frac{Y_t}{N_t}$$

$$R_{K,t} = \alpha\frac{Y_t}{K_{t-1}}$$

2.2.6 *Governments*

Government spending is financed through taxes on households, entrepreneurs, bankers, and through debt. The government budget constraint in the Periphery Country is

$$B_t - R_{t-1}(1 - p_{t-1})B_{t-1}$$
$$= G_t - \{\tau_{ct}C_t + \tau_{nt}W_tN_t + \tau_{kt}[(R_t^Z - 1)Z_{t-1}$$
$$+\Pi_t^{sb} + \Pi_t^{bb} + (R_{K,t} - \delta)K_{t-1}]\} \tag{2.39}$$

where G_t is exogenous government spending, B_t is the amount of government bonds issued in the Periphery. Public expenditure is financed at time t by raising taxes, issuing additional debt, or partially defaulting on debt issued in the past.

We assume that government spending has a counter-cyclical component seeking to stabilize the business cycle. In addition, we impose a cut on government spending when the probability of default rises

$$G_t = \rho_B G_{t-1} + (1-\rho_B)(G - \sigma(Y_t - Y) - \gamma(B_{t-1} - B)) + \varepsilon_{gt} \quad (2.40)$$

The distorsive taxes follow the rules

$$\tau_{ct} = \rho_B \tau_{ct-1} + (1-\rho_B)[\tau_c - \phi(B_t/Y_t - B/Y)] + \varepsilon_{\tau_c t}$$
$$\tau_{nt} = \rho_B \tau_{nt-1} + (1-\rho_B)[\tau_n - \phi(B_t/Y_t - B/Y)] + \varepsilon_{\tau_n t}$$
$$\tau_{kt} = \rho_B \tau_{kt-1} + (1-\rho_B)[\tau_k - \phi(B_t/Y_t - B/Y)] + \varepsilon_{\tau_k t}$$

2.2.7 *Sovereign default risk*

There are mainly two strands of literatures about sovereign default. On one hand (Eaton and Gersovitz, 1981; Arellano, 2008), and others have modeled default as a strategic decision of the government. On the other hand (Bi, 2012), considers default as the consequence of the government's inability to raise funds used to honor its debt obligations. Under both approaches, the probability of sovereign default is closely and nonlinearly related to the level of public debt to GDP. We adopt the approach from (Corsetti *et al.*, 2013), in which the *ex ante* probability of default, p_t, at a certain level of sovereign indebtedness, $b_t = B_t/(4Y_t)$, will be given by the cumulative distribution function of the beta distribution

$$p_t = F_{beta}(b_t/b_{max}, \alpha_{b^g}, \beta_{b^g}) \quad (2.41)$$

where b_{max} denotes the upper end of the support for the debt-to-GDP ratio. We focus on the *ex ante* probability of sovereign default because the *ex ante* default risk is crucial for the pricing of government debt.

2.2.8 *Equilibrium*

We assume that the Core country is characterized by similar equilibrium conditions. An equilibrium is defined as a sequence of prices and quantities such that all agents solve their optimization problems, and that prices clear the following markets

(1) Production factor markets
(2) Loan markets
(3) Bank capital markets

$$Z^P_{t-1} = \frac{L^P_{t-1}}{\Gamma^P_t \kappa^P_t} - X^P_t$$

$$Z^C_{t-1} = \frac{L^C_{t-1}}{\Gamma^C_t \kappa^C_t} - X^C_t$$

(4) The goods market

$$\begin{aligned} Y^P_t + nY^C_t = {} & (C^{H,P}_t + C^{B,P}_t + C^{E,P}_t) + n(C^{H,C}_t + C^{B,C}_t + C^{E,C}_t) \\ & (K^P_t - (1-\delta)K^P_{t-1}) + n(K^C_t - (1-\delta)K^C_{t-1}) \\ & + G^P_t + G^C_t + \text{adjustment/monitoring costs} \\ & - \text{gains from excess bank capital} \end{aligned}$$

(5) The interbank market

$$\delta^{IB,P}_t s^P_t D^P_{t-1} + n\delta^{IB,C}_t s^C_t D^C_{t-1} = D^{IB,P}_t = \frac{L^P_{t-1}}{\Gamma^P_t} - M^P_t$$

$$\begin{aligned} & n(1-\delta^{IB,C}_t)s^C_t D^C_{t-1} + (1-\delta^{IB,P}_t)s^P_t D^P_{t-1} = nD^{IB,C}_t \\ & = n\left(\frac{L^C_{t-1}}{\Gamma^C_t} - M^C_t\right) \end{aligned}$$

(6) Sovereign debt markets

$$\begin{aligned} B^P_t = {} & B^{B,P}_t + \delta^{B,P}_t[(1-s^P_t)D^P_{t-1} + Z^P_{t-1} + X^P_t] \\ & + n\delta^{B,C}_t[(1-s^C_t)D^C_{t-1} + Z^C_{t-1} + X^C_t] \\ B^C_t = {} & B^{B,P}_t + (1-\delta^{B,P}_t)[(1-s^P_t)D^P_{t-1} + Z^P_{t-1} + X^P_t] \\ & + n(1-\delta^{B,C}_t)[(1-s^C_t)D^C_{t-1} + Z^C_{t-1} + X^C_t] \end{aligned}$$

2.2.9 *Shock processes*

The economy is subject to productivity, government expenditure, interbank tension, and conventional and unconventional monetary policy shocks.

Government spending shock is given by equation (2.40). The left structural shocks follow AR(1) processes

$$\log(\Lambda_t) = (1 - \rho_\Lambda)\log(\Lambda) + \rho_\Lambda \log(\Lambda_{t-1}) + \varepsilon_{\Lambda_t}$$

where $\Lambda_t = \{A_t, \Gamma_t, \tau_{ct}, \tau_{nt}, \tau_{kt}\}$; $\Lambda \geq 0$ is the steady-state value of Λ_t; $\rho_\Lambda \in (0,1)$; and $\varepsilon_{\Lambda_t} \sim N(0, \sigma_\Lambda)$.

2.3 Calibration

We calibrate the model to the Euro Area. The time unit is a quarter. The Periphery comprises Greece, Italy, Portugal, and Spain, while the Core is made of remaining members of the monetary union. We choose the households' discount factor, β_H, to be symmetric and equal to 0.9975, implying an annual real interest rate on deposits of 1%. The inverse of the Frisch elasticity of labor supply is $\eta = 2$. The discount factors of bankers and entrepreneurs are set equal to 0.997 and 0.99, respectively.

On the production side, the depreciation rate δ is 0.03 and the capital share in production α is 0.33. We set investment adjustment costs $\phi_I^E = 2.5$ to match the relative volatility (standard deviation) of investment as much as possible. Entrepreneurs also pay a convex cost for adjusting loans; we set $\phi_L^E = 0.05$ as in (Guerrieri *et al.*, 2013). We set the parameter governing entrepreneurs' working capital constraint $\rho_E = 0.75$ m is chosen so that its value matches the ratio of outstanding loans over capital stocks.

Moving to the government, the debt ceiling parameter $\bar{b}$ is 3.4 for the Periphery bloc and 2.4 for the Core bloc. These choices imply a debt-to-GDP ratio equal to 0.85 in the Periphery and 0.6 in the Core, in line with data from the IMF Economic Outlook for 2010. Steady-state tax rates are calibrated to represent 45% of the consumption of each type of agent and remain constant over simulations. In terms of sovereign default risk, we follow (Corsetti *et al.*, 2013), and choose parameters $\alpha_{bg} = 3.70$, $\beta_{bg} = 0.54$, $b_{max} = 2.56$. In the public spending process, we assume a $\rho_B = 0.81$ persistence, the coefficient on default risk is $\gamma = 0.025$ in the Core and $\gamma = 0.05$ in the Periphery, and the coefficient on output is $\sigma = 0.25$ in the Core and $\sigma = 0$ in the Periphery. These different coefficients are set to match differences in cyclical patterns of public spending between the Core and Periphery, as well as sovereign spread volatilities.

Households pay a cost for adjusting deposits, so we set $\phi_D = 0.05$. In the banker's problem, the parameter measuring the convexity of the adjusting cost function, ϕ_B, denotes how costly it is for the bankers to adjust domestic and foreign bonds we set $\phi_B = 0.01$.

To apportion the steady-state holdings of government debt to households, Periphery, and Core banks, we adopt the calibration in (Guerrieri *et al.*, 2013), i.e. 41.7% the share of public debt of the Periphery is held by the Core bloc, 18.8% is held by Periphery households, and 39.5% is allocated to Periphery banks. For the Core government debt, 11% of their collective sovereign debt is held by households in Core countries, and 70% of the total is assigned to Core banks.

In the interbank sector, the parameter χ_s determines the ratio of bank lending to total assets held by the savings banks s_t. It is set so that the steady-state value of s_t is equal to 0.64 for the Periphery and 0.86 for the Core, which corresponds to the historical ratio observed in the data.[4] The parameter χ_κ is set so that we could have a reasonable value for ν_L, i.e. around 4.

Based on the Basel II minimum required bank capital ratio of 8%, we assume that the maximum imposed bank leverage, $\bar{\kappa}$, is 5.36 for Periphery and 4.03 for Core.[5] Similarly, we calibrate χ_{δ_D}, the parameter determining the total cost of banks' defaults on interbank borrowing, so that the probability of default in the interbank market equals 0.2% in annual term.

The parameters ν_D and ν_L, which measure the degrees of monopoly power of Savings and Borrowing banks, are set to match the historical averages of real deposit and loan rates, R^D and R^L.

For the distorsive tax rates, we follow the calibration in (Auray *et al.*, 2016) and we set the steady-state consumption tax rate

[4]This is significantly smaller than in the US (0.82), which might have helped Europe to offset the impact from the 2008 subprime crisis.

[5]Before Basel II, the maximum ratio of bank asset/capital is the reciprocal of required capital ratio, which equals to 12.5. However, loans are only a part of bank assets. The leverage ratio in our model equals to loans/bank capital.

$\tau_c = 0.19$, the labor income tax rate $\tau_n = 0.38$, and the capital income rate $\tau_k = 0.41$.

Table 2.1 summarizes the parameterization and shows the implied steady-state value of key variables in the model.

Table 2.1. Parameter and steady-state values.

	Parameter values			Steady-state values	
	Periphery	**Core**		**Periphery**	**Core**
β_H	0.9975	0.9975	A	1.00	1.21
β_B	0.997	0.997	Y	3.9860	6.1067
β_E	0.99	0.99	W	1.9249	2.5581
η	2.00	2.00	N	0.3481	0.2619
m	0.4580	0.4550	$\bar{s}$	0.5	0.75
δ	0.03	0.03	s	0.64	0.86
α	0.33	0.33	$\bar{\kappa}$	5.3619	4.0387
ρ_E	0.75	0.75	κ	4.9330	3.7156
ν_D	3.35	2.88	Γ	1.00	1.00
ν_L	3.88	3.86	R^D	1.0025	1.0025
χ_s	0.00019	0.00015	R^L	1.007	1.007
χ_κ	0.08	0.06	R^{IB}	1.004	1.004
χ_{δ_D}	128.93	84.73	$R^{P/C}$	1.0093	1.0047
ϕ_D	0.05	0.05	R^Z	1.0030	1.0030
ϕ_Z	70	70	R_E^K	1.0387	1.0387
ϕ_B	0.01	0.01	δ^D	0.0005	0.0005
ϕ_I^E	2.50	2.50	D/Y	4.55	4.80
ϕ_L^E	0.05	0.05	T^H/Y	0.2115	0.2117
$\phi_{\delta B}$	0.01	0.01	C^H/Y	0.4699	0.4704
$\phi_{\delta IB}$	0.01	0.01	Z/Y	0.7913	1.0435
ρ_B	0.81	0.81	B^B/Y	1.9168	0.4452
γ	0.05	0.025	T^B/Y	0.0079	0.0069
σ	0.00	0.25	C^B/Y	0.0175	0.0154
α_{Bg}	3.70	3.70	Π^{SB}/Y	0.0036	0.0043
β_{Bg}	0.54	0.54	Π^{BB}/Y	0.0137	0.0136
b_{max}	2.56	2.56	K^E/Y	8.5223	8.5203
$size$	1	2.58	T^E/Y	0.0146	0.0147
ϕ	0.1	0.1	L/Y	3.9035	3.8772
			C^E/Y	0.0324	0.0326
			D^{IB}/Y	3.9035	3.8772
			$G/(sizeY)$	0.2237	0.2260
			$B/(sizeY)$	3.4	2.4
			τ_c	0.19	0.19
			τ_n	0.38	0.38
			τ_k	0.41	0.41

2.4 Simulations

In this section, we simulate the effects of increasing the consumption tax, the pay-roll tax and the capital-income tax, respectively in the Periphery Country.

2.4.1 *Effects of a rise on the consumption tax*

In this part, we simulate the effects of a rise of 0.1 pp on the consumption tax in the Periphery Country (Figures 2.1–2.5). The IRFs show that the rise of consumption tax reduces the government indebtedness, releases the government bond yield, which reduced the interbank interest rate and loan's interest rate (in the short run) in the Periphery Country. The fall of consumption in the Periphery Country reduces demand in the market, then the demand of investment in

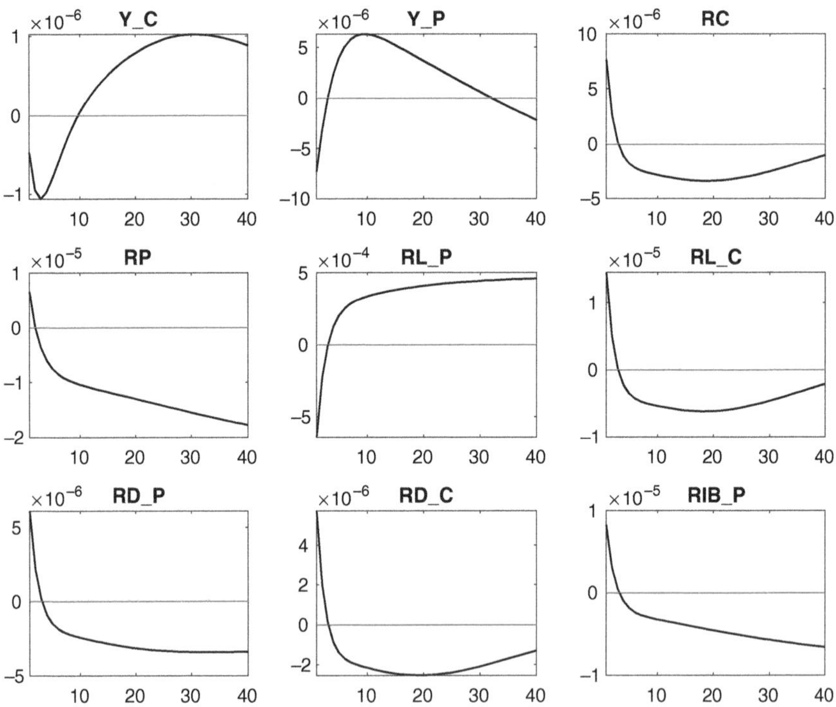

Fig. 2.1. The effects of a rise of 0.1 pp on the consumption tax in the Periphery Country — 1.

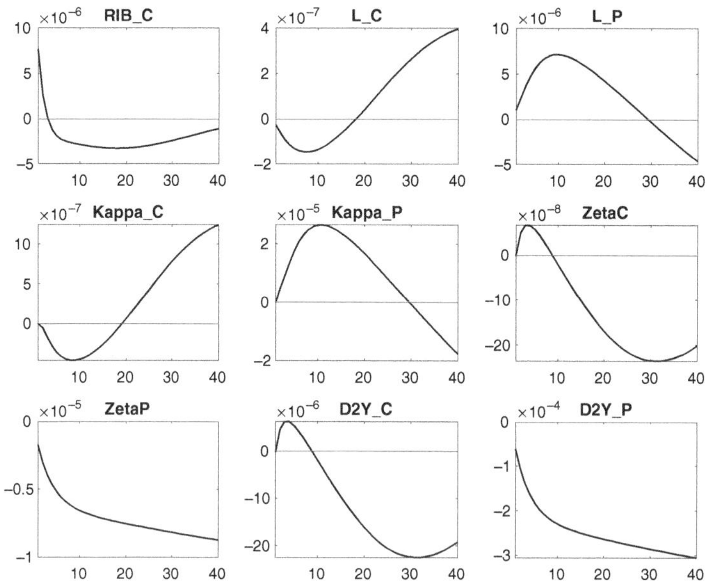

Fig. 2.2. The effects of a rise of 0.1 pp on the consumption tax in the Periphery Country — 2.

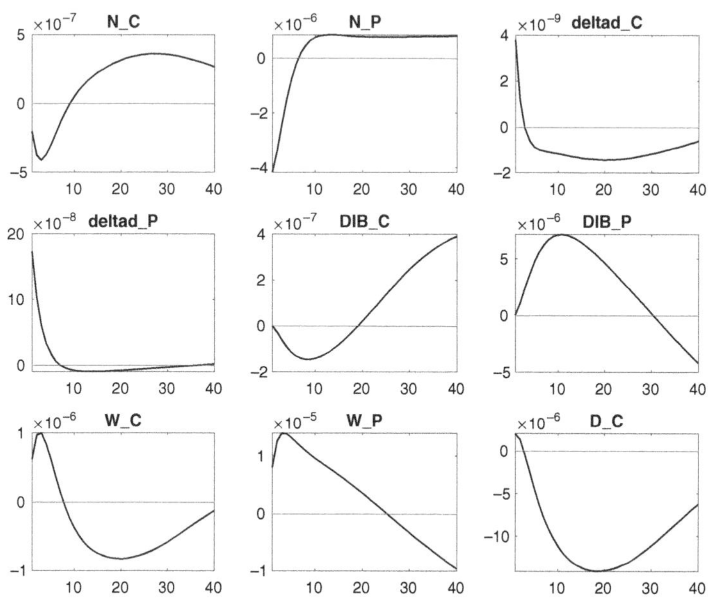

Fig. 2.3. The effects of a rise of 0.1 pp on the consumption tax in the Periphery Country — 3.

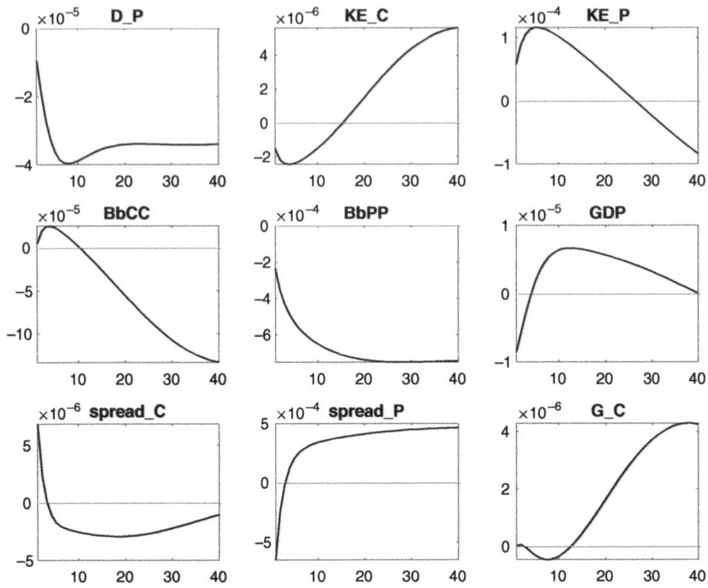

Fig. 2.4. The effects of a rise of 0.1 pp on the consumption tax in the Periphery Country — 4.

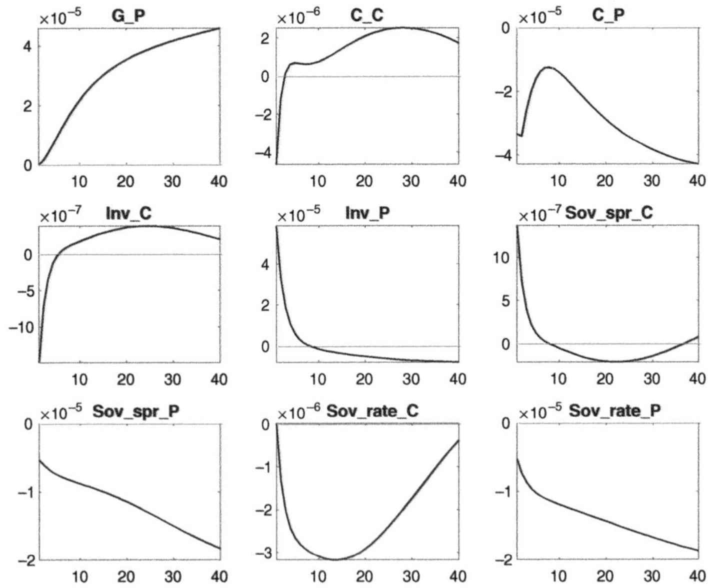

Fig. 2.5. The effects of a rise of 0.1 pp on the consumption tax in the Periphery Country — 5.

the credit market. Therefore, the loan's interest rate falls in the short run as a result of less demand and the fall of interbank interest rate. Naturally, the loans in the Periphery Country increase, which later drives up the loan's interest rate in the Periphery Country. If we look at the production, it first decreases because of the austerity measure that depresses consumption in short term, but later increases thanks to the rise of investment. The effects of austerity measures on the consumption tax in the Periphery Country are transmitted to the Core Country through the interbank market. The government bond yield in the Periphery Country first rises then falls thanks to the release of debt burden; therefore, the deposit interest rate in the Periphery Country first rises then falls as the savings banks set the deposit interest rate according to the government bond yield and the interbank interest rate. The interbank interest rate in the Periphery Country first rises and then falls because the savings banks arbitrate between interbank lending and the government bonds. As banks arbitrate between domestic interbank market and the foreign interbank market; naturally, the interbank interest rate in the Core Country follows the same movement, i.e. first rises then falls. Therefore, the loans' interest rate in the Core Country falls in the long run, which results in the rise of production in long run for the Core Country.

2.4.2 *Effects of a rise on the pay-roll tax*

In this part, we simulate the effects of a rise of 0.1 pp on the pay-roll tax in the Periphery Country (Figures 2.6–2.10). The rise of pay-roll tax first reduces the wage in Periphery Country; as the net wage decreases, the labor market becomes less attractive, as a results there are less people looking for jobs in the labor market. This demand–supply equilibrium in the labor market pushes the wage level up. The increase of wage together with the fall of sovereign debt due to the austerity measure on pay-roll tax raise the demand in the good market and in the credit market. Therefore, the production in the Periphery Country first falls then rises in the long run. The rise of wage drives up the demand, and thus the investment in the Periphery Country rises. As a result, the loan interest rate increases in the Periphery Country. The effects of the Periphery Country's austerity measures are transmitted to the Core Country through the interbank market. As there are more savings in the bank, the deposit

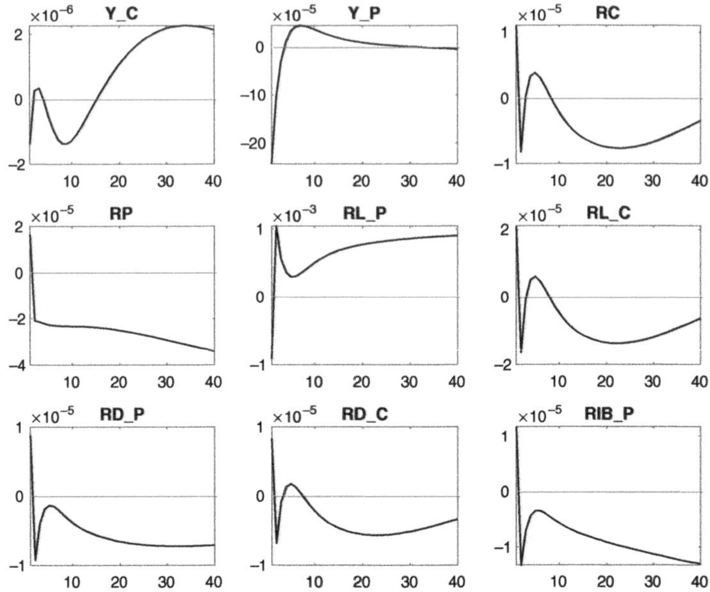

Fig. 2.6. The effects of a rise of 0.1 pp on the pay-roll tax in the Periphery Country — 1.

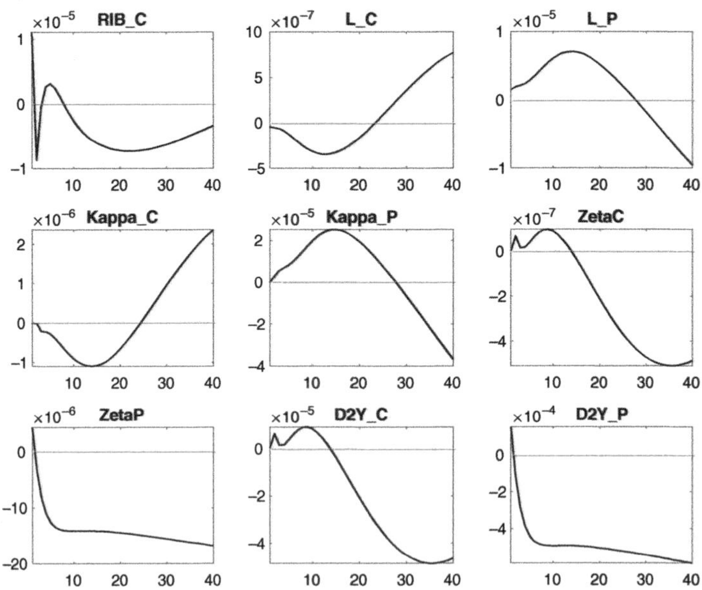

Fig. 2.7. The effects of a rise of 0.1 pp on the pay-roll tax in the Periphery Country — 2.

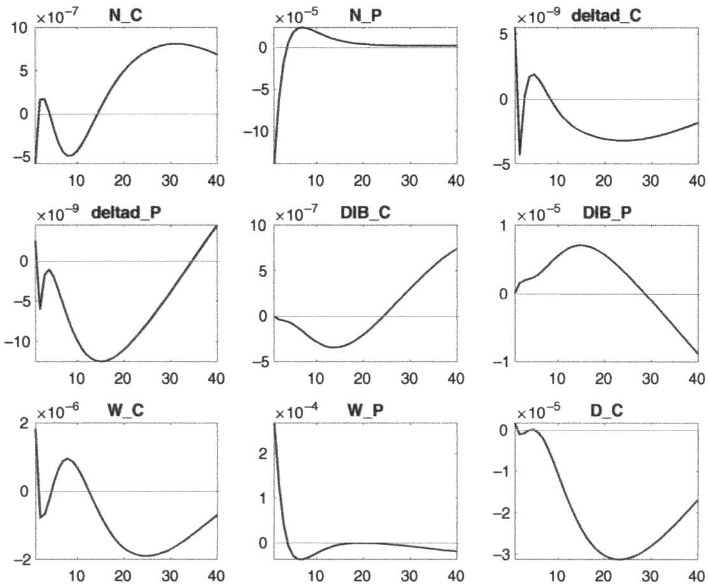

Fig. 2.8. The effects of a rise of 0.1 pp on the pay-roll tax in the Periphery Country — 3.

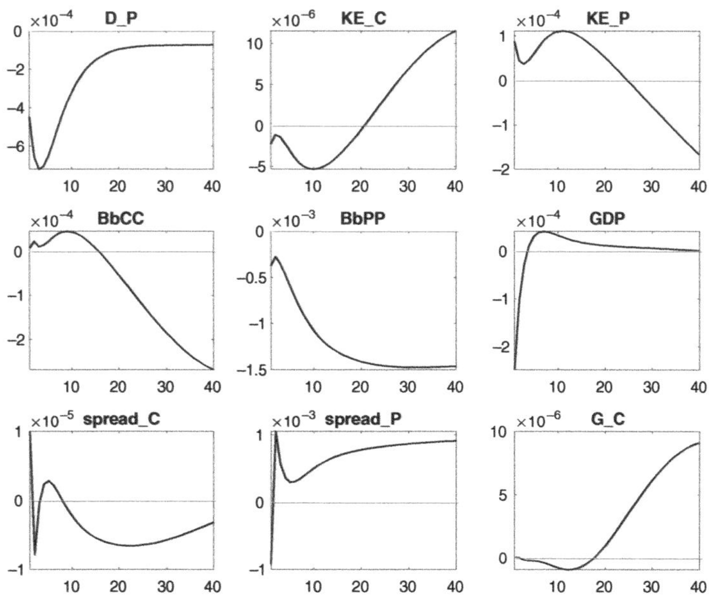

Fig. 2.9. The effects of a rise of 0.1 pp on the pay-roll tax in the Periphery Country — 4.

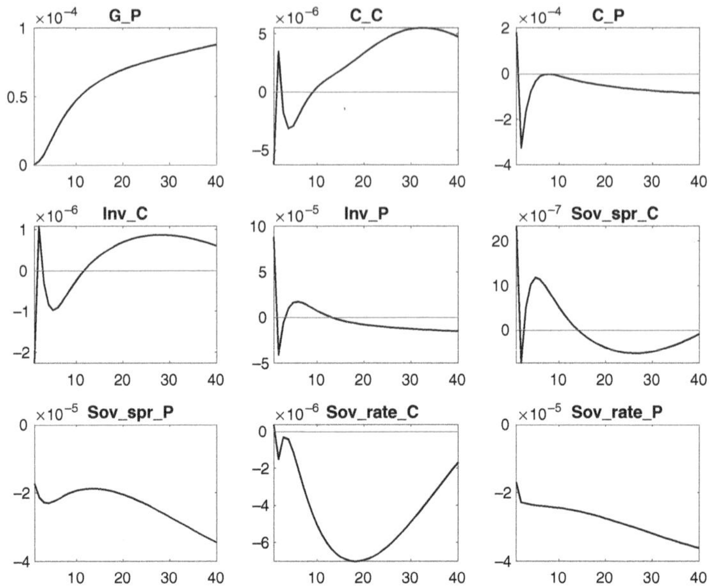

Fig. 2.10. The effects of a rise of 0.1 pp on the pay-roll tax in the Periphery Country — 5.

interest rate in the Periphery Country falls; thus the interbank interest rate in Periphery Country falls. Due to the arbitrage effect, the interbank interest rate in the Core Country falls as well. As a result, the loan interest rate in the Core Country falls in the long run, which encourages the investment in the Core Country. Therefore, the production in Core Country falls in the short run but increases in long run.

2.4.3 *Effects of a rise on the capital-income tax*

In this part, we simulate the effects of a rise of 0.1 pp on the capital-income tax (Figures 2.11–2.15). Different from the two previous policies, in this experiment with capital-income tax, the production first increases then falls in the long run. Indeed, the rise of capital-income tax reduces the demand of investment for both bankers and the banks. As a result, the interbank loans fall. The fall of investment reduces the production. As a result, the government increases its indebtedness in order to balance the fall in production. The rise of

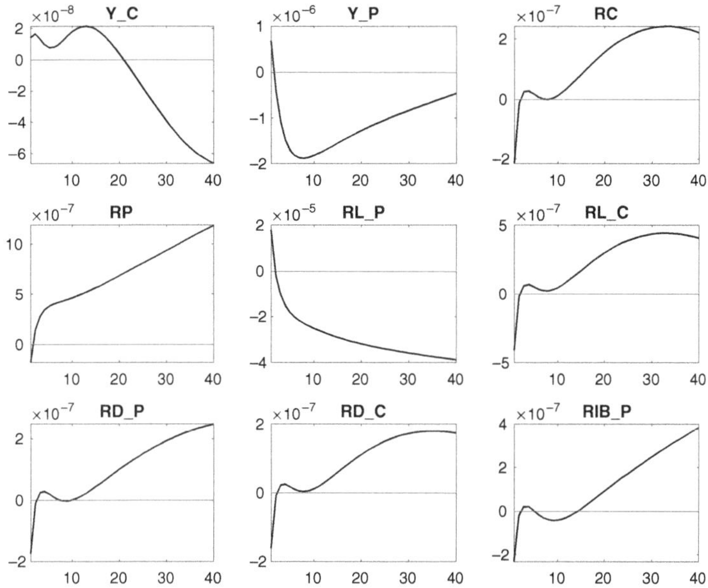

Fig. 2.11. The effects of a rise of 0.1 pp on the capital-income tax in the Periphery Country — 1.

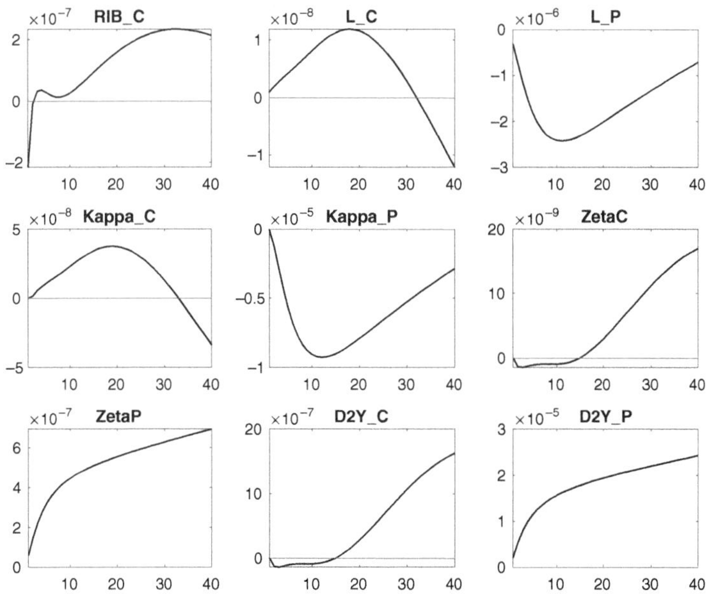

Fig. 2.12. The effects of a rise of 0.1 pp on the capital-income tax in the Periphery Country — 2.

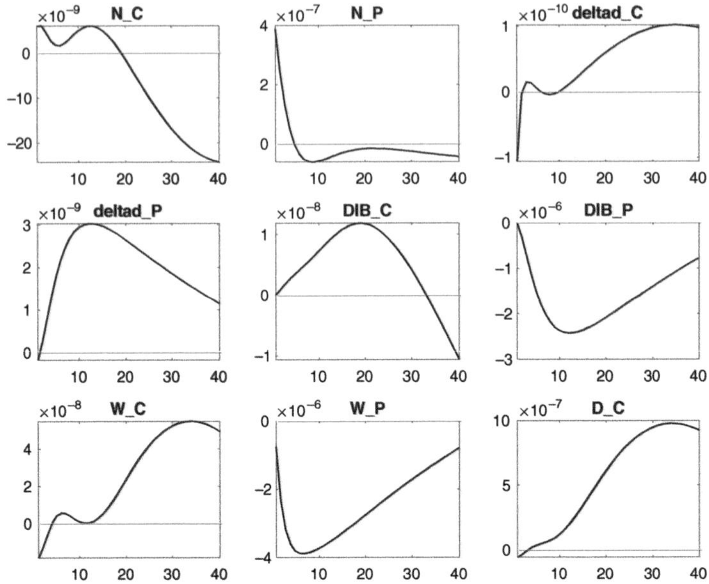

Fig. 2.13. The effects of a rise of 0.1 pp on the capital-income tax in the Periphery Country — 3.

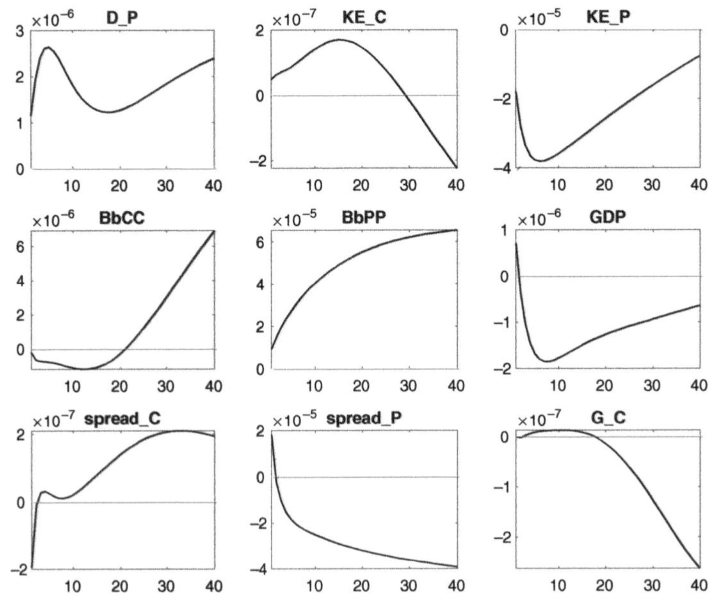

Fig. 2.14. The effects of a rise of 0.1 pp on the capital-income tax in the Periphery Country — 4.

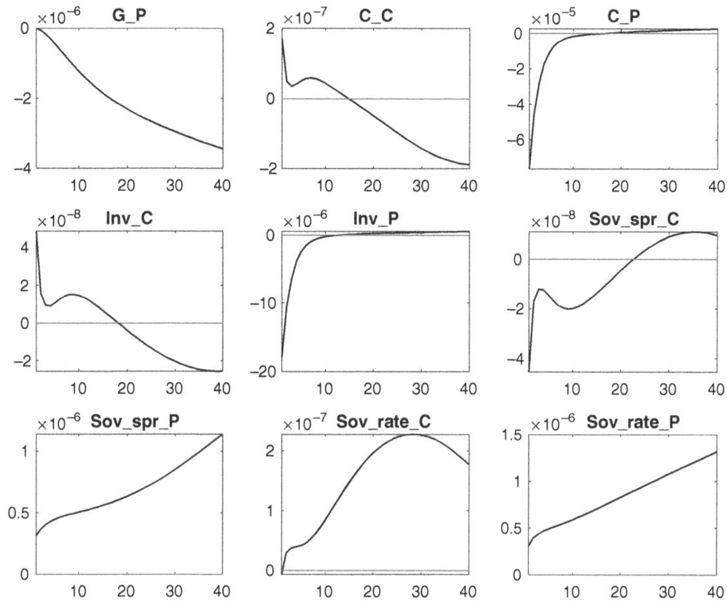

Fig. 2.15. The effects of a rise of 0.1 pp on the capital-income tax in the Periphery Country — 5.

indebtedness pushes up the government bond yield in the long run, although it decreases in the short run due to the reduction of government indebtedness in the short term. Then the interbank interest rate rises as a result, and the same happens for loan's interest rate. The rise of capital-income tax seems to be the least efficient austerity measure for the Periphery Country. We can also observe the different reactions in the Core Country. The fall of loan demand decreases the loan interest rate in the Periphery Country; meanwhile, the falling production drives up the government bond yield in the Periphery Country, which pushes up the interbank interest rate due to the savings banks' arbitrage among government bonds and interbank lending. The effects of the Periphery Country's austerity measure are transmitted through the interbank market and the rise of interbank interest rates depresses the demand of interbank borrowing from the borrowing bank, thus reducing the available loans in the credit market. Therefore, the production in the Core Country first increases in the short run, thanks to the temporary positive effects from the austerity measure, and then falls in the long run as the second effects transmitted from the interbank market touches the credit market in Core Country.

2.5 Conclusion

We developed a two-country model with an explicitly microfounded interbank market and sovereign default risk. Calibrated to the Euro Area, we used the model to qualify the potential effects of alternative austerity measures and fiscal policies on the dynamics of GDP, sovereign default risk, and public indebtedness, in the short run and the long run. Our results show that while the rise in consumption tax and pay-roll tax are beneficial for the Periphery Country's long-run growth, the rise in capital-income tax cannot cope with the government's indebtedness, thus tending to suppresses economic growth in the long run.

References

Arellano, C. (2008). Default risk and income fluctuations in emerging economies. *American Economic Review*, **98**(3): 690–712.

Auray, S., Eyquem, A., and Gomme, P. (2016). A tale of tax policies in open economies. *International Economic Review*, **57**(4): 1299–1333.

Auray, S., Eyquem, A., and Ma, X. (2018). Banks, sovereign risk and unconventional monetary policies. *European Economic Review*, **108**: 153–171.

Bi, H. (2012). Sovereign default risk premia, fiscal limits, and fiscal policy. *European Economic Review*, **56**(3): 389–410.

Corsetti, G., Kuester, K., Meier, A., and Mueller, G. J. (2014). Sovereign risk and belief-driven fluctuations in the euro area. *Journal of Monetary Economics*, **61**: 53–73.

Dib, A. (2010). Banks, credit market frictions, and business cycles, Working Papers 10–24, Bank of Canada 2010.

Eaton, J. and Gersovitz, M. (1981). Debt with potential repudiation theoretical and empirical analysis. *Review of Economic Studies*, **48**(2): 289–309.

Gertler, M. and Kiyotaki, N. (2010). Financial intermediation and credit policy in business cycle analysis. In B. M. Friedman and M. Woodford (Eds.), *Handbook of Monetary Economics*, pp. 547–599. Elsevier, Robert W. Kolb Series in Finance.

Goodhart, C., Sunirand, P., and Tsomocos, D. (2006). A model to analyse financial fragility. *Economic Theory*, **27**(1): 107–142.

Guerrieri, L., Iacoviello, M., and Minetti, R. (2013). Banks, sovereign debt and the international transmission of business cycles. *NBER International Seminar on Macroeconomics, University of Chicago Press*, **9**: 181–213.

https://doi.org/10.1142/9781786349507_0003

Chapter 3

How Do Financial Markets Listen to the Economic Policy Uncertainty?

Abir Abid

University Orléans, CNRS, LEO, FRE 2014, France
University of Tunis, Higher Institute of Management, LR. MACMA, Tunisia
abir.abid@etu.univ-orleans.fr/abir1988abid@gmail.com

3.1 Introduction

Uncertainty is a phenomenon that can be traced back to the study of Knight (1921) that theoretically distinguishes between risk and uncertainty. Hence, the "Knightian uncertainty" (risk) refers to a lack (presence) of quantifiable knowledge necessary about a possible occurrence of an event. In other words, the uncertainty translates to the inability to forecast the likelihood of a future event. From a statistical point of view, it describes an unknown probability distribution over a set of events. Conversely, the risk reflects an event with a known probability distribution. Uncertainty appears as an elusive concept because of its different definitions and measures. From an economic perspective, the uncertainty is a situation where the economic agents are not able to anticipate the future economic outcomes with sufficient confidence. Hence, the economic uncertainty has several implications for economic agents' behaviors (Bernanke, 1983; Bloom, 2009; Brograad and Detzel, 2015). Furthermore, by its non-observable nature, measuring of economic uncertainty remains one of the most discussed empirical issues in the past few years (Jurado *et al.*, 2015; Baker *et al.*, 2016).

There is a wide variety of literature that investigates how uncertainty affects economic outcomes. This is based around the idea that higher uncertainty depresses the real activity through the real option effect. In fact, uncertainty increases the option value of waiting, thereby altering a firm's investment choices and hiring (Bloom, 2009) and householders consumption and saving decisions (Bloom, 2014). Thus, the changing behavior of economic agents under uncertainty has the potential to harm the economic activity and will have prominent real but also financial effects (Pástor and Veronesi, 2012, 2013; Baker and Bloom, 2011; Jurado *et al.*, 2015; Bhattarai *et al.*, 2019; Creal and Wu, 2017).

Specifically, concerns about uncertainty effects have intensified since the global financial crisis (2007/2009) that led the world economy to experience an exceptionally high degree of economic as well as political uncertainty. In this regard, it is well established that the Economic Policy Uncertainty (EPU hereafter), a feature of the general uncertainty, is quoted as a fundamental reason for the steep downturn in the global financial crisis and the slow and weak recovery afterwards (Baker *et al.*, 2016, Ghirelli *et al.*, 2019).

Obviously, the EPU is an uncertainty created by the authority's policymaking process. It can be defined as the situation where economic agents are confused about the future outcomes of the economic policies. In such a situation, they are conscious of their limited knowledge, which leads to revision of their expectations.

In fact, government actions are motivated by both economic and non-economic objectives (Pástor and Veronesi, 2013). For instance, they attempt to ensure investors' welfare *via* undertaking several economic policies. However, the cost of a given policy is either high or uncertain. Hence, investors are not able to clearly and fully anticipate the future evolution of government policy decisions. Such an EPU is trigged by major political events. For example, it has sharply increased around the Brexit referendum and President Trump's election in the UK and the US, respectively (Kostka and Van Roye, 2017).

With the development of the EPU measures in recent years, the main focus of empirics lies in quantifying its effects on economic activity and financial conditions. Several empirical studies have investigated its impacts on investment, output, and employment (Baker *et al.*, 2016), business cycle (Baker and Bloom, 2011), among other factors. As for general uncertainty, the EPU has harmful effects on the economic prospect as economic agents might report/delay investment and consumption decisions until the uncertainty has been removed. Particularly, the EPU can (i) cost the overall economy a lot of jobs (Creal and Wu, 2017), (ii) alter companies' investment and weaken the response of investment to demand (Guiso and Parigi, 1999), (iii) command increased precautionary saving of households that dampens their consumption (Bloom, 2014), and (iv) slow economic recovery (Dakhlaoui and Aloui, 2016). In addition, the recent literature asserts that the EPU significantly poses threats for the financial environment (Arouri *et al.*, 2016; Trung, 2019).

By implementing different fiscal, monetary, and regulatory policies, governments shape the environment in which firms operate. When a change in such policies occurs, the financial markets are naturally reactive. Such a reaction is weak when the changes are anticipated by economic agents, i.e. lower EPU. However, it can be strong when the markets are surprisingly caught by the changes (Pástor and Veronesi, 2012). This behavior reflects the reaction of the financial markets to the EPU.

The modern finance theory assumes that the stock prices are the sum of the present value of the expected futures cash-flows. Therefore, any driving forces of these components translate into stock price changes. Certain economic policies strengthen the confidence of the market participant on the future economic outlook. This restores investment opportunities, which stimulate the stock market performance. Nevertheless, if market participants lack sufficient confidence to anticipate whether a given announced policy will be undertaken or not, they pessimistically regard the discount rates or expected future dividends in such a way they reduce their market participation (Phan *et al.*, 2018 among others). This may not be without effects on the stock prices/returns.

Against this background, this chapter reviews the existing literature on the asset pricing implications of the EPU to help better understand how and to what extent financial markets (stock markets) account for the uncertainties created by economic policymakers.

The rest of the chapter proceeds as follows: Section 3.2 briefly sheds light on the measuring of the EPU. Section 3.3 reviews the literature on the stock market behavior under uncertainty. We provide insight on the sensitivity of the stock market to foreign EPU spillovers in Section 3.4. Section 3.5 discusses EPU impacts on the equity premium. In Section 3.6, we analyze how the EPU acts as an influential factor of financial market co-movements. Finally, some concluding remarks are presented in the Section 3.7.

3.2 Measuring EPU: The Baker Bloom and Davis (BBD) Index

As an unobservable factor, one of challenges of the empirical literature is how to measure the economic uncertainty. Unfortunately, the available works do not provide an objective measure of this phenomenon (Jurado *et al.*, 2015). In fact, some proxies such as the implied or realized volatility of the stock market return or conditional variance of some economic variables have been used as uncertainty indicators (e.g. Bhattarai *et al.*, 2019; Wang *et al.*, 2016; Fountas, 2010; Bahloul and Gupta, 2018).

Regarding the EPU, the VIX has been used as a proxy of government-related uncertainty in several papers (Colombo, 2013; Pástor and Veronesi, 2012, 2013).[1] Unfortunately, the VIX can vary over time, even though economic fundamentals-based uncertainty remains unchanged (Jurado *et al.*, 2015). Additionally, such a proxy pertains primarily to equity returns uncertainty and covers publicly traded firms, accounting only for about one-third of private employment (Baker *et al.*, 2016). Then, how could the uncertainty surrounding the future paths of economic policies be objectively measured? Baker, Bloom and Davis, (2016) provide novelties while attempting

[1]The Volatility Index (VIX) is developed by the Chicago Board Options Exchange (CBOE). It is a measure of expected price changes in the S&P 500 Index options over the next 30 days.

to fill this gap. Hence, they developed an EPU index (BBD's index) based mainly on newspapers' coverage frequency.

The BBD index was initially developed for American data that starts in 1900. This index is a weighted average of four components: (i) the news-based uncertainty index, which accounts for about half of the overall index, (ii) tax expiration, (iii) forecasters disagreement about CPI, and (iv) government spending forecast disagreement. Note that the four components index are made available only for the US. All other indexes constructed based on developed and emerging economies data reflect the news-based index alone.[2]

The latter is calculated based on a monthly newspapers search of articles containing words related to the EPU. For each country, the articles considered appear in the leading home newspapers. To be retained in the index construction, an article should contain terms related at least to three fields (i) economy/economics [E], (ii) uncertainty/uncertain [U], and (iii) Policy, White House, Congress [P]. The computing strategy of the EPU index is as follows. First, the authors divided the number of all selected policy uncertainty articles within one month by the total number of articles published within the same month and the same newspaper. The idea is to handle the time-varying behavior of the published articles' volume. Second, the same procedure is applied to each retained newspaper. Third, the resulting series of each newspaper is normalized to a unit one standard deviation. Finally, all series are summed to obtain the monthly index.

As the most original and objective measure of the EPU, the BBD index is intensively used in the empirical literature attempting to account for the macroeconomic or financial implications of the EPU ([Christou *et al.*, 2017; Dakhlaoui and Aloui, 2016; Arouri *et al.*, 2016; Ftiti and Hadhri, 2019; Bartsch, 2019 among others, Das and Kumar, 2018, Brogaard and Detzel, 2015). This is clear with respect to its advantages for researchers. The BBD offers the possibility to access continuous data on the EPU. Moreover, such a measure is

[2]The BBD index is available for Australia, Brazil, Canada, Chile, China, France, Germany, Greece, India, Ireland, Italy, Japan, Mexico, the Netherlands, Russia, South Korea, Spain, Hong Kong, Singapore, Columbia and Croatia. For further details on the index construction, see www.policyuncertainty.com.

the most likely to capture expectations around the economic policy (Backmann and Czudaj, 2017).

3.3 The Stock Market Behavior Under EPU

Political conditions-related uncertainty poses challenges for the business environment. A firm's exposure to national and foreign political risk and instabilities in the government policies lead to a decrease of the firm's efficiency as it operates in an economic environment that is less flexible (Boutchkova *et al.*, 2013). As a result, returns may exhibit higher volatility.

News about government actions or inactions are valuable information to which financial markets are reactive (Baker *et al.*, 2016; Pástor and Veronesi, 2013). This market sensitivity to political news is naturally translated into assets price fluctuation. Unfortunately, the asset pricing implications of political news lack theoretical background in the financial literature. A notable contribution to this debate is Pástor and Veronesi (2012, 2013)'s theoretical setting (DSGE model) of the political uncertainty impacts on asset prices behavior in the United States. The authors postulate a stock returns contraction in response to higher EPU. On a similar but empirical note, Brogaard and Detzel (2015) find that the EPU is not only a source of depressive effects on equity prices but also commands risk premium. A wide array of empirical studies has thenceforward succeeded these pioneer works, especially since the advent of the BBD index. Therefore, the relationship between financial risk management and the EPU has recently taken novel dimension as research papers related to this topic seems to be the most widely viewed, downloaded and cited in financial economics (Hammoudeh and McAleer, 2015).

Regarding the EPU–stock market nexus, the literature can be split into three streams investigating (a) the reaction of the stock returns to the EPU, (b) the EPU effects on stock prices, and (c) its implications on the stock market volatility. In Table 3.1, we display further details on these literatures and provide a summary of their core research questions, applied methodologies, context of each study, and the main conclusions.

Let us first discuss some interesting econometric issues observed through Table 3.1 of the literature review. On the one hand, empirics

Table 3.1. The stock markets' implications of the EPU: A survey.

Authors	Research Question	Methodology	Country/Zone	Main Results
Christou *et al.* (2017)	Domestic and US-EPU effects on stock returns.	Panel Bayesien Vector AutoRegressive (VAR)	Australia, Canada, Japan, Korea, and China	Both home and foreign EPU foreshadow stock returns' decline in most of the studied countries. Nevertheless, the US-EPU does not exhibit a significant effect on Australian and Canadian stock returns. For example, following the US-EPU shock, the stock returns dropped by 2%, 0.5%, 1%, and 0.2% respectively in Japan, USA, China, and Korea (nearly 1 to 2 months after the shock). Similarly, domestic EPU shocks decrease the stock returns by 1%, 0.5%, 0.1%, 0.1%, and 0.5% respectively in Canada, USA, China, Korea, and Japan (nearly 1 to 2 months after the shock).
Su *et al.* (2018)	The stock market volatility's response to the foreign EPU.	Generalized Autoregressive Conditional Heteroscedasticity-Mixed Data Sampling model [GARCH-MIDAS]	France, Canada, United Kingdom, Italy, Japan, India, Russia, and China	In developed countries, the US-EPU positively affects the stock market volatility (France, Japan, United Kingdom, and Italy). However, the authors find that the volatility declines in response to the US-EPU in emerging markets (India, Russia, and China).

(*Continued*)

Table 3.1. (*Continued*)

Authors	Research Question	Methodology	Country/Zone	Main Results
Das *et al.* (2019)	The impacts on stock returns of the geopolitical risk, financial stress and the EPU in emerging markets.	Nonparametric causality in quantile test	24 Emerging Economies	Emerging stock returns are highly sensitive (size and significance) to the effects of the EPU rather than those of the financial stress or the geopolitical risk. The causality in mean outperforms the causality in variance.
Phan *et al.* (2018)	Evaluation of the stock returns predictability through EPU.	Linear regression (OLS)	16 countries including a mixture of mature and emerging markets	Both local and global EPU predict significantly the stock returns. This result is obtained through in-sample and out-of-sample estimations. The predictive power of the EPU varies with respect to positive and negative EPU shocks.
Sum (2012)	The stock returns reaction to the EPU.	Several linear regressions and Granger causality test	Brazil, Russia, India, and China (BRIC)	The stock market returns' decline is about 0.20%, 0.08%, and 0.13% respectively in Russia, India, and Brazil in response to the US-EPU increase. In the Chinese market, the reaction is negative but not significant.

Sum (2013)	US-EPU effects on stock returns.	Linear OLS regression, linear VAR, and Granger causality test	Indonesia, Malaysia, Philippines, Singapore, and Thailand	For the period spanning 1985 to 2012, the linear regression shows that following a US-EPU shock, the stock returns fall by 0.10%, 0.07%, 0.14%, 0.11%, and 0.10% in India, Philippines, Singapore, Malaysia, and Thailand, respectively. The VAR impulse response functions display an immediate decrease of the stock returns in all countries following a US-EPU shock. Causality analysis illustrates significant Granger causality running from the US-EPU to the stock returns only in Singapore and Malaysia.
Hardouvelis *et al.* (2018)	The relationship between the EPU and the stock returns in Greece.	VAR model	Greece	An increase of the home EPU is followed by a decrease in the stock market returns.
Yu and Song (2018)	Stock returns response to the global EPU.	Regime Switching Forecasting model	United States	Significant effect of the global EPU in forecasting stock returns in the United States. This effect is more pronounced during higher volatility periods rather than low volatility phases. Introducing the global EPU improves the forecasting ability of the model.

(*Continued*)

Table 3.1. (*Continued*)

Authors	Research Question	Methodology	Country/Zone	Main Results
Arouri *et al.* (2016)	Domestic EPU implications on stock returns.	Three-Regimes Markov Switching model	United States	Broadly, this study shows a stock returns decline by 1.07(0.16)% in response to the increase of the local EPU in the extreme (high) volatility regime. The effect seems to be more pronounced and persistent along extreme volatility periods.
Chiang (2019)	EPU impacts on stock returns volatility.	Threshold GARCH model	G7	Negative correlation associating the local and global EPU to the stock returns.
Balcilar *et al.* (2019)	Causality between stock markets (volatility and returns) and the domestic and global EPU (China, the European Area, Japan, and the US).	Linear Granger causality test and nonlinear causality in quantile test	Hong Kong, Malaysia, South Korea	Linear causality, main results: In Hong Kong, stock returns and volatility are neither caused by the domestic EPU nor by the global EPU. In the case of Malaysia, none of the EPUs allows predicting the stock returns. However, the volatility is significantly explained by both EPUs. In Korea, the predictive effect of the EPU on stock returns is originated from the US while the home EPU accounts more than the global EPU for the stock market volatility.

				Nonlinear causality-in-quantile, main results: Causality is running from the EPU to (a) the stock return volatility in Malaysia, (b) to both volatility and return in South Korea. In Hong Kong, there is no causality running from either the domestic or global EPU to the stock market (both returns and volatility).
Bekiros *et al.* (2016)	Causality between EPU and stock market return/volatility.	Linear and nonlinear causality tests	United States	Linear and nonlinear causalities running from the EPU to the stock returns. These results are observed within a long sample period (01:1900–02:2014). The nonlinear causality test provides evidence of a significant predictive power of the EPU on stock market volatility.
KirikKaleli (2018)	The reaction of emerging stock markets to domestic and global shocks.	Autoregressive Distributed Lag model (ARDL), OLS, and Markov switching model	Taiwan	Generally, the stock returns are negatively responsive to the global EPU. Results from ARDL specification highlight that the stock market index's decrease is about 0.2% in response to global EPU increase. Results from the nonlinear specification highlight a negative effect of the global EPU on the stock price volatility regardless of the volatility regime (higher or lower).

(Continued)

Table 3.1. (*Continued*)

Authors	Research Question	Methodology	Country/Zone	Main Results
He *et al.* (2019)	Spillover effects of the foreign EPU (Canada, Australia, China, Japan, and the United Kingdom) to the US stock market volatility.	VAR model based on the spillover model of Diebold and Yilmaz (2012)	The United States	The US stock market is significantly receptive of the foreign EPU. The US market is more sensitive to the Japanese EPU rather than other EPUs. The United Kingdom's EPU exhibits the weakest effect on the US market. Broadly, the EPU is more strongly related to the bad US stock market volatility comparing to the good one.
Das and Kumar (2018)	Relationship between the EPU (domestic and international) and the stock prices.	Multiple and Partial Wavelet Approach	Emerging and Developed Markets	The developed markets are more sensitive to the international EPU. While the emerging markets are more vulnerable to the domestic EPU, the developed markets are more sensitive to the US-EPU. Among these markets, Japan and European countries exhibit the stronger dependence on the US-EPU.
Peng *et al.* (2018)	Stock returns asymmetric dependence to the EPU.	Quantile regression	BRIC and G7	The negative effects of the EPU on stock returns are only observed in France and the United Kingdom. Except these two countries, the asymmetric dependence between the EPU and stock returns is observed in 8 out of 10 countries.

Li *et al.* (2019)	Examining the predictive power of the Global EPU on stock market volatility in China.	GARCH-MIDAS	China	Sample analysis provides evidence that (a) introducing Global EPU alone in the model does not have significant impact on the Chinese stock market volatility and (b) the Global EPU's ups and downs significantly lead the volatility to increase. The out-of-sample estimation first support that the Global EPU helps forecast the stock market volatility. Second, taking into account ups and downs of the Global EPU helps ameliorate the forecasting accuracy of the model.

Notes: This table presents a literature review on the impacts of the EPU on the stock market dynamics. This review includes papers focusing on the stock prices/returns and volatility reactions. Moreover, the studies mentioned here could investigate the home EPU effects or the foreign EPU spillovers. Note that EPU, GEPU, and US-EPU refer, respectively, to the domestic, global, and the US policy uncertainties. From a technical point of view, this literature review contains papers relying on linear and nonlinear econometric frameworks.

focus on linear or nonlinear frameworks when studying how the EPU affects the financial markets dynamics. Note that there is a substantial interest in the nonlinear approaches in almost of the recent papers. Besides, whatever linear or nonlinear methodologies are employed, extensive attention is paid to the causality linkages. When considering nonlinear causalities, we can clearly see the predominance of the quantile regression approaches. Furthermore, if we try to refine our understanding of the empirical literature by focusing on whether the studies are primarily investigating the stock prices/returns or volatility behavior, we find (i) consistent with most of the volatility based empirical works, this strand of the literature investigates the implications of the EPU from a GARCH perspective and (ii) even though Vector AutoRegressive (VAR) models are widely used when analyzing the macroeconomic shocks propagation to the stock prices or returns (e.g. Mun, 2012; Guo *et al.*, 2013 among others), such a methodology remains quite limited in the EPU-stock market literature despite its advantages. In fact, VAR analysis can provides useful information regarding the effects of EPU shocks on the stock markets (size and direction) via the implementation of Impulse Response Functions (IRFs). In addition, it can provide insights on the contribution of EPU shocks to stock returns or volatility fluctuation through the Forecast Error Variance Decomposition (FEVD).

On the other hand, another look at Table 3.1 allows us conclude that there is an increased interest in time series econometrics. Despite the importance of such a procedure in making specific recommendations for countries, it seriously lacks information regarding the interdependences between countries/markets. We contend that such an issue could be of great importance since the world economy is continuously experiencing a growing financial integration combined with increased worldwide capital account openness. Perhaps, this presents one of the drawbacks of this empirical literature. Panel data approaches might probably fill this gap and potentially provide new insights in this regard.

Turning now to the economic outcomes of this growing body of the literature, two main conclusions can be derived from the data given in Table 3.1. First, a commonly obtained finding reflects that the EPU is associated with harmful effects on financial markets. Such impacts are observed through stock prices/returns decline or volatility increase (Christou *et al.*, 2017; Arouri *et al.*, 2016; Chiang, 2019 among others). This recent literature broadly corroborates the theoretical predictions of Pástor and Veronsei (2012). In this vein, Pástor and Veronesi (2013) emphasize that stock prices decline particularly in periods of high uncertainty since investors consider the EPU in their asset pricing. Thus, the EPU can be used as a predictive factor of future returns in the financial market (Brogaard and Detzel, 2015). Similarly, Aye *et al.* (2018) find that the EPU allows the predictability of either stock returns or volatility.

Second, our literature review explicitly highlights that the negative response of the stock market to the EPU is not limited to home uncertainty but can be due to international spillover of uncertainty, especially when the latter comes from advanced economies. Further details on the international EPU spillovers will be discussed in the next section. Now, we will focus on how to interpret the negative association between the stock market performance and the EPU.

Policy uncertainty influences the effectiveness of policy intervention on the overall economy and thus negatively impacts stock returns as a transmission channel of some economic policies (Pástor and Veronesi, 2012; Tsai, 2017). When the economic environment is less predictable and uncertainty surrounding the policy results occurs, news plays a key role in adjusting investors' expectations (He *et al.*, 2019). In the short run, this can translate into higher risk aversion (Raza *et al.*, 2018), reducing the incentive of investors to hold financial assets (Gábor-Tóth and Georgarakos, 2019). Hence, the higher EPU reduces the attractiveness of financial markets to national and international investors (Ko and Lee, 2015; Christou *et al.*, 2017; Arouri *et al.*, 2016). Consequently, market participation decreases (Gábor-Tóth and Georgarakos, 2019), implying a decline of the stock prices/returns.

Moreover, one of the most important transmission channels of the EPU to financial market discussed in the literature is corporate investment. First, the EPU negatively impacts corporate investment (Dakhlaoui and Aloui, 2016; Wang *et al.*, 2014). Second, given the highly irreversible costs of investment, firms might reduce/report their investment and hiring when facing uncertainty (Bernanke, 1983), which slow down capital accumulation (Guiso and Parigi, 1999). Accordingly, EPU modifies investment behavior and business conditions of firms, which in turn impacts stock prices and returns.

For example, during election episodes, investment falls (Julio and Yook, 2012) and becomes less sensitive to the stock prices (Durnev, 2010). This confirms that when EPU is high, investments declines (Gulen and Ion, 2016; Baker *et al.*, 2016). Relatedly, the negative impact of the EPU runs through (i) future cash flows which are reduced with the deterioration of investment opportunities and (ii) impeding market expectations that induce higher volatility. This implies a rise in uncertainty premium [Chiang, 2019]. The financial implications of the EPU are then closely related to risk aversion and uncertainty premiums. Such an issue will be discussed in-depth in Section 3.5.

However, an important question arises here. Can we generalize the depressive effect of the EPU on the stock market performance? In fact, it is possible that the EPU has a positive implication on financial market dynamics. According to Pástor and Veronesi (2013), this may occur if governments respond properly to unanticipated shocks. In other words, when the EPU reaches a high degree, governments intervene in the financial market by implementing actions to put protective effects on asset prices. Such an intervention leads investors to be more confident with respect to the future evolution of economic policies. As a result, this improves the financial market performance or at least slows down its decline. Supporting this point of view, Peng *et al.* (2018) fail to provide evidence of significant negative effect of the EPU on stock returns in a large part of their sample. Alongside these studies, Koskta and Van Roye (2017) show that financial conditions have remained benign and even improved in the US and the UK when the EPU is high. In such a situation, they surprisingly observe an equity valuation increase and implied stock market volatility decreases. Two plausible explanations are advanced by the authors. Such a result is due to the countervailing effect of other shocks in the United Kingdom. Specifically, the Bank of England has sharply responded to higher uncertainty episodes by implementing both conventional and non-conventional monetary policies in order to limit the adverse effects of the EPU. For the United States, on the other hand, Koksta and Van Roye (2017) conclude that the negative effect of the post-election-related uncertainty has been absorbed by the improvement of the US macroeconomic conditions. This improvement is due to the increased level of consumer confidence regarding the government policies for future actions.

3.4 Foreign EPU Spillovers: The Role of the US

Now we know that the domestic EPU presents a risk factor which alters investors' expectations regarding the future. Accordingly, such an uncertainty plays a key role in driving the stock market performance. Nevertheless, the financial implications of the EPU are not limited to the domestic one. The empirical literature supports the idea that an EPU in one country/zone can spill over into foreign markets (among others, Das and Kumar, 2018; Li *et al.*, 2019; He *et al.*, 2019; Balcilar *et al.*, 2019; Chiang, 2019; Yu and Song, 2018; Sum, 2013; Su *et al.*, 2018; Christou *et al.*, 2017; Dakhlaoui and Aloui, 2016). For example, a given country can be victim of foreign uncertainties even though the domestic EPU level is stable (Jiang *et al.*, 2019). In this vein, almost all of the papers broadly provide evidence of significant spillovers from developed countries to less-advanced economies. Particularly, government policy turmoil originating from the US has garnered special attention among researchers. Thus, the US-EPU is regarded as a benchmark of international policy uncertainty (Das and Kumar, 2018).

Thus, a wide array of papers empirically assesses the transmission of the US-EPU to both developed and emerging markets (Balcilar *et al.*, 2019; Su *et al.*, 2018; Christou *et al.*, 2017; Dakhlaoui and Aloui, 2016; Das *et al.*, 2019). Hence, one could questions why the US-EPU plays a greater role in the international EPU spillovers? Several plausible explanations are possible. First, this may be due to the US financial market size and its international influence (Fang *et al.*, 2017). As the most important market worldwide, the US market is a barometer of the global financial conditions (Mensi *et al.*, 2014). Second, investors are extremely vigilant regarding the US financial and economics outlooks and regard the US uncertainty as an important source of information when valuing stock prices in foreign markets (Belgacem and Lahiani, 2012). Hence, their behaviors are functions of economic and financial US turbulences (Su *et al.*, 2018), which translate into demand and supply equilibrium shift inducing changes in asset prices (Das *et al.*, 2019). For example, the US monetary policy tightening presents a negative signal to numerous foreign markets (Ehrmann and Fratzscher, 2009).

Moreover, despite the consensus on the domestic EPU financial effects, empirics fail to be really conclusive regarding the transmission of foreign EPUs to domestic markets. Numerous papers documents that the US-EPU negatively spills over other stock markets returns (Christou *et al.*, 2017; Su *et al.*, 2018, Sum, 2012). Bhattarai *et al.* (2019) point that 0.372% fall of the emerging markets stock markets is due to a positive US uncertainty shocks. In this regard, we conjecture that EPUs interdependence acts as a transmission channel of the foreign EPU to the domestic financial market. In fact, there is recent literature focusing on the international interconnections between EPUs (Ko and Lee, 2015; Jiang *et al.*, 2019; Balli *et al.*, 2017). These studies found evidence of a close link between the foreign and domestic EPU. Hence, the foreign EPU can be negatively transmitted to the stock market dynamics through its effects on the domestic EPU. In a similar vein, Klößner and Sekkel (2014) conclude a significant role of the US as a net transmitter of EPU while other countries like Canada, France, the United Kingdom, Germany, and Italy are net importers.

However, interestingly some studies argue a positive impact of the US-EPU on foreign stock markets performance (e.g. Mensi *et al.*, 2014). This improvement can be explained by international diversification of investor's portfolios as a transmission channel of uncertainty (Christou *et al.*, 2017). In this sense, several studies highlight particularly the ability of emerging markets to attract capital flows in times of bad US economic conditions. Given their high level of financial and economic integration, a foreign EPU's increase leads to increased capital inflows towards emerging markets (Trung, 2019), which presents an alternative issue to manage the risk of portfolio allocation (Balcilar *et al.*, 2019). This is clear with respect to the higher US-EPU that not only weakens the attractiveness of developed markets but also induces increased portfolio allocations towards emerging markets (Gauvin *et al.*, 2014).

In addition, another potential transmission channel is the emerging market monetary policy reaction to the US-EPU. For example, the Fed's decision to reduce policy rates combined with higher US-EPU has led some emerging countries' central banks to raise their own policy rates (Choi and Shim, 2019). Such a decision stimulates the attractiveness of the home financial markets to foreign investors (seeking for higher returns of their investments) and reduces the capital outflows. Consequently, the whole stock market dynamics will improve.

Furthermore, the level of the US-EPU can play a significant role in explaining its different effects on foreign markets. When the US uncertainty is relatively calm, investors could be sufficiently confident regarding the domestic market. Accordingly, they can take riskier positions but generating higher return. This reduces capital outflows from the US financial market and naturally impacts negatively the market performance of other countries. Let us discuss a special case of the emerging markets. In such a circumstance, investors reduce their portfolio exposure in these markets (usually perceived as more risky than mature markets). This can lead to rebalancing portfolios allocation towards more secure strategies (e.g. US treasury bills). As a result, within calm US-EPU episodes (i) capital inflows into emerging markets decrease and/or (ii) capital outflows from these markets toward the US market increase (Bhattarai *et al.*, 2019; Trung, 2019). This may induce a collapse of the emerging stock markets. Closely related to this, Gauvin *et al.* (2016) suggest that tranquil periods of US-EPU have no effect on equity inflows into emerging markets. However, the negative impacts of the US-EPU are observed when the global risk is high.

Along the same line, the literature argues that the EPU implications depend, on the one hand, on the country economic strength and, on the other hand, on its financial market size (Christou *et al.*, 2017). For example, focusing on emerging markets, some recent papers postulate a remarkable influence of the EPU due to credit constraints. Nevertheless, others works highlight a weak effect of the EPU on some other emerging markets (e.g. Das and Kumar, 2018; Bhattarai *et al.*, 2019).

3.5 Risk Premium Under Uncertainty

One of the major questions in macro-financial literature is the macroeconomic driving forces of financial asset returns. In this regard, efforts have been initiated to identify the macroeconomic sources that help predict future returns by providing information beyond what is there in the current asset price.

Discussing the relationship between uncertainty and financial conditions, the recent literature establishes a link between uncertainty and risk premium. The financial conditions are the reflexion of the investors risk appetite. They measure the price required by investors to firstly compensate bearing risk and secondly to provide insurance against risk.

Given that finance theory postulates that stock prices are the sum of the actualized future dividends, economic policy news which adversely impacts investors' sentiments regarding future cashflows or discount rates may cause stock price deterioration. Naturally, equity premium increases (Raza *et al.*, 2018).

Let us start with a brief distinction between risk and uncertainty in order to understand the extent to which equity premium can be reactive to the uncertainty. According to the economic theory (see Knight, 1921 for example), the uncertainty (risk) reflects the economic agent's choices regarding the future outcomes of events with unknown (known) probability (Dimmock *et al.*, 2016 among others).

From a theoretical point of view, the pioneering work of Pástor and Veronsei (2013) is probably the first attempting to establish a link between uncertainty and risk/equity premium. They implemented a Dynamic Stochastic General Equilibrium [DSGE] government policies model in which the policy news affects the stock prices. Pástor and Veronesi (2013) document in this regard that (i) the risk premium increases with the political uncertainty and (ii) the magnitude of the risk premium is more pronounced in bad economic situation.

The EPU's effects on equity premium have been recently discussed by a handful of empirics, which generally argue either positive or negative impacts. Obviously, the positive effect is mainly explained by investor's sentiments. When EPU is high, investors are less confident regarding the future outcomes of financial markets, which could imply a revision of future cashflows or discount factor or both. Thus, a rise in the EPU reduces the attractiveness of domestic as well as foreign risk-free assets and may be destabilizing insofar as shifting the behavior of investors towards riskier strategies (Rajan, 2006). Hence, stock price fall induces higher equity premium.

Such theoretical issues were confirmed by Li (2017) who empirically showed that the EPU commanded an increase of the equity premium in the Chinese stock market.

According to Pástor and Veronesi (2013) the risk premium can be broken down into components corresponding to three types of shocks.

The first component called “capital shock” refers to shocks affecting the amount of capital; the second component is the “impact shock”, which reacts to changes in investors beliefs regarding a prevailing government policy. Finally, the third component is “political shock”, which reflects the continuous flow of political news that impact the investor’s beliefs regarding the likelihood of future government policies.

Accordingly, two main plausible explanations can be for the negative effect of the EPU on equity premium. First, in high turmoil phases, the government puts some protection on asset prices due to the unstable aspects of government policies. Hence, it implies optimistic consideration of investors regarding the behavior of the financial market. As a result, the “impact shocks” are transitory since policy decisions can be changed. Such a confidence in turn reduces the “impact shock” component, thereby decreasing the risk premium (Pástor and Veronesi, 2013).

Second, when investing in stocks that hedge against uncertainty, investors do not demand higher returns. Thus, with higher uncertainty, equity premium falls.

Trying to empirically test such a relationship, Raza *et al.* (2018) have examined the implications of the EPU on equity premium in G7 countries. Overall, this study provides evidence supporting the negative link between the equity premium and the policy-related uncertainty.

More recent works investigate the impacts of uncertainty on the premium demanded by economic agents to hold risky assets which they no longer center around risk but specifically about uncertainty. In fact, facing uncertainty, economic agents are now considered as uncertainty averse rather than risk averse. In this vein, Gábor-Tóth and Georgarakos (2018) show that the unconditional probability of owing stocks by householders significantly declines following a positive EPU shock. Therefore, economic agents are uncertainty averse in phases of high uncertainty. Then, they require an uncertainty premium, which is over and above the traditional well-known risk premium to hold assets with uncertain returns (Gábor-Tóth and Georgarakos; Dimmock *et al.*, 2016). Consequently, it is clear that the uncertainty premium rises with an increased uncertainty aversion (Maccheroni *et al.*, 2013).

3.6 Financial Market Interconnection Under Uncertainty

Despite the well-documented role of the EPU in shaping the economic outlook, its implications to the international co-movement of the financial system are yet less understood. Why is such an issue relevant? First, the role of asset market correlation in an optimal international portfolio diversification that ensures a balance between risk and return is important (Li and Peng, 2017). If investors miss the increased asset prices' correlation, portfolio diversification values could be overestimated (Li, 2011). Second, one of the lessons from the global financial crisis recently experienced is to look at the global economic shocks as a whole rather than in isolation. In fact, even the countries with strong macroeconomic features are not far from negative spillovers of economic and financial shocks (Candelon *et al.*, 2018). Accordingly, it is crucial to understand the extent to which the EPU can alter financial markets' interdependences. This will enrich our understanding of the international behavior of the financial markets.

In a similar vein, some papers have empirically explored how uncertainty drives the financial markets' co-movements. Specifically, the stock–bond correlation is among the most discussed issues in this strand of the literature. Why does uncertainty account for such a correlation?

It is recognized that discount rates and future cashflows in both markets are broadly affected by the same economic factors (Skintzi, 2019). Naturally, the stock and bond assets co-move. On the one hand, a growing literature is continuously supporting a significant reaction of the stock market to the economic uncertainty and the EPU particularly. On the other hand, uncertainty literature documents several implications of the EPU on the bond market (Trung, 2019; Gauvin *et al.*, 2014; Gauvin *et al.*, 2016 among others). Hence, the stock–bond markets' co-movement can be significantly altered by economic uncertainty.

In fact, it appears that this co-movement is significantly influenced by uncertainty surrounding macroeconomic variables such as inflation or interest rates (Li, 2002). This correlation is also likely to vary with the financial uncertainty since investors rebalance their portfolios when the market is facing higher financial turmoil. Therefore, they transfer their assets from a high-risk stock market to a secure bond-market. In this case, the correlation between the bond and stock markets is negative. Connolly *et al.* (2005) provide evidence of the significant negative effect of uncertainty shocks on the stock–bond market correlations whatever the sign of the shock is. Closely related to this, Li *et al.* (2015) have looked at the sensitivity of the stock–bond correlation to the EPU in the US. The authors assume that higher EPU leads to risky panic sentiment among investors, which translates into (i) reducing their positions on riskier assets (stock market) and (ii) taking relatively safe positions on bond markets. Such a behavior is well known as the "flight to quality phenomenon". Li *et al.* (2015) empirically confirmed such a prediction by showing that the stock–bond correlation is negatively driven by the US-EPU innovations. Interestingly, they also found that this reaction was asymmetrically influenced by the negative and positive EPU shocks. For example, a strong stock–bond correlation is observed when a negative EPU shocks occurs. However, the correlation level drops with a positive EPU shock. In periods of modest EPU (decreased EPU), the overall economic outlook improves, which fuels optimistic considerations of investors regarding future cashflows. As a result, risk aversion decreases implying a jump in market participation. Therefore, demand increases in stock markets as well as in bond markets, thereby increasing their correlations.

In a different context, Skintzi (2019) examined the influencing factors of the time-varying pattern of the dynamic co-movement between stock and bond markets in the Euro Area. Skintzi (2019) broadly supported the "flight to quality" phenomenon by documenting a crucial role of the domestic bond market uncertainty as well as the global market one (the VIX) on the stock–bond correlation.

Apart from the stock–bond correlation, the empirical investigations into EPU effects have been extended to the interconnections between home and abroad stock markets. Recent papers argue that the EPU commands the stock market co-movement between the US and China (Li and Peng, 2017). The latter has established that the US-EPU affecting the behavior of institutional investors in both countries is likely to command the joint movement of the two markets. Hence, financial market connections occur when economic agents' decisions vary with respect to foreign markets prices shocks (King and Wadhwani, 1990). Furthermore, Candelon *et al.* (2018) provide evidence of strong connectedness of equity indexes in mature as well as in emerging markets when uncertainty level is high. Conversely, they show that, in tranquil uncertainty phases, the degree of the observed interconnection declines.

3.7 Conclusion

This chapter summarizes the academic literature that focuses on the role played by the EPU in asset pricing. First, we have briefly discussed the measurement of the uncertainty in the empirical literature and emphasized the importance and advantages of the BBD's index. Second, we have summarized the theoretical and empirical backgrounds regarding the impacts of the EPU on financial markets. Our literature survey points are the following. The EPU appears to exert strong effects on financial markets. The well-documented effect is generally negative and observed through stock market prices/returns decline and volatility increase. Furthermore, the stock markets are sensitive to the local as well as the foreign EPU. In this regard, our review sheds light especially on a dominant player, i.e. the United States, that appears as net exporter of the EPU to other financial markets. Moreover, the EPU is a key influential factor of investor's sentiment, which commands movements of the equity premium. Finally, the EPU is probably an important driver of the international connection of the financial markets.

Insights offered in this chapter help both investors and policymakers understand how the EPU affects the financial environment. Therefore, they can build strategies to deal with its possible negative impacts on financial markets. This gives rise to other questions that might be interesting to future avenues of research. Given the overall strong and significant impact of the EPU, one could ask about the factors inducing a higher level of EPU. Thus, policymakers can reduce the EPU that allows for the prevention of a possible market collapse.

References

Arouri, M., Estay, C., Rault, C., and Roubaud, D. (2016). Economic policy uncertainty and stock markets: Long-run evidence from the US. *Finance Research Letters*, **18**: 136–141.

Aye, G. C., Balcilar, M., Demirer, R., and Gupta, R. (2018). Firm-level political risk and asymmetric volatility. *Journal Economic Asymmetries*, **18**: e00110.

Bahloul, W. and Gupta, R. (2018). Impact of macroeconomic news surprises and uncertainty for major economies on returns and volatility of oil futures. *International Economics*, **156**: 247–253.

Baker, S. and Bloom, N. (2011). Does Uncertainty Reduce Growth? Using disasters as natural experiment. Macro Econ & Int'L Finance Workshop.

Baker, S., Bloom, N., and Davis, S. J. (2016). Measuring economic policy uncertainty. *Quarterly Journal Economics*, **131**: 1593–1163.

Balcilar, M., Gupta, R., Kim, W. J., and Kyei, C. (2019). The role of economic policy uncertainties in predicting stock returns and their volatility for Hong Kong, Malaysia and South Korea. *International Review Economics Finance*, **59**: 150–163.

Balli, F., Uddin, G. S., Mudassar, H., and Yoon, S-M. (2017). Cross-country determinants of economic policy uncertainty spillovers. *Economic Letters*, **156**: 179–183.

Bartsch, Z. (2019). Economic Policy Uncertainty and Dollar-Pound Exchange Rate Return Volatility. *Journal of International Money and Finance*, **98**: 102067.

Bekiros, S., Gupta, R., and Kyei, C. (2016). On economic uncertainty, stock market predictability and nonlinear spillover effects. *North American Journal of Economics and Finance*, **36**: 184–191.

Belgacem, A. and Lahiani, A. (2012). More on the impact of US macroeconomic announcements: Evidence from french and german stock markets' volatility. *Economics Bull*, **32**: 1509–1526.

Bernanke, B. S. (1983). Irreversibility, uncertainty and cyclical investment. *Quarterly Journal Economics*, **98**: 95–106.

Bhattarai, S., Chatterjee, A., and Park, W. Y. (2019). Global spillover effects of US uncertainty. *Journal of Monetary Economics*, https://doi.org/10.1016/j.jmoneco.2019.05.008.

Bloom, N. (2009). The impact of uncertainty shocks. *Econometrica*, **77**: 623–685.

Bloom, N. (2014). Fluctuations in uncertainty. *Journal of Economic Perspectives — American Economic Association*, **28**: 153–176.

Boutchkova, M., Doshi, H., Durnev, A., and Molchanov, A. (2013). Precarious politics and return volatility. *The Review of Financial Studies*, **25**: 1111–1154.

Brogaard, J. and Detzel, A. (2015). The asset-pricing implications of government economic policy uncertainty. *Management Science*, **61**: 3–18.

Candelon, B., Ferrara, L., and Joëts, M. (2018). Global financial interconnectedness: A nonlinear assessment of uncertainty channel. Banque de France Working Paper. WP #661.

Chiang, T. C. (2019). Economic policy uncertainty, risk and stock Returns: Evidence from G7 stock markets. *Finance Research Letters*, https://doi.org/10.1016/j.frl.2019.03.018.

Choi, S. and Shim, M. (2019). Financial vs. Policy uncertainty in emerging market economies. *Open Economies Review*, **30**: 297–318.

Christou, C., Cunado, J., Gupta, R., and Hassapis, C. (2017). Economic policy uncertainty and stock market returns in pacific-rim countries: Evidence based on a bayesian panel VAR model. *Journal of Multinational Financial Management*, **40**: 92–102.

Colombo, V. (2013). Economic policy uncertainty in the US: Does it Matter for the Euro area? *Economics Letters*, **121**: 39–42.

Connolly, R. A., Stivers, C., and Sun, L. (2005). Stock market uncertainty and the stock-bond return correlation. *Journal of Financial and Quantitative Analysis*, **40**: 161–194.

Creal, D. D. and Wu, J. C. (2017). Monetary policy uncertainty and economic fluctuations. *International Economic Review*, **58**: 1317–1354.

Dakhlaoui, I. and Aloui, C. (2016). The interactive relationship between the US economic policy uncertainty and BRIC' stock markets. *International Economics*, **146**: 141–157.

Das, D., Kannadhasan, M., and Bhattacharyya, M. (2019). Do the emerging stock markets react to international economic policy uncertainty, geopolitical risk and financial stress Alike? *North-American Journal of Economics and Finance*, **48**: 1–19.

Das, D. and Kumar, S. B. (2018). International economic policy uncertainty and stock prices revisited: Multiple and partial wavelet approach. *Economics Letters*, **164**: 100–108.

Dimmock, S. G., Kouwenberg, R., Mitchell, O. S., and Peijnenburg, K. (2016). Ambiguity aversion and household portfolio choice puzzles: Empirical evidence. *Journal of Financial Economics*, **119**: 559–577.

Durnev, A. (2010). The real effects of political uncertainty: Elections and investment sensitivity to stock Prices. https://ssrn.com/abstract=1549714 or http://dx.doi.org/10.2139/ssrn.1549714.

Ehrmann, M. and Fratzscher M. (2009). Global financial transmission of monetary policy shocks. *Oxford Bulletin of Economics*, **71**: 739–759.

Fang, L., Y, H., and Li., L. (2017). The effect of economic policy uncertainty on the long-term correlation between US. Stock and bond markets correlation. *Economic model*, **66**: 139–145.

Fountas, S. (2010). Inflation, inflation uncertainty and growth: Are They Related? *Economic model*, **27**: 896–899.

Ftiti, Z. and Hadhri, S. (2019). Can economic policy uncertainty, oil prices, and investor sentiment predict Islamic stock Returns? A multi-scale perspective. pacific-basin finance. *Pacific-Basin Finance Journal*, **53**: 40–55.

Gábor-Tóth, E. and Georgarakos, D. (2019). Economic policy uncertainty and stock market participation. SSRN: https://ssrn.com/abstract=3006651 or http://dx.doi.org/10.2139/ssrn.3006651.

Gauvin, L., McLoughlin, C., and Reinhardt, D. (2014). Policy uncertainty spillovers to emerging markets — evidence from capital flows. Bank of England Working Paper No. 512. https://dx.doi.org/10.2139/ssrn.2502029.

Gauvin, L., McLoughlin, C., and Reinhardt, D. (2016). Economic policy uncertainty in advanced countries and portfolio capital flows to emerging markets. Rue de la Banque, Banque de France, Issue 34.

Ghirelli, C., Pérez, J. J., and Urtasun, A. (2019). A new economic policy uncertainty index for Spain. *Economics Letters*, **182**: 64–67.

Guiso, L. and Parigi, G. (1999). Investment and demand uncertainty. *Quarterly Journal of Economics*, **114**: 185–227.

Gulen, H. and Ion, M. (2016). Policy uncertainty and corporate investment. *The Review of Financial Studies*, **29**: 523–564.

Guo, F., Hu J., and Jiang, M. (2013). Monetary shocks and asymmetric effects in an emerging stock market: The case of china. *Economic model*, **32**: 532–538.

Hammoudeh, S. and McAleer, M. (2015). Advances in financial risk management and economic policy uncertainty: An overview. *The International Review of Economics & Finance*, **40**: 1–7.

Hardouvelis, G. A., Karalas, G., Karanastasis, D., and Samartzis, P. (2018). Economic policy uncertainty, political uncertainty and the greek economic crisis. Available at SSRN: https://ssrn.com/abstract=3155172 or http://dx.doi.org/10.2139/ssrn.3155172.

He, F., Wang, Z., and Yin, L. (2019). Asymmetric volatility spillovers between international economic policy uncertainty and the U.S. stock market. *North-American Journal of Economics and Finance*, 101084. https://doi.org/10.1016/j.najef.2019.101084.

Jiang, Y., Zhua, Z., Tiana, G., and Nie, H. (2019). Determinants of within and cross-country economic policy uncertainty spillovers: Evidence from US and China. *Finance Research Letters*, https://doi.org/10.1016/j.frl.2019.08.004.

Julio, B. and Yook, Y. (2012). Political uncertainty and corporate investment cycles. *J. Finance*, **67**: 45–83.

Jurado, K., Ludvigson, S. C., and Ng., S. (2015). Measuring uncertainty. *The American Economic Review*, **105**: 1177–1216.

King, M. A. and Wadhwani, S. (1990). Transmission of volatility between stock markets. *The Review of Financial Studies*, **3**: 5–33.

KirikKaleli, D. (2018). The effect of domestic and foreign risks on an emerging stock market: A time Series Analysis. *North-American Journal of Economics and Finance*, 100876. https://doi.org/10.1016/j.najef.2018.11.005.

Klößner, S. and Sekkel, R. (2014). International spillovers of policy uncertainty. *Economics Letters*, **124**: 508–512.

Knight, F. (1921). *Risk, uncertainty, and profit.* 5th ed. New York, Dover Publications.

Ko, J. H. and Lee, C. M. (2015). International economic policy uncertainty and stock prices. Wavelet Approach. *Economics Letters*, **134**: 118–122.

Kostka, T. and Van Roye, B. (2017). Assessing the decoupling of economic policy uncertainty and financial conditions. *Financ. Stab. Rev.* European Central Bank, Vol. 1.

Li, L. (2002). Macroeconomic factors and the correlation of stock and bond returns. Working paper. Yale International Center of Finance.

Li, T., Ma, F., Zhang, X., and Zhang, Y. (2019). Economic policy uncertainty and the chinese stock market volatility: Novel evidence. *Economic Model*, https://doi.org/10.1016/j.econmod.2019.07.002.

Li, X. M. (2011). How do exchange rates Co-Move? A study on currencies of five inflation-targeting countries. *Journal of Banking & Finance*, **35**: 418–429.

Li, X. M. (2017). New evidence on economic policy uncertainty and equity premium. *Pacific-Basin Finance Journal*, **46**: 41–56.

Li, X. M. and Peng, L. (2017). US economic policy uncertainty and Comovements between Chinese and US stock markets. *Economic Model*, **61**: 27–39.

Li, X. M., Zhang, B., and Gao, R. (2015). Economic policy uncertainty shocks and stock–bond correlations: evidence from the US market. *Economics Letters*, **132**: 91–96.

Maccheroni, F., Marinacci, M., and Ruffino, D. (2013). Alpha as ambiguity: Robust mean-variance portfolio analysis. *Econometrica*, **81**, 1075–1113.

Mensi, W., Hammoudeh, S., Reboredo, J. C., and Nguyen, D. K. (2014). Do global Factors Impact BRICS Stock Markets? A quantile regression approach. *Emer. Mark. Rev.* **19**: 1–17.

Mun, K. C. (2012). The joint response of stock and foreign exchange markets to macroeconomic surprises: Using US and Japanese data. *Journal of Banking and Finance*, **36**: 383–394.

Pástor, L. and Veronesi, P. (2012). Uncertainty about government policy and stock prices. *J. Finance*, **67**: 1219–1264.

Pástor, L. and Veronesi, P. (2013). Political uncertainty and risk premium. *The Journal of Financial Economics*, **110**: 520–545.

Peng, G., Huiming, Z., and Wanhai, Y. (2018). Asymmetric dependence between economic policy uncertainty and stock market returns in G7 and BRIC: A quantile regression approach. Finance. *Research Letter*, **25**: 251–258.

Phan, D. H. B., Sharma, S. S., and Tran, V. T. (2018). Can economic policy uncertainty predict stock returns? Global evidence. *Journal of International Financial Markets, Institutions & Money*, **55**: 134–150.

Rajan, R. G. (2006). Has finance made the world riskier? *European Financial Management*, **12**: 499–533.

Raza, A. S., Zaighum, I., and Shah, N. (2018). Economic policy uncertainty, equity premium and dependence between their quantiles: Evidence from quantile-on-quantile approach. *Physica. A.*, **492**: 2079–2091.

Skintzi, V. D. (2019). Determinants of the stock-bond market comovement in the eurozone under model uncertainty. *International Review of Financial Analysis*, **61**: 20–28.

Su, Z., Fanga, T., and Yin, L. (2018). Understanding stock market volatility: What is the role of U.S. uncertainty? *North-American Journal of Economics and Finance*, **48**: 582–590.

Sum, V. (2012). The reaction of stock markets in the BRIC countries to economic policy uncertainty in the United States https://ssrn.com/abstract=2094697.

Sum, V. (2013). The ASEAN stock market performance and economic policy uncertainty in the United States. *Economics Papers*, **32**: 512–521.

Trung, N. B. (2019). The spillover effects of US economic policy uncertainty on the global economy: A global VAR approach. *North-American Journal of Economics and Finance*, **48**: 90–110.

Tsai, I. C. (2017). The source of global stock market risk: A viewpoint of economic policy uncertainty. *Economic Model*, **60**: 122–131.

Wang, Y., Chen, C. R., Chen, L., and Huang, Y. S. (2016). Overinvestment, inflation uncertainty, and managerial overconfidence: Firm level analysis of Chinese corporations. *North-American Journal of Economics and Finance*, **38**: 54–69.

Wang, Y., Chen, C. R., and Huang, Y. S. (2014). Economic policy uncertainty and corporate investment. Evidence from China. *Pacific-Basin Finance Journal*, **26**: 227–243.

Yu, M. and Song, J. (2018). Volatility forecasting: Global economic policy uncertainty and regime switching. *Physica A.*, **511**: 316–323.

https://doi.org/10.1142/9781786349507_0004

Chapter 4

Regulation, Ethics, and Economic Stability Evidence from Eastern European Countries

Zaineb Hlioui[*,‡], **Sonia Boukattaya**[*,§], **and Zyed Achour**[†,¶]

[*]*University of Tunis, Tunis, Tunisia*
[†]*National Institute of Labour and Social Studies (INTES), University of Carthage, Tunis, Tunisia*
[‡]*zainebhlioui@gmail.com*
[§]*sonia.boukattaya@icloud.com*
[¶]*zyed.achour@intes.rnu.tn*

4.1 Introduction

During these past few decades, tremendous financial scandals have shaken global financial stability. Since one of the main reasons for these scandals was fraudulent and unethical corporate behaviors, governments and financial regulators have been pushed to fix high ethical standards with the aim of maintaining the financial stability and managing the risk level generated by ethically unaccepted practices. Considering some firms' incapacity to promote an internal culture based on ethical and socially responsible manners, regulators have changed their goals, aiming to improve the corporate risk-taking culture, which is a key factor of systemic financial stability. Therefore, firms can focus on financial performance while maintaining a reasonable risk level and ensuring well-being. Governments and international regulators have adapted their norms and laws to prevent financial shocks. Nevertheless, the default of large strong firms such as WorldCom,[1] ENRON,[2] Andersen,[3] Lehman Brothers,[4] and so on provides many examples and shows how lack of transparency and unethical practices lead to financial fragility and harm the corporate outlook. It outlines the loopholes of the current norms and confirms that the financial stability remains a big challenge faced by the market regulators. In other words, regulators are challenged not just to enact efficient laws but also to ensure their compliance.

Since unethical behaviors damage trust between the corporate framework's actors, its effect goes beyond the corporate scope. Hence, it harms the meso- and macroeconomic stability. According to Stiglitz (2008), the main reason behind crisis generation is trust erodibility, which caused the collapse of confidence between stakeholders. He stressed that wealth creation depends on resource allocation and concluded that we are supporting an inequality cost. Thus, to avoid it, firms should behave in a socially responsible way and think about ethics as well as profit. In the same vein and according to Reich (2008), the former US Labor secretary, the obstacle that impedes growth and stability is not the lack of financial resources but the lack of trust between the stakeholders. Markets trade in promises, and if economic actors are not able to trust each other, then the financial market cannot operate correctly.

Indeed, trust is an intangible asset that has precious value, especially during crises periods. For instance, at the beginning of 2007, the American firms, as well as the world economic systems, had been

---

[1]WorldCom: An American telecommunication enterprise that was founded in 1983 went bankrupt in 2002 after declaring fictitious revenues (11 billions $), a good example of the contaminated corporate governance and accounting results.

[2]ENRON: Was one of the biggest American firms, an energy corporation founded in 1985 by the merging of Houston Natural Gas and Internorth of Omaha. It filed for bankruptcy in 2001 after falsifying accounting.

[3]Andersen: Andersen, founded in 1913 by Arthur Andersen and Clarence DeLany, specialized in audit and financial, juridical, and fiscal advice. It was one of the most well-known firms and a part of the big five global networks until 2002, when, under ENRON default, Andersen was dismantled. This is an example that illustrates corruption and accounting fraud consequences.

[4]Lehman Brothers: A financial services firm (investment bank) founded in 1850; during the subprime crisis (2008) it failed for the same reason as above.

going at full blast. The financial system was doing well. Nevertheless, by 2009, economies faced a dramatic slowdown of the production process and financial institutions were not lending. Hence, economies were sliding into deep recession and governments had to react immediately to solve this issue. From a neoclassical economic perspective, there is no valid reason that can explain the quick development of the crisis. This financial crisis could not be explained simply by the default of an investment bank (Sapienza *et al.*, 2012). Several researchers have dug deep for the missing link that gives a clear analysis of the financial system collapse. They came to a consensus about the crucial role of trust for traders and investment. What is broken during crises is trust (Lins *et al.*, 2017). Along the same lines, Kanagaretnam *et al.* (2019) documented that trust is positively associated with financial stability through its negative effect on risk-taking. They pointed out a positive relationship between transparency, reporting conservatism, and country-level societal trust. Their study is consistent with Cui *et al.*'s (2018) research in which they investigated the simultaneous relationship between corporate social responsibility and information asymmetry. Their research provided evidence that socially responsible behaviors enhance corporate reputation. Hence, firms gain legitimacy and decrease their reputational risk through their ethical acts, which is consistent with the legitimacy theory. Trust is a key factor for stability and crisis avoidance. Moreover, it cannot be built without social and ethical behaviors. Hence, firms have to share an internal as well as an external ethical culture. Otherwise, regulators must fix the adequate norms that ensure financial system stability.

McGovern (2016) argued in his book that the primary cause of corporate unethical practices is the complexity and bureaucracy of the process. These complexities force firms to pass through unnecessary steps, which are used as a tool to create unneeded fees or bribery opportunities, in other words, corruption. Furthermore, this corruption is the driver of the trust crises and, consequently, the economic crisis. He claimed that the Greek crisis was a result of numerous legal barriers that obliged SMEs to use corrupt methods. The core of the Greek economic crisis was the complexity of processes imposed by the government. In the same vein, he took the UK citizens' attitude toward the European Union as an example to illustrate how bureaucracy drives distrust even with the presence of a great national power.

The mediation role of ethics in the regulation and economic stability link can be explained through several theories. Beyond the stakeholder theory, the legitimacy theory can explain this relation. This theory is based on a social contract that exists between organizations and society. The corporate sustainability and the license to operate depend on the ability of a company to gain legitimacy, in other words, its ability to gain trust. Thus, firms continually seek to operate within the standards of their framework and ensure regulatory compliance. Accordingly, greater regulation quality leads to more responsible behavior and thereby more trust and stability. Nevertheless, companies might adopt corrupt behavior even in the presence of laws. Based on the planned behavior theory, whether it is a natural or legal person, his behaviors are the result of interdependent factors, which are the attitude, the perceived behavioral control, and the subjective norms. Even with the intention of doing business while maintaining a sound outlook, companies might end up behaving unethically, especially in corrupt environments, which is consistent also with the institutional theory.

In this chapter, we aim to give a clearer definition of the concept of ethical culture. Moreover, we investigate the relationship between corporate ethical culture, Regulation's characteristics, and macroeconomic stability. Furthermore, we provide empirical evidence of the mediating role of ethics in the regulation and economic stability association in the Eastern European Countries (EECs) over the period 2012–2016. Indeed, these countries are characterized by higher corruption compared to western countries. Ivlevs and Hinks (2018) pointed out that after more than 25 years since the fall of the USSR and the communist rule, the presence of former communist members increases the bribe payments. In addition, those members think that bribery is expected.

Given the corruption level in these countries, in our empirical research, we shed light on the effect of corporate bribery on the regulation and economic stability link and assume the presence of a partial mediation association. To test our assumption, we use a probit, an ordered probit, as well as an ordinary least squares estimation. Our findings confirm this mediating role. We remark that the corporate unethical practices depend basically on the framework specificities rather than the corporate characteristics. Generally, those complexities are related to bureaucracy. To sum up, there is no question that trust is important. Nevertheless, for the Eastern European countries, stakeholders' relationship is based on tangible factors such as collaterals and returns more than trust.

Our study is organized as follows. In the next part, we will present the theoretical background of the corporate ethical conduct evolution and application, followed by the relationship between macroeconomic governance and corporate ethical tools. Then we will present our empirical investigation. Finally, we conclude.

4.2 Theoretical Background

4.2.1 *Corporate ethics evolution and application*

Since the second half of the 20th century, the social and ecological movements and the evolution of regulations have put high pressure on firms. The enterprises' accountability toward society increasingly gained the attention of scholars and practitioners. Therefore, currently, corporate sustainability depends on the firms' behaviors and ethics, which form the core of the corporate reputation.

4.2.1.1 *The ethical business conducts definition*

Considering the economic recession and the last financial shocks, the interested actors have become more aware of the importance of ethical behaviors. Among others, O'Toole and Warren (2009) pointed out that firms need to stop evaluating managers based on their financial wealth creation and should start considering healthier yardsticks that evaluate the social and ethical engagements, which cannot be achieved without a culture of candor. Hence, to fix the appropriate evaluation benchmarks, clear definitions of the ethical business are required. Unfortunately, despite the importance of "the business ethics" and "the social responsibility" concepts in academic research, few studies have investigated the significance and the use of these terms to researchers as well as practitioners. Omarova (2017) underlined that business "ethics", "culture", and "morals" are terms inherently hard to define precisely. She pointed out that their definition depends on the corporate framework. Thus, they can be used as synonyms or as distinct concepts according to the context. Her ascertainment is in line with Ferrell *et al.* (2019) who investigated the importance of business ethics and CSR in brand attitude identification. They pointed out that previous researches have failed to differentiate between CSR and business ethics.

According to Fischer (2004), the inconsistencies of the employment of social responsibility, morality, and ethics lead to confusion, since their use in a descriptive or normative way is not generally associated with a discussion that distinguishes the difference between the terms and the key drivers of each concept. On one hand, Kurucz *et al.* (2008) defined the roles of the key actors in driving social strategies. They reported that the main justifications of the social investments are the cost and risk reduction, the legitimacy gain, the competitive advantage creation, and so on. On the other hand, Treviño *et al.* (1999) considered that social practices and corporate ethics programs are driven by compliance and protection motivations. In fact, corporate social engagement is a subject that has been widely analyzed. Nevertheless, researchers do not share a common set of core principles that can define it. Furthermore, this lack of a single definition goes beyond the academic research sphere. Weller (2017) marked that firms seek to manage efficiently the business ethical dimensions. Yet, those companies that create and implement ethical practices, including in terms of compliance and corporate social responsibility, might not be able to understand their meaning and relationship. According to his research, senior managers define ethical practices differently and suggest diverse meanings. Even with the deep research field built through the normative as well as the empirical studies, the concepts of ethical business and the corporate social responsibility evolve and remain dynamic. Fischer (2004) indicated that the confusion is not simply due to the different ways of treating the concepts. What makes the situation complicated is the inconsistencies within the disciplines.

Thus, to provide a better understanding, Weller (2017) suggested, based on Schwartz and Carroll's (2008) integration of several complementary frameworks and Fischer's (2004) clarification in her seminal teaching texts, three basic views. The first one considers that business ethics and corporate social responsibility refer to the same concept. These terms can be used interchangeably depending on the analysis units (Joyner and Payne, 2002). More precisely in an organizational context, CSR refers to ethics.

The second view considers that whether the used term is "business ethics" or "social responsibility", each one is a part of the other. Differently stated, corporate social responsibility includes business ethics, and vice-versa. Several studies of the business and society literature have supported this view. Among others, Goodpaster (1991) considered that the firms' accountability toward their stakeholders is the bedrock of business ethics. Along the same line, Carroll (1991) presented a pyramid that organizes the corporate responsibilities to clarify the path toward moral management. In his pyramid, he included the economic, legal, ethical, and philanthropic dimensions. Dahlsrud (2008) focused on the CSR concept and the main dimensions that form it. His description defines ethics as part of corporate social responsibility.

The third stream of research admits that those terms are distinct yet related. Indeed, while philosophers have involved ethical theories to structure the business ethics conduct, the business perspective highlighted evolvement of corporate social responsibility. Epstein (1987) was one of the first researchers who distinguished between these different concepts. He underlined that business ethics, corporate social responsibility, and corporate social responsiveness are related. However, an understanding of the differences between them is required. Thus, the third view defines business ethics as a concept with moral reflection at its core; while corporate social responsibility is seen from a more business perspective and it focuses on the stakeholders' beneficial outcomes. Corporate social responsiveness refers to the decision-making processes. To put it differently, business ethics and corporate social responsibility are the main inputs of the firms' decision-making processes, which is their responsiveness. In line with this view, Schwartz and Carroll (2008) pointed out that the business ethics concept, including values, ethics, and integrity, and so on, was driven by the ethical philosophies. It concerns law and compliance. This definition could not be applied to corporate social responsibility. During these last decades, the definition of CSR moved from simply reducing stakeholders' damages to a more general notion of doing good. Currently, being socially responsible means going beyond the requirements of the law, which is not the case for business ethics. Brenkert (2019) investigated the challenges and limits of global business ethics evolvement. He supports the third view of business ethics.

In our research, we perceive business ethics as law compliance since we aim to shed light on the relationship between regulation and corporate ethical behaviors. Furthermore, we investigate the association between this and the country's financial stability. Even with theoretical successes of the business ethics development, the regulation effectiveness is still in question. Regulators should seriously consider the ethical failures not only for SMEs but also for the internationally known firms such as Volkswagen, Siemens, Mitsubishi, Wells Fargo...

4.2.1.2 *Corporate framework and ethical business application*

Given globalization, the development of new technologies and digitalization, the increase of the social issues, and the ecological crisis, institutions have been under higher pressure. According to the contemporary institutional theory, corporate growth and sustainability cannot be achieved without the satisfaction of the stakeholders. Zucker (1988) stressed that the firms' survival and persistence are the exceptions and not the rule. This survival requires providing inputs continuously to prevent decline as a firm's sustainability is subject to entropic forces. Consequently, corporate behaviors and associated resources have to be anchored in the cultural schema. Firms should behave in accordance with the framework norms and rules, which present the core of the authoritative guidelines for social behaviors. Thus, from an ethical perspective we except that firms should prioritize their ethical practices. Nevertheless, it is not realistic to always assume ethical commitment. In other words, the corporate framework can foster firms' unethical behaviors.

Previous literature presents two main streams that explain ethical business adoption. On one hand, Hoskisson *et al.* (2000) and Van Vu *et al.* (2017) focused on firms in the transition economies and pointed out that the corporate corrupt behavior might be explained by the framework influence. Considering that systems surrounding institutions shape their decisions, ethically unaccepted actions might not harm firms' reputation if those actions are shared and commonly used between the different actors. In contrast, unethical behavior can facilitate the business doing in corrupt environments. On the other hand, based on the legitimacy theory, unethical behavior damages the corporate reputation and harms the firm's growth and the development process. Namely, it erodes the stakeholders' trust. Mauro (1995),

Fisman and Svensson (2007), Méon and Weill (2010), Fungáčová *et al.* (2015), Abdixhiku *et al.* (2017), and Frimpong *et al.* (2019), among others singled the negative impact of unethical practices such as bribery and tax evasion on the growth, foreign direct investment, and the financial stability.

Thus, with the controversially empirical results and diverse theoretical explanations, scholarly literature has dug deep for a better understanding of the corporate ethical behaviors and risk-taking culture as a component of the complex economic systems. Omarova (2017) highlighted the fact that an understanding of the macro-structural lens is crucial if we aim to treat modern finance as a cultural phenomenon. She pointed out that the financial culture has the same mechanism as a Matryoshka doll. Generally, researchers shed light on their discussions by identifying and altering the norms that drive harmful practices. Nevertheless, this identification or modification is not as easy as it seems since the financial professionals interact inside financial systems characterized by organizational cultures that generate norms. Those systems operate, in turn, within the broader economies, which are nested inside polities. Thus, the cultural norms determination passes through a multi-level perspective that goes from the outermost level of the macro-system to the innermost level of economic actors.

Despite the important influence of the corporate framework on the ethical and risk-taking culture, investigations on macro-economic effects are still limited. The current literature that studies the ethical behaviors and risk-taking culture gives more attention to the micro-level "individual and firms". This might be explained by the complexity of the interactions that drive ethical conduct. Ben Khaled and Gond (2019) pointed out that little is known about the external factors such as the political systems and their trends, which make the understanding of the internal politics of ethical tools development harder. Thus, the financial stability that is directly influenced by both corporate ethics and the regulations remains in question.

4.2.2 *The relationship between macroeconomic governance and the corporate ethical tools*

After the global crisis, firms were aware that they had to rethink their risk-taking not only to guarantee their profitability but also for the stability of the economic system. Moreover, regulators reacted immediately by applying new post-crisis reforms such as strengthening mandatory limits and increasing the system vulnerability to potential shocks. They adopted macro-prudential approaches to control for the corporate financial operations and avoid system fragility. Nevertheless, in recent years, business conduct norms have gone beyond the traditional scope. Since the effect of corporate ethical behaviors on the risk-taking level is crucial, regulators increasingly focused on the firms' internal culture.

4.2.2.1 *Unethical business a key driver of financial fragility*

Business regulation, which has as a main objective the establishment of financial stability, has been developed based on empirical evidence, scandals, and crises experiences. Omarova (2017) pointed out that under the pre-sub-prime crisis' legal rules, most of the financial institutions were allowed to apply lucrative but ethical suboptimal business strategies, which was the crisis trigger. She drew attention to their corrupt behaviors, excessive risk-taking, and apathy toward public costs. Therefore, to ensure better safety of the financial system, regulators increasingly adopted ethical requirements that define corporate risk taking-culture, ethical and anti-corrupt behaviors, and their application methods such as the Congressional Ethics Reforms in the USA.

According to Argandoña (2012), society and regulators are developing their protective mechanisms against the consequences of immoral and unethical actions and not against the action itself. In his research, he supported Miller's (2009) analysis, which considers that greed is the main cause of the crisis and that we should not confuse between legitimate economic rationality and excessive desire. Furthermore, humility should temper our pride since the behaviors of arrogance and hubris among the different actors such as economists, financiers, and regulators were the engines of the crisis, which is one of the consequences. Nevertheless, Argandoña underlined that these behaviors do exist continuously in one way or another in each human activity. The real cause of crises is the generalization of these actions. Hence, to guarantee stability, regulators have to ensure that a certain threshold should not be exceeded. In fact, the failures that had accrued and led to the threshold overflow were mainly the non-control of the corporate risk analysis. Firms used rigorous mechanisms to manage their risk-taking. However, those mechanisms neglected certain realistic aspects. For instance, the anthropological model based on simplistic assumptions was widely used by the decision-makers on the different levels of the Matryoshka doll, especially by those with less financial experience. Those models perceive a rational agent as ethically neutral (Miller, 2009). Economics should be assessed objectively. It deals in facts, while ethics is related to values that are subjective Keynes (1890). Given that there are no better models,[5] no one dared criticize since no one had a better solution. Therefore, these assumptions created the illusion of the nonexistence of "black swans" Taleb (2007). However and as Harris and Freeman (2008) argued, the assumption of separation thesis[6] was empirically rejected and the crisis is the main proof. To sum up, and based on the above analysis, unethical behaviors were the main driver of financial fragility and crises.

In the same line of investigation, a large body of research has focused on the unethical behaviors' effect during the non-crisis periods. Numerous researchers have researched the effect of corrupt actions such as bribery and tax evasion on several macro-economic dimensions. Among others, Joseph *et al.* (2016) remarked that, all over the world, corruption presents a major concern. Van Vu *et al.* (2018) highlighted the negative effect of bribery on corporate financial performance. In the same vein, several studies demonstrated its negative influence on financial growth, efficiency, productivity, foreign direct investment, and lending activity (Méon and Weill, 2010; Mauro, 1995; Fungáčová *et al.*, 2015). As a matter of fact, those hidden actions influence the equality between actors and interfere with the usual process, thereby creating unexpected reactions and a certain disorder that affects the whole system and generates anarchy. Moreover, Abdixhiku *et al.* (2017) reported the positive relationship between the judicial system's low trust and corporate tax evasion. Those empirical results explain the regulators' focus on the anti-corruption law's enactment. For instance, the United Nations Convention against Corruption (2005), the French anti-corruption law

[5]Even the most complicated econometrics models need unrealistic assumptions that make them a pale imitation of our reality Keele (2008).

[6]The separation thesis assumes the separation between ethics and economics. It considers that the values do not influence decisions and that the legal validity of norms is affected only by the resources.

(the Sapin II Law) (2017), the UK Bribery Act (2010), the German Anti-Corruption Legislation, the International Federation of Accountants (IFAC) and others have placed corruption as a serious concern on their agendas.

In fact, as we have argued in the previous sections, unethical behaviors might facilitate doing things at the micro level under some framework conditions. Nevertheless, at a macro-economic level, those actions damage the financial stability and the different actors' trust. Moreover, if they are generalized and they exceed a certain threshold, the collapse of the financial system should be expected. Hence, regulators have to find the right tools and strategies that control the firms' behaviors and limit unethical actions.

4.2.2.2 *The influence of governance policies on corporate ethical tools*

Ethical Business Conduct is one of the firms' policy bedrocks. In fact, and as we argued above, corporate ethics are major determinants of the firm's decisions and risk-taking level. Hence, the control of those ethical conducts should be one of the regulators' prioritizes. Nevertheless, consistent with North (1993), institutions are composed of standards and rules of behaviors, which are combined and enforced, and this can determine the kinds of future activities that will come into existence. Furthermore, the way those institutions evolve shapes the long-term performance. Along the same line, Scott (2005) stated that enterprises are made up of various bases of compliance and orders, different logics, and varying evaluation methods. In other words, institutions are scalable combinations that change among themselves and over time, thereby they use alternative empirical indicators to set up their legitimacy. However, some crucial indicators tend to be more adopted than others according to several theories. For most of the economists, the regulative element is necessary but sometimes insufficient to gain legitimacy. Knowing that ethical culture is a stability driver, regulators have accentuated their focus on how to orient corporate ethical conduct and ensure a low level of corruption. Thus, in one way or another, they established a regulation that shapes ethical corporate behaviors. Ben Khaled and Gond (2019) studied the association between the corporate ethical internal culture's evolvement and the external regulatory trend. They uncovered the process through which this latter affects the internal ethical tools. According to them, regulation development is increasingly defining the corporate ethical components and its embodiment. Therefore, they provided more clarification on the regulation effect on corporate behaviors. In their study, a distinction between the external sourcing of ethical tools, the legalist domination, and the quasi-legal procedures was presented, since these different levels of regulators' interventions have various interrelated effects.

Bondy *et al.* (2008) highlighted the existence of an implicit general assumption in the literature that confirms the codes' encouragement of socially responsible actions. According to their research conclusion, codes and regulations are used more often as tools to govern traditional issues, such as, for example, compliance and the employees' behaviors in the workplace. Yet, the development of ethical practices and the influence of the external regulation is affected by multiple endogenous and exogenous factors such as legitimacy and public pressure (Clegg *et al.*, 2018; Weber and Waeger, 2017). In fact, the design of corporate ethical tools remains unstudied in detail. Gordon and Zaring (2017) endorsed that the capstone of regulatory reforms after the global financial crisis has had, as a main goal, making ethical conduct a primary intuitional value, thereby leading to a change in behavior. Nevertheless, to reach this aim, regulators have to understand how organizations manage the adoption of ethical regulation and compliance with the law. In the same spirit, Ben Khaled and Gond (2019) indicated that the professionals are the ones who translate the external regulations then behave according to internal policies, which are fixed based on the applied translation. This fact makes ethics a double-edged sword, as described by Gamma *et al.* (2020). Under the framework pressure, social and ethical behavior seems optional but mandatory at the same time. Hence, firms without an ethical shared culture might adopt hypocritical practices; thereby, ethical behaviors will backfire and generate losses and financial fragility. Accordingly, making hypocrisy salient to the different financial actors and the non-governmental organizations, which are employing a vast array of tools that foster ethical pro-environmental and pro-social behaviors, is required. Ojasoo (2016) developed a new ethics audit approach that provides more reliable information and helps stakeholders to prevent hypocrisy.

In fact, regulations form the foundation of the ethical behavior. Nevertheless, the influence of both hard and soft regulations is mediated by decision-makers' characteristics. Since most of the professional actors, regardless of their organizational status and positions, have a certain knowledge and background in law, an overlapping zone will be created during the law embodiment and translation. This zone enables managers to manipulate corporate ethical actions to reach their goals while satisfying the compliance condition. Furthermore, what strengthens this mediating relation is the ambiguity of the regulation that allows the construction of personal new meanings of compliance (Edelman, 1992; Lenglet, 2012; Ben Khaled and Gond, 2019). Consequently, the regulation effect depends on the regulation quality and the level of agents' trust and application of the legal rules. In other words, it depends on the governments' capacities to formulate, enact, and implement the appropriate laws and build compliance with sound policies.

4.3 Empirical Investigation

As argued previously, one of the main financial regulators' goals is ensuring macro-economic stability; thus, they have to control, through regulation, the corporate risk-taking culture and unethical behaviors, which are the key drivers of the recent financial crises. In the second part of this chapter, we contribute to the previous research by shedding light on the influence of regulation's characteristics on the financial stability through the mediating role of corporate ethical practices. In our study, we focus on the Eastern European financial stability and corporate ethical behaviors. The selection of those countries is due to their specificities as transition economies. In addition, according to Diaby and Sylwester (2015), the Eastern European countries are more corrupt compared to the western ones. Karklins (2002) interpreted the corruption level in the post-communist countries and explained it by the democratic transition process. Thus, since a corrupt framework leads firms to feel at ease using inappropriate methods, it increases the likelihood of the unethical practices' adoption. Those countries' financial stability could be in danger. Therefore, our research question is "would unethical practices mediate the association between regulatory specificities and financial stability?" This hypothesis assumes implicitly four main assumptions, which are the following:

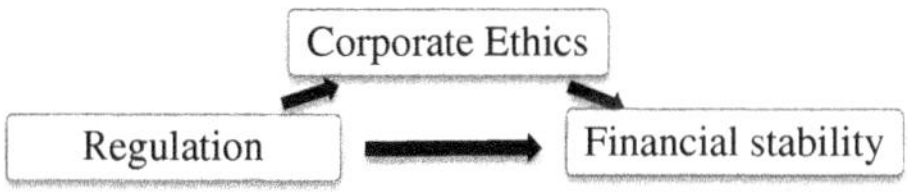

H1: Regulation significantly affects the financial stability.

H2: Regulation significantly influences the corporate ethical practices.

H3: Corporate Ethical behaviors drive financial stability.

H4: Regulation has an indirect impact on financial stability through its effect on the firms' practices.

Our empirical part is organized as follows. First, we will present our methodology and model as well as the choice of variables. Second, we will describe our sample and data sources. In the penultimate section, we will discuss our results. Finally, we will conclude.

4.3.1 *Methodology and model*

4.3.1.1 *The dependent variables: Financial system stability*

In this study, our dependent variable is the financial stability. Since the Eastern European economies are founded basically on the banking sector as demonstrated by Wiesiołek and Tymoczko (2015), following Kasman and Kasman (2015) and Noman *et al.* (2017), we opted for the Z-Score and the NPL ratio as measures to reflect financial system stability. As a first step, we consider the natural logarithm of Z-Score "ln Z_Score" of the banking sector as a proxy of financial system stability. This variable was introduced by Boyd and Graham (1986). Its formula is as follows:

$$Z\text{-Score} = \frac{\text{ROA} + (\text{Equity}/\text{Asset})}{\sigma(\text{ROA})}$$

A higher Z–score value indicates less insolvency and, thereby, greater stability. This variable was used previously by Chiaramonte *et al.* (2016); Shim (2019) and others.

The second Financial Stability measure is the Provisions to non-performing loans (%) "PNPL". Several studies have indicated that the nonperforming loans' (NPL)[7] ratios are representative indicators of financial stability. According to Zhang *et al.* (2016), the NPLs are a major obstacle that impedes the banking sector's stability and development. Hence, Provisions to nonperforming loans reduces the risk and ensures a greater financial stability.

4.3.1.2 *The independent variables: Regulation*

For the regulation characteristics measures, which are our exogenous variables, we use three proxies.

First, we consider The Regulation Quality. This variable reflects the government's ability to enact qualified and appropriate laws and to implement sound regulation that helps to promote private sector development. For the second variable, we use The Rule of law. The use of this variable allows us to test the effect of the economic actors' confidence in the applied rules. It reflects to what extent agents foster building trust in the regulatory system by respecting the rules. This variable takes into consideration factors such as the quality of contract enforcement and property rights. Finally, since we aim to understand the mediating role of corporate ethical behaviors, we use The Control of Corruption measure that underscores the degree of the public power involvement in the different forms of corruption. This means this variable highlights to what extent governmental authorities and institutions use their power for individual private gain. The estimated values of these variables are between −2.5 and 2.5. A higher value indicates better governance performance. Umar *et al.* (2019), Shaheer *et al.* (2019), and Kanas *et al.* (2019) used those variates to measure the government's and regulators' intervention characteristics.

4.3.1.3 *The mediating variables*

For our mediating variable, which is the corrupt corporate behavior, we assume that ethical behavior is reflected in the firms' compliance

[7]The Nonperforming Loans: loans are considered as nonperforming if the debtor has not made the scheduled payments (the contractual payments are delinquent) of a specified period (usually more than 90 or 180 days) that depends on loan's type and debtor's characteristics.

and respect of the law. More precisely, we verify whether the enterprise admits to paying a bribe to facilitate doing things and override the legal process or not. Hence, to measure our variable "Bribe Frequency", we use the answers to the following statement:

"Frequency of informal payments/gifts to get things done". This ordinal variable takes 1 if the firm has never paid a bribe and 6 if it admits frequent payment (1 Never; 2 Seldom; 3 Sometimes; 4 Frequently; 5 Very frequently; 6 Always).

The second variable to measure the unethical behaviors is "Bribe", which is a binary variate that takes 0 if the firm has never paid bribe and 1 otherwise. Among others, Fungáčová *et al.* (2015), Bassetti *et al.* (2015), Lopatta *et al.* (2017), Wellalage *et al.* (2019), Qi and Ongena (2019), and others have used the BEEPs data to test the bribery effects through the same defined variables.

4.3.1.4 *The controls*

In this research, we include country-level and firms-level controls. For the first, we consider the "Inflation" and "GDP growth" to control for the economic conjuncture. Besides, for the firm's unethical behavior estimation, we use the "Size" defined as the natural logarithm of the permanent employees' number and the "Age" presented by the natural logarithm of the firm's age. We assume according to the existing research that these two variables' increase should reduce the firms' unethical behaviors since large firms have less financial hurdles due to the economy of scale, and so they are able to endure more the legal processes and avoid unethical practices. Longenecker *et al.* (1989) underlined the significant ethical practice differences between large and small firms and explained it by environmental pressure and the formal control system levels.

Moreover, we consider whether the enterprise is a part of a larger firm or not "Part of a Larger Firm". This variable takes "1" if it is, and "0" otherwise. In fact, on one hand, being part of a larger firm gives the firm financial and reputational support. On the other hand, it requires the following of certain disciplines. Besides, we test the CEO gender and the dilution of property effects on the firm's ethical practices ("% Largest Owner" and "Female CEO") since these variables significantly influence the decision-making process. Plaksina *et al.* (2019) underscored the CEO gender influence on the risk-taking culture and decision-making and the agency relation. Finally, we use the percentage of employees who achieved a university education, since we expect that the educational system should improve the employees' awareness and affect their attitude toward risk-taking and unethical behaviors.

4.3.2 *Methodology*

Since illegal practices, such as bribe payments, are extremely hidden, limited databases could provide reliable and truthful information, which explains the use of BEEPs data by numerous studies. This data presents firms' answers to the questionnaire anonymously. Furthermore, after investigating the collected data, the world bank classifies answers based on their truthfulness, which grants credible responses. Therefore, we start by selecting credible and reliable answers based on the question "Truthfulness of responses to questions regarding opinions and perceptions". Then, after building our variables as defined previously, we test the mediation effect of the corporate bribe on the regulation, financial stability relationship. First, we verify the regulations' characteristics direct link with the macro-economic stability. To test this relation, we use an ordinary least squares estimation. Second, we test the effect of regulations' specificities on corporate unethical behaviors. Since the unethical behaviors' measures are binary and ordered variables, we apply, respectively, Probit and ordered Probit estimations following the variable types. The third step to estimate the mediating effect is to investigate the nexus between our dependent and mediating variables. In other words, we check the effect of corporate unethical behaviors on the macro-economic stability. Finally, we estimate the impact of an estimated Bribe "$\widehat{Bribe}$" and "$\widehat{Bribe\ Frequency}$" on economic stability.

4.3.3 *Model*

As we indicated in the methodology section, determination of the mediating effect requires the validation of various steps. Thus, to achieve the appropriate estimation process, we apply the following equations:

$$Stability = \alpha + \beta_1\ Regulation + \delta_1\ Country\ Controls + \varepsilon \tag{1}$$

In the first equation, we test the direct influence of regulation characteristics on the macro-economic financial system stability. Stability is the dependent variable presented by the ln Z-Score and the PNPL. Regulation is the independent variable that reflects the Regulations' characteristics, which are the Regulation Quality, The Rule of law, and the Control of Corruption. The Country Controls are the GDP Growth and the Inflation. α, β, and δ are the model's parameters. ε is the error term.

$$\begin{aligned} \mathit{Unethics} = \alpha' &+ \beta_2\, \mathit{Regulation} + \delta_2\, \mathit{Country\ Controls} \\ &+ \gamma_1 \mathit{Corporate\ \ Controls} + \varepsilon' \end{aligned} \tag{2}$$

$$\mathit{Stability} = \alpha'' + \beta_3\, \mathit{Unethics} + \delta_3\, \mathit{Country\ Controls} + \varepsilon'' \tag{3}$$

For the second equation, we verify the impact of the regulations characteristics on corporate bribery. Where the variable "Unethics" presents the Bribe payment act and Bribe Frequency practices. The second equation includes corporate controls already defined.

$$\mathit{Stability} = \alpha''' + \beta_4\, \widehat{\mathit{Unethics}} + \delta_4\, \mathit{Country\ Controls} + \varepsilon''' \tag{4}$$

Finally, in the last equation, we test the influence of the estimated Unethics "$\widehat{\mathit{Unethics}}$" on the financial stability. Through this regression, we examine the indirect influence of the Regulations of financial stability.

4.3.4 *Sample and data*

Through our study, and using a sample that covers 24 eastern European countries, we aim to enrich the existent literature and investigate the mediating effect of corporate ethical acts on the relationship between regulation and financial stability. To this end, we combine three main databases, which are the Business Environment and Enterprise Performance Survey (BEEPs), the Worldwide Governance Indicators (WGI), and The Global Financial Development Database (GFDD).

The first data was jointly produced by the European Bank for Reconstruction and Development (EBRD) and the World Bank (WB). This survey provides pooled cross-sectional data collected based on identical questionnaires and through the same sampling approaches. It comprised representative random samples to present detailed firm-level information. This dataset includes details about the enterprises' informal practices such as tax evasion and bribe payments. To ensure higher transparency, this data is collected anonymously, which enables firms to respond to the survey questions more honestly.

The second database is the Worldwide Governance Indicators (WGI); this data reports governance indicators that evaluate the regulation quality and implementation in over 200 countries around the world. The WGI is produced by the Daniel Kaufmann Natural Resource Governance Institute (NRGI) and Brookings Institution and Aart Kraay, the World Bank Development Research Group and Massimo Mastruzzi. It has been used by many studies to evaluate the influence of governance and regulators' intervention on financial stability (Kanas *et al.*, 2019) and on the enterprises' ethical practices (Shaheer *et al.*, 2019).

The third and last dataset is the World Bank Global Financial Development Database (GFDD). This extensive dataset is used in our research to define the macro-economic financial stability measures since it summarizes financial system characteristics and aggregates for 214 economies. More, precisely the selected macro-economic stability measures presented in the GFDD are aggregates calculated from the ORBIS Bank Focus data source named Bankscope previously and the Financial Soundness Indicators Database. Siddik *et al.* (2018) used the Global Financial Development aggregates to estimate macro-economic stability.

Our sample contains 6140 firms spread over 24 eastern European countries from 2012 to 2016. We should point out that Georgia, Armenia, and Cyprus were included in our sample for historical and cultural reasons.

4.3.5 *Empirical results*

The first graph reflects the percentage of firms that admit their bribe payment at least once (Fig. 4.1). According to the statistics, Ukraine and Greece have the highest averages among the Eastern European countries with, respectively, 80.8% and 74.6% against only 13.3% and 14% for Estonia and Georgia. These results are in line with several previous investigations. In fact, despite the Ukrainian legal evolvement of anti-corruption laws, the transparency international

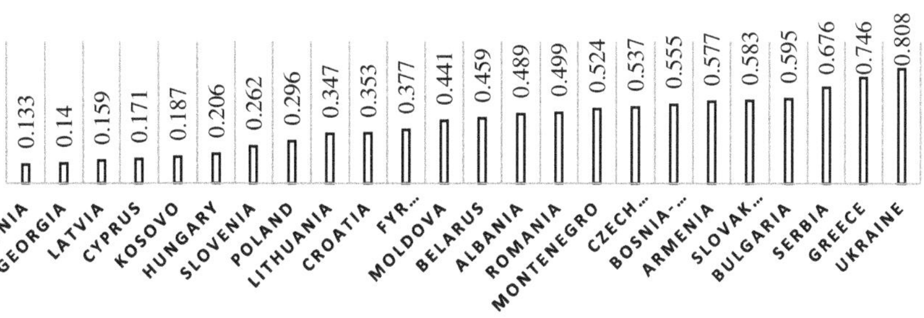

Fig. 4.1. Percentage of firms admitting to bribe payments.

Corruption Perceptions Index (CPI) ranks Ukraine as the 120th among 182 countries, which makes it the second corrupt European country after Russia. Indeed, on the 7th of December 1984, the Ukrainian Code of Administrative Offenses established an administrative liability for corruption offenses. On the 5th of April 2001, the Ukrainian Criminal code set a criminal liability for it. Moreover, on the 14th of October 2014, Ukraine enacted an anti-corruption law. Nevertheless, according to the freedom house survey, the corruption level has slightly decreased compared to that during the presidency of Viktor Yanukovych, who was removed in early 2014. Although some practitioners consider that the adopted measures are misleading, these measures focus on the perceptions, the reporting, and the public attitude. In other words, these measures form the core of the legitimacy theory, the institutional theory, and even the planned behavior theory. Regarding the corruption level in Greece, McGovern (2016) mentioned in his book the confession of a Greek small business owner, in which he declared that about a fifth of his revenue is paid as bribe. Furthermore, the owner declared that small companies are obligated to carry out business like this. McGovern pointed out that regulation and process complexities are the main reasons for such behavior and the drivers of the Greek crisis. Given that Greece has been facing a financial, ethical crisis, this result confirms an association between regulation, unethical practices, and financial stability.

Figure 4.2 regulation specifics by country. Based on our descriptive statistics, the most corrupt countries are characterized by a low control of corruption indicators. Moreover, Estonia occupies the

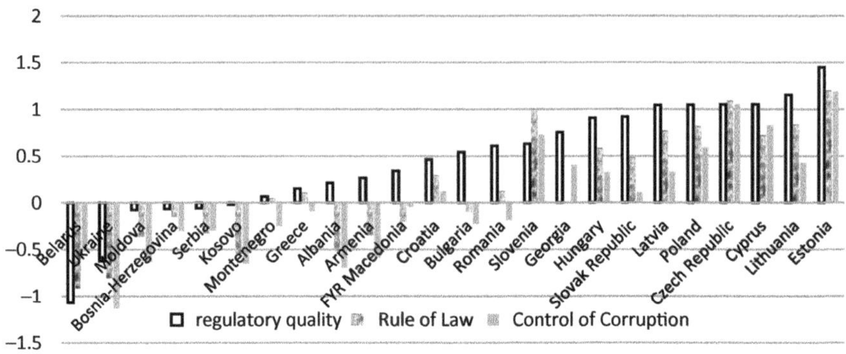

Fig. 4.2. Regulations' characteristics by country.

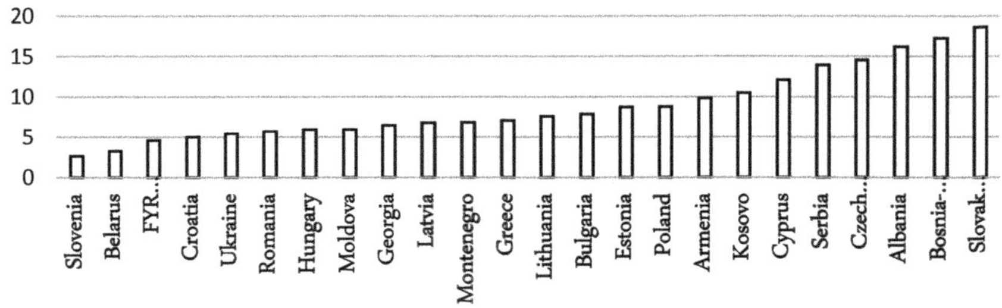

Fig. 4.3. Z-Score by country.

last position among the corrupt countries and has the best regulations characteristics, which is in line with our second assumption. Figure 4.3, we illustrate the Z-score values by country. In this graph, we select the top and least 5 corrupt countries according to the results obtained from the first graph. Unexpectedly, we find that the Slovak Republic and Serbia, which are some of the most corrupt countries, have high Z-Score. According to Taplin (2007), even with the high corruption level in the former communist era, several countries have ensured their financial stability due to foreign investments.

To clarify the characteristics of regulations and assess its relationship with and financial stability, either direct or indirect, we ran our regressions as defined previously. The findings indicate that the regulation's characteristics influence directly and significantly the systems' financial stability (see Table 4.1). While an increase

Table 4.1. The direct link between regulation and financial stability.

	ln Z-Score	PNPL
Inflation	0.311***	−0.146***
	(0.022)	(0.023)
GDP growth	0.045***	−0.110***
	(0.003)	(0.003)
Regulatory quality	0.628***	−0.053**
	(0.023)	(0.023)
Rule of law	−0.258***	0.113***
	(0.031)	(0.032)
Control of corruption	−0.221***	−0.144***
	(0.026)	(0.027)
Constant	1.490***	4.426***
	(0.017)	(0.018)
Mean dependent var	2.012	4.053
SD dependent var	0.492	0.508
R-squared	0.211	0.226
F-test	327.821	358.099
Number of obs = 6 140		

Note: $^{***}p < 0.01$, $^{**}p < 0.05$.

of the regulation quality grants a higher level of Z-Score measure, it decreases slightly the provision to nonperforming loans; this result could be explained by the trust of economic agents on the judicial system, thereby leading to a less fear of nonperforming loans. For the Rule of Law variable, which reflects the respect and the application of law, we find that it is the provisions to nonperforming loans (%) (Provisions/nonperforming loans). Hence, it increases financial stability and reduces risk. Nevertheless, based on the Z-Score measure, it harms the financial system stability. Such a result might be explained by the nonconformity between firms' practices and enacted laws. Firms use illegal practices to grant higher returns. However, with stricter law application and more respect demanded, those returns decrease and their dispersion may increase, which causes the Z-Score to decrease. Surprisingly, the "Control of Corruption" coefficients are both negatively associated with the financial stability measures. Firms in the Eastern European countries are using bribery to facilitate getting tasks done. Thereby, they are illegally improving their financial returns. Hence, with greater corporate profit generation, banks can guarantee better borrower solvency. Furthermore, we conclude based on this association the corporate framework's insensibility toward unethical behavior. Bribery is commonly used, which desensitizes the stakeholders' perception and attitude toward it. Consistent with Farra (2011), our findings prove the deep mistrust that has been developed in these developing countries. What takes the first place is not trust but tangible assets and audited financial reports. Thus, it is harder for SMEs to demonstrate their creditworthiness. Before thinking about ethics and reputation, SMEs in the sampled countries have to demonstrate solid financial abilities.

Regarding the details listed in second table, we estimate the direct effect of regulations on the firm's ethical behaviors. Our finding shows that the firms' bribery does not depend on the enterprise's characteristics such as size, age, and so on but does on the percentage of employees with a college degree variable, which is significant at the 10% significance level; its increase by 1% decreases the likelihood of bribe payment by 0.121. We find similar results for the bribe frequency measure (see Table 4.2 second regression). Among the firm's characteristics, only the size and the gender of the CEO influence the intensity of bribery. An increase in the firms' size decreases the likelihood of bribery, which is consistent with the findings of Baldini *et al.* (2018). Larger firms are more visible to the private and public economic agents. Thus, they are more likely to attract the attention of the government, regulators and public grudges; thus, they should be cautious and avoid law noncompliance. Besides, Rodríguez-Ariza (2017) underscored the female CEO's socially responsible behaviors. The Bribe Frequency likelihood tends to shrink if the CEO is female. This result is in line with Luo *et al.* (2018) interpretation. They emphasized that women show less opportunistic behaviors. Since women face more framework hurdles to develop their management career, they are more aware of the ethical scandals and danger that exists even in corrupt environments.

According to our estimations, we conclude the high influence of the institutional framework rather than the corporate characteristics on the firms' unethical behaviors. For the two bribe measures, we find that Regulatory Quality and Control of Corruption reduce the Bribery likelihood. Nevertheless, the Rule of law fosters bribe payments and intensity; unexpectedly, with a higher level of following of the law, the likelihood of bribery increases.

After verifying the first two steps, we tested the influence of the bribe on macro-economic stability. In our study and based on previous research, we assume a negative link between bribe and stability. However, this assumption is rejected in the Eastern European context. With a positive coefficient, the bribe payments improve the financial stability measures. Weill and Godlewski (2009) indicated that Eastern and Central European countries consider the lack of funding as one of the top three hurdles to business activities development and that the collateral requirements are the major obstacle to external funding. They explained this fact by the collaterals' ability to shrink the credit risk and to solve the trust issues. Banks do not fear information asymmetries. On one hand, the financial institutions think that they are immune to firms' default in the presence of guarantees. They do not need to trust borrowers. On the other hand, firms do not worry about their reputational risk since they provide high collaterals. In fact, the financial system in the former Soviet Union countries cannot be built based on trust. Habibov *et al.* (2017) mentioned that people in the post-communist countries often refer to bribe and corruption as unavoidable and even a necessary step in business activities. Hence, the efficient grease' hypothesis is accepted. The bribe might improve efficiency and stability. However, in a crisis period, the damage will be much deeper.

Table 4.4 presents the influence of estimated bribe measures on financial stability. This estimated bribe is determined based on the results of Table 4.2. It reflects how the characteristics of regulation affect macro-economic stability through the mediating role of corporate unethical practices. Consistent with the results seen in Table 4.3, the estimated firms' bribe payment increases the provisions to non-performing loans, which allow financial institutions to confront the borrowers' default. Yet those provisions' increase reflect the degree of lenders' lack of trust. For the Z-score measure, the estimated bribe shakes financial stability. Hence, an enhancement in the Regulatory Quality and the Control of Corruption strengthens the macro-economic stability by influencing the likelihood of bribery. The results of this research are in line with the intuitional theory explanation. The institutions' behaviors are a result of their environment.

Table 4.2. The direct link between regulation and firms' bribery.

	Probit regression Bribe estimation	**Ordered probit regression Bribe frequency estimation**
Inflation	−0.350***	−0.199***
	(0.070)	(0.067)
GDP growth	−0.014	0.004
	(0.009)	(0.010)
Regulatory quality	−0.395***	−0.256***
	(0.070)	(0.073)
Rule of law	0.912***	0.723***
	(0.103)	(0.108)
Control of corruption	−1.174***	−1.142***
	(0.084)	(0.086)
Size	0.002	−0.047***
	(0.015)	(0.016)
Part of a larger firm	0.015	0.030
	(0.065)	(0.065)
% largest owner	0.068	0.068
	(0.057)	(0.057)
Ln age	0.029	0.027
	(0.023)	(0.023)
Female CEO	−0.044	−0.074*
	(0.043)	(0.043)
% Employees with a university degree	0.121*	0.060
	(0.064)	(0.063)
Constant	−0.035	
	(0.108)	
Mean dependent var	0.442	1.530
SD dependent var	0.497	0.978
Pseudo r-squared	0.079	0.057
Chi-square	604.814	592.574
Number of obs	5604.000	5502.000

Note: $^{***}p < 0.01$, $^{*}p < 0.1$.

Table 4.3. The direct association between firms' bribery and financial stability.

	Ln *Z*-Score		PNPL	
Inflation	0.479***	0.478***	−0.115***	−0.126***
	(0.024)	(0.024)	(0.023)	(0.022)
GDP growth	0.049***	0.049***	−0.115***	−0.118
	(0.003)	(0.003)	(0.003)	(0.003)
Bribe	0.070***		0.130***	
	(0.013)		(0.012)	
Bribe frequency		0.016**		0.041***
		(0.007)		(0.006)
Constant	1.578***	1.583***	4.348***	4.357***
	(0.020)	(0.022)	(0.019)	(0.020)
Mean dependent var	2.006	2.006	4.045	4.045
SD dependent var	0.497	0.503	0.511	0.509
R-squared	0.083	0.082	0.233	0.225
F-test	170.251	164.804	570.347	535.015
Number of obs	5633.000	5532.000	5633.000	5532.000

Note: $^{***}p < 0.01$, $^{**}p < 0.05$.

Table 4.4. The indirect association between firms' bribery and financial stability.

	Ln *Z*-Score		PNPL	
Inflation	0.441***	0.478***	−0.104***	−0.129***
	(0.022)	(0.022)	(0.022)	(0.021)
GDP growth	0.034***	0.037***	−0.109***	−0.110***
	(0.003)	(0.003)	(0.003)	(0.003)
$\widehat{Bribe}$	−0.182***		0.122***	
	(0.014)		(0.014)	
$Bribe\widehat{Frequency}$		−0.156***		0.122***
		(0.014)		(0.014)
Constant	1.652***	1.621***	4.406***	4.426***
	(0.018)	(0.018)	(0.017)	(0.017)
Mean dependent var	2.012	2.012	4.053	4.053
SD dependent var	0.492	0.492	0.508	0.508
R-squared	0.104	0.098	0.226	0.226
F-test	238.187	221.698	595.603	595.413
Number of obs	6139.000	6139.000	6139.000	6139.000

Note: $^{***}p < 0.01$.

4.4 Conclusion

In the chapter, we defined corporate ethical behavior and its evolvement depending on corporate framework. Besides, we presented the association between financial stability, corporate ethics, and social responsibility based on the legitimacy theory, the institutional theory, and so on. Moreover, we studied the mediating role of corporate corrupt behaviors on the characteristics of regulations and the financial stability link. Our findings partially confirm the theoretical background. A greater regulatory focus is required since corporate bribery behaviors depend on the corporate frame, not the corporate characteristics.

Compliance with law illustrates the corporate risk aversion culture. Nevertheless, the application of norms has several boundaries. Despite the development of regulations that support ethical business, we cannot deny the considerable challenges and limits of their efficiency. Ethical failures and system fragility continue to appear even with the progress of the regulation evolvements due to other external factors. Besides the influence of legal norms on the firms' practices, the presence of political struggles, the external institutional environment, and so on are factors that shape the business conduction. Indeed, in Eastern European countries, the relationship between an enterprise and its stakeholders relies on several factors other than trust-building. Hence, corporate reputation and morality might not be prioritized.

Firms seek the key factors of sustainability in their environments. Even if a practice is not legally allowed, firms might tend to adopt it if they think that the risk is worth taking from their point of view. To sum up, the social culture and corporate framework should be considered through a mediation–moderation model in future investigations. Moreover, more research is required to define the optimal level of process complexity imposed by regulators to control the business ethical practices. Furthermore, it will be interesting to investigate the effect of artificial intelligence on the ethical behavior influence and on the studied link.

References

Abdixhiku, L., Krasniqi, B., Pugh, G., and Hashi, I. (2017). Firm-level determinants of tax evasion in transition economies. *Economic Systems*, **41**(3): 354–366.

Argandoña, A. (2012). Three ethical dimensions of the financial crisis. *IESE Business School — University of Navarra*, 1–18.

Baldini, M., Dal Maso, L., Liberatore, G., Mazzi, F., and Terzani, S. (2018). Role of country-and firm-level determinants in environmental, social, and governance disclosure. *Journal of Business Ethics*, **150**(1): 79–98.

Bassetti, T., Dal Maso, L., and Lattanzi, N. (2015). Family businesses in Eastern European countries: How informal payments affect exports. *Journal of Family Business Strategy*, **6**(4): 219–233.

Ben Khaled, W. and Gond, J. P. (2019). How do external regulations shape the design of ethical tools in organisations? An open polity and sociology of compliance perspective. *Human Relations*, **73**(5): 653–681.

Bondy, K., Matten, D., and Moon, J. (2008). Multinational corporation codes of conduct: Governance tools for corporate social responsibility? *Corporate Governance: An International Review*, **16**(4): 294–311.

Boyd, J. H. and Graham, S. L. (1986). Risk, regulation, and bank holding company expansion into nonbanking. *Quarterly Review*, **10**(Spr), 2–17.

Brenkert, G. G. (2019). Mind the gap! The challenges and limits of (Global) business ethics. *Journal of Business Ethics*, **155**(4): 917–930.

Carroll, A. (1991). The pyramid of corporate social responsibility: Toward the moral management of organizational stakeholders. *Business Horizons*, **34**(4): 39–48.

Chiaramonte, L., Liu, H., Poli, F., and Zhou, M. (2016). How accurately can Z-score predict bank failure? *Financial Markets, Institutions & Instruments*, **25**(5): 333–360.

Clegg, S., Geppert, M., and Hollinshead, G. (2018). Politicization and political contests in and around contemporary multinational corporations: An introduction. *Human Relations*, **71**(6): 745–765.

Cui, J., Jo, H., and Na, H. (2018). Does corporate social responsibility affect information asymmetry? *Journal of Business Ethics*, **148**(3): 549–572.

Dahlsrud, A. (2008). How corporate social responsibility is defined: An analysis of 37 definitions. *Corporate Social Responsibility and Environmental Management*, **15**: 1–13.

Diaby, A. and Sylwester, K. (2015). Corruption and market competition: Evidence from post-communist countries. *World Development*, **66**: 487–499.

Edelman, L. B. (1992). Legal ambiguity and symbolic structures: Organizational mediation of civil rights law. *American journal of Sociology*, **97**(6): 1531–1576.

Epstein, E. (1987). The corporate social policy process: Beyond business ethics, corporate social responsibility, and corporate social responsiveness. *California Management Review*, **29**(3): 99–114.

Farra, F. (2011). Competitiveness and private sector development: Eastern Europe and South Caucasus 2011. *Competitiveness Outlook. Organisation for Economic Co-operation and Development (OECD)*, Paris.

Ferrell, O. C., Harrison, D. E., Ferrell, L., and Hair, J. F. (2019). Business ethics, corporate social responsibility, and brand attitudes: An exploratory study. *Journal of Business Research*, **95**: 491–501.

Fischer, J. (2004). Social responsibility and ethics: Clarifying the concepts. *Journal of Business Ethics*, **52**(4): 381–390.

Fisman, R. and Svensson, J. (2007). Are corruption and taxation really harmful to growth? Firm level evidence. *Journal of Development Economics*, **83**(1): 63–75.

Frimpong, J., Lazarova, S., and Gyamerah, S. A. (2019). Anti-corruption instrument and economic growth: Evidence from SADC member states. *Journal of Finance and Economics*, **7**(1): 14–22.

Fungáčová, Z., Kochanova, A., and Weill, L. (2015). Does money buy credit? Firm-level evidence on bribery and bank debt. *World Development*, **68**: 308–322.

Gamma, K., Mai, R., and Loock, M. (2020). The double-edged sword of ethical nudges: Does inducing hypocrisy help or hinder the adoption of pro-environmental behaviors? *Journal of Business Ethics*, **161**: 351–373.

Goodpaster, K. (1991). Business ethics and stakeholder analysis. *Business ethics quarterly*, **1**: 53–73.

Gordon, G. and Zaring, D. (2017). Ethical Bankers. *J. Corp. L.*, **42**: 559.

Habibov, N., Afandi, E., and Cheung, A. (2017). Sand or grease? Corruption-institutional trust nexus in post-Soviet countries. *Journal of Eurasian studies*, **8**(2): 172–184.

Harris, J. D. and Freeman, R. E. (2008). The impossibility of the separation thesis: A response to Joakim Sandberg. *Business Ethics Quarterly*, **18**(4): 541–548.

Hoskisson, R. E., Eden, L., Lau, C. M., and Wright, M. (2000). Strategy in emerging economies. *Academy of Management Journal*, **43**(3): 249–267.

International Federation of Accountants. (2017). *Strengthening organizations, advancing economies.*

Ivlevs, A. and Hinks, T. (2018). Former Communist Party membership and bribery in the post-socialist countries. *Journal of Comparative Economics*, **46**(4): 1411–1424.

Joseph, C., Gunawan, J., Sawani, Y., Rahmat, M., Noyem, J. A., and Darus, F. (2016). A comparative study of anti-corruption practice disclosure among Malaysian and Indonesian Corporate Social Responsibility (CSR) best practice companies. *Journal of Cleaner Production*, **112**: 2896–2906.

Joyner, B. and Payne, D. (2002). Evolution and implementation: A study of values, business ethics and corporate social responsibility. *Journal of Business Ethics*, **41**: 297–311.

Kanagaretnam, K., Lobo, G. J., Wang, C., and Whalen, D. J. (2019). Cross-country evidence on the relationship between societal trust and risk-taking by banks. *Journal of Financial and Quantitative Analysis*, **54**(1): 275–301.

Kanas, A., Hassan Al-Tamimi, H. A., Albaity, M., and Mallek, R. S. (2019). Bank competition, stability, and intervention quality. *International Journal of Finance & Economics*, **24**(1): 568–587.

Karklins, R. (2002). Typology of post-communist corruption. *Problems of Post-communism*, **49**(4): 22–32.

Kasman, S. and Kasman, A. (2015). Bank competition, concentration and financial stability in the Turkish banking industry. *Economic Systems*, **39**(3): 502–517.

Keele, L. (2008). *Semiparametric Regression for the Social Sciences*. John Wiley & Sons.

Keynes, J. N. (1890). *The scope and method of political economy*. Macmillan, London.

Kurucz, E. C., Colbert, B. A., and Wheeler, D. (2008). *The business case for corporate social responsibility*. In The Oxford handbook of corporate social responsibility, 83–112.

Lenglet, M. (2012). Ambivalence and ambiguity: The interpretive role of compliance officers. In *Finance: The Discreet Regulator* (59–84). Palgrave Macmillan, London.

Lins, K. V., Servaes, H., and Tamayo, A. (2017). Social capital, trust, and firm performance: The value of corporate social responsibility during the financial crisis. *The Journal of Finance*, **72**(4): 1785–1824.

Longenecker, J. G., McKinney, J. A., and Moore, C. W. (1989). Ethics in small business. *Journal of Small Business Management*, **27**(1): 27.

Lopatta, K., Jaeschke, R., Tchikov, M., and Lodhia, S. (2017). Corruption, corporate social responsibility and financial constraints: International firm-level evidence. *European Management Review*, **14**(1): 47–65.

Luo, J. H., Huang, Z., Li, X., and Lin, X. (2018). Are women CEOs valuable in terms of bank loan costs? Evidence from China. *Journal of Business Ethics*, **153**(2): 337–355.

Mauro, P. (1995). Corruption and growth. *Quarterly Journal of Economics*, **110**: 681–712.

McGovern, G. (2016). *Transform: A Rebel's Guide for Digital Transformation.* Silver Beach.

Méon, P. G. and Weill, L. (2010). Is corruption an efficient grease? *World development*, **38**(3): 244–259.

Miller, R. T. (2009). Morals in a market bubble. *University of Dayton Law Review*, **35**(1): 113–137.

Noman, A. H. M., Gee, C. S., and Isa, C. R. (2017). Does competition improve financial stability of the banking sector in ASEAN countries? An empirical analysis. *PLoS One*, **12**(5): 1–27.

North, D. C. (1993). Institutions and economic performance. *Rationality, Institutions, and Economic Methodology*, **2**: 242–261.

O'Toole, J. and Bennis, W. (2009). A culture of candor. *Harvard business review*, **87**(6): 54–61.

Ojasoo, M. (2016). CSR reporting, stakeholder engagement and preventing hypocrisy through ethics audit. *Journal of Global Entrepreneurship Research*, **6**(1): 14.

Omarova, S. T. (2017). Ethical finance as a systemic challenge: Risk, culture, and structure. *Cornell JL & Public Policy*, **27**: 797.

Plaksina, Y., Gallagher, L., and Dowling, M. (2019). CEO social status and M&A decision making. *International Review of Financial Analysis*, **64**: 282–300.

Qi, S. and Ongena, S. (2019). Will money talk? Firm bribery and credit access. *Financial Management*, **48**(1): 117–157.

Reich, R. (2008). Government needs to rebuild trust in the markets. *U.S. News and World Report.*

Rodríguez-Ariza, L., Cuadrado-Ballesteros, B., Martínez-Ferrero, J., and García-Sánchez, I. M. (2017). The role of female directors in promoting CSR practices: An international comparison between family and non-family businesses. *Business Ethics: A European Review*, **26**(2): 162–174.

Sapienza, P. and Zingales, L. (2012). A trust crisis. *International Review of Finance*, **12**(2): 123–131.

Schwartz, M. and Carroll, A. (2008). Integrating and unifying competing and complementary frameworks. *Business & Society*, **47**: 148–186.

Scott, W. R. (2005). Institutional theory: Contributing to a theoretical research program. *Great Minds in Management: The Process of Theory Development*, **37**: 460–484.

Shaheer, N., Yi, J., Li, S., and Chen, L. (2019). State-owned enterprises as bribe payers: The role of institutional environment. *Journal of Business Ethics*, **159**(1): 221–238.

Shim, J. (2019). Loan portfolio diversification, market structure and bank stability. *Journal of Banking & Finance*, **104**: 103–115.

Siddik, M., Alam, N., and Kabiraj, S. (2018). Does financial inclusion induce financial stability? Evidence from cross-country analysis. *Australasian Accounting, Business and Finance Journal*, **12**(1): 34–46.

Stiglitz, J. (2008). The fruit of hypocrisy. *The Guardian*, **16**(9): 2008.

Taleb, N. N. (2007). *The Black Swan. The Impact of the Highly Improbable. New York: Random House.* Reviewed by James Iain Gow Université de Montréal, Canada.

Taplin, R. (Ed.). (2007). *Outsourcing and human resource management: An international survey.* Routledge.

Treviño, L., Weaver, G., Gibson, D., and Toffler, B. (1999). Managing ethics and legal compliance: What works and what hurts. *California Management Review*, **41**: 131–151.

Umar, M. A., Derashid, C., Ibrahim, I., and Bidin, Z. (2019). Public governance quality and tax compliance behavior in developing countries: The mediating role of socioeconomic conditions. *International Journal of Social Economics*, **46**(3): 338–351.

Van Vu, H., Tran, T. Q., Van Nguyen, T., and Lim, S. (2018). Corruption, types of corruption and firm financial performance: New evidence from a transitional economy. *Journal of Business Ethics*, **148**(4): 847–858.

Weber, K. and Waeger, D. (2017). Organizations as polities: An open systems perspective. *Academy of Management Annals*, **11**(2): 886–918.

Weill, L. and Godlewski, C. J. (2009). Collateral and adverse selection in transition countries. *Eastern European Economics*, **47**(1): 29–40.

Wellalage, N. H., Locke, S., and Samujh, H. (2019). Corruption, gender and credit constraints: Evidence from South Asian SMEs. *Journal of Business Ethics*, **159**(1): 267–280.

Weller, A. (2017). Exploring practitioners' meaning of "Ethics", "Compliance", and "Corporate Social". *Business & Society*, 1–27.

Wiesiołek, P. and Tymoczko, D. (2015). The evolution of banking sectors in Central and Eastern Europe-the case of Poland. *BIS Paper*, (83r).

Zhang, D., Cai, J., Dickinson, D. G., and Kutan, A. M. (2016). Nonperforming loans, moral hazard and regulation of the Chinese commercial banking system. *Journal of Banking & Finance*, **63**(1): 48–60.

Zucker, L. G. (1988). Where do institutional patterns come from? Organizations as actors in social systems. *Institutional patterns and organizations: Culture and Environment*, **20**(3): 23–49.

Part II:

Financial Markets: Post-crisis Challenges

https://doi.org/10.1142/9781786349507_0005

Chapter 5

Beyond the Myths: Questions for Post Modern Finance

Jean-François Boulier
French association representing institutional investors, France
jean-francois.boulier@af2i.org

Que restera t il demain des écrits des savants? Seulement le mal qu'ils ont dit de ceux qui les ont précédés
Amin Maalouf
Samarcande

5.1 Introduction

Finance theory is thriving and crumbling at the same time. The first foundations of modern finance set in the seventies and eighties have proved to be very effective: finance research has developed tremendously since then and the financial industry has grown much quicker than overall economies during the course of several decades. But a price has now to be paid for that success: the great crisis has tarnished the status of the sector, decelerated its growth, and the limits of an industry working on its own are all clear. On top of that, many hypotheses which help to build the theories behind that growth have been challenged by the researchers themselves, like the market efficiency, and by the facts, like statistical distributions or rational behaviors. Furthermore, the great crisis has shifted the paradigm to a more inclusive industry with closer connection to social and environmental issues. Regulation and political might are back to a field that has sometimes pretended to manage itself better than with rules and supervisors.

It feels then quite appropriate to step back and think of some of these foundations, or credences, that were the major hypothesis behind modern finance, with the hindsight of real-world experience and past empirical research. Since most of the hypothesis are not totally flawed, it is also useful to try to assess how to revamp them to make them more appropriate. In addition, new avenues to tackle the desire for a more inclusive finance should be tried. These are the rather immodest goals of this short paper which draws on my personal experience, thus limited by nature, and my own readings, again limited. Nevertheless it seems useful to take a rather comprehensive view at the risk of being too simple or less accurate because the variety of topics addressed by finance literature may lead to silos of knowledge, yet more specific and precise, but unable to embrace the big picture, which all practitioners face in a way or another.

The main theories whose hypothesis I would like to discuss are predominantly the ones related to pricing and investments. What is called behavioral theory is not a theory per se, but rather a set thoughts on actual behavior of market participants with empirical evidence supporting them. Asset pricing remains the cornerstone of many professional activities, and therefore most of my concerns are related to a too narrow approach of pricing by many theories. The so-called modern portfolio theory has shaped many products and helped to develop many services in asset management, but they have always been considered with some suspicion by practitioners who understood the difficulties of estimating the entrants. And other theories are also influenced by the credences I shall discuss now, even if I shall not make reference to them.

I have made a choice of some of the founding myths and shall discuss them in light of the industry practices or the experience I happened to gather during the last decades. All along my career of investor, I have been in active relationships with academics, at least those able and willing to engage with practitioners, which help me select and read relevant papers if not all. Chairman of the French Finance Association at the turn of the century, Editor of Bankers Markets and Investors, which I contributed to create in 1992, and active board member of Inquire Europe, I truly believed, and still do believe, that a better knowledge is a decisive advantage for a sound and effective practice, better for innovation, better for risk management, and a truly international language to discuss these matters with foreigners. I am therefore thankful of what I am prepared to criticize! And certainly some of my views will just reflect my lack of knowledge or understanding, so please bear with me.

The eight myths I have selected are the following: markets exists; markets are pure and perfect; markets are liquid; markets are efficient; individuals are rational; only risks are priced; markets are random walks; one cannot beat markets. Some of them hide much more than what they say; I, thus, may spend more time decrypting what lies behind in my mind. A number of other issues may be related to these eight myths which I intend to discuss even if they are not necessarily at the center of the specific hypothesis I shall discuss. In conclusion, I shall try to lay a program of what feels to me necessary for a "better future".

5.2 Markets Exist

They do not. The existence, or more precisely, the persistence of markets is more an exception than a rule. Many emerging markets, like Argentina or Russia, reopened after years of closure. Most of the financial markets are indeed intermittent. Corporate bond markets, for example, tend be active a few weeks after their issuance. Then liquidity is sparse. Moreover during the great crisis, the liquidity of even very actively traded bonds or related instruments, credit default swaps for example, all of a sudden evaporated. The mantra in the years before the crisis was to privatize markets which, in many cases, resulted in dispersion of liquidity in many venues, including the "dark pools". Besides, many so-called markets are indeed very infrequent and the transactions not always public.

Thus, markets depend on the will and capacity of participants to transact. The permanence of trading depends on the motives of the buyer and the seller, possibly helped by intermediaries or facilitated by platforms enabled by technologies. It seems that the interests of the market participants should be somewhat taken into account to build a reasonable story about markets. Empirical work done on currency and high-frequency trading has shown that there are obviously times when nobody trades, but maybe robots. Some participants, like high-frequency traders, pretended to bring liquidity. Many empirical studies (see Dacorogna *et al.*, 2001) have shown that their activity was contingent to other trading participants and that as soon liquidity stops they stop trading. This shows that the motive of the intermediaries has to be integrated into the picture. It is also clear that the legal and, above that, the political framework plays a critical role. Many stock markets disappeared during communist regimes. Many organizations depend on rules, habits, and are regulated to prevent many evils and dangers. So the existence of markets is highly dependent on these aspects. It depends on the willingness of potential participants to establish a market with the support or approval of all other stakeholders. This means, notably, legal enforcement and regulatory oversight.

The growth of private markets, in loans, equities, or property, is a challenge to the proponents of public markets. Could it be possible to see public market simply disappear? Of course not, but the equilibrium between both private and public market also has an impact on the existence and sustainability of markets.

5.3 Markets Are Pure and Perfect

Of course they are not. Starting with a more realistic assumption that there are inevitable frictions and cost associated with the transactions would certainly modify most of the reasoning and evaluation. The oversimplification was useful at the time when computing power was limited, for option pricing notably, but this is no longer a limitation. This assumption has hidden the role of intermediaries and may have blurred their benefits in the market place. There is no doubt they need profits in order to fulfill their roles and engage in the market. Too much regulation and insufficient profitability has forced a great number of banks out of the active market, making and even trading since the crisis, in particular in Europe. The liberalization of market places could also be debated in light of the great crisis debacle.

Perfection of market relates to the possibility to trade continuously. The preceding section has stated the first limit, market must exist. When they do, trading may be infrequent, and therefore liquidity becomes an issue, which we shall discuss in the next section. Of course the idea of instantaneous trading could lead one to think that transaction prices are reflecting the underlying value of what is traded. But is it still the case if we have infrequent trading? Research in less liquid markets like real estate or infrastructure has debated at length on the differences between appraisal by experts, which is often used when transactions are missing, and transactions prices, quite rare for some assets. The outcome is that there is ample differences in their probability distribution. This shows that valuation might be a much more challenging exercise than it seems. Should the mark to market dogma be revisited? This does not mean imperfect markets cannot be modeled and that we should abandon transactions values. It seems the mark to model should be further researched; such an approach has been used in practice when the liquidity has evaporated. Could it be a more reasonable way to assess valuation?

Perfection was also related to two other very important notions, the first related to information and the second to efficiency; we shall come back to these two notions later.

5.4 Markets Are Liquid

Sometimes, and for some. Reality shows that when markets exist they may not be active all the time. Volume variations are quite important even for very liquid assets. Recently, the Federal Reserve was forced to pump a few hundred billions to support the Treasury market supposed to back the short-term market in the dollar market. And we don't even know why. During the crisis, most of the corporate bonds' liquidity evaporated without any reason but the possibility of a crisis. Which somehow created the crisis! Understandably, all fancy structured products and ABS related to bad assets were in deep trouble, even though their trading was very active in the past two to three years. Euro money markets experienced a very significant and yet unforeseen liquidity crash in 2007, much before the great crisis. The explanation given to this shortage of liquidity in the money market was that banks no longer wanted to trade for fear that other banks would be hurt by the subprime ABS or related structured credit instruments. So, liquidity modeling seems quite daunting.

But why not try to model the phenomenon? There is ample evidence and good reasons to incorporate a liquidity premium in less liquid assets. But we should also include the possibility of illiquidity! A lot of efforts have been made in the last ten year to measure and manage the liquidity risk. Nevertheless, in my opinion, no real model offers a credible framework to understand and harness liquidity challenges.

Maybe physics, quantic physics, or fluid mechanics could provide interesting tools to begin the modeling of liquidity of assets. And including a view on the willingness of intermediaries to trade would certainly help, so social dynamics may be considered. When a less liquid asset is traded, the transaction value doesn't reflect the intrinsic value because a cost is incurred by the buyer. And this cost is even amplified as the market value increases.

5.5 Markets Are Efficient

It is often claimed that market prices incorporate all public information. There are, thus, two assumptions here: first, public information is disseminated immediately and, second, price adjustments are made instantaneously. Information efficiency is indeed often met, so it might seem these assumptions are close to being valid. Nevertheless, experience shows how far from reality the two assumptions are. What public information means could be questioned. Of course, procedures to issue market sensitive information are well developed and regulation frame its disclosure. Also, regulators punish the one who infringe the rules. But there is a wide body of evidence that many people use private information to trade and make profits. This means that valuation also includes some private information. And public information can also be gained from sources other than the issuer. Stakeholders may send signals or individuals may gather information that may have an impact on profits or risks, and therefore on market values. Many surveys on customers or employees have shown their impacts. The information available to the public is often used by people closer geographically to the headquarters of firm, and often with success.

Price tend to react in a variety of ways to new information as many empirical studies have demonstrated (see Schiller, 1981 in particular). First, they tend to be slow, so the reaction takes several days to stabilize. This shows there are leaders and followers in the market, and several researchers have tried to model that. Overreaction also happen, so certain news, specially macroeconomic or political news, tend to push price too quickly and too far into a direction, and then prices tend revert to a more credible equilibrium value. September 11 was such an event when not enough was known to begin to trade, and fortunately markets were shut. Even when trading resumed, most of the assumptions of the magnitude of the shocks to the US economy were exaggerated. Also price movements can occur before the news are certain, like ballots with an uncertain outcome and a possible big shift in policy have often illustrated. One of the most important outcome is finally that price volatility of assets is far too wide than the fundamental values would imply. For example, a famous paper of Schiller demonstrated that US equities were almost three times too volatile!

Gathering data and relevant information is also costly. Having the right models to guess how and when market prices will react means investment in very qualified resources. It feels information and the many new channels by which it circulates should be better modeled. Big data or simply data on transactions have also a price. Efficiency seems to be a kind of asymptotic state which will always be challenged if there are profitable trades at stake.

5.6 Individuals Are Rational

They may be rational, but their behavior is not. There is now ample evidence of bias in attitudes towards risks and profit. Behavioral finance has empirically demonstrated how large these biases could be. No doubt the biases are exploited, sometimes even very consciously. It is common wisdom that people should not trade or borrow if they do not understand. So rational behavior should not be expected from people with insufficient financial literacy. A new stream of literature goes into this direction and addresses the gap of knowledge between professionals and non-professionals. In many countries, regulators have put in place quite severe restrictions to distribution to avoid the dangers of overoptimism with lack of understanding of the risks.

But more curiously, even many well-educated individuals behave irrationally, as the famous paper on investment choices of professors of finance in a Californian university has shown. There are many other influences that may determine the portfolio choices and the willingness to trade. A new stream of papers show how extra financial data can come into play. People may act on information they understand more than on financial data they do not fully grasp. As ESG development tends to prove, individuals care about other aspects than purely financial information when they invest. Undoubtedly, climate and social aspects enter into their decisions. How much and on what elements need to be better understood. The balance between financial and extra financial criteria is probably different for different individuals and will evolve with time. But ESG risks are now in all market participants' minds. They, thus, should have an influence on prices, like the troubles VW faced in the diesel case have shown.

A less researched consideration should be better understood: individuals behave within groups, and social aspects have therefore many consequences. Herding is one of the most common. But there are certainly many others. With extra financial data, the complexity of issues and the willingness of some investors to do good to others will probably add to the diversity of situations, sometimes overwhelming the strict financial framework. Most of the standards are decided by a group of people; most decisions made by institutions and firms are made by teams, thus a better representation of group behavior could be useful. It is often claimed, and indeed there is some empirical evidence, that board diversity leads to better governance and better decisions, which shows such an approach proved to be useful. On the other hand, how beliefs are built and how fake news and rumors develop and their impacts on markets should be better taken into account.

5.7 Only Risks Are Priced

It is maybe less of a fundamental assumption than the other ones. But the argument to keep only factors in pricing that are related to risks is often claimed. There are good reason to start from risks, but it may be too restrictive. A great deal of empirical work has been dedicated to hedonic approaches in real estate valuation. It seems such an approach could be useful for financial assets. Paying high dividends or additional payments tied to loyalty may influence pricing. Bond features also have an impact on their desirability, like floating rate when rates are on the rise.

In particular, the inclusion of ESG criteria in pricing of securities needs to be addressed urgently. Will the various components be the same in all markets? Will carbon emissions only be cared for in a transitory phase or will they remain once the energy transition is completed? Are the social components stable over time, or will they just progress getting better with increased care? Many investors consider ESG as long-term risks to include into prices. But there might be preferences, in societal issues; notably, that are not directly related to risks.

A recent approach has recently being proposed by Ibbotson *et al.* (2018) which they called Popularity Asset Pricing Model. This extension of traditional CAPM goes exactly in that direction while keeping most of framework that proved useful in the restricted CAPM model. New elements like preferences in the demand for assets and heterogeneity in that demand enhance the model into a more comprehensive and realistic framework. Other aspects like statistical assumptions could add to that and make an appealing model.

5.8 Market Prices Follow Random Walks

Very strong hypothesis indeed! Made sometimes even stronger with the addition of a Gaussian structure... None of these hypothesis proved completely right. They may be about right, or right most of the time, but there is a lot of empirical evidence showing the limits of these assumptions (see Hou, 2018 for a recent survey). Of course this critique is not new, and many efforts have been dedicated to try other statistical models. None of them have succeeded to replace the good old Brownian motion!

Meanwhile market prices tend to exhibit correlations; especially, short movements tend to be positively correlated and stock prices changes seem to be negative on lower frequencies. It is sometimes due to information leakage or diffusion as I already mentioned. It can also be due to followers in the markets, either humans or even robots, in case of high-frequency trading for instance. But news and price movements may trigger more sophisticated price paths that can be somewhat predictable and therefore exploited. The success of momentum strategies is a clear indication that we are not always in a random walk situation. Even the factor momentum is now taken as a strategic component for portfolio construction.

Gaussian law is a perfect model but more suited to former Deutsche Mark banknotes than to real money markets! It is an asymptotic model for a large number of samples and thus makes a lot of sense when one looks at what is happening in markets. Nevertheless, the stability of that statistical law remains questionable, since the number of trades fluctuate widely depending on news and other factors. Many studies have shown indeed that the behavior of prices tended to be heteroskedastic and that ARCH, GARCH models were more suitable than constant volatility processes to describe past data. Other researchers have pushed for stable laws, which indeed stick to two characteristics of price movements: higher tendency of no changes than expected with a Normal law and much higher probability of very large movements, which has often be a difficulty for stress testing.

5.9 One Cannot Beat the Market

Everyone can! Theoretically, many studies showed how one could beat markets and, in practice, many providers have performed much better than markets on a risk-adjusted basis. Which of course does not means it is easy...and cannot necessarily be done on a very large scale. There are limits to the possibility, as the capacity of certain strategies are limited and also the majority of investors cannot obviously beat the rest of the market players on an asset-weighted basis.

A recent paper has summarized the many anomalies that have been found and empirically demonstrated. Its count is over a thousand! Fama (1965), who was among the first to state market could not be beaten, reversed his claim in showing that factors could drive market valuation. University of Chicago researchers were quite quick to contradict their fellow member. Nobody would nowadays claim or teach that to anymore.

And many investors have shown they were actually able to beat markets in a systematic manner. The hedge funds industry has grown in size to over three trillion and proved that the claim was wrong. But there are obviously risks associated with these returns. Even a strategy with a very high Sharpe ratio, say above one (three times asset classes' average Sharpe ratio), can involve hidden risks, but with a different probability distribution and measurable with other metrics. Credit strategies, for example, exhibit performances with asymmetric distributions. And even very powerful strategies can fail overnight.

But good performance, above market benchmarks, are indeed hard to achieve. It is one major of the arguments of ETF or passive funds providers.

5.10 In Conclusion

A reassessment of the most common hypotheses in finance needs to be done. Many products, regulations, and habits were based on some of the assumptions I have listed. In a oversimplified way, they could all come from the belief market prices are representative of true asset value and that their fluctuations were the proper measure of their risk. Market comes first was the mantra. In my mind, this starting point is flawed. Or more precisely, transaction prices are a result; starting from the motives of the market participants with their biases seems more appropriate. Knowing what I know, here is a suggestion for building a more realistic framework.

I would start by reassessing participants' utility functions. They are probably different if there are end users or intermediaries. Their motives should include some preferences on social, governance, and political aspects, like climate nowadays. These preferences should have individual and group components.

Then I would try to consider valuation as a quantic value that may be revealed by transaction prices but with some deviation, due to the many biases and costs. The possibility of a trade should also be modeled and liquidity seen as the outcome of participants motives, not as a characteristic of securities. The valuation would include fundamental elements, financial and extra financial items, and transaction-related items.

Given the availability of computing power, I do not think imposing statistical structures is necessary. Risks should then be looked at from different angles. Valuation risks would therefore be different from volatilities. Even future market prices risks and volatilities, should include intrinsic components and market components. There may be feedback loops between them, but I think the former are dominant and that market components are more temporary and influenced by intrinsic components.

Professionals would gain from having more realistic frameworks, and the loss of too simplistic and heroic assumptions could have more relevance if not more accuracy. They would also have more inclusive tools to manage their portfolios, balance sheet, or the like of their clients, with hopefully more confidence that the hypothesis are not bringing unwanted biases. The myths were truly helping some but not all market participants. In particular, it seems assets should be considered primarily for being held rather than for being traded. Responsible investments and corporate responsibility would be better suited than they are in the present existing framework.

In this new setup, market prices would no longer be at the center and no longer be the only reference as far as valuations are concerned. The belief markets "know" would be replaced by a more realistic view that anyone knows the market prices, at least when there are transactions. The usefulness of intermediaries should be acknowledged, but their influence must be recognized. Finance would then be thought in a more inclusive way.

Easier said than done, one may think. A great amount of resources is presently dedicated to research and publication, with often wrong implicit hypothesis. Isn't it time to spend more effort in a direction, albeit more difficult, that makes more sense?

References

Fama, E. (1965). Random walks in stock market prices. *Financial Analyst Journal*, **21**(5): 55–59.

Gencay, R., Dacorogna, M., Muller, U., Pictet, O., and Olsen, R. (2001). *An introduction to high frequency finance*, Elsevier.

Hou, K., Xue, C. and Zhang, L. (2018). Replicating anomalies. *Review of Financial Studies*, **33**(5): 2019–2133.

Ibbotson, R., Idsorek, T., and Kaplan, P. (2018). Popularity: A bridge between classical and behavioral finance. *CFA Research.*

Kahneman, D. and Tversky, A. (1979). Prospect theory: An analysis of decision under risk. *Economica*, **47**(2): 263–291.

Mandelbrot, B. (1960). The Pareto Levy law and the distribution of income. *International Economic Review*, **1**(2): 79–106.

Schiller, R. (1981). Do stock prices move too much to be justified by subsequent changes in dividends? *American Economic Review*, **71**(3): 421–436.

https://doi.org/10.1142/9781786349507_0006

Chapter 6

Contagion Effect Between Financial Markets and Collectibles Markets: A Review of Empirical Research

Eric Le Fur

INSEEC Grande Ecole, CS 63089, 33000 Bordeaux, France
elefur@inseec.com

6.1 Introduction

A wealth of studies has examined the returns and volatility on collectibles and expected gains to portfolio diversification in the past 20 years. All kinds of collectibles are studied, though these include mainly art and wine. For example, according to the Art Market 2018 report, which was published by Art Basel and UBS, the total sales of the international fine art trade was estimated to be in excess of $63.7 bn in 2017, which is over 150 times the value that was recorded in 1970 (Artprice, 2018). The US, China, and the UK accounted for 83% of the total sales by value. This is explained by the presence of major auction houses in New York, London, Hong Kong, and Beijing. China maintains the lion's share of the Asian market by value. Together, Japan, South Korea, India, and Indonesia account for more than 20% of the market, and the EU accounts for 33%. Furthermore, online art sales reached a new high of USD 5.4 billion in 2017, or 8% of the global art market by value. Indeed, the Internet has allowed the market to reach new clients. Forty percent of the clients that bought online through top-tier auction houses were new customers. Galleries reported that 45% of online buyers were new to their business in 2018. Investment in fine wines has also become quite fashionable in recent years. This passion has been accompanied by an increase in the volume of auctions and by record prices. The worldwide turnover from major auction houses climbed from US$90 million in 2003 to US$346 million in 2015. To follow market trends, investors, collectors, and brokers have access to several indices (Masset and Weisskopf, 2018). In recent years, the emergence of wine funds has also allowed people to invest without directly holding the bottles. Finally, between 2009 and 2016, according to the Historic Automobile Group International (HAGI), which tracks collectible automobile prices, the HAGI Top Index, which measures the rare collector's automobile market, grew by more than 200%.

Several facts may explain this enthusiasm for the purchase of collectibles. For example, there is an economic and political opening of some countries (China in particular) that allows the populations of those countries to adopt Western consumer traits. Furthermore, the growing number of wealthy households in the world may explain this craze for investing in collectibles. Indeed, according to Knight Frank's 2018 Wealth Report, the number of ultra-high net worth individuals (UHNWI)[1] increased by 20.25% between 2012 and 2017 to reach 2,535,480 individuals; the projection for 2022 is 3,617,550 individuals. The strongest growth has occurred on the Asian continent. In 2017, there were 686,820 high net worth individuals (HNWI), an increase of 39% between 2012 and 2017. During the same period, the increase was 96% in China, 56% in India, 43% in Hong Kong, and 41% in South Korea. These new wealthy households have financial liquidity and are, therefore, looking for alternative products to consume and save.

Thus, investors consider collectibles suitable alternative assets and an additional way to diversify their portfolios (Jorda *et al.*, 2017). For several years, new specialized investment funds have provided the opportunity to invest in this type of alternative assets without

[1]The UHNWI are defined as those having a net worth of at least US$50 million, and the HNWI are defined as those whose net worth exceeds US$5 million, excluding their primary residence. Among these individuals, demi-billionaires have a net worth exceeding US$500 million.

acquiring the asset directly. Beyond the financial potential, this increasing popularity is also due to the passion and hobby elicited by these alternative assets. Indeed, some collectors are passionate and even obsessive about purchasing unique objects in one way or another (Belk, 2013). They may be taxonomic (i.e. they have one copy of each type of a series of objects) or aesthetic (i.e. they simply collect a few copies of a particular type of object) (Belk, 1991). They can also be classified into four other categories: passionate collectors (obsessive and willing to pay irrationally high prices), acquired collectors (who buy collectibles as an investment), amateur collectors (who simply collect for pleasure), and expressive collectors (who build collections that confirm their identity) (Saari, 1997). In the United States, the Internal Revenue Service distinguishes three categories of actors: collectors (who buy items primarily for fun), investors (who want to make a long-term profit), and dealers (who buy and sell for the sole purpose of making a short-term profit) (Dale, 2008). Conversely, some observers give a more restrictive definition, in which a collector is motivated to accumulate a series of similar objects whose instrumental function is not important and does not intend to dispose of them immediately.

However, the collectibles market is characterized by specific features, such as heterogeneity, illiquidity, market segmentation, information asymmetries, behavioral abnormalities, absence of basic value, specific taxes, insurance, commissions for intermediaries, and transport costs (Baumol, 1986; Burton and Jacobsen, 1999). As a result of these specificities, the market is faced with high structural uncertainty. This raises the question of whether this uncertainty is related to the transmission of volatility from other markets. In other words, are collectibles isolated from financial markets, commodities, and other alternative assets and, therefore, an asset for risk diversification? This question is crucial for practitioners and individual investors because their investment strategies are both based and developed on three distinct categories of assets: traditional financial assets (shares, bonds), commodities, and alternative real assets that include real estate and collectibles (Baumol, 1986). Knowledge of volatility for heterogeneous assets is crucial information for private and institutional investors in their investment decision-making, especially in times of uncertainty. When a market becomes very volatile and agents become increasingly uncertain about the future trend of certain economic variables relevant to their decision-making, market activities can be altered, depressed, or even stopped. At the other extreme, high market volatility can dry up a market's liquidity (Jones and Manuelli, 2001).

Financial theory contrasts conventional and alternative assets. The literature proposes several classifications of these alternative assets, which include financial assets and real assets. Finally, real alternative assets are divided into three main classes: real estate (residential, non-residential), commodities, and collectibles. It is these latter real alternative assets that we present in this article. First, we present the methodology used to conduct this study. Then, the three main collectibles studied in the literature (art, wine, and stamps) are presented, as well as a section devoted to other collectibles. Finally, we conclude.

6.2 Methodology: Identification of Papers and Selection Process

This research covers empirical papers published in academic journals, books, and working papers on collectibles from 1971 to 2019. We performed two main steps to identify and select the papers covered in this review. The selection process has been carefully designed to assure that we cover the complete collectibles finance literature. We refer to the research structure proposed in the management literature (Siebels and zu Knyphausen-Aufseß, 2012; Pindado and Requejo, 2015).

In the first step, we searched for different electronic libraries (EBSCO Host, Google Scholar, ScienceDirect) using different keyword combinations (each collectibles combined with contagion, finance, investment, portfolio, prices, and returns) in the title, abstract, or list of keywords. At this stage, we retained all papers without restriction.

In the second step, we eliminated the duplicates as well as the substantive irrelevant articles by selective reading of the title and abstract. Regarding the working papers and books, we use the number of citations in academic journals. Finally, Table 6.1 indicates the final sample per category of journals and Fig. 6.1 presents the number of articles per year. There is an increasing number of papers

Table 6.1. List of journals.*

Agricultural economics (16)	
Agricultural Economics	Wine (2)
European Review of Agricultural Economics	Wine (1)
International Journal of Wine Business Research	Wine (2)
Journal of Wine Economics	Wine (11)
Book and working papers (15)	
Book	Ceramics (1), coins (1), rare book (1), whisky (1), wine (1).
Working papers	Art (1), Lego (2), metlach beer steins (1), stamps (1), violins (1), whisky (2), wine (2)
Development economics (1)	
Emerging Markets Review	Wine (1)
Econometrics (1)	
Empirical Economics	Art (1)
Economic theory (1)	
Journal of Economic Theory	Wine (1)
Finance (23)	
Accounting and Finance	Art (1)
Bankers, Markets & Investors	Art (1)
Finance Economic Letters	Diamonds (1)
Financial Analysts Journal	Stamps and violins (1)
Geneva Papers on Risk and Insurance	Art (1)
International Review of Financial Analysis	Wine (1)
Journal of Alternative Investments	Stamps (1), wine (2)
Journal of Finance	Stamps (1)
Journal of Finance and Investment Analysis	Art (1)
Journal of Financial Economics	Stamps (1), wine (1)
Journal of Investments	Wine (1)
Quarterly Review of Economics and Finance	Cars (1)
Journal of Financial Service Professionals	Stamps (1)
Journal of Wealth Management	Cars (2)
Journal of Portfolio Management	Coins (1)

(*Continued*)

Table 6.1. (*Continued*)

Pacific Basin Finance Journal	Wine (1)
Quantitative Finance	Wine (1)
Review of International Business & Finance	Wine (2)
General economy (32)	
American Economic Review	Art (5)
Applied Economics	Wine (1)
Australian Economic Papers	Wine (1)
Business & Economic Research	Diamonds (1)
Chance	Wine (1)
Cosmopolitan Canvases	Art (1)
Economic Inquiry	Art (2), diamonds (1), violins (2), wine (1)
Economic Record	Wine (1)
Economie et Prévisions	Wine (1)
European Economic Review	Art (4)
Journal de la Société Statistiques de Paris	Wine (1)
Journal of Economic Behavior Organization	Coins (1)
Journal of Economic Literature	Art (1)
Journal of Economic Perspectives	Beanie Babies (1)
Journal of Political Economy	Art (1), ceramics (1)
Management Science	Art (1)
Southern Economic Journal	Antique furniture (1), stamps (2)
Industrial organization (3)	
Business : Theory and Practice	Wine (1)
Journal of Cultural Economics	Antique firearms (1), art (1)
Innovation (1)	
International Journal of Entrepreneurship and Small Business	Wine (1)
Macroeconomics (3)	
Journal of International Financial Markets, Institutions & Money	Cars (1)
Economic Modelling	Wine (2)
Spatial economics (1)	
Land Economics	Timber (1)

*In brackets, the number of articles per category of economic classification and per collectibles.

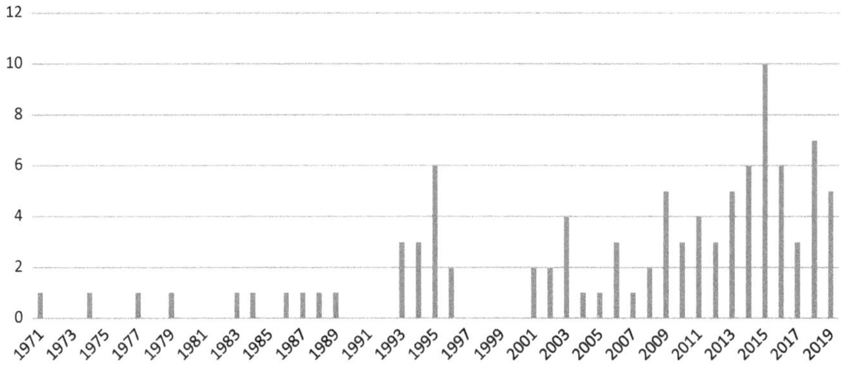

Fig. 6.1. Number of papers per year.

since the beginning of the millennium. The number of journals is high. More than half of the articles are published in journals of general economics or finance. A second large share of papers is published in agricultural economics, books, and working papers.

6.3 Art

6.3.1 *Returns of art*

The first studies on determining the returns on investment in art[2] date back to the mid-1970s (Anderson, 1974; Stein, 1977). Two main methods are used to calculate the rate of return on works of art: the repeat sales method (Goetzmann, 1993; Pesando, 1993; Mei and Moses, 2002) and the hedonic approach (Buelens and Ginsburgh, 1993; Chanel *et al.*, 1996; Ashenfelter and Graddy, 2003; Renneboog and Spaenjers, 2013, 2015). It is customary to think that investing in art is profitable. This seems to be confirmed by some auctions with record amounts. However, over a longer period of time, high prices are only partially reflected in the high rates of return on investment in art. For example, considering all the additional risks and frictions in the art market, the return on investments in art does not

[2]For a review of the literature on the determinants of art prices, anomalies in price formation in the art market, art auctions and price indices, see Ashenfelter and Graddy (2003) and Ginsburgh *et al.* (2006).

exceed their opportunity cost (Baumol, 1986). In addition, over the period 1957–2007, the real annual rate of return on investment in art was 3.9%. In some years it was even negative, with the lowest rate being −32% in 1991 (Renneboog and Spaenjers, 2013). Between 1900 and 2012, the annualized real return was 2.4% (6.4% in nominal terms). There were strong price appreciations in the late 1960s, early 1970s, late 1980s, and between 2004 and 2006. Prices fell significantly during the First World War, during the Great Depression, in the years following the 1973 oil crisis, during the recession of the early 1990s, and during the financial crisis of 2008 (Dimson and Spaenjers, 2014).

6.3.2 *Return on art in relation to other assets*

Over the period 1977–1995, investments in art earned on average a lower rate of return than equity markets (Frey and Eichenberger, 1995). These results are confirmed over the period 1995–2007, when the average annual return on art was 4% lower, while it was 6.6% for equities. However, the rate of return for art is higher than for government bonds (2.7%) and corporate bonds (4.0%). Compared to gold, art offers a higher return for a much lower risk (Renneboog and Spaenjers, 2013). Similarly, between 1900 and 2012, the nominal annual rate of art was 6.4% (2.4% in real terms) lower than that of American equities (9.4% and 5.2%) and higher than that of bonds (5.5% and 1.5%) (Goetzmann *et al.*, 2011; Dimson and Spaenjers, 2014).

6.3.3 *Relationship between art market and financial markets*

It may take some time for the wealth created in the financial markets to trickle down to the art markets. There is no consensus on the link between financial markets and investments in art. For example, there were short-term influences of the stock markets on the hedonic price indexes of the great masters and American painters in London, Paris, and New York over the period 1963–1992. However, this relationship was not significant in the long term (Ginsburgh and Jeanfils, 1995). Over the 1976–2001 period, the level of integration of international art markets was high in the short and long term.

There are also significant interrelations between art and the main stock markets (Worthington and Higgs, 2003, 2004). Some studies also conclude that it is difficult to make long-term forecasts for art prices and that these prices follow a random walk (Chanel *et al.*, 1994; Chanel, 1995). Finally, it seems that art markets are weakly to moderately integrated with each other and that art prices on the American market influence prices on the European market without any feedback (Bakhouche, 2013). Between 1998 and 2016, there seem to be feedback phenomena between a few art markets and moderate causal links between art market indices, which would indicate that there are many possibilities for diversification for practitioners, investors, and collectors (Le Fur, 2019).

6.3.4 *Art and portfolio diversification*

The majority of academic studies show weakly positive correlation indices between art and financial markets, especially with the S&P500 (Mei and Moses, 2002; Pesando and Shum, 2008). It also seems that this correlation is higher between a global art price index and the returns of a global stock market index than between the same art index and the S&P500 (Renneboog and Spaenjers, 2009).

6.4 Wine

6.4.1 *What is a fine wine?*

On October 13, 2018, during an auction organized by Sotheby's in New York, a bottle of 1945 Romanée-Conti was sold for $558,000. A few minutes later, at the same auction, another bottle of 1945 Romanée-Conti was auctioned for $496,000. The previous record for a regular bottle of wine was recorded in Hong Kong, in 2010, for an 1869 Château Lafite Rothschild for $304,000. These prestigious wines represent only a part of the total market. They are often called fine wines. A fine wine is a wine for investment with a potential return, as opposed to a non-fine wine that investors call a "normal wine" (Baldi *et al.*, 2013; Introvigne *et al.*, 2017). The term fine wine is reserved for exceptional wines from the best vineyards in the world, prestigious châteaux, and the best winemakers. Over the years, they have achieved a kind of "blue chip" status. They represent a very large part of the main auctions held at Acker Merall, Butterfield, Christie's, Sotheby's, and Zachy's. The best known and most renowned are the five first growths of Bordeaux: Haut-Brion, Lafite Rothschild, Latour, Margaux, and Mouton Rothschild. There are others in Bordeaux (Angelus, Ausone, Cheval Blanc, Léoville Las Case, Mission Haut Brion, Petrus, Yquem...) and in other regions or countries such as Australia (Penfolds Grange), Burgundy (Echezeaux, Grand Echezeaux, Richebourg, Romanee Conti, Romanee St Vivant, Tache), California (Dominus, Mondavi), Champagne (Krug, Moet & Chandon, Ruinart, Taittinger), Italy (Gaja, Masseto, Ornella), Portugal (Dow's Vintage), or Spain (Vega Sicilia).

6.4.2 *Databases and methodologies to analyze the fine wine returns*

Several data sources are available, such as specialized wine indices, auction prices from different auction houses, "en primeur" prices, private data providers, and famous wine guides. Many prices are suggested prices and not actual prices. In the fine wine market, the law of one price is imperfect (Cardebat *et al.*, 2017), and there are price differences between auction houses (Masset *et al.*, 2016). In addition, many studies on wine returns use hedonic functions and more particularly log-linear or mixed log-linear functional forms. Some studies also use the method of repeated sales.

6.4.3 *Wine returns in within-wine asset class portfolio*

This section presents the returns on fine wines in a wine-only portfolio. The portfolios selected are most often composed of Bordeaux wines and more particularly of the top five growths. Some studies also compare the returns of Bordeaux wines with those of other regions such as Australia, California, Italy, Rhône, and Spain as well as returns of indirect investment via wine funds.

Studies show that regardless of the wine-growing region, returns are always positive. The annual returns of Bordeaux Premiers Crus vary over a very long period (1900–2012) by 4.1% (Dimson *et al.*, 2015). The average annual variation was higher (8.7%) over the period 1988–2000 (Bentzen *et al.*, 2002). The first five growths had annual returns on average of 4.25% over the period 1995–1999 (Hadj Ali and Nauges, 2003). It seems that the returns of Australian wines are more moderate, estimated for example at 3.9% per year for Penfold's Grange over the 1952–1980 period (Byron and Ashenfelter, 1995) and between 2.2% and 4.3% depending on the vintage (Wood and Anderson, 2006). However, Australian wines may also be comparable, if not superior, to Bordeaux wines in terms of returns (Fogarty, 2006). During the period 1996–2007, we observed the same thing with the Rhone in comparison to the Bordeaux wines (Lucey and Devine, 2015). The academic literature also indicates the positive effect of portfolio diversification. For example, the correlation between wines from Australia, France, Italy, and Portugal remains low enough to offer investors significant diversification potential (Kourtis *et al.*, 2012). However, the benefits of diversification depend on the index used. Indeed, over the period 2001–2010, the Liv-ex Fine Wine 1000, which is an index composed of wines from several regions and countries, offered diversification benefits while the Liv-ex Bordeaux 500 did not (Chu, 2014). Finally, the returns on indirect investments via wine funds are higher than for direct investments. However, the selectivity and valuation methods used by the managers of these funds, their ability to anticipate the market, and the volatility of the funds raise questions about the relevance of these returns (Bocart and Hafner, 2015; Lucey and Devine, 2015; Masset and Weisskopf, 2015).

6.4.4 *Wine returns in a mixed-asset portfolio*

This section deals with the inclusion of a fine wine in a portfolio of traditional assets such as stocks and bonds. The academic literature on wine returns in a mixed-asset portfolio context does not conclude on the supremacy of any asset. Indeed, results depend on the period under study, the methodology used, and type of assets considered in the portfolio. However, it seems that portfolios with wine are more efficient than portfolios without wine. In addition, the higher the proportion of wine, the higher the portfolio's return (Aytaç and Mandou, 2016). Most of the studies are focusing on Bordeaux wines, more specifically on the Bordeaux five first growths, while other studies perform the wine returns in Australia and California.

In general, the returns of fine wines are positive. For example, over the period 1990-1991, Bordeaux wines presented an annual real rate of return of 2.4% (Ashenfelter *et al.*, 1995), over the period 1980–1994 of 3% (Jones and Storchmann, 2001), and between 4.1% and 6% over the period 1996–2009 (Masset and Henderson, 2010). Bordeaux wine returns can be higher and reached an annual rate of 7.9% between 1986 and 1996 (Burton and Jacobsen, 2001) and between 7.5% and 9.5% for the period 1996–2003 (Sanning *et al.*, 2008). In the same vein, Californian wines reached 8% between 1998 and 2003 (Haeger and Storchmann, 2006). Exceptionally, an increase can be followed by a slight decrease. For example, between 1981 and 1985, the Bordeaux wine prices increased by close to 75% and then declined by 15% between 1986 and 1992 (Di Vittorio and Ginsburgh, 1996).

There is no consensus on the under or overperformance of wines compared to listed and unlisted shares. The returns on great wines can sometimes be lower than the returns on listed shares. This is the case for Bordeaux wines compared to the DJIA (Ashenfelter *et al.*, 1995; Burton and Jacobsen, 2001) and for American wines (California and Oregon) still compared to the DJIA (Haeger and Storchmann, 2006). This result can be further reduced by the presence of insurance and storage costs, liquidity problems, and the difficulty of obtaining certain wines. However, the returns on fine wines can sometimes be higher than those from stock markets (Sanning *et al.*, 2008; Masset and Weisskopf, 2010). In general, academic literature indicates that fine wines outperform bonds. Indeed, only two studies carried out over short periods indicate lower yields of wines compared to US Treasury Bonds (Krasker, 1979; Ashenfelter *et al.*, 1995).

6.4.5 *Diversification effects in a mixed-asset portfolio*

The role of wine as an alternative asset class has been the subject of controversial discussion for several decades (Storchmann, 2012). Two main trends emerge from these studies. First, many studies agree on the interest of including wine in a mixed-asset portfolio (Kumar, 2005; Sanning *et al.*, 2008; Masset and Henderson, 2010; Masset and Weisskopf, 2010; Fogarty and Jones, 2011; Bouri *et al.*, 2018). Second, wine is considered as a safe haven (Bouri, 2014, 2015; Jurevičienė and Jakavonytė, 2015; Bouri and Roubaud, 2016; Bouri *et al.*, 2018).

While all studies conclude that including wine in a portfolio increases returns, investors should remain cautious about the true benefits of wine for portfolio diversification purposes (Fogarty and Jones, 2011; Fogarty and Sadler, 2014). Indeed, the benefits can be misleading depending on the construction of the index and the method used to measure diversification. In addition, the relevance of hedonic estimates is questioned because most hedonic coefficients are unstable (Faye and Le Fur, 2018).

6.4.6 *Analysis of cointegration and contagion effect with the financial markets and macroeconomic variables*

There is a controversial interpretation of the co-integration between financial markets and fine wine markets. For example, there seems to be an asymmetric reverse volatility in the market measured by the impact of negative shocks on the wine market (Bouri, 2014). In addition, some indicate a high impact of financial markets on wine prices and short-term causality for some wines (Faye *et al.*, 2015). On the other hand, others indicate that there is a possible diversification advantage due to the lack of co-integration between fine wines, normal wine, and the MSCI World (Introvigne *et al.*, 2017).

There seems to be a contagion effect from financial market volatility to the fine wine markets. However, this finding is highly dependent on the indices used. Indeed, the different wine indices are not affected in the same way by financial market volatility and there is a proximity or regional effect that favors the transmission by contagion of financial market volatility to fine wine indices (Le Fur *et al.*, 2016a). Bordeaux wines present the greatest systematic risk among the world's greatest wines (Le Fur *et al.*, 2016b). In the short term, volatility is transmitted to the wine market with a negative effect via the financial and commodity markets and with a positive effect via the art, residential real estate, and credit markets. In the long term, the wine market is affected by all other markets (Ben Ameur and Le Fur, 2019). The knowledge of these channels of transmission of volatility to the wine market allows us to anticipate future volatility and the consequences of a shock on the wine market, to develop investment strategies, and to diversify risk.

Macroeconomic variables could also explain variations in the price of wine. Indeed, under the influence of common macroeconomic factors, the prices of fine wines do not behave differently from those of commodities (Cevik and Sedik, 2014). Due to the process of financialization of the fine wine market, prices have become more volatile. Factors such as money supply, real interest rates, and the growth of investment funds influence the price of fine wines (Jiao, 2017; Aytaç *et al.*, 2018).

6.5 Stamps

Stamp dealer and catalogue publisher Stanley Gibbons is the reference for the construction of price indices for collector stamps. For example, in 2002 he launched a global index, the SIG 100, and two years later he launched the Stanley Gibbons Great Britain 30 Rarities (SG GB30) index. The SG GB30 aggregates the list prices of 30 rare British stamps. These indices meet the needs of stamp collectors and investors. Despite the financial values involved, the returns on stamps have been studied relatively less by researchers over the long term. Most studies use US data. Between 1947 and 1980, the prices of US stamps sold at auction followed an upward (and accelerating) trend, with prices rising five times between 1976 and 1980 (Cardell *et al.*, 1995). Thus, over the period 1963–1976, the average annual return on stamps sold at auction was 12.2% (Taylor, 1983). Indeed, in the United Kingdom, philately reached its peak in the 1960s and 1970s. Thereafter, prices declined and stabilized. Despite the collapse of the 1980s and the declining interest of younger generations, philately remains one of the most popular pastimes in the world, especially among the wealthiest (Satchell and Auld, 2009). Year-to-year changes in prices of postage stamps are predictable based on age of the stamp and quantity printed (Schnitzel, 1979). Tens of millions of stamp collectors around the world spend up to $10 billion annually on their hobby. Over the period 1900–2008, the annualized return on British collector stamps was 7.0% in nominal terms and 2.9% in real terms. These returns are higher than those of bonds but lower than those of equities. Stamp returns are influenced by equity market movements, but the systematic risk of stamps remains low. The volatility of stamp prices is similar to that of equities

(Dimson and Spaenjers, 2011). Over the period 1900–2012, the average annual return of British stamps was 7.6% (3.5% in real terms). These returns underperformed those of equities but were slightly higher than those of bonds (Dimson and Spaenjers, 2014). Returns on US stamps are positively related to expected inflation functioning as a hedge (Cardell *et al.*, 1995; Grable and Chen, 2015). There is also evidence that British stamps could have advantages in a portfolio composed of financial assets by reducing the overall risk of the portfolio (Veld and Veld-Merkoulova, 2007).

6.6 Other Collectibles

There are many other collectibles that can be considered possible investment opportunities such as antique firearms (Avery and Colonna, 1987), beanie babies (Burton and Jacobsen, 1999), ceramics (Keen, 1971; Stein, 1977), metlach beer steins (Kelly, 1994), and timber (Redmond and Cubbage, 1988). In this section, we focus on those most studied in the academic literature.

6.6.1 *Antique furniture*

For 1967–1986, the estimated annual rate of return on American antique furniture was 6.97%, slightly less than the 90-day T-bill yields. However, in the decade 1967–1976, the antique furniture earned 8.24% while T-bills' yield was only 5.66% (Graeser, 1993).

6.6.2 *Classic cars* (*Collectible automobile*)

Despite the increased interest of investors and collectors in classic cars, academic research on the characteristics of this alternative asset as an investment is little studied. Two initial studies (Martin, 2016, 2018) focused on classic cars as an alternative asset in the context of portfolio diversification. Based on a sample of 96 vintage cars from six different categories over the period 2006–2017, the results indicated that classic cars offer attractive returns compared to traditional investments such as equities, bonds, and gold. Another study (Le Fur, 2019) analyzed the long-term relationship between the classic car market and stock markets, from the global level to specific countries, applying a co-integration approach on a monthly basis between 1995 and 2018. The results showed significant co-integration between the conventional car markets and the markets in the Asia, Asia-Pacific, Far East, and Pacific regions. Porsche is influenced by the Asia, Europe, and the Far East regions, while Ferrari is mainly influenced by the developed markets. Finally, between 1998 and 2017, classic cars (built between 1888 and 1907) appreciated annually by 3.37% and 5.63%, respectively, in real and nominal terms before transaction costs. Investments in first-class classic cars (12,50%) and Italian classics (11,28%) generate the highest annual nominal returns. Returns on classic cars outperformed those of equities and art, but underperformed bonds and gold (Laurs and Renneboog, 2019).

6.6.3 *Diamonds*

Diamonds are valued because of the consumer utility they provide (Scott and Yelowitz, 2010) and also because they are a store of value. Their prices have been available regularly for several centuries. Over the period 1999–2010, average yields were 10.0%, 5.5%, and 6.8% for white diamonds, colored diamonds, and other gemstones, respectively (Renneboog and Spaenjers, 2012). Over the period 1999–2012, the annual nominal profitability in US dollars for white diamonds was 8.1% (5.5% in real terms). The annual nominal profitability for colored diamonds was 7.4% (4.8% in real terms). The returns for white and colored diamonds are about 1.3% lower for an investor in Euros than for an investor in dollars. However, euro returns still beat inflation by 3.5% per year. The returns on rubies, emeralds, and sapphires are 4.5% in nominal terms and 2.1% in real terms. There is a low positive correlation between diamonds and equity markets, indicating possible benefits in terms of portfolio diversification (Renneboog, 2013).

6.6.4 *LEGO*

The secondary market for Lego collectibles is an internationalized market in about 100 countries and represents about $15 million annually. Large economies and countries with higher per capita incomes and less income inequality are the most active in this market. The LEGO market has an important advantage over other collectibles: the low number of counterfeits. Indeed, all sets are easily identifiable at a low cost. However, the secondary LEGO market is characterized by high transaction costs. Recent studies have analyzed the value of introducing LEGOs into an asset portfolio. Over the period 1987–2015, the average annual real return of 2322 LEGO packages was 8.0% (Dobrynskaya and Kishilova, 2018). However, during the largest period (1966–2018), the LEGO index built from 10588 units had an inflation-adjusted return of 1.20% per year, much lower than equities (5.54%). However, the inclusion of 5–25% LEGO in a diversified portfolio is beneficial in terms of risk (Shimkus *et al.*, 2019).

6.6.5 *Rare books*

Rare books have increased in value steadily over the last 30 to 50 years, although short-term risk has been high. The increase in value appears not to have been structurally connected with other asset markets or inflation. Books appear to have been relatively immune to the risks and episodic crises (Rudd, 2009).

6.6.6 *Rare coins*

The market for rare coins is active, well organized, an economically relevant market, a potent inflation hedge, and a source of portfolio diversification (Kane, 1984; Koford and Tschoegl, 1998). At the beginning of 1990, annual sales of US coins were estimated at $5 billion (Dickie *et al.*, 1994), an amount estimated by the Professional Numismatists Guild (PNG) to have exceeded $4 billion in sales in 2018, not including sales of newly minted coins or the sales of bullion coins. Thus, over 80 million coins have been rated by the top ratings companies combined. For example, the Professional Coin Grading Service (PCGS) states that it has rated more than 40 million coins with a combined total market value of over $35 billion while its largest competitor, Numismatic Guaranty Corporation (NGC), indicates that it has rated over 26 million US coins. However, there is little academic research on coin returns, despite their importance as an alternative asset class with notably large diversification benefits. Between 1967 and 2015, US collectable coins had a 9.7% annualized nominal return and a 5.5% real return (Maslar *et al.*, 2019). Between 1979 and 2011, US rare coins had an average annual return of between 10.7% and 12.6%, identical to that of equities and much higher than bonds (between 5.4% and 9%) and gold (6.8%) (Lombra, 2003).

6.6.7 *Violins*

Very few studies have analyzed the evolution of prices, returns, and the interest of introducing musical instruments into an asset portfolio. Between 1803 and 1982, the average real return of Stradivarius instruments was about 2%, equal to the long-term real interest rate (Ross and Zondervan, 1989). Since 1980, the real returns of a portfolio composed of violins made in Italy between 1580 and 1850, the Italian Modern School, and the French School, have averaged about 3.3%. Since 1850, returns have averaged 3.5%. These violins have a slightly negative correlation with stocks and bonds, making them a candidate for inclusion in a diversified portfolio. In addition, they have a relatively low variance of return (Graddy and Margolis, 2011, 2013). Between 1900 and 2012, the average nominal returns of violins was 7.0% and only 2.8% in real terms. These violin returns underperform those of equities but are slightly higher than those of bonds (Dimson and Spaenjers, 2014).

6.6.8 *Whisky*

Whisky is produced worldwide, with distillers located in Scotland, Ireland, the United States and, more recently, in Japan, India, Australia, Sweden, and France. This market includes a variety of subcategories of products, such as bourbon, rye whisky, cask strength, etc. (Murray, 2018). The reputation of the distiller, the age of the whisky, and the vintage have a positive effect on the price. There is also a negative effect for bottling not done by the distiller and a positive "collector" effect for bottles identified as rare (Moroz and Pecchioli, 2018). Whisky is now seen as an investment opportunity by investors with a rate of return for single malt vintages between 2015 and 2017 of 102.23% (Page, 2013).

6.7 Conclusion

The purpose of this chapter was to present a descriptive review of about one hundred studies published on collectibles returns and the sensibility of these assets with the financial markets over the last fifty years. The selection process has been carefully designed to assure that we cover the complete literature of these issues. Given the high number of different collectibles, we opted to present the literature per category of collectibles. Not all collectibles are studied with the same frequency. Art is the most studied collectible and has been for a long time. Then, wine has also been widely studied for about fifteen years with a strong increase in recent years. Stamps are also analyzed with particular attention. Many other collectibles are studied with very limited frequency. Some were studied several decades ago, such as antique firearms, beanie babies, ceramics, or timber. Some have only been studied for a few years, such as vintage cars, diamonds, or rare whiskies. Finally, some are not even studied like autographs, guitars, watches, or handbags. These collectibles that are little or not studied open up many avenues of research into the analysis of the returns on these real assets and the opportunities for investment and integration into a diversified portfolio.

References

Ali, H. H. and Nauges, C. (2003). Vente en primeur et investissement: Une étude sur les grands crus de Bordeaux. *Economie Prévision*, **3**: 93–103.

Ameur, H. B. and Le Fur, E. (2019). Volatility transmission to the fine wine market. *Economic Modelling*, **85**: 307–316.

Anderson, R. C. (1974). Paintings as an investment. *Economic Inquiry*, **12**(1): 13–26.

Ashenfelter, O., Ashmore, D., and Lalonde, R. (1995). Bordeaux wine vintage quality and the weather. *Chance*, **8**(4): 7–14.

Artprice (2018). Artprice's 2017 Global Art Market Annual Report. Paris.

Ashenfelter, O. and Graddy, K. (2003). Auctions and the price of art. *Journal of Economic Literature*, **41**(3): 763–787.

Avery, A. E. and Colonna, C. M. (1987). The market for collectible antique and reproduction firearms: An economic and financial analysis. *Journal of Cultural Economics*, **11**(2): 49–64.

Aytaç, B., Coqueret, G., and Mandou, C. (2018). Herding behavior among wine investors. *Economic Modelling*, **68**: 318–328.

Aytaç, B. and Mandou, C. (2016). Wine: To drink or invest in? A study of wine as an investment asset in French portfolios. *Research in International Business and Finance*, **36**: 591–614.

Bakhouche, A. (2013). The examination of the degree of integration among art markets. *Journal of Finance and Investment Analysis*, **2**(1): 101–120.

Baldi, L., Peri, M., and Vandone, D. (2013). Investing in the wine market: A country-level threshold cointegration approach. *Quantitative Finance*, **13**(4): 493–503.

Baldi, L., Vandone, D., and Peri, M. (2010). Is wine a financial parachute? *Proceedings in Food System Dynamics*, 472–487.

Baumol, W. J. (1986). Productivity growth, convergence, and welfare: What the long-run data show. *The American Economic Review*, **76**: 1072–1085.

Belk, R. W. (1991). Possessions and the Sense of Past, in Highways and Buyways: Naturalistic Research from the Consumer Behavior Odyssey, Russell W. Belk, ed. Provo, UT: Association for Consumer Research, 114–130.

Belk, R. W. (2013). *Collecting in a consumer society*. Routledge.

Bentzen, J., Smith, V., and Leth-Sorensen, S. (2002). *Prices of French Icon Wines and the Business Cycle: Empirical Evidence from Danish Wine Auctions*. Centre for International Economic Studies.

Bocart, F. Y. and Hafner, C. M. (2015). Fair revaluation of wine as an investment. *Journal of Wine Economics*, **10**(2): 190–203.

Bouri, E. I. (2014). Beyond the negative relation between return and conditional volatility in the wine market. *International Journal of Wine Business Research*, **26**(4): 279–294.

Bouri, E. I. (2015). Fine wine as an alternative investment during equity market downturns. *The Journal of Alternative Investments*, **17**(4): 46–57.

Bouri, E., Gupta, R., Wong, W. K., and Zhu, Z. (2018). Is wine a good choice for investment? *Pacific-Basin Finance Journal*, **51**: 171–183.

Bouri, E. I. and Roubaud, D. (2016). Fine wines and stocks from the perspective of UK investors: Hedge or safe haven? *Journal of Wine Economics*, **11**(2): 233–248.

Buelens, N. and Ginsburgh, V. (1993). Revisiting Baumol's "art as floating crap game". *European Economic Review*, **37**(7): 1351–1371.

Burton, B. J. and Jacobsen, J. P. (1999). Measuring returns on investments in collectibles. *Journal of Economic Perspectives*, **13**(4): 193–212.

Burton, B. J. and Jacobsen, J. P. (2001). The rate of return on investment in wine. *Economic Inquiry*, **39**(3): 337–350.

Byron, R. P. and Ashenfelter, O. (1995). Predicting the quality of an unborn Grange. *Economic Record*, **71**(1): 40–53.

Cardebat, J. M., Faye, B., Le Fur, E., and Storchmann, K. (2017). The law of one price? Price dispersion on the auction market for fine wine. *Journal of Wine Economics*, **12**(3): 302–331.

Cardell, N. S., Kling, J. L., and Petry, G. (1995). Stamp returns and economic factors. *Southern Economic Journal*, **12**: 411–427.

Cevik, S. and Sedik, T. S. (2014). A barrel of oil or a bottle of wine: how do global growth dynamics affect commodity prices? *Journal of Wine Economics*, **9**(1): 34–50.

Chanel, O. (1995). Is art market behaviour predictable? *European Economic Review*, **39**(3–4): 519–527.

Chanel, O., Gérard-Varet, L. A., and Ginsburgh, V. (1994). Prices and returns on paintings: An exercise on how to price the priceless. *The Geneva Papers on Risk and Insurance Theory*, **19**(1): 7–21.

Chanel, O., Gérard-Varet, L. A., and Ginsburgh, V. (1996). The relevance of hedonic price indices. *Journal of Cultural Economics*, **20**(1): 1–24.

Chu, P. K. K. (2014). Study on the diversification ability of fine wine investment. *The Journal of Investing*, **23**(1): 123–139.

Dale, A. (2008). If you collect, the IRS will collect from you: Whether category is collector, dealer or investor matters. *Wall Street Journal*, February **15**: B1.

Dickie, M., Delorme Jr, C. D., and Humphreys, J. M. (1994). Price determination for a collectible good: The case of rare US coins. *Southern Economic Journal*, **61**(1): 40–51.

Dimson, E., Rousseau, P. L., and Spaenjers, C. (2015). The price of wine. *Journal of Financial Economics*, **118**(2): 431–449.

Dimson, E. and Spaenjers, C. (2011). Ex post: The investment performance of collectible stamps. *Journal of Financial Economics*, **100**(2): 443–458.

Dimson, E. and Spaenjers, C. (2014). Investing in emotional assets. *Financial Analysts Journal*, **70**(2): 20–25.

Di Vittorio, A. and Ginsburgh, V. (1996). Pricing red wines of Medoc vintages from 1949 to 1989 at Christie's auctions. *Journal de la Société Statistique de Paris*, **137**(1): 19–49.

Dobrynskaya, V. and Kishilova, J. (2018). LEGO-The Toy of Smart Investors. *Available at SSRN 3291456.*

Faye, B. and Le Fur, E. (2018). On the Constancy of Hedonic Wine Price Coefficients over time, *Journal of Wine Economists*, **14**(2): 182–207.

Faye, B., Le Fur, E., and Prat, S. (2015). Dynamics of fine wine and asset prices: Evidence from short-and long-run co-movements. *Applied Economics*, **47**(29): 3059–3077.

Fogarty, J. J. (2006). The return to Australian fine wine. *European Review of Agricultural Economics*, **33**(4): 542–561.

Fogarty, J. J. and Jones, C. (2011). Return to wine: A comparison of the hedonic, repeat sales and hybrid approaches. *Australian Economic Papers*, **50**(4): 147–156.

Fogarty, J. J. and Sadler, R. (2014). To save or savor: A review of approaches for measuring wine as an investment. *Journal of Wine Economics*, **9**(3): 225–248.

Frey, B. S. and Eichenberger, R. (1995). On the rate of return in the art market: Survey and evaluation. *European Economic Review*, **39**(3–4): 528–537.

Ginsburgh, V. and Jeanfils, P. (1995). Long-term comovements in international markets for paintings. *European Economic Review*, **39**(3–4): 538–548.

Goetzmann, W. N. (1993). Accounting for taste: Art and the financial markets over three centuries. *The American Economic Review*, **83**(5): 1370–1376.

Goetzmann, W. N., Renneboog, L., and Spaenjers, C. (2011). Art and money. *American Economic Review*, **101**(3): 222–26.

Grable, J. E. and Chen, X. (2015). Collectible, investment, or both: Evaluating the attractiveness of collectible stamps. *Journal of Financial Service Professionals*, **69**(5): 78–87.

Graddy, K. and Margolis, P. E. (2011). Fiddling with value: Violins as an investment? *Economic Inquiry*, **49**(4): 1083–1097.

Graddy, K. and Margolis, P. (2013). *Old Italian violins: A new investment strategy* (No. 7). Brandeis University, Rosenberg Institute of Global Finance, International Business School.

Graeser, P. (1993). Rate of return to investment in American antique furniture. *Southern Economic Journal*, **59**(4): 817–821.

Haeger, J. W. and Storchmann, K. (2006). Prices of American Pinot Noir wines: Climate, craftsmanship, critics. *Agricultural Economics*, **35**(1): 67–78.

Introvigne, S., Bacchiocchi, E., and Vandone, D. (2017). A cointegration analysis of wine stock indexes. *Risk Governance and Control: Financial Markets & Institutions*, **7**(4): 178–188.

Jiao, L. (2017). Macroeconomic determinants of wine prices. *International Journal of Wine Business Research*, **29**(3): 234–250.

Jones, L. E. and Manuelli, R. E. (2001). Volatile policy and private information: The case of monetary shocks. *Journal of Economic Theory*, **99**(1–2): 265–296.

Jones, G. V. and Storchmann, K. H. (2001). Wine market prices and investment under uncertainty: An econometric model for Bordeaux Crus Classés. *Agricultural Economics*, **26**(2): 115–133.

Jordà, Ò., Schularick, M., and Taylor, A. M. (2017). Macrofinancial history and the new business cycle facts. *NBER Macroeconomics Annual*, **31**(1): 213–263.

Jurevičienė, D. and Jakavonytė, A. (2015). Alternative investments: Valuation of wine as a means for portfolio diversification. *Business: Theory and Practice*, **16**(1): 84–93.

Kane, A. (1984). Coins: anatomy of a fad asset. *The Journal of Portfolio Management*, **10**(2): 44–51.

Keen, G. (1971). *The sale of works of art.* Nelson, London.

Kelly, F. S. (1994). A rate of return analysis of Mettlach Beer Steins. In *Mimeo.* Department of Economics, Ohio University Athens, OH.

Koford, K. and Tschoegl, A. E. (1998). The market value of rarity. *Journal of Economic Behavior & Organization*, **34**(3): 445–457.

Kourtis, A., Markellos, R. N., and Psychoyios, D. (2012). Wine price risk management: International diversification and derivative instruments. *International Review of Financial Analysis*, **22**: 30–37.

Krasker, W. S. (1979). The rate of return to storing wines. *Journal of Political Economy*, **87**(6): 1363–1367.

Kumar, M. (2005). *Wine investment for portfolio diversification: How collecting fine wines can yield greater returns than stocks and bonds.* Wine Appreciation Guild.

Laurs, D. and Renneboog, L. (2019). My kingdom for a horse (or a classic car). *Journal of International Financial Markets, Institutions and Money*, **58**: 184–207.

Le Fur, E. (2020). Dynamics of the global fine art market prices. *The Quarterly Review of Economics and Finance*, **76**: 167–180.

Le Fur, E. (2019). The long-term relationship between the classic cars market prices and financial markets. *Bankers, Markets & Investors*, **152–153**: 2–20.

Le Fur, E., Ameur, H. B., Braune, E., and Faye, B. (2016a). Financial market contagion and fine wines: The evidence of the ADCC GARCH model. *International Journal of Entrepreneurship and Small Business*, **29**(4): 583–601.

Le Fur, E., Ameur, H. B., and Faye, B. (2016b). Time-varying risk premiums in the framework of wine investment. *Journal of Wine Economics*, **11**(3): 355–378.

Lombra, R. E. (2003). The investment performance of rare US Coins. Penn State University, Pennsylvania.

Lucey, B. M. and Devine, L. (2015). Was wine a premier CRU investment? *Research in International Business and Finance*, **34**: 33–51.

Martin, S. G. (2016). The road less traveled: The case for collectible automobiles as an asset class. *The Journal of Wealth Management*, **19**(3): 131–139.

Martin, S. G. (2018). Driving returns: Determinants of the returns associated with collectible automobiles. *The Journal of Wealth Management*, **21**(1): 110–123.

Masset, P. and Henderson, C. (2010). Wine as an alternative asset class. *Journal of Wine Economics*, **5**(1): 87–118.

Masset, P. and Weisskopf, J. P. (2010). Raise your glass: Wine investment and the financial crisis. *Available at SSRN 1457906.*

Masset, P. and Weisskopf, J. P. (2015). Wine funds: An alternative turning sour? *The Journal of Alternative Investments*, **17**(4): 6–20.

Masset, P., Weisskopf, J. P., Faye, B., and Le Fur, E. (2016). Red obsession: The ascent of fine wine in China. *Emerging markets review*, **29**: 200–225.

Mei, J. and Moses, M. (2002). Art as an investment and the underperformance of masterpieces. *American Economic Review*, **92**(5): 1656–1668.

Moroz, D. and Pecchioli, B. (2018). America, Association of Wine Economists. Working Paper.

Murray, J. (2018). *Jim Murray's Whisky Bible 2018.* Dram Good Books.

Obaid, K., Pukthuanthong, K., and Maslar, D. A. (2019). US Coins Market: Historical Performance and Anomalies. Available at SSRN 3492347.

Page, I. B. (2013). Why do distilleries produce multiple ages of whisky? ageconsearch.umn.edu.

Pesando, J. E. (1993). Art as an investment: The market for modern prints. *The American Economic Review*, **83**: 1075–1089.

Pesando, J. E., and Shum, P. M. (2008). The auction market for modern prints: Confirmations, contradictions, and new puzzles. *Economic Inquiry*, **46**(2): 149–159.

Pindado, J. and Requejo, I. (2015). Family business performance from a governance perspective: A review of empirical research. *International Journal of Management Reviews*, **17**(3): 279–311.

Redmond, C. H. and Cubbage, F. W. (1988). Portfolio risk and returns from timber asset investments. *Land Economics*, **64**(4): 325–337.

Renneboog, L. (2015). Investing in diamonds. *Business and Economic Research*, **5**(1): 166–195.

Renneboog, L. D. R. and Spaenjers, C. (2009). *Buying beauty: On prices and returns in the art market* (pp. 2–30). Tilburg University.

Renneboog, L. and Spaenjers, C. (2012). Hard assets: The returns on rare diamonds and gems. *Finance Research Letters*, **9**(4): 220–230.

Renneboog, L. and Spaenjers, C. (2013). Buying beauty: On prices and returns in the art market. *Management Science*, **59**(1): 36–53.

Renneboog, L. and Spaenjers, C. (2015). Investment returns and economic fundamentals in international art markets. *Cosmopolitan Canvases: The Globalization of Markets for Contemporary Art*, 129–146.

Ross, M. H. and Zondervan, S. (1989). Capital gains and the rate of return on a Stradivarius. *Economic Inquiry*, **27**(3): 529–540.

Rudd, A. (2009). Investing in Rare Books. In *Collectible Investments for the High Net Worth Investor* (pp. 175–192). Academic Press.

Saari, L. (1997). Those crazy collectors. *The Orange County Register*, D1.

Sanning, L. W., Shaffer, S., and Sharratt, J. M. (2008). Bordeaux wine as a financial investment. *Journal of Wine Economics*, **3**(1): 51–71.

Satchell, S. and Auld, J. F. (2009). Collecting and investing in stamps. In *Collectible Investments for the High Net Worth Investor* (pp. 215–230). Academic Press.

Schnitzel, P. (1979). A note on the philatelic demand for postage stamps. *Southern Economic Journal*, **49**(4): 1261–1265.

Scott, F. and Yelowitz, A. (2010). Pricing anomalies in the market for diamonds: Evidence of conformist behavior. *Economic Inquiry*, **48**(2): 353–368.

Shimkus, N., Shanaev, S., Sharma, S., and Ghimire, B. (2019). Children's Toy or Grown-Ups' Gamble? LEGO Sets as an Alternative Investment. (September 20, 2019).

Siebels, J. F., & zu Knyphausen-Aufseß, D. (2012). A review of theory in family business research: The implications for corporate governance. *International Journal of Management Reviews*, **14**(3): 280–304.

Stein, J. P. (1977). The monetary approach of paintings. *Journal of Political Economy*, **85**(5): 1021–35.

Storchmann, K. (2012). Wine economics. *Journal of Wine Economics*, **7**(1): 1–33.

Taylor, W. M. (1983). The estimation of quality-adjusted rates of return in stamp auctions. *The Journal of Finance*, **38**(4): 1095–1110.

Veld, C. and Veld-Merkoulova, Y. V. (2007). Portfolio diversification benefits of investing in stamps. *The Journal of Alternative Investments*, **10**(1): 56–61.

Wood, D. and Anderson, K. (2006). What determines the future value of an icon wine? New evidence from Australia. *Journal of Wine Economics*, **1**(2): 141–161.

Worthington, A. C. and Higgs, H. (2003). Art as an investment: Short and long-term comovements in major painting markets. *Empirical Economics*, **28**(4): 649–668.

Worthington, A. C. and Higgs, H. (2004). Art as an investment: Risk, return and portfolio diversification in major painting markets. *Accounting & Finance*, **44**(2): 257–271.

https://doi.org/10.1142/9781786349507_0007

Chapter 7

Machine Learning, Computational Techniques, and Reporting Processes: Risk Exposure in GCC Markets in the Wake of the 2007–2009 Global Financial Meltdown

Mazin A. M. Al Janabi
Finance and Banking and Financial Engineering,
Tecnologico de Monterrey,
EGADE Business School, Santa Fe Campus,
Mexico City, Mexico
mazin.aljanabi@tec.mx/
mazinaljanabi@gmail.com

7.1 Introduction

The 2007–2009 global financial crisis has emphasized the necessity of a proper identification and computation of embedded liquidity risk in financial trading portfolios. In essence, liquidity trading risk arises due to the inability of financial entities to liquidate their holdings, at reasonable prices, as time lapses throughout the liquidation (closeout) period. Undeniably, certain collapses in some well-known financial entities and the consequential financial turmoil were caused, to some degree, by the impact of trading liquidity risk on structured equity portfolios (Al Janabi, 2013). To that end, the key objectives of this chapter are first to develop and test a robust modeling technique for the measurement and reporting of market and liquidity price risk exposure for financial trading portfolios that contain a number of illiquid equity multiple assets, under regular and crisis-driven circumstances. Second, to propose a novel modeling algorithm for the determination of maximum risk-threshold limits, under both regular and stressed markets outlooks, for emerging financial markets.

Risk management has become of paramount importance in the financial industry and a major endeavor by academics, practitioners, and regulators. As such, a cornerstone of recent interest is a class of models called Value at Risk (VaR) techniques. The concepts of VaR and other advanced risk management techniques are not new and are based — with some modifications — on modern portfolio theory. Notwithstanding VaR is one of many — both quantitative and qualitative — dynamics that should be integrated into a cohesive risk management method, it is remarkably a vital one.

In fact, VaR is not the maximum loss that will occur, but rather a loss level threshold that will be pierced some percentage of the time (Al Janabi, 2008, 2013). The actual loss that occurs could be much higher than the VaR estimates. As such, VaR should be used in conjunction with other risk measures such as stress-testing, scenario analysis, and other asset/business-specific risk processes. The most common VaR models estimate variance/covariance matrices of multiple-asset returns using historical time series, under the assumption that asset returns are normally distributed and that portfolio risk is a function of the risk of each asset and the correlation factors the returns of all trading multiple assets. The VaR is then computed from the standard deviation of the portfolio, given the appropriate investment/liquidation horizon, and the most fitting confidence interval (Al Janabi, 2008, 2013).

To measure and report the risks involved in their trading operations, major financial institutions are increasingly exploiting Value at Risk (VaR) simulation models. Since financial institutions differ in their individual characteristics, tailor-made internal risk models are more appropriate. Fortunately, and in accordance with Basel II and Basel III capital adequacy accords, financial institutions are permitted to develop their own internal risk models for risk assessment and reporting. Furthermore, internal risk models can be used in the determination of economic capital (or risk-capital cushion) that financial entities must hold to endorse their trading of multiple-asset securities. The benefit of such an approach is that it takes into account the relationship between various multiple asset types and can accurately evaluate the overall risk for a whole combination of trading assets (Al Janabi, 2013, 2014).

Despite many criticisms and limitations of the VaR method, it has proven to be a very useful measure of market risk and is widely used in financial and non-financial markets. The *RiskMetrics*^{TM} system (Morgan Guaranty Trust Company, 1994), developed and popularized by J.P. Morgan, has provided a tremendous impetus to the growth in the use of VaR concept and other modern risk management techniques and processes. Since then, the VaR concept became well known and scores of specific applications were adapted to credit risk management and mutual funds investments. The general recognition and use of large-scale VaR models has initiated a considerable literature including statistical descriptions of VaR and the assessments of different modeling techniques. For a comprehensive survey, and the different VaR analysis and techniques, one can refer to Jorion (2006).

In their research paper, Berkowitz and O'Brien (2001), question how accurate VaR models are at commercial banks. Because trading accounts at large commercial banks have considerably grown and become increasingly diverse and complex, the authors present statistics on the trading revenues from such activities and on the associated VaR forecasts internally estimated by banks. Several other authors have attempted to tackle the issues of extreme events and fat tails phenomena in the distribution of returns. Nonetheless, most of their approaches and techniques are good exercises for academic purposes, but they do lack evidence of real-world applications with tangible market portfolios.

On another front, Garcia *et al.* (2007) tackle a specific issue within the VaR, and that is the subadditivity property required for the VaR to be a coherent measure of risk. The authors argue that, in the context of decentralized portfolio management, central management possesses only a fraction of information that belongs to each specialist (trader). In such a context, a distribution appears always thicker to the central unit than to the specialist. Therefore, because of a lack of information, VaR may appear fallaciously nonsubadditive to the central management unit. Despite evidence to the contrary, the authors show that decentralized portfolio management with a VaR allocation to each specialist will work, and furthermore VaR remains subadditive in many situations of practical interest.

In his research papers, Al Janabi (2008, 2012, 2013, 2014) establishes a robust and practical modeling technique for the measurement, management, and control of trading risk and tackles the issue of adverse market price impact on liquidity trading risk and coherent portfolio optimization using a closed-form parametric LVaR algorithm. The effects of illiquid multiple assets, which are dominant characteristics of emerging markets, are also incorporated in the risk modeling algorithms. These literatures provide solid real-world risk quantitative management techniques and strategies (drawn from a practitioner viewpoint) that can be applied to equity trading portfolios in emerging markets. The intent is to propose a robust technique for including of liquidation trading risk in standard VaR analysis and to examine the liquidity risk arising due to illiquid trading positions by obtaining an LVaR estimation. The proposed adverse price unwinding approach comprises a liquidation multiplier that can adjust the impact of unfavorable price movement throughout the closeout period, along with an optimization algorithm that allocates multiple assets subject to imposing meaningful financial and operational constraints.

Furthermore, in their research paper Madoroba and Kruger (2014) introduced a VaR model that incorporates intraday price movements on high–low spreads and adjusts for a trade impact measure, a novel sensitivity measure of price movements due to trading volumes. Furthermore, the authors compare and contrast 10 worldwide-recognized liquidity risk management models including the "*Al Janabi model*", which is used in this chapter for liquidly risk modeling and for optimizing the maximum permitted LVaR trading limits.

In a different modeling technique, Al Janabi *et al.* (2017) propose a portfolio optimization methodology based on the integration of DCC (dynamic conditional correlation) *t*-copula and LVaR models to enhance asset allocation decisions under illiquid market conditions.

Their empirical findings prove the superiority of the DCC-copula-LVaR modeling technique over the traditional Markowitz (1959) optimization procedure for a portfolio composed of international stock market indices, gold, and crude oil across various trading scenarios.[1]

Set against this background, the objective of this research study is to provide robust modeling techniques and optimization algorithms for the measurement and reporting of market and liquidity risk exposures for emerging market equity trading portfolios (it is often called, trading, investment, or price risk). As such, the key aim is to examine a robust modeling algorithm that can aid in the establishment of sound liquidity risk management practices (for equity portfolios that contain both long-only and long-/short-sales trading positions) and within a prudential regulatory framework of rules and policies.

To that end, in this chapter, the risk parameters required for the construction of robust liquidity-adjusted VaR (or LVaR) and stress-testing methods are reviewed from previous work and adapted to the specific applications of these methods to emerging markets. Moreover, a robust modeling technique for the incorporation of illiquid assets, in daily trading risk management practices, is defined and is appropriately incorporated into LVaR and stress-testing methods. Effectively, the developed methodology and risk computation algorithms can aid in evolving risk management, portfolio selection, and financial engineering practices in emerging markets, largely in light of the aftermath of the 2007–2009 sub-prime credit crunch and the consequential financial turmoil.

In addition, the proposed computational techniques and risk reporting process can have key uses and applications in machine learning and artificial intelligence, expert systems, smart financial functions, and financial technology (FinTech) in big data

[1]For other relevant literature on liquidity risk, internal risk models, asset pricing and portfolio choice and diversification one can refer as well to Al Janabi (2020a); Al Janabi (2020b); Asadi and Al Janabi (2020); Ruozi and Ferrari (2013); Roch and Soner (2013); Bangia *et al.* (2002); Angelidis and Benos (2006); Berkowitz (2000); Madhavan *et al.* (1997); Hisata and Yamai (2000); Le Saout (2002); Amihud *et al.* (2005); Takahashi and Alexander (2002); Arreola-Hernandez and Al Janabi (2020); Arreola-Hernández *et al.* (2017); Arreola-Hernández *et al.* (2015); Grillini *et al.* (2019); Al Janabi *et al.* (2019); Cochrane (2005); and Meucci (2009), among others.

environments. Similarly, it can aid in the progress of regulatory technology (RegTech) for the global financial services industry and can be of interest to professionals, regulators, and researchers working in the field of machine learning, Internet of Things (IoT), data analytics, financial engineering and FinTech, and for those who want to advance their understanding of the impact of innovative risk computational techniques and reporting processes on regulatory challenges for the financial services industry and its effects on global financial stability.

The remainder of the chapter is organized as follows. The next section lays out the quantitative foundations of LVaR technique using Al Janabi model and the optimization algorithms that incorporates the effects of illiquid multiple assets in daily market risk management. The outcomes of the empirical tests, simulations panels, and the optimization end results are drawn in the third section. The last section provides concluding remarks and recommendations.

7.2 Computation of Liquidity Adjusted Value-at-Risk (LVaR) with a Closed-Form Parametric Process Using Al Janabi Model

A robust and simplified computational process for the estimation of VaR risk factors (using a closed-form parametric process) for a single and multiple assets positions is explained as follows (Al Janabi, 2013).

For a single trading asset, the absolute value of VaR can be defined in monetary terms as follows:

$$VaR_i = |(\mu_i - \alpha * \sigma_i)(Asset_i * Fx_i)| \tag{1}$$

where μ_i is the expected return of the asset, α is the confidence level (or in other words, the standard normal variant at confidence level α), and σ_i is the forecasted standard deviation (or conditional volatility) of the return of the security that constitutes the single position. The $Asset_i$ is the mark-to-market value of the trading asset and specifies the monetary amount of equity position in asset i and Fx_i denotes the unit foreign exchange rate of asset i.

Trading risk in the presence of multiple risk factors is determined by the combined effect of individual risks. Magnitude of the total risk is determined not only by the magnitudes of the individual risks but also by their correlations parameters. As such, portfolio effects are crucial in risk management not only for large diversified portfolios but also for individual instruments that depend on several risk factors. For multiple assets or portfolio of assets, VaR is a function of each individual security's risk and the dependence measure or correlation factors $[\rho_{i,j}]$ between the returns on the different securities, detailed as follows[2]:

$$VaR_P = \sqrt{\sum_{i=1}^{n}\sum_{j=1}^{n} VaR_i\, VaR_j \rho_{i,j}} = \sqrt{[VaR]^T[\rho][VaR]} \tag{2}$$

This formula is a general one for the computation of VaR for any portfolio of multiple assets regardless of the number of securities. It should be noted that the second term of this formula is presented in terms of a matrix-algebra technique — a useful form to avoid mathematical complexity, as more and more securities are added. This approach can simplify the algorithmic programming process and can permit a straightforward incorporation of short-sales positions in the market risk assessment process. As such, in order to compute the VaR (of a portfolio of any number of securities), one needs to first create a vector $|VaR|$ of the individual VaR positions — explicitly n rows and one column ($nx1$) vector — a transpose vector $|VaR|^T$ of the individual VaR positions — an ($1xn$) vector, and hence the superscript "T" indicates transpose of the vector — and finally a matrix, $|\rho|$, of all correlation factors (ρ) — an (nxn) matrix. Consequently, as one multiplies the two vectors and the correlation matrix and then takes the square root of the result, one ends up with the VaR_P of any portfolio with any n-number of securities. This simple number summarizes the portfolio's exposure to market risk. Investors and senior managers can then decide whether they feel comfortable with this level of risk. If the answer is no, then the process that led to the estimation of VaR can be used to decide where to reduce redundant risk. For instance, the riskiest securities can be sold, or one

[2]The dependence measure function can take different forms. For liner dependence, it can be represented by the typical Pearson's correlation coefficients. However, for nonlinear and non-normal distributions, Kendall's tau and other forms of copulas functions can be used to replace the dependence measure function.

can use derivative securities, such as futures and options, to hedge undesirable risk.

Illiquid securities such as foreign exchange rates and equities are very common in emerging markets. Customarily, these securities are traded infrequently (at very low volume). Their quoted prices should not be regarded as a representative of the traders' consensus vis-à-vis their real value but rather as the transaction price that is arrived at by two counter parties under special market conditions. This of course represents a real dilemma to anybody who seeks to measure the market risk of these securities with a methodology that is based on volatilities and correlation matrices. The main problem arises when the historical price series is not available for some securities or when it is available but not fully reliable due to the lack of liquidity.

The methodology proposed and used by *J.P. Morgan* in their earlier *RiskMetrics*^{TM} method (Morgan Guaranty Trust Company, 1994) implicitly assumes that liquidation occurs in one block sale at the end of the holding (closeout) period and that there is one holding period for all assets, regardless of their inherent trading liquidity structure. Unfortunately, this approach does not consider real-life trading situations, where traders can liquidate (or re-balance) small portions of their trading portfolios on a daily basis. Moreover, this could generate unreliable risk assessments and can lead to considerable overestimates of LVaR figures, especially for the purposes of economic capital allocation between trading and/or investment units.

The assumption of a given holding period for orderly liquidation inevitably implies that assets' liquidation occurs during the holding period. Accordingly, scaling the holding period to account for orderly liquidation can be justified if one allows the assets to be liquidated throughout the holding period. In order to perform the calculation of LVaR under more realistic illiquid market conditions, we can define the following liquidity risk modeling parameter throughout the close-out period:[3]

$$LVaR_{adj} = VaR\left(\sqrt{\frac{(2t+1)(t+1)}{6t}}\right) \tag{3}$$

[3]The mathematical approach, modeling algorithms, and robust optimization techniques presented herein are largely drawn from Al Janabi (2012, 2013, 2014),

where, t is the number of liquidation days (t–*day* to liquidate the entire asset fully), VaR = Value at Risk under liquid market environments (as presented formerly in equation [1]) and $LVaR_{adj}$ = Value at Risk under illiquid market environments. The latter equation clearly indicates that $LVaR_{adj} > VaR$, and for the special case when the number of days to liquidate the entire multiple assets is one trading day, then we get the equality of $LVaR_{adj} = VaR$. Consequently, the difference between $LVaR_{adj} - VaR$ should be equal to the residual market risk due to the illiquidity of multiple assets under illiquid markets conditions. Actually, the number of liquidation days (t) necessary to liquidate the entirety of multiple assets is related to the choice of the liquidity threshold; however, the size of this threshold is likely to change under severe market circumstances. Indeed, the choice of the liquidation horizon can be estimated from the total trading position size and the daily trading volume that can be unwound into the market without significantly disrupting market prices. Effectively, a linear liquidation procedure of assets is assumed in the above formula, i.e. selling equal parts of each asset every day until the last trading day (t), where the entire asset is sold. The above model is more appropriate for daily trading circumstances where traders can unwind part of their positions on a daily basis.

Furthermore, the closeout period can be estimated in this manner:

$$t = |\,Total\,Market\,Value\,of\,Asset_i / Average\,Daily\,Volume\,of\,Asset_i|,\quad st.\ t \geq 1.0 \tag{4}$$

In order to calculate the $LVaR$ for the entire multi-assets portfolio (i.e. $LVaR_{P_{adj}}$), the next model, which is an expansion of Eq. (2), can be implemented to yield:

$$LVaR_{P_{adj}} = \sqrt{\sum_{i=1}^{n}\sum_{j=1}^{n} LVaR_{i_{adj}} LVaR_{j_{adj}} \rho_{i,j}} = \sqrt{[LVaR_{adj}]^T[\rho][LVaR_{adj}]} \tag{5}$$

---

and Al Janabi *et al.* (2017) research papers. In addition, in this research study, the modeling techniques and the non-linear robust optimization algorithms are based on Al Janabi model (Al Janabi, 2008; Madoroba and Kruger, 2014).

Once the model to evaluate LVaR for a multi-assets portfolio is identified, we examine the portfolio management approach and optimization algorithms that integrate LVaR and multi-asset dependence measures. This proposed portfolio management model can maximize and/or minimize the LVaR objective function conditional on implementing a number of financial and operational constraints. Basically, the proposed optimization algorithm represents an enhancement of the classical Markowitz (1959) Mean-Variance (MV) method, where the risk measure is substituted by the LVaR optimization algorithm. Thus, by considering various expected returns, an LVaR frontier can be generated. The maximization and/or minimization portfolio optimization problem is formulated as follows:

$$\begin{aligned} Max\,and/or\,Min{:}\,LVaR_{P_{adj}} &= \sqrt{\sum_{i=1}^{n}\sum_{j=1}^{n} LVaR_{i_{adj}} LVaR_{j_{adj}} \rho_{i,j}} \\ &= \sqrt{[LVaR_{adj}]^T[\rho][LVaR_{adj}]} \end{aligned} \tag{6}$$

The maximization or the minimization process of the objective risk-function (Eq. 6) really depends on the sought application for either risk management or portfolio management purposes. For instance, if the aim is to set upper limits of LVaR for trading units to comply with internal and external risk management regulatory issues, then we need to maximize the objective function subject to operational and financial constraints. In contrast, if the goal is to optimize the asset allocation process and determine risk–return tradeoffs for portfolio management applications, then we ought to minimize the objective risk-function subject to realistic boundary limits.

To that end, the above objective risk-function can be maximized and/or minimized subject to satisfying the following operational and financial boundary limits:

$$\sum_{i=1}^{n} R_i x_i = R_P; \quad l_i \leq x_i \leq u_i \; i = 1, 2, \ldots, n \tag{7}$$

$$\sum_{i=1}^{n} x_i = 1.0; \quad l_i \leq x_i \leq u_i \; i = 1, 2, \ldots, n \tag{8}$$

$$\sum_{i=1}^{n} V_i = V_P \quad i = 1, 2, \ldots, n \tag{9}$$

$$[LF] \geq 1.0; \quad \forall i = 1, 2, \ldots, n \tag{10}$$

where LF is the liquidation factor, which is defined for any asset i as:

$$LF_i = \left[\sqrt{\frac{(2t_i + 1)(t_i + 1)}{6t_i}} \right] \geq 1.0; \quad i = 1, 2, \ldots, n \tag{11}$$

In Eqs. (7)–(10), R_P and V_P denote the target portfolio mean expected return and total volume of the multi-assets portfolio, respectively, and x_i is the weight for each asset. The values l_i and u_i, for $i = 1, 2, \ldots, n$ in Eqs. (7)–(8) indicate the lower and upper limits for the portfolio weights x_i. Furthermore, $[LF]$ represents a $(n \times 1)$ vector of the particular liquidation period for each asset of the portfolio.

7.3 Computation and Controlling of Market and Liquidity Risk Exposures — A Practical and Real-World Trading Case Study of Multiple-Assets Portfolios

In this background, a number of Arab countries have started the implementation of modified versions of the Basel II and Basel III capital adequacy accords. In fact, the Gulf Cooperation Council (GCC) financial markets, in general, are in progressive stages of implementing advanced quantitative risk management regulations and techniques. Furthermore, in recent years, outstanding progress has been made in cultivating the culture of risk management among local financial entities and regulatory institutions. In the Middle East, the majority of banking assets is expected to be covered by Basel III regulations by 2020. By and large, capital ratios are fairly strong in the GCC region, though they have fallen lately as banks have expanded their products and operations. Within the GCC, there have been negotiations for common application of Basel II and Basel III capital adequacy requirements, though with different timeframes. This is because some GCC countries are more diverse, for instance, in terms of the presence of foreign banks than others (Al Janabi, 2013).

In this research study, datasets of daily price returns of the six GCC stock market main indicators (indices) are gathered, filtered, and effectively adjusted for the computation of relevant input parameters for the calculation of all risk factors. The total numbers of indices that are considered in this work are nine, seven local indices for the six GCC stock markets (including two indices for the UAE markets) and two benchmark indices, as follows[4]:

- DFM General Index (United Arab Emirates, Dubai Financial Market General Index)
- ADSM Index (United Arab Emirates, Abu Dhabi Stock Market Index)
- BA All Share Index (Bahrain, All Share Stock Market Index)
- KSE General Index (Kuwait, Stock Exchange General Index)
- MSM30 Index (Oman, Muscat Stock Market Index)
- DSM20 Index (Qatar, Doha Stock Market General Index)
- SE All Share Index (Saudi Arabia, All Share Stock Market Index)
- Shuaa GCC Index (Shuaa Capital, GCC Stock Markets Benchmark Index)
- Shuaa Arab Index (Shuaa Capital, Arab Stock Markets Benchmark Index).

For this particular research study, we have chosen a confidence interval of 95% (or 97.5% with "one-tailed" loss side) and a number of liquidation time horizons to compute LVaR. Historical database (of more than six years) of daily closing index levels, for the period 17/10/2004–22/05/2009, are assembled for the purpose of carrying out this research and further for the construction of market liquidity risk management parameters and maximum risk limits (or risk-budgeting). In fact, the selected time-series datasets fall within the

[4]In this chapter, a database of the six GCC states indices is utilized whose behavior is presumably more diverse than if equity assets of any particular stock market had been employed, as other authors have done heretofore. The basic argument is that specific country indices may have, compared to individual stocks, a more predictable structure due to aggregation. The composition and the calculation method of each index can be obtained from the websites of each GCC stock market.

period of the most severe part of the 2007–2009 sub-prime financial crunch. The analysis of data and discussions of relevant empirical findings and results of this research are organized and explained as follows.

7.3.1 *Stochastic properties of the returns series and testing for non-normality forms*

To investigate the stochastic properties of the data, we have computed the log returns of each series. As such, Table 7.1 illustrates the daily volatility of each of the stock markets indices under normal (regular) market and adverse (stressed, event or crisis) market conditions.

Table 7.1. Stochastic properties of returns dataset: Daily and annual volatility and systematic risk factor.

Stock Market Indices	Daily Volatility (Regular Market) %	Daily Volatility (Stressed Market) %	Annual Volatility (Regular Market) %	Annual Volatility (Stressed Market) %	Systematic Risk Factor (Beta Coefficient)
DFM General Index	1.93	12.16	31.05	196.03	0.58
ADSM Index	1.42	7.08	22.83	114.09	0.40
BA All Share Index	0.59	3.77	9.50	60.76	0.06
KSE General Index	0.76	3.74	12.28	60.25	0.14
MSM30 Index	0.84	8.70	13.58	140.27	0.10
DSM20 Index	1.53	8.07	24.65	130.19	0.31
SE All Share Index	2.08	11.03	33.50	177.90	0.98
Shuaa GCC Index	1.45	8.10	23.36	130.56	1.05
Shuaa Arab Index	1.28	7.57	20.62	122.11	1.00

Notes: This table illustrates the daily and annual volatility of each stock market index under regular and stressed market conditions and the systematic risk factor (beta sensitivity coefficient) for each market.

Crisis market volatilities are computed by implementing an empirical distribution of the past returns for all stock market indices and, hence, the maximum negative returns (i.e. potential losses), which are witnessed in the historical time series, are selected for this purpose. This approach can aid in overcoming some of the limitations of normality assumption and can provide a better analysis of LVaR, especially under severe and illiquid market settings.

From Table 7.1 we can observe that the index with the highest volatility is the SE All Share Index (that is, under normal market condition), whereas the DFM General Index has demonstrated the highest volatility under adverse market circumstances. Annualized volatilities are depicted in Table 7.1, and this is performed by adjusting (multiplication) the daily volatilities with the square root of 260 — assuming there are 260 trading days in the calendar year.

An interesting outcome of the study of systematic risk dynamics (beta sensitivity factors) is the manner in which the results are varied across the sample indices as indicated in Table 7.1. SE All Share Index appears to have the highest systematic risk factor (0.98) vis-à-vis the Shuaa Arab Index (that is, the highest beta coefficient) and the BA All Share Index seems to have the lowest beta factor (0.06). Moreover, and in accordance with general beliefs, Shuaa GCC Index (with a sensitivity risk factor of 1.05) is the best index among the entire sample indices that appears to move very closely with respect to the benchmark Shuaa Arab Index (with a beta factor of 1.0).

In another study, the measurements of skewness and kurtosis are performed on the sample stock markets indices. The results are depicted in Table 7.2. It is seen, in general, that all indices have shown asymmetric behavior i.e. (both positive and negative values). Moreover, kurtosis studies have shown similar patterns of abnormality (i.e. peaked/flat distributions). At the upper extreme, MSM 30 Index has shown a negative skewness (–0.57), which is combined with a high kurtosis — that is, a peakedness of (18.40). Some stock markets indices, such as in the case of DSM30 Index, have shown the closest relationship to normality (i.e. skewness of −0.11 and kurtosis of 5.59). Nonetheless, the Jarque–Bera (JB) test shows an obvious general deviation from normality and, thus, rejects the hypothesis that GCC stock markets time series returns are normally distributed. As evidenced in Table 7.2 the above results of general departure from normality are also confirmed with the Jarque–Bera (*JB*) test.

Table 7.2. Stochastic properties and descriptive statistics of data: Returns, skewness, kurtosis, and Jarque–Bera Test of non-normality.

Stock Market Indices	Maximum %	Minimum %	Median %	Arithmetic Mean %	Skewness	Kurtosis	Jarque-Bera (JB) Test
DFM General Index	9.9	−12.2	0.01	0.12	0.01	7.86	955**
ADSM Index	6.6	−7.1	0.00	0.07	0.12	7.26	734**
BA All Share Index	3.6	−3.8	0.00	0.05	0.43	10.24	2142**
KSE General Index	5.0	v3.7	0.00	0.09	−0.18	8.38	1173**
MSM30 Index	5.2	−8.7	0.00	0.12	−0.57	18.40	9617**
DSM20 Index	6.2	−8.1	0.00	0.06	−0.11	5.59	273**
SE All Share Index	9.4	−11.0	0.07	0.03	−0.97	8.47	1361**
Shuaa GCC Index	11.1	−8.1	0.00	0.06	−0.66	14.00	4949**
Shuaa Arab Index	9.4	−7.6	0.00	0.07	−0.61	13.79	4758**

Notes: This table demonstrates descriptive statistics of daily returns and the JB test for non-normality. The JB test clearly indicates that all stock markets exhibit non-normal behavior. Asterisks **denote statistical significance at the 0.01 levels.

The interesting outcome of this non-normality study suggests the necessity of combining VaR computation — which assumes normal distributions of returns — with other methods such as stress-testing and scenario analysis to get a detailed examination of other remaining risks (i.e. fat-tails in the probability distribution) that cannot be captured with the simple assumption of normality.

7.3.2 *Computation of the maximum LVaR limit for a typical financial trading entity*

Maximum LVaR risk limits (or allowable risk-budgeting thresholds) are an important element for any trading risk management unit, and it should be defined clearly and used wisely to ensure control on the trading/investment unit's exposure to risk. To that end, the risk management unit, independently from the front office's traders, should perform all LVaR limit setting and control, monitoring, and reporting.

How should we set risk limits to safeguard against maximum loss amounts? These are some of the central questions risk managers must envisage. In this chapter, a robust — however practical modeling technique — is presented for the setting of maximum LVaR trading limits. To that end, varieties of optimization case studies with different LVaR computations have been examined in order to set up procedures for the establishment of maximum LVaR limits. This is with the objective of setting adequate policies and procedures for handling situations in which the trading/investment units are above the authorized LVaR limits. These LVaR limits methodology and procedure must be examined and approved by the board of directors of the financial entity. All trading/investment units need to have such upper limits of LVaR as practical trading rules and as a strict policy for their risk takings. Any excess of LVaR beyond the ratified upper limits must be reported to senior management by the risk management unit. Moreover, traders/asset managers need to give full and justified explanations of why their LVaRs are beyond the approved limits (Al Janabi, 2009).

The objective of this chapter is to showcase an optimization algorithm that maximizes LVaR upper limits for contemporary risk management application. For this purpose, the optimization process is set by maximizing the objective function (i.e. Eq. 6). As such,

Table 7.3. LVaR maximum daily trading limits in AED for different correlation factors (ρ), with 5 days closeout period, and under regular (normal) market outlooks.

Correlation Factors (ρ)	Optimization Case Study 1: Closeout Period = 5 Days	Optimization Case Study 2: Closeout Period = 5 Days	Optimization Case Study 3: Closeout Period = 5 Days	Optimization Case Study 4: Closeout Period = 5 Days
$\rho = 0$	1,951,897	5,711,650	4,132,885	**6,428,020**
$\rho = +1$	4,293,009	**5,711,650**	5,208,534	4,672,152
$\rho =$ Empirical	2,594,910	5,711,650	4,177,090	**6,668,592**

Notes: This table illustrates the optimization results of the maximum daily LVaR trading limits for four optimization case studies with different correlation factors, 5 days closeout period, and under regular market settings. As a result, optimization case studies 4 and 2 denote the highest LVaR limits for different correlation parameters.

to set LVaR upper limits for typical trading units to comply with internal and external risk management regulatory issues, we need to maximize the objective function subject to operational and financial constraints, as indicated in Eqs. (7)–(11).

To that end, Tables 7.3–7.6 represent four optimization case studies for the setting of rational maximum LVaR trading limits, under both regular and stressed market outlooks and with different closeout horizons. In all four optimization case studies, the effects of various asset allocations (with or without short-selling) are examined for the purpose of setting of acceptable LVaR threshold limits. As such, in all optimization case studies, the optimization dynamics is based on the definition of LVaR as the maximum possible loss over a specified time horizon within a given confidence level. The optimization technique solves the problem by finding the market positions (i.e. asset allocations) that maximize the loss, subject to the fact that all constraints are satisfied within their boundary values. In addition, we used different closeout periods of 5 and 10 days in the individual optimization case studies, and for both simulations under regular (normal) and stressed (event) markets outlooks, respectively. For the sake of generalization of the optimization process and, thereafter, the analysis of empirical results, a volume trading limit of AED 100,000,000 is

Table 7.4. LVaR maximum daily trading limits in AED for different correlation factors (ρ), with 10 days closeout period, and under regular (normal) market outlooks.

Correlation Factors (ρ)	Optimization Case Study 1: Closeout Period = 10 Days	Optimization Case Study 2: Closeout Period = 10 Days	Optimization Case Study 3: Closeout Period = 10 Days	Optimization Case Study 4: Closeout Period = 10 Days
$\rho = 0$	2,582,117	7,555,803	5,467,293	**8,503,471**
$\rho = +1$	5,679,117	**7,555,803**	6,890,242	6,180,677
$\rho =$ Empirical	3,432,744	7,555,803	5,525,770	**8,821,719**

Notes: This table illustrates the optimization results of the maximum daily LVaR trading limits for four optimization case studies with different correlation factors, 10 days closeout period, and under regular market settings. As a result, optimization case studies 4 and 2 denote the highest LVaR limits for different correlation parameters.

Table 7.5. LVaR maximum daily trading limits in AED for different correlation factors (ρ), with 5 days closeout period, and under stressed (event) market outlooks.

Correlation Factors (ρ)	Optimization Case Study 1: Closeout Period = 5 Days	Optimization Case Study 2: Closeout Period = 5 Days	Optimization Case Study 3: Closeout Period = 5 Days	Optimization Case Study 4: Closeout Period = 5 Days
$\rho = 0$	11,056,427	36,064,278	22,688,503	**38,551,576**
$\rho = +1$	24,805,676	**36,064,278**	26,734,021	27,650,267
$\rho =$ Empirical	14,767,065	36,064,278	22,735,864	**39,563,095**

Notes: This table illustrates the optimization results of the maximum daily LVaR trading limits for four optimization case studies with different correlation factors, 5 days closeout period, and under stressed market settings. As a result, optimization case studies 4 and 2 denote the highest LVaR limits for different correlation parameters.

assumed as a constraint — that is, the financial entity (or trading unit) must keep a maximum overall market value of stocks of no more than AED 100,000,000 (between long-only and/or long-/short-sales multiple assets).

Table 7.6. LVaR maximum daily trading limits in AED for different correlation factors (ρ), with 10 days closeout period, and under stressed (event) market outlooks.

Correlation Factors (ρ)	Optimization Case Study 1: Closeout Period = 10 Days	Optimization Case Study 2: Closeout Period = 10 Days	Optimization Case Study 3: Closeout Period = 10 Days	Optimization Case Study 4: Closeout Period = 10 Days
$\rho = 0$	14,626,278	47,708,556	30,014,069	**50,998,941**
$\rho = +1$	32,814,825	**47,708,556**	35,365,786	36,577,865
$\rho =$ Empirical	19,534,991	47,708,556	30,076,721	**52,337,055**

Notes: This table illustrates the optimization results of the maximum daily LVaR trading limits for four optimization case studies with different correlation factors, 10 days closeout period, and under stressed market settings. As a result, optimization case studies 4 and 2 denote the highest LVaR limits for different correlation parameters.

While in optimization case study 1, distinct asset allocation percentages are assumed, in case study 2 all equity trading position is concentrated in one stock market that has, under severe market conditions, the highest daily return volatility — that is, the Dubai Financial Market (DFM) General Index. Finally, in case study 3 and case study 4, the effect of short-selling of stocks is also considered by randomly short-selling some of the sample stocks.

The principal effect of portfolio diversification on LVaR upper limits setting seems to be through optimization case study 1, that is, with unequal asset allocation proportions. The highest computed LVaR numbers are generally for optimization case study 4 (under both empirical and zero correlation parameters) and for optimization case study 2 (merely under 100% positive correlation factor). As indicated earlier, optimization case study 4 is obtained when the trading budget is allocated between long- and short-sales equity trading assets, whereas case study 2 is attained when the budget is assigned to the asset with the highest daily volatility.[5] In fact, in accordance with general risk management intuition, short-selling of assets should decreases LVaR figures and, hence, the overall LVaR upper trading

[5]The upper LVaR computed limits are highlighted in Tables 7.3–7.6 in bold.

limits. However, in the case of the GCC stock markets, the above phenomena (of high LVaR figures for optimization case study 4) can be explained by the nature of the diminutive correlation factors that we have witnessed in the entire GCC stock markets. These tiny correlation factors have led to grand diversification benefits for long-only equity trading positions and vice-versa for short-sales positions.

As a conclusion of these four optimization case studies using Tables 7.3–7.6, the senior management and board of directors of the financial trading entity can set the maximum daily LVaR threshold limits for their multiple-assets equity trading portfolios as follows.

1. **Panel A: Optimization Results with 5 Days Closeout Period**

   - Maximum approved daily LVaR threshold limit under regular market outlooks = 6,428,020 AED, with zero correlations parameters.
   - Maximum approved daily LVaR threshold limit under regular market outlooks = 5,711,650 AED, with 100% positive correlations parameters.
   - Maximum approved daily LVaR threshold limit under regular market outlooks = 6,668,592 AED, with empirical correlations parameters.
   - Maximum approved daily LVaR threshold limit under stressed or event market outlooks = 38,551,576 AED, with zero correlations parameters.
   - Maximum approved daily LVaR threshold limit under stressed or event market outlooks = 36,064,278 AED, with 100% positive correlations parameters.
   - Maximum approved daily LVaR threshold limit under stressed or event market outlooks = 39,563,095 AED, with empirical correlations parameters.
   - Maximum approved daily volume limit = AED 100,000,000 (between long-only and long/short-sales multiple trading assets).
   - The maximum liquidation horizons for all multiple-assets is 5 trading days.

2. **Panel B: Optimization Results with 10 Days Closeout Period**
   - Maximum approved daily LVaR threshold limit under regular market outlooks = 8,503,471 AED, with zero correlations parameters.
   - Maximum approved daily LVaR threshold limit under regular market outlooks = 7,555,803 AED, with 100% positive correlations parameters.
   - Maximum approved daily LVaR threshold limit under regular market outlooks = 8,821,719 AED, with empirical correlation parameters.
   - Maximum approved daily LVaR threshold limit under stressed or event market outlooks = 50,998,941 AED, with zero correlation parameters.
   - Maximum approved daily LVaR threshold limit under stressed or event market outlooks = 47,708,556 AED, with 100% positive correlation parameters.
   - Maximum approved daily LVaR threshold limit under stressed or event market outlooks = 52,337,055 AED, with empirical correlation parameters.
   - Maximum approved daily volume limit = AED 100,000,000 (between long-only and long-/short-sales multiple trading assets).
   - The maximum liquidation horizons for all multiple assets is 10 trading days.

It should be noted here that the above maximum permitted LVaR trading threshold limits are in their converted (or equivalent) UAE dirham (AED) values at the current or prevailing foreign exchange rates of GCC countries versus the UAE dirham.

7.4 Concluding Remarks and Recommendations

Trading risk management units are responsible for monitoring all risks related to proprietary trading. The market risk of a trading asset is the risk of experiencing changes in the value of the position due to unexpected changes in market variables or factors that affect the valuation of the position, such as the level of stock market indices or the impacts of specific stocks. The market variables that affect the value of a trading position are referred to as market risk factors.

In fact, there are many methods, modeling techniques, and ways to identify, to measure, to control, and to report market liquidity risk, and trading risk managers have the task to ascertain the identity of the one that suits their needs. In fact, there is no right or wrong way to measure, manage, and report liquidity trading risk; it all depends on each entity's objectives, lines of business, risk appetite, and the availability of funds for investment in trading risk management and IT projects. Regardless of the methodology chosen, the most important factors to consider are the establishment of sound risk practices, modeling algorithms, policies, standards, and the consistency in the implementation process across all lines of businesses and risks.

Under special conditions when changes in market risk factors are normally distributed, Liquidity-Adjusted Value at Risk (LVaR) can be computed using a closed-form parametric methodology. For LVaR maximum limit setting and daily trading risk measurement purposes, these assumptions are made for the sake of simplifying the computational process. However, for emerging market environments, one needs to supplement the closed-form parametric approach with other analyses such as stress-testing and simulation scenarios. This is done with the objective of estimating the impact of assumptions that are made under the LVaR method. Likewise, the effects of illiquidity of trading assets, in emerging markets, must be dealt with more wisely and should be brought into existence within the LVaR modeling algorithms.

Our results suggest that in almost all empirical tests, there are clear asymmetric behaviors in the distribution of returns of the sample indices and the two benchmark indices. The appealing outcome of this research study suggests the inevitability of combining LVaR computation with other quantitative techniques such as stress-testing and scenario analysis to grasp an in-depth view of other remaining risks (such as, fat-tails in the probability distribution of returns) that cannot be revealed with the plain assumption of normality.

Against this backdrop, the maximum LVaR threshold limit setting is an important theme as part of daily risk management and reporting processes for strategic decision-making within trading financial entities. To that end, a meaningful procedure for an optimization engine with a robust algorithm is developed to illustrate a practical modeling technique for the setting of maximum LVaR threshold limits for an equity trading unit. As such, in all four optimization case studies, the volume trading limit of 100,000,000 AED in UAE dirham is assumed constant and is used as a constraint (on the complex matrix-algebra algorithm) for the calibration of acceptable and practical LVaR threshold limits. For this particular research study, LVaR threshold limits were obtained for regular and stressed market outlooks and under the notion of different correlation factors and closeout periods. To that end, quite a few structured optimization case studies and simulation patterns were performed, with different asset allocations (i.e. with or without short-selling of multiple assets) and with the objective of setting an optimum LVaR threshold limits structure for an equity market risk management unit, under regular and event market circumstances.

In fact, the implications of the findings of this research study on the GCC stock markets suggest that although there is a clear departure from normality in the distribution of multiple-asset returns, this issue can be tackled without the need of complex mathematical algorithms and computational processes. In effect, it is possible to handle these issues for equity cash assets with the simple use of a robust closed-form parametric method (in the form of matrix-algebra algorithms), along with the incorporation of a credible stress-testing methodology (under adverse crisis-market outlooks), as well as by incorporating a robust illiquidity risk factor (or multiplier) that takes into account real-world trading circumstances, in the risk computational engine. In this research study, a robust modeling algorithm for the measurement of illiquidity of both short-selling and long-only trading positions is incorporated. In contrast to other commonly used liquidity models, the liquidity modeling algorithm that is applied in this work is more appropriate for real-world trading practices since it considers selling small fractions of long-only and different combinations of long-/short-sales trading assets on a daily basis. In essence, this liquidity modeling technique can be implemented for the entire multiple-assets portfolio or for each individual asset within the equity trading portfolio. Indeed, the developed quantitative methodology and risk computational algorithms can aid in advancing risk management practices in emerging markets, above all in the wake of the 2007–2009 credit crunch and the ensuing financial upheavals.

To that end, in this chapter, the risk parameters required for the construction of robust Liquidity-adjusted VaR (or LVaR) and stress-testing methods were reviewed from previous work and adapted to the specific applications of these methods to emerging markets. Moreover, a robust modeling technique for the incorporation of illiquid asset, in daily trading risk management practices, was defined and appropriately incorporated into LVaR and stress-testing methods. Effectively, the developed methodology and risk computation algorithms can aid in evolving risk management practices in emerging markets, largely in light of the aftermath of the 2007–2009 sub-prime credit crunch and the consequential financial turmoil. In addition, the proposed computational techniques and risk reporting process can have key uses and applications in machine learning and artificial intelligence, expert systems, smart financial functions, and financial technology (FinTech) in big data environments. Similarly, it can aid in the progress of regulatory technology (RegTech) for the global financial services industry and can be of interest to professionals, regulators, and researchers working in the field of machine learning for the policymaking process, machine learning techniques for the Internet of Things (IoT) data analytics, financial engineering and FinTech, and for those who want to advance their understanding of the impact of innovative risk computational techniques and reporting processes on regulatory challenges for the financial services industry and its effects on global financial stability.

References

Al Janabi, M. A. M. (2020a). Multivariate Portfolio Optimization under Illiquid Market Prospects: A Review of Theoretical Algorithms and Practical Techniques for Liquidity Risk Management. *Journal of Modelling in Management*, EarlyCite Articles: https://doi.org/10.1108/JM2-07-2019-0178.

Al Janabi, M. A. M. (2020b). Commodity markets asset allocation with robust liquidity risk management optimization parameters, In Goutte, S., and Guesmi, K. (Eds.), *Risk Factors and Contagion in Commodity Markets and Stock Markets*, World Scientific Publishing, Singapore, ISBN: 978-981-121-023-5.

Al Janabi, M. A. M. (2014). Optimal and investable portfolios: An empirical analysis with scenario optimization algorithms under crisis market prospects. *Economic Modelling*, **40**: 369–381.

Al Janabi, M. A. M. (2013). Optimal and coherent economic-capital structures: Evidence from long and short-sales trading positions under illiquid market perspectives. *Annals of Operations Research*, **205**(1): 109–139.

Al Janabi, M. A. M. (2008). Integrating liquidity risk factor into a parametric value at risk Method. *Journal of Trading*, **3**(3): 76–87.

Al Janabi, M. A. M., Ferrer, R., and Shahzad, S. J. H. (2009). Liquidity-adjusted value-at-risk optimization of a multi-asset portfolio using a vine copula approach. *Physica A: Statistical Mechanics and its Applications*, **536**: 122579.

Al Janabi, M. A. M., Arreola-Hernández, J. A., Berger, T., and Nguyen, D. K. (2017). Multivariate dependence and portfolio optimization algorithms under illiquid market scenarios. *European Journal of Operational Research*, **259**(3): 1121–1131.

Amihud, Y., Mendelson, H., and Pedersen, L. H. (2005). Liquidity and asset prices. *Foundations and Trends in Finance*, **1**(4): 269–364.

Asadi, S. and Al Janabi, M. A. M. (2020). Measuring market and credit risk under Solvency II: Evaluation of the standard technique versus internal models for stock and bond markets. *European Actuarial Journal*. Online First Articles: https://doi.org/10.1007/s13385-020-00235-0.

Angelidis, T. and Benos, A. (2006). Liquidity adjusted value-at-risk based on the components of the bid-ask spread. *Applied Financial Economics*, **16**(11): 835–851.

Arreola-Hernandez, J. and Al Janabi, M. A. M. (2020). Forecasting of dependence, market and investment risks of a global index portfolio. *Journal of Forecasting*, **39**(3): 512–532.

Arreola-Hernandez, J., Hammoudeh, S., Khuong, N. D., Al Janabi, M. A. M., and Reboredo, J. C., (2017). Global financial crisis and dependence risk analysis of sector portfolios: A vine copula approach. *Applied Economics*, **49**(25): 2409–2427.

Arreola-Hernández, J., Al Janabi, M. A. M., Hammoudeh, S., and Nguyen, D. K. (2015). Time lag dependence, cross-correlation and risk analysis of U.S. energy and non-energy stock portfolios. *Journal of Asset Management*, **16**(7): 467–483.

Bangia, A., Diebold, F. X., Schuermann, T., and Stroughair, J. D. (2002). Modeling liquidity risk with implications for traditional market risk measurement and management, In Figlewski, S. and Levich, R. M. Risk Management: The State of the Art. Amsterdam: Kluwer Academic Publishers.

Berkowitz, J. and O'Brien, J. (2001). How accurate are value-at-risk models at commercial banks? Working paper, US Federal Reserve Board's Finance & Economic.

Berkowitz, J. (2000). Incorporating liquidity risk into VAR models, Working Paper, Graduate School of Management, University of California, Irvine.

Cochrane, J. H. (2005). *Asset pricing.* Princeton University Press, Princeton, New Jersey.

Garcia, R., Renault, E., and Tsafack, G. (2007). Proper conditioning for coherent VaR in portfolio management. *Management Science*, **53**(3): 483–494.

Grillini, S., Sharma, A., Ozkan, A., and Al Janabi, M. A. M. (2019). Pricing of time-varying illiquidity within the Eurozone: Evidence using a Markov switching liquidity-adjusted capital asset pricing model. *International Review of Financial Analysis*, **64**: 145–158.

Hisata, Y. and Yamai, Y. (2000). Research toward the practical application of liquidity risk evaluation methods. Discussion Paper, Institute for Monetary and Economic Studies, Bank of Japan.

Jorion, P. (2006). *Value-at-Risk: The New benchmark for Controlling Market Risk.* McGraw-Hill, Chicago.

Le Saout, E. (2002). Incorporating liquidity risk in VaR models, Working Paper, Paris 1 University.

Madhavan, A., Richardson, M., and Roomans, M. (1997). Why do security prices change? A transaction-level analysis of NYSE stocks. *Review of Financial Studies*, **10**(1): 1035–1064.

Madoroba, S. B. W. and Kruger, J. W. (2014). Liquidity effects on value-at-risk limits: Construction of a new VaR model. *Journal of Risk Model Validation*, **8**: 19–46.

Markowitz, H. (1959). *Portfolio selection: Efficient diversification of investments.* John Wiley, New York.

Meucci, A. (2009). Managing diversification. *Risk*, **22**(5): 74–79.

Morgan Guaranty Trust Company (1994). *RiskMetrics-Technical Document.* New York: Morgan Guaranty Trust Company, Global Research.

Roch, A. and Soner, H.M. (2013). Resilient price impact of trading and the cost of illiquidity. *International Journal of Theoretical and Applied Finance*, **16**(6): 1–27.

Ruozi, R. and Ferrari, P. (2013). Liquidity risk management in banks: Economic and regulatory issues, Springer Briefs in Finance, DOI: 10.1007/978-3-642-29581-2.

Takahashi, D. and Alexander, S. (2002). Illiquid alternative asset fund modeling. *Journal of Portfolio Management*, **28**(2): 90–100.

https://doi.org/10.1142/9781786349507_0008

Chapter 8

On the Performances of Dynamic Conditional Correlation Models in the Sovereign CDS Market and the Corresponding Bond Market

Saker Sabkha
LEGO: Laboratoire d'Economie et de Gestion de l'Ouest
University of South Brittany, Brittany, France
saker.sabkha@univ-ubs.fr

8.1 Introduction

The Mathematical formalization of stock market fluctuations has been developed for the first time by Bachelier (1900) who mathematized the evolution of speculative values as a Brownian-motion (Walter, 2013). The probabilistic analysis of the variation of assets' prices proposed by Bachelier (1900) seems not to be valid in the long-run and discords with the efficient-market assumptions. In fact, the random walk equation that Bachelier (1900) obtained from this model is based on the hypothesis that the instantaneous and non-constant volatility is independent, linear, and follows a Gaussian marginal distribution.[1] De facto, this model presents some shortcomings: Empirical studies easily show that financial time series exhibit

[1]These are the fractal properties of the random walk and Brownian-motion paths. For more details, see Walter (2013).

kurtosis coefficients in excess, rejecting the distribution under normality. Also, asset prices in levels are obviously non-stationary and, over time, non-linear dependence is clearly observed between financial returns.

In order to consider for the non-linearity, the non-stationarity, and the extreme fluctuations of stock prices, a new class of financial models was proposed by Engle (1982), called Autoregressive Conditional Heteroscedasticity (ARCH). A generalization of this ARCH model (GARCH) was suggested by Bollerslev (1986), enabling for more flexibility and simplicity in the lag structure and the estimation process.[2] Several extensions and restrictive versions of GARCH-type have followed, allowing to take into account further financial market properties and specifications (Baillie *et al.*, 1996; Bollerslev and Mikkelsen, 1996; Davidson, 2004; Ding *et al.*, 1993; Engle and Bollerslev, 1986; Engle, 1987; Glosten *et al.*, 1993; Hentschel, 1995; Higgins and Bera, 1992; Klüppelberg *et al.*, 2004; Nelson, 1991; Sentana, 1995; Tse, 1998; Zakoian, 1994).

Numerous applications of the univariate GARCH models to financial data have been done by researchers as well as by finance practitioners. Even though they have been a good toll for financial managers in risk assessment, these volatilities models are inadequate when it comes to estimating a portfolio risk with several and different underlying assets. Because of the interdependence between stock market variables, the estimation of correlations and covariance matrix turns out to be a requisite to financial markets' investors, so they can pursue optimal risk allocation and hedging policies. Thus, portfolio optimization motivates the work of Bollerslev *et al.* (1988) who propose the first multivariate framework for Generalized Autoregressive Conditional Heteroscedastic models (MV-GARCH). Although it is considered as a considerable theoretical contribution, empirical application of this MV-GARCH — as it is initially proposed — is problematic due to the high-dimension of the parameters and the number of necessary restrictions.

In order to circumvent this estimation complexity, Engle (2002) introduce a new class of multivariate models called Dynamic

[2]A simple GARCH(1,1) could be an alternative for a long lag length of an ARCH model.

Conditional Correlation (DCC, hereafter) allowing for correlations to vary over time. This model keeps up with the flexibility of the univariate GARCH models and yet simplifies the parameterization and the empirical estimation. Another DCC-GARCH model was suggested by Tse and Tsui (2002) whereby the correlation computing is also done in two steps: a first step for estimating the univariate GARCH model for each time series and a second step for estimating the conditional covariance (see Engle and Sheppard (2001) for further details about technical differences between the two previous models). Engle and Kelly (2012) also proposed a time-varying correlation model considering more financial data specifications known as a dynamic equicorrelation model (DECO). In fact, the DCC-DECO model assumes that whenever the time is, correlations' pairwise across markets are equals based on an arbitrary estimation of the covariance matrix (Cai *et al.*, 2016; Engle and Kelly, 2012).[3]

Based on the aforementioned considerations, DCC models constitute a reliable tool for estimating interconnections between several assets, markets, and/or countries. It is obvious thus that this class of model was used in previous research to investigate financial phenomena such as contagion, risk spillover (Cai *et al.*, 2016; Lee, 2006) or co-movement (Coudert and Gex, 2010), given the considerable number of reasons making correlation an important variable in financial and economic studies.

This chapter aims to extend previous works — comparing the performance of GARCH models — to the multivariate dimension.[4] An extensive set of linear and non-linear DCC-GARCH models are estimated: 9 volatility model specifications are considered, taking into account the clustering volatility, the volatility persistence, the dependence between the mean and the conditional variance, the asymmetry of the error distribution, the leverage effect, the long memory property, the slow hyperbolic rate of decay of the volatility persistence, the long-run mean reverting property, and the fractionally integrated specifications. These models (GARCH-DCC, IGARCH-DCC,

---

[3]Cai *et al.* (2016) empirically compare the reliability of dynamic conditional correlation models using both conventional DCC and DECO estimates.

[4]We extend the work of Fantazzini (2011) on the univariate GARCH models and we transmit the same idea to the multivariate volatility models.

EGARCH-DCC, APARCH-DCC, GJR-GARCH-DCC, FIGARCH-DCC, FIEGARCH-DCC, FIAPARCH-DCC, HYGARCH-DCC) are estimated using both Engle (2002) and Tse and Tsui (2002) propositions. Also, results of the models are presented for both Gaussian and Student marginal distributions.

Owing to the noteworthy role played by the credit market during the recent two financial crises, the interest of the scientific community to bonds and to credit derivatives (CDS, CDO, ABX...) is ever increasing. Therewith, modeling multivariate volatilities of credit assets is a high-priority concern among policy makers, portfolio managers, and hedge funds. That is why, our studied models are applied to credit risk data (sovereign CDS spreads and the underlying bond yields) over a relatively long period covering the last two recent financial and economic crises and spanning from January 2006 until April 2014.

Our chapter contributes to the extant literature in several ways. First, while there exists a considerable number of studies using the DCC model to estimate multivariate volatilities, the literature comparing the empirical performance of different Dynamic Conditional Correlation models is still not developed, especially when it comes to using the credit assets as an application reference. As far as we are concerned, there is no study comparing the 9 dynamic conditional correlation GARCH models for the credit market. Second, the assessment of the interconnectedness between credit markets in an international context puts forward the fact that countries from different regions present different features. This suggests improving the standard method commonly applied to comovement studies by using rather flexible approaches with individual readjustment for each country and each set of data. Third, studying the multivariate modeling framework in the credit markets presents accurate results since it improves the predictive ability of financial tools in terms of future evolution in sovereign borrowing conditions.

The rest of the chapter is organized as follows: Sections 8.2 and 8.3 give some background information about the literature on the comparison of GARCH performances and discuss the methodology approach used in this chapter. Section 8.4 is dedicated to sample description and the descriptive statistics. Empirical results and discussion are covered in Section 8.5. Section 8.6 concludes the chapter and outlines possible directions for future work.

8.2 Literature Review

Unlike volatility models, not many studies have been conducted to assess the performance of the multivariate GARCH-type models.[5] The few works dealing with the time-varying correlation are only interested in straightening out the model's shortcomings by developing some extensive forms that takes into account more financial data features.

Evaluating the conditional covariance of 100 companies' assets from the S&P 500 and the Dow Jones American indices, Engle and Sheppard (2001) develop a framework where the time-varying correlation converges easily and presents a strong estimation. The authors propose a simplified method in which correlation coefficients are estimated through two steps[6] and give some theoretical and empirical evidence of the estimator consistency. In a more theoretical framework, Degiannakis and Xekalaki (2004) summarize the existing literature on ARCH processes and present the most useful multivariate Autoregressive Conditional Heteroscedasticity models, their respective properties, and the different estimating techniques.

Using 45 daily stock returns from the DAX and the FTSE, Hafner and Franses (2003) propose a generalized form of the DCC model that controls for heterogeneity. Results show that the GDCC has a superior performance and fits better financial data. One of the DCC issues discussed by Billio *et al.* (2006) is the restrictive hypothesis of mutual dynamics between different class of assets. The authors propose a flexible Dynamic Conditional Correlation model (fDCC) where each group of assets is allowed to have a different dynamic. By applying the fDCC to three sectors from the Italian stock market, they show that this model provides a better portfolio allocation with a lesser risk and a greater yield. Furthermore, Billio and Caporin (2009) generalize the DCC and the fDCC model and propose a Quadratic Flexible DCC model allowing for interaction between assets' correlations.

Based on a Monte Carlo simulation, Hafner and Reznikova (2012) study the performance and the estimators consistency of the DCC

---

[5]See Bollerslev *et al.* (1992) for a complete theoretical and empirical survey on the use of univariate ARCH processes in financial studies.

[6]More details about the two-stage estimation method are given in the next section.

models. The authors find some estimation bias with a large sample size and show that the shrinkage technique, as an alternative to the maximum likelihood one, can be a solution. Through a theoretical study, Caporin and McAleer (2013) study the estimating and forecasting limits of the time-varying covariance and correlation models. Among the ten discussed shortcomings, the authors argue that the variance misspecification — due to some financial markets properties (leverage and asymmetry effects) — leads to biased correlation estimator parameters. This research line is followed by Boudt *et al.* (2013) who propose an extensive form of the DCC model (BIP-cDCC) to overcome the forecasting issue. Application of this new class of models to the exchange rate returns of the euro and the yen against the dollar shows that the BIP-cDCC outperforms the standard DCC in terms of forecasting.

In the same context, Aielli (2013) discusses a particular limit of the DCC model and argue that the second-stage estimator is biased, leading to inappropriate conclusions. Application to simulated and real data shows that the alternative model (cDCC) is more consistent with slightly better forecasting performances.

More recently, García de la Fuente *et al.* (2014) propose an extension of the DCC model that take into account the non-normality features of financial time series while modeling DCC models. A Bayesian DCC with multivariate skew-slash distribution is applied to simulated data and real data sets from three worldwide stock market indices (CAC40, DAX, Nikkei). The authors show that even though this new class of model allows a better capture of the slight skewness and the high kurtosis characterizing stock returns, it doesn't outperform the standard normal-distributed DCC model. Moreover, Cai *et al.* (2016) compare the estimators' accuracy of the dynamic conditional correlation and the dynamic equicorrelation (DECO)[7] on 9 stock markets from East Asia nd the USA during the Global Financial Crisis. Results of the DECO model are consistent and confirm those of the standard DCC.

[7]The DECO-MGARCH model, as proposed by Engle and Kelly (2012), supposes that the time-varying conditional correlation between markets (or assets) is constant whatever the time is.

8.3 Methodology

Even though they have been abundantly developed and examined in the theoretical and empirical literature, several correlation models are so sophisticated and over-parameterized with a complicated optimization, making them rarely used by practitioners. Unlike these models, the DCC nonlinear model, proposed by Engle (2002) and Tse and Tsui (2002), is a more reliable estimator of correlation with a limited number of parameters to estimate and an easy estimation method. The flexibility of this class of model lies in the fact that the estimation needs to go through a two-step process: the conditional volatility of each time series is estimated from a traditional univariate GARCH model in the first step, then in the second step, the multivariate conditional volatility is estimated using the Quasi-Maximum Likelihood function.

8.3.1 *Marginal volatility processes: Univariate ARCH-type models*

As an extension of the ARCH model proposed by Engle (1982), Bollerslev (1986) propose a generalized ARCH model given by:

$$\begin{aligned} x_{i,t} &= \mu_{i,t} + a_{i,t}/a_{i,t} = \sigma_{i,t}\varepsilon_{i,t}, \quad \varepsilon_{i,t}/\mathcal{F}_{t-1} \rightsquigarrow \mathcal{N}(0,1); \\ \sigma_{i,t}^2 &= E(x_{i,t}/\mathcal{F}_{t-1}) = \alpha_{i,0} + \sum_{k=1}^{q} \alpha_{i,k} a_{t-1}^2 + \sum_{h=1}^{p} \beta_{i,h} \sigma_{t-1}^2, \end{aligned} \tag{8.1}$$

with x_t is a time series, i is a given country from the sample and μ_t and σ_t are, respectively, the conditional mean and the conditional volatility. To satisfy the positive-definite condition, some restrictions are imposed: $p >= 0$, $q > 0$, $\alpha_k >= 0$ for $k = 1 \ldots q$, $\beta_h >= 0$ and $\alpha_0 >= 0$ for $h = 1 \ldots p$.

For the sake of simplicity and suitability, only models with process orders (p and q) equal to 1 are estimated. In fact, the simplest GARCH (1,1) specification is the most useful and fitted for financial time series (Bollerslev, 1986; Wei *et al.*, 2010).

The GARCH (1,1) process, as proposed by Bollerslev (1986) is given by the following formula:

$$\sigma_{i,t}^2 = \alpha_{i,0} + \alpha_{i,1} + \alpha_{i,1} a_{t-1}^2 + \beta_{i,1} \sigma_{i,t-1}^2. \tag{8.2}$$

In addition to the previous model restrictions, the parameters α_1 and β_1 must satisfy the condition of $\alpha_1 + \beta_1 < 1$ to comply with the stationarity in the broad sense.

A more restrictive version of the GARCH (1,1) is proposed by Engle and Bollerslev (1986) where the equivalent of the unit root in the mean included in the variance so we can handle for the stationarity of the variance. The Integrated GARCH (1,1) takes into account the persistence of conditional volatilities.[8] The main difference with the GARCH (1,1) is that the IGARCH require the parameters α_1 and β_1 to respect the equality of $\alpha_1 + \beta_1 = 1$. Thus, the IGARCH (1,1)[9] can be written as follows:

$$\sigma_{i,t}^2 = \alpha_{i,0} + \alpha_{i,1} a_{t-1}^2 + (1 - \alpha_{i,1})\sigma_{i,t-1}^2. \tag{8.3}$$

Besides the aforementioned linear models, there exist some nonlinear GARCH-class of models that consider the other financial market properties. The Exponential GARCH, as proposed by Nelson (1991), is one of these models: it takes into account the leverage effect and the asymmetry of the error distribution. While the nonnegativity of linear GARCH model is ensured by several parameters restrictions, the EGARCH model proposes another formulation allowing for a positive volatility without any restrictive constraints. The EGARCH (1,1) is expressed as follows:

$$\begin{aligned} \ln(\sigma_{i,t}^2) &= \alpha_{i,0} + \alpha_{i,1-1} ln(\sigma_{i,t}^2) + \beta_{i,1} g(\varepsilon_{i,t-1}), \\ \text{where} \quad g(\varepsilon_t) &= \theta\varepsilon_t + \gamma[\mid \varepsilon_t \mid - E(\mid \varepsilon_t \mid)]. \end{aligned} \tag{8.4}$$

The asymmetric relation between assets' fluctuation and volatility changes is depicted by the θ and γ representing, respectively, the sign and the magnitude of ε_t.

Glosten *et al.* (1993) propose a model that allows the sign and the amplitude of the innovations (ε_t) to affect the conditional volatility separately. The asymmetric leverage effect[10] is represented in the

[8]Today's shocks on a financial asset have a significant impact on the conditional volatility several periods in the future.

[9]The IGARCH(1,1) is equivalent to the Exponentially Weighted Moving Average (EWMA) model developed by Morgan (1997).

[10]Positive and negative financial shocks revamp asymmetrically the variance. Furthermore, bad news (shocks) generate greater volatility than good news.

following formulation of the GJR-GARCH(1,1)[11] model:

$$\sigma_{i,t}^2 = \alpha_{i,0} + \alpha_{i,1}a_{i,t-1}^2 + \gamma_i I_{i,t-1}a_{i,t-1}^2 + \beta_{i,1}\sigma_{i,t-1}^2, \tag{8.5}$$

with I_t being a dummy variable equals to 0 when a_t is positive and 1 otherwise.

The first model accounting for the long-range persistence of financial assets variance is developed by Ding *et al.* (1993). This asymmetric power ARCH model allows the volatility to be long memory.[12] The APARCH (1,1) model is:

$$\sigma_{i,t}^2 = \alpha_{i,0} + \alpha_{i,1}(\mid a_{i,t-1} \mid -\gamma_i a_{i,t-1})^\delta + \beta_{i,1}\sigma_{i,t-1}^\delta, \tag{8.6}$$

where δ depicts the Box-Cox power transformation of the conditional volatility (σ_t) and satisfies the condition of $\delta >= 0$.

A more flexible class of GARCH models is proposed by Baillie *et al.* (1996) who introduce a new feature of the unit root for the variance. In fact, the fractionally integrated GARCH model (FIGARCH) highlights the fact that — unlike stationary processes where the persistence of volatility shocks is finite — in unit root processes, the impact of lagged errors occurs at a slow hyperbolic rate of decay. The FIGARCH model allows, thus, to capture the long memory in financial volatility with a complete flexibility regarding the persistence degree. In fact, the FIGARCH (1,d,1) formulation depends on fractional integration parameter (d) as follows:

$$\sigma_{i,t}^2 = \alpha_{i,0} + [1 - (1 - \beta_i(L))^{-1}(1 - \phi(L))(1 - L)^d]a_{i,t}^2 + \beta\sigma_{i,t-1}^2, \tag{8.7}$$

with $0 < d < 1$. When $d = 1$, the FIGARCH (1,d,1) is equivalent to an IGARCH (1,1) where the persistence of conditional variance is supposed to be complete, while when $d = 0$, it is rather equivalent to a GARCH (1,1) and no volatility persistence is taken into consideration. L is the lag operator and $(1 - L)^d$ is the financial fractional differencing operator.

[11]The volatility's different reactions to signs and sizes of past innovations are also suggested in the Threshold Heteroskedastic model (TGARCH) of Zakoian (1994). The major difference is that, in the TGARCH model, the conditional standard deviation (σ_t) is considered rather than the conditional variance (σ_t^2).

[12]The autocorrelation function of time series returns decreases gradually.

Other ARCH formulations are extended to the fractionally integrated GARCH, including asymmetric leverage effect presented in the EGARCH model. Bollerslev and Mikkelsen (1996) propose a new class of model combining characteristics of the FIGARCH and the EGARCH models so-called FIEGARCH (p,d,q). Financial assets' volatilities are, thus, better explained and depicted by a mean-reverting fractionally integrated process. The FIEGARCH(1,d,1) model is written as follows:

$$\ln(\sigma_{i,t}^2) = \alpha_{i,0} + \phi(L)^{-1}(1-L)^{-d}[1+\psi(L)]g(\varepsilon_{i,t-1}), \tag{8.8}$$

where $\phi(L)$ and $\psi(L)$ are lag polynomials, and — as in the EGARCH (1,1)[13] — $g(\varepsilon_t)$ is a quantization function of information flows such as:

$$g(\varepsilon_t) = \theta\varepsilon_t + \gamma[|\ \varepsilon_t\ | - E(|\ \varepsilon_t\ |)].$$

An extension of the conventional fractionally integrated GARCH model is proposed by Tse (1998) so-called FIAPARCH (1,d,1). The new approach combines the long-range dependencies feature and the asymmetric impact of lagged positive and negative shocks on future volatilities in one fractionally integrated model. The FIAPARCH (1,d,1) is written as follows:

$$\sigma_{i,t}^{\delta} = \alpha_{i,0}(1-\beta)^{-1} + [1-(1-\beta(L))^{-1}\phi(L)(1-L)^d] \\ \times (|\ a_{i,t}\ | - \gamma a_{i,t})^{\delta}. \tag{8.9}$$

More recently, another linear GARCH model, called hyperbolic GARCH (HYGARCH) is proposed by Davidson (2004) who argues that the impact of lagged errors on the conditional variance discloses near-epoch dependence feature. The main contribution of this model is that the fractional integration parameter is negative $(-d)$ instead of positive and that d increases when it approaches zero.[14] The statistical properties included in the HYGARCH make it the most successful and used approach by financial practitioners in modeling time series volatilities. The HYGARCH (1,d,1) is defined under

[13]When the memory parameter, $d = 0$, the FIEGARCH formulation is equivalent to the conventional EGARCH (1,1) (FIEGARCH (1,0,1) $\simeq$ EGARCH (1,1)).

[14]When d of the HYGARCH is positive, it is considered as a unit root process.

the following formulation:

$$\sigma_{i,t}^2 = \alpha_{i,0} + [1 - (1 - \beta(L))^{-1}(1 - \phi(L))[1 + \alpha((1 - L)^d - 1)]]a_{i,t}^2. \tag{8.10}$$

As mentioned before, the 9 GARCH-class models, cited above, are estimated in the first step through a univariate process to capture the apparent conditional univariate standard deviations. Then, a multivariate process is estimated in the second step so we can have the conditional bivariate volatilities (and so the conditional correlations).

8.3.2 *Joint volatility processes: Multivariate ARCH-type models*

In the second step, the multivariate specification is introduced to each one of the GARCH-class models in order to estimate the bivariate dynamic conditional correlations. Following the propositions of Engle (2002) and Tse and Tsui (2002), the DCC model is defined as a time varying structure:

$$Var(x_t/\mathcal{F}_{t-1}) = \sigma_t^2 = \Omega_t = D_t H_t D_t, \tag{8.11}$$

where $\mathcal{F}_{t-1}$ is the information set available at the time $(t-1)$. D_t is a diagonal matrix $N \times N$ such as $D_t = diag\{\sigma_{ii,t}\} = diag(\sigma_{11,t}...\sigma_{NN,t})$, $\sigma_{NN,t}$ is the conditional standard deviation obtained from the univariate models. H_t is the time-varying correlation matrix of the standardized residuals ε_t (of x_t).

Engle (2002) and Tse and Tsui (2002) propose two DCC models presenting some similarities and divergences. For Engle (2002),

$$H_t = diag(q_{11,t}^{-1/2} \cdots q_{NN,t}^{-1/2}) Q_t diag(q_{11,t}^{-1/2} \cdot q_{NN,t}^{-1/2}), \tag{8.12}$$

where $\overline{q_{ij}} = \overline{\rho_{ij}}$ ($\overline{\rho_{ij}}$ is the unconditional correlation between $\varepsilon_{i,t}$ et $\varepsilon_{j,t}$). Q_t is a symmetric covariance $N\times N$ matrix that can be written as follows:

$$Q_t = \overline{Q_{ij}}(1 - \alpha - \beta) + \alpha(\varepsilon_{t-1}\varepsilon_{t-1}') + \beta Q_{ij,t-1}, \tag{8.13}$$

with $\overline{Q}$ is a symmetric time-invariant unconditional correlation matrix. α and β parameters are positive and respect the constraint of

$\alpha + \beta < 1$. The bivariate dynamic conditional correlation coefficient of Engle (2002) is, thus, defined as:

$$\rho_{12,t} = \frac{\overline{q_{12}}(1-\alpha-\beta) + \alpha(\varepsilon_{1,t-1}\varepsilon_{2,t-1}) + \beta q_{12,t-1}}{\sqrt{(\overline{q_{11}}(1-\alpha-\beta) + \alpha\varepsilon_{11,t-1}^2 + \beta q_{11,t-1})(\overline{q_{22}}(1-\alpha-\beta) + \alpha\varepsilon_{22,t-1}^2 + \beta q_{22,t-1})}}. \tag{8.14}$$

For Tse and Tsui (2002), $H_t = \{\rho_{ij,t}\}$ is assumed to follow a univariate GARCH process and is obtained from the recursion of:

$$H_t = (1-\theta_1-\theta_2)H + \theta_1 H_{t-1} + \theta_2 \Xi_{t-1}, \tag{8.15}$$

where the parameters θ_1 and θ_2 are supposed to satisfy the non-negativity constraint and the inequality $\theta_1 + \theta_2 <= 1$. H is a symmetric time-invariant $N\times N$ with $\rho_{ii} = 1$ (a unit diagonal element). Ξ_{t-1} is the correlation matrix of the lagged standardized residuals ε_t such as $\varepsilon_{i,t} = \frac{a_t}{\sigma_{i,t}}$. Since Ξ_{t-1} depends on the lagged residuals, and analogously to the x_{t-1}^2 in the GARCH (1,1) representation, Ξ_{t-1} can be specified by the following formula:

$$\Xi_{ij,t-1} = \frac{\sum_{m=1}^{M} \varepsilon_{i,t-m}\varepsilon_{j,t-m}}{\sqrt{\left(\sum_{m=1}^{M}\varepsilon_{i,t-m}^2\right)\left(\sum_{m=1}^{M}\varepsilon_{j,t-m}^2\right)}}, \quad 1 \le i < j \le N \le M. \tag{8.16}$$

$N \le M$ is a necessary condition for ψ_{t-1} and H_t to be nonnegative definite. Thus, in the bivariate case, the conditional correlation coefficient of Tse and Tsui (2002) is defined as:

$$\rho_{12,t} = (1-\theta_1-\theta_2)\rho_{12} + \theta_1\rho_{12,t-1} + \theta_2 \frac{\sum_{s=1}^{S}\varepsilon_{1,t-s}\varepsilon_{2,t-s}}{\sqrt{\left(\sum_{s=1}^{S}\varepsilon_{1,t-s}^2\right)\left(\sum_{s=1}^{S}\varepsilon_{2,t-s}^2\right)}}. \tag{8.17}$$

In this chapter, dynamic conditional correlation coefficients are estimated using both models proposed by Engle (2002) and Tse and Tsui (2002). For each of the estimated model, time series are assumed to follow an AR(1) process with a normal and t-student marginal distributions. Models' performances comparison is made upon the value of the Akaike information criterion (AIC) and some multivariate diagnostic tests: Vector normality test and Hosking's Multivariate Portmanteau Statistics on standardized residuals (and on squared standardized residuals) are used to investigate the reliability of the multivariate GARCH specifications.

8.4 Data

The models detailed above are estimated using daily price changes data from the credit market of 33 worldwide countries belonging to four different economic levels (low economic growth, developed countries, newly industrialized countries, and emerging countries). DCC models are estimated on both credit spreads of sovereign CDS market and the corresponding government bond market, during a period spanning from January, 2nd 2006 to April, 3th 2014. CDS spreads and bond yields are extracted from Bloomberg® and Thomson Reuters®.

During the studied period (2006–2014), the world economy has been affected by two major crises — namely the Global Financial Crisis and the European Debt Crisis — and the borrowing costs of countries greatly fluctuated whatever their economic level or their geographical position. Thus, evaluating and comparing the performances of multivariate volatility models is particularly relevant during this period.

For the sake of homogeneity, bond yields are transformed into spreads regarding the risk-free interest rate. Several studies are interested in the issue of the appropriate choice of this riskless rate. A first strand of the literature suggests the use of the US treasury yield (Longstaff *et al.*, 2005) or the swap rate of the same maturity (Blanco *et al.*, 2005). Another strand promotes the use of the bond rate issued by the country considered as the least risky of the zone (government bond yield curves of Deutsch Bundesbank, the Federal Reserve Board and the bank of England) (Gilchrist and Mojon, 2016; Norden and Weber, 2009). In this paper, the 5 year German federal government bond is chosen as a reference rate for European countries, and the United States sovereign bonds for American and Asian countries. In order to not reduce our sample, for Germany, euro-area generic bond is used as a benchmark yield, and the US Treasury Zero-Coupon Yield Curve for the United States.

Results of the descriptive statistics[15] show that CDS and Bond spreads exhibit similar statistical properties. The average daily spreads are almost always positive (except for Germany, the USA, and Japan where the bond spreads mean is negative). Negative credit spreads can be explained by the fact that during recessions markets participants are willing to pay government for riskless investments, making bonds of some countries (Germany among others) issued with negative yields (Dolvin, 2012). This phenomenon can be caused, likewise, by a temporary liquidity factors (Beber *et al.*, 2009; Bhanot and Guo, 2011). Another explanation is that these negative spreads are due to a mis-choice of the risk-free rate. The high levels of standard deviations show that our data is widely spread and not centered around the mean.

The Jarque–Bera test confirms the non-normality of the data distribution at the 1% significance level. Theses findings are confirmed by the significant excess kurtosis and the positive skewness coefficients. As expected, the Augmented Dickey–Fuller test confirms the null hypothesis of the unit-root presence. Both CDS spreads and bond spreads are non-stationary. The ARCH-LM test and the Q statistics of Ljung-Box both confirm the presence of ARCH effect and reject the null hypothesis of no serial correlation in the CDS and bond spreads.

8.5 Empirical Results

For each of the 33 countries composing our sample, 9 DCC models are estimated following Engle (2002) and Tse and Tsui (2002). Results of the conditional multivariate volatility models are not reported here due to space limits but are available upon request. Table 8.1 reports diagnostic checking tests for different models of some chosen countries.

DCC-FIGARCH, DCC-FIAPARCH, and DCC-HYGARCH are the most difficult models to estimate with mis-convergences in at least 14 among the 33 countries. On the other hand, the models that perform well with to strong numerical convergence and

[15]Descriptive statistics are not reported here but can be presented upon request.

Table 8.1. Diagnostic checking tests for different models.

Countries			Austria				Spain				Brazil				Russia			
Dynamic correlation models (*DCC-GARCH (1,1)*)			DCC (Engle)		DCC (Tse and Tsui)		DCC (Engle)		DCC (Tse and Tsui)		DCC (Engle)		DCC (Tse and Tsui)		DCC (Engle)		DCC (Tse and Tsui)	
Distribution			Gauss	Student	Gauss	Student	Gauss	Student	Gauss	Student	Gauss	Student	Gauss	Student	Gauss	Student	Gauss	Student
Numerical convergence			Yes	Yes	Yes	Yes	Yes	Yes	Yes	Yes	Yes	Yes	Yes	Yes	Yes	Yes	Yes	Yes
Information criterion		AIK	9,287	8,691	9,286	8,691	12,504	11,619	12,515	11,619	13,747	12,400	13,746	12,400	13,024	12,245	13,015	12,248
Multivariate diagnostic tests	*Vector normality test*	Chi^2(4)	2140,6 ***	2161,1 ***	2139,6 ***	2144,4 ***	5753,6 ***	8313,3 ***	7212,2 ***	9465,4 ***	2,1 ***	21419,0 ***	21323,0 ***	21419,0 ***	4535,7 ***	4581,7 ***	4530,4 ***	4517,2 ***
	Hosking's Multivariate Portmanteau Statistics on standardized residuals	5	61,845 ***	59,946 ***	63,639 ***	62,915 ***	68,982 ***	70,408 ***	72,748 ***	69,354 ***	45,116 ***	44,475 ***	44,273 ***	44,475 ***	78,465 ***	74,480 ***	80,472 ***	80,112 ***
		10	86,663 ***	85,059 ***	87,524 ***	87,110 ***	82,492 ***	83,633 ***	86,052 ***	82,740 ***	64,472 ***	65,230 ***	65,548 ***	65,230 ***	98,707 ***	95,172 ***	100,348 ***	99,892 ***
		20	124,682 ***	123,461 ***	125,525 ***	125,545 ***	127,578 ***	130,453 ***	130,133 ***	127,668 ***	94,396	95,395	94,824	95,395	140,639 ***	135,520 ***	143,794 ***	142,658 ***
		50	238,177 **	235,964 **	237,767 **	237,607 **	242,304 **	248,300 **	246,113 **	244,775 **	241,293 **	248,345 **	246,638 **	248,345 **	256,031 ***	250,422 ***	257,080 ***	255,635 ***
	Hosking's Multivariate Portmanteau Statistics on squared standardized residuals	5	8,369	7,766	7,797	7,753	3,727	3,259	3,413	3,320	2,993	3,279	2,932	3,279	16,136	16,159	16,202	16,168
		10	17,068	16,507	16,645	16,547	7,079	6,298	5,958	6,211	8,461	8,651	8,278	8,651	20,862	20,570	20,901	20,876
		20	36,90	36,38	36,36	36,20	59,705	66,107	55,626	63,492	13,875	14,310	13,675	14,310	51,302	48,761	51,590	51,754
		50	126,34	123,56	123,34	122,81	96,601	103,240	91,824	100,938	136,426	140,120	131,720	140,120	85,666	81,152	86,598	86,878

The Hosking's Portmanteau test is the mutivariate version of the Box-Pierce Q statistic under the null hypothesis of no serial correlation. ** and *** denotes the rejection of the null hypothesis at the 5% and 10% level of significance.

Countries			Belgium				Italy				Turkey				Hungary			
Dynamic correlation models (*DCC-IGARCH (1,1)*)			DCC (Engle)		DCC (Tse and Tsui)		DCC (Engle)		DCC (Tse and Tsui)		DCC (Engle)		DCC (Tse and Tsui)		DCC (Engle)		DCC (Tse and Tsui)	
Distribution			Gauss	Student	Gauss	Student	Gauss	Student	Gauss	Student	Gauss	Student	Gauss	Student	Gauss	Student	Gauss	Student
Numerical convergence			Yes	Yes	Yes	Yes	Yes	Yes	Yes	Yes	Yes	Yes	Yes	Yes	Yes	Yes	Yes	Yes
Information criterion		AIK	10,583	9,784	10,584	9,785	11,246	10,929	11,267	10,938	15,182	14,983	15,182	14,982 ***	14,062	13,623	14,061	13,623
Multivariate diagnostic tests	*Vector normality test*	Chi^2(4)	1135,0 ***	11362,0 ***	11333,0 ***	11327,0 ***	1197,7 ***	1233,0 ***	1212,0 ***	1233,6 ***	932,1 ***	946,9 ***	954,6 ***	958,7 ***	2896,3 ***	3035,3 ***	2801,6 ***	3017,4 ***
	Hosking's Multivariate Portmanteau Statisticds on standardized residuals	5	98,674 ***	98,440 ***	99,201 ***	99,748 ***	94,736 ***	99,781 ***	104,750 ***	105,510 ***	126,473 ***	126,153 ***	128,036 ***	127,658 ***	113,192 ***	116,127 ***	117,225 ***	119,705 ***
		10	116,302 ***	116,103 ***	116,392 ***	117,075 ***	110,940 ***	116,331 ***	121,276 ***	122,166 ***	143,777 ***	143,222 ***	144,961 ***	144,575 ***	132,288 ***	134,514 ***	136,604 ***	138,121 ***
		20	155,775 ***	155,309 ***	156,018 ***	156,766 ***	181,443 ***	186,748 ***	189,093 ***	190,494 ***	188,842 ***	187,851 ***	188,940 ***	188,505 ***	173,692 ***	177,086 ***	178,060 ***	181,455 ***
		50	291,862 ***	290,224 ***	292,699 ***	293,245 ***	356,740 ***	362,413 ***	365,798 ***	367,116 ***	296,192 ***	295,874 ***	297,636 ***	297,450 ***	276,710 ***	283,619 ***	281,020 ***	286,444 ***
	Hosking's Multivariate Portmanteau Statisticds on squared standardized residuals	5	16,140	16,245	15,955	16,078	25,044	25,071	24,480	24,573	28,142 *	27,884 *	27,096 *	27,172 *	33,234 **	35,206 **	37,697 **	40,530 **
		10	27,907	27,846	27,768	27,804	48,637	49,465	48,904	49,286	42,102	41,900	40,992	41,116	52,620 *	54,559 *	58,334 *	57,760 *
		20	88,67	87,89	88,99	89,12	97,378 *	99,019 *	97,311 *	98,042 *	87,236	86,173	85,678	84,763	73,289	74,412	79,721	77,375
		50	238,40 **	235,51 **	238,64 **	238,27 **	240,069 **	243,570 **	238,583 **	239,994 **	165,690	164,886	163,999	163,452	133,906	133,078	141,468	136,202

The Hosking's Portmanteau test is the mutivariate version of the Box-Pierce Q statistic under the null hypothesis of no serial correlation. *, ** and *** denotes the rejection of the null hypothesis at the 1%, 5% and 10% level of significance.

Countries			Finland				Portugal				Latvia				Romania			
Dynamic correlation models (*DCC-EGARCH (1,1)*)			DCC (Engle)		DCC (Tse and Tsui)		DCC (Engle)		DCC (Tse and Tsui)		DCC (Engle)		DCC (Tse and Tsui)		DCC (Engle)		DCC (Tse and Tsui)	
Distribution			Gauss	Student	Gauss	Student	Gauss	Student	Gauss	Student	Gauss	Student	Gauss	Student	Gauss	Student	Gauss	Student
Numerical convergence			Yes	Yes	Yes	Yes	Yes	Yes	Yes	Yes	Yes	Yes	Yes	Yes	Yes	Yes	Yes	Yes
Information criterion		AIK	7,616	6,571	7,616	6,572	13,240	12,837	13,270	12,848	13,220	10,878	13,215	10,855	13,126	12,310	13,124	12,308
Multivariate diagnostic tests	*Vector normality test*	Chi^2(4)	5279,9 ***	5265,7 ***	5275,2 ***	5268,7 ***	222,7 ***	2294,2 ***	2337,0 ***	2336,2 ***	50128,0 ***	39111,0 ***	49566,0 ***	17828,0 ***	5289,4 ***	5527,2 ***	5284,6 ***	5648,0 ***
	Hosking's Multivariate Portmanteau Statisticds on standardized residuals	5	37,736 ***	37,098 ***	37,887 ***	37,800 ***	109,444 ***	112,479 ***	127,546 ***	116,353 ***	56,330 ***	42,397 ***	53,599 ***	50,762 ***	63,228 ***	62,052 ***	62,877 ***	60,605 ***
		10	51,113 *	50,277 *	51,145 *	51,032 *	137,712 ***	140,620 ***	154,723 ***	143,215 ***	111,421 ***	72,175 ***	105,111 ***	91,847 ***	165,047 ***	162,170 ***	163,004 ***	162,048 ***
		20	109,511 **	108,398 **	109,439 **	109,610 **	178,501 ***	181,290 ***	193,954 ***	183,167 ***	339,245 ***	364,768 ***	329,854 ***	441,145 ***	245,127 ***	240,489 ***	243,095 ***	239,530 ***
		50	228,053 *	227,045 *	228,321 *	228,242 *	301,254 ***	304,544 ***	319,241 ***	306,360 ***	475,888 ***	436,216 ***	455,480 ***	513,120 ***	483,721 ***	474,735 ***	480,532 ***	471,585 ***
	Hosking's Multivariate Portmanteau Statisticds on squared standardized residuals	5	1,442	1,442	1,444	1,449	8,083	7,947	8,958	8,080	2,784 ***	0,294 ***	2,722	1,668	13,692	13,696	13,772	13,676
		10	3,113	3,104	3,112	3,105	17,593	17,500	18,907	17,646	3,532	0,478	3,434	2,535	69,457 ***	72,134 ***	66,303 ***	80,338 ***
		20	7,601	75,791	75,365	75,041	118,285 ***	120,495 ***	124,375 ***	121,804 ***	1143,380	1430,520	1152,630 ***	1621,130 ***	108,545 **	111,592 **	105,417 **	119,874 **
		50	162,616	161,413	161,360	160,936	212,402	212,600	212,535	211,250	1146,400 ***	***	1155,620 ***	1622,060 ***	169,150	171,709	166,092	179,283

The Hosking's Portmanteau test is the mutivariate version of the Box-Pierce Q statistic under the null hypothesis of no serial correlation. *, ** and *** denotes the rejection of the null hypothesis at the 1%, 5% and 10% level of significance.

(*Continued*)

Table 8.1. (*Continued*)

Countries			Denmark				Ireland				Turkey				Croatia			
Dynamic correlation models (*DCC-CJR(1,1)*)			DCC (Engle)		DCC (Tse and Tsui)		DCC (Engle)		DCC (Tse and Tsui)		DCC (Engle)		DCC (Tse and Tsui)		DCC (Engle)		DCC (Tse and Tsui)	
Distribution			Gauss	Student	Gauss	Student	Gauss	Student	Gauss	Student	Gauss	Student	Gauss	Student	Gauss	Student	Gauss	Student
Numerical convergence			Yes	Yes	Yes	No	Yes	Yes	No	Yes	Yes	Yes	Yes	Yes	Yes	Yes	Yes	Yes
Information criterion		AIK	8,135	7,026	8,135	—	12,784	11,683	—	11,662	15,143	14,974	15,141	14,973	11,812	10,690	11,819	10,693
Multivariate diagnostic tests	*Vector normality test*	Chi^2(4)	13450,0 ***	13438,0 ***	13450,0 ***	—	15533,0 ***	20846,0 ***	—	16054,0 ***	753,3 ***	763,4 ***	757,7 ***	763,5 ***	14672,0 ***	14349,0 ***	14681,0 ***	14726,0 ***
	Hosking's Multivariate Portmanteau Statisticds on standardized residuals	5	25,641	25,703	25,641	—	114,831 ***	88,525 ***	—	102,185 ***	123,968 ***	123,918 ***	126,657 ***	126,171 ***	52,276 ***	52,144 ***	51,902 ***	51,320 ***
		10	3,794	35,855	35,794	—	142,999 ***	108,844 ***	—	128,761 ***	143,495 ***	143,279 ***	145,848 ***	145,352 ***	67,483 ***	67,058 ***	66,947 ***	65,972 ***
		20	74,185	74,153	74,185	—	171,544 ***	132,305 ***	—	155,772 ***	190,138 ***	189,811 ***	191,219 ***	190,880 ***	113,752 ***	113,536 ***	114,435 ***	112,570 ***
		50	249,156 ***	249,397 ***	249,156 ***	—	287,530 ***	237,662 ***	—	276,710 ***	299,412 ***	299,739 ***	302,245 ***	302,171 ***	207,720	208,437	208,111	206,004
	Hosking's Multivariate Portmanteau Statisticds on squared standardized residuals	5	0,295	0,295	0,295	—	1,382	0,693	—	1,204	26,298 *	26,254 *	26,623 *	26,377 *	4,991	4,781	4,684	4,681
		10	0,716	0,714	0,716	—	2,776	1,495	—	2,695	42,967	42,769	42,834	42,519	5,868	5,697	5,586	5,613
		20	1,343	1,341	1,343	—	7,631	3,723	—	7,352	88,262	87,891	88,935	88,190	11,046	10,788	10,883	10,873
		50	36,188	36,083	36,188	—	19,991	14,756	—	31,482	169,364	169,313	170,099	169,461	23,518	23,034	23,229	23,309

The Hosking's Portmanteau test is the mutivariate version of the Box-Pierce Q statistic under the null hypothesis of no serial correlation. * and *** denotes the rejection of the null hypothesis at the 1% and 10% level of significance.

Countries			Netherlands				Italy				China				Latvia			
Dynamic correlation models (*DCC-APARCH (1,1)*)			DCC (Engle)		DCC (Tse and Tsui)		DCC (Engle)		DCC (Tse and Tsui)		DCC (Engle)		DCC (Tse and Tsui)		DCC (Engle)		DCC (Tse and Tsui)	
Distribution			Gauss	Student	Gauss	Student	Gauss	Student	Gauss	Student	Gauss	Student	Gauss	Student	Gauss	Student	Gauss	Student
Numerical convergence			Yes	Yes	Yes	Yes	Yes	Yes	Yes	Yes	Yes	Yes	Yes	Yes	Yes	No	Yes	Yes
Information criterion		AIK	8,012	7,113	8,013	7,114	11,179	10,887	11,210	10,897	11,580	11,175	11,580	11,175	13,221	—	13,222	9,182
Multivariate diagnostic tests	*Vector normality test*	Chi^2(4)	4354,7 ***	4322,6 ***	4333,8 ***	4317,0 ***	1141,7 ***	1202,7 ***	1217,3 ***	1235,3 ***	4805,7 ***	4807,2 ***	4781,6 ***	4807,2 ***	45335,0 ***	—	45335,0 ***	22289,0 ***
	Hosking's Multivariate Portmanteau Statisticds on standardized residuals	5	40,982 ***	42,966 ***	44,766 ***	44,129 ***	90,634 ***	97,912 ***	101,122 ***	101,896 ***	80,935 ***	80,920 ***	81,130 ***	80,920 ***	36,511 ***	—	36,631 ***	23,147 ***
		10	56,147 **	57,923 **	60,317 **	59,358 **	106,885 ***	114,677 ***	118,711 ***	119,357 ***	97,976 ***	97,962 ***	98,190 ***	97,962 ***	76,027 ***	—	76,330 ***	30,217 ***
		20	101,669 **	103,311 **	105,809 **	105,103 **	173,437 ***	181,126 ***	184,057 ***	184,948 ***	146,242 ***	146,223 ***	146,400 ***	146,223 ***	247,921 ***	—	248,380 ***	537,273 ***
		50	236,249 **	238,154 **	239,801 **	240,149 **	342,986 ***	351,243 ***	354,714 ***	355,381 ***	259,661 ***	259,628 ***	259,665 ***	259,628 ***	368,742 ***	—	369,120 ***	561,496 ***
	Hosking's Multivariate Portmanteau Statisticds on squared standardized residuals	5	9,836	9,828	9,876	9,779	37,925 ***	38,503 ***	38,790 ***	38,698 ***	15,132	15,124	15,173	15,124	8,864	—	8,840	0,269
		10	13,329	13,279	13,375	13,249	60,599 **	62,305 **	62,375 **	62,665 **	19,740	19,725	19,840	19,725	13,490	—	13,472	0,503
		20	26,266	26,254	26,515	26,279	100,213 **	102,322 **	101,702 **	102,055 **	54,857	54,833	54,951	54,833	978,449	—	977,667	1733,110
		50	90,096	89,942	90,505	89,943	222,544	225,654	224,032	224,598	127,619	127,561	128,159	127,561	986,215	—	985,441	1734,090

The Hosking's Portmanteau test is the mutivariate version of the Box-Pierce Q statistic under the null hypothesis of no serial correlation. ** and *** denotes the rejection of the null hypothesis at the 5% and 10% level of significance.

Countries			Japan				Portugal				Brazil				Czech			
Dynamic correlation models (*DCC-FIGARCH (1,1)*)			DCC (Engle)		DCC (Tse and Tsui)		DCC (Engle)		DCC (Tse and Tsui)		DCC (Engle)		DCC (Tse and Tsui)		DCC (Engle)		DCC (Tse and Tsui)	
Distribution			Gauss	Student	Gauss	Student	Gauss	Student	Gauss	Student	Gauss	Student	Gauss	Student	Gauss	Student	Gauss	Student
Numerical convergence			Yes	Yes	Yes	Yes	Yes	Yes	Yes	Yes	Yes	Yes	Yes	Yes	Yes	Yes	Yes	Yes
Information criterion		AIK	23,208	22,428	23,207	22,428	13,358	12,935	13,352	12,930	14,814	13,624	14,814	13,644	11,475	11,023	11,476	11,026
Multivariate diagnostic tests	*Vector normality test*	Chi^2(4)	7082 ***	7088 ***	6812 ***	7087 ***	1628,4 ***	1572,6 ***	1603,0 ***	1603,7 ***	59755,0 ***	56828,0 ***	60191,0 ***	59517,0 ***	2610,5 ***	2630,0 ***	2610,6 ***	2641,2 ***
	Hosking's Multivariate Portmanteau Statisticds on standardized residuals	5	195,419 ***	193,301 ***	189,269 ***	193,292 ***	137,815 ***	126,498 ***	142,484 ***	139,866 ***	25,772	24,880	27,185	26,522	36,204 ***	36,678 ***	36,409 ***	36,371 ***
		10	231,197 ***	229,332 ***	223,627 ***	229,324 ***	160,892 ***	149,616 ***	164,504 ***	161,699 ***	42,957	40,767	44,395	43,985	52,257 *	52,804 *	52,408 *	52,491 *
		20	291,837 ***	289,809 ***	285,916 ***	289,801 ***	191,467 ***	179,757 ***	193,807 ***	191,021 ***	101,029 **	98,520 **	102,077 **	103,737 **	87,308	87,593	87,123	87,980
		50	416,201 ***	413,917 ***	410,050 ***	413,909 ***	305,794 ***	295,635 ***	306,386 ***	303,939 ***	280,811 ***	275,699 ***	280,553 ***	284,254 ***	224,118	224,458	224,665	224,626
	Hosking's Multivariate Portmanteau Statisticds on squared standardized residuals	5	93,443 ***	99,667 ***	98,377 ***	99,696 ***	10,281	10,344	10,449	10,635	5,286	2,539	5,118	4,919	21,193	21,284	21,258	21,771
		10	108,210 ***	114,823 ***	113,056 ***	114,855 ***	20,934	21,087	21,635	21,912	12,526	7,523	12,071	12,064	32,032	32,149	32,079	32,381
		20	177,133 ***	184,612 ***	183,667 ***	184,651 ***	102,146 **	102,289 **	103,635 **	104,681 **	24,064	16,261	23,948	23,686	73,456	73,196	73,712	74,442
		50	308,321 ***	315,740 ***	314,098 ***	315,783 ***	217,324	217,543	218,916	219,345	223,059	148,552	208,718	212,225	169,490	169,883	169,305	170,089

The Hosking's Portmanteau test is the mutivariate version of the Box-Pierce Q statistic under the null hypothesis of no serial correlation. *, ** and *** denotes the rejection of the null hypothesis at the 1%, 5% and 10% level of significance.

Table 8.1. *(Continued)*

Countries			Slovenia				Ireland				China				Ukraine			
Dynamic correlation models (*DCC-FIEGARCH (1,1)*)			DCC (Engle)		DCC (Tse and Tsui)		DCC (Engle)		DCC (Tse and Tsui)		DCC (Engle)		DCC (Tse and Tsui)		DCC (Engle)		DCC (Tse and Tsui)	
Distribution			Gauss	Student	Gauss	Student	Gauss	Student	Gauss	Student	Gauss	Student	Gauss	Student	Gauss	Student	Gauss	Student
Numerical convergence			Yes	Yes	Yes	Yes	Yes	Yes	Yes	Yes	Yes	Yes	Yes	Yes	Yes	Yes	Yes	Yes
Information criterion		AIK	13,374	11,656	13,400	11,634	12,156	11,249	12,196	11,264	11,556	11,167	11,556	11,167	13,735	11,770	13,735	11,770
Multivariate diagnostic checking	*Vector normality test*	Chi^2(4)	9783,5 ***	16826,0 ***	9781,2 ***	13371,0 ***	15618,0 ***	15724,0 ***	16006,0 ***	14888,0 ***	6685,6 ***	6686,5 ***	6638,1 ***	6686,5 ***	21194,0 ***	21236,0 ***	21268,0 ***	21236,0 ***
	Hosking's Multivariate Portmanteau Statisticds on standardized residuals	5	70,015 ***	66,408 ***	71,311 ***	65,536 ***	112,332 ***	111,050 ***	109,099 ***	105,710 ***	81,820 ***	81,808 ***	82,089 ***	81,808 ***	172,521 ***	173,449 ***	172,860 ***	1473,449 ***
		10	105,848 ***	100,770 ***	105,643 ***	98,580 ***	154,133 ***	152,679 ***	149,444 ***	146,488 ***	107,736 ***	107,727 ***	108,177 ***	107,727 ***	277,286 ***	278,032 ***	277,587 ***	278,032 ***
		20	199,377 ***	195,761 ***	193,670 ***	199,797 ***	198,749 ***	198,330 ***	198,699 ***	199,174 ***	159,318 ***	159,310 ***	159,641 ***	159,310 ***	333,756 ***	334,536 ***	334,083 ***	334,537 ***
		50	367,991 ***	366,017 ***	364,747 ***	391,678 ***	393,563 ***	394,530 ***	406,354 ***	412,436 ***	283,599 ***	283,577 ***	283,995 ***	283,577 ***	468,567 ***	468,720 ***	468,171 ***	468,720 ***
	Hosking's Multivariate Portmanteau Statisticds on squared standardized residuals	5	3,155	8,017	3,271	3,589	2,123	2,114	1,967	1,767	10,799	10,798	10,837	10,798	23,129	23,502	23,514	23,502
		10	5,505	10,079	5,821	5,690	3,422	3,395	3,093	2,739	20,751	20,746	20,853	20,746	39,781	40,109	40,173	40,109
		20	38,728	28,761	42,306	26,739	21,292	21,344	22,509	24,167	45,062	45,057	45,307	45,057	70,474	70,761	70,764	70,761
		50	67,809	52,945	72,633	112,481	136,346	137,025	139,518	143,043	128,979	128,913	129,811	128,913	175,215	175,567	175,572	175,567

The Hosking's Portmanteau test is the mutivariate version of the Box-Pierce Q statistic under the null hypothesis of no serial correlation. *** denotes the rejection of the null hypothesis at the 10% level of significance.

Countries			Sweden				Greece				Turkey				Poland			
Dynamic correlation models (*DCC-FIAPARCH (1,1)*)			DCC (Engle)		DCC (Tse and Tsui)		DCC (Engle)		DCC (Tse and Tsui)		DCC (Engle)		DCC (Tse and Tsui)		DCC (Engle)		DCC (Tse and Tsui)	
Distribution			Gauss	Student	Gauss	Student	Gauss	Student	Gauss	Student	Gauss	Student	Gauss	Student	Gauss	Student	Gauss	Student
Numerical convergence			Yes	Yes	Yes	Yes	Yes	Yes	Yes	Yes	Yes	Yes	Yes	Yes	Yes	Yes	Yes	Yes
Information criteria		AIK	7,655	6,776	7,655	6,776	16,643	15,064	16,653	15,025	15,106	14,942	15,102	14,940	11,713	11,529	11,718	11,537
Multivariate diagnostic tests	*Vector normality test*	Chi^2(4)	3008,7 ***	3008,4 ***	3011,0 ***	3013,6 ***	10907,0 ***	10794,0 ***	10968,0 ***	11434,0 ***	705,6 ***	709,8 ***	693,3 ***	699,0 ***	1022,1 ***	1020,1 ***	1012,1 ***	1015,6 ***
	Hosking's Multivariate Portmanteau Statisticds on standardized residuals	5	41,755 ***	41,481 ***	41,669 ***	41,180 ***	126,337 ***	105,698 ***	121,428 ***	102,031 ***	127,922 ***	124,841 ***	127,481 ***	127,282 ***	63,961 ***	63,852 ***	63,549 ***	63,762 ***
		10	69,052 ***	68,606 ***	69,017 ***	68,496 ***	208,221 ***	185,072 ***	204,933 ***	186,068 ***	145,578 ***	145,336 ***	147,710 ***	147,506 ***	79,417 ***	79,470 ***	78,609 ***	78,901 ***
		20	128,905 ***	128,602 ***	128,925 ***	128,481 ***	307,803 ***	283,329 ***	303,129 ***	281,371 ***	194,792 ***	194,434 ***	195,815 ***	195,780 ***	141,211 ***	140,899 ***	141,712 ***	141,675 ***
		50	251,374 ***	250,921 ***	250,706 ***	249,869 ***	595,438 ***	563,512 ***	589,652 ***	574,956 ***	307,092 ***	306,915 ***	309,303 ***	309,249 ***	229,279 *	228,690 *	231,321 *	231,248 *
	Hosking's Multivariate Portmanteau Statisticds on squared standardized residuals	5	4,641	4,624	4,631	4,617	143,552 ***	108,661 ***	144,335 ***	94,906 ***	24,065	23,652	24,019	23,732	14,496	14,248	13,587	13,377
		10	10,698	10,673	10,687	10,654	157,071 ***	120,461 ***	156,861 ***	103,713 ***	38,084	37,646	37,933	37,600	24,282	23,987	23,154	22,834
		20	17,434	17,398	17,382	17,308	171,928 ***	133,787 ***	171,287 ***	115,507 ***	86,548	85,375	86,787	85,823	48,170	47,643	47,382	46,828
		50	52,454	52,327	52,407	52,256	296,042 ***	241,469 ***	290,054 ***	203,759 ***	167,972	166,812	169,010	167,838	154,473	154,229	153,020	152,916

The Hosking's Portmanteau test is the mutivariate version of the Box-Pierce Q statistic under the null hypothesis of no serial correlation. * and *** denotes the rejection of the null hypothesis at the 1% and 10% level of significance.

Countries			Finland				Ireland				Norway				Lithuania			
Dynamic correlation models (*DCC-HYGARCH (1,1)*)			DCC (Engle)		DCC (Tse and Tsui)		DCC (Engle)		DCC (Tse and Tsui)		DCC (Engle)		DCC (Tse and Tsui)		DCC (Engle)		DCC (Tse and Tsui)	
Distribution			Gauss	Student	Gauss	Student	Gauss	Student	Gauss	Student	Gauss	Student	Gauss	Student	Gauss	Student	Gauss	Student
Numerical convergence			Yes	Yes	Yes	Yes	Yes	Yes	No	Yes	Yes	Yes	Yes	Yes	Yes	Yes	Yes	Yes
Information criteria		AIK	25,774	24,192	25,772	24,192	12,561	11,547	–	11,513	22,029	20,812	22,027	20,812	14,859	13,542	14,854	13,541
Multivariate diagnostic checking	*Vector normality test*	Chi^2(4)	3866,4 ***	3865,4 ***	3121,2 ***	3865,2 ***	12755,0 ***	13258,0 ***	–	12907,0 ***	4084,5 ***	4626,1 ***	4190,7 ***	4624,7 ***	6055,9 ***	6097,6 ***	6179,9 ***	6031,3 ***
	Hosking's Multivariate Portmanteau Statisticds on standardized residuals	5	67,495 ***	67,545 ***	55,216 ***	67,553 ***	110,461 ***	112,673 ***	–	108,010 ***	111,048 ***	38,968 ***	19,378 ***	38,882 ***	61,640	61,527	61,586	61,839
		10	89,029 ***	89,074 ***	73,094 ***	89,081 ***	145,623 ***	147,495 ***	–	143,181 ***	161,022 ***	80,469 ***	56,278 ***	80,404 ***	98,653 ***	98,647 ***	98,794 ***	98,,5572 ***
		20	153,155 ***	153,200 ***	136,713 ***	153,204 ***	172,657 ***	173,584 ***	–	168,293 ***	215,205 ***	112,314 ***	100,070 ***	112,206 ***	132,728 ***	132,576 ***	132,892 ***	132,426 ***
		50	298,260 ***	298,334 ***	280,239 ***	298,349 ***	287,436 ***	287,895 ***	–	284,058 ***	423,003 ***	281,108 ***	224,093 ***	280,985 ***	244,347 **	243,969 **	245,918 **	243,436 **
	Hosking's Multivariate Portmanteau Statisticds on squared standardized residuals	5	398,057 ***	398,331 ***	562,141 ***	398,334 ***	0,889	0,851	–	0,899	574,787 ***	597,550 ***	67,623 ***	597,806 ***	25,106 ***	24,934 ***	25,114 ***	24,501 ***
		10	631,940 ***	632,431 ***	829,486 ***	632,486 ***	1,574	1,504	–	1,674	867,268 ***	886,829 ***	110,580 ***	887,759 ***	167,567 ***	164,611 ***	170,734 ***	164,344 ***
		20	1111,300 ***	1111,960 ***	1248,550 ***	1112,030 ***	6,082	5,997	–	6,367	1280,460 ***	1163,640 ***	213,166 ***	1164,660 ***	182,094 ***	178,979 ***	185,472 ***	178,618 ***
		50	2360,940 ***	2361,960 ***	2671,270 ***	2362,030 ***	16,259	16,184	–	18,971	2470,900 ***	1923,520 ***	398,211 ***	1925,200 ***	234,936 **	232,898 **	239,021 **	232,115 **

The Hosking's Portmanteau test is the mutivariate version of the Box-Pierce Q statistic under the null hypothesis of no serial correlation.** and *** denotes the rejection of the null hypothesis at the 5% and 10% level of significance.

computing-time delay are the DCC-GARCH, the DCC-IGARCH and the fractional model DCC-FIEGARCH. Among fractionally integrated models, the DCC-FIAPARCH is the most miss-specified model with a non-convergence in 18 countries.

Taking into account different financial markets' properties (long memory behavior, shock persistence and asymmetric leverage effects...) does not necessarily improve the models' performances. The complexity of the model's statistical specifications cannot be justified in all cases, which leads to inconsistent and inaccurate estimator parameters. However, the opposite may be true since the more the model is over-parametrized the more its computation and convergence are complicated.

The Akaike information criterion (AIK) doesn't allow us to select only one optimal model. AIK results of the studied models are mitigated across each country of the sample. The only conclusion that can be drawn is that the information criterion is almost always lower for the student marginal distribution. Without knowing the facts, allowing the data to follow a student rather than a Gaussian distribution law makes a better fit of the dynamic conditional correlation models. This confirms the heavy tails and the slightly skewed data distributions suggested by the Jarque-Bera preliminary test.

The vector normality tests reject the null hypothesis of the linearity of combinations between innovations of all models and for all countries under study. This means that combinations between CDS and bond spreads have too many extreme values (significant excess kurtosis) and a fat-tailed distribution. The assumption of a multivariate student marginal distribution of our time series is once again preferred.

Results of the diagnostic tests on the standardized residuals show that there is an obvious misspecification in the conditional mean equations of all the estimated models (the multivariate Q-statistics is almost always significant at 5% whatever the number of lags is). One explanation is that 1 is not the optimal order number of AR(.), which suggests a more persistent (less quickly) shocks' integration in the credit markets. The autoregressive terms can be allowed to vary from zero to three so we can better control for the serial correlation of CDS and bond spreads times series.

Mispecification are also detected in the conditional multivariate variance of some DCC models. ARCH effects are still present

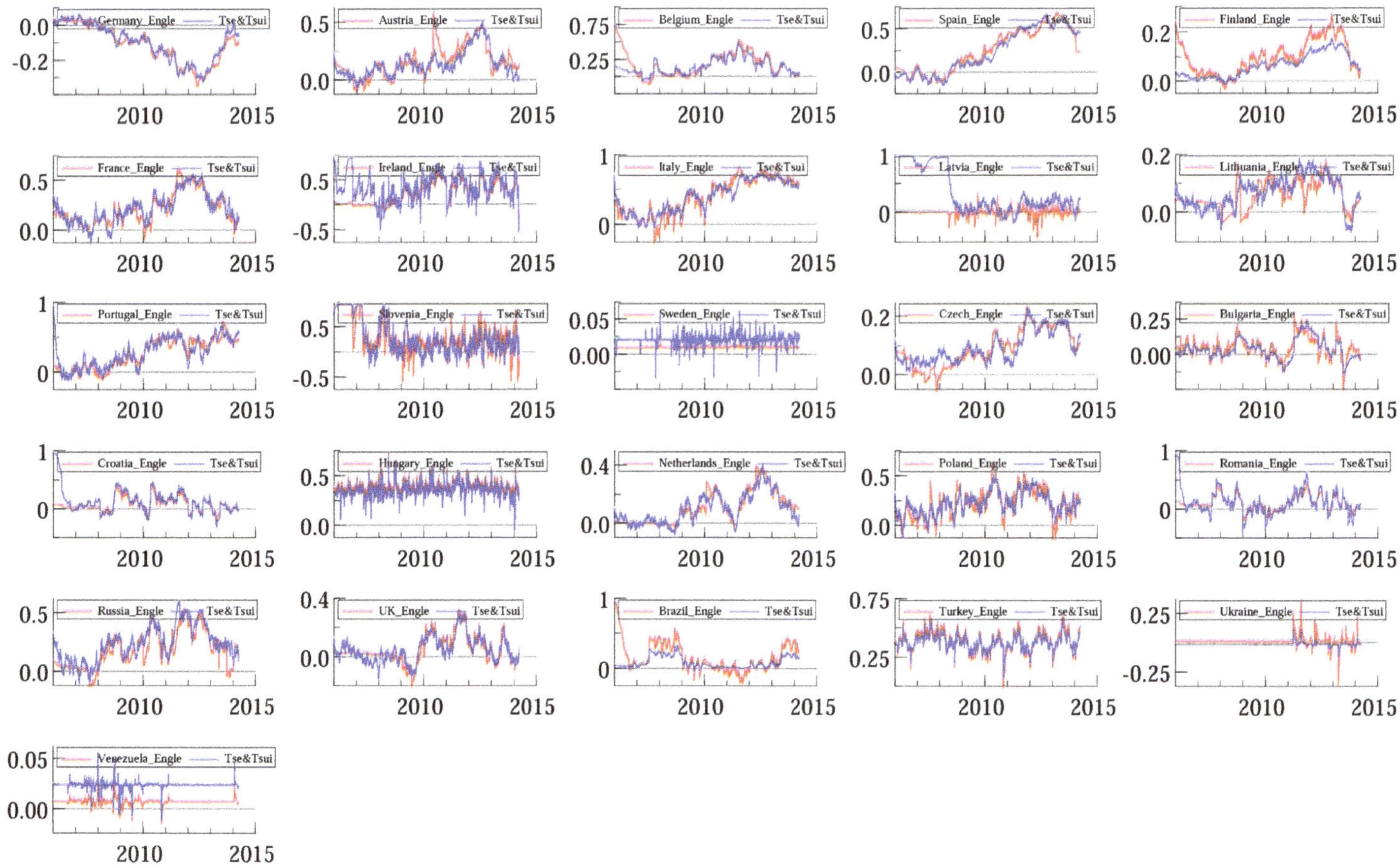

Fig. 8.1. Engle and Tse&Tsui's GARCH(1,1)-DCC correlation plots of some chosen countries.

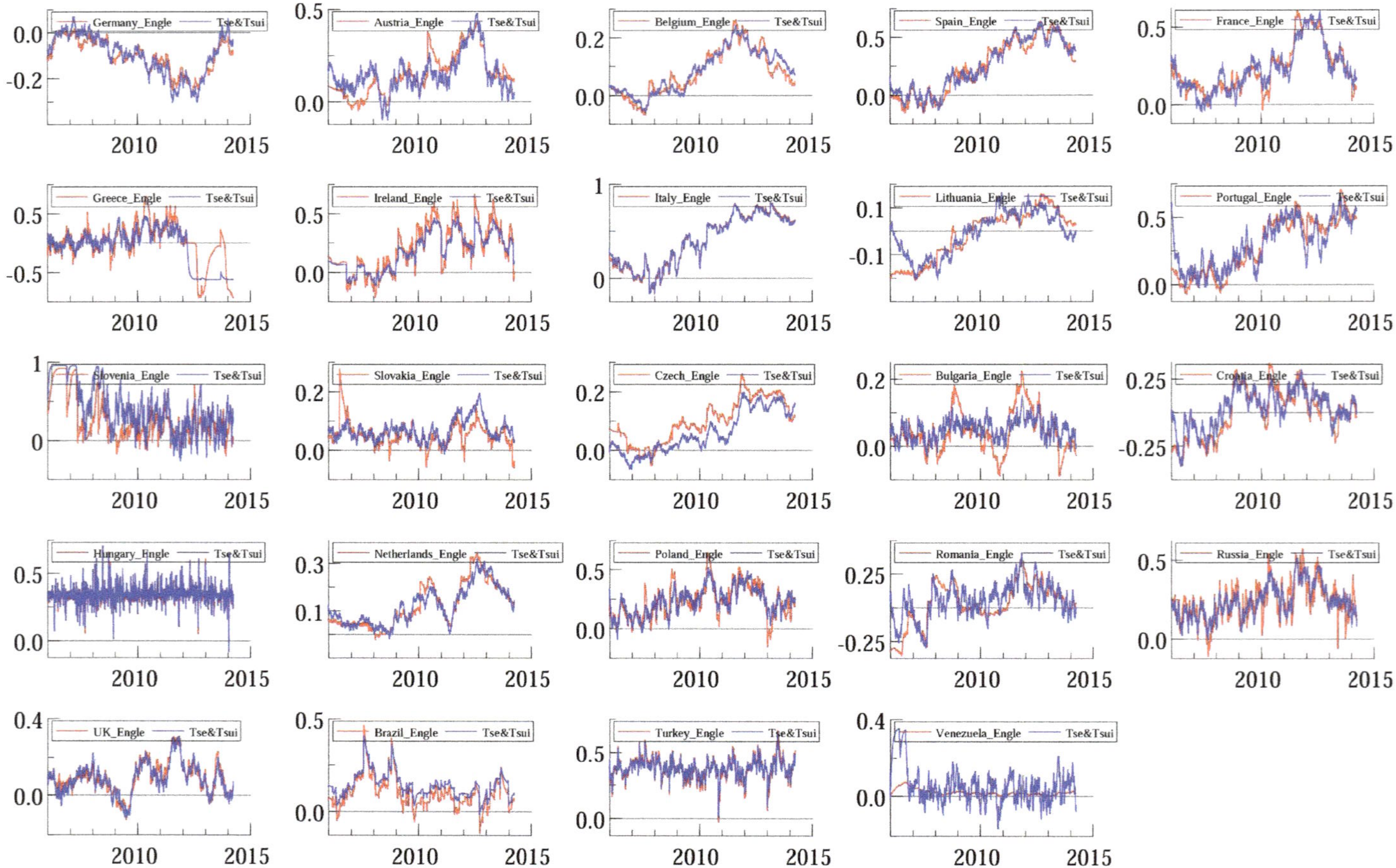

Fig. 8.2. Engle and Tse&Tsui's FIEGARCH(1,1)-DCC correlation plots of some chosen countries.

in the squared standardized residuals even after controlling for the heteroscedasticity. The best fitted models, in terms of autocorrelation in the time series, are DCC-GARCH and the DCC-FIEGARCH. The Hoskings' multivariate portmanteau statistics, up to 10th, 20th and 50th order of lags, accept the null hypothesis of no correlation in the sovereign credit assets. However, in the same context, the APARCH does not perform well with serial correlations detected in all combinations of innovations for all countries.

The last striking finding is that the Engle's DCC and Tse and Tsui's DCC present very close results and no significant divergence is detected. Focusing on the DCC plots of the Engle and the Tse and Tsui, Figs. 8.1 and 8.2, it is clearly seen that the correlation's dynamic evolution of both estimation techniques is almost the same for all the countries (except for Japan, Denmark, Norway and China).

To sum up, the global CDS market is characterized by the same stylized facts as the stock market: volatility clustering, nonlinearity, asymmetric leverage effects, and long-memory behavior. Results support that allowing flexibility regarding the persistence degree of variance shocks significantly improves the model's suitability to sovereign CDS spreads. Furthermore, in most of the studied countries, the improvement of the fitting power of the studied multivariate models depends on their ability to capture a maximum of financial stylized facts while estimating the CDS volatility.

8.6 Conclusion

This chapter aimed to assess the performances of 9 Dynamic Conditional Correlation models. Using sovereign CDS and bond data, DCC-GARCH, DCC-IGARCH, DCC-EGARCH, DCC-GJR, DCC-APARCH, DCC-FIGARCH, DCC-FIEGARCH, DCC-FIAPARCH, and DCC-HYGARCH were estimated, allowing to take into account different financial markets' properties such as the leverage effect, the asymmetric reaction to good and bad news, and the long-range persistence. The performance comparison being made upon the information criteria and several multivariate diagnostic tests, a certain number of conclusions can be drawn.

First, although the CDS and bond data exhibit long memory behavior, shock persistence, and asymmetric leverage effects, models that take into account all these specifications do not necessarily provide better estimation results. In fact, the straightforward DCC-GARCH model seems to provide the most relevant estimator parameters in terms of diagnostic tests. Second, the innovations distribution assumption significantly impacts the statistical fit of the model since the information criterion is almost always lower for models with student marginal distribution compared to models with Gaussian distribution. Third, all models present serial correlation in the standardized residuals, indicating a mispecification in the conditional mean equation. This might be due to the low order of the AR process and/or the persistence of shocks in worldwide credit markets. Finally, the results suggest the necessity of a constantly time-varying hedging positions for countries that present dissimilar financial characteristics.

In this constantly evolving worldwide credit market, the study of the CDS spreads needs to keep pace with this change. Since modeling correlation is of paramount importance in assessing diversification risk, in dynamic asset pricing theory, and in optimization of portfolio allocation, the economic implication of our findings concerns particularly policymakers, financial practitioners, and financial market participants generally. Even though no model clearly outperforms all the others, our results show that the basic DCC-GARCH and the DCC-FIEGARCH models seem to better fit the studied data. Thus, after taking into account the transaction costs, investors could eventually take advantage of the comovement predictability of sovereign credit markets and generate extra profits by putting in place a simple trading strategy. However, results are mitigated and differ from one country to another, which implies that no multivariate volatility model should be selected in an arbitrary way. The model selection should rather be based on the particular features of the used data and the countries composing the studied sample. These dissimilarities between markets' financial characteristics should be taken into account by finance practitioners in upgrading trading strategies, readapting portfolio management techniques, and implementing beneficial speculative and arbitrage operations. Our results on the comovement between the CDS market and its underlying bond market could also be used by regulators in order to anticipate financial turmoil and appropriately control the risk transmission between the CDS and the underlying bond markets by putting in place different economic and regulatory policies depending on each country's financial characteristics.

Many interesting avenues regarding the global sovereign CDS markets' main behaviors are still left for future works and our research line can thus be pursued in several ways. First, a further investigation on the performances of the Dynamic Conditional Correlation models can be done by carrying out a comparative study based on the predictive reliability rather than on diagnostic tests as in our case. Second, our study can be generalized to other financial markets, namely the primary equity markets, in order to assess whether the nature of the asset impact the performances of the studied models. Third, since there is a dynamic segmentation in financial markets, it can be interesting to check the robustness of our findings using a different sample from other regions and/or a CDS term structure with different maturities. This might reveal more details about the markets' dynamics and could be beneficial for CDS portfolio construction and markets, economic regulations.

References

Aielli, G. P. (2013). Dynamic conditional correlation: On properties and estimation. *Journal of Business & Economic Statistics*, **31**(3): 282–299.

Bachelier, L. (1900). *Théorie de la spéculation* (Gauthier-Villars).

Baillie, R. T., Bollerslev, T., and Mikkelsen, H. O. (1996). Fractionally integrated generalized autoregressive conditional heteroskedasticity. *Journal of Econometrics*, **74**(1): 3–30.

Beber, A., Brandt, M. W., and Kavajecz, K. A. (2009). Flight-to-quality or flight-to-liquidity? Evidence from the euro-area bond market. *Review of Financial Studies*, **22**(3): 925–957.

Bhanot, K. and Guo, L. (2011). Negative credit spreads: Liquidity and limits to arbitrage. *The Journal of Fixed Income*, **21**(1): 32–41.

Billio, M. and Caporin, M. (2009). A generalized dynamic conditional correlation model for portfolio risk evaluation. *Mathematics and Computers in Simulation*, **79**(8): 2566–2578.

Billio, M., Caporin, M., and Gobbo, M. (2006). Flexible dynamic conditional correlation multivariate GARCH models for asset allocation. *Applied Financial Economics Letters*, **2**(02): 123–130.

Blanco, R., Brennan, S., and Marsh, I. W. (2005). An empirical analysis of the dynamic relation between investment-grade bonds and credit default swaps. *The Journal of Finance*, **60**(5): 2255–2281.

Bollerslev, T. (1986). Generalized autoregressive conditional heteroskedasticity. *Journal of Econometrics*, **31**(3): 307–327.

Bollerslev, T., Chou, R. Y., and Kroner, K. F. (1992). Arch modeling in finance: A review of the theory and empirical evidence. *Journal of Econometrics*, **52**(1-2): 5–59.

Bollerslev, T., Engle, R. F., and Wooldridge, J. M. (1988). A capital asset pricing model with time-varying covariances. *Journal of Political Economy*, **96**(1): 116–131.

Bollerslev, T. and Mikkelsen, H. O. (1996). Modeling and pricing long memory in stock market volatility. *Journal of Econometrics*, **73**(1): 151–184.

Boudt, K., Danielsson, J., and Laurent, S. (2013). Robust forecasting of dynamic conditional correlation GARCH models. *International Journal of Forecasting*, **29**(2): 244–257.

Cai, X. J., Tian, S., and Hamori, S. (2016). Dynamic correlation and equicorrelation analysis of global financial turmoil: Evidence from emerging east asian stock markets. *Applied Economics*, **48**(40): 3789–3803.

Caporin, M. and McAleer, M. (2013). Ten things you should know about the dynamic conditional correlation representation. *Econometrics*, **1**(1): 115–126.

Coudert, V. and Gex, M. (2010). Contagion inside the credit default swaps market: The case of the gm and ford crisis in 2005. *Journal of International Financial Markets, Institutions and Money*, **20**(2): 109–134.

Davidson, J. (2004). Moment and memory properties of linear conditional heteroscedasticity models, and a new model. *Journal of Business & Economic Statistics*, **22**(1): 16–29.

Degiannakis, S. and Xekalaki, E. (2004). Autoregressive conditional heteroscedasticity (arch) models: A review. *Quality Technology & Quantitative Management*, **1**(2): 271–324.

Ding, Z., Granger, C. W., and Engle, R. F. (1993). A long memory property of stock market returns and a new model. *Journal of Empirical Finance*, **1**(1): 83–106.

Dolvin, S.D. (2012). Negative Bond Yields. All Chapters. 28. https://digitalcommons.butler.edu/jmdallchapters/28.

Engle, R. F. (1982). Autoregressive Conditional Heteroscedasticity with Estimates of the Variance of United Kingdom Inflation. *Econometrica*, **50**(4): 987–1007.

Engle, R. (2002). Dynamic conditional correlation: A simple class of multivariate generalized autoregressive conditional heteroskedasticity models. *Journal of Business & Economic Statistics*, **20**(3): 339–350.

Engle, R. and Kelly, B. (2012). Dynamic equicorrelation. *Journal of Business & Economic Statistics*, **30**(2): 212–228.

Engle, R. F. and Bollerslev, T. (1986). Modelling the persistence of conditional variances. *Econometric Reviews*, **5**(1): 1–50.

Engle, R. (1987). Estimating time varying risk premia in the term structure: the Arch-M model. *Econometrica*, **55**(2): 391–407.

Engle, R. F. and Sheppard, K. (2001). Theoretical and empirical properties of dynamic conditional correlation multivariate GARCH. Tech. rep., National Bureau of Economic Research.

Fantazzini, D. (2011). Fractionally integrated models for volatility: a review. In Nonlinear Financial Econometrics: Markov Switching Models, Persistence and Nonlinear Cointegration (pp. 104–123). Palgrave Macmillan, London.

García de la Fuente, C., Wiper, M. P., Galeano, P. *et al.* (2014). Bayesian estimation of a dynamic conditional correlation model with multivariate skew-slash innovations. Tech. rep., Universidad Carlos III de Madrid. Departamento de Estadística.

Gilchrist, S. and Mojon, B. (2018). Credit risk in the euro area. *The Economic Journal*, **128**(608): 118–158.

Glosten, L. R., Jagannathan, R., and Runkle, D. E. (1993). On the relation between the expected value and the volatility of the nominal excess return on stocks. *The Journal of Finance*, **48**(5): 1779–1801.

Hafner, C. and Franses, P. H. (2003). A generalized dynamic conditional correlation model for many asset returns. Tech. rep.

Hafner, C. M. and Reznikova, O. (2012). On the estimation of dynamic conditional correlation models. *Computational Statistics & Data Analysis*, **56**(11): 3533–3545.

Hentschel, L. (1995). All in the family nesting symmetric and asymmetric GARCH models. *Journal of Financial Economics*, **39**(1): 71–104.

Higgins, M. L. and Bera, A. K. (1992). A Class of Nonlinear ARCH Models. *International Economic Review*, **33**(1): 137–158.

Klüppelberg, C., Lindner, A., and Maller, R. (2004). A continuous-time GARCH process driven by a lévy process: Stationarity and second-order behaviour. *Journal of Applied Probability*, **41**(03): 601–622.

Lee, J. (2006). The comovement between output and prices: Evidence from a dynamic conditional correlation GARCH model. *Economics Letters*, **91**(1): 110–116.

Longstaff, F. A., Mithal, S., and Neis, E. (2005). Corporate yield spreads: Default risk or liquidity? New evidence from the credit default swap market. *The Journal of Finance*, **60**(5): 2213–2253.

Morgan, J. P. (1997). *RiskMetrics Technical Documents* (Fourth Edition). New York: J. P. Morgan Co.

Nelson, D. B. (1991). Conditional Heteroskedasticity in Asset Returns: A New Approach. *Econometrica: Journal of the Econometric*, **59**(2): 347–370.

Norden, L. and Weber, M. (2009). The co-movement of credit default swap, bond and stock markets: An empirical analysis. *European Financial Management*, **15**(3): 529–562.

Sentana, E. (1995). Quadratic arch models. *The Review of Economic Studies*, **62**(4): 639–661.

Tse, Y. K. (1998). The conditional heteroscedasticity of the yen-dollar exchange rate. *Journal of Applied Econometrics*, **13**(1): 49–55.

Tse, Y. K. and Tsui, A. K. C. (2002). A multivariate generalized autoregressive conditional heteroscedasticity model with time-varying correlations. *Journal of Business & Economic Statistics*, **20**(3): 351–362.

Walter, C. (2013). Les origines du modèle de marche au hasard en finance, FMSH-WP-2013-33.

Wei, Y., Wang, Y., and Huang, D. (2010). Forecasting crude oil market volatility: Further evidence using GARCH-class models. *Energy Economics*, **32**(6): 1477–1484.

Zakoian, J.-M. (1994). Threshold heteroskedastic models. *Journal of Economic Dynamics and Control*, **18**(5): 931–955.

https://doi.org/10.1142/9781786349507_0009

Chapter 9

Development of Socially Responsible Investing (SRI) — Evidence from the Mutual Funds Industry

Warwick Anderson*, Jędrzej Białkowski†, and Moritz Wagner‡

Department of Economics and Finance,
University of Canterbury, New Zealand
**warwick.anderson@canterbury.ac.nz*
†*jedrzej.bialkowski@canterbury.ac.nz*
‡*moritz.wagner@canterbury.ac.nz*

9.1 Introduction: A Short History of SRI and Its Development Globally

Over the last two decades, the idea of SRI has become increasingly popular, attracting an ever-growing share of investor flows and has advanced from a niche to a mainstream investment strategy.[1] According to well-known industry bodies, worldwide SRI assets have multiplied to several trillion USD under management.[2]

[1]See Davidson (2016). https://www.wsj.com/articles/sustainable-investing-goes-mainstream-145248273.

[2]For example, the US Social Investment Forum (USSIF) 2018 report (https://www.ussif.org/) shows that SRI assets have increased 18-fold from $639 bn in 1995 to about $12,000 bn at the start of 2018, which represents about 26% of all US assets under professional management. The PRI (Principles of Responsible Investment, https://www.unpri.org/) organization reports that as of 2019, more than $80 trillion in worldwide assets are under management of institutions that

Prior research shows that the mutual fund industry as a whole is larger in countries with well-developed capital markets, where rules and regulations are strong (in particular where investor's rights are protected), barriers to entry are low, and where the level of education as well as per-capita income are higher (e.g. Khorana *et al.* (2005) and Klapper *et al.* (2004)). In addition, equity funds tend to dominate in Anglo-American countries while bond funds do so in Continental Europe and in middle-income countries. Although very insightful, these studies are based on data around 2000, i.e. before much of the innovation in SRI funds took hold. We complement the findings by using data on 49,094 mutual funds,[3] encompassing both SRI funds and conventional funds from a cross-section of 25 developed and emerging countries around the world to examine the size, structure, and growth pattern of both fund categories separately.[4],[5] We obtain data on open-end mutual funds for all countries available from Morningstar Asset Flows over the period 1999 through 2018.[6] Bekaert and Harvey (2002) date the opening of capital markets in emerging countries to the late 1980s and early 1990s. Therefore, this expanded sample covers the entire (or most of the) life of the majority

---

have signed on to their principles, an increase of twentyfold from the $4 trillion at the organization's start in 2006.

[3]Number of funds as per end of 2018 free of survivorship bias (i.e. including obsolete or defunct funds).

[4]To avoid an inflated number of funds, the data is obtained at the fund level. Most funds usually offer different share classes with different fee structures and purchase and redemption restrictions attached, but refer to the same underlying portfolio. Share class and fund level data can be identified in Morningstar using either the security or performance ID ("SecID" or "PerformanceID") for the former, or fund ID ("FundID") for the latter.

[5]Morningstar categorizes funds with SRI or ESG objectives as "socially conscious" and includes any fund that invests according to non-economic guidelines. According to this definition, "such funds may make investments based on such issues as environmental responsibility, human rights, or religious views. A socially conscious fund may take a pro-active stance by selectively investing in, for example, environmentally-friendly companies, or firms with good employee relations. This group also includes funds that avoid investing in companies involved in promoting alcohol, tobacco, or gambling, or in the defence industry".

[6]Data on mutual funds in developed countries is available for a longer historical period but for the purpose of comparison, we start the sample period when the first data on EM funds in Morningstar Asset Flows is available.

of SRI funds as well as conventional emerging market funds (EM funds) and includes equity, bond, allocation, alternative, and other funds such as money market and property funds. Since Morningstar Asset Flows reports data in local currencies, we obtain exchange rates from Datastream to convert total net assets (TNA) and fund flows into USD. In addition, we obtain data on GDP from the World Bank (World Development Indicators, WDI) and the International Monetary Fund (IMF), which ensures consistency and comparability across countries.

Table 9.1 provides an overview of the aggregate data. The number of both SRI and conventional funds has increased in each year from 232 and 8,661 in 1999 to 2,141 and 46,953 at the end of 2018, respectively. The change in TNA shows that SRI funds were, on average, much larger than conventional funds at the beginning of the period. However, average net assets have decreased over time from a few larger funds to numerous funds that follow a responsible investment strategy, including smaller funds, resulting in SRI funds overall having an average size comparable to that of conventional funds. We conjecture that this development is mainly related to the supply side of the market, i.e. the increasing number of fund companies trying to get a share of the growing demand for socially responsible investing schemes. Table 9.1 also shows how the impact of the last two major crises is reflected in decreases in the average fund size and overall fund assets, during or in the aftermath of the dot-com bubble (2000–2002) and the global financial crisis (2008–2009). The decrease in assets in 2018 was associated with the large sell-off during the fourth quarter in that year largely driven by geopolitical risks, global trade tensions (in particular between the US and China) as well as concerns of a severe slowdown in economic growth.[7] At the end of 2018, the TNA of SRI funds and conventional funds of the 25 countries covered in this section account to USD 1.08 trillion and USD 24.88 trillion, respectively.[8] Relative to GDP, SRI and conventional mutual

[7]For example, both the S&P 500 and the MSCI World Index decreased by 15–20% between the end of September and the end of December 2018. Markets recovered subsequently during 2019.

[8]We discuss fund assets on the country level in more detail in Table 9.2.

Table 9.1. Overview of SRI and conventional open-end mutual funds worldwide between 1999–2018.

	Number of funds		TNA (USDbn)		Average fund size (USDm)		TNA/GDP (in%)	
Year	SRI	Conventional	SRI	Conventional	SRI	Conventional	SRI	Conventional
1999	232	8,661	230	4,637	989.6	535.3	0.84	16.97
2000	269	9,419	217	4,561	807.6	484.2	0.79	16.52
2001	323	9,901	255	4,276	788.3	431.9	0.93	15.65
2002	349	10,321	218	4,028	624.0	390.3	0.73	13.53
2003	372	11,110	304	5,331	817.3	479.9	0.90	15.82
2004	409	12,051	368	6,326	898.7	524.9	0.99	17.01
2005	705	14,790	477	7,629	676.9	515.8	1.29	20.56
2006	817	16,761	591	9,624	723.0	574.2	1.43	23.36
2007	912	18,635	676	11,640	740.9	624.6	1.45	25.04
2008	1,113	25,354	454	8,751	408.0	345.2	0.97	18.78
2009	1,204	27,653	612	12,029	508.0	435.0	1.27	25.08
2010	1,248	29,381	706	13,873	565.6	472.2	1.35	26.63
2011	1,316	30,974	676	13,507	513.9	436.1	1.24	24.80
2012	1,347	32,228	761	15,795	564.7	490.1	1.34	27.89
2013	1,406	34,491	904	18,486	643.2	536.0	1.56	31.91
2014	1,484	37,184	958	19,993	645.4	537.7	1.67	34.96
2015	1,588	39,858	927	20,299	583.8	509.3	1.65	36.09
2016	1,709	42,488	958	21,638	560.7	509.3	1.67	37.80
2017	1,905	44,448	1,154	26,547	605.7	597.3	1.82	41.90
2018	2,141	46,953	1,083	24,883	505.8	530.0	1.68	38.55

Notes: This table reports the number of funds and total net assets (TNA) of SRI (socially responsible investing) and conventional (all other) open-end mutual funds. SRI funds are designated as "socially conscious" in Morningstar. Year refers to the 31 December of each year. Number of funds are those for which TNA are available. Average fund size is measured across mutual funds at the end of each year (in millions). The last two columns measure TNA as percent of global GDP, where the latter is total GDP of the countries for which TNA are available. The sample period is December 1999 through December 2018.

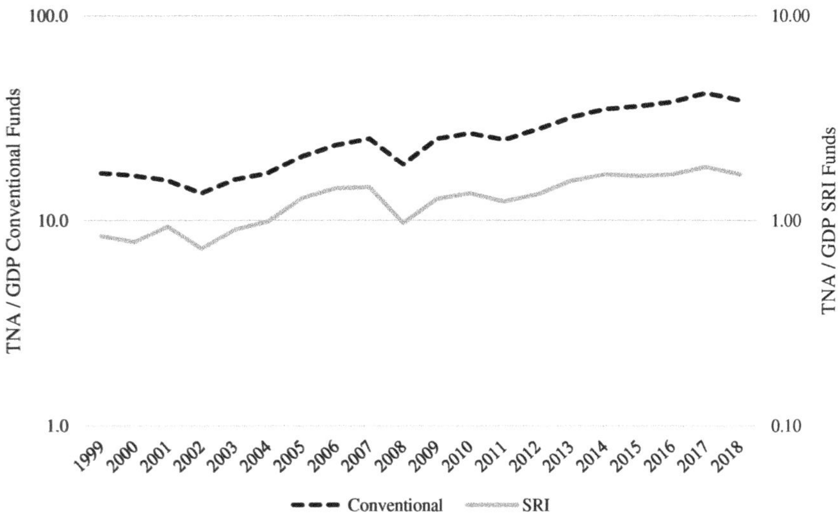

Fig. 9.1. Global fund assets as percent of GDP.

Notes: This figure plots aggregate mutual fund assets of SRI (grey line) and conventional funds (black line) as percent of GDP (logarithmic scale). The sample period is from December 1999 through December 2018.

fund assets increased from below 1% and about 17% in 1999 to 1.7% and 38.6% in 2018.

The growth pattern of global fund assets is illustrated in Fig. 9.1. While SRI funds have a much smaller starting point, both fund categories display a similar trajectory. However, plotting SRI and conventional fund assets relative to GDP by region separately reveals some interesting findings (Fig. 9.2).

The growth in assets of conventional funds in the developed and emerging world do follow a similar pattern (Panel A), but are very different in the case of SRI funds (Panel B). In emerging markets, net assets increased at a faster pace until 2007 but have since decreased, whereas in developed countries SRI fund assets have steadily increased over time.

Table 9.2 reports TNA on the country level and by asset class at the end of 2018. It shows that countries vary substantially in the structure of their mutual fund sectors. The US (71.6%) and China (63.4%) account for the largest fraction of the fund industry among developed and emerging countries, with USD 16.7 trillion and

Panel A — Conventional fund assets by region as percent of GDP

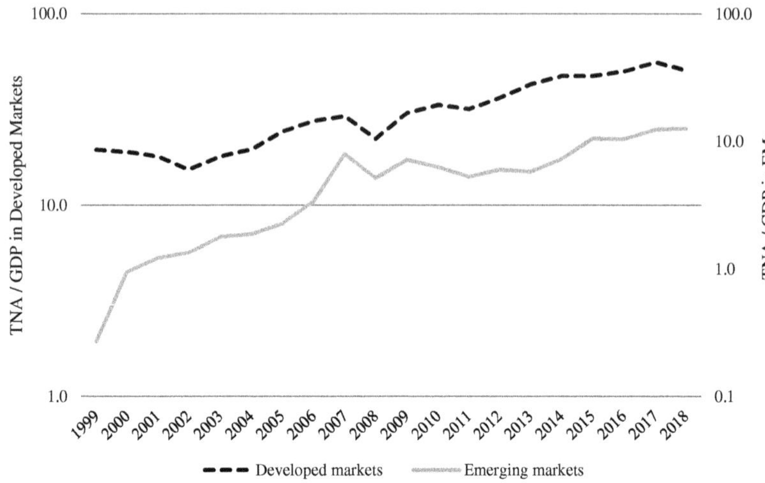

Panel B — SRI fund assets by region as percent of GDP

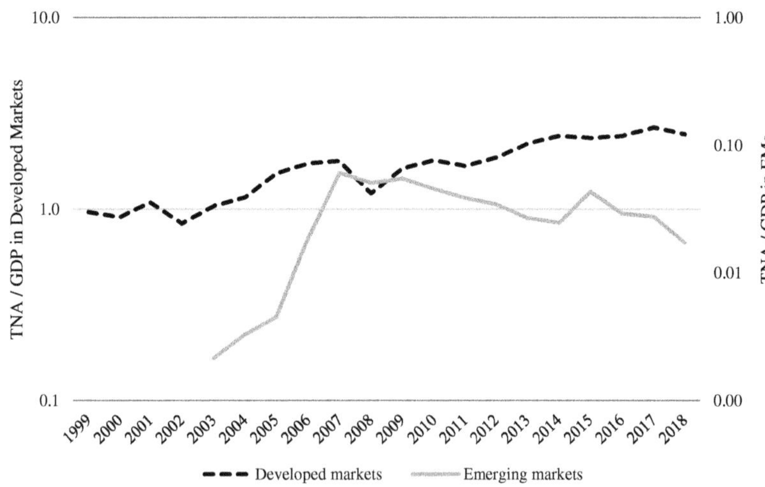

Fig. 9.2. Conventional and SRI fund assets as percent of GDP by region.
Notes: This figure plots conventional and SRI fund assets relative to GDP by region separately (logarithmic scale). Developed countries are depicted by the black line; emerging markets (EMs) by the grey line. Aggregate mutual fund assets of conventional funds are shown in Panel A and of SRI funds in Panel B. The sample period is from December 1999 through December 2018, except for SRI funds in EMs, which starts in 2003.

Table 9.2. Structure of mutual funds industry by major categories 2018.

Country	TNA (USDbn)	TNA/GDP (in %)	No. of funds	Avg fund size (USDm)	Fund categories: Allocation (%) Conventional	SRI	Alternative (%) Conventional	SRI	Equity (%) Conventional	SRI	Bonds (%) Conventional	SRI	Other (%) Conventional	SRI
Developed countries														
Australia	895	67.3	4,546	197	54.1	1.46	1.47	0.14	23.34	3.01	9.93	0.47	5.88	0.16
Canada	777	47.4	2,466	315	23.98	0.06	1.20	—	46.63	0.46	26.54	0.22	0.92	—
Switzerland	412	58.4	1,016	405	7.39	1.53	0.10	—	44.81	1.83	35.83	0.76	7.71	0.03
Germany	492	12.7	1,645	299	17.97	1.94	1.95	0.01	38.13	0.50	12.89	0.42	26.15	0.05
Denmark	129	37.7	593	217	7.60	0.72	1.40	—	40.17	2.15	45.60	2.25	0.10	—
Spain	306	22.1	4,137	74	48.88	0.71	4.54	0.00	15.42	0.05	24.22	0.02	6.15	—
Finland	19	41.8	469	40	20.38	1.17	0.53	0.01	29.89	3.00	35.41	1.86	7.63	0.12
France	898	33.3	2,870	313	11.28	0.77	3.58	0.00	19.46	3.78	13.71	1.89	37.69	7.85
Israel	59	16.8	1,439	41	42.13	—	0.21	—	12.51	0.05	34.43	—	10.67	—
Italy	269	13.4	1,082	249	58.47	2.04	3.23	—	9.11	0.20	23.25	0.40	3.30	—
Japan	541	10.7	5,592	97	14.45	0.00	1.54	—	54.92	0.67	27.77	0.01	0.63	—
Norway	132	31.9	361	365	4.14	0.52	0.12	0.11	27.34	24.81	30.90	12.06	—	—
Sweden	405	74.9	636	637	18.58	3.16	3.70	0.82	44.73	12.23	10.58	6.09	0.12	—
Singapore	28	8.1	199	139	24.87	—	0.05	—	39.26	—	35.65	0.03	0.14	—
United Kingdom	1,287	48.2	2,351	548	16.67	0.62	5.42	0.01	53.42	2.51	15.41	0.39	5.47	0.08
United States	16,734	81.6	8,672	1930	7.06	0.12	1.07	0.04	62.30	3.06	25.01	0.72	0.61	0.00
Mean	1461	37.9	2380	366.5	23.6	0.9	1.9	0.1	35.1	3.6	25.4	1.7	7.1	0.5
Emerging markets														
Chile	36	13.3	405	89	28.74	—	0.31	—	13.30	0.01	55.74	—	1.90	—
China	1,647	12.8	4,178	394	10.46	0.12	0.02	—	3.65	0.01	18.05	0.05	67.64	—

(Continued)

Table 9.2. (*Continued*)

					Fund categories									
					Allocation (%)		Alternative (%)		Equity (%)		Bonds (%)		Other (%)	
Country	TNA (USDbn)	TNA/ GDP (in %)	No. of funds	Avg fund size (USDm)	Conventional	SRI	Conventional	SRI	Conventional	SRI	Conventional	SRI	Conventional	SRI
India	290	10.8	752	386	15.10	—	2.75	—	32.25	0.02	26.63	—	23.26	—
Brazil	155	8.75	1,345	115	4.06	—	18.85	—	6.73	0.04	70.32	—	0.00	—
Mexico	89	7.5	462	193	7.37	—	—	—	10.06	—	77.81	—	4.77	—
Malaysia	35	10.0	635	54	12.84	0.00	—	—	69.75	0.11	16.62	0.02	0.54	0.12
Thailand	122	24.3	1,386	88	8.99	—	—	—	28.21	0.01	47.05	—	15.75	—
Taiwan	84	14.2	851	98	8.30	—	7.00	—	25.09	0.27	30.64	—	28.70	—
South Africa	126	36.8	1,006	125	50.00	0.02	0.16	—	27.88	0.02	21.38	0.01	0.52	0.00
Mean	287	15.4	1224	171.5	16.2	0.0	3.2	0.0	24.1	0.1	40.5	0.0	15.9	0.0

Notes: This table reports the number of funds and total net assets (TNA) of SRI (socially responsible investing) and conventional (all other) open-end mutual funds at the end of 2018 in 16 developed countries and 9 emerging markets. The countries are grouped based on the most recent MSCI Market Classification Review (2019). TNA is given in billion USD and TNA as percent of GDP is based on the GDP of each individual country. The fund categories, Allocation, Alternative, Equity, Bonds, and Other are shown as percent of total assets (columns add to 100%). Other funds include money market funds, property funds and convertible funds.

USD 1.6 trillion in net assets, respectively.[9] TNA as a function of GDP are, on average, 37.9% in developed and 15.4% in emerging countries, but with a wide range between the individual countries. For example, TNA in the US account for as much as 81.6% and in Sweden for 74.9%,[10] whereas only for 8.1% and 7.5% in Singapore and Mexico. Overall, ten developed and only one emerging country (South Africa) have mutual fund sectors with net assets exceeding 30% of GDP. Equity and bond funds represent about two-third of global fund assets, most of which is still invested in conventional funds.[11] In five developed (Japan, Norway, Sweden, UK and the US) and one emerging country (Malaysia) equity funds represent more than 50% of total fund assets. Equity funds account for almost the entire SRI sector in emerging markets, yet still below 1% of total assets in each country. By contrast, in developed countries SRI equity funds represent on average 3.6% of total assets and even 24.8% and 12.2% in Norway and Sweden, respectively.

Furthermore, there is a notable tilt toward bond funds in emerging markets with an average share of total fund assets of 40.5%, compared to 24.1% for equity funds. In three countries (Chile, Brazil and Mexico) bond funds account for more than 50% of total net assets. Virtually all of the assets are invested in conventional funds. Denmark shows the highest allocation to bond funds among developed countries, again most is held by conventional funds (45.6%). The dominance of conventional bond funds is less surprising considering that "green" bonds or bonds issued for social or sustainable (e.g. housing etc.) projects are rather a recent occurrence.[12]

---

[9]Based on total net assets of USD 23.38 trillion in developed and USD 2.58 trillion in emerging countries.

[10]Morningstar Asset Flows includes funds available for sales (designated as "AFS") in case of Germany and Israel. To avoid that net assets are overstated, we exclude all funds that are domiciled outside of these countries.

[11]Sum of SRI and conventional fund net assets. In 16 countries, the sum of bond and equity fund assets account for two-third or more and in three countries even above 90% (Denmark, Norway and the US).

[12]The World Bank issued the first green bond in 2008 after being approached by Swedish pension funds, while the first green corporate bond was issued in 2013. For more details see World Bank News, 18 March 2019, *"10 Years of Green Bonds: Creating the Blueprint for Sustainability Across Capital Markets"* or the

Allocation funds (or balanced funds) hold portfolios invested in stocks, bonds, and cash depending on how "aggressive" the asset allocation is. Investors often use such funds in order to save for retirement. These funds are commonly referred to as life cycle funds, as they adjust the allocation into safer assets (e.g. bonds and cash) as the date of retirement gets closer. In three developed and one emerging country, conventional allocation funds account for around 50% or more of total fund assets (Australia, Spain, Italy and South Africa). SRI allocation funds are again smaller by comparison, accounting between 1.2% and 3.2% in six developed countries (Australia, Switzerland, Germany, Finland, Italy and Sweden), while there are almost none present in emerging countries.

Alternative funds invest in non-traditional asset classes including private equity, commodities, art, antiques and derivative contracts. Both conventional and SRI alternative funds have a relatively small share of total fund assets.[13] Other funds include mainly money market funds and, to a very small extent, property funds. Interestingly, in France, conventional and SRI money market funds account for about twice as much of total fund assets as corresponding equity funds, 37.7% and 7.9%, respectively, whereas in Germany conventional money market funds represent 26.2% of the sector. As pointed out by Klapper *et al.* (2004), money market funds tend to thrive more in countries with tight regulation on banks and bank deposit rates.[14] Similarly, in China conventional money market funds are by far the largest fund category representing two-thirds of the total.

Although conventional mutual funds still hold a larger share of the global fund industry, Table 9.3 shows that in some countries TNA held by SRI funds have grown much faster over time compared to conventional funds. In terms of equity mutual funds, this is the case in eight out of 16 developed countries, which also have a well-established mutual fund sector in general. In particular, Scandinavian countries experienced rapid growth. Norway and Sweden, where SRI

Climate Bond Initiative (Market Intelligence Service) https://www.climatebonds.net/market.

[13]Apart from Brazil, where conventional alternative funds account for about 19% of total assets.

[14]In addition to the general demand of institutional or retail investors to "park" their liquid funds.

Table 9.3. Net assets of SRI and conventional mutual funds and annual growth rates.

	Time period — Conventional	Time period — SRI	TNA (USDm)		Growth p.a. (%)		
Country	**Start End**	**Start End**	**Conventional**	**SRI**	**Conventional**	**SRI**	
Panel A — Equity funds							
Developed countries							
Australia	12/1999–12/2018	12/1999–12/2018	208,992	26,979	7.7	18.1	+
Canada	12/2002–12/2018	12/2002–12/2018	362,216	3,546	8.7	5.1	–
Switzerland	12/2006–12/2018	12/2006–12/2018	184,445	7,533	12.1	9.4	–
Germany	12/2008–12/2018	12/2008–12/2018	187,771	2,476	8.4	4.7	–
Denmark	12/2005–12/2018	12/2005–12/2018	51,753	2,770	8.0	14.3	+
Spain	12/2008–12/2018	12/2008–12/2018	47,189	156	17.5	13.7	–
Finland	12/2005–12/2018	12/2005–12/2018	5,594	561	27.0	27.9	+
France	12/2005–12/2018	12/2005–12/2018	174,640	33,895	5.7	8.0	+
Israel	12/1999–12/2018	12/2005–12/2018	7,320	28	11.4	7.4	–
Italy	12/2006–12/2018	12/2006–12/2018	24,525	551	−2.7	2.4	+
Japan	12/1999–12/2018	12/1999–12/2018	297,119	3,649	7.1	3.4	–
Norway	12/2005–12/2018	12/2005–12/2018	35,985	32,651	9.6	17.8	+
Sweden	12/2005–12/2018	12/2005–12/2018	181,190	49,530	10.5	12.3	+
Singapore	12/2009–12/2018	n/a–12/2018	10,825	—	2.0	—	n/a
United Kingdom	12/2008–12/2018	12/2008–12/2018	687,631	32,356	8.0	9.5	+
United States	12/1999–12/2018	12/1999–12/2018	10,425,348	511,272	6.3	4.9	–
Mean	—	—	805,784	44,247	9.2	9.9	+
Emerging markets							
Chile	12/1999–12/2018	12/2018–12/2018	4,797	4	16.2	—	–
China	12/2006–12/2018	12/2010–12/2018	60,138	208	37.9	2.3	–
India	12/2002–12/2018	12/2008–12/2018	93,527	58	80.4	4.6	–

(Continued)

Table 9.3. (*Continued*)

Country	Time period — Conventional (Start–End)	Time period — SRI (Start–End)	TNA (USDm) Conventional	TNA (USDm) SRI	Growth p.a. (%) Conventional	Growth p.a. (%) SRI	
Brazil	12/1999–12/2018	12/2004–12/2018	10,453	56	18.5	21.1	+
Mexico	12/2004–12/2018	n/a–12/2018	8,957	—	30.5	—	n/a
Malaysia	12/2009–12/2018	12/2009–12/2018	24,113	39	9.3	24.8	+
Thailand	12/2006–12/2018	12/2007–12/2018	34,489	7	24.1	−17.6	−
Taiwan	12/2000–12/2018	12/2006–12/2018	21,031	228	8.0	−3.6	−
South Africa	12/2003–12/2018	12/2006–12/2018	35,066	30	13.2	−10.7	−
Mean	—	—	32,508	70	26.5	2.3	−
Panel B — Bond funds							
Developed countries							
Australia	12/1999–12/2018	12/1999–12/2018	88,875	4,229	7.4	42.2	+
Canada	12/2002–12/2018	12/2002–12/2018	206,151	1,724	14.9	18.3	+
Switzerland	12/2006–12/2018	12/2006–12/2018	147,468	3,121	13.5	21.9	+
Germany	12/2008–12/2018	12/2008–12/2018	63,460	2,065	4.1	21.9	+
Denmark	12/2005–12/2018	12/2005–12/2018	58,746	2,899	6.7	24.0	+
Spain	12/2008–12/2018	12/2017–12/2018	74,104	68	8.2	4,824.1	+
Finland	12/2005–12/2018	12/2009–12/2018	6,628	348	30.6	24.7	−
France	12/2005–12/2018	12/2005–12/2018	123,053	16,938	5.9	14.3	+
Israel	12/1999–12/2018	n/a–12/2018	20,144	—	16.3	—	n/a
Italy	12/2006–12/2018	12/2006–12/2018	62,609	1,064	−1.2	−0.2	+
Japan	12/1999–12/2018	12/2010–12/2018	150,211	62	11.1	−17.0	−
Norway	12/2005–12/2018	12/2005–12/2018	40,675	15,880	8.8	19.3	+
Sweden	12/2005–12/2018	12/2005–12/2018	42,849	24,676	14.9	18.1	+
Singapore	12/2009–12/2018	12/2009–12/2018	9,830	9	18.1	−9.9	−
United Kingdom	12/2008–12/2018	12/2008–12/2018	198,315	5,055	7.1	15.2	+

United States	12/1999–12/2018	12/1999–12/2018	4,184,547	121,205	9.2	11.4 +
Mean	—	—	—	—	11.0	314.3 +
Emerging markets						
Chile	12/1999–12/2018	n/a–12/2018	20,101	—	16.5	— n/a
China	12/2006–12/2018	12/2008–12/2018	297,315	862	51.1	−5.9 −
India	12/2002–12/2018	n/a–12/2018	77,245	—	54.5	— n/a
Brazil	12/1999–12/2018	n/a–12/2018	109,151	—	15.5	— n/a
Mexico	12/2004–12/2018	n/a–12/2018	69,291	—	22.1	— n/a
Malaysia	12/2009–12/2018	12/2018–12/2018	5,745	6	12.0	— n/a
Thailand	12/2006–12/2018	12/2008–12/2018	57,523	10	21.1	6.5 −
Taiwan	12/2000–12/2018	n/a–12/2018	25,680	—	31.6	— n/a
South Africa	12/2003–12/2018	12/2003–12/2018	26,894	14	14.1	−11.7 −
Mean	—	—	—	—	26.5	−1.2 −
Panel C — Allocation funds						
Developed countries						
Australia	12/1999–12/2018	12/1999–12/2018	484,769	13,053	10.6	24.6 +
Canada	12/2002–12/2018	12/2002–12/2018	186,235	428	11.1	2.7 −
Switzerland	12/2006–12/2018	12/2006–12/2018	30,424	6,279	4.6	32.4 +
Germany	12/2008–12/2018	12/2008–12/2018	88,505	9,560	17.1	20.2 +
Denmark	12/2005–12/2018	12/2005–12/2018	9,788	932	25.7	26.7 +
Spain	12/2008–12/2018	12/2008–12/2018	149,566	2,164	17.4	30.5 +
Finland	12/2005–12/2018	12/2005–12/2018	3,815	220	32.3	26.2 −
France	12/2005–12/2018	12/2005–12/2018	101,230	6,934	10.1	16.0 +
Israel	12/1999–12/2018	n/a	24,646	—	18.8	— n/a

(*Continued*)

Table 9.3. (*Continued*)

Country	Time period — Conventional Start End	Time period — SRI Start End	TNA (USDm) Conventional	TNA (USDm) SRI	Growth p.a. (%) Conventional	Growth p.a. (%) SRI	
Italy	12/2006–12/2018	12/2006–12/2018	157,423	5,487	8.2	22.7	+
Japan	12/1999–12/2018	12/2000–12/2018	78,179	24	14.3	3.7	–
Norway	12/2005–12/2018	12/2005–12/2018	5,448	686	25.2	33.2	+
Sweden	12/2005–12/2018	12/2005–12/2018	75,282	12,801	14.4	8.1	–
Singapore	12/2009–12/2018	n/a	6,857	—	18.9	—	n/a
United Kingdom	12/2008–12/2018	12/2008–12/2018	214,512	7,956	17.4	20.0	+
United States	12/1999–12/2018	12/1999–12/2018	1,182,209	20,705	7.5	8.7	+
Mean	—	—	15.8	17.2	+		
Emerging markets							
Chile	12/1999–12/2018	n/a	10,365	—	32.2	—	n/a
China	12/2006–12/2018	12/2006–12/2018	172,253	2,029	11.0	19.8	+
India	12/2004–12/2018	n/a	43,791	—	64.2	—	n/a
Brazil	12/1999–12/2018	n/a	6,307	—	19.0	—	n/a
Mexico	12/2004–12/2018	n/a	6,562	—	12.9	—	n/a
Malaysia	12/2009–12/2018	12/2018–12/2018	4,440	0	9.9	—	n/a
Thailand	12/2006–12/2018	n/a	10,995	—	21.8	—	n/a
Taiwan	12/2000–12/2018	n/a	6,954	—	12.6	—	n/a
South Africa	12/2003–12/2018	12/2003–12/2018	62,885	21	27.0	6.9	–
Mean	—	—	—	—	23.4	3.0	–

Notes: This table reports the total net assets (TNA) and annual growth rates of SRI (socially responsible investing) and conventional (all other) open-end mutual funds at the end of 2018 in 16 developed countries and 9 emerging markets. The countries are grouped based on the most recent MSCI Market Classification Review (2019). TNA is given in million USD. The plus and minus signs in the last column indicate where SRI fund assets have grown faster compared to conventional fund assets. The sample periods vary across countries and fund category as shown in columns 2–5.

equity funds already account for a large share of the total, registered growth rates of 17.8% and 12.3% per year, while Finland even experienced a growth of 27.9% per year. Other countries with double-digit growth rates are Australia and Denmark. At the lower end, SRI funds in Italy recorded a relatively small growth rate of 2.4%, yet conventional funds decreased by almost the same magnitude −2.7% per year over the same period. In emerging markets, only two countries (Brazil and Malaysia) achieved high growth, but from very small starting points. In three countries, SRI fund assets even decreased (Thailand, Taiwan, and South Africa). Consistent with past research, our findings suggest that general equity market and mutual fund sector development is important for the adoption and implementation of responsible investment strategies.

Panel B of Table 9.3 shows a similar picture with higher growth of SRI bond fund assets in 12 developed countries, most notably Australia, Switzerland, Germany, and Denmark, with annual growth rates between 21.9% and 42.2%. In the US, which has the largest (bond) mutual fund sector, growth averaged 11.4% per year. Ten of those countries also recorded higher growth rates in case of allocation funds, almost all of which recorded a growth of 20% or more per year (Panel C). Across all three main fund categories equity, bond and allocation, SRI funds grew faster compared to conventional funds in Australia, Denmark, France, Italy, Norway, and the UK.[15]

We now move on to discuss existing literature concerning relative performance and investment pattern differences in the next section as well as record-keeping and oversight body development in the section following that.

9.2 Comparisons with Conventional Funds: Performance and Investor Behavior

The research record on SRI begins in the 1970s with small-scale studies of the performance of companies deemed to be socially responsible (Moskowitz, 1972; Vance, 1975; Alexander and Buchholz, 1978)

[15]For the sake of brevity and due to the lack of a meaningful SRI sector, we do not discuss the growth pattern of alternative and other funds in detail. Results are available from the authors upon request.

and an early discussion of SRI in a funds context (and call for research) can be found in Rudd (1981). Rudd conjectured that constraints laid on investment may, in particular by excluding sin stocks (liquor, tobacco, armaments) or country boycotts, reduce a portfolio's profitability and undermine the fiduciary responsibility owed to its shareholders. However, a lack of information made undertaking quantitative analysis difficult in the 1980s, since for much of that time there were only six funds in existence in the US. Research started fairly small in terms of data sets and simple methodology in the early 1990s.

Hamilton, Jo, and Statman (1993) used monthly excess returns derived from the CAPM from data provided by Lipper Analytical, covering a mere 32 all-equity mutual funds (1981–1990) to compare with the excess returns of 220 conventional funds. The difference was statistically insignificant. The authors interpreted this as implying "the market does not price social responsibility characteristics" (p. 66). Hamilton *et al.* explained SRI mutual funds as having a number of goals. These include fair and equitable hiring practices with respect to gender, race, ethnicity, commitment to employee well-being, care for the environment, and the adoption of a "corporate conscience" (p. 62) that might help a firm be profitable. An early example of such a fund was the Calvert Social Investment Fund, which also had negative screens for avoidance of investment in weapons manufacturers, nuclear power, and any connection with South African business (an Apartheid era restriction that disappeared with the end of Apartheid in 1994).

In the decade leading to the turn of the millennium, SRI really caught on and the research record expanded too. On UK data, Luther, Matatko and Corner (1992) found weak positive outperformance on a small sample of 15 ethical unit trusts, but there was a small-cap bias in their study. Again on UK data, Luther and Matatko (1994) ran a comparison employing a small-cap index, yielding similar results. Using matched pairs on UK data, Mallin, Saadouni and Briston (1995) again found positive outperformance for SRI funds. Meanwhile on US data, Diltz (1995), Guerard (1997), Sauer (1997), and Goldreyer and Diltz (1999) followed Hamilton *et al.* (1993) in finding no statistically significant differences between screened and unscreened portfolios. Investigations were also made for possible confounding factors, and in the US any outperformance was found to be driven by large-cap stocks and growth stocks rather than by SRI stocks (Guerard,1997; Kurtz, 1997).[16] In the UK, Gregory, Matatko and Luther (1997) still not satisfied with existing control for the small-cap bias, employed a two-factor Jensen's alpha approach. The outperformance detected in earlier studies disappeared. This was corroborated by Havemann and Webster (1999), who pointed out that successful performance was not so much a matter of a fund being an SRI fund, but on how well the fund manager operated within the relevant SRI prescription.

By 1998, Morningstar was listing 64 socially conscious funds. In his 2000 paper, Statman chose 31 of these (based on a 70% equity requirement) for comparison with the performance of the S&P 500 over the period 1990–1998. He also matched each SRI fund with pairs of conventional funds. The S&P 500 outperformed the SRI portfolios, but the difference was statistically insignificant as were the differences in performance between the matched funds. These results were robust across two methodologies: Jensen's alpha and a modified version of the Sharpe ratio, the excess standard-deviation-adjusted return.

As part of the above process, Statman discussed and made use of the Domini 400 Social Index (DSI)[17] founded in 1990 by Kinder, Lyndenberg, Domini and Company (KLD). The DSI is a value-weighted index of 400 stocks, 250 of which were S&P 500 firms, with 100 further firms from elsewhere providing representation from a range of industries and a final 50 non-S&P 500 firms providing a strong infusion of positive SRI characteristics. The 400 were selected by use of exclusionary screens (screening out firms with more than 2% investment in weaponry, tobacco, alcohol, for instance). The 50 SRI champion firms were also selected via positive screening on items such as the diversity of employees, employee relations, and the firm's relationship with the environment. Statman (2000) also noted that the Social Investment Forum (SIF, 1998) reported that negative screening entailed having no investment in tobacco for 84% of SRI funds, none in gambling for 72%, eschewing weapons manufacturers for 69%,

---

[16]The outperformance here by large-cap stocks is in the context of comparing SRI with investment in conventional funds and not more generally.

[17]This index is now known as the MSCI KLD 400 Social Index.

and 68% of SRI funds totally excluding brewers and distillers.[18] With respect to comparing the DSI with the S&P 500 (1990–1998), Statman found that the DSI trailed by 14 basis points, but when it was compared with a socially responsible version of the S&P 500, there was no statistically significant difference in risk-adjusted returns.

After 2000, research had moved into usage of multi-regional datasets. Bauer *et al.* (2005) addressed the relative performance question on a dataset of 103 US, UK, and German ethical equity mutual funds measured, in each country respectively, against all other equity mutual funds, employing Cahart's (1997) four-factor model and provided results for purely domestic as well as international investment.

After controlling for growth bias and small-cap bias, market risk, size, book-to-market, and momentum, the authors found the difference in return between conventional and SRI funds remained statistically insignificant in all three countries, both before and after consideration of fees.

Bauer *et al.* also found that ethical mutual funds tend to be less exposed to market variability than conventional funds, and tended to be more growth-oriented than value-oriented. They also noted the difference in investment focus between the Europeans and the Americans in that the UK and German funds were small-cap focused while in the US they were large-cap focused. Two of the authors went on to cover SRI in the Australian context (Bauer *et al.*, 2006) and in Canada (Bauer *et al.*, 2007), finding similar results.

Benson, Brailsford and Humphrey (2006) investigated three research questions. These were, first, are SRI funds more profitable? Second, do SRI funds put weight their investment across sectors differently? Third, are SRI fund managers better stock pickers? The authors employed bootstrapping methodology to compare 155 SRI funds in the US with the available population of conventional funds (1994–2003) and found that, in nine out of the ten years, the difference in returns was statistically insignificant, and in just one, conventional funds did better. Similarly, based on Sharpe ratios, the authors

[18]The Social Investment Forum (SIF) subsequently changed its name to US SIF: The Forum for sustainable and Responsible Investing. This organization is discussed in the final section of this chapter. The URL for US SIF's website is: https://www.ussif.org/.

found very little difference in the risk-adjusted returns between SRI and conventional funds. Interestingly, conventional funds tended to have higher fees. There were also differences in weightings of allocations across industries, but the authors were unable to find any consistent pattern in this. With respect to the stock-picking abilities of fund managers, Benson *et al.* found that any differences between the two types of fund manager lacked statistical significance.

A number of studies have reported evidence that a mutual fund's reported performance has a downstream effect on subsequent investment inflows and outflows. See, for instance, Chevalier and Ellison (1997) and Sirri and Tufano (1998), among others. Sirri and Tufano cite research costs as a reason why SRI investors might tend not to switch funds as these costs may be higher for them than for investors in conventional funds. On much the same theme, Geczy, Stambaugh and Levin (2005) furnish anecdotal information to the effect that SRI investors tend to take money out of funds at a slower rate than do conventional investors.

This point was picked up by Bollen (2007), who posited that a tardier withdrawal rate might imply SRI investors had a conditional utility function which incorporated personal values or societal concerns. If their utility function lacked that conditional factor, then as rational investors, they should demonstrate rates of investment and disinvestment no different from those of conventional investors.

Bollen found evidence in support of this conditional utility function. Using annualized flows and performance of a sample of 205 US SRI funds matched with conventional funds (1991–2002), he showed that SRI fund flows increase more in response to positive prior-year returns, and decrease less in response to negative prior-year returns. Consistent with this dampening of negative flows, Bollen found on monthly data that SRI funds in his sample tended to display lower flow volatility than conventional funds. Further, using Carhart's (1997) four-factor model, Bollen corroborated Bauer *et al.* (2005) in finding that SRI investors were less exposed than conventional investors to the size factor (the funds being largely invested in larger stocks) and were also less exposed to momentum stocks.

Benson and Humphry (2008) followed Bollen's lead and expanded on it. They used 144 SRI funds and 4449 conventional funds (January 1991–September 2005) to analyze the relationship between investment flow and past investment flows, and between flow and current and past returns. They controlled for age, size, and fund expense and distinguished SRI funds from conventional ones with a dummy. They employed current returns, 1-, 2-, and 3-month lagged returns and 1-year lagged returns (all obtained from Morningstar), and a GMM methodology.

On conventional funds, they found that investment flow was a positive function of current and past returns, with strongly significant relations between flows and current, one-month lagged returns and one-year lagged returns. But the relation with respect to SRI funds was either negative and significant (current, two-month lag and one-year lag) or just not significant. Benson and Humphrey interpreted this as suggesting that investors were not so fast to invest more or to take out investment as conventional investors were on current or earlier return figures. In other words, the SRI investors were "gaining additional utility from their non-financial criteria" (Benson and Humphrey, 2008, p. 1855). In addition, the coefficient for investment flow lagged one year was strongly significant and positive for both fund categories. However, its size with respect to SRI investment was three times bigger than that for conventional investment. This suggests SRI investors tend to invest further in funds in which they have already invested. Further work on the return-flow relation was performed by El Ghoul and Karoui (2017), who corroborated the persistence of SRI investment flows.

Motivated by the argument that investors who would be willing to sacrifice some performance to satisfy personal ethical considerations might accept lower performance by SRI funds than from conventional funds, Renneboog, Ter Horst and Zhang (2008a) investigated whether SRI fund returns were superior or inferior to conventional fund returns in 17 countries (1991–2003). They found that in the US and UK, and in many, but not all European and Asia-Pacific countries, SRI funds underperform domestic counterparts by 2.2% to 6.5% on a raw return basis, but in risk-adjusted terms, the differences are statistically insignificant. In addition, they found ethical factors individually are statistically insignificant with respect to SRI performance.

Renneboog, Ter Horst and Zhang (2008b) provide a meta-study along with an excellent background to the development of the market for SRI, mentioning among other things, the seventeenth century Quaker colonists in North America who refused to profit from any trading in guns or slaves. Renneboog *et al.* cover the research record from Luther *et al.* (1992) in the UK and Hamilton *et al.* (1993) in the US through to Bollen (2007). Table 4 of their paper provides a summary of sample sizes, reference groups, and findings (Renneboog *et al.*, 2008b, pp. 1736–1737). A further more quantitative meta-analysis of 85 studies and 190 experiments was performed by Revelli and Vivani (2015). They reaffirmed that SRI was neither superior nor inferior to conventional investing. A third meta-analysis performed by Jedynak (2017) arrived at the same conclusion.

Statman and Glushkov (2009) analyzed stock returns 1992–2007 for portfolios based on social responsibility characteristics ratings provided by KLD Research and Analytics (KLD). Using adjusted returns derived from the CAPM, Fama and French's (1992) three-factor model, and Carhart's (1997) four-factor model, they found that firms with higher social responsibility scores yielded higher returns than did firms with lower scores.

However, overall, this tended to be cancelled by the disadvantage of non-inclusion of "shunned companies" in socially responsible portfolios. The two opposing effects left the returns SRI portfolios similar in size to those of conventional portfolios, implying "...the advantages of some social responsibility criteria are offset by the disadvantages of other social criteria". (Statman and Glushkov, 2009, p. 44).

In terms of social responsibility, KLD rates firms positively on their strengths and negatively on their shortcomings ("concerns"). Each item has a binary value (1 or zero, if not present). The sum of the concerns is subtracted from the sum of the strengths.[19] The strengths, in brief, are charitable giving, innovative giving (to not-for-profits), non-US charitable giving, support for housing, support for education, indigenous peoples relations, volunteer programs, and "other" community activity. The concerns are investment controversies, negative economic impact, indigenous people's relations (negative), tax disputes, and "other" concerns.

Investors opt for best-in-class investments, whether SRI or conventional. However, there is no universal consensus on what is most

[19]Statman and Glushkov provide more details in an appendix explaining their employment of KLD ratings.

important or most socially desirable, or where to draw a boundary. For instance, should a tobacco company be rated as a shunned firm because its product is health-harming or could the firm be deemed socially responsible because it donates to charity and maintains excellent employment practices? With respect to corporate governance and stock returns, the authors found no statistically significant relationship.

For the next few papers, we drop down from fund level to company level to explore underlying phenomena that would impact on the value of SRI investment and SRI fund managers' choices.

Operating on the interface between finance and marketing, Luo and Bhattacharya (2009) construct and test a model that sets out to predict the impact of corporate social performance (CSP) on a firm's idiosyncratic risk and how this is influenced by advertising and by the firm's commitment to research and development. Using data from Fortune's MAC surveys (2002 and 2003), COMPUSTAT, and CRSP on 541 companies, they found that firms that have a reputation for higher quality CSP than their industry peers will enjoy relatively lower levels of stock price volatility. However, the simultaneous pursuit of CSP, intensive advertising, and research and development turns out to be counter-productive, as in this context, stock price volatility tends to rise.

Hong and Kacperczyk (2009) focused on the shareholder composition of sin stocks (alcohol, tobacco, and gambling) and the returns on holding these stocks, which they compute with Carhart's (1997) four-factor model on data (1965–2006). Such firms enjoy less investment from large institutional investors such as pension funds than firms outside the sinful industry but otherwise possessing similar financial characteristics, and tend to have less coverage from analysts. Hong and Kacperczyk found that sin firms tend to be up to 20% lower priced (as a result of lack of large institutional investors demand) and outperform non-sin firms by 29 basis points per month. This may be viewed as an opportunity cost for SRI investors.

Greenwald (2010) with quite a different methodology set out to determine if firms with high environmental, social, and governance (ESG) factors enjoy incrementally superior earnings performance over those with low ratings. Using ASSET4 ESG scores (available from DataStream) for US firms in the period, 2004–2010, he compared published earnings with analysts' earnings estimates on data from I/B/E/S. He found that firms with ESG scores in the top quartile outperformed analysts' estimates 70% of the time, which was roughly ten percent more often than did the lowest quartile. Greenwald equated this outperformance with a stronger managerial focus on the longer term predicated on commitment to environmental and social values.

Renneboog *et al.* (2011) focused on SRI fund characteristics. They examined the role of nonfinancial attributes in the SRI investment process by comparing the pattern of investment cash flow/returns relationship of SRI funds with relationship found with respect to conventional funds. They hypothesized that, relative to conventional funds, the flow-return relation of SRI funds would be weaker and be affected by the type and intensity of screening; and that the screening would also influence SRI performance relative to conventional funds (Renneboog *et al.*, 2011, pp. 565–566).

The authors found that SRI investors are less likely to withdraw cash in response to past negative earnings than are investors in conventional funds. The presence of negative screening in the SRI fund selection process lessened this further. But unlike Bollen (2007), Renneborg *et al.* also found that SRI investors' positive response to positive past earnings may be watered down when compared with how conventional investors react. This muting effect occurs in the presence of social screening of potential investments (on business practices, labor relations, diversity, human rights, and corporate governance). However, environmental screening heightens the positive response by SRI investors to past announced positive earnings, increasing inward cash flows. The authors also estimated that SRI funds in the UK employed, on average, 9.1 screens each while in the rest of the world, it was 5.6 screens (Renneboog *et al.*, 2011, pp. 572–573).

Moreover, they explored the capacity of SRI investors to pick winners, based on ex-post analysis of future returns and found they had similar odds of being consistent winner pickers as other investors. Indeed, the authors found no statistically significant relationship between fund flows and the next month's return for either SRI or conventional funds. Further, the deployment of funds by investors was likely to be a function of their lack of portfolio investment education in conjunction with marketing efforts by funds soliciting cash and media attention.

With a shift of focus on to the nature of returns alone, the authors found SRI funds employing negative screens tend to underperform matched conventional funds, but European SRI funds employing in-house financial analysts earn, on average, a premium of 25 basis points per month. In the US, SRI funds engaging in shareholder activism also earn higher returns.

Clacher and Hagendorff (2012) performed an event study on a sample of 356 announcements made when London Stock Exchange firms were included in the FTSE4Good index over the period 2001–2008 and obtained a strongly significant positive abnormal return and an increased volume of trading on the day of the announcement. The next day and thereafter, statistical significance disappeared. While this could be viewed as a nice demonstration of market efficiency, the authors interpreted this rapidity of adjustment as failing to provide sufficient evidence that shareholders consider the classification of firms as being socially responsible to be a value enhancement. On the other hand, the classification did not negatively affect firm value either.

Nofsinger and Varma (2014) examined differences in performance of SRI and conventional funds over the business cycle. In particular, they contrast the return differential obtained during periods of economic prosperity with what is apparent during economic crises. They tracked their sample of 240 US SRI funds, each matched with US conventional funds, over the years 2000–2011. In terms of Carhart's (1997) four-factor alpha, the difference between SRI and conventional returns was statistically insignificant during the years of prosperity. But during crisis years, the outperformance by SRI funds of conventional funds was 1.66%, significant at the five percent level (Nofsinger and Varma, 2014, Table 4, p. 186). The authors relate their findings to prospect theory (Kahneman and Tversky, 1979) in which financial decision-makers are more willing to avoid losses than forego gains. This connection with Kahneman and Tversky also fits with the patterns of investment flows discussed by Bollen (2007) and Benson and Humphrey (2008) and may underlie the findings by Cox, Brammer and Millington (2004) that pension funds and life insurance firms in the UK prefer to invest in companies with strong ESG credentials.

Hawn, Chatterji and Mitchell (2018) performed another, broader event study on announcements of firms being added to, continuing on, or deleted from the Dow Jones global sustainability index, DJSI World. Their sample covered announcements of 321 additions, 215 deletions, and 1,646 retentions from 27 countries in the period

1999–2015. Overall, the investor response to the announcement events was minimal, although there was some strengthening in positive reactions to additions for announcements occurring later in the sample period. The authors related this time trend phenomenon to "a changing institutional logic concerning the benefits of CSR" (Hawn *et al.*, 2018, p. 971).

The power of social values and of social signaling was investigated by Riedl and Smeets (2017) with quite a different conclusion. These authors found in a set of laboratory experiments that SRI investors were prepared to forego higher financial returns and put up with higher management fees in order to invest in accordance with their personal beliefs and values. They concluded that social signaling and social preferences provided a better explanation for SRI investing than did pursuit of profit.

Story and Neaves (2015) explored the relationship between perceptions of a firm's corporate social responsibility (CSR) rating and the performance of its employees. While efforts by firms to be socially responsible may be intrinsic (sincere and ingrained in the firm's ethos) or extrinsic (imposed as an obligation to avoid negative outcomes), both sources of CSR were associated with increases in employee productivity.

Bialkowski and Starks (2016) examined the possible nexus between fund profile characteristics and investment cash flows. They establish that the profiles of SRI funds, as laid out in their prospectuses, differ from those conventional funds in terms of investments held and their weightings, and in terms of fund objectives. They found, on their sample of 117 US SRI domestic equity funds and 1,617 conventional domestic equity funds, that investors paid attention to these details and that there was a statistically significant connection between cash flows and fund profiles. Funds with a greater number of ESG screens disclosed in their investment strategy attracted significantly higher cash inflows. In addition, the authors found that SRI funds tend to maintain their ESG scores over time, which suggests that managers pay attention to keeping their weighting allocations true to their published profiles. Further, Bialkowski and Starks found that funds that were members of the US Social Investment Forum enjoyed cash inflows greater than for both conventional funds and for those SRI funds that were non-members.

The authors used differences-in-differences analysis to analyze the changes in pattern of cash flows into and out of SRI and conventional funds associated with exogenous shocks to financial markets. Several of these were business-related (for instance, the global financial crisis of 2008–2009) and another two were economic shocks brought on by environmental disasters (the Deepwater Horizon oil-spill in the Gulf of Mexico in 2010 and the Fukushima Daiichi nuclear meltdown in 2011). In the case of the global financial crisis, when there were large cash outflows from conventional funds symptomatic of heightened risk aversion and loss of trust in big corporations, the net cash flow of SRI funds shrank slightly for four quarters only and then became positive, fitting with the returns performance record reported by Nofsinger and Varma (2014). In the aftermath of the two environmental disasters, the SRI fund inflows became significantly greater relative to conventional fund inflows, which is evidence suggesting that investors were influenced by environmental concerns.

Gibson *et al.* (2019) analyzed different ESG implementation strategies and the associated effects on ESG scores and returns using data obtained from the organization, Principles for Responsible Investment (PRI). They mapped ESG scores to their use in SRI investment in North America, Europe, and in the Asia-Pacific region for 2013–2017, which are the first five years for which score data has been made available.[20] A description of PRI is provided in the next section. Evidence from the mapping procedure showed that institutional investors and funds that had become PRI signatories tend mostly to base their investment strategies on the use of exclusionary screening, shareholder activism, proxy voting, and a requirement that SRI be discussed in a prospective investment's financial accounts. Over time, however, norms-based and best-in-class screening and thematic placement have become increasingly popular. Gibson *et al.* noted that if signatories made a choice between no strategy and a single strategy adoption, then either negative screening, integration, or proxy voting were the likely choices. When multiple strategies were to be adopted, signatories added shareholder activism to the mix. The authors also found that larger signatories were more likely to adopt any given strategy than were smaller signatories. In terms of the effect of strategies on ESG outcomes, negative and best-in-class screening,

[20]This paper is possibly the first use of this major new resource.

along with individual shareholder activism had the greatest positive impact, while proxy voting was the least useful. With respect to the range of regions covered in the study, European investors tended to exhibit higher ESG scores on governance than did North American investors. European investors were also more likely to prefer negative and positive and norm-based screening than were North American investors. Another item of interest was that early signatories tended to have a stronger commitment to PRI principles than later signatories and this could be and was identified by the greater effectiveness of the early adopters' ESG strategies.

Kim (2019) has performed the most recent meta-analysis available on SRI. On a sample of 51 quantitative studies (1978–2016), the author used standardized measures of impact, effect size (ES), and absolute value of effect size (AES) to report what the magnitude of effects might be for returns in various categories of study. Of note, Kim found that ESs tended to be positive in the early years of the record, but then become smaller in absolute value terms, and variable in sign. Kim interpreted this to mean that investors initially gained benefit from including SRI stocks in their portfolios, but that this benefit has waned somewhat. Kim also found that domestic SRI funds had higher ESs than did international funds, and SRI mutual funds tended to have smaller ESs than did portfolios collated by individual investors.

In summary, a number of trends have become apparent in the literature. Investments in SRI equity mutual funds have increased markedly over time, and the differences in risk-adjusted returns have repeatedly been found to be insignificant. Furthermore, no single SRI ethical screen has been shown, over time and across samples, to be consistently influential on returns. However, there are two clear differences in investment flow behavior: SRI investment is more muted in response to past and current positive returns and existing SRI investment tends not to decline in response to negative returns.

9.3 Movements Towards Facilitating Socially Responsible Investing

There is scope for the reduction of investor search costs through the provision of a regulatory entity that could provide better, faster assessments of SRI funds. This, in the first instance, is a matter of providing one uniform set of definitions of SRI types, which would lead to the development and acceptance of standardized quantitative measures of exposure to non-financial values. In addition, it would foster insistence on clarity and transparency about funds' goals and the assets under their management.

Arguably, the evolution of such standardization is already underway with the advent of US SIF and PRI, both mentioned earlier in the chapter and further discussed in this section. However, at the present point on the evolutionary path, there is no one universally recognized body with full regulatory oversight. The existing initiatives are largely advisory, playing an advocacy role.

The US SIF, Forum for Sustainable and Responsible Investment (earlier known simply as SIF), has been publishing biennial trends reports on SRI in accordance with ESG principles since 1995, with the most recent of these in 2018. These reports present data from questionnaire surveys on the numbers of institutional investors, money management firms, and mutual funds identified as employing ESG principles in their financial activities, and also refines this information with respect to specific ESG items. Given that ESG stands for "environmental, social, and governance", the executive summary to the 2018 report itemizes climate change, human rights, the quality of corporate governance, and eschewal of the armaments industry as such items. The 2018 Trends Report also examines the degree to which pension funds subject to the US Employment Retirement Income Security Act (1974) have taken heed of the US Department of Labor's guidance disclosure in 2015 in support of investment in accordance with ESG values. In addition to biennial trends reports, US SIF runs annual conferences and publishes on a range of topics within SRI. Two recent publications are "Investing to Advance Women: A Guide for Investors" (February 2020) and "Sustainable Investor Poll on TCFD Implementation"[21] (December 2019). US SIF's mission statement is to "rapidly shift investment practices towards sustainability, focusing on long-term investment

[21]TCFD is the Task force on Climate-related Financial Disclosures, founded and currently chaired by Michael Bloomberg. Its purpose is to improve the quality of firms' financial reports and other disclosures with respect to reporting on climate change risks to financial markets (see: www.fsb-tcfd.org).

and the generation of positive social and environmental impacts" and its stated vision is to see that "environmental, social and governance impacts are meaningfully assessed in all investment decisions resulting in a more sustainable and equitable society" (US SIF, 2020).

Principles for Responsible Investment (PRI), an international network set up with United Nations support in 2006, performs a similar role with a strong emphasis on investor education. PRI's website provides publications in PDF format on a range of SRI topics including guides to dealing with ESG issues in listed equities, private equity, and when considering fixed income investment. With respect to environmental and social issues, among its current offerings are "Implementing TCFD recommendations for oil and gas methane disclosure", "Growing water risk resilience: An investor guide on agricultural supply chains" and "How investors can promote responsible cobalt sourcing practices" (PRI, 2020). The organization also regularly runs forums and webinars.

By 2018, when information on the 2017 year became available, PRI had more than 2,000 signatories who collectively controlled $80 trillion of assets under management and had become strongly influential globally. At the start of 2020, there were in excess of 2,000 investment manager signatories and 500 asset owner signatories.[22] PRI requires signatories to make mandatory annual disclosures on the ESG-related principles they make use of in their investment practices. The network's six guiding principles, binding on the signatories, are, as follows (Gibson *et al.*, 2019, p. 5):

1. Incorporate ESG issues into both investment analysis and the resulting decisions.
2. Incorporate ESG issues into ownership policies and practices.
3. Require appropriate disclosure of ESG matters by entities invested in.
4. Work for the acceptance and implementation of these six principles in the investment industry.
5. Work collectively to enhance overall effectiveness in implementing the principles.

[22]The greatest number of asset owner signatories, by country, at this point were Japanese and French, and the largest concentrations of assets under management were in the Nordic countries and in Britain and Ireland (PRI, 2020).

6. Report on activities and progress towards implementing the principles.

The range of strategies by which criteria are met is slightly longer with eight items (Gibson *et al.*, 2019, pp. 16–17):

1. Negative or exclusionary screening (of sectors or firms deemed unacceptable).
2. Positive or best-in-class screening (of companies with ESG attributes superior to those of others in a particular industry).
3. Norms-based screening (measurement against a benchmark standard accepted as an international norm).
4. Integration (where funds are allocated to firms where ESG factors are brought explicitly into financial analysis).
5. Thematic (investment according to a favored type of SRI investment, such as wind and solar energy production).
6. Individual shareholder activism (the use of voting power to access, communicate with and influence company decisions).
7. Collaborative shareholder activism (relating to the fifth guiding principle listed above).
8. Proxy voting (annual general meetings of firms in which PRI signatories invest).

It is important for the growth of SRI that investors are satisfied by the flow of information concerning fund strategies, and it is clear that PRI and US SIF understand that. Both are moving to address the need for investment professionals and organizations to be more candid about their processes for screening potential assets.

9.4 Concluding Remarks

Socially responsible investment (SRI) in equity-based mutual funds now has a history going back over more than a quarter of a century and it is clear that investment in accordance with ESG principles is becoming increasingly integrated into the mainstream investment industry. In this context, it is worth noting that the performance of SRI funds tends to be statistically indistinguishable from that of conventional mutual funds, although the behavior of the two types of investor is distinctively different. Unlike conventional investors,

SRI investors tend to prefer putting more cash into their existing investments rather than diversifying elsewhere. SRI investors are also slower than conventional investors to withdraw funds in response to a fund's underperformance. This suggests a greater degree of loyalty based on ESG principles and a greater degree of stability — or potentially a reduced propensity for panic. A further consideration is that money invested according to ESG principles, especially with respect to environmentally green mutual funds, are likely to be investments supporting research into and the development of renewable energy sources and environmentally sustainable technologies.

A further consideration is the growing sense of urgency, felt worldwide, concerning out-of-control global carbon dioxide emissions and the possible triggering of irreversible (at least in the short-term) global warming. Given that the "E" in ESG stands for environment, increased attention to technological change that mitigates or entirely removes the global greenhouse threat is highly likely to foster an ever stronger focus on SRI by investors in general. Therefore, in the future, one could predict a strong degree of convergence between SRI and conventional funds. This convergence could occur in two manners. It could be driven by more funds taking on SRI characteristics, or it could be driven at firm level by more listed companies conforming to ESG best practice. Will it be either of these, or both? We leave this as an open question.

Over the past quarter century, the growth of SRI has also seen the development of oversight organizations whose purpose is to foster SRI in accordance with ESG principles, to provide clarity on what constitutes ESG and quality ratings. As the bodies which have currently gained credence (US SIF and PRI) have regulatory authority only over investment managers and financial institutions who have signed up to them, the development of a single set of definitions and a single set of standards is yet a work in progress. However, an increasing sense of urgency felt by populations and governments in the matter of climate change may well foster both the popularity of SRI among investors and the adoption of an eventual universal set of ESG standards that are measurable and enforceable. But currently, such thinking is optimistic speculation. Governments, however, can influence where superannuation funds lodge their investments and there is some evidence that this is already happening. The French government, for instance, invests retirement funds only in SRI funds.

In the US, the Department of Labor published guidance suggesting that US superannuation funds follow a similar approach. Further, the existing SRI oversight bodies can and do advocate shareholder activism.

As a coda to this chapter, we suggest some avenues for future research. First, determining why the SRI sector has flourished in some countries more than in others warrants attention. Possible extensions should go beyond the economic and capital market development factors discussed in past research. First, the relation to changes in regulations and the adoption of SRI policies by large institutional investors is enticing. However, regulation might be a (partial) driver of growth as much as it might be a response to the changing landscape of available investment products and therefore, is endogenous.

Another research avenue is to examine the role of non-financial information or motivation. Financial literature suggests that social signaling and preferences, the growing awareness of social and environmental issues, and related factors such as religious characteristics and (perceived) climate change might all affect investor behavior and decisions (see e.g. Choi *et al.*, 2019; Riedl and Smeets, 2017; Hood *et al.*, 2013; Bollen, 2007; and Statman, 2004).

The above considerations are very broad. A narrower, but potentially productive line of investigation might be to examine the cultural and political characteristics of investors in order to determine more accurately the nature of the sticky money idea — the observed phenomenon that SRI investors, in general, are slower to disinvest from loss-making funds and have a greater existing fund loyalty. The key words here that signal currently insufficient focus are "in general". Would a closer examination of the demographics reveal a richer pattern of systematic differences?

Research to date has also largely focused on the mature markets of North America and Western Europe because these are where SRI have become a noteworthy phenomenon. As shown in Table 9.2, SRI is relatively small in emerging markets, but this is not likely to remain the case. It would therefore be interesting to document the evolution of SRI investment in emerging markets. This is not just a matter of the bare mechanics of the growth trajectory. There may be salient differences in investment practices between developed and emerging markets based on the preferences of the growing middle classes of the latter. As yet, the picture is not clear. Do investors in emerging markets look beyond risk and return to broader ethical considerations?

A final possibility, in this far from exhaustive list, is research concerning SRI relative to conventional fund investment in the context of financial crises. Over the past twenty years, the financial world has experienced two long bull runs and the global financial crisis, and at the time of writing, is entering a second recessionary phase brought on by the COVID-19 virus. What changes in relative investment growth, relative performance, and investor behavior characteristics can we determine in the context of these wildly differing market conditions?

In summary, SRI is a phenomenon worthy of interest. In this chapter, we have covered its development up till the present. It is rich with possibilities for future research.

References

Alexander, G. T. and Buchholz, R. A. (1978). Corporate social responsibility and stock market performance. *Academy of Management Journal*, **21**(3): 479–486.

Bauer, R., Derwall, J., and Otten, R. (2007). The ethical mutual fund performance debate: New evidence from Canada. *Journal of Business Ethics*, **70**(2): 111–124.

Bauer, R., Koedijk, K., and Otten, R. (2005). International evidence on ethical mutual fund performance and investment style. *Journal of Banking and Finance*, **29**: 1751–1767.

Bauer, R., Otten, R., and Tourani Rad, A. (2006). Ethical investing in Australia: Is there a financial penalty? *Pacific-Basin Finance Journal*, **14**(1): 33–48.

Bekaert, G. and Harvey, C. R. (2002). Research in emerging markets finance: Looking to the future. *Emerging Markets Review*, **3**: 429–448.

Benson, K. L., Brailsford, T. J., and Humphrey, J. E. (2006). Do socially responsible fund managers really invest differently? *Journal of Business Ethics*, **65**: 337–357.

Benson, K. L. and Humphrey, J. E. (2008). Socially responsible investment funds: Investor reaction to current and past returns. *Journal of Banking and Finance*, **32**: 1850–1859.

Białkowski, J. and Starks, L. T. (2016). SRI funds: Investor demand, exogenous shocks and ESG profiles, Proc American Finance Association Conf., San Francisco, 2016.

Bollen, N. (2007). Mutual fund attributes and investor behaviour. *Journal of Financial and Quantitative Analysis*, **42**: 683–708.

Carhart, M. M. (1997). On persistence in mutual fund performance. *Journal of Finance*, **52**: 57–82.

Chevalier, J. and Ellison, G. (1997). Risk taking by mutual funds as a response to incentives, *Journal of Political Economy*, **105**: 1167–1200.

Choi, D, Gao, Z., and Jiang, W. (2019). Attention to global warming. *Review of Financial Studies*, **33**(3): 1112–1145.

Clacher, I. and Hagendorff, J. (2012). Do announcements about corporate social responsibility create or destroy shareholder wealth? Evidence from the UK. *Journal of Business Ethics*, **106**(3): 253–266.

Cox, P., Brammer, S., and Millington, A. (2004). An empirical examination of institutional preferences for corporate social performance. *Journal of Business Ethics*, **52**: 27–43.

Davidson, A. (2016). Sustainable investing goes mainstream: Do-good investing took a step forward in 2015, with Wall Street ramping up interest. *Wall Street Journal*, January 13th.

Diltz, J. D. (1995). Does social screening affect portfolio performance? *Journal of Investing*, **1**: 64–69.

El Ghoul, S. and Karoui, A. (2017). Does corporate social responsibility affect mutual fund performance and flows? *Journal of Banking and Finance*, **77**: 53–63.

Fama, E. F. and French, K. R. (1993). Common risk factors in the returns of stocks and bonds. *Journal of Financial Economics*, **33**: 3–53.

Geczy, C., Stambaugh, R. F., and Levin, D. (2005). Investing in socially responsible mutual funds, Working paper available at SSRN 416380.

Gibson, R., Glossner, S., Krueger, P., Matos, P., and Steffen, T. (2019). Responsible institutional investing around the world, Working paper retrieved from https://editorialexpress.com/cgi-bin/conference/download.cgi?db_name$=$AFA2020&paper_id$=$685.

Goldreyer, E. and Diltz, J. D. (1999). The performance of socially responsible mutual funds: Incorporating sociopolitical information in portfolio selection. *Managerial Finance*, **25**: 23–36.

Gregory, A., Matatko, J., and Luther, R. (1997). Ethical unit trust financial performance: Small company effects and fund size effects. *Journal of Business Finance and Accounting*, **24**(5): 705–724.

Greenwald, C. (2010). ESG and Earnings Performance, *Thomsonreuters*, Retrieved from https://www.thomsonreuters.com/content/dam/openweb/documents/pdf/tr-com-financial/case-study/esg-and-earnings-performance.pdf.

Guerard, J. B. (1997). Is there a cost to being socially responsible in investing? *Journal of Forecasting*, **16**: 475–490.

Hamilton, S., Jo, H., and Statman, M. (1993). Doing well while doing good? The investment performance of socially responsible mutual funds. *Financial Analysts Journal*, **49**: 62–66.

Havemann, R. and Webster, P. (1999). Does ethical investment pay? *EIRIS Report*, retrieved from http://www.eiris.org/files/research%20publications/doesethicalinvestmentpay99.pdf.

Hawn, O., Chatterji, A. K., and Mitchell, W. (2018). Do investors actually value sustainability? New evidence from investor reactions to the Dow Jones Sustainability Index (DJSI). *Strategic Management Journal*, **39**(4): 949–976.

Hong, H. and Kaperczyk, M. (2009). The price of sin: The effects of social norms on markets. *Journal of Financial Economics*, **93**: 5–36.

Hood, M., Nofsinger, J., and Varma, A. (2014). Conservation, discrimination, and salvation: Investors' social concerns in the stock market. *Journal of Financial Services Research*, **45**: 5–37.

Jedynak, T. (2017). Is it worth being good? — The efficiency and risk of socially responsible investing in light of various empirical studies. *e-Finance*, **13**(3): 1–14.

Kahneman, D. and Tversky, A. (1979). Prospect theory: An analysis of decision under risk. *Econometrica*, **46**: 263–292.

Khorana, A., Servaes, H., and Tufano, P. (2005). Explaining the size of the mutual fund industry around the world. *Journal of Financial Economics*, **78**: 145–185.

Kim, C.-S. (2019). Can socially responsible investments be compatible with financial performance? A meta-analysis. *Asia-Pacific Journal of Financial Studies*, **48**: 30–64.

Klapper, L., Sulla, V., and Vittas, D. (2004). The development of mutual funds around the world. *Emerging Markets Review*, **5**: 1–38.

Kurtz, L. (1997). No effect, or no net effect? Studies on socially responsible investing. *Journal of Investing*, **6**(4): 37–49.

Luo, X. and Bhattacharya, C. B. (2009). The debate over doing good: Corporate social performance, strategic marketing levers, and firm-idiosyncratic risk. *Journal of Marketing*, **73**(6): 198–213.

Luther, R. G. and Matatko, J. (1994). The performance of ethical unit trusts: Choosing an appropriate benchmark. *British Accounting Review*, **26**: 77–89.

Luther, R. G., Matatko, J., and Corner, D. (1992). The investment performance of U.K. ethical unit trusts. *Accounting, Auditing and Accountability Journal*, **5**, 57–70.

Mallin, C. A., Saadouni, B., and Briston, R. J. (1995). The financial performance of ethical investment funds. *Journal of Business, Finance and Accounting*, **22**(4): 483–496.

Moskowitz, M. R. (1972). Choosing socially responsible stocks. *Business and Society Review*, **1**: 71–75.

Nofsinger, J. and Varma, A. (2014). Socially responsible funds and market crises. *Journal of Banking and Finance*, **48**: 180–193.

PRI. (2020). Principles for Responsible Investment, *PRI Association*, accessible at: https://www.unpri.org/.

Renneboog, L., Ter Horst, J., and Zhang, C. (2008a).The price of ethics and stakeholder governance: The performance of socially responsible mutual funds. *Journal of Corporate Finance*, **14**(3): 302–328.

Renneboog, L., Ter Horst, J., and Zhang, C. (2008b). Socially responsible investments: Institutional aspects, performance, and investor behavior. *Journal of Banking & Finance*, **32**(9): 1723–1742.

Renneboog, L., Ter Horst, J., and Zhang, C. (2011). Is ethical money financially smart? Nonfinancial attributes and money flows of socially responsible investment funds. *Journal of Financial Intermediation*, **20**: 562–588.

Revelli, C. and Viviani, J. L. (2015). Financial performance of socially responsible investing (SRI): What have we learned? A meta-analysis. *Business Ethics: A European Review*, **24**(2): 158–185.

Riedl, A. and Smeets, P. (2017). Why do investors hold socially responsible mutual funds? *Journal of Finance*, **72**: 2505–2550.

Rudd, A. (1981) Social responsibility and portfolio performance. *California Management Review*, **23**: 55–61.

Sauer, D. A. (1997). The impact of social responsibility screens on investment performance: Evidence from the Domini 400 social index and Domini equity mutual fund. *Review of Financial Economics*, **6**(2): 137–149.

Sirri, E. and Tufano, P. (1998). Costly search and mutual fund flows. *Journal of Finance*, **53**: 1589–1622.

Social Investment Forum (1998). 1997 Report on Responsible Investing Trends in the United States. Social Investment Forum (SIF), Washington DC, November.

Statman, M. (2000). Socially responsible mutual funds. *Financial Analysts Journal*, **56**: 30–39.

Statman, M. (2004). What do investors want? *Journal of Portfolio Management 30th Anniversary Issue*, **30**: 153–161.

Statman, M. (2006). Socially responsible indexes. *Journal of Portfolio Management*, **32**(3): 100–109.

Statman, M. and Glushkov, D. (2009). The wages of social responsibility. *Financial Analysts Journal*, **65**(4): 33–46.

Story, J. and Neaves, P. (2015). When corporate social responsibility (CSR) increases performance: Exploring the role of intrinsic and extrinsic CSR attribution. *Business Ethics: A European Review*, **24**(2): 111–123.

US SIF (2018). 2018 Report on US sustainable, Responsible and Impact Investing Trends. *Forum for sustainable and Responsible Investment*, retrieved from: https://www.ussif.org/trends.

US SIF (2020). US SIF: The Forum for Sustainable and Responsible Investment. Retrieved from: https://www.ussif.org/trends.

Vance, S. C. (1975). Are socially responsible corporations good investment risks? *Management Review*, **64**: 18–24.

Part III:

CSR, Sustainability, and Ethical Finance: New Trends

https://doi.org/10.1142/9781786349507_0010

Chapter 10

The Relationship Between CSR Disclosure and CSR Performance: A Western European Sample

Lan-Phuong Nguyen[*,†,§], **Lionel Touchais**[†,‡,¶], **and Jean-Laurent Viviani**[†,‡,||]

[*] *Danang University of Economics, 59000 Danang, Vietnam*
[†] *Université de Rennes 1, CNRS, CREM — UMR 6211, F-35000 Rennes, France*
[‡] *IGR-IAE Rennes, 11 rue Jean Macé, 35708 Rennes Cedex 7, France*
[§] *phuongnl@due.edu.vn*
[¶] *lionel.touchais@parisnanterre.fr*
[||] *jean-laurent.viviani@univ-rennes1.fr*

10.1 Introduction

The question why firms should engage in social and environmental disclosure and what its impacts will be on the various stakeholder groups have been unsolved in the literature (Ullmann, 1985). To answer it, many studies have been conducted to see the relationship between corporate social responsibility (CSR) reporting and the firm's financial performance, market value, or systematic risk. In this study, we will investigate the association between CSR disclosure and non-financial performance (CSRD). What is the essence of this link? Does this relationship run in both directions? These questions have been unsolved in social and environmental accounting.

Our explanations initially come from the economic-based and the social-political theories of disclosure that predict two opposite signs for the relationship between reporting and performance (Clarkson *et al.*, 2008; Verrecchia, 1983; Patten, 2002). The economic-based theory of disclosure predicts a positive relation between the two. It says that firms doing good CSR performance will disclose more CSR information to convey their proactive CSR type so that they can differentiate themselves from the inferior firms and potentially increase firm valuation. The socio-political theories predict a negative association between the two. It suggests that CSR disclosure is a function of social and political pressures that firms face. Particularly, due to the greater pressures from social and political parties, firms with poor CSR performance may tend to produce more voluntary disclosure to change the perceptions on their performance.

From the two perspectives presented above, CSR performance may affect CSR disclosure positively or negatively. The relationship between CSR disclosure and CSR performance can also run in the reverse direction. As a measurable activity visibly to stakeholders, CSR reporting can improve CSR performance as a signal of good corporate governance, signaling less engagement in the future misconduct. Yet, it might be a cover-up to hide poor performance in other activities or for purely presentation purposes rather than for achieving the sustainability target.

In this empirical study, we develop an aggregate measure of CSR performance, the total net CSR index (CSP). This index is constructed by taking into account five categories of CSR activities: (1) Human Rights, (2) Community, (3) Employee, (4) Diversity, (5) Environment. For CSRD we used the Bloomberg index ranging from 0.1 for companies that disclose the minimum amount of social/environmental data to 100 for those that disclose every data point. Following Nelling and Webb (2009), the fixed-effect models incorporated with the Ganger causality using both CSP and CSRD as dependent variables are applied to examine the relationship between the two as well as to see whether there is Granger-causality relationship between them. Our sample includes large public companies from seventeen Western European countries that have at least ten entities and disclosed the social and environmental information continuously during the period between 2007 and 2015. This selection aims to ensure the stability of ESG disclosure across nations and comparability in data. The final sample includes 2,894 firm-year observations from 424 companies in eleven countries.

In brief, our main results are as follows. We found a positive relationship between CSR disclosure and CSR performance. This relation runs from both sides where the CSP → CSRD is stronger in magnitude than the CSRD → CSP. In other words, superior CSR performance was more forthcoming in CSR disclosure channels as predicted by the economic-based voluntary disclosure theory. Also, the increase in reporting CSR information would force firms to improve the quality of CSR activities for fear of negative actions from stakeholders as firms perform badly. The chapter is organized as follows. Section 10.2 discusses the literature review and hypothesis development. Section 10.3 describes the sample, data, and methodology. Section 10.4 displays the results. Section 10.5 is the conclusion.

10.2 Literature Review and Hypotheses Development

In this section, we review the origin and definition of corporate social responsibility disclosure and social capital. Besides, a review of theories and empirical researches on the relationship between environmental disclosure and environmental performance are presented to develop our hypotheses.

10.2.1 *Corporate social responsibility disclosure*

Corporate social responsibility (CSR) is a broad concept that does not have a unified and precise definition yet (Wood, 2010; Scherer and Palazzo, 2007). According to The World Business Council for Sustainable Development (WBCSD), CSR refers to firm's commitment to balance the benefit between companies and community in order to improve the quality of life and ensure a sustainable economic development. CSR activities are based on the triple bottom line: economic, social, and environmental (Carroll, 1999; McWilliams and Siegel, 2001; Whetten and Mackey, 2002). According to Harjoto and Jo (2015), there are two major groups of CSR activities.

First, CSR activities that can be considered as following the laws and regulations (legal CSR) such as tax disputes, accounting concerns, non-representation, regulatory problems, labor rights, antitrust, product safety, etc. Second, voluntary CSR activities that can be considered as following social norms (normative CSR) such as charitable giving, transparency concern, employment of the disabled, work–life benefits, benefits to economically disadvantage, etc. In this case, a firm can go beyond legal constraints and commit to bear the cost of more ethical behavior in a variety of practices (McWilliams and Siegel, 2001).

CSR reporting or CSR disclosure is the process of communicating the social and environmental impacts of economic activities of the organization to specific groups of stakeholders and society as a whole (Mathews, 1995). Ernst and Ernst (1978) defined it as the amount of information related to firm's activities, programs, and application of resources deemed to affect both the public in general and particular stakeholder groups like the environment, energy usage, employees, products, community services, and fair business practices. In CSR reports, most companies focus on some categories such as environment, employees, and consumers issues and disregard community involvement issues. The historical development of sustainability reporting was charted by Hahn and Kühnen (2013). In the early 20th century, firms in UK and US focused on social values and conditions and safety for workers much more than environmental issues such as pollution (Hogner, 1982; Maltby, 2004). In the 1970s, "social reports" were sometimes introduced to supplement conventional financial reports, with more attention to environmental issues including emission and waste. By the late 1990s, following to the Global Reporting Initiative (GRI), both environmental and social information began to be detailed to financial reports (Kolb, 2010). Recently, South Africa has produced fully integrated reports that incorporate economic, social, and environmental information in a single document to provide a complete picture of the firm's activities (Adams and Simnett, 2011). CSR disclosure has several roles, such as assessing the impacts of CSR activities, measuring the effectiveness of CSR programs, and reporting on CSR and external and internal information system, thus allowing the comprehensive assessment of all corporate resources and sustainability impacts (Jenkins and Yakovleva, 2006; Gray *et al.*, 2001; Gray *et al.*, 1996; Mathews, 1997).

CSR disclosure may be compulsory or voluntary. Countries with mandatory sustainability reporting are China, Hong Kong, India, Malaysia, Brazil, South Africa, and Denmark, currently. However, their disclosure regulations limit at a "complex and explain" basis where firms are able to make disclosures or not provided that they justify their position (Ioannou and Serafeim, 2016). Despite this, the United Nations is recommending that all large firms be mandated to publish sustainability reports by 2030 (UN Panel Call for Global Sustainability Reporting). Beyond mandatory requirements, firms can either be proactive — voluntarily going beyond minimal stakeholder expectation or — reactive — responding to social pressures when they occur.

The main question is why firms should make voluntary CSR disclosure beyond that required by law. According to Mathew (1997), there are three possible motivations: making a sense of "social contract", enhancing their legitimacy, and improving their financial valuation. Legitimacy relates to the notion of a "social contract", which limits the activities of an organization within the boundaries set by the society (Gray *et al.*, 1996). Organizations are expected to act in a socially acceptable manner so as to access resources, gain approval of their goals and place in the society, and guarantee continued existence (Guthrie and Parker, 1989). Hahn and Kühnen (2013) provided a list of potential benefits that firms may achieve when disclosing sustainability information such as enhancing transparency, improving reputation and brand value, motivating employees, and supporting the firm's control process. It seems that reporting CSR information that meets or exceeds stakeholder expectations would create the impression of the firm doing good. This leads to the suspicion on the purpose of CSR disclosure: for purely presentation reasons rather than improving the sustainability or even for hiding poor performance on other activities. Indeed, Brammer and Pavelin (2006) argued that the main purpose of corporate disclosure is to "influence perceptions regarding the future financial prospects of the firm in the minds of external, primarily financial, stakeholders' rather than to genuinely attempt to reduce environmental and social damage". Holder-Webb *et al.* (2009) provided evidence that firms only select a portion of information that improve their image in the self-congratulatory way when undertaking voluntary disclosure. This line of argument refers to the fact that sustainability reporting does more harm than good (Gray, 2010).

10.2.2 *CSR performance — Concept and measurement*

Thus, CSR performance can be considered as the results that a company achieves from its CSR program. A properly implemented CSR can lead to a variety of competitive advantages, such as enhanced access to capital and markets, increased sales and profits, operational cost savings, improved productivity and quality, efficient human resource base, improved brand image and reputation, enhanced customer loyalty, and better decision-making and risk management processes.

In the empirical studies, scholars have mostly used the Kinder, Lydenberg, and Domini (KLD) ratings database to construct a composite measure of CSP (Waddock and Graves, 1997; Kinder and Domini, 1997; Nelling and Webb, 2009; Barnett and Salomon, 2012; Gao and Zhang, 2015). KLD is an independent rating service that focuses exclusively on assessment of corporate social performance across a range of dimensions related to stakeholder concerns. It employs a widely accepted set of CSR measures that fit Carroll (1979)'s proposed model, which describes a firm's social obligations as economic, legal, ethical, and discretionary responsibilities. In particular, the KLD database takes a comprehensive approach by examining eight dimensions related to social performance: corporate governance, community, diversity, employee relations, environment, human rights, product characteristics, and controversial business issues. After collecting information from surveys, financial statements, articles on companies in the popular press, academic journals (especially law journals), and government reports, they classify such information into strengths and weakness. CSP would be computed by aggregating the strength and weakness ratings.

In the meanwhile, CSR performance includes three main dimensions, environmental, social, and governance, with five inclusive categories, (1) community, (2) diversity, (3) employee relations, (4) environment, and (5) human rights (Lins *et al.*, 2017) that cover the aspects of nonfinancial performance. In essence, CSR actions are nonfinancial activities that are on issues of customers, employees, regulators, competitors, community, and society. CSR performance is therefore able to represent the nonfinancial performance of the company.

10.2.3 *Relationship between CSR disclosure and CSR performance*

Based on the concept of corporate social responsibility, CSR disclosure may be relative to CSR performance. CSR performance is the result that a company achieves from its CSR program or strategy. CSR disclosure is the process of communicating the social and environmental impacts of economic activities of the organization to specific groups of stakeholders and the society (Mathews, 1995). Reporting CSR information is actually a criterion to evaluate a firm's CSR performance. So, what is the nature of their relationship? Does CSR disclosure lead to CSR performance or vice versa?

First, what is the true nature of the relationship between CSR disclosure and CSR performance: positive, negative, or irrelative? At the beginning, the literature in environmental accounting research presented mixed results on the relation between environmental disclosure and environmental performance. Some studies using the CEP environmental performance rankings[1] and the Wiseman environmental disclosure index rankings[2] found no association between the two, for example, Ingram and Frazier (1980), Wiseman (1982), Freedman and Wasley (1990). Some presented a negative relationship between environmental disclosure and environmental performance after changing the methodology of measuring environmental disclosure and performance index, (Bewley and Li, 2000; Hughes *et al.*, 2001; Patten, 2002). By using simultaneously equation approach, Al-Tuwaijri *et al.* (2004) found a positive association between environmental performance and non-discretionary environmental disclosure. Brammer and Pavelin (2006) showed that firms with poor environmental performance had less incentives to

[1]The Council on Economic Priorities (CEP) is a nonprofit organization specializing in the analysis of corporate social responsibility.

[2]Wiseman (1982) constructed an environmental disclosure index basing on 18 items in four categories: economic factors (5 items), environmental litigation (2 items), pollution abatement activities (5 items), and environmental disclosures that do not stand in the other three (6 items). He assigned a score to each item on the notion that the disclosure is quantitative or qualitative, particularly 3 for quantitative disclosure, 2 for non-quantitative disclosure, 1 for general terms, 0 for no disclosure).

make environmental disclosure than the others, and when they did, they would be careful to minimalize the ability of adverse selection. Clarkson *et al.* (2008) said that these mixed results were due to the choice of non-discretionary disclosure channels and the use of the Wiseman (1982) index. They suggested to use the purely discretionary environmental disclosure and develop a content analysis index based on the GRI[3] sustainability reporting guidelines to measure environmental disclosure and environmental performance.

According to Clarkson *et al.* (2008) and Clarkson *et al.* (2011), there are two streams of theories that present opposite signs for the link between environment disclosure and environmental performance: the economics based and the socio-political theories of voluntary disclosure. The economic-based theory of voluntary disclosure (Verrecchia, 1983) predicts a positive relationship between environmental performance and the discretionary environmental disclosure. This theory proposes that firms tend to disclose "good news" to differentiate themselves from the inferior firms to avoid the adverse selection problem. Further, firms with superior environmental performance tend to show more objective environmental performance indicators that firms with poor performance cannot imitate. By providing voluntary disclosure, they can signal their proactive environmental performance "type" to investors and other stakeholders and then gain competitive advantages such as an enhanced corporate reputation and a reduction in the cost of capital (Mahoney *et al.*, 2013; Luo and Tang, 2014; Lys *et al.*, 2015). Producing sustainability disclosures require expending resources to put the appropriate mechanisms in place to measure, collect, and report relevant information (Buhr, 2002), so firms would select to make sustainability disclosures if the expected benefits outweigh the costs. From this point of view, firms with superior CSR performance would select more voluntary disclosures whereas the inferior firms would disclose less or be silent for fear of stakeholders' negative reaction towards "bad" news.

Inversely, socio-political theories, including political economy, legitimacy theory, and stakeholder theory, predict a negative

[3]The Global Reporting Initiative (GRI) principally focus on the environmental and social pillars with the conventions for presenting the economic dimension left largely to the conventional financial report.

relationship between the two. According to the legitimacy theory, legitimacy is required for organizational survival. A company can get legitimacy when it is perceived to operate within a socially constructed system of norms, values, and bounds of which the entity is a part. When companies do not satisfy public expectations and requirements, they must face increased public pressure, scrutiny, and monitoring as well as greater risks to legitimacy (Patten, 2002; Hrasky, 2011; Alrazi *et al.*, 2015). In an effort to address these issues, companies may exploit communication strategies including the use of voluntary corporate disclosures to distract attention and change societal perceptions, expectations, and values (Lindblom, 1994; Gray *et al.*, 1995; Hooghiemstra, 2000). Thus, firms with poor environmental performance face more political and social pressures and threatened legitimacy, so they tend to select a high level of discretionary disclosure to change stakeholders' perceptions about their performance.

In short, doing "good" CSR performance may encourage firm to disclose a higher CSR information subsequently because it can improve the relationships with key stakeholder groups (Freeman, 1984), resulting in better overall performance and greater competitive advantages. On the other hand, doing "bad" CSR performance enable firms to face more social and political pressures, and therefore firms need to disclose more voluntary CSR information to change stakeholders' perceptions on their performance. Thus, the relationship between CSR disclosure and CSR performance may run from CSR performance to CSR disclosure in either the positive or negative direction.

Second, does a "virtuous circle" relationship between CSR disclosure and CSR performance exist? In the literature, there are some suggestions that sustainability reporting improves CSR performance as it is considered a measurable activity (Topping, 2012). Christensen (2015) found that firms making voluntary disclosures tend to engage less in misconduct behaviors in the future. They found that such firms would suffer a worse loss if they are involved in a misconduct scandal because their previously good behavior granted them a degree of protection. CSR disclosure is one of communication channels that can reduce the information asymmetry between a company and its stakeholders; it can be considered as a signal of "good" management skill (Alexander and Buchholz, 1978; Bowman and Haire, 1975). CSR reporting may develop as a myth incorporated in the organization structure. Thanks to CSR, the organization will gain legitimacy, resources, stability and enhances its survival prospects (Meyer and Rowan, 1977; Dimaggio and Powell, 1983; Suchman, 1995). It thus enables to create the competitive advantages for company. CSR disclosure is an increasing trend in businesses, concerning both individual organizations and authority. It therefore forces the company to involve in CSR activities at a broader scope of content and implementation. From this point of view, CSR reporting can increase the subsequent CSR performance due to the pressure of informing about "good news". Inversely, CSR disclosure might be a self-congratulatory way to polish a firm's image or hide poor performance in other activities, rather than improving sustainability (Brammer and Pavelin, 2006; Hodder-Webb *et al.*, 2009). Firms that face great public pressures such as the highly polluting companies might take risks to disclose hard performance indicators when public scrutiny is strong. In this context, stakeholders may detect whether companies undertook CSR disclosure to disguise bad CSR performance. This detection may damage the firm's reputation and perceived integrity, reducing its legitimacy and increasing the likelihood of outside intervention. CSR reporting therefore does more harm than good (Gray, 2010). In addition, a high CSRD does not indicate superior CSP. Given that CSRD is a costly process, it may be assumed that companies that are either relatively good or bad environmental performers use CSRD as a management tool to enhance corporate value, as long as the expected marginal benefits outweigh the marginal costs (McWilliams and Siegel, 2001; Matsumura *et al.*, 2014). In an unregulated setting with the absence of certain governance structures, it is difficult to distinguish between the two types of firms because it is hard to observe whether a company conveys a true and fair view of its environmental performance or provides a misleading representation that may be not indicative of company's actual CSR performance. For this reason, bad CSR performers, which likely experience threatened legitimacy, could use extensive CSRD as a risk management tool to reduce public pressure and prevent intervention. The link between CSRD and CSP now is negative rather than positive.

The relationship between CSR disclosure and CSR performance can run in both directions, with either a positive or a negative sign. Therefore, we hypothesize the following:

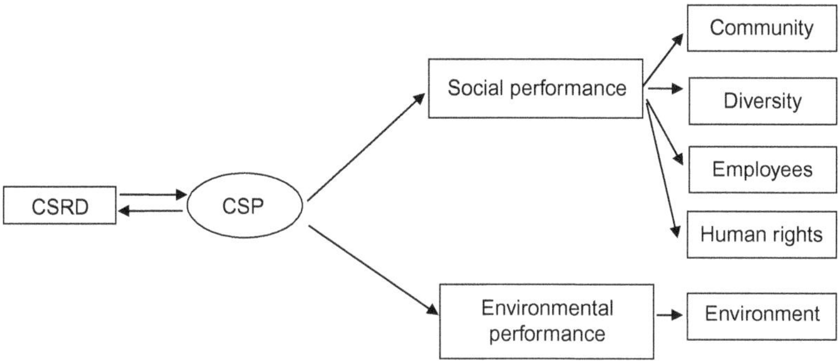

Fig. 10.1. Conceptual framework.

H1: CSP is positively related to CSRD.
H2: CSP is negatively related to CSRD.

If this relationship runs from both sides, we suspect that there would be a causal relationship between CSR disclosure and CSR performance. This chapter goes further into the issue of precedence in order to capture the interaction between two items. It is hypothesized that either CSR disclosure precedes CSR performance or vice versa, then:

H3: CSP precedes CSRD.
H4: CSRD precedes CSP.

The null hypothesis in both cases is that there is no causal relationship (see Fig. 10.1).

10.3 Sample, Variables, and Models

This section provides information about sample, data selection, and the measurement of main variables such as CSR disclosure, CSR performance, and control variables. The empirical models are introduced in this part as well.

10.3.1 *Sample and data*

To observe a general pattern of the mutual relationship between CSR disclosure and CSR performance, it is better to choose a sample of organizations or companies disclosing CSR information frequently and stably. To ensure the stability of ESG disclosure across nations, we chose Western European countries that follow a similar CSR reporting policy or regulation. We select a sample of listed companies from seventeen Western European countries including Norway, Finland, Netherlands, Belgium, Austria, Italy, Spain, Portugal, Ireland, Greece, France, Germany, Luxembourg, Switzerland, Sweden, Denmark, and the United Kingdom. However, to ensure the comparability in data, we only choose countries that have at least 10 entities and disclose the social and environmental information continuously during the period between 2007 and 2015. The initial sample included 3,816 firm-year observations from 424 companies in 11 countries. Our selection also relies on a survey on the number of ESG companies in Western Europe based on Bloomberg ESG data to finalize which countries and which time duration should be used. As in previous studies, we only choose "large" "public interest entities" ("PIEs") with more than 500 employees and a balance sheet total of at least €20 million or a net turnover of at least €40 million.[4] We also excluded firms that have missing data of all explanatory variables, noting the possibility of the outlier's effect. The final sample consisted of 2,894 firm-year observations.

10.3.2 *Variables*

10.3.2.1 *Corporate social responsibility performance (CSP)*

In previous studies, CSP has been computed by aggregating the strengths and weaknesses ratings from Kinder, Lydenberg, and Domini (KLD) ratings database (now is the MSCI) to create a firm's overall net score across thirteen social performance criteria (Barnett *et al.*, 2012; Nelling and Webb, 2009). Yet, this database does not cover our sample, which focuses on the CSR performance of Western European countries' companies. Besides, because of using ESG disclosure score from Bloomberg, we decided to measure CSP by using ESG information gathered by Bloomberg as well. The use of

[4]Non-financial reporting Directive, Preamble pt14, the Accounting Directive Arts 2(1) and 3.4.

these data are in our view the most reliable estimation of the effective level of CSR because it ensures the matching of ESG issues between two measures CSRD and CSP. Bloomberg ESG database (see Appendix B for details) covers six categories of CSR activities: (1) Human Rights, (2) Community, (3) Employee, (4) Diversity, (5) Environment, and (6) Corporate Governance. Due to the elimination of corporate governance in measuring CSR disclosure score, we do not include the corporate governance domain in our main tests as in Lins *et al.* (2017). In consequence, our self-constructed CSP variable is a composite measure covering the performance of the five first CSR categories cited above. Each category includes CSP indicators collected from Bloomberg ESG database. We relied on such information to rate those as "strengths" and "concerns". "Strength" indicates that the firms are engaged in some socially responsible actions that may have positive effects on society, and "Concern" implies that firm's socially responsible actions may have negative impacts on society. Then, how do we rate CSP indicators? If ESG data are numeric, we compared a firm's CSP to its industry's CSP value to evaluate whether the performance of that CSR activity is a strength or concern. We will assign it as 1 if it is strength and 0 otherwise. On the other hand, if ESG data are in the form of dummies (0 or 1), we rely on the Bloomberg variable definition to decide whether that CSP is strength (1) or concern (0). For example, basing on Bloomberg's ESG database, there are four CSP indicators to present the activities related to "Human rights" in which the equal opportunity policy indicates whether the company has made a proactive commitment to ensure non-discrimination against any type of demographic group. This indicator is a dummy which returns a "1" if Yes or "0" if No, so we follow such definition to assign 1 (strength) for firm having this policy and 0 (concern) for firm without this policy. In another case, the number of employee representatives on the board, one of the CSP indicators in "Employee" category, is a numeric data. It presents the number of employee representatives on the board when companies have non-executive employee representatives. This indicator refers to the ability of employee involvement in the company, whether the company strongly encourages worker involvement and/or ownership. Thereby, we compared the number of employee representatives on the board of each firm to the median value of industry that the firms belongs to, if firm-value is larger than industry-median-value, we assign 1 for this CSP indicator (strength) and 0 (concern) for otherwise.

In doing so, CSP will contain both elements: strength and concern. However, the number of strengths and concerns for any given category differs over time, so we construct a strength (concerns) index of firm i at year t for each category as follows:

$$\begin{aligned}\mathrm{Strength\_index_{i,t}} &= \mathrm{Number\_of\_strengths_{i,t}} \\ &\quad \times \frac{\mathrm{Number\_of\_disclosed\_CSP_{i,t}}}{\mathrm{Median\_of\_disclosed\_CSP_{j,t}}} \\ \mathrm{Concern\_index_{i,t}} &= \mathrm{Number\_of\_concerns_{i,t}} \\ &\quad \times \frac{\mathrm{Number\_of\_disclosed\_CSP_{i,t}}}{\mathrm{Median\_of\_disclosed\_CSP_{j,t}}}\end{aligned}$$

where:

- $\mathrm{Number\_of\_strengths}_{i,t}$ ($\mathrm{Number\_of\_concerns}_{i,t}$) is the number of strengths (concerns) of firm i at year t;
- $\mathrm{Number\_of\_disclosed\_CSP}_{i,t}$ is the total number of CSP disclosed by firm i at year t;
- $\mathrm{Median\_of\_disclosed\_CSP}_{j,t}$ is the median value of total number of CSP disclosed at year t within industry j where firm i belongs.

As a result, we got the strengths (concerns) indices for each category-year. Then, the net CSP in each category-year was computed by taking the difference between strengths index and concern index. For example, the net CSP of Human rights activities of firm i at year t is as follows:

$$\begin{aligned}\mathrm{Net\ CSP}_{\mathrm{Humanrights},i,t} &= \mathrm{strength\_index}_{\mathrm{Humanrights},i,t} \\ &\quad - \mathrm{concern\_index}_{\mathrm{Humanrights},i,t}\end{aligned}$$

Our primary explanatory variable is the total net CSP of five CSR categories, and it is computed as follows:

$$\begin{aligned}\mathrm{CSP}_{i,t} = \sum \big(&\mathrm{Net\ CSP}_{\mathrm{Humanrights},i,t} + \mathrm{Net\ CSP}_{\mathrm{Community},i,t} \\ &+ \mathrm{Net\ CSP}_{\mathrm{Employee},i,t} + \mathrm{Net\ CSP}_{\mathrm{Diversity},i,t} \\ &+ \mathrm{Net\ CSP}_{\mathrm{Environment},i,t}\big)\end{aligned}$$

10.3.2.2 *CSR disclosure*

To gauge the degree of corporate social responsibility disclosure (CSRD), we employ ESG disclosure score obtained from Bloomberg. More specifically, we use the social disclosure score (S-score) and environmental disclosure score (E-score). The two scores range from 0.1 for companies that disclose minimum amount of social data to 100 for those that disclose every data point collected by Bloomberg. Each data point is weighted in terms of importance, with, for S-score, workforce data carrying greater weight than other disclosures and, for E-score, data such as Greenhouse Gas Emissions carrying greater weight than other disclosures. Both scores are tailored to different industry sectors by which each company is only evaluated in terms of the data that is relevant to its industry sector. Then, we construct a single scale of CSR disclosure by taking the average of social disclosure and environmental disclosure indices.

10.3.2.3 *Control variables*

Previous studies have suggested size, risk, R&D investment, and industry to be factors that affect CSR performance (Ullmann, 1995; Waddock and Graves, 1997), we use them as control variables. Firm size (*Size*) is widely recognized as determinant of CSR performance. There is some evidence that larger firms may exhibit many overt socially responsible behaviors more than smaller firms because of the more attention from external parties and the greater pressure from stakeholders. We approximated it by using total assets on a log scale in order to reduce skewness. Risk tolerance (*Risk*) affects a firm's willingness to adopt CSR activities that can incur both cost and benefit in the long term; we use the level of debt held by the firm, which is the ratio of total debt to total assets. R&D investments enable firms to incorporate the stakeholders' preferences into production and services that may lead to a higher stakeholders' satisfaction and the firm's CSR as a result. Therefore, we use R&D intensity (*RD*) as a control, which is the ratio of R&D expenditures to total revenues. Since the idiosyncratic characteristics of country and industry may influence firm's social arena, we control for country and industry to take these differences into account. We include country, industry, and year dummies in the model.

10.3.3 *Models*

First, the FEM approach is applied to test the relationship between CSR disclosure and CSR performance (Hypothesis 1 and 2) so that we can control the difference in CSR reporting regulations and implementation across countries and industry. The OLS regressions with country, industry, and time fixed effects are as follows:

$$\begin{aligned}\text{CSRP}_{it} &= \alpha_1 + \alpha_2\text{CSRD}_{it} + \alpha_3 \ln\_\text{tasset}_{it} + \alpha_4\text{debt\_ratio}_{it} \\ &\quad + \alpha_5 rd_{it} + \gamma_t + \varepsilon_{it} \qquad (1)\end{aligned}$$

$$\begin{aligned}\text{CSRD}_{it} &= \chi_1 + \chi_2\text{CSRP}_{it} + \chi_3 \ln\_\text{tasset}_{it} + \chi_4\text{debt\_ratio}_{it} \\ &\quad + \chi_5\text{rd}_{it} + \gamma_t + \varepsilon_{it} \qquad (2)\end{aligned}$$

where CSRD_{it} and CSRP_{it} represent CSR disclosure and CSR performance of firm i in year t; ln_tasset, debt_ratio, rd are control variables which represent firm size, firm risk, R&D intensity respectively; $\gamma_t = \beta_0 + \beta_1 Z_i$ and Z_i represents the unobserved variable that varies across country and firm but does not change over time; ε_{it} is an error term that is assumed to be uncorrelated over time. The signs of coefficients α_2 and χ_2 indicate the relationship between CSR disclosure and CSR performance.

We address the causal links between CSR disclosure and social capital in the context of Granger causality. The Granger causality approach (Granger, 1969) actually concerns precedence more than causation in the usual sense (Leamer, 1985). With this test, what we really know is whether a particular variable (X) comes before another (Y) in the time series. If X causes Y, lags of X should be significant in the equation for Y. In this case, it would be said that X "Granger-causes" Y. If Y causes X, lags of Y should be significant in the equation for X. In this case, it would be said that Y "Granger-causes" X. If both set of lags are significant, there is a "bi-directional causality" between X and Y (Brooks, 2014). So, Granger-causality really addresses the correlation between the current value of one variable and the past values of others. It just focuses on lead–lag relationships rather than the true cause-and-effect relationship as in the standard notions of causation.

However, Granger-causality test is only applied for time series data, whereas our data is a panel. Thereby, we follow Nelling and Webb (2009) to incorporate both fixed effects and Granger causality using CSP and CSRD as dependent variables to test the hypotheses. The model now includes n intercepts (where n is the number of firms in the panel data) that are represented by a set of indicator variables such that:

$$\mathrm{CSP}_{it} = a_0 + a_1\mathrm{CSP}_{i,t-1} + a_2\mathrm{CSRD}_{i,t-1} + \sum_{n=3}^{\infty} a_n X_{it} + \gamma_t + \varepsilon_{it} \quad (3)$$

$$\mathrm{CSRD}_{it} = b_0 + b_1\mathrm{CSRD}_{i,t-1} + b_2\mathrm{CSP}_{i,t-1} + \sum_{n=3}^{\infty} b_n X_{it} + \gamma_t + \varepsilon_{it} \quad (4)$$

where CSP_{it} and CSP_{it-1} represent CSR performance of firm i in year t and $t-1$; CSRD_{it} and CSRD_{it-1} represent CSR disclosure of firm i in year t and $t-1$; X_{it} are control variables of firm i in year t, including size, risk, R&D intensity; $\gamma_t = \beta_0 + \beta_1 Z_i$ and Z_i represents the unobserved variable that varies across country, firm but does not change over time; ε_{it} is an error term that is assumed to be uncorrelated over time.

If the coefficients a_2 are significantly different from zero, we can conclude that CSRD Granger causes CSR performance. Similarly, if coefficients b_2 are significant, we say that CSR performance precedes CSR disclosure. If coefficients a_2 and b_2 are both significantly different from zero, we infer a "bi-directional causality" between CSR disclosure and CSR performance, or the "virtuous circle" relationship does exist.

10.4 Results

The empirical results are presented in this section.

10.4.1 *Summary statistics*

Table 10.1 presents the summary statistics for the entire sample. **Panel A** reports the descriptive statistics of the main variables used in the analysis. First, the variation of CSRD and CSP is high across firms (36.430 ± 14.980 and -0.18 ± 0.68, respectively). All the scores do not suffer from excessive skewness or Kurtosis. **Panel B** reports the distribution of observations across countries. Nearly 40%

Table 10.1. Summary statistics.

Variable	N	Mean	S.D.	Min	Mdn	Max	Skewness	Kurtosis
Panel A: Descriptive statistics — Full sample								
CSRD	3,816	36.430	14.980	3	35.80	80.76	0.14	2.26
Sscore	3,816	41.100	15.970	3.33	38.60	86.67	0.09	2.40
Escore	3,816	31.760	16.750	1.55	31.78	84.50	0.19	2.31
Gscore	3,816	54.910	10.970	8.930	55.36	85.71	−0.61	3.87
ESGscore	3,816	39.450	13.200	7.850	38.84	80.58	0.13	2.30
CSP	3,816	−0.180	0.680	−3.38	−0.2	3.84	1.13	9.11
S_perf	3,816	0.010	0.380	−1.460	−0.03	2.780	1.23	9.53
E_perf	3,816	−0.190	0.450	−2.170	−0.15	2.7400	0.61	9.86
ln_tasset	3,816	8.960	2.030	3.940	8.66	14.740	0.54	2.99
Debt_ratio	3,816	25.580	19.300	0.000	23.45	245.550	2.67	24.68
RD	2,894	2.220	4.100	0	0.27	19.4	2.59	9.46

Country	Freq.	Percent	Cum.
Panel B: Number of obs across countries			
Denmark	117	3.07	3.07
Finland	171	4.48	7.55
France	522	13.68	21.23
Germany	333	8.73	29.95
Italy	171	4.48	34.43
Netherlands	135	3.54	37.97
Norway	126	3.3	41.27
Spain	180	4.72	45.99
Sweden	279	7.31	53.3
Switzerland	252	6.6	59.91
United Kingdom	1, 530	40.09	100
Total	3, 816	100	

(Continued)

Table 10.1. (*Continued*)

Variables	CSRD	Sscore	Escore	Gscore	ESGscore	CSP	S_perf	E_perf	ln_tasset	Debt_ratio	RD
Person correlation (obs = 2,894)								**Spearman correlation (obs = 2,894)**			
Panel C: Correlation											
CSRD	1	0.9134*	0.9207*	0.5229*	0.9784*	0.3275*	0.5651*	0.0433#	0.5911*	0.1459*	0.1928*
Sscore	0.9112*	1	0.6877*	0.5077*	0.8434*	0.3113*	0.5306*	0.0392#	0.5146*	0.1360*	0.1343*
Escore	0.9219*	0.6805*	1	0.4518*	0.9498*	0.2911*	0.5083*	0.0373#	0.5667*	0.1341*	0.2171*
Gscore	0.4853*	0.4842*	0.4079*	1	0.6283*	0.2414*	0.3275*	0.0688*	0.3617*	0.0501*	0.0242
ESGscore	0.9774*	0.8384*	0.9503*	0.6067*	1	0.3314*	0.5556*	0.0522*	0.5933*	0.1385*	0.1817*
CSP	0.3422*	0.3092*	0.3181*	0.2361*	0.3504*	1	0.7339*	0.7770*	0.4725*	0.0413#	0.0193
S_perf	0.4806*	0.4527*	0.4291*	0.2919*	0.4772*	0.7835*	1	0.2722*	0.5342*	0.0469	0.1204*
E_perf	0.1176*	0.0908*	0.1238*	0.1140*	0.1327*	0.8575*	0.3522*	1	0.2839*	0.0502*	−0.0749*
ln_tasset	0.5901*	0.5086*	0.5713*	0.3166*	0.5917*	0.4823*	0.5086*	0.3054*	1	0.2019*	0.0995*
Debt_ratio	0.1338*	0.1329*	0.1129*	0.0368#	0.1219*		0.0196	−0.0134	0.1767*	1	−0.1109*
RD	0.0735*	0.0367#	0.0962*	−0.0212	0.0696*	0.0579*	0.1333*	−0.0232	−0.0137	−0.1769*	1

Note: $^{*}p < 0.01$, two tailed; # $p < 0.05$, two tailed.

of sample came from the United Kingdom. France and Germany account for the second and third position, with 13.67% and 8.73%, respectively. **Panel C** reports the correlation results between CSR disclosure (CSRD, Sscore, Escore, Gscore), CSR performance (CSP, S_perf, E_perf), and other main controls. Notably, there was a highly positive correlation between CSR disclosure and CSR performance, either overall measure or dimensional measures. Furthermore, we observe a positive and significant correlation between CSR disclosure scores and CSR performance. It seems that CSR disclosure promotes more social performance than environmental performance (correlation of 48.06% vs 11.76%).

10.4.2 *Univariate test results*

The relationship between CSRD and CSP can be revealed by observing the trend of CSRD and CSP (and their components) during the period between 2007 and 2015. Figure 10.2 shows that the increasing trend of CSRD and CSP was similar from 2007 to 2014 except for 2015 when CSRD increases slightly but CSP decreases. The slight increase of CSRD in 2015 was driven by the reduction of environmental disclosure; meanwhile, social disclosure still climbed up. This is a preliminary for the potential correlation between CSRD and CSP. The movement of CSP and social performance was quite the same over 9 years, increasing from 2007 to 2014 and moderately decreasing in 2015. However, the environmental performance was not the same, it fluctuated and dramatically reduced from 2012 to 2015. From the graphs, we can see that most of social activities are the "good" actions that can make positive impacts on society (strengths) while firm's environmental actions can bring concerns to society. Thus, the improvement of CSR performance over time was primarily contributed by the social actions.

10.4.3 *Empirical results*

Table 10.2 presents the FEM results of testing the relationship between CSR disclosure and CSR performance (Hypotheses 1 and 2)

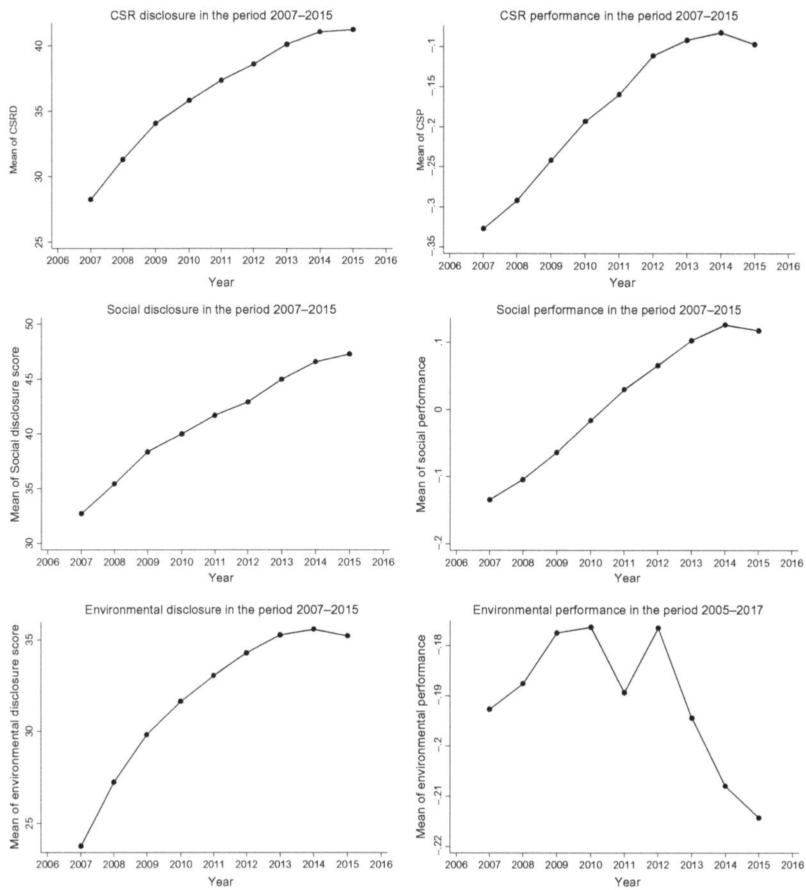

Fig. 10.2. CSR disclosure and CSR performance in the period 2007–2015.

as well as the FEM estimates of Granger causality models (Hypotheses 3 and 4). First, the coefficients on CSRD in model 1 and CSP in model 2 are positive and significant. In other words, the association between the two is positive, and furthermore this positive relation runs from both sides: CSRP → CSRD and CSRD → CSRP. These results are consistent with the predictions of economic-based voluntary disclosure theory: superior CSR performance is more forthcoming in CSR disclosure channels, and firms with high level of

Table 10.2. The relationship between CSR disclosure and CSR performance.

	Dependent variable			
Independent/ Control	**CSP**	**CSRD**	**CSP**	**CSRD**
variables	**Model 1**	**Model 2**	**Model 3**	**Model 4**
CSP_{it}		3.5679^{***}		
		(0.000)		
CSP_{it-1}			0.4414^{***}	0.3443
			(0.000)	(0.368)
$CSRD_{it}$	0.0065^{***}			
	(0.000)			
$CSRD_{it-1}$			0.0003	0.5484^{***}
			(0.682)	(0.000)
ln_tasset_{it}	−0.0218	2.9691^{***}	−0.0076	2.2866^{***}
	(0.265)	(0.000)	(0.722)	(0.000)
$Debt\_ratio_{it}$	0.0009	0.0073	−0.00003	0.0044
	(0.223)	(0.658)	(0.968)	(0.784)
RD_{it}	-0.0097^{*}	0.2939^{**}	-0.0107^{*}	0.0042
	(0.098)	(0.033)	(0.087)	(0.975)
Constant	-0.3163^{*}	3.3278	−0.0541	3.7371
	(0.053)	(0.386)	(0.759)	(0.329)
Industry FE	Yes	Yes	Yes	Yes
Country FE	Yes	Yes	Yes	Yes
Time FE	Yes	Yes	Yes	Yes
Observations	2,894	2,894	2,667	2,667
R-squared	0.0235	0.3756	0.8501	0.8366
F-test	23.37^{***}	123.17^{***}	66.78^{***}	217.53^{***}

Notes: This table presents the results of tests regarding to the relationship between CSRD and CSP. Model 1 and Model 2 are the FEM, whereas Model 3 and Model 4 are the Granger causality model using the fixed time, country, and industry. All variables are as defined in Appendix A. ***, **, * denote the regression coefficients that are statistically significant at the two-tailed 1%, 5%, and 10% levels, respectively.

CSR disclosure have many incentives to be good at performing CSR activities. Besides, the coefficients of CSP are much higher than of CSRD in magnitude, suggesting a possible stronger effect of CSP to CSRD than the inversed direction.

The results of Granger causality models also show a positive relationship between CSR disclosure and CSR performance, but it is not causality. Particularly, the coefficient of 1-year lagged CSRD in model 3 is positive but insignificant, suggesting that CSRD does not lead to CSP. Similarly, the coefficients of 1-year lagged CSP in model 4 is positive but insignificant, showing that CSP does not precede CSRD. Thus, there is no lead–lag relationship between CSR disclosure and CSR performance.

10.5 Conclusion

This chapter contributes to the CSR study by examining the relationship between CSR disclosure and CSR performance. A long history of CSR study shows that firms with high CSR performance tend to disclose more CSR to increase its competitive advantage; in turn, CSR disclosure meets the demand of stakeholders on voluntary information to resolve the information asymmetry, which can create trust and cooperation between firms and outsiders. Their relationship therefore might be positive. However, the socio-political theories predict a potentially negative association between the two. Therefore, we questioned what the true nature of this relation is and if it runs from both directions: CSRD $\rightarrow$ CSP and/or CSP $\rightarrow$ CSRD. Due to the potential circle correlations, we further suspect a causality relationship between CSRD and CSP.

Using the fixed-effect models incorporated with the Granger causality test with present and 1-year lagged CSP and CSRD, our results support a positive relationship between the two. Besides, we found that the CSP $\rightarrow$ CSRD is stronger than the inverse direction, showing that firms with good CSR performance tend to inform more, perhaps to get more rewards from society and polish their image; these are intangible assets that increases the firm's competency. However, there is no evidence for the lead–lag relationship between CSR disclosure and CSR performance.

Appendix A: Description of Variables

Variables	Symbol	Definition/Measurement
CSR performance	CSP	The total performance of five CSR categories: Human Rights, Community, Employee, Diversity, and Environment, using environmental, social, and governance database (ESG) from Bloomberg
Environmental disclosure	Escore	Environmental disclosure score over [0.1, 100]
Social disclosure	Sscore	Social disclosure score over [0.1, 100]
CSR disclosure	CSRD	The average of social disclosure and environmental disclosure indices, ranging from 0.1 to 100
Firm size	ln_tasset	ln of total assets
Risk	Debt_ratio	Total debt/total assets
R&D intensity	RD	R&D expenses/net sales
Industry profile	Industry	Dummy variables according to GICS four-digit classification
Country profile	Country	Dummy variables
Time fixed effect	Year	Dummy variables

Appendix B: Environmental and Social Issues with Bloomberg Fields

Categories	Indicators	Categories	Indicators
Community		*Environment*	
1	Community Spending	58	Total GHGs/Sales
2	SRI Assets Under Management (AUM)	59	Total GHGs/Energy
3	Percentage SRI AUM	60	Total GHGs/Employees
4	Business Ethics Policy	61	Total GHGs/BOE
5	Political donations	62	Energy/Sales
6	Political donations/Profit before tax	63	Energy/Employees
7	PRI Signatory	64	Energy/BOE
8	Equator principle signatory	65	Water/Sales
9	Consumer data protection policy	66	Water/Employees
10	Quality assurance and recall policy	67	Water/BOE
11	Intellectual property rights protection policy	68	Total Incident Tate
12	Donate to gender equality	69	Lost Time Incident Rate
13	Offer products for women health and well-being	70	Fatalities/1,000 Emp.
14	Lobby in support for gender quality	71	Greenhouse Gas Emission
15	Sponsors financial education programs for women	72	Direct (Scope 1) Emissions
16	Sponsors health education programs for women	73	Indirect (Scope 2) Emission

(*Continued*)

(*Continued*)

Categories	Indicators	Categories	Indicators
Human rights		74	Scope 3 Emissions
17	Equal Opportunity Policy	75	Energy Use
18	Human Rights Policy	76	Electricity Use
19	Policy Against Child Labor	77	Renewable Energy Use
20	UN Global Compact Signatory	78	Water Consumption
Employee		79	Water usage efficiency rate
21	Employee Turnover	80	Waste Total Generation
22	Workforce Accidents	81	Hazardous Waste
23	Lost Time from Accidents	82	Waste Recycled
24	Total Fatalities	83	Waste Landfilled
25	Employee Fatalities	84	Number of Spills
26	Contractor Fatalities	85	Amount of Spills
27	Number of employee representatives on the board	86	Gas Flaring
28	Employee Average Age	87	Business Travel CO2/ Employee
29	Number of employees-CSR	88	Business Travel CO2
30	% Employees Unionized	89	NOx Emissions
31	Employee Training Cost	90	SOx Emissions
32	3rd Party Fatalities	91	SO2 Emissions
33	# of Suppliers Audited	92	VOC Emissions
34	# of Supplier Audits Conducted	93	CO Emissions
35	# of Supplier Facilities Audited	94	Methane Emissions
36	Health and Safety Policy	95	ODS Emissions
37	Training Policy	96	Particulate Emissions
38	Fair Remuneration Policy	97	% Water Recycled

(*Continued*)

Categories	Indicators	Categories	Indicators
39	Employee CSR Training	98	Discharges to Water
40	Employee Protection/ Whistle Blower Policy	99	Coal Use
41	Anti-Bribery Ethics Policy	100	Natural Gas Use
42	Offers Flexible Work Schedule	101	Oil and Distillates Use
43	Offers Flexible Work Location	102	PaperConsumption
44	Offers Elder Care Support	103	Paper Recycled
45	Investigator for sexual harassment	104	% Capacity Fossil Fuels
46	Has formal employee development programs	105	% Capacity Nuclear
Diversity		106	% Capacity Hydroelectric
47	Women in Management	107	% Capacity Renewables
48	Women in the Workforce	108	% Generation Nuclear
49	% Employees Minorities	109	% Generation Solar
50	% Management Minorities	110	Number of Environmental Fines
51	% Employees Disabled	111	Value of Environmental Fines
52	Social Supply Chain Management	112	Energy Efficiency Policy
53	Sustain Sup Guidelines Encomp ESG Area Pub Disclosed	113	Emissions Reduction Initiatives

(*Continued*)

(Continued)

Categories	Indicators	Categories	Indicators
54	Has supplier diversity program	114	Environmental Supply Chain Management
55	Requires gender divers candidates for management	115	Green Building Policy
56	Board has at least one female director	116	Waste Reduction Policy
57	Women promoted percentage of total promoted percentage	117	Sustainable Packaging
		118	Environmental Quality Management Policy
		119	New Products — Climate Change
		120	Climate Change Policy
		121	GRI Criteria Compliance
		122	Biodiversity Policy
		123	Climate Change Opportunities Discussed
		124	Risks of Climate Change Discussed
		125	Water Policy
		126	ISO 14001 Certified sites
		127	Number of sites
		128	% Sites certified
		129	Verification type
		130	Assured ESG data

References

Adams, S. and Simnett, R. (2011). Integrated reporting: An opportunity for Australia's not-for-profit sector. *Australian Accounting Review*, **21**(3): 292–301.

Al-Tuwaijri, S. A., Christensen, T. E., and Hughes Ii, K. (2004). The relations among environmental disclosure, environmental performance, and economic performance: A simultaneous equations approach. *Accounting Organizations Society*, **29**(5–6): 447–471.

Alexander, G. J. and Buchholz, R. A. (1978). Corporate social responsibility and stock market performance. *Academy of Management Journal*, **21**(3): 479–486.

Alrazi, B., De Villiers, C., and Van Staden, C. J. (2015). A comprehensive literature review on, and the construction of a framework for, environmental legitimacy, accountability and proactivity. *Journal of Cleaner Production*, **102**: 44–57.

Barnett, M. L. and Salomon, R. M. (2012). Does it pay to be really good? Addressing the shape of the relationship between social and financial performance. *Strategic Management Journal*, **33**(11): 1304–1320.

Bewley, K. and Li, Y. (2000). Disclosure of environmental information by Canadian manufacturing companies: A voluntary disclosure perspective *Advances in Environmental Accounting & Management* (pp. 201–226). Emerald Group Publishing Limited.

Bowman, E. H. and Haire, M. (1975). A strategic posture toward corporate social responsibility. *California Management Review*, **18**(2): 49–58.

Brammer, S. and Pavelin, S. (2006). Voluntary environmental disclosures by large UK companies. *Journal of Business Finance & Accounting*, **33**(7–8): 1168–1188.

Brooks, C. (2014). *Introductory econometrics for finance*, Cambridge University Press, USA.

Buhr, N. (2002). A structuration view on the initiation of environmental reports. *Critical Perspectives on Accounting*, **13**(1): 17–38.

Carroll, A. B. (1999). Corporate social responsibility: Evolution of a definitional construct. *Bus Soc*, **38**(3): 268–295.

Christensen, D. M. (2015). Corporate accountability reporting and high-profile misconduct. *Account Review*, **91**(2): 377–399.

Clarkson, P. M., Li, Y., Richardson, G. D., and Vasvari, F. P. (2008). Revisiting the relation between environmental performance and environmental disclosure: An empirical analysis. *Accounting Organizations Society*, **33**(4–5): 303–327.

Clarkson, P. M., Overell, M. B., and Chapple, L. J. A. (2011). Environmental reporting and its relation to corporate environmental performance. *Abacus*, **47**(1): 27–60.

DiMaggio, P. and Powell, W. (1983). The iron cage revisited: Institutional isomorphism and collective rationality in organizational fields. *American Sociological Review*, **48**(2): 147–160.

Ernst and Ernst (1978), Social Responsibility Disclosure: 1978 Survey, Survey of Fortune 500 Annual Reports, Ernst and Ernst, Cleveland, OH.

Freedman, M. and Wasley, C. (1990). The association between environmental performance and environmental disclosure in annual reports and 10Ks. *Advances in Public Interest Accounting*, **3**(2): 183–193.

Freeman, R. E. (1984). *Strategic Management: A Stakeholder Approach*. Pitman, Boston, MA.

Gao, L. and Zhang, J. H. (2015). Firms' earnings smoothing, corporate social responsibility, and valuation. *Journal of Corporate Finance*, **32**: 108–127.

Granger, C. W. (1969). Investigating causal relations by econometric models and cross-spectral methods. *Econometrica*, **37**(3): 424–438.

Gray, R. (2010). A re-evaluation of social, environmental and sustainability accounting: An exploration of an emerging trans-disciplinary field? *Sustainability Accounting, Management and Policy Journal*, **1**(1): 11–32.

Gray, R., Javad, M., Power, D. M., and Sinclair, C. D. (2001). Social and environmental disclosure and corporate characteristics: A research note and extension. *Journal of Business Finance and Accounting*, **28**(3–4): 327–356.

Gray, R., Kouhy, R., and Lavers, S. (1995). Constructing a research database of social and environmental reporting by UK companies. *Accounting Auditing & Accountability Journal*, **8**(2): 78–101.

Gray, R., Owen, D., and Dams, C. (1996). *Accounting and Accountability: Changes and Challenges in Corporate Social and Environmental Reporting*, Prenctice Hall Europe, Hemel Hempstead.

Guthrie, J. and Parker, L. D. (1989). Corporate social reporting: A rebuttal of legitimacy theory. *Accounting and Business Research*, **19**(76): 343–352.

Hahn, R. and Kühnen, M. (2013). Determinants of sustainability reporting: A review of results, trends, theory, and opportunities in an expanding field of research. *Journal of Cleaner Production*, **59**: 5–21.

Harjoto, M. A. and Jo, H. (2015). Legal vs. normative CSR: Differential impact on analyst dispersion, stock return volatility, cost of capital, and firm value. *Journal of Business Ethics*, **128**(1): 1–20.

Hogner, R. H. (1982). Corporate social reporting: Eight decades of development at US Steel. *Research in Corporate Performance and Policy*, **4**(1): 243–250.

Holder-Webb, L., Cohen, J. R., Nath, L., and Wood, D. (2009). The supply of corporate social responsibility disclosures among US firms. *Journal of Business Ethics*, **84**(4): 497–527.

Hooghiemstra, R. (2000). Corporate communication and impression management–new perspectives why companies engage in corporate social reporting. *Journal of Business Ethics*, **27**(1–2): 55–68.

Hrasky, S. (2011). Carbon footprints and legitimation strategies: Symbolism or action? *Accounting Auditing and Accountability Journal*, **25**(1): 174–198.

Hughes, S. B., Anderson, A., and Golden, S. (2001). Corporate environmental disclosures: Are they useful in determining environmental performance? *Journal of Accounting and Public Policy*, **20**(3): 217–240.

Ingram, R. W. and Frazier, K. B. (1980). Environmental performance and corporate disclosure. *Journal of Accounting Research*, **18**(2): 614–622.

Ioannou, I. and Serafeim, G. (2016). The consequences of mandatory corporate sustainability reporting: Evidence from four countries (Harvard Business School Research Working Paper No. 11–100, August). Boston, MS: Harvard Business School.

Jenkins, H. and Yakovleva, N. (2006). Corporate social responsibility in the mining industry: Exploring trends in social and environmental disclosure. *Journal of Cleaner Production*, **14**(3–4): 271–284.

Kinder, P. D. and Domini, A. L. (1997). Social screening: Paradigms old and new. *Journal of Investing*, **6**(4): 12–19.

Leamer, E. E. (1985). *Vector autoregressions for causal inference?* Carnegie-rochester conference series on Public Policy.

Lindblom, C. K. (1994). *The implications of organizational legitimacy for corporate social performance and disclosure*. Critical Perspectives on Accounting Conference, New York, 1994.

Lins, K. V., Servaes, H., and Tamayo, A. (2017). Social capital, trust, and firm performance: The value of corporate social responsibility during the financial crisis. *Journal of Finance*, **72**(4): 1785–1824.

Luo, L. and Tang, Q. (2014). Does voluntary carbon disclosure reflect underlying carbon performance? *Journal of Contemporary Accounting & Economics*, **10**(3): 191–205.

Lys, T., Naughton, J. P., and Wang, C. (2015). Signaling through corporate accountability reporting. *Journal of Accounting and Economics*, **60**(1): 56–72.

Mahoney, L. S., Thorne, L., Cecil, L., and LaGore, W. (2013). A research note on standalone corporate social responsibility reports: Signaling or greenwashing? *Critical Perspectives on Accounting*, **24**(4–5): 350–359.

Maltby, J. (2004). Hadfields Ltd: Its annual general meetings 1903–1939 and their relevance for contemporary corporate social reporting. *British Accounting Review*, **36**(4): 415–439.

Mathews, M. R. (1995). Social and environmental accounting: A practical demonstration of ethical concern? *Journal of Business Ethics*, **14**(8): 663–671.

Mathews, M. R. (1997). Twenty-five years of social and environmental accounting research: Is there a silver jubilee to celebrate? *Accounting Auditing & Accountability Journal*, **10**(4): 481–531.

McWilliams, A. and Siegel, D. (2001). Corporate social responsibility: A theory of the firm perspective. *Academy of Management Review*, **26**(1): 117–127.

Meyer, J. W. and Rowan, B. J. (1977). Institutionalized organizations: Formal structure as myth and ceremony. *American Journal of Sociology*, **83**: 340–363.

Nelling, E. and Webb, E. (2009). Corporate social responsibility and financial performance: The "virtuous circle" revisited. *Review of Quantitative Finance and Accounting*, **32**(2): 197–209.

Patten, D. M. (2002). The relation between environmental performance and environmental disclosure: A research note. *Accounting, Organizations and Society*, **27**(8): 763–773.

Scherer, A. G. and Palazzo, G. (2007). Toward a political conception of corporate responsibility: Business and society seen from a Habermasian perspective. *Academy of Management Review*, **32**(4): 1096–1120.

Suchman, M. C. (1995). Managing legitimacy: Strategic and institutional approaches. *Academy of Management Review*, **20**(3): 571–610.

Topping, N. (2012). How does sustainability disclosure drive behavior change? *Journal of Applied Corporate Finance*, **24**(2): 45–48.

Ullmann, A. A. (1985). Data in search of a theory: A critical examination of the relationships among social performance, social disclosure, and economic performance of US firms. *Academy of Management Review*, **10**(3): 540–557.

Verrecchia, R. E. (1983). Discretionary disclosure. *Journal of Accounting and Economics*, **5**: 179–194.

Waddock, S. A. and Graves, S. B. (1997). The corporate social performance-financial performance link. *Strategic Management Journal*, **18**: 303–319.

Whetten, D. A. and Mackey, A. (2002). A social actor conception of organizational identity and its implications for the study of organizational reputation. *Bus Soc*, **41**(4): 393–414.

Wiseman, J. (1982). An evaluation of environmental disclosures made in corporate annual reports. *Accounting, Organizations and Society*, **7**(1): 53–63.

Wood, D. J. (2010). Measuring corporate social performance: A review. *International Journal of Management Reviews*, **12**(1): 50–84.

https://doi.org/10.1142/9781786349507_0011

Chapter 11

Corporate Social Responsibility and Corporate Governance: A Cognitive Approach

Rania Béji[*,†,‡], **Ouidad Yousfi**[*,§], **and Abdelwahed Omri**[†,¶]

[*] *MRM, University of Montpellier, France*
[†] *GEF2A, ISG Tunis, University of Tunis, Tunisia*
[‡] *r.beji@montpellier-bs.com*
[§] *fouidad.yousfi@umontpellier.fr*
[¶] *abdelomri@gmail.com*

11.1 Introduction

Since the start of the new millennium, researchers have been looking for an alternative way to achieve sustainable development and better utilization of the firms' natural resources (Carvalho *et al.*, 2018). Companies have become more aware of the negative impacts of many business operations on the environment and society, specifically long-term effects. To overcome the short-term thinking, many firms have become more involved in socially and environmentally responsible strategies to improve their social, environmental and financial performances. This leads to the emergence of a more inclusive philosophy in businesses going beyond stockholders: CSR.

According to Ashrafi *et al.* (2018), CSR is a long-term approach that aims to bring a multi-dimensional added value to social, environmental, and economic spheres. Nowadays, responsible companies not only fully meet the applicable legal obligations, but also go beyond by extending their efforts to promote more socially responsible projects. For instance, companies, such as Starbucks and Orange, have become more concerned about the protection of human rights, employees' conditions, environmental issues, and communities' expectations.

According to Bocquet *et al.* (2017), Zerbini (2017), and Goyder (2003), there are two CSR strategies: (1) strategic CSR, which ties in with the highest level of commitment and implies a more comprehensive implementation of CSR within a firm and (2) responsive CSR where CSR involvement is mainly determined by external expectations and reporting standards and corresponds to the lowest level of commitment.

CSR has been considered as one of the most important challenges of corporate governance. Companies and their boards of directors have to integrate socially responsible investment into their overall approach (Jamali *et al.*, 2008). Due to the increasing attention paid to CSR, scholars have examined the various antecedents of CSR.

On the one hand, there is an extensive literature on how CSR could influence the firm's performance and risks. Some CSR-related studies have shown evidence that CSR activities lead to financial and non-financial benefits (Famiyeh, 2017; Hategan and Curea-Pitorac, 2017; Reverte *et al.*, 2016). For instance, various empirical studies have concluded that socially responsible firms tend to have better social ratings and consequently are able to reduce their financial risk (Bouslah *et al.*, 2016; Harjoto and Jo, 2015; Benlemlih *et al.*, 2014). Other studies have provided evidence on the existence of a negative correlation between CSR and financial performance (Galant and Cadez, 2017; Kim *et al.*, 2014; Lee *et al.*, 2013; Baird *et al.*, 2012). We notice, however, that several emerging evidence shows insignificant relationships between the firm involvement in CSR activities and financial performance (Javed *et al.*, 2016; Reverte *et al.*, 2016; Barnett and Salomon, 2012).

On the other hand, there is an emerging brand of the literature on the role of boards of directors in managing the firm's corporate image and shaping strategic orientations (Schepker *et al.*, 2018; Schulze *et al.*, 2001; Walsh and Seward, 1990). In fact, CSR seems to be influenced by the choices, motivations, and values of those involved in the decision-making process. Accordingly, taking into account demographic attributes of directors, such as gender, age, nationality, educational background, and multiple directorships, could be very helpful to better understand the board's dynamics and how they could influence the firm performances from different perspectives (Won-Yong *et al.*, 2019; Tasheva and Hillman, 2018; Haniffa and Cooke, 2005; Gibbins *et al.*, 1990). For instance, more diverse attributes on the board could lead to better organizational outcomes (Won-Yong *et al.*, 2019). Besides, the resource dependence (Pfeffer and Salancik, 1978), resource-based view (Wernerfelt, 1984; Barney and Tyler, 1991), social categorization (Tajfel, 1981), upper echelons (Hambrick and Mason, 1984), and agency theories provide strong arguments on how more diverse boards could lead to superior monitoring and advisory capabilities, and therefore a more strategic involvement in CSR (Aggarwal *et al.*, 2019; Tasheva and Hillman, 2018).

Along the same vein, there is an emerging literature on board organization and the way boards conduct their roles and their influence on financial and CSR performances. More specifically, the role and the composition of specialized committees such as sustainable development, CSR, nomination, and compensation committees seem to be key determinants of CSR performance and CSR-related issues. For instance, Peters and Romi (2015) and Rodrigue *et al.* (2013) argue that CSR committees could be an essential part of the corporate governance structure. They aim to guide the company towards CSR actions, as well as to promote and implement firms' CSR initiatives, which decreases CSR risks and achieve new opportunities. Moreover, Khan (2017) argues that the existence of CSR committees acts as an effective mechanism to enhance CSR performance. For instance, it can provide new incentives to CEOs to promote CSR strategies and to fulfill, therefore, sustainable development goals. Similarly, according to Hussain *et al.* (2018a), CSR committees establish the rules required to promote CSR activities. They control the impacts of companies' activities that affect or are affected by their operations on different stakeholders' groups such as environmentalists, the community, employees, consumers, and suppliers.

The main aim of the current chapter is to cover these challenging issues based on a critical state of the art. In particular, this chapter stresses how board features could be a determinant key to CSR decision-making processes. Also, it provides new perspectives to improve our understanding of the role of diversity in boards in

CSR performance. From a managerial angle, it helps to assess how the board strategies and human resources could drive the firms to achieve a better CSR performance and more competitive advantages (Galbreath, 2010; Porter and Reinhardt, 2007; Hart, 1995).

This chapter is structured as follows. First, we analyze how board composition could influence the CSR and financial performances. We distinguish between diversity in boards and diversity of boards. We identify the main features of strategic CSR and responsive CSR activities. Section 11.3 focuses on the board functioning and sheds some light on the impact of the committee's boards, specifically CSR committees, and their role on CSR strategies and CSR-related decisions. A critical analysis is provided in Section 11.4. The last section of the chapter provides concluding insights.

11.2 Corporate Social Responsibility: Could Ethics Rebuild Financial Performance?

11.2.1 *On the confounded link between social performance and financial performance*

The debate over the relationship between corporate social performance (CSP) and corporate financial performance (CFP) has dominated the empirical research during the last 40 years (Wood, 2010; Preston and O'Bannon, 1997; Wood, 1991).

The results of recent empirical studies remain very mixed (Rost and Ehrmann, 2017). More than 200 empirical studies have been reviewed in previous research (Lu *et al.*, 2014; Nelling *et al.*, 2009; Margolis *et al.*, 2007; Allouche and Laroche, 2005; Margolis and Walsh, 2003; Orlitzky *et al.*, 2003). The majority of studies show the existence of a positive association between social performance and financial performance (see among others Nelling *et al.*, 2009; Margolis *et al.*, 2007; Orlitzky *et al.*, 2003).

In fact, three theoretical models have been developed. The first model describes a positive association between CSP and CFP. The results of several meta-analyses confirm the existence of a positive relationship (Rost and Ehrmann, 2017; Endrikat *et al.*, 2014; Albertini, 2013; Dixon-Fowler *et al.*, 2013; Margolis *et al.*, 2009; Orlitzky and Swanson, 2008). This model is based essentially on the theory of social impact (Cornell and Shapiro, 1987) rooted in the stakeholder theory of Freeman (1984). It is based on the assumption that a company creates a competitive advantage through the ability to acquire resources, which leads to the establishment of a long-term synergy between the CSP and the CFP (Barney and Tyler, 1991). Furthermore, previous studies point out that meeting the needs of the different stakeholders acts as an insurance tool covering reputation risk during crises (Peloza, 2006; Schnietz and Epstein, 2005; Ziglidopoulos, 2001; Orlitzky and Benjamin, 2001). Also, Lu *et al.* (2014) reported an inconclusive overall result of the CSP-CFP link through a meta-analysis of 84 empirical studies from 2002 to 2011. They find a significant positive relationship between CSP reputation ratings and CFP. Several other studies rooted in the social impact theory and the slack resources theory, such as Waddock and Graves (1997), state that better CFP is a source of social performance. Although companies follow the normative rules of good corporate citizenship, their actual behavior may depend on the resources available. Accordingly, profitability can increase a company's ability to fund social performance projects.

The second model describes a negative link between CSP and CFP (Shane and Spicer, 1983; Freedman and Jaggi, 1982; Vance, 1975).

Based on the trade-off hypothesis and the hypothesis of the opportunism of managers, CSR decreases financial performance.

The first hypothesis states that the investments in CSR activities may worsen a firm's profitability by inhibiting optimal resource allocation, thus creating a competitive disadvantage (Kang *et al.*, 2010). The second hypothesis assumes that corporate executives can pursue their private benefits at the expense of shareholders and stakeholders' interests (Weidenbaum and Vogt, 1987, Williamson, 1985, 1967). One explanation could be that when financial performance is high, managers can seize the opportunity to increase their gains by reducing social spending (Bénabou and Tirole, 2010; McWilliams *et al.*, 2006).

The third model points out that the costs and benefits of CSR cancel each other out (McWilliams *et al.*, 1999). In fact, previous studies argue that the link between CSP and CFP may not exist (Germann *et al.*, 2015; Guiral, 2012; Goll and Rasheed, 2004; McWilliams and Siegel, 2000; Aupperle *et al.*, 1985). In fact, CSP-CFP relationship could be powered by many confounding variables, such as environmental and social regulations stringency, R&D expenses, advertising expenditures, labor market conditions, etc.

Besides, Allouche and Laroche (2005a) and Orlitzky *et al.* (2003) show the existence of a virtuous circle, where a financially successful company is prone to be able to spend more on social activities, and better CSP provides a superior long-term economic return.

CSR literature has begun to question the validity of previous studies on the relationship between CSP and CFP since many researchers have displayed discrepancies (Shahzad and Sharfmann, 2017; Crane *et al.*, 2017; Jean *et al.*, 2016; Endrikat *et al.*, 2014; Schreck, 2011; Garcia-Castro *et al.*, 2010). For instance, Crane *et al.* (2017) and Shahzad and Sharfmann (2017) point out that endogeneity could be the main reason for the ambiguity of the results, specifically in structural equation modeling (SEM) studies using regression analysis to extract causal inferences (Jean *et al.*, 2016). This may change the direction and the amplitude of CSR-CFP relationship, and distort result interpretation (Ketokivi and McIntoch, 2017; Zaefarian *et al.*, 2017).

The mixed results on CSP-CFP relationship could be explained to a large extent by the difference in terms of CSR strategies adopted by firms. In fact, CSR practices vary significantly according to the firm's degree of involvement in CSR behavior. Some firms are involved in strategic CSR: they are pioneers and want to achieve a better CSP by going beyond mandatory rules and standards. Some other firms adopt responsive CSR strategies and get involved only in what is legally expected or compliant with stakeholders' demand.

Hereafter, we analyze the differences between the two strategies and how they could shape CFP and firms' strategies.

11.2.2 *Strategic CSR versus responsive CSR*

Recently, CSR has been directly associated with firms' performance (see among others Vilanova *et al.*, 2009; Porter and Kramer, 2006). According to Amin-Chaudhry (2016) and Bagnoli and Watts (2003), firms engage in profit-maximizing CSR, this being their lead motivation. Therefore, the proponents of CSR are convinced that investment in CSR enhances the firm's long-term revenue and reputation (Manzano and Fernandez, 2016; Burke and Logsdon, 1996). In fact,

Porter and Kramer (2006) point out that when firms integrate CSR activities into their practices, this would help them in achieving competitive advantages. In consequence, according to Zerbini (2017), Bocquet *et al.* (2017), Porter and Kramer (2006), Goyder (2003), and Burke and Logsdon (1996), the following two opposite views of CSR emerge:

1. Strategic CSR, where CSR and the firm's core competencies and resources are aligned. According to Burke and Logsdon (1996), CSR becomes strategic when the company considers social and environmental issues as a high priority and goes beyond the implementation of best practices. It consists of aligning all considerate acts towards people and the natural environment in the organizational context beyond the legal minimum, with the overall objectives and actions of a company. Besides, Bansal *et al.* (2015) argue that the strategic CSR comprises activities with long time horizons and large resource commitments. It also allows the firm to achieve a distinctive position as compared to competitors (Burke and Logdson, 1981).
2. Responsive CSR, where CSR involvement is mainly determined by external expectations and reporting standards. The basic aim of firms is image-building to gain legitimacy in the eyes of their stakeholders (Ruggiero *et al.*, 2018). Porter and Kramer (2006) define responsive CSR as mitigating existing or potential adverse effects of organizational activities. Indeed, responsive CSR is, most often, associated with a limited level of commitment and more adaptive behavior.

In fact, several relevant theoretical perspectives provide an understanding of the strategic CSR (Bhattacharyya *et al.*, 2008; McAlister and Ferrell, 2002; Burke and Logsdon, 1996).

The first framework is the natural resource-based view proposed by Hart (1995). Specifically, Hart (1995) classifies product stewardship, pollution prevention and sustainable development as three interconnected strategies to support a natural resource-based view. He also points out that achieving sustainable development is the most demanding. It requires good stakeholder integration and good planning. In fact, this framework argues that by integrating sustainability and technological innovation into their strategies, firms could acquire a competitive advantage.

The second framework is the strategic CSR proposed by Burke and Logsdon (1996). In fact, the authors propose five strategy dimensions to differentiate strategic CSR from responsive CSR: (1) centrality ("the closeness of fit to the firm's mission and objectives"); (2) proactivity ("the degree to which the program is planned in anticipation of emerging social trends and the absence of crisis"); (3) voluntarism ("the scope for discretionary decision-making and the lack of externally imposed compliance requirements"); (4) visibility ("observable, recognizable credit by internal and/or external stakeholders for the firm"); (5) specificity ("the ability to capture private benefits by the firm"). Burke and Logsdon (1996) point out when firms' CSR initiatives meet these features, they are more likely to generate economic benefits. Accordingly, strategic CSR could positively impact firm financial performance.

The third framework is provided by Porter and Kramer (2002, 2006, 2011). They argue that strategic CSR goes beyond best practices and provides a competitive advantage, while responsive CSR concerns acting as a good corporate citizen and responding to stakeholders' demands. Accordingly, choosing strategic or responsive CSR produces varied benefits (Bocquet *et al.*, 2019; Martinez-Conesa *et al.*, 2017; Chang, 2015; Bocquet *et al.*, 2013). In fact, if a company combines effectively its resources and expertise with the competitive context, CSR could drive an integral part of its profitability and its competitive positioning (Porter and Kramer, 2002, 2006, 2011). The strategic CSR approach suggested by the authors aims to achieve convergence between social and economic objectives, by requiring firms to use their attributes to meet social needs. Specifically, this model encourages companies to be more selective in terms of CSR engagement.

The final theoretical framework is the stakeholder theory (Freeman *et al.*, 2004). In fact, managing complex stakeholder relationships is considered as one of the main reasons why a firm should be more concerned about CSR and the opportunities that stakeholders could bring to the business (Post, 2003). The instrumental theory of stakeholders considers CSR as a strategic driver of wealth creation (Garriga and Melé, 2004; Jones, 1995). Also, according to Jamali (2008) and Turker (2009), strategic CSR studies are aligned with the stakeholder perspective of CSR. This could serve as useful guidance for managers in their pursuit of CSR, by providing an easier explanation of stakeholder issues.

All of the above theories on the link between CSP and CFP provide strong support for the positive association between corporate governance and CSR activities.

In fact, the academic debates surrounding this approach argue that the association between good CSR policy and the appropriate behavior of board directors could improve financial profitability (Kaufman and Englander, 2011; Choi *et al.*, 2010; Pesqueux and Damak-Ayadi, 2005; Donaldson, 1999; Jones and Wicks, 1999; Preston and Donaldson, 1999; Sternberg, 1999; Freeman, 1984). For instance, according to Cuervo (2002), corporate governance is a specific mechanism where the board of directors plays a relevant role in advising management on taking the most appropriate decisions and ensuring the long-term viability of the company. Consequently, the decisions taken by the board could lead to the possible implementation of CSR policies (Ingley *et al.*, 2011) and influence, therefore, CFP.

Moreover, Choi *et al.* (2010) argue that the level of effort in terms of CSR depends on the relative importance given by the company to its interest groups. The company establishes an order of priority among them and favors those who are best positioned (Surroca *et al.*, 2010).

Thus, it becomes imperative to introduce good corporate governance recommendations as an important element of CSR.

In the next section, we analyze how governance features could be influential to different extents on the degree of involvement in CSR strategies. Specifically, we focus on board characteristics.

11.3 Corporate Governance and CSR

Research and scholarship on board diversity have been one of the most prolific topics in recent years, appearing as one of the most significant current themes in corporate governance research (Tasheva and Hillman, 2018; Jizi, 2017; Harjoto *et al.*, 2015; Hafsi and Turgut, 2013; Ben-Amar *et al.*, 2013; Mahadeo *et al.*, 2012; Bear *et al.*, 2010; Kang *et al.*, 2007).

Prior literature has focused on the role of board diversity on cognitive impacts such as creativity, innovation and the generation of new ideas (Tasheva and Hillman, 2018; Adams *et al.*, 2015; Miller and Triana, 2009; Kang *et al.*, 2007; Ruigrok *et al.*, 2007; Carter *et al.*, 2003; Robinson and Dechant, 1997). These studies show that diversity fosters creativity, innovation, and independence of thought processes. For instance, Carter *et al.* (2003) argue that board diversity allows a company to better understand her marketplace, which improves market penetration ability.

According to several studies (Mahadeo *et al.*, 2012; Kang, 2007; Erhardt *et al.*, 2003; Milliken and Martin, 1996), board diversity refers to the heterogeneity of a board across different demographic characteristics such as age, educational level, gender, and nationality, as well as the heterogeneity across different structural characteristics such as duality and independence. For instance, Mahadeo *et al.* (2012) and Carter *et al.* (2003) argue that diversity can be considered as an ethical objective, which brings to the company several advantages, such as greater creativity, a better understanding of the market, and better problem-solving. Therefore, it provides a competitive advantage for the company as well as several beneficial long-term results (Erhardt *et al.*, 2003; Siciliano, 1996).

Furthermore, Hemmingway and Maclagan (2004) argue that individuals' beliefs and values could influence board discussion related to CSR, as there is no mandatory standard for CSR (Deegan *et al.*, 2006). Also, Hambrick *et al.* (1996) and Nielsen (2010) put forward that, in high uncertainty contexts, diverse teams are more successful, while, in stable contexts, less diverse teams achieve better performance.

In fact, many theories have highlighted the effective role of board members to implement effective CSR strategies. For instance, the upper echelons theory (Hambrick and Mason, 1984) provides strong arguments on how more diverse boards could lead to superior monitoring and, thus, more strategic involvement in CSR (Aggarwal *et al.*, 2019; Tasheva and Hillman, 2018). This theory suggests that the characteristics of directors, such as age, gender, educational level, knowledge, skills, values, professional experience, and tenure, influence their interpretations of the situations they face, which affects, therefore, their strategic choices (Hambrick, 2007).

Based on agency theory (Jensen and Meckling, 1976), one of the main functions of a board of directors is to act as fiduciaries of shareholders by monitoring top management on behalf of shareholders. According to Jo and Harjoto (2011, 2012), the effectiveness of corporate governance practices is closely related to the board's composition. For instance, corporate transparency practices are determined by board directors to improve management practices and to ensure the involvement of a company in more ethical projects.

Furthermore, another important theoretical perspective for diversity is the resource dependence theory (Pfeffer and Salancik, 1978). In fact, several studies point out that board diversity allows the firm to acquire critical resources, policy advice, knowledge, and networks and to widen the range of choices when making strategic decisions (Locke and Reddy, 2015; Taljaard *et al.*, 2015; Al-Musalli *et al.*, 2012; Goodstein *et al.*, 1994; Pfeffer, 1972; Pfeffer and Salancik, 1978). According to Bear *et al.* (2010), diversity enhances the internal and external resources of the board, such as the new skills and competencies. This helps companies to better respond to stakeholders' expectations. They become more sensitive to CSR issues due to the variety of resources given by board diversity (Davis and Cobb, 2010; Susan Vinnicombe *et al.*, 2003; Pfeffer and Salancik, 1978).

11.3.1 *Board diversities: Diversity in boards and diversity of boards*

Much of the prior literature has focused on the impact of board composition on a firm's behavior (Lehn *et al.*, 2009; Linck *et al.*, 2008; Fich and Shivdasani, 2006). The level of diversity could be considered as one of the key aspects of board composition.

Prior research on board diversity distinguishes between structural and demographic diversity of boards (Aggarwal *et al.*, 2019; Jizi, 2017; Harjoto *et al.*, 2015; Hafsi and Turgut, 2013). The structural diversity of boards is linked to dissimilarities in board attributes, which are related to boards' formal structure, such as size, the non-separation between management and control functions, board independence, and board committees (Tasheva and Hillman, 2018). Demographic diversity, however, is given by the individual attributes of directors such as gender, age, nationality, educational level, educational background, multiple directorships, culture, tenure, nationality, and experience. Hafsi and Turgut (2013) highlight that the structural diversity of boards does not allow to differentiate among firms or to explain their differences, while demographic diversity does. Table 11.1 summarizes the findings from this literature review.

11.3.1.1 *Diversity of boards*

Diversity of boards stems from the structural differences that could exist between boards. It has several attributes.

First, board size is considered as a critical factor that determines the effectiveness of board oversight. However, the literature provides no consensus regarding the effect of board size on firm performance. The resource dependency theory holds that large boards are likely to have better information and more knowledge, which allows them to provide more oriented advice on strategic decisions (De Villiers *et al.*, 2011; Siciliano, 1996; Provan, 1980; Pfeffer, 1972, 1973). For instance, Kabir *et al.* (2017) put forward that large boards can increase the firm's involvement in CSR investments and have a better CSR performance as they have more resources provided for consulting and monitoring roles. Moreover, prior studies show that large boards are more likely to constitute a specific social capital and have more effective communication. Therefore, they are prone to contribute more to the efficiency of the ethical decision-making process than small boards, which could lead to a better CSR performance (Hillman *et al.*, 2001; Clarkson 1995; Pfeffer and Salancik, 1978).

For instance, the mean board size of a firm is around 9 members in European firms and US firms (Haque and Jones, 2020; Madden *et al.*, 2020).

Table 11.2 presents descriptive statistics of the study of Beji *et al.* (2020) on the association between boards' characteristics and globally CSR and specific areas of CSR, conducted on French companies listed on the SBF 120[1] index between 2003 and 2016. It uses Bloomberg, Factset IODS, and Thomson Reuters for financial and corporate governance data, and VigeoEiris[2] for CSR scores.

---

[1]The SBF120 index consists of the largest 120 capitalizations listed on the French Stock Exchange market (SBF: Société des Bourses Françaises).

[2]http://vigeo-eiris.com/fr/.

Table 11.1. Summary of studies on the impact of board diversity on CSR.

Author(s)	Aim	Method	Diversity measure	Sample and time period	Key findings
Olthuis and van den Oever (2020)	The impact of the ideological diversity on CSR performance.	Quantitative (regression)	Board Ideological diversity	Dutch firms (2014–2017)	A negative relationship between board ideological diversity and CSR performance.
Cordeiro *et al.* (2019)	The impact of ownership structure and board gender diversity on corporate environmental performance.	Quantitative (regression)	Gender diversity Ownership structure	US firms (2010–2015)	The majority of family owners and dual-class owners interact with board gender diversity to positively influence corporate environmental performance.
Harjoto *et al.* (2019)	The impact of the nationality and educational background diversity on CSR.	Quantitative (regression)	Board nationality Educational background diversity	US firms (2000–2013)	Improving director nationality diversity and educational background increase firms' social performance.
Galbreath (2018)	The impact of board gender diversity on financial and social performance.	Quantitative (regression)	Gender diversity	Australian firms (2004–2005)	Gender diversity influences firms' prosocial actions, which results in higher levels of CSR.

(*Continued*)

Table 11.1. (*Continued*)

Author(s)	Aim	Method	Diversity measure	Sample and time period	Key findings
Cuadrado-Ballesteros *et al.* (2017)	The impact of the board of directors on CSR practices.	Quantitative (regression)	Board size Board independence Diversity of gender and nationality	Firms from Canada, Denmark, Finland, France, Italy, the Netherlands, Norway, the UK, the USA, Germany, Spain, and Sweden (2003–2009)	Board size is positively associated with CSR practices; however, when the number of directors is excessively high, the CSR commitment decreases. board diversity increases the level of CSR practices.
Ben Barka and Dardour (2015)	The impact of board interlocks, director's profile on CSR.	Quantitative (regression)	Director's background Nationality diversity Age Gender Tenure Board size Ownership Duality Independence	France (2010)	Director's background and nationality diversity are the most relevant attributes to discerning firms with high CSR scores.
Boulouta (2013)	The impact of female directors on CSR.	Quantitative (regression)	Female directors	US firms (1999–2003)	More gender-diverse boards exert a stronger influence on CSR performance.
Hafsi and Turgut (2013)	The impact of board diversity on CSP.	Quantitative (regression)	Director ownership CEO duality Board independence Director tenure	US firms (2005)	A significant relationship between demographic diversity and social performance, which is moderated by the

			Director ethnicity Director age Director experience Gender diversity		structural diversity of boards. In particular, gender, and age have a significant effect on corporate social performance.
Post *et al.* (2011)	The impact of Board composition on environmental performance.	Quantitative (regression) (disclosure-proxy)	Age Gender diversity Outside directors Cultural background Educational attainment	US firms (2006–2007)	A higher proportion of outside board directors is associated with better environmental performance and higher KLD strengths scores. Firms with boards composed of three or more female directors have higher KLD strengths scores. And, boards whose directors average closer to 56 years are likely to implement environmental governance structures.
Jo and Harjoto (2011)	The impact of CG on the choice of CSR.	Quantitative (regression)	Board independence Board leadership	US firms (1993–2004)	CSR choice is positively associated with board leadership and board independence.

(*Continued*)

Table 11.1. (*Continued*)

Author(s)	Aim	Method	Diversity measure	Sample and time period	Key findings
De Villiers *et al.* (2011)	The impact of board characteristics on environmental performance.	Quantitative (regression)	Board diversity Board size Board independence Legal experts Active CEO CEO duality	US firms (2003–2004)	Larger boards, higher board independence, lower duality, more legal experts on the board, and larger representation of active CEOs on the board increase environmental performance.
Bear *et al.* (2010)	The impact of diversity of board resources and the number of women on boards on CSR ratings.	Quantitative (regression)	Gender diversity Director resource diversity: variety of experience and knowledge	US firms and international firms (2009)	Gender diversity increases CSR ratings.

Table 11.2. Descriptive statistics.

Variable	N	Mean	Std. Dev.	Min	Max
Board size	937	12.8943	3.5268	3	23
Independency	937	52.5293	21.4000	0	100
Duality	937	.33617	.4726	0	1
Gender	937	22.1631	13.9675	0	63.6363
Age	937	.6247	.1068	0	.7901
Foreign nationality	937	23.5345	21.1733	0	100
Educational-level	937	69.6529	22.2949	0	100
Business-education	937	63.2988	18.4547	14.2857	100
Multiple-directorships	937	73.30	16.7990	9	100

However, the agency theory holds that agency problems can become more severe with larger boards, specifically when they suffer from coordination and communication problems (Hermalin and Weisbach, 2003; Bushman and Smith, 2001; Yermack, 1996). In fact, it is easier for the CEO to control and influence the smaller boards as they can reach consensus more easily in comparison with large boards (Cheng, 2008).

Another board characteristic is the presence of independent directors on boards (Hermalin and Weisbach, 2003). Harjoto and Jo (2011) point out that independent directors have stronger stakeholder orientation and better management quality, which leads to a successful CSR implementation (Shaukat *et al.*, 2015; Li *et al.*, 2012; Harjoto and Jo, 2011; Ho and Wong, 2001). Also, independent directors are prone to reduce agency conflicts and to ensure effective monitoring. In the same vein, Adams and Ferreira (2009) and Walsh and Seward (1990) point out that independent directors help to monitor executives' agency behavior, as they tend to check managers' self-serving decisions and to solve attendance problems on the board.

Also, previous studies argue that the duality structure on the board is prone to decrease corporate investment in CSR. According to Jizi *et al.* (2014) and Surroca and Tribo (2008), the concentration of management and control functions in the CEO's hands is likely to have negative impacts on the engagement in CSR activities.

Furthermore, in line with agency theory, duality increases the CEO power and, therefore, CEO-chair could enjoy private benefits at the expense of CSR investments. In fact, CEOs who also act as the chair may pursue opportunistic strategies to protect their interests at the expense of shareholders (Jizi *et al.*, 2014; Firth *et al.*, 2007). They are also prone to prefer short-term financial projects and to marginalize value-enhancing projects, specifically long-term projects such as CSR ones (Surroca and Tribo, 2008; Firth *et al.*, 2007).

Focusing only on the diversity of boards does not help to fully assess the most influential factors of CSP. We need also to address its interaction with other forms of diversity, such as diversity in boards.

11.3.1.2 *Diversity in boards*

There is emerging literature, specifically on cognitive governance, on the influence of board members on CSP. It shows that, under specific conditions, the diversity of directors' profiles could be a valuable resource for the business, particularly on CSR area (see among others Conyon and He, 2017; Rodriguez Ariza *et al.*, 2016; Pucheta *et al.*, 2016; Boulouta, 2013).

Gender diversity on boards has attracted increasing interest in the last years. According to the social role theory (Eagly, 1987; Eagly and Wood, 1991), women are more likely to be oriented toward others' welfare, more concerned with personal relationships, and more socially skilled than men. They are prone to show communal qualities, while men are likely to display agentic qualities (Eagly and Wood, 1991). Moreover, in line with the cognitive moral reasoning theory (Kohlberg, 1969, 1976), women and men are different in terms of moral reasoning (Jaffee and Hyde, 2000). In fact, previous studies show that women have higher cognitive moral reasoning scores and more ethical perceptions than men (Elm *et al.*, 2001; Eynon *et al.*, 1997; Forte, 2004).

Also, consistent with the upper echelons theory (Hambrick and Mason, 1984), women and men on board display different cognitive features. They have different norms, attitudes, perspectives, experiences, and knowledge (Sundarasen *et al.*, 2016; Pelled *et al.*, 1999). For instance, prior studies show that female directors could bring to light new perspectives, which improves, therefore, the governance quality (Conyon and He, 2017; Pucheta *et al.*, 2016; Krishnan and Parsons, 2008).

Furthermore, in line with the resource dependence theory (Pfeffer and Salancik, 1978) and the social identity theory (Ashforth and Mael, 1989), female directors are more engaged in social activities and more likely to undertake non-profit activities. Besides, they could provide new perspectives and many resources to the board which improves, therefore, the governance quality (Conyon and He, 2017; Rodriguez Ariza *et al.*, 2016; Pucheta *et al.*, 2016; Boulouta, 2013; Zhang and Juelin, 2012; Post *et al.*, 2011; Nielsen and Huse, 2010; Krishnan and Parsons, 2008).

Previous studies put forward that socially responsible firms are associated with a higher percentage of female directors (Harjoto *et al.*, 2015; Hafsi and Turgut, 2013; Zhang and Juelin, 2012; Carter *et al.*, 2003). For instance, Carter *et al.* (2003) find that gender-diverse boards perform better than less diverse ones. Further, Rodriguez Ariza *et al.* (2016), Braun (2010), and Nielsen and Huse (2010) point out that female directors are prone to be more engaged in green activities and more concerned about environmental issues than men. However, low gender quotas cannot influence CSP. For example, Post *et al.* (2011) show that environmental strength scores increases in the presence of at least three female members on the board.

In fact, using a dataset of listed firms from India, China, and Russia over the period 2007–2014, Saeed and Sameer (2017) find that board gender diversity had increased in each country. Specifically, gender diversity on boards had increased from 5.6% to 10.3% in India, and 4.7–9.5% for Russia. The highest increase has been noticed in China where the percentage of female directors has more than doubled (from 7.6% to 14.4%). This could be explained by many reasons such as globalization and the proliferation of cross-border trade, communities' pressure (feminist groups), and the emerging of standards and norms for acceptable governance practices conducted by international organizations (the UN and the OECD). In addition, there is a regulatory pressure of governments all over the world to increase gender diversity. Moreover, between 2009 and 2011, the GMI Ratings' (2012) Women on Boards Survey.[3] shows low percentages of women on boards: only 12.9% in Germany, and 12.6% in the USA. In France,

[3]https://www.boardagender.org/files/GMI-Ratings-2012-Women-on-Boards-Survey-F.pdf

the parliament introduced in 2011, a gender quota law to have more gender-balanced boards: the gender quota law of Copé-Zimmermann. "French listed firms must appoint at least 20% of women to their boards by the end of 2010 and at least 40% by the end of 2017". Consequently, many firms have suddenly increased gender diversity in their boards to comply with this law.

Another dimension of diversity in boards is the director's age. Prior studies suggest that age diversity enhances CSR performance (Ferrero *et al.*, 2015; Hafsi and Turgut 2013; Post *et al.*, 2011, and Harrison and Klein, 2007). According to Ouma *et al.* (2017), age diversity could reflect directors' knowledge, experience, and openness to new ideas. Besides, Ferrero-Ferrero *et al.* (2015) argue that age diversity helps to avoid the threat of "narrow group thinking".

Regarding the influence of age diversity on CSR performance, results are mixed. Hafsi and Turgut (2013) and Kets de Vries *et al.* (1984) argue that as directors mature, their generational behavior increases, and therefore, older directors are more likely to be sensitive to society. However, other studies document a negative association between the director's age and CSR performance. For instance, Post *et al.* (2011) argue that younger directors show more concern about environmental issues and tend to be more sensitive to ethical issues.

Also, the presence of foreign directors could be a valuable resource for businesses, specifically on CSR areas (Hafsi and Turgut, 2013; Tihanyi *et al.*, 2005; Oxelheim and Randoy, 2003; Eskeland and Harrison, 2002). For instance, according to Tihanyi *et al.* (2005) and Eskeland and Harrison (2002), foreign directors are more concerned about philanthropic contributions and local social development. Most often, they have access to broader social networks, diversified and international expertise, and may prefer using technologies producing less waste and pollution. In addition, foreign directors could take advantage of their cultural values on the role of corporations in society to benefit the business (see among others Hafsi and Turgut, 2013 and Oxelheim and Randoy, 2003).

Another dimension of diversity is the educational level diversity (Rupley *et al.*, 2012; Goll and Rasheed, 2004; Hillman and Dalziel, 2003; Geletkanycz and Black, 2001). For instance, Geletkanycz and Black (2001) and Hambrick and Mason (1984) argue that directors with high educational levels contribute to the firm's success, as they have a better capacity to benefit from opportunities and to learn more about new trends. Moreover, Finkelstein *et al.* (2009), Goll and Rasheed (2004); Grimm and Smith (1991) suggest that highly educated directors are more likely to adjust their strategies in response to deregulation and other change, and display different and rational decision-making processes, in comparison with other directors. Furthermore, several studies argue that highly educated directors tend to be more concerned about environmental issues and international markets, to better understand problems that may affect the environment (Shahgholian, 2017; Ewert *et al.*, 2001; Hines *et al.*, 1987). For instance, Shahgholian (2017) put forward that highly educated directors are more likely to help the board to develop environmental activities, as they have more knowledge of environmental issues.

Previous research also shows evidence that multiple directorships could be a key determinant of the involvement in CSR activities (Rupley *et al.*, 2012). In fact, according to Rupley *et al.* (2012), directors who are sitting on multiple boards could bring to the board information about unfamiliar practices, based on their experience on other firms. Therefore, they could help the company to adopt policies of other companies, and increase environmental performance. They are more likely to have access to more information about environmental initiatives and to help to shape more proactive environmental strategies (De Villiers *et al.*, 2011). Having different experiences could increase CSR sensitivity directors with multiple directorships. Accordingly, they could show more ethical behavior and become more involved in CSR practices.

Finally, despite the fact that there is a growing number of studies on diversity in boards and diversity of boards, to the best of our knowledge, the interaction between the two forms of diversity and how it could influence CSR is not yet fully explored.

11.3.2 *CSR performance and CSR committees*

According to Godos-Díez *et al.* (2018), companies establish specialized committees to better deal with a wide range of board functions. For instance, firms concerned about being socially and environmentally responsible, create CSR committees (CSRC) in charge of CSR strategies. Several emerging papers show that companies establish CSRCs to signal their transparency in the field of CSR and their commitment towards sustainable development (Hussain *et al.*, 2018a;

Mallin and Michelon, 2011; Eccles *et al.*, 2011). These committees are prone to shape the strategies required to promote and implement firms' CSR initiatives and to decrease CSR risks (Hussain *et al.*, 2018a; Peters and Romi, 2015; Rodrigue *et al.*, 2013). Prior literature shows that the presence of CSRCs on boards increases CSR performance (Cucari *et al.*, 2018; Helfaya and Moussa, 2017; Khan, 2017; Peters and Romi, 2015; Walls *et al.*, 2012, and Mallin and Michelon, 2011). For instance, Sánchez *et al.* (2019) and Khan (2017) point out that the existence of CSRCs allows for a better understanding of the key strategic problems facing the board of directors. CSRCs aim to promote CSR strategies and provide new incentives to CEOs to get the business actively involved in CSR projects.

A survey of the literature shows that CSRCs could be also called environmental committees (Liao *et al.*, 2015; Walls *et al.*, 2012; Adnan *et al.*, 2010). Environmental committees are established to increase the firm's proactivity in handling environmental issues (Walls *et al.*, 2012). For instance, using a sample of 4,013 firm-year observations from listed companies in 13 European countries from 2002 to 2016, Haque and Jones (2020) find that 63% of the firms maintain CSR committee of the board. Moreover, Eberhardt-Toth (2017) points out that, in 2012, the proportion of firms with CSRCs on boards represents 25.42% in UK, and 16.38% in the USA.

The state of art on CSRC composition shows that most of the current studies have focused on the analysis of structural and demographic characteristics of CSRC members.

11.3.2.1 *Structural characteristics of CSRC*

Turning to the CSRC attributes, to the best of our knowledge, few studies have investigated the CSRC composition. For instance, some papers have analyzed how the presence of independent members in CSRC could affect CSR performance (Danvila del Valle *et al.*, 2013; Adams *et al.*, 2010). According to Lovdal *et al.* (1977), in order to maintain a critical view of management operations, 80% of CSRC's directors should be independent.

Also, Danvila del Valle *et al.* (2013), and Aboody and Lev (2000), independent members of CSRCs are more likely to ensure effective monitoring and better management quality, as they provide more objective feedback on firms' activities. Accordingly, their presence could prevent stakeholders from the opportunistic behavior of managers, which could enhance social performance. Another set of papers shows that the presence of independent directors could decrease CSR performance. One explanation is that independent members could suffer from a lack of information about the day-to-day operations of the business and the company's strategies (Adams *et al.*, 2010).

They may face limited-access to firm-specific information. Their decisions could be, therefore, largely based on information provided by the managers (De Villiers *et al.*, 2011; Donnelly *et al.*, 2008; Adams and Ferreira, 2007).

Another interesting feature of CSRC is CEO membership. In fact, Graham *et al.* (2017) argue that the CEO is prone to care more about profitable projects than environmental and social projects, and could, therefore, avoid risks and uncertainty related to CSR activities. Also, Danvila del Valle *et al.* (2013) point out that it could be difficult to challenge the CEO on CSR issues if he or she is a member of the CSRC, which may affect negatively CSR performance. According to the agency theory, CEOs could adopt an opportunistic behavior to increase their private benefits at the expense of shareholders. Powerful CEOs could be tempted to manipulate information on CSR investments, particularly when they are entrenched (Bebchuk *et al.*, 2011; Bartov and Mohanram, 2004; Aboody and Lev, 2000). In fact, they could influence committees' discussions by sharing their personal views in order to maximize their benefits (Clune Richard *et al.*, 2014).

Some studies have focused on the relationship between CSRC size and CSR performance. According to Golden *et al.* (2001), significant strategic changes are related to smaller board sizes. This idea can be extended to the CSRC. In fact, strong strategic changes are needed to achieve CSR performance. In a small committee, each director's decision is less likely to depend on the other director's decision. Therefore, directors make more individual effort to fulfill their responsibilities. However, in line with the resource dependence theory (Pfeffer and Salancik, 1978), more directors imply more resources and larger networks, which could be valuable to enhance CSR strategies (Mangena and Pike, 2005; DeFond and Francis, 2005). Additionally,

Bedard *et al.* (2004) put forward that a larger committee has the necessary strength, diversity of expertise, and views to ensure appropriate monitoring', which leads to higher CSR performance.

Not only has the CSRC size been discussed in the literature but also the committee functioning has been analyzed as it could matter in CSR.

For instance, previous studies show that the number of meetings organized could be considered as a proxy for directors' monitoring effort (Nurulyasmin *et al.*, 2017; Ponnu et Karthigeyan, 2010; Vafeas, 1999). According to Vafeas (1999), meetings' frequency could be a remedy to asymmetric information problems. For instance, Nurulyasmin *et al.* (2017) and Ponnu and Karthigeyan (2010) put forward that with a high-frequency meeting committee, directors could be more informed about existing and appropriate strategies. Accordingly, they become more likely to use their knowledge to help managers to enhance their decision-making process. A higher frequency of board meetings allows the directors to better carry out their duties in line with shareholders' expectations (see among others Salim *et al.*, 2016; Chou *et al.*, 2013).

Another interesting feature of CSRC functioning is directors' assiduity in CSRC meetings. In fact, Huilong *et al.* (2014) argue that directors' assiduity shows the level of commitment to the job, which could have an impact on a firm's corporate governance. This could enhance information sharing between firm management and CSRC, which may increase CSR performance.

11.3.2.2 *Demographic characteristics*

Regarding the demographic characteristics of CSRC, very little evidence has been provided. In fact, the most discussed feature is the presence of female members on CSRC.

If gender diversity is valuable in boardrooms, there is some evidence that it could be also valuable in CSRCs: Appointing more female members on CSRC committees could be another way for directors to get actively involved in CSR activities and to effectively enhance social and financial performances (Pucheta-Martínez *et al.*, 2016; Krishnan and Parsons, 2008; Carter *et al.*, 2003). For instance, Pucheta-Martínez *et al.* (2016) and Carter *et al.* (2003) point out that female directors are more prone to improve the performance of the CSRC, by increasing the creativity and innovation of the committee. In fact, they could bring important resources such as skills and constituencies and external networks (Krishnan and Parsons, 2008).

Besides, previous studies also show that the significant roles of boards are usually attributed to the more interactive and participative style of leadership by female directors (Conyon and He, 2017; Elstad and Ladegard, 2012). The firms rely more on female directors' skills, especially when the chair committee is a woman (Peterson and Philpot, 2007; Mattis, 2000).

To the best of our knowledge, there is a huge gap in the literature on the influence of other demographic features of CSRCs, such as age, the educational level, the professional experience, and ethnic diversity on CSR performance.

11.4 Discussion

The current chapter shed light on urgent and critical issues on boards and their functioning when it comes to CSR-related concerns.

From a managerial perspective, it shows the relevance of the board composition in CSR strategies. Boards have to prioritize structural and demographic diversities to bring new meaningful insights, specifically in terms of more ethical behavior. Increasing diversity could boost overall corporate visibility and develop a more proactive and comprehensive CSR strategy and orientation.

First, the emerging studies on the Board-CSR relationship show how the diversity of boards and diversity in boards could help the firm to achieve a double target: improving the governance quality and getting better social and financial performances.

In practice, there is a huge debate on the way to achieve more diverse-balanced boards. Some studies stand for the role of regulation to increase diversity in boards (for example, gender quota law). However, this could lead to the increase of multiple directorships and raises, therefore, several questions on the extent to which directors sitting on different boards could be and stay independent.

For instance, in France and Spain, many firms have appointed non-business women members to their boards to comply with the gender quota law. Some non-regulation defenders highlight the side effects of appointing non-expert profiles and its influence on the business. Accordingly, as a response, many countries, have preferred to rely on recommendations and voluntary quotas, instead of laws to increase the involvement of minorities in top management positions.

Besides, when minority groups are not supported in their choices, this could worsen the board dynamics, and slowed therefore, the decision-making process. For instance, Erkut *et al.* (2008) show that when only one or two female members are appointed to the board, they cannot influence the boards' decisions. A critical number of female board members is needed in order to exert a positive influence on the boards' decisions.

Furthermore, women are more likely than men to serve in precarious management positions and continue to be underrepresented in leadership positions. This is explained by the "glass ceiling" that prevents women from gaining access to such positions (Singh and Vinnicombe, 2004; Arfken *et al.*, 2004; Maume, 2004) and the "glass escalator", which means that men are accelerated through the organizational ranks (Maume, 1999; Williams, 1992).

Also, the current chapter shows that most of the existing studies on Board-CSR relationship are more likely to explore one direction of this association, according to which governance features, and therefore CSR committees, help to achieve higher social and financial performances. However, the question of the potential reversal effect of financial performance on governance quality, more specifically on the effectiveness of CSR committees and their compositions, is not yet analyzed. To the best of our knowledge, no studies have examined how financial performance could influence board composition and functioning.

Finally, identifying the timely role of CSR committees in improving CSR strategies should not be taken without consideration of the role of other board committees, specifically nomination committees (NC) that are in charge of selecting new board member candidates. NC have definitely influential effects on diversity in (and of) boards and therefore on CSRC composition. To the best of our knowledge, studies on NC role and composition are still scarce.

Shedding more light on the cognitive and individual characteristics of committee members is valuable to understand the board dynamics and how they influence firms' strategies (see Fig. 11.1).

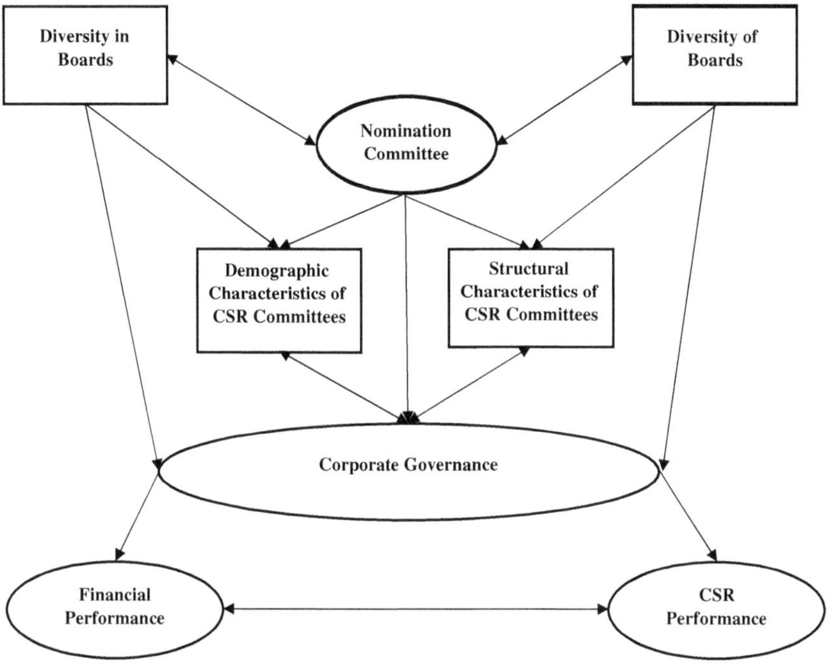

Fig. 11.1. Theoretical model.

11.5 Conclusion

Companies have become more concerned about the protection of human rights, employees' conditions, environmental issues, and communities' expectations. They manage their business according to specific ethical standards. Enhancing governance quality is also among the challenging issues in CSR. The main aim of the current chapter is to put forward the influence of governance features on CSR. It covers these challenging issues.

First, the results of recent empirical studies remain very mixed, and the majority of these studies show the existence of a positive association between social performance and financial performance (Rost and Ehrmann, 2017; Endrikat *et al.*, 2014; Albertini, 2013; Dixon-Fowler *et al.*, 2013; Margolis *et al.*, 2009; Orlitzky and Swanson, 2008). This could be explained by the difference in terms of CSR strategies adopted by firms.

Second, previous studies show that strategic CSR is a source of original and pioneering actions, where interactions with stakeholders are the key to sustainable performance. Strategic CSR aims to create resources and capabilities that can lead to superior economic performance. While responsive CSR reflects more adaptive behavior. Companies try to gain legitimacy in the eyes of the firm's stakeholders to appear socially responsible (Ruggiero *et al.*, 2018).

Third, there is an emerging literature on how board diversity could be an advantage for the decision-making process and the key to strategic CSR (Bocquet *et al.*, 2019). This heterogeneity can promote diversified exchanges and relationships, offer new perspectives, and influence the board's functioning, which in turn can influence its performance (see among others Isidro and Sobral, 2015; Aggarwal and Dow, 2012). Specifically, taking into account structural characteristics of boards such as size, duality structure, and board independence, and director's profile such as gender, age, foreign directors, and educational level, could be very helpful to better understand how boards of directors influence firm performance from different perspectives (Haniffa and Cooke, 2005; Gibbins *et al.*, 1990).

Finally, CSR committees have attracted increasing interest (Khan, 2017; Peters and Romi, 2015; Rodrigue *et al.*, 2013). Specifically, previous studies show that the presence of CSR committees acts as an effective mechanism to enhance CSR performance (Khan, 2017). They could help to promote and implement firms' CSR initiatives, which decreases CSR risks and achieve new opportunities (Perters and Romi, 2015; Rodrigue *et al.*, 2013).

In future research, it could be interesting to focus on the financial and strategic risk-taking in a responsive or strategic form of CSR.

References

Aboody, D. and Lev, B. (2000). Information asymmetry, R&D, and insider gains. *Journal of Finance*, **55**: 2747–2766.

Adams, R. and Ferreira, D. (2007). A theory of friendly boards. *Journal of Finance*, **62**: 217–250.

Adams, R., Hermalin, B., and Weisbach, M. (2010). The role of boards of directors in corporate governance: A conceptual framework and survey. *Journal of Economic Literature*, **48**: 58–107.

Adnan, S. M., Van Staden, C., and Hay, D. (2010). Do culture and governance structure influence CSR reporting quality: Evidence from China, India, Malaysia and the United Kingdom. *In Proceedings of the 6th Asia Pacific Interdisciplinary Research in Accounting Conference*, Sydney, Australia, 12–13 July 2010.

Aggarwal, R., Jindal, V., and Seth, R. (2019). Board diversity and firm performance: the role of business group affiliation. *International Business Review*, **28**(6): 1–17.

Al-Musalli, M. A. K. and Ismail, K. N. I. K. (2012). Intellectual capital performance and board characteristics of GCC banks. *Procedia Economics and Finance*, **2**: 219–226.

Albertini, E. (2013). Does environmental management improve financial performance? A meta-analytical review. *Organization and Environment*, **26**: 431–457.

Allouche, J. and Laroche, P. (2005). A meta-analytical investigation of the relationship between corporate social and financial performance. *Revue Française de Gestion des Ressources Humaines*, **57**: 18–40.

Amin-Chaudhry, A. (2016). Corporate social responsibility-from a mere concept to an expected business practice. *Social Responsibility Journal*, **12**(1): 190–207.

Arfken, D. E., Bellar, S. L., and Helms, M. M. (2004). The ultimate glass ceiling revisited: The presence of women on corporate boards. *Journal of Business Ethics*, **50**(2): 177–186.

Ashforth, B. E. and Mael, F. (1989). Social identity theory and the organization. *Academy of Management Review*, **14**(1): 20–39.

Ashrafi, M., Adams, M., Walker, T. R., and Magnan, G. (2018). How corporate social responsibility can be integrated into corporate sustainability: a theoretical review of their relationships. *International Journal of Sustainable Development and World Ecology*, **25**: 672–682.

Bagnoli, M. and Watts, S. (2003). Selling to socially responsible consumers: Competition and the private provision of public goods. *Journal of Economics and Management Strategy*, **12**: 419–445.

Bansal, P., Jiang, G. F., and Jung, J. C. (2015). Managing responsibly in tough economic times: Strategic and tactical CSR during the 2008–2009 global recession. *Long Range Plan*, **48**: 69–79.

Barney, J. B. and Tyler, B. (1991). *The attributes of top management teams and sustained competitive advantage*. In M. Lawless and Gomez-Mejia (Eds.), Managing the high technology firm: JAI Press, in press.

Bartov, E. and Mohanram, P. (2004). Private information, earnings manipulations and executive stock–option exercises. *The Accounting Review*, **79**: 889–920.

Bear, S., Rahman, N., and Post, C. (2010). The impact of board diversity and gender composition on corporate social responsibility and firm reputation. *Journal of Business Ethics*, **97**(2): 207–221.

Bebchuk, L., Cremers, M., and Peyer, U. (2011). The CEO pay slice. *Journal of Financial Economics*, **102**: 199–221.

Bedard, J., Chtourou, S. M., and Courteau, L. (2004). The effect of audit committee expertise, independence, and activity on aggressive earnings management. *Auditing: A Journal of Practice and Theory*, **23**(2): 13–35.

Beji, R., Yousfi, O., Loukil, N., and Omri, A. (2020). Board diversity and corporate social responsibility: Empirical evidence from france. *Journal of Business Ethics*, 1–23. DOI: https://doi.org/10.1007/s10551-020-04522-4.

Ben-Amar, W., Francoeur, C., Hafsi, T., and Labelle, R. (2013). What makes better boards? A closer look at diversity and ownership. *British Journal of Management*, **24**(1): 85–101.

Ben Barka, H. and Dardour, A. (2015). Investigating the relationship between director's profile, board interlocks and corporate social responsibility. *Management Decision*, **53**: 553–570.

Bhattacharyya, S. S., Sahay, A., Arora, A. P., and Chaturvedi, A. (2008). A toolkit for designing firm level strategic corporate social responsibility (CSR) initiatives. *Social Responsibility Journal*, **4**(3): 265–282.

Bocquet, R., Le Bas, C., Mothe, C., and Poussing, N. (2013). Are firms with different CSR profiles equally innovative? An empirical analysis with survey data. *European Management Journal*, **31**(6): 642–654.

Bocquet, R., Le Bas, C., Mothe, C., and Poussing, N. (2017). CSR, innovation, and firm performance in sluggish growth contexts: A firm-level empirical analysis. *Journal of Business Ethics*, **146**(1): 241–254.

Bocquet, R., Le Bas, C., Mothe, C., and Poussing, N. (2019). Strategic CSR for innovation in SMEs: Does diversity matter? *Long Range Planning*, **52**(6): 101913.

Braun, P. (2010). Going green: women entrepreneurs and the environment. *International Journal of Gender and Entrepreneurship*, **2**(3): 245–259.

Burke, L. and Logsdon, J. M. (1996). How corporate social responsibility pays off. *Long Range Planning*, **29**(4): 495–502.

Carter, D. A., Simkins, B. J., and Simpson, W. G. (2003). Corporate governance, board diversity, and firm value. *Financial Review*, **38**(1): 33–53.

Carvalho, F., Santos, G., and Gonçalves, J. (2018). The disclosure of information on sustainable development on the corporate website of the certified portuguese organizations. *International Journal for Quality Research*, **12**(1): 253–276.

Chang, C. H. (2015). Proactive and responsive corporate social responsibility: Antecedent and consequence. *Management Decision*, **53**(2): 451–468.

Choi, J., Kwak, Y., and Choe, C. (2010). Corporate social responsibility and corporate financial performance: Evidence from Korea. *Australian Journal of Management*, **35**(3): 291–311.

Chou, H. I., Chung, H., and Yin, X. (2013). Attendance of board meetings and company performance: Evidence from Taiwan. *Journal of Banking and Finance*, **37**(11): 4157–4171.

Clune, R., Hermanson, R. D., Tompkins, J., and Shelly, Y. Z. (2014). The nominating committee process: A qualitative examination of board independence and formalization. *Contemporary Accounting Research*, **31**(3): 748–786.

Conyon, M. J. and He, L. (2017). Firm performance and boardroom gender diversity: A quantile regression approach. *Journal of Business Research*, **79**: 198–211.

Cordeiro, J. J., Profumo, G., and Tutore, I. (2019). Board gender diversity and corporate environmental performance: The moderating role of family and dual-class majority ownership structures. *Business Strategy and the Environment*, **29**(3): 1127–1144.

Crane, A., Henriques, I., Husted, B. W., and Matten, D. (2017). Measuring corporate social responsibility and impact: Enhancing quantitative research design and methods in business and society research. *Business and Society*, **56**(6): 787–795.

Cuadrado-Ballesteros, B., García-Sánchez, I. M., and Martínez-Ferrero, J. (2017). The impact of board structure on CSR practices on the international scale. *European Journal of International Management*, **11**(6): 633–659.

Cucari, N., Esposito De Falco, S., and Orlando, B. (2018). Diversity of board of directors and environmental social governance: Evidence from Italian listed companies. *Corporate Social Responsibility and Environmental Management*, **25**: 250–266.

Cuervo, A. (2002). Corporate governance mechanisms: A plea for less code of good governance and more market control. *Corporate Governance: An International Review*, **10**(2): 84–93.

Danvila del Valle, I., Diez Esteban, J. M., and Lopez de Foronda, O. (2013). *Corporate social responsibility and sustainability committee inside the board.* Working paper SSRN no. 2260382, University of Burgos, Burgos.

Davis, G. F. and Cobb, J. A. (2010). Corporations and economic inequality around the world: The paradox of hierarchy. *Research in Organizational Behavior*, **30**: 35–53.

Deegan, C. and Blomquist, C. (2006). Stakeholder influence on corporate reporting: An exploration of the interaction between WWF-Australia and the Australian minerals industry. *Accounting, Organizations and Society*, **31**(4–5): 343–372.

DeFond, M. and J. Francis. (2005). Audit research after Sarbanes-Oxley. *Auditing: A Journal of Practice and Theory*, **24**: 5–30.

De Villiers, C., Naiker, V., and Van Staden, C. J. (2011). The effect of board characteristics on firm environmental performance. *Journal of Management*, **37**(6): 1636–1663.

Dixon–Fowler, H. R., Slater, D. J., Johnson, J. L., Ellstrand, A. E., and Romi, A. M. (2013). Beyond "does it pay to be green?" A meta-analysis of moderators of the CEP-CFP relationship. *Journal of Business Ethics*, **112**(2): 353–366.

Donaldson, L. (1999). Making stakeholder theory whole. *Academic Management Review*, **24**(2): 237–241.

Donnelly, R. and Mulcahy, M. (2008). Board structure, ownership, and voluntary disclosure in Ireland. *Corporate Governance: An International Review*, **16**(5): 416–429.

Eagly, A. H. (1987). *Sex Differences in Social Behaviour: A Social-Role Interpretation*. Erlbaum, Hillsdale, NJ.

Eagly, A. H. and Wood, W. (1991). Explaining sex differences in social behavior: A meta-analytic perspective. *Personality and Social Psychology Bulletin*, **17**(3): 306–315.

Eccles, R.G., Ioannou, I., and Serafeim, G. (2011). *The impact of a corporate culture of sustainability on corporate behavior and performance*, Working paper SSRN no. 1964011, Harvard Business School, Allston, MA.

Eberhardt-Toth, E. (2017). Who should be on a board corporate social responsibility committee? *Journal of Cleaner Production*, **140**: 1926–1935.

Erkut, S., Kramer, V. W., and Konrad, A. M. (2008). 18. Critical mass: does the numberof women on a corporate board make a difference. *Women on Corporate Boards of Directors: International Research and Practice*, 222.

Elm, D. R., Kennedy, E. J., and Lawton, L. (2001). Determinants of moral reasoning: Sex role orientation, gender, and academic factors. *Business and Society*, **40**(3): 241–265.

Elstad, B. and Ladegard, G. (2012). Women on corporate boards: Key influencers or tokens? *Journal of Management and Governance*, **16**(4): 595–615.

Endrikat, J., Guenther, E., and Hoppe, H. (2014). Making sense of conflicting empirical findings: A meta-analytic review of the relationship between corporate environmental and financial performance. *European Management Journal*, **32**(5): 735–751.

Erhardt, N. L., Werbel, J. D., and Shrader, C. B. (2003). Board of director diversity and firm financial performance. *Corporate Governance: An International Review*, **11**(2): 102–111.

Eskeland, G. A. and Harrison, A. E. (2002). *Moving to Greener Pastures? Multinationals and the Pollution Haven Hypothesis*, National Bureau of Economic Research: Cambridge, MA, USA.

Ewert, A. and Baker, D. (2001). Standing for Where You Sit: An exploratory analysis of the relationship between academic major and environment beliefs. *Environment and Behavior*, **33**(5): 687–707.

Eynon, G., Hills, N. T., and Stevens, K. T. (1997). Factors that influence the moral reasoning abilities of accountants: Implications for universities and the profession. *Journal of Business Ethics*, **16**(12–13): 1297–1309.

Famiyeh, S. (2017). Corporate social responsibility and firm's performance: Empirical evidence. *Social Responsibility Journal*, **13**(2): 390–406.

Ferrero-Ferrero, I., Fernández-Izquierdo, M. Á., and Muñoz-Torres, M. J. (2013). Integrating sustainability into corporate governance: An empirical study on board diversity. *Corporate Social Responsibility and Environmental Management*, **22**: 193–207.

Ferrero-Ferrero, I., Fernández-Izquierdo, M. Á., and Muñoz-Torres, M. J. (2015). Board diversity: An empirical study in the board of Directors. *Cybernetics and Systems*, **46**(3–4): 249–270.

Fich, E. M. and Shivdasani, A. (2006). Are busy boards effective monitors? *The Journal of Finance*, **61**(2): 689–724.

Finkelstein, S., Hambrick, D. C., and Cannella, A. A. (2009). *Strategic Leadership: Theory and Research on Executives, Top Management Teams and Boards*, Oxford University Press, Oxford.

Firth, M., Fung, P. M., and Rui, O. M. (2007). Ownership, two–tier board structure, and the informativeness of earnings–Evidence from China. *Journal of Accounting and Public Policy*, **26**(4): 463–496.

Forte, A. (2004). Business ethics: A study of the moral reasoning of selected business managers and the influence of organizational ethical climate. *Journal of Business Ethics*, **51**(2): 167–173.

Freeman, R. (1984). *Strategic management: A stakeholder approach*, Pitman Publishing Inc., Massachusetts.

Freeman, R. E., Wicks, A. C., and Parmar, B. (2004). Stakeholder theory and the corporate objective revisited. *Organization Science*, **15**(3): 364–369.

Galant, A. and Cadez, S. (2017). Corporate social responsibility and financial performance relationship: A review of measurement approaches. *Economic Research-Ekonomska Istraživanja*, **30**: 676–693.

Galbreath, J. (2010). Corporate governance practices that address climate change: An exploratory study. *Business Strategy and the Environment*, **19**(5): 335–350.

Galbreath, J. (2018). Is board gender diversity linked to financial performance? The mediating mechanism of CSR. *Business and Society*, **57**(5): 863–889.

Garcia-Castro, R., Arino, M. A., and Canela, M. A. (2010). Does social performance really lead to financial performance? Accounting for endogeneity. *Journal of Business Ethics*, **92**(1):107–126.

Garriga, E. and Melé, D. (2004). Corporate social responsibility theories: Mapping the territory. *Journal of Business Ethics*, **53**: 51–71.

Geletkanycz, M. A. and Black, S. S. (2001). Bound by the past? Experience-based effects on commitment to the strategic status quo. *Journal of Management*, **27**: 3–21.

Godos-Díez, J. L., Cabeza-García, L., and Fernández-González, C. (2018). Relationship between Corporate Social Responsibility (CSR) and Internationalisation Strategies: A descriptive study in the spanish context. *Administrative Sciences*, **8**: 1–57.

Golden, B. R. and Zajac, Z. J. (2001). When will boards influence strategy? Inclination × power = strategic change. *Strategic Management Journal*, **22**: 1087–1111.

Goll, I. and Rasheed, A. A. (2004). The moderating effect of environmental munificence and dynamism on the relationship between discretionary social responsibility and firm performance. *Journal of Business Ethics*, **49**(1): 41–54.

Goodstein, J., Gautam, K., and Boeker, W. (1994). The effects of board size and diversity on strategic change. *Strategic Management Journal*, **15**(3): 241–250.

Goyder, M. (2003). *Redefining CSR: From the Rhetoric of Accountability to the Reality of Earning Trust*, Tomorrow's Company, London.

Graham, J. R., Kim, H., and Leary, M. T. (2017). CEO power and board dynamics. *SSRN Electronic Journal.*

Hafsi, T. and Turgut, G. (2013). Boardroom diversity and its effect on social performance: Conceptualization and empirical evidence. *Journal of Business Ethics*, **103**(3): 385–402.

Hambrick, D. C. and Mason, P. A. (1984). Upper echelons: The organization as a reflection of its top managers. *Academy of Management Review*, **9**: 193–206.

Hambrick, D. C., Cho, T. S., and Chen, M. J. (1996). The influence of top management team heterogeneity on firms' competitive moves. *Administrative Science Quarterly*, 659–684.

Haque, F. and Jones, M. J. (2020). European firms' corporate biodiversity disclosures and board gender diversity from 2002 to 2016. *The British Accounting Review*, **52**(2): 100893.

Harjoto, M., Laksmana, I., and Lee, R. (2015). Board diversity and corporate social responsibility. *Journal of Business Ethics*, **132**(4): 641–660.

Harrison, D. A. and Klein, K. J. (2007). What's the difference? Diversity constructs as separation, variety, or disparity in organizations. *Academy of Management Review*, **32**(4); 1199–1228.

Hart, S. L. (1995). A natural-resource-based view of the firm. *Academy of Management Review*, **20**(4): 986–1014.

Hategan, C. D. and Curea-Pitorac, R. I. (2017). Testing the correlations between corporate giving, performance and company value. *Sustainability*, **9**: 1210.

Helfaya, A. and Moussa T. (2017). Do board's corporate social responsibility strategy and orientation influence environmental sustainability disclosure? UK Evidence, *Business Strategy and the Environment*, **26**(8): 1061–1077.

Hillman, A. J. and Dalziel, T. (2003). Boards of directors and firm performance: Integrating agency and resource dependence perspectives. *Academy of Management Review*, **28**(3): 383–396.

Hines, J. and Hungerford, H. (1987). Analysis and synthesis of research on responsible environmental behavior: A meta–analysis. *Journal of Environmental Education*, **18**(2): 1–8.

Huilong, L., Hong, W., and Liansheng, W. (2014). Removing vacant chairs: Does independent directors' attendance at board meetings matter? *Journal of Business Ethics*, **133**(2): 375–393.

Hussain, N., Rigoni, U., and Orij, R. P. (2018). Corporate governance and sustainability performance: Analysis of triple bottom line performance. *Journal of Business Ethics*, **149**: 411–432.

Ingley, C., Mueller, J., and Cocks, G. (2011). The financial crisis, investor activists and corporate strategy: Will this mean shareholders in the boardroom? *Journal of Management and Governance*, **15**(4): 557–587.

Jaffee, S. and Hyde, J. S. (2000). Gender differences in moral orientation: A meta–analysis. *Psychological Bulletin*, **126**(5): 703–726.

Jamali, D., Safieddine, A. M., and Rabbath, M. (2008). Corporate governance and corporate social responsibility: Synergies and interrelationships. *Corporate Governance: An International Review*, **16**(5): 443–459.

Jean, R.-J. B., Deng, Z., Kim, D., and Yuan, X. (2016). Assessing endogeneity issues in international marketing research. *International Marketing Review*, **33**(3): 483–512.

Jensen, M. C. and Meckling, W. H. (1976). Theory of the firm: Managerial behavior, agency costs and ownership structure. *Journal of Financial Economics*, **3**(4): 305–360.

Jizi, M. (2017). The influence of board composition on sustainable development disclosure. *Business Strategy Environment*, **26**: 640–655.

Jizi, M. I., Salama, A., Dixon, R., and Stratling, R. (2014). Corporate governance and corporate social responsibility disclosure: Evidence from the US banking sector. *Journal of Business Ethics*, **125**(4): 601–615.

Jo, H. and Harjoto, M. A. (2011). Corporate governance and firm value: The impact of corporate social responsibility. *Journal of Business Ethics*, **103**: 351–383.

Jones, T. M. (1995). Instrumental stakeholder theory: A synthesis of ethics and economics. *Academy of Management Review*, **20**(2): 404–437.

Jones, T. M. and Wicks, A. C. (1999). Convergent stakeholder theory. *Academic Management Review*, **24**(2): 206–221.

Kang, H., Cheng, M., and Gray, S. J. (2007). Corporate governance and board composition: Diversity and independence of Australian boards. *Corporate Governance: An International Review*, **15**(2): 194–207.

Kang, K. H., Lee, S., and Huh, C. (2010). Impacts of positive and negative corporate social responsibility activities on company performance in the hospitality industry. *International Journal of Hospitality Management*, **29**(1): 72–82.

Kaufman, A. and Englander, E. (2011). Behavioral economics, federalism and the triumph of stakeholder theory. *Journal of Business Ethics*, **102**(2): 421–438.

Ketokivi, M. and McIntosh, C. N. (2017). Addressing the endogeneity dilemma in operations management research: Theoretical, empirical, and pragmatic considerations. *Journal of Operations Management*, **52**: 1–14.

Kets de Vries, M. and Miller, D. (1984). *The Neurotic Organization: Diagnosing and Changing Counterproductive Styles of Management*, Jossey Bass Business and Management Series.

Kim, Y., Li, H. and Li, S. (2014). Corporate social responsibility and stock price crash risk. *Journal of Banking and Finance*, **43**(1): 1–13.

Kohl, S. (1976). *Working Together: Women and Family in Southwestern Saskatchewan*, Holt, Rinehart and Winston of Canada, Toronto.

Kohlberg, L. (1969). *Stage and sequence: The cognitive development approach to socialization*. In D. A. Goslin (Ed.). Handbook of socialization theory, Chicago, IL, Rand McNally, pp. 347–480.

Krishnan, G. V. and Parsons, L. M. (2008). Getting to the bottom line: An exploration of gender and earnings quality. *Journal of Business Ethics*, **78**(1–2): 65–76.

Lee, E. M., Park, S. Y., and Lee, H. J. (2013). Employee perception of CSR activities: Its antecedents and consequences. *Journal of Business Research*, **66**: 1716–1724.

Lehn, K. M., Patro, S., and Zhao, M. (2009). Determinants of the size and composition of US corporate boards: 1935–2000. *Financial Management*, **38**(4): 747–780.

Liao, L., Luo, L., and Tang, Q. (2015). Gender diversity, board independence, environmental committee and greenhouse gas disclosure. *British Accounting Review*, **47**: 409–424.

Linck, J. S., Netter, J. M., and Yang, T. (2008). The determinants of board structure. *Journal of Financial Economics*, **87**(2): 308–328.

Lovdal, M. L., Bauer, R. A., and Treverton, N. H. (1977). Public responsibility committees of the board. *Harvard Business Review*, **55**(3): 40–181.

Lu, W., Chau, K., Wang, H., and Pan, W. (2014). A decades debate on the nexus between corporate social and corporate financial performance: A critical review of empirical studies. *Journal of Cleaner Production*, **79**: 195–206.

Madden, L., McMillan, A., and Harris, O. (2020). Drivers of selectivity in family firms: Understanding the impact of age and ownership on CSR. *Journal of Family Business Strategy*, 100335.

Mahadeo, J. D., Soobaroyen, T., and Hanuman, V. (2012). Board composition and financial performance: Uncovering the effects of diversity in an emerging economy. *Journal of Business Ethics*, **105**(3): 375–388.

Mallin, C. and Michelon, G. (2011). Board reputation attributes and corporate social performance: An empirical investigation of the US Best Corporate Citizens. *Accounting and Business Research*, **41**(2): 119–144.

Mangena, M. and Pike, R. (2005). The effect of audit committee shareholding, financial expertise and size on interim financial disclosures. *Accounting and Business Research*, **35**(4): 327–49.

Margolis, J. D., Elfenbein, H. A., and Walsh, J. P. (2007). *Does it pay to be good? What a meta-analysis of CSP and CFP can (and cannot) tell us*, In: 67th Meeting of the Academy of Management, Philadelphia, Pennsylvania.

Martinez-Conesa, I., Soto-Acosta, P., and Palacios-Manzano, M. (2017). Corporate social responsibility and its effect on innovation and firm performance: an empirical research in SMEs. *Journal of Cleaner Production*, **142**(4): 2374–2383.

Mattis, M. (2000). Women corporate directors in the United States. In Burke, R. and Mattis, M. (Eds.) *Women on Corporate Boards of Directors: International Challenges and Opportunities*, pp. 43–55, Kluwer Academic Publishers, Dordrecht, The Netherlands.

Maume Jr, D. J. (1999). Glass ceilings and glass escalators: Occupational segregation and race and sex differences in managerial promotions. *Work and Occupations*, **26**(4): 483–509.

Maume Jr, D. J. (2004). Is the glass ceiling a unique form of inequality? Evidence from a random-effects model of managerial attainment. *Work and Occupations*, **31**(2): 250–274.

McAlister, D. and Ferrell, L. (2002). The role of strategic corporate philanthropy in marketing strategy. *European Journal of Marketing*, **36**(5): 689–708.

Milliken, F. J. and Martins, L. L. (1996). Searching for common threads: Understanding the multiple effects of diversity in organizational groups. *Academy of Management Review*, **21**: 402–433.

Nekhili, M., Nagati, H., Chtioui, T., and Nekhili, A. (2017). Gender-diverse board and the relevance of voluntary CSR reporting. *International Review of Financial Analysis*, **50**: 81–100.

Nelling, E. and Webb, E. (2009). Corporate social responsibility and financial performance: the "virtuous circle" revisited. *Review of Quantitative Finance and Accounting*, **32**(2): 197–209.

Nielsen, S. and Huse, M. (2010). The contribution of women on boards of directors: Going beyond the surface. *Corporate Governance: An International Review*, **18**(2): 136–148.

Nurulyasmin, A., Ju, B., Afzalur, R., and Jeff, G. (2017). Board Independence and Corporate Social Responsibility (CSR) reporting in Malaysia. *Australasian Accounting, Business and Finance Journal*, **11**(2): 61–85.

Olthuis, B. R. and van den Oever, K. F. (2020). The board of directors and CSR: How does ideological diversity on the board impact CSR? *Journal of Cleaner Production*, **251**: 119532.

Orlitzky, M., Schmidt, F. L., and Rynes, S. L. (2003). Corporate social and financial performance: a meta-analysis. *Organization Studies*, **24**(3): 403–441.

Ouma, C. A. and Webi, R. Y. (2017). Effect of age diversity of board members on performance of non–governmental organizations in Kenya. *International Journal of Novel Research in Marketing Management and Economics*, **4**(2): 101–123.

Oxelheim, L. and Randoy, T. (2003). The impact of foreign board membership on firm value. *Journal of Banking and Finance*, **27**(12): 2369–2392.

Pelled, L. H., Eisenhardt, K. M., and Xin, K. R. (1999). Exploring the black box: An analysis of work group diversity, conflict and performance. *Administrative Science Quarterly*, **44**(1): 1–28.

Pesqueux, Y. and Damak-Ayadi, S. (2005). Stakeholder theory in perspective. *Corporate Governance International Review*, **5**(2): 5–21.

Peters, G. and Romi, A. (2015). The association between sustainability governance characteristics and the assurance of corporate sustainability reports. *Auditing: A Journal of Practice and Theory*, **34**(1): 163–198.

Peterson, C. A. and Philpot, J. (2007). Women's roles on U.S. Fortune 500 boards: Director expertise and committee memberships. *Journal of Business Ethics*, **72**: 177–196.

Peterson, C. A., Philpot, J., and O'Shaughnessy, K. C. (2007). African American diversity in the boardrooms of the US Fortune 500: Director presence, expertise and committee membership. *Corporate Governance: An International Review*, **15**: 558–575.

Pfeffer, J. and Salancik, G. R. (1978). *The External Control of Organisations: A Resource Dependence Perspective*, Harper and Rob Publishers, New York, NY.

Ponnu, C. and Karthigeyan, R. (2010). Board independence and corporate performance: Evidence from Malaysia. *African Journal of Business Management*, **4**(6): 858–868.

Porter, M. E. and Kramer, M. R. (2002). The competitive advantage of corporate philanthropy. *Harvard Business Review*, **80**(12): 56–68.

Porter, M. E. and Kramer, M. R. (2006). The Link Between Competitive Advantage and Corporate Social Responsibility. *Harvard Business Review*, **12**: 78–92.

Porter, M. E. and Kramer, M. R. (2011). Creating shared value. *Harvard Business Review*, **89**(1/2): 62–77.

Porter, M. E. and Reinhardt, F. L. (2007). A strategic approach to climate change. *Harvard Business Review*, **85**(10): 22–23.

Post, C., Rahman, N., and Rubow, E. (2011). Green governance: Boards of directors' composition and environmental corporate social responsibility. *Business and Society*, **50**(1): 189–223.

Post, F. R. (2003). The social responsibility of management: A critique of the shareholder paradigm and defense of stakeholder primacy. *American Journal of Business*, **18**(2): 57–61.

Preston, L. E. and Donaldson, T. (1999). Stakeholder management and organizational wealth. *Academic Management Review*, **24**(4): 619–625.

Preston, L. E. and O'Bannon, D. P. (1997). The corporate social-financial performance relationship. *Business Society*, **36**: 419–429.

Pucheta-Martínez, M. C., Bel-Oms, I., and Olcina-Sempere, G. (2016). Corporate governance, female directors and quality of financial information. *Business Ethics: A European Review*, **25**(4): 363–385.

Reverte, C., Gomez-Melero, E., and Cegarra-Navarro, J. G. (2016). The influence of corporate social responsibility practices on organizational performance: evidence from eco–responsible Spanish firms. *Journal of Cleaner Production*, **112**: 2870–2884.

Rodrigue, M., Magnan, and Cho, C. H. (2013). Is environmental governance substantive or symbolic? An empirical investigation. *Journal of Business Ethics*, **114**: 107–129.

Rodriguez-Ariza, L., Martínez-Ferrero, J., and Bermejo-Sánchez, M. (2016). Consequences of earnings management for corporate reputation: Evidence from family firms. *Accounting Research Journal*, **29**(4): 457–474.

Rost, K. and Ehrmann, T. (2017). Reporting biases in empirical management research: The example of win–win corporate social responsibility. *Business and Society*, **56**(6): 840–888.

Ruggiero, P. and Cupertino, S. (2018). CSR Strategic Approach, Financial Resources and Corporate Social Performance: The Mediating Effect of Innovation. *Sustainability*, **10**: 3611.

Ruigrok, W., Peck, S., and Tacheva, S. (2007). Nationality and gender diversity on Swiss corporate boards. *Corporate Governance: An International Review*, **15**(4): 546–557.

Rupley, K. H., Brown, D., and Marshall, R. S. (2012). Governance, media and the quality of environmental disclosure. *Journal of Accounting and Public Policy*, **31**(6): 610–640.

Saeed, A. and Sameer, M. (2017). Impact of board gender diversity on dividend payments: Evidence from some emerging economies. *International Business Review*, **26**(6): 1100–1113.

Salim, R., Arjomandi, A., and Seufert, J. H. (2016). Does corporate governance affect Australian banks' performance? *Journal of International Financial Markets, Institutions and Money*, **43**: 113–125.

Sánchez, I., Gómez-Miranda, M., David, F., and Lázaro, C. (2019). Board independence and GRI-IFC Performance Standards: The mediating effect of the CSR committee. *Journal of Cleaner Production*, **225**: 554–562.

Schreck, P. (2011). Reviewing the business case for corporate social responsibility: new evidence and analysis. *Journal of Business Ethics*, **103**: 167–188.

Shahgholian, A. (2017). The Effect of Board Roles on Firm Environmental Governance. *Academy of Management Proceedings*.

Shahzad, A. M. and Sharfman, M. P. (2017). Corporate social performance and financial performance. *Business and Society*, **56**: 889–918.

Siciliano, J. I. (1996). The relationship of board member diversity to organizational performance. *Journal of Business Ethics*, **15**(12): 1313–1320.

Singh, V. and Vinnicombe, S. (2004). Why so few women directors in top UK boardrooms? Evidence and theoretical explanations. *Corporate governance: An international review*, **12**(4): 479–488.

Smith, K. G., Grimm, C. M., Gannon, M., and Chen, M. (1991). Organizational information processing, competitive responses, and performance in the U.S. domestic airline industry. *Academy of Management Journal*, **34**(1): 60–85.

Sternberg, E. (1999). The stakeholder concept: A mistaken doctrine. *Foundation for Business Responsibilities, Issue Paper*, (4).

Sundarasen, S. D. D., Je-Yen, T., and Rajangam, N. (2016). Board composition and corporate social responsibility in an emerging market. *Corporate Governance: The International Journal of Business in Society*, **16**(1): 35–53.

Surroca, J. and Tribó, J. A. (2008). Managerial entrenchment and corporate social performance. *Journal of Business Finance and Accounting*, **35**(5–6): 748–789.

Surroca, J., Tribó, J. A., and Waddock, S. (2010). Corporate responsibility and financial performance: The role of intangible resources. *Strategic Management Journal*, **31**(5): 463–490.

Tajfel, H. (1981). *Human groups and social categories*, Cambridge University Press, Cambridge.

Taljaard, C. C., Ward, M. J., and Muller, C. J. (2015). Board diversity and financial performance: A graphical time-series approach. *South African Journal of Economic and Management Sciences*, **18**(3): 425–447.

Tasheva, S. and Hillman, A. (2018). Integrating diversity at different levels: Multi–level human capital, social capital, and demographic diversity and their implications for team effectiveness. *Academy of Management Review*, **44**(4): 746–765.

Tihanyi, L. D., Griffith, A., and Russel, C. J. (2005). The effect of cultural distance on entry mode choice, international diversification, and MNE performance: A meta–analysis. *Journal of International Business Studies*, **36**(1): 270–283.

Turker, D. (2009). Measuring corporate social responsibility: A scale development study. *Journal of Business Ethics*, **85**(4): 411–427.

Vafeas, N. (1999). Board meeting frequency and firm performance. *Journal of Financial Economics*, **53**(1): 113–142.

Vilanova, M., Lozano, J. M., and Arenas, D. (2009). Exploring the nature of the relationship between CSR and competitiveness. *Journal of Business Ethics*, **87**(1): 57–69.

Vinnicombe, S. and Singh, V. (2003). Locks and keys to the boardroom. *Women in Management Review*, **18**(6): 325–333.

Walls, J. L., Berrone, P., and Phan, P. H. (2012). Corporate governance and environmental performance: Is there really a link? *Strategic Management Journal*, **33**: 885–913.

Wernerfelt, B. (1984). A resource-based view of the firm. *Strategic Management Journal*, **5**(2): 171–180.

Williams, C. L. (1992). The glass escalator: Hidden advantages for men in the "female" professions. *Social Problems*, **39**(3): 253–267.

Wood, D. J. (1991). Corporate social performance revisited. *Academic Management Review*, **16**(4): 691–718.

Wood, D. J. (2010). Measuring corporate social performance: A review. *International Journal of Management Review*, **12**(1): 50–84.

Zaefarian, G., Kadile, V., Henneberg, S. C., and Leischnig, A. (2017). Endogeneity bias in marketing research: Problem, causes and remedies. *Industrial Marketing Management*, **65**: 39–46.

Zerbini, F. (2017). CSR initiatives as market signals: A review and research agenda. *Journal of Business Ethics*, **146**(1): 1–23.

Zhang, Y. and Juelin, Y. (2012). Institutional dynamics and corporate social responsibility (CSR) in an emerging country context: Evidence from China. *Journal of Business Ethics*, **111**(2): 301–316.

https://doi.org/10.1142/9781786349507_0012

Chapter 12

ESG Performance and ESG Rating: A Critical Review of the Screening Methodologies and the Way Forward

Anissa Naouar
Assistant professor and researcher at HEC Sfax University, Tunisia
anissanaouar@yahoo.fr

12.1 Introduction

The financial sector plays a crucial role in the economy. It invests capital in other economic sectors, which indirectly negatively impact the environment (among others through waste production) and social and economic development (through inefficient utilization of available resources). The impact can also be direct through the resources/energy consumed by the financial enterprises, which can be reduced through energy consumption control, measures to conserve water, and focusing procurement on environmental-friendly suppliers, etc. The indirect impact is higher than the direct impact and, as such, can be targeted by the financial sector in its quest for higher sustainability.

Commercial banks for instance can be negatively impacted by environmental risk. For example, banks can extend financing to environmentally harmful projects that could default as a result of more stringent environmental regulations. On the contrary, being more alert to environmental risk could help banks improve their performance. Taken at a strategic level, opportunities related to the transition to a cleaner global economy could drive banks' future profitable and sustainable growth. With an increasing number of investors committing to the Principle of Responsible Investments, ethical investments and Environmental, Social and Governance (ESG) factors, financial and non-financial corporates are now more alert to ESG factors. This has created a market for ESG information. In fact, the number of investment funds incorporating ESG criteria grew from 260 in 2007 to more than 1000 in 2016. More recently, Fitch Ratings asserts that ESG sector increased by 15% to $52 billion in the first half of 2019 compared to 1% in 2018. Thus, responsible investing is of particular interest to the next generation of investors, who are expected to inherit more than US$30 trillion in wealth by 2050 (Accenture, 2014).

From a regulatory point of view, policymakers are also starting to take notice of ESG issues as well, particularly in the European Union and Asia. For years, the Nordic and Baltic regions led the world in sustainable investing practices, but this is now spreading across the globe.

Currently, there are numerous providers of ESG ratings and data services to investors and asset managers. Their business is booming as interest in ESG surges and sustainable and social investing is entering the mainstream. At the end of 2019, according to the Global Initiative for Sustainability Ratings, there were more than 600 ESG data providers operating globally. These include both well-established, global data providers like MSCI, Bloomberg, FTSE, and, recently, S&P Dow Jones; and ESG specialists like Sustainalytics, VigeoEiris, and TruValue Labs; Trucost (focused on carbon data). However, while disclosures on ESG matter, there is very little correlation between the data collected, the estimated missing data, how the different ESG factors are accounted for, and ultimately the ratings produced. As such, ESG scores show inconsistencies that potentially undermine their usefulness to investors. In addition, as rating agencies play a role in capital allocation, it is crucial to understand how ESG ratings agencies integrate sustainability principles in their assessment and whether there is any need for a supra authority to regulate and provide comprehensive global criteria to the ESG rating agencies industry.

Despite much academic literature on the link between performance and various aspects of corporate social responsibility, researchers and practitioners often acknowledge that existing academic literature does not attempt to critically review practitioner guidelines or practices (Dumay *et al.*, 2016).

In light of these shortcomings, this chapter has two main objectives. First, it offers an extensive literature review of the recent developments of sustainable performance in the non-financial and financial sector. Second, it presents a comprehensive qualitative screening of ESG rating methodologies of the main providers of these assessments. Finally, it offers a summary of the main challenges and opportunities related to the ESG rating methods and a critical view of the ESG ratings practices. The reminder of this chapter is structured as follows: Section 12.2 describes the concept of performance in the financial sector and how it evolved with regards to ESG goals. Then, Section 12.3 describes the ESG performance across the world. Section 12.4 provides a literature review of the recent literature on sustainable performance and Section 12.5 provides a comparative qualitative screening of main ESG rating methodologies. Finally, the Section 12.6 concludes.

12.2 The Performance in the Financial Sector

The concept of financial performance of the banks based on the financial ratios has been applied by different researchers. There is a huge number of studies that examined bank performance in an effort to isolate the factors that explain differences in profitability. These studies fall generally into several categories. One group has focused broadly on the link between banks' earnings and various aspects of banks' operating performance. A second set of studies has focused on the relationship between banks' earnings performance and their balance sheet structure.

Another body of literature has examined the impact of some regulatory, macroeconomic or structural factors on overall bank performance. The term bank structure is frequently used when referring to the characteristics of individual institutions. Individual bank characteristics such as its loan portfolio composition, and the scale and scope of its operations, can affect the costs at which it produces financial services. External determinants of banks' profitability relate to factors that are not influenced by a specific bank's decisions and policies, but by events outside the influence of the bank itself. Several external determinants are included separately in the performance examination to isolate their influence from that of bank structure so the impact of the former on profitability may be more clearly discerned. These factors include the scale of regulations (Jayaratne and Strahan (1998)), the market structure, GDP growth, inflation, etc.

The last economic crisis in 2008 put in serious doubt the reputation of the financial sector. Due to the collapse of the markets in some developed countries, other markets, both in developed and developing countries, were inevitably dragged down. As a result of this global financial crisis, there is a growing consensus that the financial system should not only be solid and stable but also sustainable.

12.2.1 *New paradigm for performance: From ECR to ESG performance*

Performance measurement allows the management to assess the success of the firm's adaptation to a changing environment. Traditional management tools are built on financially driven performance measurement systems. Financial statements are the main source of information when assessing a company's financial situation. But, under the current competitive conditions, successful evaluation of a company cannot rely solely on the financial indicators. When changing market and competitive conditions are taken into account, managers need to consider non-financial performance goals as well as economic goals. Increased awareness of stakeholders on environmental and social issues necessitated environmental and social performance measures to be taken into consideration within the set of non-financial performance measures.

The paradigm of non-financial performance measures is not a new phenomenon. Socially responsible investing gained momentum during the 1960s as societal concerns surrounding civil rights, women's rights, the Vietnam War, and the environment all empowered political activists to align their investment strategies with their political and social beliefs. Following that, Kaplan and Norton (1992) proposed the Balanced Scorecard (BSC) as a management tool that integrates financial and non-financial performance measures and builds a connection between organizational strategy and operational activity. Also, after the publication of John Elkington's book Cannibals with

Forks: The Triple Bottom Line (TBL) for the 21st Century Business, the TBL accounting system became popular (Elkington (1997), Turan *et al.* (2008)). TBL accounting means expanding the traditional reporting framework to an integrated perspective for measuring sustainability that takes into account environmental and social performance in addition to financial performance and expands stakeholders' knowledge of the company (Goel (2010), Jackson *et al.* (2011)).

A Forum for the Future (2002) defines "sustainability as building a successful business today and delivering value over the long run". According to the African Institute of Corporate Citizenship (2004), "Sustainability is about ensuring long term business success, while contributing to society's present and future social, environmental and economic needs. This approach requires ethical, environmental, social and economic considerations to be integrated into all aspects of the business, reflecting the principles of sustainable development". Therefore, there are three broad components of sustainability. They are sometimes referred to as "people, planet and prosperity", or the "social, environmental and economic dimensions". The need for businesses to address all three has been encapsulated in the concept of the "triple bottom line" by assessing these three aspects of sustainability: economic, social, and environmental performance.

From that period, modern ESG investing took shape following the 2005 publication of the United Nations-supported Principles for Responsible Investment (PRI). These principles aimed to develop a more sustainable global financial system by incorporating ESG issues into investment practices and laid the groundwork for ESG investing as a common practice.

With regard to financial firms, for a long time, most of the banks did not consider the social and environmental problems as relevant for their operations. The banking industry holds a unique position with regard to sustainable development because of its intermediation function between depositors and borrowers. As Finger *et al.* (2018) indicate, banks are often excluded from samples in empirical work due to their special characteristics — different accounting requirements, reporting incentives, or risk exposures — compared to other industries, and they also operate under unique codes. One of the most known publication in this field is "The do's and don'ts of sustainable banking", which was written by Jan Willem van Gelder, a member of BankTrack in 2006. The manual provides an overview of actions that the banking sector can do and can't to become more sustainable through achieving a performing sustainable banking management. It also presents the methods and guidelines for implementing the principles and commitments of sustainable banking in practice.

According to Bouma *et al.* (2001), sustainable banking can be defined as a decision by banks to provide products and services only to customers who take into consideration the environmental and social impacts of their activities.

The UNEP Statement of Commitment by Financial Institutions on Sustainable Development argues that sustainability in banking is about meeting the financial needs of the present without compromising the ability of future generations to meet their needs. It is not only about preserving the environment and biodiversity for future generations but also about guaranteeing human rights and a life in dignity, free from poverty. Sustainable finance is defined as the provision of financial capital and risk management products to projects and businesses that promote, or do not harm, economic prosperity, environmental protection, and social justice.

12.3 The Rise of ESG Investment and Worldwide Evolution

As discussed before, the sustainable performance of a company is commonly measured by assessing three aspects of sustainability: economic, social, and environmental performance. Economic performance encompasses issues conventionally reported in a company's annual financial report and also involves investments in human capital, research and development, wages and benefits paid, community development initiatives, etc. Environmental performance includes the amount of resources that companies use in their operations such as energy, land, water, and the results of its activities like waste, air emissions, and chemical residues. The environmental performance of companies is measured mainly by assessing their externalities to society and the environment, or by measuring their "environmental footprint". Social performance encompasses the impact of companies (and their suppliers) on the communities they are operating in. It includes employees' relations, health and safety, ratio of wages to cost of living, non-discrimination, employee turnover rate, education, etc.

12.3.1 *Defining ESG components?*

ESG as a term and concept was first proposed in June 2004 by the UN Global Compact's "Who Cares Wins" initiative to focus mainstream investors and analysts on the materiality of and interplay between environmental, social, and governance issues. Key issues for consideration typically include the following: E: climate change, carbon emissions, pollution, resource efficiency, biodiversity; S: human rights, labor standards, health & safety, diversity policies, community relations, development of human capital (health & education); G: corporate governance, corruption, rule of law, institutional strength, and transparency. A definitive list of ESG issues does not exist — and it looks impossible to agree on.[1] Markets, technologies, policies, values, and social preferences change all the time, and vary from region to region, country to country, and even within countries. Nonetheless, investors and analysts consider ESG performance in their fundamental analysis of companies with the underlying premise that companies that proactively manage ESG issues are better placed than their competitors to generate long-term tangible (direct) and intangible (indirect) results. While corporate governance assesses mostly general management quality, which has a direct impact on the company's performance, E and S tend to capture risk and opportunities linked to a specific industry or region. Understanding environmental aspects, for example, is more important when analyzing utility companies, rather than banks. The connection between performance and behavior is also more indirect and longer term for social and environmental factors than it is for corporate governance.

The following section provides some insight on how ESG rating evolved across the globe and how it could evolve further over the next few years.

[1] Appendix A summarizes the main ESG issues.

12.3.2 *State-of-the-art: Where do we stand?*

An unprecedented agreement around sustainable development priorities among 193 Member States was made by the UN Member States at the United Nations Conference on Sustainable Development (Rio+20) in 2012. The Sustainable Development Goals (SDGs) are the result of a three-year long transparent, participatory process inclusive of all stakeholders' views. These Goals and targets will stimulate action over the next 20 years in areas of critical importance: People, Planet, Prosperity, Peace, and Partnership.[2] The 17 Sustainable Development Goals (SDGs) and 169 targets are "global" in nature taking into account different national realities, capacities, and levels of development and respecting national policies and priorities. The SDGs call for building peaceful, inclusive, and well-governed societies with responsive institutions as the basis for shared prosperity. They realize that we cannot reach our development goals without addressing human rights and complex humanitarian issues at the same time. Besides, the SDGs are people-centered and planet-sensitive. They are universal, applying to all countries while recognizing different realities and capabilities. The goals are not independent from each other; they need to be implemented in an integrated manner. Accordingly, various ESG-related initiatives have taken place in many countries during the last decades. European countries have led the way in terms of implementing sustainable business practices. This is due, among other reasons, to the recommendations of the European Union. Specifically, in its 2011 directive, the European Commission specified that companies should integrate social, environmental, and ethical issues into their basic management strategy in order to maximize the creation of shared value for their shareholders, the remainder of their stakeholders, and society in general. According to The European Sustainable Investment Forum, SRI incorporates

[2]There are 17 SDGs and 169 targets (1. No poverty, 2. Zero hunger, 3. Good health and wellbeing, 4. Quality education, 5. Gender equality, 6. Clear water and sanitation, 7. Affordable and clean energy, 8. Decent work and economic growth, 9. Industry, innovation, infrastructure, 10. Reduced inequalities, 11. Sustainable cities and communities, 12. Responsible consumption and production, 13. Climate action, 14. Life below water, 15. Life on land peace, 16. Justice and strong institutions, 17. Partnerships for the goals).

ESG issues as well, as criteria linked to a values-based approach. In addition, according to the UN, SDGs are expected to be a roadmap for innovation, with revenue and savings opportunities, mostly in emerging markets, estimated at over $12 trillion through 2030.

In the US, investors and companies, however, only shifted their attention to SDGs in the last few years. In 2018, one in every four dollars invested in the US was aligned with a SRI strategy. While ESG approach is better suited to developed economies, which have benefitted from the general trend of governance, oversight and regulation issues, it would be more relevant in emerging markets, particularly from a corporate governance risk perspective and would even be considered from a country risk perspective. More importantly, the environment factor and specifically the climate change would impact the macroeconomy through the negative impact on the labor supply growth and productivity growth as well as the level of output.

In the context of financial firms, Douglas (2008) find that (a) banks are increasingly discussing climate change business opportunities in their annual reports, (b) many have calculated and disclosed their greenhouse gas (GHG) emissions from operations, (c) growing demand for climate-friendly financial products and services is leading banks into new markets, and (d) investment banks have taken a leading role in supporting emissions trading mechanisms and introducing new risk management products.

Therefore, various approaches towards sustainability and "green banking" have been adopted by banks worldwide (Yeung (2011)). Broadly, four stages of recognition of and response to sustainability issues can be identified. Banks can be classified according to their stage of awareness, and most will pass through the four phases on their journey towards 'Sustainability Finance'. They will move from:

- A defensive phase of basic environmental risk management, where broader sustainability issues are overlooked or ignored, to
- A protective or reactive phase where there is more systematic management of environmental and social risk, to
- A more proactive or offensive phase, where there is strategic management of environmental and social risk, and even, limited environmental and social value added, to
- The ultimate sustainability banking phase, where the triple bottom line approach (people, planet and prosperity) is integrated

into the bank's core business strategy, and is no longer limited to risk avoidance, but is now seen as a potential part of every type of financial risk management and decision-making process. Sustainability related issues are recognized as drivers for developing new products and services, generating additional revenue, and increasing market share, and consequently the organization becomes environmental value driven.

The main business case for integrating ESG is twofold: it can help banks to manage risks and it can help them to capitalize on opportunities. Understanding the main ESG drivers[3] that come under these two tenets can help banks establish a clear business case for developing and implementing an ESG strategy. However, some incidents relating to negative ESG outcomes caused by the bank lending, client relationships, and advisory decisions can affect their financial performance. First, these incidents may cause reputational and brand damage. Second, they may potentially have direct financial impact, such as increased non-performing loans due to credit/default issues and client inability to comply with loan agreements.[4] In addition, they can induce increased risk of litigation due to lack of appropriate disclosure on ESG risks for equity and debt issuance activities. Finally, they can induce higher cost of capital for the bank itself, related to: (1) equity and debt holders requiring higher returns due to perceived weak risk management capabilities and quality of loan book; (2) loss of a low-cost source of capital for banks with retail operations if depositors shift their funds away due to concerns about the bank's ESG impacts. Consequently, the cost concern of the CSR-ESG initiatives to the banks do not stop only at this operational stage but also affect credit portfolios and provisions for loan losses. Thus, banks have to allocate more on their provision of loan losses, which therefore affects profitability of the banks substantially.

---

[3]Four key drivers can be advanced: (1) Increasing regulatory expectations, (2) Reputation management and license to operate from shareholders and other stakeholders, (3) Enhanced risk management, (4) Value creation for the bank.

[4]Since many CSR-ESG firms developed in recent years, assessing their business model and cash flows are hard because their products and sales are very elastic given the competition from existing firms.

12.4 Sustainable Performance and Financial Performance: Antecedents and Recent Developments

Today, more and more companies are focusing on different levels — economic, social, and environmental — trying to maintain a balance in the short, medium, and long term. Many scholars and practitioners, in recent years, have discussed the need for organizations to guarantee their own economic sustainability through profit and reinvestment into human and social spheres as well as into the protection of the planet. Moreover, CSR[5] projects have received an increased interest from many companies who are looking at their advantages in terms of brand image, new investments, better reputation, and customer loyalty. Moreover, ESG principles are now increasingly recognized as central to the growth of financial markets. In the banking sector, this represents both a demand for greater social and environmental responsibility as well as a new landscape of business opportunity. Recently, the banks began to realize the major impact of the sustainable development over the way of ulterior development of the society and, implicitly over the way of creating the banking value in the future. Banks are increasing their social responsibility practices, reinforcing their credibility and the trust that their stakeholders have in them.

Due to the debate regarding CSR and its potential value creating capabilities, the question of whether firms should incorporate social responsibility practices into their management strategies designed to meet the expectations of their different stakeholders leads to theoretical positions in favor and against. Several empirical studies have explored the cause and effect relationship between Corporate Social Performance (CSP) and Corporate Financial Performance (CFP) for both financial and non-financial companies. This literature analyzing the relationship between CSR and value creation is very extensive,

[5]The concept Corporate Social Responsibility (CSR), originally referred to as Social Responsibility (SR), was discussed as early as the 1930's (Carroll, 1999). However, Carroll (1999) argues, it was not until the publication of Bowen's Social Responsibilities of the Businessman in 1953 that the concept became popularized and discussed in similar terminology as it is today. Although, there is no consensus to one standard definition of SRIs due to its wide range of screening criteria.

but the results are not conclusive. The most exhaustive overview study of academic research on this topic was performed by Friede *et al.* (2015). They have shown aggregated evidence for more than 2000 empirical studies suggesting that almost 90% of these studies find a nonnegative ESG–corporate financial performance relation. More importantly, the large majority of studies report positive findings and that the results are different when differentiating between emergent and developed markets (see Appendix C).

In the specific case of the banking industry, studies regarding the impact of CSR-ESG performance are not abundant, and conclusions are mixed. Mostly, they are conducted at a country level, a limited time period, or a specific socially responsible aspect. Simpson and Kohers (2002) provided evidence of a positive and significant relationship between CSR activities and the performance of the company. However, more recently, Soana (2011) concluded that there is no statistically significant link between the two measures of performance for a sample of Italian banks. Wu and Shen (2013) observed, on the basis of a sample of 162 banks from 22 countries covering the period 2003–2009, that CSR is positively associated with financial performance in terms of asset, capital, net interest income, and non-financial income. On the contrary, CSR is negatively associated with unproductive loans. Their results were subsequently affirmed by Fange *et al.* (2016) where they expanded their sample to 6,125 banks in 18 countries. These studies show that banks can use CSR-ESG to benefit financially from the environmental and social awareness of their stakeholders. Shen *et al.* (2016), on the other hand, analyzed 65 socially responsible banks corresponding to 18 countries during the period 2000–2009. The results reveal that socially responsible banks have significantly higher financial performance than non-socially responsible banks. In the US banks context, Cornett *et al.* (2014) analyzed the relationship between CSR and financial performance during the 2008 financial crisis. Their results indicate that larger banks perform significantly more CSR activities than smaller banks. The same authors expanded their research in 2016 by incorporating data from 2003 to 2011 and 2010 to 2013. They demonstrated that the improvement in financial performance did not come at the expense of the CSR-ESG investments. That said that a higher CSR-ESG investment doesn't necessarily result in a lower financial performance for banks (Cornett *et al.*, 2016).

Additionally, Esteban-Sánchez *et al.* (2017) analyzed the effect of different CSR dimensions on the financial performance of 154 banks in 22 countries, before and during the years of financial crisis, obtaining mixed results, depending on the dimension analyzed.

Other studies such as Weshah *et al.* (2012), Pradhan (2011), Dorasamy and Abdel-Baki (2014) arrived also at the same results. However, the opposite relationship between CSR-ESG and financial performance was demonstrated by few other authors. Yýlmaz (2013) used content analysis and panel regression for a sample of Turkish banks to show a negative relationship between banks' return on equity and CSR-ESG. Interestingly Yylmaz showed that ROA and CSR-ESG indicators are independent. Other examples such as Abeysinghe and Basnayake (2015), who used a sample of banks in Sri Lanka, showed the same negative relationship between banks' performance and CSR-ESG. Abu Baker (2018) studied the impact of CSR-ESG performance on the financial performance of US banks. He found that only management quality and CSR-ESG have direct impact on financial performance and both are negatively significant. On the other hand, he found that CSR-ESG has an indirect positive impact on financial performance through asset quality. To our knowledge, there is no empirical paper studying the linkage between ESG performance and the financial performance of banks in emergent markets.

Finally, Miralles-Quirós *et al.* (2019) studied the relationship between ESG performance and shareholders value creation in a larger sample of 166 internationally listed commercial banks from 2010 to 2015. Taken into account the level of development, legal systems, and the geographic area, they conclude that there is no homogeneity in the value relevance of environmental, social, and governance practices adopted by the selected banks over the entire sample period. For instance, there exists a positive and significant relationship between banks' environmental and corporate governance performance with Tobin's Q and, therefore, on shareholder value creation, after controlling for bank specific variables. In contrast, social performance does not have a direct relationship with the bank's financial stakeholders.

Within the Islamic industry, many researchers focused on the compatibility and complementarities between SDGs and Islamic banking principles. As Islamic firm is based on the principles of fairness, equality, and ethics that lead to social well-being, it seeks social justice and economic prosperity of the society and encourages sustainable economic activity. On the other hand, Socially Responsible Investing (SRI) has a similar rationale. SRI is sometimes referred to as "sustainable", "socially conscious", "mission", "green", or "ethical" investing. Therefore, SDG values have parallels relevance and application with Islamic Finance practice and provide banks an opportunity to redefine their role pertaining to people empowerment, socio-economic development, and the preservation of the environment.[6] However, there are challenges too, as Islamic Finance should also comply with Maqasid al Shariah.[7]

Comparing the Shariah compliance versus ESG compliance impact on Islamic bank performance, many studies tested if compliance leads to an advantage in terms of performance. In general, they show that there is no empirical evidence to prove that SRI screening or Shariah compliance screening lead to lower or better performance of Islamic banks compared to their conventional peers (see for instance Abdullah *et al.* (2007), Hassan *et al.* (2010) and Mansor and Bhatti (2011), Elfakhani and Hassan (2005) and Hassan *et al.* (2010)).

In relation to non-financial firms, some of them found a negative or mixed relationship (Vance, 1975, Alexander and Buchholz, 1978; Wright and Ferris, 1997; Stanwick and Stanwick, 1998; Peng and Yang, 2014; Hirigoyen and Poulain-Rehm, 2015; Cui *et al.*, 2016). Hirigoyen and Poulain-Rehm (2015), for instance, examined the causal relationships between the various dimensions of corporate social responsibility (human resources, human rights in the workplace, societal commitment, respect for the environment, market behavior, and governance) and financial performance (return on equity, return on assets, market to book ratio) of 329 listed companies in three geographical areas (the United States, Europe, and the Asia-Pacific region) between 2009 and 2010. They conclude that greater social responsibility does not result in better financial performance

[6]Appendix B provides the similarities and differences between Shariah compliance criteria and the SDGs.

[7]As known, there are two commandments of major importance in the Shariah, which have an immense bearing on the sustainable development issue. These two are the command to pay zakah and the prohibition of usury (riba).

but also that financial performance negatively impacts corporate social responsibility. According to this "traditionalist" hypothesis, social responsibility implies that business managers must act in some way that is not in the interest of his employers Friedman (1970). Managers are experts at producing and delivering products and/or services, so they do not necessarily possess expertise in managing social projects. In addition, they have no business advantage when implementing social programs. Managers, acting as agents of the shareholders, have no mandate to embark on socially responsible projects that do not enhance the income-generating ability of the firm. By pushing a social mission, they reduce a firm's ability to maximize shareholder value. Therefore, the responsibility of the company is to use its resources on activities aimed at maximizing its profits, acting in accordance with the basic rules of society incorporated into the law and ethical customs. When this is achieved, the contribution of the company to society will be optimized according to Friedman (1970). In contrast to this position, some authors found no relationship (Patten, 1991; McWilliams and Siegel, 2001; Nelling and Webb, 2009; Soana, 2011; Makni *et al.*, 2009), while others found a positive relationship (Russo and Fouts, 1997; Simpson and Kohers, 2002; Orlitzky *et al.*, 2003; Lai *et al.*, 2010; Saeidi *et al.*, 2015; Clark *et al.*, 2015). This view has been expanded by the so-called "stakeholder theory" (Freemen, 1984) which argues that managers have a responsibility to shareholders — the owners of the corporation — to maximize firm value, and that the better they satisfy stakeholder's interest, the more successful the firm will be in the long run. Engaging in socially responsible behaviors is one of the primary mechanisms through which a firm may foster and maintain trusting stakeholder relationships, reducing the transaction costs of those relationships (Wicks *et al.*, 1999; Barnett and Salomon, 2012). Following this theory, some authors such as Post *et al.* (2002) argue that companies should apply social, environmental, and corporate governance aspects that are necessary, regardless of the costs incurred or the income they produce. Others like Barnett and Salomon (2006); Brammer and Millington (2008); McWilliams and Siegel (2000); Cheng *et al.* (2014) and Lu and Abeysekera (2015) in CEE countries, Fisher and Sawczyn (2013) for Germain listed banks, and Yussof and Adamu (2016) for Malaysian listed companies, provided some support for the existence of a statistical correlation between some types of CSP and CFP.

They focused on the firm-level relationship between CSP and CFP (see also Brammer and Millington (2008); McWilliams and Siegel (2001)) or the investment portfolio Barnett and Salomon (2006), and likewise found that the highest and lowest levels of CSP were associated with the highest levels of CFP, hypothesizing in some cases a U-shaped relationship (while others assume a more linear correlation). Therefore, the company must be understood considering the plurality of agents involved in it and its objective should not be to maximize value for the shareholder, but instead, create value for all the stakeholders including employees, consumers, local communities, natural or environmental resources, etc.

Many other scholars, for instance, Margolis and Walsh (2003) and Barnett (2007) have claimed that we cannot conclude, after years of study, if investments into social causes return benefits to stakeholders. Barnett (2007), for instance, asserts that after more than thirty years of research, we cannot clearly conclude whether a one-dollar investment in social initiatives returns more or less than one dollar in benefit to the shareholder.

Although research indicates that any causal effect of social performance on economic performance is likely to be limited and difficult to detect with common measures, it is argued that the better a firm's social performance, the better it can attract resources (capital, human) and market its products and services. According to Porter and van der Linde (1995), social responsibility is a source of competitive advantage. Barnett (2007), building on the premise of the instrumental stakeholder theory that social responsibility can be beneficial to firms, developed the concept of SIC (Stakeholder Influence Capacity), which he defined as "the ability of a firm to identify, act on, and profit from opportunities to improve stakeholder relationships through CSR". Despite the fact that spending on social performance is costly, firms that have accrued adequate SIC through significant social performance may earn financial returns that offset and come to exceed the costs (Barnett and Salomon, 2012).

Thus, research has shown how business strategies rooted in social causes can create a virtuous circle seen in the value created in the local community, the satisfaction of its stakeholders, the company reputation, and the company sustainability (in the long term). In other words, the value is continuously created and enforced by mutual relationships. However, social and responsible investments are not free from the possibility of failure and incorrect implementation. These problems can neutralize the normally positive impact on the business and on the firm's overall performance. It is therefore important to know whether these measures are profitable for the company, in the sense that they allow shareholder value to be maximized. Particularly, measuring performance of the company against these performance measures is not an easy task because there are various multiple criteria which are qualitative. It is indeed difficult to evaluate criteria that are verbally evaluated, informally reported, cover different cycles, and are set based on various units of measurement.

As evidenced by several surveys, the assessment of environmental performance is still very limited since it is mainly based on primary environmental impacts such as natural resource depletion, pollution emissions, and energy consumption and waste generation — but not on the long-term environmental impacts of firms' operations. The assessment of the social impact of companies, however, seems a more difficult task and much less developed than the assessment of economic and environmental performance. Companies today tend to focus and report on their philanthropic initiatives and improved labor practices (i.e. reducing accidents at work, hiring more women, and employing a more ethnically diverse workforce) (Goel (2010), Hubbard (2009); Székely and Knirsch (2005)).

Overall, a growing body of research shows that ESG factors are truly material credit risk for investors. The evidence suggests that incorporating ESG into investing strategies should be part of the overall credit risk analysis and should contribute to more stable financial returns. It also dispels the myth that incorporating ESG means having to sacrifice financial returns. ESG investing is increasingly becoming part of the mainstream investment process for investors. In this context, several academic studies agree that companies with high ratings for corporate social responsibility and ESG factors have a lower cost of capital in terms of debt (loan and bonds) and equity. Besides, companies with high ESG ratings[8] are found to

[8]ESG ratings are evaluations of a company based on a comparative assessment of their quality, standard or performance on environmental, social or governance (ESG) issues.

exhibit a better market-based performance than an accounting-based outperformance (e.g. higher return on assets, return on equity).

Given that ESG investment is increasingly gaining a foothold in mainstream financial market, the role of ESG ratings providers is becoming challenging. ESG scores should reflect accurately the ESG commitment of any firm. Consistency between rating agencies is also crucial to help global investors in identifying ESG risks and opportunities and in their decision-making process when looking to the long-term sustainability of their portfolios within their portfolios.

12.5 Qualitative ESG Screening Methodologies by Main Rating Providers

The number of ESG ratings has grown significantly in the last decade. It is estimated that there are now over 600 ESG ratings globally. Driven by increasing investor interest in and demand for ESG-linked products and portfolios, asset managers are looking to ESG data and ratings providers to produce products that inform and improve investment decision-making.

Parallel to this rapid growth in the overall number of ratings, some agencies have been consolidating. For example, MSCI acquired GMI Ratings, Vigeo and Eiris merged, Sustainalytics acquired Solaron Sustainability Services, and ISS bought Oekom. Recently, the prominent credit ratings agencies S&P, Moody's, and Fitch entered the race to provide ESG scores.

Today, experts from different sectors (corporate, think tanks, academic, NGOs) rank ratings providers differently. A recent study run by SustainAbility (2019) states that MSCI and Sustainalytics and Reprisk remain the leaders in the sustainability ratings field compared to all other ratings providers. For Corporates, Sustainalytics, MSCI, and ISS-QualityScore are the next highest, while Bloomberg, Thomson Reuters, and FTSE round out the top five for academic/think tank/NGO respondents. RobecoSAM, ISS E&S Quality Score, Sensofolio, and Refinitivare also identified as eminent ESG scores providers for companies. The next section provides a qualitative screening of the methodologies used by the main ESG providers.

12.5.1 *ESG ratings screening: Comparison of the main criteria's*

It clearly appears from the Table 12.1 that individual agencies' ESG ratings can vary dramatically. An individual company can carry vastly divergent ratings from different agencies simultaneously, due to differences in methodology, subjective interpretation, or an individual agency's agenda. In fact, each rating agency has a customized scoring method that evaluates different non-financial metrics that frequently disagree about the various dimensions of ESG. Determining which ESG topics and metrics to evaluate is not a straightforward exercise — certainly not when compared to traditional financial metrics. Core ESG metrics vary from as few as 11 performance indicators to as many as 1,000 for other agencies. In addition, ESG rating agencies do not fully disclose the indicators they evaluate or the material impact of selected indicators. There are also inherent biases from market capitalization size to location, to industry or sector — all rooted in a lack of uniform disclosure. The qualitative evaluation of the ESG rating agencies would support investors in understanding the current state of play in the ESG ratings industry.

12.5.2 *Shortcomings and limits of current individual ratings methodologies*

We count a number of significant shortcomings and disparities in the individual ESG ratings methodologies. They include the following:

The disclosure limitations and quality of the methodology: Disclosure-based rating methodology provides ample room for companies to manipulate the disclosure process. Self-reported and unaudited sustainability reports invariably present companies in the best possible light, and rarely do they alert investors of looming problems. Besides, usually there is a company size bias in the ESG methodology. Companies with higher market capitalization tend to be awarded ratings in the ESG space that are meaningfully better than lower market-capitalization peers, such as mid-sized and small businesses.

Table 12.1. Overview of major ESG ratings agencies.

ESG agency	Overview	Main criteria and methodology	Rating scale
MSCI	Launched in 2010, it provides ESG ratings for 6000+ global companies and 400000+ equity and fixed income securities.	10 themes and 37 ESG Key Issues 1. Environment: Climate Change, Natural Ressources, Pollution &Waste, Environmental Opportunities 2. Social: Human Capital, Product Liability, Stakeholder Opposition, Social Opportunities 3. Governance: Corporate Governance, Corporate Behavior	AAA (highest) to CCC (lowest).
FTSE Russell's	Launched in 1995 and wholly owned by London Stock Exchange Group. The ESG Ratings include 7,200 securities in 47 Developed and Emerging markets.	All 17 SDGs are reflected in the 14 Themes under the ESG framework including the 3 pillars (1) Environment (Biodiversity, Climate Change, Pollution & Resources and Water Security), (2) Social (Customer Responsibility, Health & Safety, Human Rights & Community, and Labor Standards), (3) Governance (Anti-Corruption, Corporate Governance, Risk Management, and Tax Transparency). The Pillars and Themes are built on over 300 individual indicator assessments that are applied to each company's unique circumstances. Also over 100 indicators are sector specific.	A cumulative calculation of total ESG performance from 0 (lowest) to 100 (highest).

Sustainalytics	Created in 2008 after the consolidation of DSR (Netherlands), Scores (Germany) and AIS (Spain). Covers internationally 7000+ companies across 42 sectors. In 2017, Morningstar acquired a 40% ownership stake in Sustainalytics.	ESG pillars are split into key indicators (at least 70) that include corporate governance, business ethics, human capital, data privacy and security, carbon own operations, and product governance. It also breaks down ESG indicators into three distinct dimensions: preparedness, disclosure, and performance.	100 (highest) to 0 (lowest) using sector and industry based comparisons.
RepRisk	Founded in 1998. It provides ESG reports for 84000+ private and public companies in 34 sectors globally.	It combines a company's own ESG risk exposure with the ESG risk exposure of the countries and sectors in which the company has been exposed to risks. It focuses on 28 ESG issues connected to the Ten Principles of the UN Global Compact.[a] It divides these into environmental, community relations, employee relations, and corporate governance issues. RepRisk also includes ESG risk exposure for both a two-year and a ten-year timeframe using a scope of 28 ESG issues and 45 "hot topic" tags.	AAA (highest) to D (lowest).

(Continued)

Table 12.1. (*Continued*)

ESG agency	Overview	Main criteria and methodology	Rating scale
ISS E&S Quality Score	Launched in 2018. It covered 5000+ companies across multiple industries.	It evaluates 380+ factors (at least 240 for each industry group) divided into environmental and social factors. Areas include management of environmental risks and opportunities, human rights, waste and toxicity, and product safety, quality, and brand. The offering is touted as being very similar to the company's well-known governance score.	10 (highest) to 0 lowest for overall Environment and Social, as well as sub-issues.
Sensefolio	Launched in 2015, it has a global coverage of more than 80 countries and 30000+ companies.	It utilizes Machine Learning and Natural Language Processing (NLP) techniques. The E, S, and Governance scores are provided, as well as their 11 sub-categories and 51 ESG topics. It includes also a way to filter out companies based on controversial activities — e.g. Alcohol, Tobacco, Gambling, or Fossil Fuel use. *Environment* indicators include climate change, sustainability and biodiversity and water. *Social* indicators include health safety, employee standards, community responsibility, and human rights. *Governance* indicators include leadership and management structure, business innovation and performance, outside activities, and business ethics.	All the indicators are mapped to 50 ESG sub-categories and then the scores are normalized. The final weighting depends on the Industry the company operates in. In this way, on Sensefolio's 5-point scale, positive news and information are scored above 2.5, and negative news and information are scores below 2.5.

Refinitiv	Launched in 2018 and covers companies across 87 countries including companies across 47 developed and emerging markets.	ESG Score ranges across 10 main themes. Environmental indicators include emissions, environmental product innovation, and resource use. Social indicators include workforce, human rights, community, and product responsibility. Governance indicators include management, shareholders, corporate social and responsibility strategy (CSR) based on company-reported data. Then, the all 10 categories are aggregated in one category score.	Grades from A+ (the highest) to D− (the lowest).

Source: Author's own construction from the ratings providers' websites.

[a] ***Human Rights*** • Principle 1: Businesses should support and respect the protection of internationally proclaimed human rights; and • Principle 2: make sure that they are not complicit in human rights abuses. ***Labour*** • Principle 3: Businesses should uphold the freedom of association and the effective recognition of the right to collective bargaining; • Principle 4: the elimination of all forms of forced and compulsory labor; • Principle 5: the effective abolition of child labor; and • Principle 6: the elimination of discrimination in respect of employment and occupation. ***Environment*** • Principle 7: Businesses should support a precautionary approach to environmental challenges; • Principle 8: undertake initiatives to promote greater environmental responsibility; and • Principle 9: encourage the development and diffusion of environmentally friendly technologies. ***Anti-Corruption*** • Principle 10: Businesses should work against corruption in all its forms, including extortion and bribery.

***Lack of standardization, geographic and industry sector bias*:** There are no standardized rules and frameworks for Environmental and Social disclosures, or a disclosure auditing process to verify reported data. Instead, agencies must apply assumptions, which only add to the subjective nature of ESG ratings. Moreover, regulatory reporting requirements vary widely by region and jurisdiction — with two companies active in the same industry, doing the same general thing, often assigned different scores based on where they are headquartered. Companies domiciled in Europe, in particular, often receive much higher ESG ratings than peers based in the United States and elsewhere. In addition, company-specific risks and differences in business models are not accurately captured in composite ratings. Because of significant differences in business models and risk exposure, companies in the same industry are unfairly evaluated under the same model.

***Inconsistency and incomparability across rating methodologies*:** Individual company ratings are not comparable across agencies, due to a lack of uniformity of rating scales, criteria, and objectives. Also, another barrier to integration is the inconsistent coverage across asset classes or data gaps that prevent scenario analysis. This bias is related to the access to data and the difficulty to evaluate it accurately. The challenge is finding the right data in the right format and knowing how to use it.

***Failure to identify risk*:** One of the purposes of ESG ratings is to evaluate risk profiles and identify misconduct. ESG ratings do not properly function as warning signs for investors in companies that experience serious mismanagement issues as larger companies obtain higher ESG ratings. One of the reasons is that ESG agencies oversimplify industry weighting and company alignment. Ratings agencies claim to normalize ratings by industry. However, more often than not, agencies assign E, S, and G weights to companies without factoring in company-specific risks. This can result in a biased rating for an entity based on their industry, as opposed to entity-specific risks.

***Consolidation of ESG ratings*:** ESG ratings fail to represent a global marketplace. There is a geographical bias towards companies in regions with high reporting requirements. Besides, comparing ESG ratings across geographies is no easy task, especially in a global market. Though the observable differences between company ratings show a clear distinction — most notably between Europe (the best) and North America (the worst). But the source of this bias may not fully reflect the quality of ESG practices, but instead the quality of reporting. In Europe, for example, the EU requires companies with 500 employees or more to publish a "non-financial statement" as well as additional disclosures around diversity policy. North America has no such requirement for disclosure, which is one source for the positive bias toward European companies.

12.6 Conclusion

Nowadays, ESG investing has increasing popularity not only for their "feel-good" factor but also for its potential to spot financial risks that often cannot be identified in a company's quarterly results. For instance, the threats that climate change pose to a supply chain or the scandals that could arise from a discriminatory workplace may have a dramatic impact on a company's future performance.

Consequently, ESG has become a requirement for all financial and non-financial firms, and therefore stakeholders increasingly demand it, regardless of its possible positive or negative impact on financial performance.

In the current business landscape, policies and requirements for environmental and social disclosure can vary significantly. They can even be conflicting and confusing. Moreover, there is no jurisdiction that has any auditing practice on these varying non-financial investment factors which would distort the information available to both ratings agencies and investors. Also, by integrating financial and non-financial data, globally integrated reporting would help businesses take more sustainable decisions and enable investors and other stakeholders to transparently understand an organization's true performance Dumay *et al.* (2016).

Given these limitations in the ratings processes and ESG evaluation weaknesses, it worth mentioning that a number of key measures need to be undertaken in order to push the industry to a higher quality standard. They include the following:

1. an improved and relevant data quality and disclosure of methodology,

2. a greater consistency and comparability across rating methodologies,
3. the consolidation of ratings and a standard ESG framework,
4. a greater commitment of rated entities in the evaluation process, and
5. a better linkage to financial performance.

From a regulatory perspective, the regulation is still weak and heterogeneous across countries. For example, countries such as Finland and Sweden have mandated sustainability reporting for state-owned enterprises. The EU requires large companies to regularly publish reports on the social and environmental impacts of their operations. Also, a number of measures are already set to be fully enforced by the New European taxonomy by the end of 2022. They include disclosure requirements on their ESG indexes, notably, regarding methodologies and data sourcing but also the commitment to follow clear guidelines around the criteria implemented according to the asset classes being included in the index. France was among the first countries to pass legislation addressing climate change risk requiring French institutional investors to disclose their carbon footprint as well as their green investments. South Africa's Pension Fund Act calls on funds to consider ESG criteria in the investment process, and the Code for Responsible Investment in South Africa provides guidelines for institutional investors on how to integrate ESG factors into investment processes. The China Securities Regulatory Commission is making it mandatory for all listed companies and bond issuers to disclose ESG risks by 2020. However, in the United States, the US Securities and Exchange Commission doesn't require corporate disclosure of material ESG data. The SASB, whose mission is to develop and spread sustainability accounting standards has recently published a comprehensive set of industry-specific sustainability accounting standards covering financially material issues but reporting is, for the most part, entirely voluntary and there is not one recognized set of standards.

Consequently, just like how financial reporting and analysis is conducted, ESG rating providers need a common core benchmark reporting that would serve as the basis of a standardized ESG framework. Furthermore, the preparedness of the firm, and specifically the willingness of the board of directors to implement ESG-related business strategies, is a key information that ESG ratings providers should incorporate in the company assessment, even though this could result in giving away some of the financial performance.

Future lines of research would be aimed at producing a framework for understanding how ESG links to value creation and analyzing the direct impact on the creation of value for the shareholder and society of more specific measures of internal and external ESG factors. In this way, we could go further into the essential aspects that should be taken into account by companies for the creation of shared value and therefore contribute to sustainable development.

Appendices

Appendix A: Examples of ESG performance issues.

Environmental issues	**Social issues**	**Governance issues**
Climate change and carbon emissions	Customer satisfaction	Board composition
Air and water pollution	Data protection and privacy	Audit committee structure
Biodiversity	Gender and diversity	Bribery and corruption
Deforestation	Employee engagement	Executive compensation
Energy efficiency	Community relations	Lobbying
Waste management	Human rights	Political contributions
Water scarcity	Labor standards	Whistleblower schemes

Appendix B: Islamic finance principles versus SDGs.

Knowledge about Islamic finance in Al Shariah	**Convergent Sustainable Development Goal**
The role of fiscal policy	SDG 1, 2, 3, 4, 5, 6, 7, 8, 9, 10, 11, 13, 16
Interest, bounty/income	SDG 1, 2, 8, 10
Public debt	SDG8, 10
Lending as moral phenomenon	SDG17 (no moral values)
Prohibition of interest	SDG1, 2, 8, 10, SDG17
Social relations vis-à-vis interest	SDG17 (Social capital)
Debtor-creditor relationship	SDG1, 10, 12, 17
Impact of interest to social economic	SDG1, 3, 12
Productive activities	SDG8, 9
Trade	SDG8, 9, 10, 12
Objective of economic activities	SDG1, 3, 8
Moral values of economic activities	SDG12
The wealth	SDG1, 8, 10
The money	SDG1, 10
Human behavior towards money	SDG12
The contract	SDG12
Business conduct	SDG3
Business profit	SDG1, 3
Philanthropy	SDG1, 2, 3, 4, 6, 8, 10, 11, 12
Zakat	SDG1, 3, 4, 5, 6, 7, 8, 9, 11, 13, 17
Waqf	SDG1, 3, 4, 5, 6, 7, 8, 9, 11, 13, 17
Inheritance	SDG3
Shadaqah	SDG1, 3, 4, 5, 6, 7, 8, 9, 11, 13, 17
Revenue	SDG1, 4

Source: A.G Ismail (2016). Islamic Economic Studies and Thoughts Centre.

Appendix C: E, S and G categories and their relation to CFP.

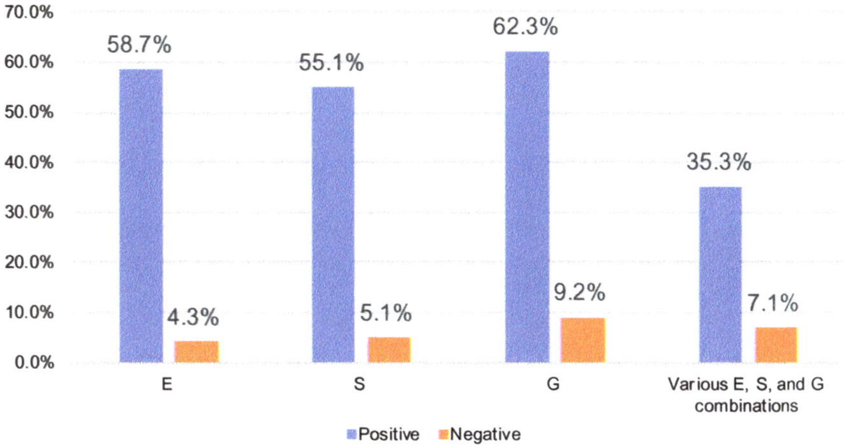

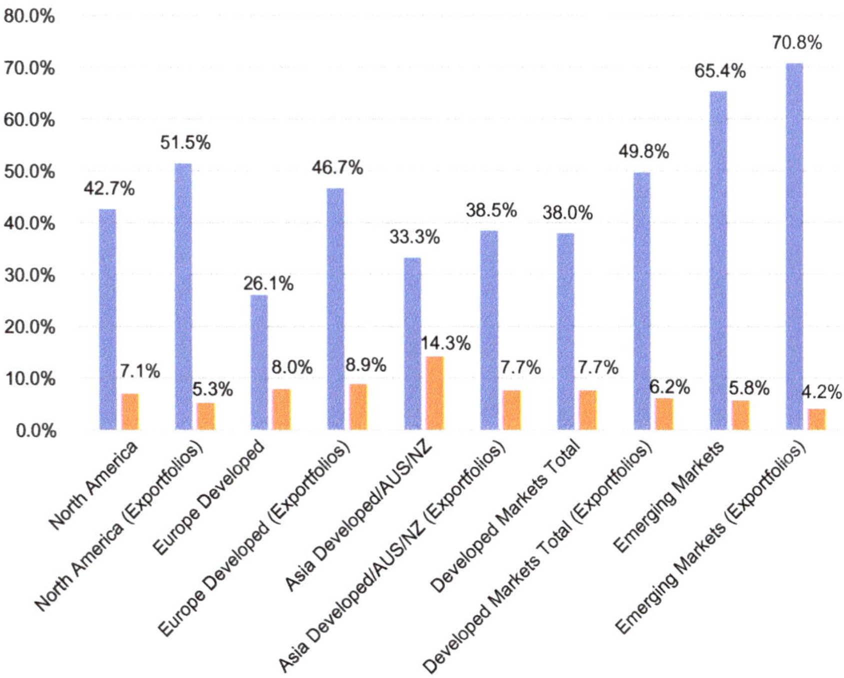

Source: Friede *et al.* (2015).

References

Abdullah, F., Hassan, T., and Mohamad, S. (2007). Investigation of performance of Malaysian Islamic unit trust funds. *Managerial Finance*, **33**(2): 142–153.

Abeysinghe, A. and Basnayake, W. (2015). Relationship between corporate social responsibility disclosure and financial performance in Sri Lankan Domestic Banking Industry, *6th International Conference on Business & Information ICBI* 111–128. Sri Lanka: Faculty of Commerce and Management Studies, University of Kelaniya.

Alexander, G. J. and Rogene, A. Buchholz (1978). Corporate social responsibility and stock market performance. *Academy of Management Journal*, **21**(3): 479–486.

Banktrack (2006). Shapping the future of sustainable finance, *moving from paper promises to Performance*, Banktrack, Amesterdam.

Barnett, M. L. and Salomon, R. M. (2012). Does it Pay to Be Really Good? Addressing the shape of the relationship between social and financial performance. *Strategic Management Journal*, **33**: 1304–1320. https://doi.org/10.1002/smj.1980.

Bouma, J. J., Jeucken, M., and Kilkers, L. (2001). Sustainable banking: The greening of finance, *Sheffield*, Greenleaf Publishing, UK.

Brammer, S. and Millington, A. (2008). Does it pay to be different? An analysis of the relationship between corporate social and financial performance. *Strategic Management Journal*, **29**(12): 1325–1343. https://doi.org/10.1002/smj.714.

Carroll, A. B. (1999). CSR: Evolution of a definitional construct. *Business and Society*, **38**: 268.

Cheng, B., Loannou, L., and Serafeim, G. (2014). Corporate social responsibility and access to finance. *Strategic Management Journal*, **35**(1): 1–23.

Clark, G. L., Feiner, A., and Viehs, M. (2015). From the stockholder to the stakeholder — How sustainability can drive financial outperformance. *University of Oxford, available at SSRN.*

Cornett, M. M. Erhemjamts, O. Tehranian, H. Greed or good deeds (2016). An examination of the relation between corporate social responsibility and the financial performance of U.S. commercial banks around the financial crisis. *Journal of Banking and Finance*, **70**: 137–159.

Cui, J., Cai, L., and Jo, H. (2016). Corporate environmental responsibility and firm risk. *Journal of Business Ethics*, **139**(3): 563–594.

Dorasamy, N. and Abdel-Baki, M. (2014). The inception of ethical banking: An imperative transformation in post-revolution Egypt. *International Business & Economics Research Journal*, **13**(3): 513–524.

Douglas, A. (2008). Corporate governance and climate change: The Banking Sector, http://www.ceres.org/Document.Doc?id$=$269.

Dumay, J., Bernardi, C., Guthrie, J., and Demartini, P. (2016). Integrated reporting: A structured literature review. *Accounting Forum*, **40**(3): 166–185.

Elfakhani, S. and Hassan, M. K. (2005). Performance of Islamic mutual funds. *Economic Research Forum*, 12th Annual Conference, Cairo, Egypt, 1–33.

Elkington, J. (1997). *Cannibals with forks — Triple bottom line of 21st century business, Stoney Creek*, New Society Publishers, CT.

Esteban-Sánchez, P. de la Cuesta-González, M., and Paredes-Gazquez, J. D. (2017). Corporate social performance and its relation with corporate financial performance: International evidence in the banking industry. *Journal of Cleaner Production*, **162**: 1102–1110.

Friede, G., Busch, T., and Bassen, A. (2015). ESG and financial performance: Aggregated evidence from more than empirical studies. *Journal of Sustainable Finance and Investment*, **5**(4): 210–233.

Friedman, M. (1970). The social responsibility of business is to increase its profits, New York Times Magazine, September 13: 32–33, 122, 124, 126.

Goel, P. (2010). Triple bottom line reporting: An analytical approach for corporate sustainability. *Journal of Finance, Accounting, and Management*, **1**(1): 27–42.

Hassan, M. K., Khan, A. N. F., and Ngow, T. (2010). Is faith-based investing rewarding? The case for Malaysian Islamic unit trust funds. *Journal of Islamic Accounting and Business Research*, **1**(2): 148–171.

Hirigoyen, G. and Poulain-Rehm, T. (2015). Relationships between Corporate Social Responsibility and Financial Performance: What is the Causality? *Journal of Business and Management*, **4**(1): 18–43.

Hubbard, Graham (2009). Measuring organizational performance: Beyond the triple bottom line. *Business Strategy and the Environment*, **18**(3): 177–191.

Ismail, A.G. (2016). Islamic Economic Studies and Thoughts Centre Paper delivered at the 2016 Quarterly Islamic Finance Public Lecture IRCIEF-IRTI, Kolej Universiti Islam Antarabangsa Selangor, 4 November 2016, Bangi, Malaysia.

Jackson, A., Boswell, K., and Davis, D. (2011). Sustainability and Triple Bottom Line Reporting — What is it all about? *International Journal of Business Humanities and Technology*, **1**(3): 55–59.

Jan Willam, V. G (2016). The do's and don'ts of Sustainable Banking, *A Bank Track manual*, Johan Frijns editing.

Kaplan, R. S. and Norton, D. P. (1992). The balanced scorecard: Measures that drive performance. *Harvard Business Review*, (January-February), pp. 71–79.

Lu, Y. and Abeysekera, I. (2015). What Do Stakeholders Care About? Investigating corporate social and environmental disclosure in China. *Journal of Business Ethics*, online first, **144**(1): 169–184.

Makni, R., Francoeur, C., and Bellavance, F. (2009). Causality between corporate social performance and financial performance: Evidence from Canadian firms. *Journal of Business Ethics*, **89**(3): 409–422.

Mansor, F. and Bhatti, I. M. (2011). Risk and return analysis on performance of the Islamic mutual funds: Evidence from Malaysia. *Global Economy and Finance Journal*, **4**(1): 19–31.

Margolis, J. and Walsh, J. (2003). Misery loves company: Rethinking social initiatives by business. *Administrative Science Quarterly*, **48**: 268–305. https://doi.org/10.2307/3556659.

McWilliams, A. and Siegel, D. (2001). Corporate social responsibility: A theory of the firm perspective. *Academy of Management Review*, **26**(1): 117–127.

Miralles-Quirós, M. M., Miralles-Quirós, J. L., and Hernández, J. R. (2019). ESG performance and shareholder value creation in the banking industry. *International Differences, Sustainability*, **11**(5): 1404.

Nelling, E. and Webb, E. (2009). Corporate social responsibility and financial performance: The "virtuous circle" revisited. *Review of Quantitative Finance and Accounting*, **32**(2): 197–209.

Orlitzky, M., Schmidt, F. L., and Rynes, S. L. (2003). Corporate social financial performance: A meta — Analysis' *Organization Studies*, **24**(3): 403–441.

Peng, C.-W. and Yang, M.-L. (2014). The effect of corporate social performance on financial performance: The moderating effect of ownership concentration. *Journal of Business Ethics*, **123**(1): 171–182.

Porter, M. and van der Linde, C. (1995). Green and competitive. *Harvard Business Review*, **73**(5): 121–134.

Post, J. E., Preston, L. E., and Sachs, S. (2002). Managing the extended enterprise: The new stakeholder view. *California Management Review*, **45**(1): 6–28.

Russo, M. V. and Fouts, P. A. (1997). A resource-based perspective on corporate environmental performance and profitability. *The Academy of Management Journal*, **40**(3): 534–559.

Saeidi, S. P., Sofian, S., Saeidi, P., Saeidi, S. P., and Saaeidi, S. A. (2015). How does corporate social responsibility contribute to firm financial performance? The mediating role of competitive advantage, reputation, and customer satisfaction. *Journal of Business Research*, **68**(2): 341–350.

Shen, C. H., Wu, M. W., Chen, T. H., and Fang, H. (2016). To engage or not to engage in corporate social responsibility: Empirical evidence from global banking sector. *Economic Model*, **55**: 207–225.

Simpson, W. G. and Kohers, T. (2002). The link between corporate social and financial performance: Evidence from the banking industry. *Journal of Business Ethics*, **35**(2): 97–109.

Soana, M. G. (2011). The relationship between corporate social performance and corporate financial performance in the banking sector. *Journal of Business Ethics*, **104**(1): 133–148.

Stanwick, P. A. and Stanwick, S. D. (1998). The relationship between corporate social performance and organizational size, financial performance, and environmental performance: An empirical examination. *Journal of Business Ethics*, **17**(2): 195–204.

Székely, F. and Knirsch, M. (2005). Responsible leadership and corporate social responsibility: Metrics for sustainable performance. *European Management Journal*, **23**(6): 628–647.

Turan, Fikret K., Scala, Natalie M., Kamrani, Akram., and Needy, Kim LaScola (2008). Organizational sustainability: A new project portfolio management approach that integrates financial and non-financial performance measures. *IIE Annual Conference and Expo (IERC)*, Vancouver, BC, Canada, May 17–21: 1025–1030.

Vance, S. C. (1975). Are socially responsible corporations' good investment risks? *Management Review*, **64**: 18–24.

Weshah, S. R., Dahiyat, A. A., Abu Awwad, M. R., and Hajjat, E. S. (2012). The impact of adopting corporate social responsibility on corporate financial performance: Evidence from Jordanian Banks. *Interdisciplinary Journal of Contemporary Research In Business*, **4**(5): 34–45.

Wicks, A. C., Berman, S. L., and Jones, T. M. (1999). The structure of optimal trust: Moral and strategic implications. *Academy of Management Review*, **24**(1): 99–116.

Wright, P. and Ferris, S. P. (1997). Agency conflict and corporate strategy: The effect of divestment on corporate value. *Strategic Management Journal*, **18**(1): 77–83.

Wu, M. W. and Shen, C. H. (2013). Corporate social responsibility in the banking industry: Motives and financial performance. *Journal of Banking & Finance*, **37**: 3529–3547.

Yeung, S. (2011). The role of banks in corporate social responsibility. *Journal of Applied Economics and Business Research*, **1**(2): 103–115.

Yilmaz, I. (2013). Social Performance vs. Financial Performance. *International Journal of Finance & Banking Studies (2147-4486)*, **2**(2): 53–65.

Yusoff, W. F. W. and Adamu, M. S. (2016). The relationship between corporate social responsibility and financial performance: Evidence from Malaysia. *International Business Management*, **10**(4): 345–351.

https://doi.org/10.1142/9781786349507_0013

Chapter 13

Corporate Social Responsibility and Firm Risk: Evidence from France

Zyed Achour[*,‡], **Zaineb Hlioui**[†,§], **and Sonia Boukattaya**[†,¶]

[*] *National Institute of Labour and Social Studies (INTES), University of Carthage, Tunis, Tunisia*
[†] *University of Tunis, Tunis, Tunisia*
[‡] *zyed.achour@intes.rnu.tn*
[§] *zainebhlioui@gmail.com*
[¶] *sonia.boukattaya@icloud.com*

13.1 Introduction

Recent years have been marked by an abundance of researches, both theoretical and empirical, dealing with the relationship between Corporate Social Responsibility (CSR) and Financial Performance (FP). Nevertheless, results have often remained mixed, and the mechanisms by which CSR could affect financial performance remain ambiguous and not fully understood. However, much less attention has been devoted to the association of CSR with Corporate Risk although it has been theoretically argued that CSR is an instrument that reduces risk. Several prior empirical analyse have found a negative link between CSR and firm risk (Orlitzky and Benjamin, 2001; Oikonomou *et al.*, 2012; Sun and Cui, 2014; Lee *et al.*, 2016). Thus, in this chapter, we address the following question: Does CSR mitigates firm risk?

The previous literature presents three managerial theories that are likely to support the link between CSR and firm risk: Signaling theory (Spence, 1973; Ross, 1977), stakeholder theory (Feeman, 1984), and legitimacy theory (Dowling and Pfeffer, 1975). First, the Signaling theory states that CSR can be perceived as a positive signal to stakeholders. It improves the firm's reputation and increases its value. Accordingly, a high level of CSR disclosure carried out by the company leads to lower risk (Thanay and Widanaputra, 2019; Cheng and Christiwan, 2011). Wiśniewski (2015) noted that CSR can be used as a tool for risk management, emphasizing that CSR should be integrated into the risk management process by identifying the issues that are important to stakeholders and assessing and prioritizing their importance in order to provide a proactive response according to Deming cycle (Plan-Do-Check-Act).

Second, the Stakeholder theory suggests that maintaining good relationships with stakeholders is a real option to mitigate firm risk. On one hand, it reduces operational costs, and thereby decreases the operational risk (Husted, 2005). On the other hand, CSR investments can generate moral capital, which creates a "reservoir of goodwill" (Ducassy, 2013), therefore preserving the financial performance and reducing risk exposure (Godfrey, 2005; Godfrey *et al.*, 2009; Luo and Battacharya, 2009). Finally, reducing the firm's risk through CSR activities would be a legitimization mechanism (Cai *et al.*, 2016; Jamali *et al.*, 2017). Public support can be gained as long as firm externalities comply with prevailing norms and society expectations. CSR activities likely reinforce the organizational legitimacy and its "License to Operate".

In the literature, the common argument for CSR engagement is that "doing well by doing good" improves profitability and value creation (Ferrell *et al.*, 2016; Lins *et al.*, 2017). From the perspective of risk management, CSR promotes the stability of cash flows (Luo and Bhattacharya, 2006) and plays the corporate shield role companies during crises. In other words, CSR-oriented firms will be less exposed to the various risks since CSR initiatives can be seen as an insurance premium (Minor and Morgan, 2011; Sui and Zhang, 2019). In a recent study, Liu and Lu (2019) argue that the firm's reputation is a comprehensive indicator of the CSR effect on firm risk mitigation.

The link between CSR and financial performance oscillates between two main rationales: a first stream, mobilizing essentially the stakeholder theory (Freeman, 1984), suggests that CSR is likely to have a positive impact on corporate firm performance, which, in return, would affect the risk level and the corporate competitive position (Bacq and Eddleston, 2018; Ting and Yin, 2018; Preston and O'Bannon, 1997). CSR engagement can improve the satisfaction of all stakeholders, consequently, enhancing the reputation and reducing the risk level. For example, CSR approaches are supposed to minimize the implicit costs associated with "irresponsible" actions that can potentially generate significant explicit costs (to repair negative externalities) (Hollandts and Valiorgue, 2011). In a context of high information asymmetry, CSR reporting is perceived as an instrument that grants transparency. Hence, socially responsible firms could be able to attract more investors and are more likely to preserve financial performance. Thus, CSR policies can be implemented to minimize risks (Tran *et al.*, 2019; Casado-Diaz *et al.*, 2014; Monti *et al.*, 2019).

Conversely, a second stream supports the liberal current defending the hypothesis of a negative relation between CSR and FP invoking the risk of deviation from shareholders' objective, which should be profit maximization. This stream of research judges CSR investments as extra–costs that drain the company's financial resources and could put the company in a situation of competitive disadvantages (Tanggamani *et al.*, 2018). According to Agency theory (Jensen and Meckling, 1976) CSR investments could be "a waste of financial resources"; various researches show that CSR is motivated by agency problems (for instance, Chang *et al.*, 2018; Ferrel *et al.*, 2016; Benabou and Tirole, 2010). Krüger (2015) argues that exercising CSR promotes the interests of managers to the detriment of shareholders.

The present chapter aims to contribute to the literature dealing with the impact of corporate social responsibility on firm risk in two ways. First, on a theoretical level, it aims to reinforce the hypothesis of a negative link between social performance and firm risk. Indeed, two hypotheses seem to be defensible: a first hypothesis mainly supported by the stakeholder theory and the legitimacy theory advocates that CSR initiatives would be a form of immunization for companies against reputational risk and a means of reducing operational costs. A second hypothesis, invoking essentially Friedman's argument, considers that CSR initiatives would be a form of value destruction and a waste of scarce resources from a shareholder's perspective. Such initiatives incurs different costs for the company and would increase earnings volatility (Göçer *et al.*, 2019), suggesting a positive relationship between CSR and firm risk due to managerial entrenchment (Utz, 2018). Furthermore, the relationship between CSR and risk is likely to be a new avenue to explore in order to demystify the CSR-FP link.

Second, on an empirical level, this research conducted on the French context constitutes a contribution to researches carried out mainly in the United States and South East Asia and which remain mixed as to their conclusions oscillating between a positive link (Nguyen *et al.*, 2015; Barnea and Rubin, 2010), the absence of a link (Humphrey *et al.*, 2012), and a negative link (Albuquerque *et al.*, 2014; Jo *et al.*, 2016; Cai *et al.*, 2016).

In this research, and due to the absence of a consensus and sole conclusion, we will contribute to the previous studies and investigate the influence of CSR on the corporate global risk in French companies. The choice of the French case is not arbitrary given that the French parliament has enacted a CSR reporting law since 2010 "the Grenelle Acts", whereby companies have been under increasing pressure and higher transparency has been required.

The remainder of this chapter will be organized as follows: Section 13.2 analyzes the theoretical foundations of the relationship between CSR and risk. In Section 13.3, we discuss the methodology used and justify the measurement indicators for the empirical validation of the negative link between risk and CSR. Section 13.4 discusses the results. Finally, Section 13.5 presents the conclusions as well as the theoretical and managerial implications of the research.

13.2 Literature Review and Hypothesis Development

Three main theories are likely to elucidate the impact of CSR activities on firm risk levels.

Signaling theory (Spence, 1973; Ross, 1977) starts from the fact, that information is unequally shared by everyone at the same time. This theory could be used to explain the voluntary disclosure in company reports. Companies report CSR information to stakeholders (sometimes beyond what is required by the regulations) to prove a higher transparency level and show their particular strengths. They aim to show that they are better than their competitors in the market in order to attract investment and strengthen their reputation

(Verrecchia, 1983; Liu and Lu, 2019). CSR activities and their disclosure are generally perceived as a positive signal which leads to an increase in stock trading activities (Astuti and Nugrahanti, 2015). Therefore, CSR commitment would allow conveying a better brand depiction. Besides, it could be perceived as a form of differentiation that creates a competitive advantage and strengthens the firm's position. Thus, CSR has been integrated into risk management strategies (Kytle and Ruggie, 2005; Yuan *et al.*, 2011; Shad *et al.*, 2019).

Among others, Jo and Na (2012) found a negative relationship between CSR engagement and firm risk. Similarly, Cai *et al.* (2016) concluded that CSR programs improve corporate image and therefore reduce risk. The Signal theory explains the different actors' behavior by their access to the information. On one hand, the signal transmitter is supposed to choose how to disclose information. On the other hand, the receiver is supposed to choose how to interpret the signal (Connelly *et al.*, 2011). The Signaling theory states that companies intentionally send signals to the market in the hope that the market will be able to distinguish between good and bad firms. Moreover, according to Thanaya and Widanaputra (2019), this theory reveals how CSR can influence financial performance. In the literature, there is an omnipresent belief that CSR disclosure is commonly used by firms to gain reputation. CSR disclosure can be considered as a tool for reputational management (Axjonow *et al.*, 2018; Odriozola and Baraibar-Diez, 2017). By acting responsibly, and showing it off, companies can obtain the trust of consumers (Donney and Canonn, 1997), pride, and commitment of their employees (Lee *et al.*, 2012). Park *et al.* (2014) showed that in supplier–buyer relationships, the reputation of the supplier would be affected by the consumer perception of the supplier's CSR activities. In the same vein, Wang *et al.* (2018) highlighted the managers' use of the CSR disclosure based on the Signaling theory. In fact, managers can manipulate information (the emitted signal) while preparing the CSR report. In addition, the report's clarity is positively associated with social performance. Thus, bad performance can be hidden through the report's ambiguity. Kanagaretnam *et al.* (2019) denoted that financial reporting conservatism and transparency are associated with social trust. They indicated that this association provides supplementary information and reduces managers' risk-taking. Cui *et al.* (2018) indicated that CSR reporting decreases informational asymmetry. Moreover, they confirmed that CSR engagement is negatively related to the reputational risk.

The second theory that might explain the CSR and corporate risk association is the Stakeholder theory (Freeman, 1984). According to this theory, companies should be concerned with the interests of any person, institution, organization, formal, or non-formal group that may affect or be affected by the company's activities and decisions (Florea and Florea, 2013). Hasan *et al.* (2018) examined the effect of CSR on employees' productivity. They underlined that the social considerations of the key stakeholders are precious and crucial for firms that dispose of high-discretionary cash levels or revenue uncertainty. Therefore, CSR can be defined as a mechanism that builds trust and establishes cooperative relationships with the key stakeholders, while ensuring a positive link with financial performance. The CSR activities allow having the support of stakeholders, especially those interested in the social, environmental, and governance issues. When companies are more involved in CSR activities and building relationships with a diverse set of stakeholders, they can gain access to new information used to reduce the specific risk. Besides, they might acquire a better position to decrease the volatility of their returns. Jo and Na (2012) pointed out that CSR activities (such as pollution prevention, employees safety programs, and fair trade policies ...) are usually designed to avoid harm imposed on stakeholders and to mitigate directly firm risk. According to Cui *et al.* (2018), firms that adopt efficient social strategies are characterized by less information asymmetry, which allows them to gain the stakeholders' trust, thus adding to higher social investment freedom. Moreover, developing close relationships with the stakeholders through CSR activities would encourage firms to share the information, which gives warring signals in a precocious way (Ortiz-de-Mandojana and Bansal, 2016). Privileged relationships with stakeholders allow companies to anticipate foreseeable risks (Ortiz-de-Mandojana and Bansal, 2016; Porter and Kramer, 2006).

The last mobilized theory in this research is the Legitimacy theory (Dowling and Pfeffer, 1975). Organizational legitimacy can be defined as a social judgment applied to the action of an entity to classify it as desirable, suitable, and appropriate within a socially constructed system of norms, values, and beliefs (Bitektine, 2011).

Campbell (2003, p. 574) argues that: "legitimacy theory is the most widely used theory to explain CSR disclosures". Legitimacy theory postulates that organizations continually seek to ensure that they operate within the limits and according to the standards of their respective Societies. According to Chiu and Sharfman (2011), any social institution — firms in particular — operates in the Society based on an explicit or implicit contract by which its survival and growth depend on the achievement of certain socially desirable ends that provide economic, social, or political benefits to the groups from which it derives its power. Companies are looking to secure "License to Operate" acting within the bounds that society deems to be acceptable. A positive reaction would be given by public power when the CSR activities show compliance with prevailing standards and values as well as public expectations (Branco and Roduguez, 2008). According to Cai *et al.* (2016), risk reduction through CSR activities can be an important legitimization mechanism. More recently, Liu and Lu (2019) have shown empirically the role of firms' ESG performance in financial risk mitigation, emphasizing the mediating role of the firm reputation.

Based on the previous literature review and the results of the large body of research that confirm the negative association between CSR and firm's risk (Orlitzky and Benjamin, 2001; Luo and Bhattacharya, 2009; El Ghoul *et al.*, 2011; Oikonomou *et al.*, 2012; Jo and Na, 2012; Bouslah *et al.*, 2018; Harjot and Laksmana, 2018), we assume the existence of a significant negative impact of CSR on the corporate global risk. Hence, we formulate our main hypothesis as follows:

H: Corporate Social Responsibility has a negative effect on firm risk

13.3 Research Methodology

13.3.1 *Sample and data*

Our sample consists of French companies belonging to the SBF 120 index over the period 2008–2017. Our main data source in this investigation is the DataStream database. On one hand, the 10-year analysis period makes it possible to constitute a large panel, which enriches the results and improves the econometric estimates and tests. On the

Table 13.1. Distribution of companies in the sample by industry.

Sector	Number	%
1. Oil and gas	6	6.8
2. Basic materials	4	4.5
3. Industrial	22	25.0
4. consumer goods	16	18.1
5. Health	9	10.2
7. Consumer services	17	17.0
8. Telecommunications	1	1.1
9. Utilities	4	6.8
10. Technology	9	10.2
Total	88	100.0

other hand, the SBF120 index groups the 120 largest companies in terms of market capitalization and trading volumes on the Euronext Paris market. These large companies, mostly groups, remain very "visible" when it comes to their societal achievements and are subject to permanent "monitoring" by both rating organizations and the media. They are of especial interest to investors. We should note that financial firms such as banks, insurance companies, investment firms, brokerage firms, and portfolio managers were excluded from our sample. Indeed, financial institutions have specific financial and accounting structures that differ from the industrial and commercial enterprises. Besides, companies with a lot of missing data were also removed from the sample. Our final sample includes 88 companies over the period 2008–2017, i.e. 880 observations. Table 13.1 presents the distribution of companies in the sample by industry.

13.3.2 *Variables' description*

In financial theory, total risk is made up of idiosyncratic risk inherent to firm's operations and its management expertise and, market risk, which may result from external factors that can affect firm profitability. Factors such as fluctuations in demand, interest rates, and exchange rates, and commodity prices can affect firm profitability. Following extant literature, we measure firm risk by the total risk. This risk of an investment is commonly measured by the standard deviation of its return (Jordan *et al.*, 2011; Elsaid *et al.*, 2018). Lin *et al.* (2019) stated that the total risk of a firm can be measured by the standard deviation of monthly stock returns over a one-year period. The standard deviation is a measure of dispersion, or a statistical measure of the risk, where greater standard deviation value reflects higher risk. In this research, **RISK** measure is estimated by the standard deviation of the monthly stock returns formulated as follows.

$$\sigma R_{it} = \sqrt{\frac{\sum_{i=1}^{n}(R_{it} - m)^2}{n - 1}}$$
$$\text{where: } \quad \sigma R_{it} = \frac{P_t - P_{t-1}}{P_{t-1}} \quad \text{and} \quad m = \frac{\sum_{i=1}^{n} R_{it}}{n} \tag{1}$$

σR_{it} = Standard deviation of company's monthly stock return,
R_{it} = Company's monthly stock return,
m = Company's average monthly stock return,
n = Amount of data,
P_t = Closing price of company stock at time t,
P_{t-1} = Closing price of company stock a month before time t.

The independent variable (CSR) is a multidimensional construct whose operationalization remains delicate. Several measures, obeying various methodologies, have been developed and used by researchers. The majority of these consist of "ratings" giving rise to a score. However, the methodologies developed by different CSR rating agencies carry a subjective weighting by assigning a score to each of the dimensions of CSR. For example, the KLD agency bases its rating criteria on seven qualitative areas: community, diversity, labor relations, human rights, environment, governance, and product safety. The dimensions below are noted according to qualitative descriptions (strengths/weaknesses) and do not necessarily imply numbers. Given the multidimensional nature of CSR and taking into account that the weights of the different dimensions must consider cross-sectoral specificities and socio-cultural differences, we retain in this research a measure including three fundamental dimensions of CSR (Environmental, Societal, and Governance: ESG). We used secondary data drawn from the Thomson Reuters Inc. database on the French companies in our sample. The agency periodically produces credible and objective data evaluated by experts (Galbreath, 2013). ESG scores range from 0 (the lowest) to 100 (the highest). The factors taken into account by Thomson Reuters when assigning these scores are as follows: Environmental performance (3 items): reduction of emissions, innovation, and reduction of resource consumption, Social performance (4 items): Community, human rights, quality and safety of employment products, training and development of human resources, Governance performance (4 items): board structure, executive compensation policy, vision and social strategy.

Following prior–related studies, we control for a number of variables that can affect the firm's risk. First, we control for firm size (SIZ). Firm size is an important control variable because small firms tend to face higher business and financial risks (Flammer, 2015; Oikonomo *et al.*, 2012; Perrault and Quinn, 2018). Previous researches provide evidence of a negative relation between firm size and risk (e.g. Chakraborty *et al.*, 2019a,b) suggesting that large firms are less exposed to risk, as they are more able to manage risk especially in times of high volatility (e.g. Jo and Na, 2012). Furthermore, large firms face, in general, greater pressures from external stakeholders for increasing CSR engagement since they are more visible (Brower and Mahajan, 2013; Udaysankar, 2008). We expect a negative relationship between size and the firm's risk. We control for the corporate size by the natural logarithm of total assets.

Second, we control for leverage (LEV), measured by total debt to total assets ratio. Prior evidence suggests higher leverage to be associated with higher firm risk (Abdelghany, 2005). An excessively high ratio of leverage has been associated with higher risk (Frammer, 2015; Perrault and Quinn, 2018). According to Oliveira *et al.* (2011), high leverage ratio tends to make firms more risky and speculative. Thus, a positive link is expected between the firm's leverage and risk.

Third, we also control for industry (IND). Previous research argues that firms from different industry sectors operate under different framework pressure. Thus, they face different competitive environments which affect the CSR engagement (Choi and Wang, 2009; Perraut and Quinn, 2018). According to the Industry Classification Benchmark (ICB), presented in Table 13.1, we classify the firms into two main groups. The first (IND1) includes those in the Oil and gas, Basic materials, Industrial, consumer goods, and utilities sectors. The rest of the firms are in the second group (IND2). Hence, our variable IND takes '1' if the enterprise belongs to the first category and '0' otherwise. Indeed, previous research (Tan *et al.*, 2016; Solikhah, 2016) underlines that firms in the first group are more sensitive toward social and environmental issues. They are more visible and face higher social pressure due to their natural resources overexploitation and their ecological externalities deemed negative.

Finally, according to agency theory (Jensen and Meckling, 1976), when the capital is relatively dispersed, the directors would be sheltered from the owners' control and could thus be motivated to invest in social actions compromising shareholder wealth. Hence, we consider the Ownership structure (OWN) as a continuous variable that reflects the shares' dilution. This variable is measured by the percentage of capital held by the three largest shareholders.

13.3.3 *Model*

In order to empirically test our hypothesis, we use panel data regression method. The advantage of using panel data is that it deals with individual and temporal effects. This double individual and temporal dimension makes it possible to separate the effects of individual characteristics from the temporal evolutions common to all individuals.

We run the following model:

$$RISK_{it} = f(CSR_i^t, IND_i^t, SIZ_i^t, OWN_i^t, LEV_i^t)$$

$$RISK_{it} = \beta_0 + \beta_1 CSR_{it} + \beta_2 SIZ_{it} + \beta_3 IND_{it} + \beta_4 OWN_{it} + \beta_5 LEV_{it} + \mu_i + e_{it}$$

The index t presents the year of the observation while the index i refers to the company. The variable RISK is our dependent variable. CSR is the firm's ESG score. SIZ, IND, OWN, and LEV are our controls as defined above. The β_j with $j = 0 \ldots 5$ are the model parameters. μ is the time fixed effect and e is our idiosyncratic error term.

13.4 Results and Discussion

Table 13.2 presents the descriptive statistics of our variables defined previously. The second column of this table confirms the number of observations presented in our sample, which is 880 obs. Our sample

Table 13.2. Descriptive statistics results.

Variable	Obs.	Mean	Std. Deviation	Max	Min
RISK	880	0.0309	0.1381	0.9603	0.013
ESG	880	0.5185	0.1852	0.9200	0.220
OWN	880	0.4566	0.3500	0.8200	0.042
SIZ	880	9.1960	1.8020	14.5700	8.887
LEV	880	37.2800	22.8140	50.6000	10.100
IND	Obs.	Freq			
IND1	52	59%			
IND2	36	41%			

is composed of 88 companies divided into two main industry sectors, with 52 companies in the first one (IND1) against 36 in the second (IND2). Besides, this table provides the averages of each variable. First, for the variable RISK, we register an average of 3.09% with a high spread around the mean presented by its standard deviation (0.1381). It is clear that the overall risk of French companies in our sample seems to be slightly lower than that of European companies. Indeed, Sassen *et al.* (2016), using a risk measure similar to ours, observed average total risk of around 0.3377 on a large sample of 8752 European firms with a standard deviation of 0.1734.

ESG scores range between 0 and 1, with high scores indicating strong performance in the category. The mean scores in our sample are 51.85%, with a maximum of 92% and a minimum of 22%. As an international comparison, the average ESG score observed on a sample of 94 Korean companies listed on the KOPSI (Korea Stock Exchange) over the 2008–2014 periods is close to 46%. According to the rating agency Novethic, the average ESG score of European companies is 45.4/100 (2017). However, these comparisons should be taken with great caution given the heterogeneity of ESG scoring approaches.

The average of our control variable OWN is 45.6%. It presents the mean of the percentage of the three largest shares, with 82% as maximum and 42% as a minimum. These findings are in line with those found by other research on the ownership structure of listed French companies (SBF120), (Faccio and Lang, 2002; Labelle and Schatt, 2005; Mard *et al.*, 2014). We conclude a high concentration of those companies' ownership, which limits the manager's authority.

Moreover, we considered the leverage ratio of the firms. According to the Table 13.2, this ratio has an average of 37.28%, judged reasonable for those firms. It remains, however, slightly below the debt rate of the Euro Zone (62% in 2015). Finally, and as our sample is made up of SFB 120 companies (the 120 largest market capitalizations), all companies are characterized by a large size (the average of total assets is 20,794 million Euros).

To reach our purpose and test the link between CSR and RISK, we started by testing the exogenous variables' choice. Thus, using the correlation matrix we verified the absence of correlation problems. The higher correlation value between the exogenous variables is 0.5325 for the SIZ and CSR variables. Besides, Table 13.3 shows a negative correlation between the CSR variable and the RISK, which in line with our assumption. Obviously a firm's higher ESG score is associated with lower total risk. Table 13.3 matrix reflects a negative correlation between the variables OWN and the ESG. Indeed, the increase in the percentage of capital held by the three largest shareholders means greater shareholders' control. Thus, managers will try to select social actions that grant higher shareholders value to avoid agency conflicts, which might reduce social investments. Moreover, the correlation between the IND measure and the ESG is positive, which is expected since firms in the IND1 group are more affected by social scandals, especially environmental ones. Hence, these companies try to generally protect their image and reduce their reputational risk through social engagement. Especially, after the French law of the energy transition for the green growth, the ESG information had to be reported by institutions (Khenissi *et al.*, 2019).

To have reliable validation, we run our least squares regressions; then we selected the appropriate estimation according to our

Table 13.3. Pearson correlation coefficient between the variables.

Variables	RISK	ESG	IND	OWN	SIZ	LEV
RISK	1					
ESG	−0.6666*	1				
IND	0.0851	0.0225**	1			
OWN	0.2225**	−0.1075**	0.0511	1		
SIZ	0.0844	0.5325**	−0.2610**	−0.2442**	1	
LEV	0.2004*	−0.1630**	0.0412**	−0.1988	0.1922	1

Note: $^{*}p < 0.10$, $^{**}p < 0.05$.

Table 13.4. ESG and firm risk.

Variable	Coefficient	t-student ($p > \|1\|$)
ESG	-0.2086^{***}	-6.667 (0.001)
SIZ	0.0291^{**}	2.370 (0.018)
IND	0.3670^{**}	2.350 (0.020)
OWN	-0.1179^{**}	-4.090 (0.017)
LEV	0.0091^{**}	1.980 (0.048)
observations	880	
R^2 (within)	23.9%	

Note: $^{**}p < 0.05$, $^{***}p < 0.01$.

regression tests. Our estimation fulfills the basic assumption of normality. Besides, we apply the Durbin–Watson autocorrelation test to verify the independency between the error terms. Moreover, we test the heteroscedasticity by the Breusch–Pagan test. Furthermore, we used the F-test for the individual effect issue. Hence, we conclude that the fixed-effect estimation is the most appropriate (see Table 13.4). This estimation method solves the time unobserved heterogeneity issue.

According to the Table 13.4 results, the explanatory power of our model is acceptable with an R^2 (within) equal to 23.9%. We register a negative significant association between CSR and RISK. An increase of 1% in the global CSR score decreases the dependent variable by -0.2086. Thus, our assumption is accepted. The CSR engagements reduce corporate global risk. This result is in line with the three main theories presented in our theoretical background. CSR reduces the reputational risk and reinforces the stakeholders' relationship.

Among others, Sharfman and Fernando (2008) and Salama *et al.* (2011) supported this negative association. Ashwin Kumar *et al.* (2016) stressed that ESG affects firms differently since the rule of less risk leads to lower returns is not applied. Social engagement not only reduces risk but also grants higher returns. This fact can be explained by the investors' preferences in the European context. More specifically, large institutional investors show their interest in specific CSR activities (Sassen *et al.*, 2016). Furthermore, France has a step forward compared to several other European countries since regulators required the extra financial reporting since 2010 after enacting the "Grenelle" law while this reporting was established in 2014 by the European Commission. According to the (IPP) Innovation Policy Platform statistics, since 2010 France has had a higher social performance than The Organization for Economic Co-operation and Development (OECD) average. The environmental performance index gap between France and OCED countries had dramatically increased, to 126.67 in France against 116.67 in the OECD countries.

Other than the CSR effect, we find a positive association (under the 10% error risk) between the corporate size and the firms' global risk. Indeed, larger firms can benefit from the economy of scale; thereby, they can hold more cash which reduces their liquidity risk. The positive coefficient of the variable IND confirms the increases of the global corporate risk by 36.7% if the firm operates in the first group sector, which is expected due to the reputational risk associated with these companies' activities.

In addition, we find a negative link between the shareholders' concentration and corporate risk. An increase of 1% of the corporate largest shares leads to less risk level. In fact, with the absence of the shareholders' control due to ownership dilution, managers grant higher power, and this might increase the agency conflicts. Those conflicts are able to increase the corporate risk and costs. In addition, with less control, managers who are the most informed can take advantage of the situation, which diminishes trust between stakeholders. Hence, increasing the shareholders' authority through their ownership concentration can help risk reduction.

Finally, a similar negative influence is presented between the leverage ratio and corporate risk. An increase in corporate debt can reduce risk, which confirms the favorable leverage and solvency for our sampled companies.

13.5 Conclusion

In this chapter, we attempted to add new insights to the literature on CSR by focusing on the relationship between CSR performance and the firm's global risk. In the first part of this chapter, we provided a theoretical background of the CSR and corporate risk nexus. We mobilized three main theories, which are the signalling theory, stakeholder theory, and legitimacy theory. Moreover, we explained the negative influence of the CSR disclosure on the corporate reputational risk, and thereby its effect on the global risk. Indeed, with greater information sharing, CSR disclosure grants higher transparency that reinforces the stakeholders' trust. It is considered as a positive signal sent to the key stakeholders. On the one hand, through the disclosure of their social achievements, firms are likely to reduce the degree of information asymmetry between the company and various market participants; therefore, social performance "exhibition" would be a positive signal enhancing a firm's notoriety and reputation, inducing better financial performance and mitigating the risk. On the other hand, CSR engagement would be able to gain stakeholders trust and support, making it possible to anticipate the risks and build up "CSR capital" to protect against the various risks, especially during crisis and scandals.

To verify the application of these theories in the French context, we provided in the second part an empirical analysis. Our results are in line with the theories and confirm the negative association between corporate global risk and CSR engagement. Our findings also highlight some policy implications. CSR initiatives and extra-financial disclosure are likely to enhance a firm's reputation by building trust-based relationships with different stakeholders and consequently mitigating stock return volatility. Managers should consider CSR as an effective tool for risk management. So, it is recommended that the management consider "strategically" CSR in decision-making-process both in managing various risks and in investment decision insofar "CSR-driven-investment" is likely to allow value creation and competitive positional betterment.

Even with the large body of research and robust theoretical background that defends the negative association between CSR and risk, several empirical evidences have disproved it. Indeed, the CSR effect depends on its strategic application. Using non-strategic CSR might give a hypocritical depiction, which influences the corporate social license to operate. Furthermore, inappropriate CSR engagement leads to extra–costs that impede corporate development and put the firm in a disadvantageous position. Hence, research should go beyond the simple CSR concept and provide a deeper understanding.

References

Abdelghany, K. E. (2005). Informational content of the cost of equity capital: empirical evidence. *Managerial Auditing Journal*, **20**(9): 928–935.

Ashwin Kumar, N. C., Smith, C., Badis, L., Wang, N., Ambrosy, P., and Tavares, R. (2016). ESG factors and risk-adjusted performance: a new quantitative model. *Journal of Sustainable Finance & Investment*, **6**(4): 292–300.

Astuti, C. W. and Nugrahanti, Y. W. (2015). Pengaruh pengungkapan corporate social responsibility terhadap reaksi pasar. *Dinamika Akuntansi Keuangan dan Perbankan*, **4**(2): 90–105.

Axjonow, A., Ernstberger, J., and Pott, C. (2018). The impact of corporate social responsibility disclosure on corporate reputation: a non-professional stakeholder perspective. *Journal of Business Ethics*, **151**(2): 429–450.

Bacq, S. and Eddleston, K. A. (2018). A resource-based view of social entrepreneurship: how stewardship culture benefits scale of social impact. *Journal of Business Ethics*, **152**(3): 589–611.

Bénabou, R. and Tirole, J. (2010). Individual and corporate social responsibility. *Economica*, **77**(305): 1–19.

Bouslah, K., Bouslah, L., and M'Zali, B. (2018). Social performance and firm risk: impact of the financial crisis. *Journal of Business Ethics*, **149**(3): 643–669.

Branco, M. C. and Rodrigues, L. L. (2008). Factors influencing social responsibility disclosure by Portuguese companies. *Journal of Business Ethics*, **83**(4): 685–701.

Brower, J. and Mahajan, V. (2013). Driven to be good: A stakeholder theory perspective on the drivers of corporate social performance. *Journal of Business Ethics*, **117**(2): 313–331.

Cai, L., Cui, J., and Jo, H. (2016). Corporate environmental responsibility and firm risk. *Journal of Business Ethics*, **139**(3): 563–594.

Campbell, D. (2003). Intra- and intersectoral effects in environmental disclosures: Evidence for legitimacy theory? *Business Strategy and the Environment*, **12**(6): 357–371.

Casado-Díaz, A. B., Nicolau-Gonzálbez, J. L., Ruiz-Moreno, F., and Sellers-Rubio, R. (2014). The differentiated effects of CSR actions in the service industry. *Journal of Services Marketing*, **28**(7): 558–565.

Chakraborty, A., Gao, L. S., and Sheikh, S. (2019a). Does size affect the relation between option compensation and managerial risk taking?

Evidence from Canadian listed companies. *International Journal of Finance & Economics*, **24**(1): 20–32.

Chakraborty, A., Gao, L. S., and Sheikh, S. (2019b). Managerial risk taking incentives, corporate social responsibility and firm risk. *Journal of Economics and Business*, **101**: 58–72.

Chang, Y., Chen, T. H., and Shu, M. C. (2018). Corporate social responsibility, corporate performance, and pay-performance sensitivity' — Evidence from Shanghai Stock Exchange Social Responsibility Index. *Emerging Markets Finance and Trade*, **54**(5): 1183–1203.

Cheng, M. and Christiawan, Y. J. (2011). Pengaruh pengungkapan corporate social responsibility terhadap abnormal return. *Journal Akuntansi dan Keuangan*, **13**(1): 24–36.

Chiu, S. C. and Sharfman, M. (2011). Legitimacy, visibility, and the antecedents of corporate social performance: An investigation of the instrumental perspective. *Journal of Management*, **37**(6): 1558–1585.

Choi, J. and Wang, H. (2009). Stakeholder relations and the persistence of corporate financial performance. *Strategic Management Journal*, **30**(8): 895–907.

Connelly, B. L., Certo, S. T., Ireland, R. D., and Reutzel, C. R. (2011). Signaling theory: A review and assessment. *Journal of Management*, **37**(1): 39–67.

Cui, J., Jo, H., and Na, H. (2018). Does corporate social responsibility affect information asymmetry?. *Journal of Business Ethics*, **148**(3): 549–572.

Doney, P. M. and Cannon, J. P. (1997). An examination of the nature of trust in buyer–seller relationships. *Journal of Marketing*, **61**(2): 35–51.

Dowling, J. and Pfeffer, J. (1975). Organizational legitimacy: Social values and organizational behavior. *Pacific Sociological Review*, **18**(1): 122–136.

Ducassy, I. (2013). Does corporate social responsibility pay off in times of crisis? An alternate perspective on the relationship between financial and corporate social performance. *Corporate Social Responsibility and Environmental Management*, **20**(3): 157–167.

El Ghoul, S., Guedhami, O., Kwok, C. C., and Mishra, D. R. (2011). Does corporate social responsibility affect the cost of capital? *Journal of Banking & Finance*, **35**(9): 2388–2406.

Elsaid, E. and Ursel, N. D. (2018). Re-examining the glass cliff hypothesis using survival analysis: the case of female CEO tenure. *British Journal of Management*, **29**(1): 156–170.

Faccio, M. and Lang, L. H. (2002). The ultimate ownership of Western European corporations. *Journal of Financial Economics*, **65**(3): 365–395.

Ferrell, A., Liang, H., and Renneboog, L. (2016). Socially responsible firms. *Journal of Financial Economics*, **122**(3): 585–606.

Flammer, C. (2015). Does corporate social responsibility lead to superior financial performance? A regression discontinuity approach. *Management Science*, **61**(11): 2549–2568.

Florea, R. and Florea, R. (2013). Stakeholders interests analyze and harmonization-starting point of strategic approach. *Economy Transdisciplinarity Cognition*, **16**(1): 130–135.

Freeman, R. E. (1984). *Stakeholder management: A strategic approach.* New York: Pitman.

Göçer, A., Jin, Y. H., and Fawcett, S. E. (2019). How Does the Contingent Sustainability–Risk–Cost Relationship Affect the Viability of CSR? An Emerging Economy Perspective. *Sustainability*, **11**(19): 1–25.

Godfrey, P. C. (2005). The relationship between corporate philanthropy and shareholder wealth: A risk management perspective. *Academy of Management Review*, **30**(4): 777–798.

Godfrey, P. C., Merrill, C. B., and Hansen, J. M. (2009). The relationship between corporate social responsibility and shareholder value: An empirical test of the risk management hypothesis. *Strategic Management Journal*, **30**(4): 425–445.

Harjoto, M. and Laksmana, I. (2018). The impact of corporate social responsibility on risk taking and firm value. *Journal of Business Ethics*, **151**(2): 353–373.

Hasan, I., Kobeissi, N., Liu, L., and Wang, H. (2018). Corporate social responsibility and firm financial performance: The mediating role of productivity. *Journal of Business Ethics*, **149**(3): 671–688.

Hollandts, X. and Valiorgue, B. (2011). La RSE comme processus entrepreneurial de conversion de valeurs sociales en valeur marchande: un examen empirique du lien entre engagements sociétaux et performance économique des entreprises françaises cotées entre 1999 et 2009. *Revue de l' Organisation Responsable*, **6**(2): 20–37.

Husted, B. W. (2005). risk management, real options, corporate social responsibility. *Journal of Business Ethics*, **60**(2): 175–183.

Jamali, D., Lund-Thomsen, P., and Khara, N. (2017). CSR institutionalized myths in developing countries: An imminent threat of selective decoupling. *Business & Society*, **56**(3): 454–486.

Jensen, M. and Meckling, W. (1976). Theory of the firm: Management behavior, agency costs and capital structure. *Journal of Financial Economics*, **3**(4): 305–60.

Jo, H. and Na, H. (2012). Does CSR reduce firm risk? Evidence from controversial industry sectors. *Journal of Business Ethics*, **110**(4): 441–456.

Jordan, B. D., Westerfield, R. W., and Ross, S. A. (2011). *Corporate finance essentials.* McGraw-Hill Irwin.

Kanagaretnam, K., Lobo, G. J., Wang, C., and Whalen, D. J. (2019). Cross-country evidence on the relationship between societal trust and risk-taking by banks. *Journal of Financial and Quantitative Analysis*, **54**(1): 275–301.

Khenissi, M., Serret, V., and Khemir, S. (2019). L'influence du système de gouvernance sur l'intégration des critères de responsabilité sociétale de l'entreprise dans la rémunération variable des dirigeants des sociétés de l'indice boursier SBF 120. *Revue de Gestion des Ressources Humaines*, **113**(3): 47–68.

Krüger, P. (2015). Corporate goodness and shareholder wealth. *Journal of Financial Economics*, **115**(2): 304–329.

Kytle, B. and Ruggie, J.G. (2005). "Corporate social responsibility as risk management: a model for multinationals", Corporate Social Responsibility Initiative Working Paper No. 10, John F. KennedySchool of Government, Harvard University, Cambridge, MA.

Lee, S., Kim, Y. K., and Kim, K. (2016). Corporate governance, firm risk, and corporate social responsibility: Evidence from Korean firms. *Journal of Applied Business Research*, **32**(1): 303–316.

Lee, Y. K., Lee, K. H., and Li, D. X. (2012). The impact of CSR on relationship quality and relationship outcomes: A perspective of service employees. *International Journal of Hospitality Management*, **31**(3): 745–756.

Lin, C. M., Chan, M. L., and Fang, W. S. (2019). Do Taiwanese Family Firms Have a Lower Propensity to Pay Cash Dividends? The Roles of Corporate Governance, Product Market Competition and Corporate Social Responsibility. *Journal of Economics*, **15**(1): 3–33.

Lins, K. V., Servaes, H., and Tamayo, A. (2017). Social capital, trust, and firm performance: The value of corporate social responsibility during the financial crisis. *The Journal of Finance*, **72**(4): 1785–1824.

Liu, M. and Lu, W. (2019). Corporate social responsibility, firm performance, and firm risk: the role of firm reputation. *Asia-Pacific Journal of Accounting and Economics*, **26**(2): 1–21.

Luo, X. and Bhattacharya, C. B. (2006). Corporate social responsibility, customer satisfaction, and market value. *Journal of Marketing*, **70**(4): 1–18.

Luo, X. and Bhattacharya, C. B. (2009). The debate over doing good: Corporate social performance, strategic marketing levers, and firm-idiosyncratic risk. *Journal of Marketing*, **73**(6): 198–213.

Mard, Y., Marsat, S., and Roux, F. (2014). Structure de l'actionnariat et performance financière de l'entreprise: le cas français. *Revue Finance Contrôle Stratégie*, **17**(4): 59–83.

Minor, D. and Morgan, J. (2011). CSR as reputation insurance: Primum non nocere. *California Management Review*, **53**(3): 40–59.

Monti, A., Pattitoni, P., Petracci, B., and Randl, O. (2019). Does Corporate Social Responsibility Impact Equity Risk? International Evidence. *International Evidence*. (January 31, 2019).

Odriozola, M. D. and Baraibar-Diez, E. (2017). Is corporate reputation associated with quality of CSR reporting? Evidence from Spain. *Corporate Social Responsibility and Environmental Management*, **24**(2): 121–132.

Oikonomou, I., Brooks, C., and Brooks, S. (2012). The impact of corporate social performance on financial risk and utility: A longitudinal analysis. *Financial Management*, **41**(2): 483–515.

Oliveira, J., Rodrigues, L. L., and Craig, R. (2011). Risk-related disclosures by non-finance companies: Portuguese practices and disclosure characteristics. *Managerial Auditing Journal*, **26**(9): 817–839.

Orlitzky, M. and Benjamin, J. D. (2001). Corporate social performance and firm risk: A meta-analytic review. *Business & Society*, **40**(4): 369–396.

Ortiz-de-Mandojana, N. and Bansal, P. (2016). The longterm benefits of organizational resilience through sustainable business practices. *Strategic Management Journal*, **37**(8): 1615–1631.

Park, J., Lee, H., and Kim, C. (2014). Corporate social responsibilities, consumer trust and corporate reputation: South Korean consumers' perspectives. *Journal of Business Research*, **67**(3): 295–302.

Perrault, E. and Quinn, M. A. (2018). What have firms been doing? Exploring what KLD data report about firms' corporate social performance in the period 2000–2010. *Business & Society*, **57**(5): 890–928.

Porter, M. E., and Kramer, M. R. (2006). The link between competitive advantage and corporate social responsibility. *Harvard business review*, **84**(12): 78–92.

Preston, L. E. and O'bannon, D. P. (1997). The corporate social-financial performance relationship: A typology and analysis. *Business and Society*, **36**(4): 419–429.

Ross, S. A. (1977). The determination of financial structure: the incentive-signalling approach. *The Bell Journal of Economics*, **8**(1): 23–40.

Salama, A., Anderson, K., and Toms, J. S. (2011). Does community and environmental responsibility affect firm risk? Evidence from UK panel data 1994–2006. *Business Ethics: A European Review*, **20**(2): 192–204.

Sassen, R., Hinze, A. K., and Hardeck, I. (2016). Impact of ESG factors on firm risk in Europe. *Journal of Business Economics*, **86**(8): 867–904.

Shad, M. K., Lai, F. W., Fatt, C. L., Klemeš, J. J., and Bokhari, A. (2019). Integrating sustainability reporting into enterprise risk management and its relationship with business performance: A conceptual framework. *Journal of Cleaner Production*, **208**: 415–425.

Sharfman, M. P. and Fernando, C. S. (2008). Environmental risk management and the cost of capital. *Strategic Management Journal*, **29**(6): 569–592.

Solikhah, B. (2016). An overview of legitimacy theory on the influence of company size and industry sensitivity towards CSR disclosure. *International Journal of Applied Business and Economic Research (IJABER)*, **14**(5): 3013–3023.

Spence, A. M. (1973). Time and communication in economic and social interaction. *The Quarterly Journal of Economics*, **87**(4): 651–660.

Sui, W., Yang, C., and Zhang, H. (2019). Is corporate social responsibility used to mask corporate speculation? evidence from emerging China. *Sustainability*, **11**(12): 3375.

Sun, W. and Cui, K. (2014). Linking corporate social responsibility to firm default risk. *European Management Journal*, **32**(2): 275–287.

Tan, A., Benni, D., and Liani, W. (2016). Determinants of corporate social responsibility disclosure and investor reaction. *International Journal of Economics and Financial Issues*, **6**(4S): 11–17.

Tanggamani, V., Amran, A., and Ramayah, T. (2018). The corporate social responsibility and corporate financial performance virtuous loop: A theoretical framework. *Global Business and Management Research*, **10**(1): 331–343.

Thanaya, S. A. and Widanaputra, A. A. G. P. (2019). The effect of CSR disclosure on firm risk in mining companies listed on $IDXa^2$. *E-Jurnal Akuntansi*, **29**(2): 93–107.

Ting, P. H. and Yin, H. Y. (2018). How do corporate social responsibility activities affect performance? The role of excess control right. *Corporate Social Responsibility and Environmental Management*, **25**(6): 1320–1331.

Tran, H., Bui, V., Phan, T., Dau, X., Tran, M., and Do, D. (2019). The impact of corporate social responsibility and risk management on financial performance: The case of Vietnamese textile firms. *Management Science Letters*, **9**(7): 1029–1036.

Utz, S. (2018). Over-investment or risk mitigation? Corporate social responsibility in Asia-Pacific, Europe, Japan, and the United States. *Review of Financial Economics*, **36**(2): 167–193.

Verrecchia, R. E. (1983). Discretionary disclosure. *Journal of Accounting and Economics*, **5**(1): 179–194.

Wang, Z., Hsieh, T. S., and Sarkis, J. (2018). CSR performance and the readability of CSR reports: too good to be true? *Corporate Social Responsibility and Environmental Management*, **25**(1): 66–79.

Wiśniewski, M. (2015). CSR risk management. *Forum Scientiae Oeconomia*, **3**(4): 17–24.

Yuan, W., Bao, Y., and Verbeke, A. (2011). Integrating CSR initiatives in business: An organizing framework. *Journal of Business Ethics*, **101**(1): 75–92.

https://doi.org/10.1142/9781786349507_0014

Chapter 14

Does Board Structure Matter for Innovation?

Meriam Attia[*,†,‡], **Ouidad Yousfi**[*,¶], **and Abdelwahed Omri**[†,‖]

[*] *Montpellier Research in Management (MRM), University of Montpellier, France*
[†] *University of Tunis, GEF2A Lab, Tunisia*
[‡] *meriam.attia@etu.umontpellier.fr*
[¶] *ouidad.yousfi@umontpellier.fr*
[‖] *abdelomri@gmail.com*

14.1 Introduction

Innovation is defined as a creative and complex activity that needs human capacities such as imagination, ingenuity, and creativity (Torchia *et al.*, 2011). However, to face the increasingly tough competition and maintain a sustainable competitive advantage, firms are forced to innovate and increase their capacity to integrate individuals displaying diverse types of knowledge, abilities, and networking. In recent years, policymakers have shown that innovation performance varies according to market regulation and governance mechanisms. Several initiatives and programs have been introduced in order to increase diversity in the board, such as gender quota laws and the presence of minorities in top management positions. These laws are intended to push companies to renew the composition of their board of directors, to select new profiles, and to detect the profiles of women, make them visible. Moreover, many decisions have been introduced to foster innovation and R&D activities (The EU agency for disruptive innovation, 2017). For instance, OECD countries, the United States (Paff, 2005; Wu, 2005), Japan (Kobayashi, 2014), China, (Chen *et al.*, 2019), and Canada (Czarnitzki *et al.*, 2011) tend to rely on tax incentives to promote R&D spending in the business sector. In order to facilitate access to financial resources and stimulate innovation activities, the government provides public R&D funding as public subsidies or R&D tax credit to innovative firms. The R&D tax credits and subsidies are two of the most popular instruments for governments to support R&D activities (Hall and Van Reenen, 2000).

Over the last fifteen years, a significant number of studies have analyzed the influence of corporate governance on innovation (Lodh *et al.*, 2014; George and Lin, 2016; Lu *et al.*, 2018; Wang *et al.*, 2017). Innovation literature has investigated several aspects of innovation such as how innovation affects firm performance (Hitt *et al.*, 1996), how leaders affect employees' innovativeness (Scott and Bruce, 1994), and how CEO (chief executive officer) and top management characteristics could lead to more innovations (Hirshleifer *et al.*, 2012; Chemmanur *et al.*, 2014; Vincent, 2002; Sariol and Abebe, 2017; Sheikh, 2018; Cho and Kim, 2017). Moreover, several studies have focused, especially, on the impact of ownership structure on innovation decisions (Chang *et al.*, 2006; Belloc, 2012; Choi *et al.*, 2012; Shapiro *et al.*, 2013; Lodh *et al.*, 2014; Diéguez-Soto *et al.*, 2016; Yi *et al.*, 2017; Villalonga, 2006). For instance, Choi *et al.* (2012), Shapiro *et al.* (2013) show that the ownership structure is a critical factor in helping companies realize innovative projects. Belloc (2012) shows that concentrated ownership is important for innovation activities because it provides effective monitoring mechanisms. Chang *et al.* (2006) confirm that the majority of shareholders have positive effects on firms' innovation performance, while Chen *et al.* (2011), Lodh *et al.* (2014), and Shapiro *et al.* (2013) argue that foreign ownership has a positive influence on innovation performance.

Furthermore, innovation literature has strongly shown how directors could have a positive impact on innovation (Torchia *et al.*, 2011 and Pathan and Faff, 2013). Empirical evidence has largely supported the idea that the board involvement is a key factor in innovation projects (Torchia *et al.*, 2011; Pathan and Faff, 2013; Galia and Zenou, 2013; Galia *et al.*, 2015). Beyond its role of ensuring the alignment of interests between shareholders and managers, dominated by agency theory and focusing on the monitoring and controlling role of boards (Daily *et al.*, 2003), research brings evidence that another crucial role of the board of directors is to provide strategic advice, knowledge, resources and networking to the company (Hillman *et al.*, 2000; Huse, 2007), which could be value-enhancing for innovation (Talke *et al.*, 2010). In fact, according to resource dependence theory (Pfeffer and Salancik, 1978), the personal characteristics of CEOs and directors affect a firm's innovation investment and value. Specifically, the educational background is an important cognitive variable for a firm to undertake complex corporate strategies. Moreover, drawing on upper-echelons and the human capital theories (Westphal and Zajac, 1995), directors may bring to the board different backgrounds, experiences, and opinions which may lead to better performance. Consequently, corporate governance mechanisms, particularly board member attributes [demographic characteristics, culture, experiences], influence and increase managerial risk-taking. So, innovation strategies can be influenced by the personal traits of directors (Barker and Mueller, 2002; Kor, 2006).

However, several areas in innovation literature are not yet fully explored: First, beyond the traditional role of monitoring and control (Ruigrok *et al.*, 2006) and the alignment of shareholders and managers' interests, mostly explained by agency theory (Daily *et al.*, 2003), studies did not focus on the analysis of the directors' characteristics and their influence on the decision-making process. Actually, few studies have examined the relationship between demographic characteristics of directors and innovation. Most of them confirm the fact that independent directors could influence innovation strategies. The literature has taken into account the influence of independent directors but has neglected the influence that foreign directors might have on innovation strategies due to their different nationalities and cultures. Moreover, some papers provide evidence that the educational level of board members is positively associated with innovation (Kuo *et al.*, 2018); however, previous studies have ignored the influence of academic degree type and the professional background of directors on innovation. Another group of studies has analyzed the impact of female directors on innovation these studies have focused on one specific pattern of diversity (Gender) (see among others Torchia *et al.*, 2011; Turner, 2009; Østergaard *et al.*, 2011; Díaz-García *et al.*, 2013; Galia and Zenou, 2013; Pathan and Faff, 2013; Galia *et al.*, 2015). Focusing on the existing finding, we notice that literature marginalizes several forms of diversity in boards, such as age, nationality, academic background, and professional experience. There is not enough evidence on the effects of different board characteristics of innovative firms.

Then, despite the central role of boards in corporate governance, there is relatively little understanding of how the internal organization of boards, specifically the structure of board committees, could shape strategic decisions such as innovation. In fact, governance literature has strongly underlined the importance of committees in the functioning of the board (Adams, 2003; Adams *et al.*, 2010; Guo and Masulis, 2015). The composition and functions of committees have a strong influence on the board's composition as well as committee's activities. Turning to studies which discuss the composition of board committees, the literature focuses, especially, on audit committee: it shows how composition of audit committees could influence the quality of financial disclosure, internet reporting, earnings management, and financial performance (Karamanou and Vafeas, 2005; Mangena and Pike, 2005, Kelton and Yang, 2008; Bédard *et al.*, 2004; Klein, 2002; Zhou *et al.*, 2018). Moreover, most of papers have studied the effect of appointing independent members in committees (Deli and Gillan, 2000; Klein, 2002; Zhang *et al.*, 2007; Krishnan, 2005; Choi *et al.*, 2007). We point out that the literature neglects several forms of directors' attributes in key committees and their influence on the firm's activities. To the best of our knowledge, the effects of diversity on committees have not been fully established.

To fulfill this gap in the literature, this contribution aims to investigate how diverse attributes could influence corporate innovation. In the next section, we focus on individual characteristics and their influence on innovation effort and performance. Then, we examine how the internal organization of boards, specifically the committees' roles and their composition and to what extent they could be meaningful to innovation processes. Specially, we discuss the influence of the committee size, the frequency of meetings, and the presence of independent and female members. Finally, the chapter sheds light on the effectiveness of initiatives and programs introduced to increase diversity on boards.

14.2 Do Directors' Attributes in Boards Influence Innovation?

14.2.1 *Board diversity: Theoretical perspectives*

The most commented functions of the board in the literature are monitoring the senior management to protect the company against opportunistic behavior and advising the management on strategic decisions (Agency theory, Fama and Jensen, 1983). However, beyond these functions, the board provides necessary resources, competencies, and networking to the firms (Hillman *et al.*, 2000; Huse, 2007). According to the resource-dependence theory (Pfeffer and Salancik, 1978), members of the board constitute a source of knowledge, expertise, and skills, and therefore a source of a better performance. In fact, personal cognition and knowledge are important corporate governance variables for a firm to perform complex investments. Therefore, the personal characteristics of CEOs and directors could affect a firm's innovation investment.

Moreover, based on the theory of human capital (Westphal and Zajac, 1995), directors with different experiences and sets of educational backgrounds may lead to more diverse boards, and thus benefit the overall performance of the firms (Terjesen *et al.*, 2009). In addition, boards with varied skills and perspectives may lead a better quality of management, and hence better innovation performance (Torchia *et al.*, 2011; Pathan and Faff, 2013; Galia and Zenou, 2013; Galia *et al.*, 2015). In the same vein, many studies highlight that diversity on the board has been associated with positive cognitive effects such as creativity, new ideas, and insights, which could influence the ideas and types of innovation in the firm (Deutsch, 2005; Torchia *et al.*, 2011; Pathan and Faff, 2013; Galia and Zenou, 2013; Galia *et al.*, 2015). Therefore, human capital theory brings new insights supported also by the resource dependence theory: under specific conditions, board diversity is a valuable mechanism to improve innovation performance (Torchia *et al.*, 2011).

However, the social-psychological concept of minority status, which is derived from social impact theory (Latané, 1981), states that majority status groups are powerful and more influential over the decision-making process (Carter *et al.*, 2010). Therefore, females, being usually considered as minorities on diverse boards, may not have the power to influence the board as the result of the internal group dynamics of the board (Westphal and Milton, 2000). Moreover, more diverse boards may lead to more conflict and divergent opinions, which make the decision-making process time-consuming and less effective (Campbell and Vera, 2008, and Carter *et al.*, 2010).

14.2.2 *Board composition and innovation*

Early research on board diversity focused on task-related director attributes such as educational and functional background, as well as organizational and board tenure factors (Goodstein *et al.*, 1994; Sharma, 2016; Prencipe, 2016; Westphal and Zajac, 1995). However, with the wider acceptance of the value in diversity proposition and the greater pressures to increase diversity on corporate boards (Daily and Dalton, 2003), new dimensions of diversity in board composition are emerging. For instance, in North America, attention is increasingly paid to race, ethnicity, and gender of corporate directors (Carter *et al.*, 2003; Daily *et al.*, 1999; Erhardt *et al.*, 2003), while in Europe, nationality (Ruigrok *et al.*, 2007) and gender (Singh and Vinnicombe, 2004; Singh *et al.*, 2001) appear to be important dimensions of board diversity. In fact, research based on the European context confirms that the introduction of gender and/or nationality diversity on boards has important implications for board dynamics (Galia and Zenou, 2013; Galia *et al.*, 2015).

Indeed, diversity as well as board composition vary according to the country, market regulation such as gender quota laws, and governance mechanisms (Hoskisson *et al.*, 2002).

For instance, referring to the (Table 14.1), which shows the descriptive statistics of the boards composition of companies listed on the SBF120 index between 2002 and 2016[1,2] the average board size

---

[1]Board structure datasets are hand-collected from annual reports available on the firms' websites.

[2]This work supported by a partnership between the University of Montpellier and CASD [reference: ANR-10-EQPX-17 - Center d' secure data access — CASD].

Table 14.1. Board composition: French context.

Variables	Obs	Mean	Std. Dev	Min	Max
B-Gen	1468	17.45547	14.15293	0	63.6363
B-Ind	1466	49.03985	22.28997	0	100
B-For	1470	20.32871	20.43091	0	100
B-Size	1502	12.37617	3.568168	3	24
B-Age	1470	59.87434	5.4997	21	81
B-Edu	1470	64.0529	22.29494	0	100
B-Bus	1470	63.29881	18.45479	0	100

Note: B-Gen: Percentage of female directors on board. B-Ind: Percentage of independent directors on board. B-For: Percentage of foreign directors on board. B-Size: Total number of directors on board. B-Age: Average age of directors. B-Edu: Percentage of directors who have Master, MBA or PhD degree. B-Bus: Percentage of directors who have a business/management/ corporate law education.

is almost 12, which is larger than boards in other countries: Torchia *et al.* (2011) find an average board size of 7 in Norwegian companies, Kang (2007) find an average board size of 8 in Australian companies, and Godard and Schatt (2005) also notice a higher average board size on French firms [more than 11] in 2002. These differences can vary significantly among countries.

Moreover, despite the introduction of gender quota law, very few women are in board positions; the percentage of female directors on boards almost is 17.5%, since, most often, males are appointed to director positions (82.5%). This low level is consistent with other countries: Kang *et al.* (2007) showed a percentage of 10% on Australian firms, and Mahadeo *et al.* (2012) showed it as only 3% on Mauritanian firms.

In addition, in line with Godard and Schatt (2005), Table 14.1 shows that the average board consists of 12 members, half of them (49%) are independent and two of them (20%) have a foreign nationality. The percentages of independent and foreign directors significantly vary among firms, particularly in multinational companies [between 0 and 100%]. However, Lu *et al.* (2018), using panel data on United States public firms, found that almost 70% of the board are independent directors. Regarding the academic background, 64% of the directors are highly educated (Master, MBA, or PhD degree), and 63% of directors are business or management educated. In fact,

France is well known for its elitist world based on prestigious education (Ecole Nationale de l'Administration, engineer's schools: Mines, Ponts, Centrale, ENSAE, Télécoms..., and business schools: HEC, ESSEC, ESCP, and INSEAD). People who graduated from these schools run the biggest French firms and accumulate directorships in large public and private firms. Most of them had governmental functions or worked in ministries for several years.

Turning to innovation, only 15.38% of firms have introduced a new or a significantly improved product or service, and 14.46% have implemented a new or a significantly improved process. For patents, there are on average, 27.48 patents filed. Regarding the R&D team structure, almost 80 hours on average is dedicated to R&D projects.[3,4]

Regarding studies that have examined the relationship between board composition and innovation, most of them confirm the fact that independent directors could influence innovation strategies. Based on panel data on the largest German companies, Balsmeier *et al.* (2014) show a positive influence of external executives on the performance of innovative firms, measured by patent applications. Using panel data on US public firms, Lu *et al.* (2018) found a positive effect of board independence on corporate innovation, whereas Sena *et al.* (2018), based on a sample of manufacturing subsidiaries controlled by British multinationals, tested the hypothesis that independent boards can insulate a company from the detrimental impact of corruption on innovation. The literature has taken into account the influence of independent directors but has neglected the influence that foreign directors might have on innovation strategies due to their different nationalities and culture.

Also, some papers provide evidence that the educational level of board members is positively associated with innovation in the Taiwanese context (Lin *et al.*, 2011). Moreover, Kuo *et al.* (2018), based on a sample of 437 Taiwanese listed firms, concluded that the

[3]Statistics of innovation are provided by the surveys on Innovation conducted by the INSEE [Project Governance and Innovation in France 2016]. This work is supported by a public grant overseen by the French National Research Agency [ANR] as part of the "Investissements d'avenir" program, specifically Governance and Innovation in France GOUINFR, 2016.

[4]https://www.insee.fr/en/metadonnees/source/serie/s1001.

directors' education does affect R&D firm investment and suggested that highly educated directors lead the firm to invest more in R&D projects. However, previous studies have ignored the influence of academic degree type and the professional background of directors on innovation: to the best of our knowledge, drawn on Asian data, Lin *et al.* (2011); Kuo *et al.* (2018) are among the rare papers to address this question.

Another group of studies has analyzed the impact of female directors on innovation in Spain (Diaz-Garcia *et al.*, 2013). Women on board improves interaction and dynamics in R&D teams (Teruel *et al.*, 2015), and specifically fosters the firm's ability to introduce organizational innovations (Torchia *et al.*, 2011). All these studies, however, have focused on one specific pattern of diversity (gender) and one specific form of innovation (organizational innovation). Very few studies have investigated the effect of gender diversity on innovation (Miller and Triana, 2009). In fact, the existing literature marginalizes other forms of diversity in boards and the impact of directors' attributes on different forms of innovations.

14.2.2.1 *Presence of outside directors on board and innovation: Independent, foreign directors*

In the past few years, many studies have examined how outside board members could impact innovation performance (see among others Chen and Hsu, 2009; Choi and Lee, 2011; Choi *et al.*, 2012; Shapiro *et al.*, 2013; Chen 2013, Lodh *et al.*, 2014; Balsmeier *et al.*, 2014; Lu *et al.*, 2018; Faleye *et al.*, 2011). Drawing on agency theory, a higher proportion of independence may lead to a better monitoring function of the board. Therefore, boards should include the appropriate mix of experience and backgrounds to better exercise their monitoring role and to evaluate management and assess business strategies (Hillman and Dalziel, 2003 and Adams and Ferreira, 2009). In fact, independent directors increase monitoring, which helps companies to effectively allocate their R&D budget and to provide access to resources for technological innovation activities (Shapiro *et al.*, 2013). They have a wide range of resources that could boost innovation activities (Choi *et al.*, 2012). Based on a sample of Taiwanese business, Chen (2013) found that the presence of independent directors has a positive moderating effect on the director's contribution to innovation. One explanation could be that independent directors exercise better monitoring of managers and facilitate access to the resources needed for innovation. In the same vein, recent results support that external knowledge and expertise on boards are especially valuable resources when complex operations are considered (Chen and Hsu, 2009). External directors on boards can provide specific monitoring and advising competencies needed to improve innovative performance because of their own proven leadership skills and market experiences.

Furthermore, the management literature points out that the monitoring and advising competences of outside directors, or generally the human capital they bring to the board, strongly depend on their specific professional experiences (see among others Kor and Sundaramurthy, 2009; Kor and Misangyi, 2008). Hence, in terms of innovation, firms might benefit particularly from having an external director who is experienced in similar technological areas (Carpenter and Westphal, 2001). Directors might also bring valuable organizational capital to the board by providing insights on suitable ways of organizing innovative activities. Nevertheless, the negative influence of outside directors is still conceivable. In fact, the financial economics literature provides evidence suggesting that outside board members might be more concerned about their private benefits than about the performance of the firms they are supposed to monitor and advise (Fahlenbrach *et al.*, 2010a). Independent directors are not the only outside directors that could be appointed to boardrooms. For instance, more foreign members are sitting on boards, specifically in large corporations.

On the one hand, in line with dependence resource theory (Pfeffer and Salancik, 1979), foreign directors may provide diverse perspectives, valuable ideas, and problem-solving abilities and may facilitate the achievement of optimal and creative solutions. They may stimulate a firm to improve or develop new products sold abroad as they also possess knowledge about global markets and customers' tastes (Kerr and Lincoln, 2010). In fact, the heterogeneity of people is likely to be a necessary driver for the creation of new ideas (Barker and Mueller, 2002) and to stimulate innovation (Berliant and Fujita, 2011). In addition, foreign directors of the same educational level are imperfectly substitutable groups because of cultural differences. Fujita and Weber (2004) argue that cultural diversity of the labor force might be a key determinant for R&D activity. In fact, the generation of new products and ideas heavily relies on individual talents and skills from diverse educational and cultural environments. Fujita and Weber (2004) note also that knowledge production relies heavily on the talents and skills of members coming from a wide range of cultural backgrounds. The nature of R&D activity calls for interaction between different individuals and the pooling of different ideas and abilities. Likewise, Alesina and La Ferrara (2005) argue that ethical and cultural diversity may lead to innovation and creativity since it involves a variety of abilities and knowledge. Berliant and Fujita (2008) also refer to the significance of cultural diversity for knowledge creation and transfer. The heterogeneity of people is important for the creation of new ideas (Cox *et al.*, 1991). On the other hand, ethnic diversity could provide diverse perspectives, but not automatically valuable for innovation and solving problems (Berliant and Fujita, 2011). Foreign directors, directors of different ethnic and cultural backgrounds and different nationalities seem to stimulate a firm to improve or develop new products sold abroad as they also possess knowledge about global markets and customers' tastes (Kerr and Lincoln, 2010).

14.2.2.2 *How does directors' education influence innovation?*

Directors' education levels have been the subject of a number of researches; most of them concluded that a high educational level is positively correlated with managerial capabilities and innovation (see among others Lin *et al.*, 2011; Kuo *et al.*, 2018). In fact, board members with postgraduate degrees have the ability to better analyze complex information (Escriba-Esteve *et al.*, 2009), to efficiently solve problems, and to adopt new technologies (Dalziel *et al.*, 2011). In the same order of ideas, Wincent *et al.* (2010) show that the number of directors who have degrees from elite institutions and who have a rich academic background[5] positively impact innovation. Similarly,

[5]Wincent *et al.* (2010) show that the degree of board diversity and interlocking directorates primarily influence incremental innovation, whereas education level influences radical innovation. They find that a network board's diversity of expertise and education level are important for improving all components of innovative performance [total, radical and incremental].

Lundvall *et al.* (2002) show that educational level reflects personality traits, cognitive styles, and values. Therefore, a firm where directors have a higher educational level is more likely to invest in innovation projects.

However, the diversity of educational degrees leads to exposure to different knowledge and may lead to different and divergent ways of thinking so that making a decision becomes time-consuming and communication less effective and slower than in a more homogenous groups. This could decrease investments in R&D projects, resulting in a negative impact on innovation. Unlike Daellenbach *et al.* (1999) and Barker and Mueller (2002), who did not find any significant association between director's education level and R&D investment, Dahlin *et al.* (2005) argue that educational diversity will enhance the information use, while too much diversity will reduce the ability to diffuse the information between members.

Turning to the type of academic degree, science, engineering, or technology degree holders will have a better ability to understand technology and innovation and are more likely to support a higher level of R&D spending (Tyler and Steensma, 1998). In fact, directors with science and engineering degrees have better skills when they have to use new technologies or to adopt new ideas. They could increase the probability of accepting and introducing new changes. However, management and business-educated directors have business skills, specifically in finance and on accounting areas (Nekhili and Gatfaoui, 2013; Gendron and Bedard, 2006). In fact, MBA programs attract more conservative and risk-averse students who acquire analytic skills to avoid losses (Finkelstein and Hambrick, 1996). Consequently, management and business-educated directors have better skills to handle risks but prefer short-term profitable investments at the expense of risky and long-term investments such as innovative projects.

14.2.3 *Gender diversity on board*

In the fields of management and economics, the number of studies on gender has increased in the last few years (Ali *et al.*, 2014; Loukil and Yousfi, 2015; Sastre, 2015; Kang, 2007; Mahadeo *et al.*, 2012; Østergaard *et al.*, 2011; Torchia *et al.*, 2011; Galia and Zenou, 2013; Pathan and Faff, 2013; Galia *et al.*, 2015). For instance, studies have discussed how the presence of women on boards could influence a firm's financial and social performance (see among others: Carter *et al.*, 2010; Carter *et al.*, 2003; Belghiti Mahut *et al.*, 2010), corporate governance (Carter *et al.*, 2003; Adams and Ferreira, 2009), identifying resource dependency (Hillman *et al.*, 2000), and network ties (Hillman *et al.*, 2007). According to the resource dependence theory, the appointment of women directors brings new skills and qualifications to the firm. The presence of female directors helps to better understand the marketplace, particularly customers and employees, as they are themselves gender diverse. It could improve the firm's image in the market, particularly for stakeholders, and potential and current employees, customers, and investors (Hillman *et al.*, 2007).

Moreover, many studies provide evidence that appointing women to board positions changes the decision-making dynamics of the board (Elstad and Ladegard, 2012). In fact, women on boards bring different perspectives, expertise, and working styles from their male counterparts (Daily *et al.*, 2003; Hillman *et al.*, 2002). Moreover, Nielsen and Huse (2010) identify another aspect, that the presence of women on board contributes to reducing the level of interest conflicts and ensures a high quality of development activities.

Turning to innovation, gender diversity may deliver a broad range of perspectives, increase the search for information, enhance the quality of brainstormed ideas, facilitate creativity, and generate more strategic alternatives (Post and Byron, 2015). For instance, Torchia *et al.* (2018) show that women directors contribute positively and significantly to organizational innovation. They notice that some decision-making culture dimensions mediate the positive relationship between women directors and the level of organizational innovation: among these dimensions, there are the degree of cognitive conflict and the degree of preparation, and involvement during board meetings. As organizational innovation is related to cognitive and learning processes (Nonaka and Takeuchi, 1995) and is the output of various intervening mental processes (Hodgkinson, 2003), gender diversity boosts all these aspects and could be positively related to the organizational innovation.

In addition, gender diversity influences a firm's risk-taking; female directors are labelled as more risk-averse than men (Croson and Gneezy, 2009). Therefore, they invest less in risky projects such as innovation. In the same vein, Niederle and Vesterlund (2007) conclude that women are less competitively inclined and less overconfident than men. Consequently, women avoid risky and challenging situations. However, Nählinder (2010) shows that men and women have different approach when they innovate: For instance, women conduct innovations that are largely inspired by local needs to achieve social ends. Therefore, women have specific knowledge of consumer markets, consumer behavior, and customer needs (Kang *et al.*, 2007; Torchia *et al.*, 2011; Díaz-García *et al.*, 2013; Teruel *et al.*, 2015). Their presence on the board can contribute to broadening the range of new products and services.

14.2.4 *Directors' age*

Social and professional experiences of directors are closely related to their age. The age will change the individual's vision, beliefs, attitudes, and interpersonal networks. In fact, director's career comes with age, and it can influence corporate governance (Jackling and Johl, 2009). For example, young directors are more concerned about their reputation and have shorter prior professional experience while old directors are more skillful in business decision-making. Moreover, Mahadeo *et al.* (2012) show that age diversity improves learning abilities and helps to develop new and innovative ideas. Therefore, age diversity among board members can help the board to consider a variety of perspectives and to better target consumers' needs in different age groups, with a greater variety of products and services (Kang *et al.*, 2007). In addition, age could influence risk-taking. Old groups are less risk-tolerant (Bucciol and Miniaci, 2011). They invest in more routine and less risky investments than young directors, particularly when they are entrenched. However, based on their experience, their knowledge, and their background, old directors can detect and identify the most profitable projects and are more prone to introduce successful innovations, despite their risk aversion (Mahadeo *et al.*, 2012). However, unlike stated by Kang *et al.* (2007), age diversity can lead to a lack of cohesion in decision-making, worsen the communication process, and decrease trust among board members (Mahadeo *et al.*, 2012). Torchia *et al.* (2011) provide evidence that there is a negative relationship between age diversity and organizational innovation.

Finally, we notice that diversity in boardrooms is a booming area of research. In fact, governance literature has strongly shown how the board of directors could provide large and diverse resources to the firm, such as strategic advice, knowledge, and networking, which could be value-enhancing for innovation (Talke *et al.*, 2010; Torchia *et al.*, 2011; Pathan and Faff, 2013; Galia and Zenou, 2013; Galia *et al.*, 2015). These studies conclude that the composition of board is a determinant for innovation strategy. However, despite a large number of studies on board committees, the question of diversity in committees is not yet fully explored. Hereafter, we analyze how board committees could influence innovation and to what extent.

14.3 Does Diversity in Board Committees Favor Innovation?

14.3.1 *Role of board committees and innovation*

Governance literature has strongly underlined the importance of committees in the functioning of the board (Adams, 2003; Adams *et al.*, 2010; Guo and Masulis, 2015). It provides a means and structure for effective governance by facilitating special tasks and addressing important corporate concerns (Adams, 2003). In fact, the most influential board decisions are taken at the committee level (Kesner, 1988; Klein, 1998; Adams, 2003; Guo and Masulis, 2015). For instance, the audit committee oversees the integrity and compliance of the firm's financial reporting. The compensation committee focuses on human resource policies and procedures, most notably the compensation of top executives. The governance committee recommends new candidates for the board and other top executive positions and sets general governance procedures; directors are usually assigned to committees at the recommendation of the governance committee (Adams, 2003). Klein (1998) considers committee membership to be a proxy for the duties and functions of a director on the board. Directors have a stronger and more direct impact on executive compensation, director selection, and other important actions that significantly affect corporate performance; under specific conditions, such committees members have to serve on board committees with primary responsibility for these functions.

Moreover, committees are important mechanisms to monitor corporate activities and play a valuable role in the protection of shareholders' wealth (Kesner, 1988). From an agency perspective, committees can allow directors to better perform their control role. The specialization of committees and the large amount of information that directors can share during meetings increase the potential to monitor executives and protect shareholders' wealth. Furthermore, from a resource-based-perspective, committees can enhance the involvement of directors in innovation activities (Harrison, 1987). They can better inform the whole board about the resources they can provide for firm growth (Gabrielsson and Winlund, 2000). They can also provide advice on how to use the resources required for innovation opportunities, which could lead to an increase in shareholders' wealth.

Board committees offer knowledge specialization, task-division efficiency, and accountability. The nature of the monitoring and advising tasks of boards are complex and require significant firm-specific knowledge; its accumulation requires personal investment from directors. In fact, committee members could provide large and diverse resources to the firm, such as strategic advice and networking, which could be value-enhancing for innovation (Talke *et al.*, 2010). Accordingly, in order to perform their role effectively, board committees should have adequate resources and authority to discharge their increasing responsibilities and stimulate innovative' activities (see among others FRC, 2008; Mangena and Pike, 2005).

14.3.2 *Committee composition and innovation*

Board committees have become more regulated and formal components of the board of directors over time. Beginning in 1940, the Securities and Exchange Commission (SEC) recommended that outside directors should be appointed to audit committees. In the 1970s, SEC adopted rules requiring firms to disclose audit committee composition (Reeb and Upadhyay, 2010). In 2002, the major stock exchanges NYSE and NASDAQ mandated that firms have compensation and governance committees. In fact, the last accounting and executive pay scandals had shed light on the role and effects of committees on financial performance (Klein, 2002; Kelton and Yang, 2008; Sun *et al.*, 2009). Governance literature has, first, focused on audit committee and how its composition could influence governance quality. For instance, Deli and Gillan (2000), Klein (2002), Krishnan (2005), and Zhang *et al.* (2007) have examined the impact of audit committee characteristics such as the audit committee independence, the financial expertise of audit committee members, and the committee's size (Deli and Gillan, 2000; Klein, 2002, Zhang *et al.*, 2007; Krishnan, 2005). Some studies have also examined how the composition of audit committee could influence the quality of financial disclosure (Karamanou and Vafeas, 2005; Mangena and Pike, 2005), internet reporting (Kelton and Yang, 2008), earnings management (Bédard *et al.*, 2004; Klein, 2002), and financial performance (Zhou *et al.*, 2018).

Moreover, turning to the composition of board committees shows that most studies have covered the effect of appointing independent members (Deli and Gillan, 2000; Klein, 2002; Zhang *et al.*, 2007; Krishnan 2005; Choi *et al.*, 2007). In fact, independent committees help to improve managerial monitoring (Xie *et al.*, 2003). They could also improve financial performance (Choi *et al.*, 2007). Ruigroki *et al.* (2006) find that firms with nomination committees are more likely to have a higher number of independent and foreign directors and a lower number of female members. When the CEO is on the nomination committee, firms appoint fewer independent directors (Shivdasani and Yermack, 1999). Moreover, Guo and Masulis (2015) conclude that greater board independence and full independence of nominating committees lead to more rigorous CEO monitoring and discipline. However, the literature neglects several forms of directors' attributes in committees and their influence on the firm's activities. Despite this booming number of studies on committees, to the best of our knowledge, the effects of diversity on board committees have not been considered, yet.

14.3.2.1 *What do women bring to committees?*

Prior research has pointed out several reasons to hire more women on corporate boards as well as on board committees (Zalata, 2018). For instance, Daily and Dalton (2003) state that boards are increasingly appointing female members. In fact, the absence of gender diversity on board may result in a negative market image. Moreover, Kesner (1988) argued that firms are prone to elect the most powerful and influential women in their committees. Most often, they are concerned about the firm image, without consideration of the women's potential contributions (Tokenism, Kanter, 1977).

However, Elstad and Ladegard (2012) show that the presence of female directors changes the decision-making dynamics inside the board. In fact, in line with the dependence resource theory, women have different experiences and qualifications from their male counterparts; they could, therefore, have different values and analysis perspectives. This leads to more interactive dynamics in boardrooms (Peterson and Philpot, 2007). They have, most often, more connections to external sources, which make them highly sought after in boards and on specific board committees, such as audit, governance, ethics, and environment committees (Singh and Vinnicombe, 2004; Adams and Ferreira, 2009).

Despite the introduction of gender quota law, female directors are not appointed to strategic committees on the board, such as development and remuneration committees. In fact, very few women are in committee board positions, particularly in male-dominated companies. Female directors are still prevented from moving up into management and leadership positions and are facing significant barriers (glass ceiling theory, ILO, 2001).[6] Moreover, the complexity of the board selection process (Peterson and Philpot, 2007), in addition to many gender stereotypes, still makes it more difficult for a woman to be nominated on boards as well as on committees (Singh and Terjesen, 2008; Brière and Rinfret, 2010).

Besides, female directors display greater diligence in monitoring and are most often appointed to corporate governance committees (Adams and Ferreira, 2009). Gender-diverse committees can provide better advice, legitimacy, effective communication, and resources (Hillman *et al.*, 2007) than male-dominated committees. Female directors exhibit more independent thinking (Adams *et al.*, 2010), which facilitates decision-making and increases transparency (Adams *et al.*, 2010; Srinidhi *et al.*, 2011). Thus, the appointment of female directors to committees can be a source of competitive advantage.

---

[6]The glass ceiling was identified in the 1980s by the International Labor Organization and Catalyst4. The glass ceiling theory is about "those artificial barriers based on an attitudinal or organisational bias that prevents qualified individuals from advancing upward into management level positions" (ILO, 2001).

Moreover, many studies have strongly supported that their presence on board can contribute to broadening the range of new products and services (Østergaard *et al.*, 2011; Teruel *et al.*, 2015) as women have specific knowledge of consumer markets, consumer behavior, and customer needs (see among others Kang *et al.*, 2007; Torchia *et al.*, 2011; Díaz-García *et al.*, 2013; Teruel *et al.*, 2015); thus, they are likely to identify the most successful innovations. For instance, when female directors are appointed to the strategic committees, they can contribute to broadening the range of new products and services.

However, turning to nomination committees, female members will be inclined to prefer and encourage the nomination of other female candidates. They may recommend more female candidates to increase their feelings of security, identity, and self-esteem (Singh and Vinnicombe, 2004). Therefore, by appointing more female directors, women seem to select members who share similar demographic characteristics and not necessarily skillful directors who have the necessary qualifications to fulfil their responsibilities. Furthermore, there is consensus in the literature arguing that women are risk-averse (Faccio *et al.*, 2016; Crosen and Gneezy, 2009). Female directors are labelled as more risk-averse than men (Croson and Gneezy, 2009), which could drastically decrease long-term profitable and uncertain activities, such as innovation projects. Therefore, women in strategic committees avoid challenging situations, which could marginalize investments with unknown outcomes, such as R&D activities.

14.3.2.2 *Why should more independent directors be appointed to committees?*

In the 1990s, the Cadbury Report (Cadbury Committee, 1992) and several studies recommended the appointment of more independent directors to corporate boards and to their key committees (i.e. audit, compensation, and nomination committees) to improve the boards' and the committees' effectiveness (Klein, 1998). In fact, board's independence could enhance board's effectiveness and improve, therefore, the firm's performance (Choi *et al.*, 2007), as well as innovation performance (Chen and Hsu, 2009; Choi and Lee, 2011; Lodh *et al.*, 2014; Shapiro *et al.*, 2013; Balsmeier *et al.*, 2014; Sena *et al.*, 2018).

Most of the papers confirm that independent committees provide more effective monitoring of managerial decisions and activities (Xie *et al.*, 2003; Guo and Masulis, 2015). Independent directors are prone to reduce agency conflicts and to ensure management. In fact, the high attendance rate among independent members can be explained by their essential role in complying with the good practices of governance (Adams and Ferreira, 2009). Furthermore, in line with resource-based theory, outsiders can be seen as providers of access to scarce or strategic resources (Lynall *et al.*, 2003; Tuggle *et al.*, 2010). Independent members can also increase the awareness of implementing new projects and bring new opportunities from their industries (Hillman and Dalziel, 2003; Tuggle *et al.*, 2010). They have outside contacts and typically bring a broader range of experience due to their address book (Chen, 2013). They have a good knowledge of many businesses, and they are more concerned about the firm's internal development (Choi *et al.*, 2012). Therefore, independent directors in strategic committees are likely to have enough knowledge and skills to offer different perspectives on innovative investments and growth opportunities. They could also mobilize new resources coming from their networks. Also, independent directors in nomination committees are likely to have enough knowledge and skills to appoint new members, who have the required qualifications for innovative activities.

Finally, we conclude that the positive outcomes of board diversity help to relate board diversity to innovation (Miller and Triana 2009). Board diversity provides the firm with human and social capital resources that help the board to generate ideas, allocate resources, and find opportunities, thereby increasing innovation (Østergaard *et al.*, 2011; Talke *et al.*, 2010; Carter *et al.*, 2010). In fact, in order to push companies to renew the composition of their board of directors and to select diverse profiles, several initiatives and recommendations have been introduced as laws on gender quotas and the presence of minorities in leadership positions.

14.3.3 *Committees size*

Large committees could provide the necessary and diversity of views to ensure effective monitoring (Bédard *et al.*, 2004). They could lead to more successful innovations due to the members' multiple resources (Zona *et al.*, 2013). However, they could suffer interest conflicts, leading to unnecessary debate and delay in making decisions. Consequently, they slow down communication and decision-making processes (Linck *et al.*, 2008); this environment can inhibit creativity and innovation opportunities (Jensen, 1993). In the same vein, Linck *et al.* (2008) stress that large boards may have more resources and knowledge, which positively contributes to firm performance and agility; however, they could delay communication inside the board (Jensen, 1993). Committee size could, therefore, inhibit creativity and innovation. In addition, large committees are prone to suffer from process losses and diffusion of responsibilities, specifically in long-term and uncertain projects, such as R&D projects (Karamanou and Vafeas, 2005; Yang and Krishnan, 2005; Cornett *et al.*, 2009).

14.3.4 *Committees functioning and innovation*

Committee meetings represent the place where directors can discuss the firm's opportunities and management's operations in more detail (Demb and Neubauer, 1992). Committee meetings are quite useful to disclose information and to discuss views. They are also a proxy for the members' involvement (Tuggle *et al.*, 2010). For instance, audit committees that meet more often would have more time to perform the role of monitoring (Karamanou and Vafeas, 2005) and are more likely to be well informed, more diligent, and more knowledgeable about the current problems (Raghunandan *et al.*, 2001). The frequency of meetings has a positive influence on the strategic role of board committees, specifically on how they perform their roles. It improves, therefore, the quality of control (Kaczmarek *et al.*, 2012; Demb and Neubauer, 1992). From a resource-based perspective, frequent meetings can help outside directors interact with insiders and to be well informed about firm activities. A large frequency of meetings can stimulate entrepreneurial thinking; particularly, outside directors could suggest innovative initiatives when they are given the opportunity in committees meetings.

14.4 Board Quota: Gender Quota Laws

The literature on board members' selection is growing (Bennouri *et al.*, 2018; Boulouta, 2013; Nekhili and Gatfaoui, 2013). The most visible illustration of diversity pressure on board members' selection criteria is on gender diversity. In fact, there are several reasons why increasing the quota of women directors might be associated with better performance (see among others: Carter *et al.*, 2003; Belghiti-Mahut *et al.*, 2010). First they tend to bring diverse viewpoints to the boardroom and encourage greater discussions and arguments over board decisions (Daily *et al.*, 2003, Hillman *et al.*, 2002; Elstad and Ladegard, 2012). In addition, they possess unique skill sets such as greater familiarity with consumer products or a better understanding of stakeholder issues (Kang *et al.*, 2007; Torchia *et al.*, 2011; Díaz-García *et al.*, 2013; Teruel *et al.*, 2015). Finally, female directors can contribute to the creativity or innovativeness of board discussions and solutions considered in the board meetings (Torchia *et al.*, 2018). Accordingly, increasing the number of women on boards can improve board decision-making through the unique contributions women can make to the board.

However, women's talents are being underutilized at decision-making levels, in particular at the top level. Very few women are in leading positions, particularly in male-dominated companies. Women have failed to attain equal representation on corporate boards of directors (Torchia *et al.*, 2011; European Commission, 2012). Women are still prevented from moving up into management and leadership positions and are facing significant barriers. These barriers are discussed in the "glass ceiling" theory (ILO, 2001). Moreover, women might be subject to discrimination before being appointed to boards; board roles are different for men and women (Bilimoria and Piderit, 1994; Kesner, 1988; Peterson and Philpot, 2007), and the board selection process is often analyzed as a 'male club' or "old boy's network". The complexity of the board selection process (Peterson and Philpot, 2007), in addition to many gender stereotypes, still makes it more difficult for a woman to be nominated on boards (Brière and Rinfret, 2010).

Over the last few years, several initiatives and programs have been introduced, to increase diversity in the board, such as gender quota laws and the presence of minorities in top management positions. In fact, gender quota legislation constrained companies to rethink their board composition and select new profiles, which needed also to be able to detect women profiles and make them visible. Moreover, board-level mandatory gender quotas, as enacted over the last decade by several countries, have, to a large extent, succeeded in breaking the glass ceiling at the top of listed companies (ILO, 2001). They have done so by forcing companies to open their board to a new population of female directors, with no prior board experience. Hence, gender quotas force firms to respond quickly to identify, develop, promote, and retain suitable female talent for the corporate board leadership structure.

Across countries, enacted legislation takes a variety of forms but generally consists of setting gender quotas, usually 33–50%, (European Commission, 2012). In 2003, Norway became the first country to implement a quota law. Following this, other countries, such as Spain, Iceland, France, Italy, Belgium, the Netherlands, and Germany, have implemented some kind of quota laws for board positions. However, what is apparent is that, over time, each country has adopted and introduced an individualized and distinct approach.

The different quota laws vary according to the country's practices, contexts, and realities. For instance: Some of the national quota laws refer to supervisory boards only (Norway, Iceland, France, and Germany), while others prescribe a quota for both supervisory and executive boards (the Netherlands, Belgium, Italy, and Spain). The first countries to implement these regulations aimed to achieve more gender-balanced boards with at least of 40% women members (Norway, Spain, Iceland, and France). Other countries have lower gender percentages: in Italy and Belgium, the gender quota is specified at 33%, while in the Netherlands and Germany, quotas are set to at least 30%. In fact, gender quotas have dealt with women underrepresentation in board seats; however, they did not attempt to regulate the distribution of positions and salaries across gender, (European Commission, 2012).

Studies on the boards' committees show that women directors most often serve on specific committees: they face a second ceiling barrier in boardrooms while they are supposed to achieve high top management positions: the glass cliff (Smith and Parrotta, 2018, and Ryan and Haslam, 2005). For instance, they can easily join audit, CSR, and corporate governance committees while they are unlikely to be appointed to the strategic, nominating, and compensation committees (Adams and Ferreira, 2009). In a recent study, Bugeja *et al.* (2016) highlight that when women sit on these committees, CEO salaries, bonuses, and total compensation are decreased.

Their presence on these committees could lead to an increase in transparency.

Another limit of gender quota laws is that they substantially increased female multiple directorships. Hillman *et al.* (2007) provide evidence that firms that have strong business relationships with other firms that have already appointed women to their boards are likely to increase women representation on their boards. In France, the gender quota law, specifically the urgent need to achieve the quota of 40%, the limited pool of talent, and the strong connection between family-controlled/owned firms in France (Sraer *et al.*, 2007; Konig *et al.*, 2013), has increased female multiple directorships.

In family-controlled firms, most often, women directors are recruited within families, without carrying out an external and neutral selection process (Campbell and Minguez-Vera, 2008). In fact, being a member of the founding family helps women to overcome barriers they usually face to achieve higher positions. In that sense, family firms could offer better career opportunities (Curimbaba, 2002). Consequently, highly qualified women who are able to sit on boards suffer from a lack of visibility because of weak networking and social circles. Indeed, firms pretend to have a limited pool of talents (Sheridan and Milgate, 2005). Hence, social ties and contacts, specifically family connections, are critical to the appointment of women to the director's positions. This could increase the risk of recruiting unqualified female directors (Claessens *et al.*, 2000).

Finally, we notice that only gender diversity has been fostered through quota law. To the best of our knowledge, there are only some recommendations to promote other forms of diversity, such as ethnic and minority diversity. The Securities and Exchange Commission (SEC), and New York Stock Exchange (NYSE)[7] recommend the appointment of independent directors on corporate boards and key corporate committees [e.g. audit, compensation, and nomination committees]. Moreover, the German Corporate Governance Code (DCGK)[8] recommends appointing an adequate number of

[7]NYSE requires an independent nominating committee. NASDAQ requires director nominees selected or recommended for board's selection by an independent nominating committee or by a majority of the independent directors.

[8]the German Corporate Governance Code as amended on May 13, 2013, Articles 5.4.1, 5.4.2.

outside board members, taking into account the specific requirements of the firm. It recommends that supervisory boards should "possess the knowledge, ability and expert experience required to properly complete its tasks". The importance of sufficient professional qualifications and leadership experience of non-executive board members, emphasized by the European Commission,[9] point to a similar direction.

14.5 Discussion and Conclusion

The influence of board structure on the performance of a company is one of the most active research areas in corporate finance (Black and Khanna, 2007). In fact, beyond its role of ensuring the alignment of interests between shareholders and managers, and monitoring and controlling (Daily *et al.*, 2003), the board could provide valuable resources to the firm, dole out strategic advice, and help the firm to develop knowledge and networks (Goodstein *et al.*, 1994; Ruigrok *et al.*, 2007; Kang *et al.*, 2007; Miller and Triana, 2009).

As R&D and innovation activities are typically associated with new technology or new products, we highlight that better-educated directors tend to have better cognitive ability to absorb new ideas, which therefore could increase the probability of introducing innovations (Barker and Mueller, 2002, Dalziel *et al.*, 2011; Lin *et al.*, 2011; Kuo *et al.*, 2018), while the education level of diversity caused by exposure to different knowledge may lead to different ways of thinking, resulting in a negative impact on innovation. In addition, we underline in this contribution that the type of academic degree can have a different influence on innovation activities. For instance, business-educated directors are more conservative and risk-averse, and they seem to marginalize innovation investments as they are more likely to focus on activities with short-term financial returns; however, directors with science and engineering degrees have better skills when they have to take risky decisions. They could increase the probability of accepting and introducing new changes.

[9]European Commission, Green Paper: The EU corporate governance framework, COM [2011] 164 final, April 5, 2011, Article 1.1.7.

On the other hand, we notice that outside directors on board have good knowledge of the business and valuable social network and resources in innovation activities. They are more prone to encourage innovative projects that could lead to the implementation of new products and processes. However, directors who have different cultural backgrounds could provide diverse perspectives, though not automatically valuable for innovation and solving problems. Directors of different nationalities seem to increase firms to improve or develop new products sold abroad as they also possess knowledge about global markets and customers' tastes (Kerr and Lincoln, 2010). Furthermore, we show that the presence of independent directors in decision-making committees could have a positive contribution on innovation: They could provide more effective monitoring of managerial decisions and activities in committees, and they are likely to have enough knowledge and skills to offer different perspectives on innovative investments and growth opportunities.

Turning to committee functioning, we show that when committees meet often, board committees seem to have more information about the current problems and are more concerned about R&D investments. Frequent meetings can help outside directors interacting with insiders. Therefore, they could be better informed about firm activities. When it comes to committee structures, we notice that large committees are prone to have a valuable diversity of views, which increases innovation investments. However, large committees could suffer interest conflicts and lead to unnecessary debate and delay in making decisions. We notice also that large committees are prone to suffer from process losses and diffusion of responsibilities, specifically in long-term and uncertain projects, such as R&D projects (Karamanou and Vafeas, 2005; Yang and Krishnan, 2005; and Cornett *et al.*, 2009). Consequently, it could influence negatively the communication and decision-making processes.

The complexity of the board selection process (Peterson and Philpot, 2007), in addition to many gender stereotypes, still makes it more difficult for a woman to be nominated on boards (Brière and Rinfret, 2010). The absence of females in corporate boards has become the focus of legislators and regulators in many countries, especially with women being more risk-averse and adopting a trust-building approach than men, as proven in prior research (Daily and Dalton, 2003). Women's talents are still being underutilized at decision-making levels. However, through this chapter, we try to show how the presence of females could change the dynamics of the board as well as the various board committees, which could influence innovative activities. We notice that gender diversity in board seems to help firms to diversify knowledge and to improve discussion, which generates new ideas. They can contribute to broadening the range of new products (Østergaard *et al.*, 2011; Torchia *et al.*, 2011; Díaz-García *et al.*, 2013; Teruel *et al.*, 2013), and introduce more organizational innovation. However, due to the feature of risk-aversion, women on board as well as on committees tend to avoid challenging situations, which could marginalize investments with unknown outcomes, such as innovation projects.

By looking at the impact of various types of directors' characteristics on innovation and by taking into account various types of innovation, this chapter brings practical insights on board structure issues. We highlight the urgent need to increase the firms' capacity to appoint, on the board as well as on board committees, individuals displaying diverse types of knowledge, abilities, skills, and networking that could drive more innovations. This chapter contributes to the current debate on how boards should be organized. It shows that boards should pay attention to the committee features as they could undermine innovation projects, specifically in innovation-sensitive industries.

The state of art provided by the current chapter has investigated how boards' characteristics could influence innovation project. It shows, however, that many areas in boardrooms and how they could influence innovation have not yet been explored. For instance, to the best of our knowledge, most of studies have focused on CEO remuneration and how it could influence CEO's incentives to get involved in innovative project, but there are no studies on board members' remuneration. Moreover, in our analysis, we have neglected the market characteristics such as competitiveness or sector affiliation, which provide significant incentive to serve as innovation projects. These issues are left for future papers.

References

Adams, J. (2003). Statement of the Public Affairs Committee of the Teratology Society on the importance of smoking cessation during pregnancy. *Birth Defects Research Part A: Clinical and Molecular Teratology*, **67**(11): 895–899.

Adams, R. B., Hermalin, B. E., and Weisbach, M. S. (2010). The role of boards of directors in corporate governance: A conceptual framework and survey. *Journal of Economic Literature*, **48**(1): 58–107.

Adams, R. B. and Ferreira, D. (2009). Women in the Boardroom and Their Impact on Governance and Performance. *Journal of Financial Economics*, **94**(2): 291–309.

Anderson, R. C., Duru, A., and Reeb, D. M. (2009). Founders, heirs, and corporate opacity in the United States. *Journal of Financial Economics*, **92**(2): 205–222.

Alesina, A. and La Ferrara, E. (2005). Ethnic diversity and economic performance. *Journal of Economic Literature*, **43**(3): 762–800.

Ali, M., Lu, Y., and Kulik, C. (2014). Board age and gender diversity: A test of competing linear and curvilinear predictions. *Journal of Business Ethics*, **125**(3): 497–512.

Arregle, J. L., Hitt, M. A., Sirmon, D. G., and Very, P. (2007). The development of organizational social capital: Attributes of family firm. *Journal of Management Studies*, **44**(1): 73–95.

Balsmeier, B., Buchwald, A., and Stiebale, (2014). Outside directors on the board and innovative firm performance. *Research Policy*, **43**(10): 1800–1815.

Balsmeier, B., Fleming, L., and Manso, G. (2017). Independent boards and innovation. *Journal of Financial Economics*, **123**(3): 536–557.

Barker, V. L. and Mueller, G. (2002). CEO Characteristics and Firm R&D Spending. *Management Science*, **48**(6): 711–820.

Bedard, J., Chtourou, S. M., and Courteau, L. (2004). The effect of audit committee expertise, Independence, and Activity on Aggressive Earnings Management. *Auditing: A Journal of Practice & Theory*, **23**(2): 13–35.

Belghiti-Mahut, S. and Lafont, A.-L. (2010). Lien entre présence des femmes dans le top management et performance financière des entreprises en France. *Gestion 2000*, **27**: 131–146.

Belloc, F. (2012). Corporate governance and innovation: a survey. *Journal of Economic Surveys*, **26**(5): 835–864.

Bennouri, M., Chtioui, T., Nagati, H., and Nekhili, M. (2018). Female board directorship and firm performance: What really matters? *Journal of Banking & Finance*, **88**: 267–291.

Berliant, M. and Fujita, M. (2008). Knowledge creation as a square Dance on the Hilbert cube. *International Economic Review*, **49**(4): 1251–1295.

Berliant, M. and Fujita, M. (2011). The dynamics of knowledge diversity and economic growth. *Southern Economic Journal*, **77**(4): 856–884.

Bilimoria, D. and Piderit, S. K. (1994). Board committee membership: Effects of sex-board bias. *Academy of Management Journal*, **37**(6): 1453–1477.

Black, B. S. and Khanna, V. S. (2007). Can Corporate Governance Reforms Increase Firm Market Values? Event Study Evidence from India. *Journal of Empirical Legal Studies*, **4**(4): 749–796.

Boubaker, S. and Labegorre, F. (2008). Ownership structure, corporate governance and analyst following: A study of French listed firms. *Journal of Banking & Finance*, **32**(6): 961–976.

Boulouta, I. (2013). Hidden Connections: The link between board gender diversity and corporate social performance. *Journal of Business Ethics*, **113**(2): 185–197.

Bucciol, A. and Miniaci, R. (2011). Household portfolios and implicit risk preference. *Review of Economics and Statistics*, **93**(4): 1235–1250.

Cadbury Committee, (1992). *Report on the Financial Aspects of Corporate Governance*. Gee, London.

Campbell, K. and Minguez-Vera, A. (2008). Gender diversity in the boardroom and firm financial performance. *Journal of Business Ethics*, **83**: 435–451.

Carter, D. A., Simkins, B. J., and Simpson, W. G. (2010). The gender and ethnic diversity of US boards and board committees and firm financial performance. *Corporate Governance: An International Review*, **18**(5): 396–414.

Carter, D. A., D'souza, F. P., Simkins, B. J., and Simpson, W. G. (2007). The diversity of corporate board committees and firm financial performance. *SSRN Electronic Journal*. doi:10.2139/ssrn.972763.

Carpenter, M. A. and Westphal, J. D. (2001). The strategic context of external network ties: Examining the impact of director appointments on board involvement in strategic decision making. *Academy of Management Journal*, **44**: 639–660.

Chang, S. J., Chung, C., and Mahmood, I. P. (2006). When and how does business group affiliation promote firm innovation? A tale of two emerging economies. *Organization Science*, **17**: 637–656.

Chemmanur, T. J., Elena, L., and Xuan, T. (2014). Corporate venture capital, value creation, and innovation. *Review of Financial Studies*, **27**: 2434–2473.

Chen, C. and Bou-Wen, L. (2016). Ownership structure, independent board members and innovation performance: A contingency perspective. *Journal of Business Research*, **69**(9): 3371–3379.

Chen, H. L. and Hsu, W. T. (2009). Family ownership, board independence, and R&D investment. *Family Business Review*, **22**(4): 347–362.

Chen, H. L. (2013). CEO tenure, independent directors and corporate innovation. *Journal of Applied Finance and Banking*, **3**: 187–197.

Chen, J., Leung, W. S., and Evans, K. P. (2018). Female board representation, corporate innovation and firm performance. *Journal of Empirical Finance*, **48**: 236–254.

Chen, L. and Yang, W. (2019). R&D tax credits and firm innovation: Evidence from China. *Technological Forecasting and Social Change*, **146**: 233–241.

Chen, V. Y. S., Tsao, S-M., and Chen, G-Z. (2013). Founding family ownership and innovation. *Asia-Pacific Journal of Accounting & Economics*, **20**: 429–456.

Cho, S. and Kim, S. (2017). Horizon problem and firm innovation: The influence of CEO career horizon, exploitation and exploration on breakthrough innovations. *Research Policy*, **46**(10): 1801–1809.

Choi, J. J., Park, S. W., and Yoo, S. S. (2007). The value of outside directors: Evidence from corporate governance reform in Korea. *Journal of Financial and Quantitative Analysis*, **42**: 941– 962.

Choi, S, B., Lee, S., and Wiliams, C. (2011). Ownership and firm innovation in a transition economy: Evidence from China. *Research Policy*, **40**(3): 441–452.

Choi, S, B., Park, B., and Hong, P. (2012). Does ownership structure matter for firm technological innovation performance? The case of Korean firms. *Corporate Governance: An International Review*, **20**(3): 267–288.

Claessens, S., Djankov, S., and Lang, L. H. (2000). The separation of ownership and control in East Asian Corporations. *Journal of Financial Economics*, **58**: 81–112.

Cox, T, H., Lobel, S, A., and Mcleod, P. (1991). Effects of Ethnic Group Cultural Differences on Cooperative and Competitive Behavior a Group Task. *Academy of Management Journal*, **34**(4): 827–847.

Croson, R. and Gneezy, U. (2009). Gender differences in preferences. *Journal of Economic Literature*, **47**(2): 448–74.

Curimbaba, F. (2002). The Dynamics of Women's Roles as Family Business Managers. *Family Business Review*, **15**(3): 239–252.

Czarnitzki, D., Hanel, P., and Rosa, J. M. (2011). Evaluating the impact of R&D tax credits on innovation: A microeconometric study on Canadian firms. *Research Policy*, **40**(2): 217–229.

Daellenbach, U. D., Mccarthy, A. M., and Schoenecker, T. S. (1999). Commitment to innovation: The impact of top management team characteristics. *R&D Management*, **29**(3): 199–208.

Daily, C. M., Dalton, D. R., and Cannella, A. A. (2003). Corporate Governance: Decades of Dialogue and Data. *Academy of Management Review*, **28**(3): 371–382.

Dalziel, T., Gentry, R. J., and Bowerman, M. (2011). An integrated agency–resource dependence view of the influence of directors' human and relational capital on firms' R&D spending. *Journal of Management Studies*, **48**(6): 1217–1242.

De Massis, A., Frattini, F., and Lichtenthaler, U. (2013). Research on technological innovation in family firms: Present debates and future directions. *Family Business Review*, **26**(1): 10–3.

Deli, D. N. and Gillan, S. L. (2000). On the Demand for Independent and Active Audit Committees. *Journal of Corporate Finance*, **6**(4): 427–445.

Demb, A. and Neubauer, F.-F. (1992). The corporate board: Confronting the paradoxes. *Long Range Planning*, **25**(3): 9–20.

Deutsch, Y. (2005). The impact of board composition on firms' critical decisions: A Meta-Analytic Review. *Journal of Management*, **31**(3): 424–444.

Diaz-Garcia, C., Gonzalez-Moreno, A., and Saez-Martinez, F. (2013). Gender Diversity within R&D Teams: Its Impact on Radicalness of Innovation. *Innovations: Management, Policy & Practice*, **15**(2): 149–160.

Elstad, B. and Ladegard, G. (2012). Women on corporate boards: Key influencers or tokens? *Journal of Management & Governance*, **16**(4): 595–615.

European Commission (2011). Green Paper: The EU corporate governance framework, 164 final, April 5, 2011, article 1.1.7.

European Commission (2012). Proposal for a directive of the european parliament and of the council on improving the gender balance among Non-executive directors of companies listed on stock exchanges and related measures. https://eur-lex.europa.eu/legalcontent/EN/TXT/?uri$=$CELEX%3A52012PC0614 (Accessed May 16, 2019).

European Commission (2014). Report on equality between women and men. Retrieved from http://ec.europa.eu/justice/gender-equality/files/annualreports/150324_annual_report_2014_web_en.pdf. (Accessed 1 Mar 2017).

Faccio, M., Marchica, M. T., and Mura, R. (2016). CEO Gender, Corporate Risk-Taking, and the Efficiency of Capital Allocation. *Journal of Corporate Finance*, **39**: 193–209.

Fahlenbrach, R., Low, A., and Stulz, R. M. (2010). Why Do Firms Appoint CEOs as Outside Directors? *Journal of Financial Economics*, **97**(1): 12–32.

Faleye, O., Hoitash R., and Hoitash, U. (2011). The Costs of Intense Board Monitoring. *Journal of Financial Economics*, **101**(1): 160–181.

Fama, E. F. and Jensen, M. C. (1983). Separation of ownership and control. *Journal of Law and Economics*, **26**: 301–325.

Finkelstein, S., Reeger, R., and Hambrick, D. C. (1996). Strategic Leadership: Top Executives and Their Effects on Organizations. *The Academy of Management Review*, **22**(3): 802–805.

Fujita, M., and Weber, S. (2004). Strategic immigration policies and welfare in heterogeneous countries. FEEM Working Paper No. 2.

Gabrielsson, J. and Winlund, H. (2000). Boards of directors in small and medium-sized industrial firms: Examining the effects of the board's working style on board task performance. *Entrepreneurship & Regional Development*, **12**(4): 311–330.

Galia, F. and Zenou, E. (2013). La diversité du conseil d'administration influence-t-elle l'innovation? L'impact de la diversité de genre et d'âge sur les différents types d'innovation. *Management & Avenir*, **66**(8): 152.

Galia, F., Zenou, E., and Ingham, M. (2015). Board composition and environmental innovation: Does gender diversity matter? *International Journal of Entrepreneurship and Small Business*, **24**(1): 117.

Gendron, Y. and Bedard, J. (2006). On the constitution of audit committee effectiveness. *Accounting, Organizations and Society*, **31**(3): 211–239.

George, G. and Lin, Y. (2016). Analytics, Innovation and Organizational Adaptation. *Innovation*, **19**(1): 16–22.

Godard, L. and Schatt A. (2005). Characteristics and operation of the French boards of directors. An inventory survey. *Revue Française de Gestion*, **158**: 69–87.

Goodstein, J., Gautam, K., and Boeker, W. (1994). The effects of board size and diversity on strategic change. *Strategic Management Journal*, **15**: 241–250.

Guo, L. and Masulis, R. W. (2015). Board structure and monitoring: New evidence from CEO turnovers. *Review of Financial Studies*, **28**(10): 2770–2811.

Hall, B. H. and Van Reenen, J. (2000). How effective are fiscal incentives for R&D? A review of the evidence. *Research Policy*, **29**: 449–469.

Hampel, R. (1998). *Committee on corporate governance: Final Report*. Gee, London.

Harrison, J. R. (1987). The strategic use of corporate board committees. *California Management Review*, **30**(1): 109–125.

Hillman, A. J., Shropshire, C., and Cannella, A. A. (2007). Organizational predictors of women on corporate boards. *Academy of Management Journal*, **50**(4): 941–952.

Hillman, A. J., Cannella, A. A., and Harris, I. C. (2002). Women and racial minorities in boardroom: How do directors differ? *Journal of Management*, **28**(6): 747–763.

Hillman, A. J. and Dalziel, T. (2003). Boards of directors and firm performance: Integrating Agency and Resource Dependence Perspectives. *Academy of Management Review*, **28**(3): 383–396.

Hirshleifer, D., Angie, L., and Siew, H. T. (2012). Are overconfident CEOs better innovators? *Journal of Finance*, **67**: 1457–1498.

Hitt, M. A., Hoskisson, R. E., Johnson, R. A. and Moesel, D. D. (1996). The market for corporate control and firm innovation. *Academy of Management Journal*, **39**(5): 1084–1119.

Hodgkinson, G. P. (2003). The interface of cognitive and industrial, work and organizational psychology. *Journal of Occupational and Organizational Psychology*, **76**(1): 1–25.

Hoskisson, R. E., Hitt, M. A., Johnson, R. A., and Grossman, W. (2002). Conflicting voices, the effects of institutional ownership heterogeneity and internal governance on corporate innovation strategies. *Academy of Management Journal*, **45**(4): 697–716.

Hsu, P.-H., Huang, S., Massa, M., and Zhang, H. (2014). The new lyrics of the old folks: The role of family ownership in corporate innovation. INSEAD Faculty & Research Working Paper.

Huse, M. (2007). *Boards, governance and value creation: The human side of corporate governance*. Cambridge University Press, 392.

ILO (2001). *Breaking through the Glass Ceiling: Women in Management*, International Labour Office, Geneva, Switzerland.

Jackling, B. and Johl, S. (2009). Board Structure and Firm Performance: Evidence from India's Top Companies. *Corporate Governance: An International Review*, **17**(4): 492–509.

Jensen, M. C. (1993). The modern industrial revolution, exit, and the failure of internal control systems. *Journal of Finance*, **48**(3): 831–880.

Jiao, H., Koo, C. K., and Cui, Y. (2015). Legal environment, government effectiveness and firms' innovation in China: Examining the moderating influence of government ownership. *Technological Forecasting and Social Change*, **96**: 15–24.

Kang, H., Cheng, M., and Gray, S. J. (2007). Corporate governance and board composition: Diversity and independence of Australian boards. *Corporate Governance: An International Review*, **15**(2): 194–207.

Kanter, R. M. (1977). *Men and women of the corporation*. New York: Basic Books.

Karamanou, I. and Vafeas, N. (2005). The association between corporate boards, audit committees, and management earnings forecasts: An empirical analysis. *Journal of Accounting Research*, **43**(3): 453–486.

Kelton, A. S. and Yang, Y. (2008). The impact of corporate governance on Internet financial reporting. *Journal of Accounting and Public Policy*, **27**(1): 62–87.

Kerr, W. and Lincoln, W. (2010). The supply side of innovation: H-1B Visa Reforms and US Ethnic Invention. *Journal of Labor Economics*, **28**: 3.

Kesner, I. F. (1988). Directors' characteristics and committee membership: An investigation of type, occupation, tenure, and gender. *Academy of Management Journal*, **31**(1): 66–84.

Khaled, S., Hichem, K., and Khaled, H. (2015). The impact of board and audit committee characteristics on voluntary disclosure: A meta-analysis. *Journal of International Accounting, Auditing and Taxation*, **24**: 13–28.

Klein, A. (1998). Firm performance and board committee structure. *The Journal of Law and Economics*, **41**(1): 275–304.

Klein, A. (2002). Audit committee, board of director characteristics, and earnings management. *Journal of Accounting and Economics*, **33**(3): 375–400.

Kobayashi, Y. (2013). Effect of R&D tax credits for SMEs in Japan: A microeconometric analysis focused on liquidity constraints. *Small Business Economics*, **42**(2): 311–327.

Konig, A., Kammerlander, N., and Enders, A. (2013). The family innovator's dilemma: How family influence affects the adoption of discontinuous technologies by incumbent firms. *Academy of Management Review*, **38**: 418–441.

Kor, Y. Y. (2006). Direct and interaction effects of top management team and board compositions on R&D investment strategy. *Strategic Management Journal*, **27**(11): 1081–1099.

Kor, Y. Y. and Misangyi, V. F. (2008). Outside directors' industry-specific experience and firms' liability of newness. *Strategic Management Journal*, **29**: 1345–1355.

Kor, Y. Y. and Sundaramurthy, C. (2008). Experience-based human capital and social capital of outside directors. *Journal of Management*, **35**(4): 981–1006.

Krishnan, J. (2005). Audit committee quality and internal control: An empirical analysis. *The Accounting Review*, **80**: 649–675.

Kuo, H. C., Wang, L. H., and Yeh, L. J. (2018). The role of education of directors in influencing firm R&D investment. *Asia Pacific Management Review*, **23**(3): 108–120.

Lee, P. M. and O'neill, H. M. (2003). Ownership structures and R&D investments of U.S. and Japanese firms, agency and stewardship perspectives. *Academy of Management Journal*, **46**(2): 212–225.

Leung, S., Richardson, G., and Jaggi, B. (2014). Corporate board and board committee independence, firm performance, and family ownership concentration: An analysis based on Hong Kong firms. *Journal of Contemporary Accounting & Economics*, **10**(1): 16–31.

Lin, C., Lin, P., Song, F. M., and Li, C. (2011). Managerial incentives, CEO characteristics and corporate innovation in China's private sector. *Journal of Comparative Economics*, **39**(2): 176–190.

Lin, P., Hutchinson, M. R., and Percy, M. (2009). The role of the audit committee and institutional investors in constraining earnings management: evidence from Chinese firms listed in Hong Kong. *Proceedings of Accounting & Finance Association of Australia & New Zealand Annual Conference 2009*, 5–7 July 2009.

Linck, J., Netter, M., and Yang, T. (2008). The determinants of board structure. *Journal of Financial Economics*, **2**: 308–328.

Lodh, S., Nandy, M., and Chen, J. (2014). Innovation and family ownership: Empirical evidence from India. *Corporate Governance: An International Review*, **22**(1): 4–23.

Loukil, N. and Yousfi, O. (2015). Does Gender Diversity on Board Lead to Risk-Taking? Empirical Evidence from Tunisia. *Canadian Journal of Administrative Sciences*, doi:10.1002/cjas.1326.

Lu, J. and Wang, W. (2018). Managerial conservatism, board independence and corporate innovation. *Journal of Corporate Finance*, **48**: 1–16.

Lundvall, B. A, Johnson, B., Andersen, E. S., and Dalum, B. (2002). National systems of production, innovation and competence building. *Research Policy*, **31**(2): 213–231.

Lynall, M. D., Golden, B. R., and Hillman, A. J. (2003). Board composition from adolescence to maturity: A multitheoretic view. *The Academy of Management Review*, **28**(3): 416.

Mahadeo, J.-D., Soobaroyen, T., and Hanuman, V. (2012). Board composition and financial performance: Uncovering the effects of diversity in an emerging economy. *Journal of Business Ethics*, **105**(3): 375–388.

Manso, G. (2011). Motivating innovation. *The Journal of Finance: The American Finance Association*, **66**(5): 51823–1860.

Miller, T. and Del Carmen Triana, M. (2009). Demographic diversity in the boardroom: Mediators of the board diversity-firm performance relationship. *Journal of Management Studies*, **46**(5): 755–786.

Nahlinder, J. (2010). Where are All the Female Innovators? Nurses as Innovators in a Public Sector Innovation Project. *Journal of Technology Management & Innovation*, **5**(1). doi:10.4067/s0718-27242010000100002.

Nekhili, M. and Gatfaoui, H. (2013). Are demographic attributes and firm characteristics drivers of gender diversity? Investigating women's positions on french boards of directors. *Journal of Business Ethics*, **118**(2): 227–249.

Niederle, M., Vesterlund, L. (2007). Do women shy away from competition? Do men compete too much? *Quarterly Journal of Economics*, **122**(3): 1067–1101.

Nielsen, S. and Huse, M. (2010). The contribution of women on boards of directors: Going beyond the Surface. *Corporate Governance: An International Review*, **18**(2): 136–148.

Nonaka, I. and Takeuchi, H. (1995). *The knowledge-creating company: How japanese companies create the dynamics of innovation.* Oxford University Press, New York.

Østergaard, C., Timmermans, B., and Kristinsson, K. (2011). Does a different view create something new? The effect of employee diversity on innovation. *Research Policy*, **40**(3): 500–509.

Paff, L. A. (2005). State-level R&D tax credit: A firm-level analysis, *Topics in Economic Analysis & Policy*, **5**, Article 17.

Pathan, S. and Faff, R. (2013). Does board structure in banks really affect their performance? *Journal of Banking and Finance*, **37**(5): 1573–1589.

Peterson, C. A. and Philpot, J. (2007). Women's roles on U.S. Fortune 500 boards: Director expertise and committee memberships. *Journal of Business Ethics*, **72**: 177–196.

Pfeffer, J. and Salancik, G. R. (1979). The external control of organizations: A resource dependence perspective. *The Academy of Management Review*, **4**(2): 309.

Post, C. and Byron, K. (2015). Women on boards and firm financial performance: A Meta-Analysis. *Academy of Management Journal*, **58**(5): 1546–1571.

Prencipe, A. (2016). Board composition and innovation in university. Spin-offs. Evidence from the Italian Context. *Journal of Technology Management and Innovation*, **11**(3): 33–39.

Raghunandan, K. Dasaratha, V. Rama, William J. Read. (2001). Audit committee composition, "Gray Directors", and interaction with internal auditing. *Accounting Horizons*, **15**(2): 105–118.

Reeb, A. and Upadhyay, A. (2010). Subordinate board structures. *Journal of Corporate Finance*, **16**(4): 469–486.

Ruigrok, W., Peck, S. Tacheva, S Greve, P., and Hu, Y. (2006). The determinants and effects of board nomination committees. *Journal of Management & Governance*, **10**(2): 119–148.

Ruigrok, W., Peck, S., and Tacheva, S. (2007). Nationality and gender diversity on swiss corporate boards. *Corporate Governance: An International Review*, **15**: 546–557.

Ruigrok, W., Peck, S. I., and Keller, H. (2006). Board characteristics and involvement in strategic decision making: Evidence from Swiss companies. *Journal of Management Studies*, **43**(5): 1201–1226.

Ruiqi, W., Wang, F, Xu, L., and Yuan, C. (2017). R&D expenditures, ultimate ownership and future performance: Evidence from China. *Journal of Business Research*, **71**: 47–54.

Ruiz-Jime Nez, J. M., Fuentes, M. D., and Ruiz Arroyo, M. (2016). Knowledge combination capability and innovation: The effects of gender diversity on top management teams in technology-based firms. *Journal of Business Ethics*, **135**(3): 503–515.

Ryan, M. K., and Haslam, S. A. (2005). The glass cliff: Evidence that women are over-represented in precarious leadership positions. *British Journal of Management*, **16**(2): 81–90.

Sariol, A. M. and Abebe, M. A. (2017). The influence of CEO power on explorative and exploitative organizational innovation. *Journal of Business Research*, **73**: 38–45.

Sastre, J. F. (2015). The impact of R&D teams' gender diversity on innovation outputs. *International Journal of Entrepreneurship and Small Business*, **24**(1): 142.

Scott, S. G. and Bruce, R. A. (1994). Determinants of innovative behavior: A path model of individual innovation in the workplace. *Academy of Management Journal*, **37**: 580–607.

Sena, V., Duygun, M., Lubrano, G., Marra, M., and Shaban, M. (2018). Board independence, corruption and innovation. Some evidence on UK subsidiaries. *Journal of Corporate Finance*, **50**: 22–43.

Shapiro, D., Tang, Y., Wang, M., and Zhang, W. (2013). The effects of corporate governance on the innovation performance of Chinese SMEs. *European Economic Review*, **50**: 155–183.

Sharma, Z. (2016). Board composition and innovation. *Applied Finance Letters*, **5**(2): 12–31.

Sheikh, S. (2018). The impact of market competition on the relation between CEO Power and firm innovation. *Journal of Multinational Financial Management*, **44**: 36–50.

Shivdasani, A. and Yermack, D. (1999). CEO involvement in the selection of new board members: An empirical analysis. *The Journal of Finance*, **54**(5): 1829–1853.

Singh, V. and Vinnicombe, S. (2004). Why so few women directors in top UK boardrooms? Evidence and theoretical explanations. *Corporate Governance*, **12**(4): 479–488.

Singh, V. and Vinnicombe, S. (2008). Newly appointed directors in the boardroom: How do women and men differ? *European Management Journal*, **26**(1): 48–58.

Smith, N. and Parrotta, P. (2015). Why so few women on boards of directors? Empirical evidence from danish companies in 1998–2010. *Journal of Business Ethics*, **147**(2): 445–467.

Srinidhi, B., Gul, F. A., and Tsui, J. (2011). Female directors and earnings quality. *Contemporary Accounting Research*, **28**(5): 1610–1644.

Sun, J., Cahan, S. F., and Emanuel, D. (2009). Compensation committee governance quality, chief executive officer stock option grants, and future firm performance. *Journal of Banking & Finance*, **33**(8): 1507–1519.

Talke, K., Salomo, S., and Rost, K. (2010). How top management team diversity affects innovativeness and performance via the strategic choice to focus on innovation fields. *Research Policy*, **39**(7): 907–918.

Terjesen, S., Sealy, R., and Singh, V. (2009). Women directors on corporate boards: A review and research agenda. *Corporate Governance: An International Review*, **17**(3): 320–337.

Teruel, M., Parra, M. D., and Segarra, A. (2015). Gender diversity and innovation in manufacturing and service firms. Working Papers 2072/249234, Universitat Rovira i Virgili, Department of Economics.

Torchia, M., Calabro, A., and Huse, M. (2011). Women directors on corporate boards: From tokenism to critical mass. *Journal of Business Ethics*, **102**(2): 299–317.

Torchia, M., Calabro, A., Gabldon, P., and Kanadli, S. B. (2018). Women directors contribution to organizational innovation: A behavioral approach. *Scandinavian Journal of Management*, **34**(2): 215–224.

Tuggle, C. S., Schnatterly, K., Johnson, R. A. (2010). Attention patterns in the boardroom: How board composition and processes affect discussion of entrepreneurial issues. *Academy of Management Journal*, **53**(3): 550–571.

Turner, L. (2009). Gender diversity and innovative performance. *International Journal Innovation and Sustainable Development*, **4**(2/3): 123–134.

Tyler, B. and Steensma, H. (1998). The effects of executives' experiences and perceptions on their assessment of potential technological alliances. *Strategic Management Journal*, **19**(10): 939–965.

Upadhyay, A. D., Bhargava, R., and Faircloth, S. D. (2014). Board structure and role of monitoring committees. *Journal of Business Research*, **67**(7): 1486–1492.

Van Den Berghe, L. A. A., and Levrau, A. (2004). Evaluating boards of directors: What constitutes a good corporate board? *Corporate Governance*, **12**(4): 461–478.

Villalonga, B. and Amit, R. H. (2006). How Do Family Ownership, Control, and Management Affect Firm Value? *Journal of Financial Economics*, **80**(2): 385–417.

Vincent, B. and George, M. (2002). CEO characteristics and Firm R&D Spending. *Management Science*, **48**: 782–801.

Voordeckers, W., Van Gils, A., and Van Den Heuvel, J. (2007). Board composition in small and medium-sized family firms. *Journal of Small Business Management*, **45**(1): 137–156.

Wang, S., Zhang, S., Li, and Bobo, (2017). Effect of diversity on top management team to the bank's innovation ability-based on the nature of ownership perspective. *Procedia Engineering*, **174**: 240–245.

Westphal, J. D. and Milton, L. P. (2000). How experience and network ties affect the influence of demographic minorities on corporate boards. *Administrative Science Quarterly*, **45**(2): 366.

Westphal, J. D. and Zajac, E. J. (1995). Who shall govern? CEO/board power, demographic similarity, and new director selection. *Administrative Science Quarterly*, **40**(1): 60–83.

Wincent, J., Anokhin, S., and Ortqvist, D. (2010). Does network board capital matter? A study of innovative performance in strategic SME network. *Journal of Business Research*, **63**(3): 265–275.

Wu, Y. (2005). The effects of state R&D tax credits in stimulating private R&D expenditure: A cross-state empirical analysis. *Journal of Policy Analysis and Management*, **24**(4): 785–802.

Xie, B., Davidson, W. N., and Dadalt, P. J. (2003). Earnings management and corporate governance: The role of the board and the audit committee. *Journal of Corporate Finance*, **9**(3): 295–316.

Xu, X. and Wang, Y. (1999). Ownership structure and corporate governance in chinese stock companies. *China Economic Review*, **10**(1): 75–98.

Yang, J. S., and Krishnan, J. (2005). Audit committees and quarterly earnings management. *International Journal of Auditing*, **9**(3): 201–219.

Yi, J., Hong, J., Hsu, W. Chung., and Wang, C. (2017). The role of state ownership and institutions in the innovation performance of emerging market enterprises: Evidence from China. *Technovation*, 62–63, 4–13.

Yuan, R., and Wen, W. (2018). Managerial foreign experience and corporate innovation. *Journal of Corporate Finance*, **48**: 752–770.

Zalata A. M., Tauringana, V., and Tingbani, I. (2018). Audit committee financial expertise, gender, and earnings management: Does gender of the financial expert matter? *International Review of Financial Analysis*, **55**: 170–183.

Zhang, Y., Zhou, J., and Zhou, N. (2007). Audit committee quality, auditor independence, and internal control weaknesses. *Journal of Accounting and Public Policy*, **26**(3): 300–327.

Zhou, H., Owusu-Ansah, S., and Maggina, A. (2018). Board of directors, audit committee, and firm performance: Evidence from Greece. *Journal of International Accounting, Auditing and Taxation*, **31**: 20–36.

Zona, F., Zattoni, A., and Minichilli, A. (2013). A contingency model of boards of directors and firm innovation: The moderating role of firm size. *British Journal of Management*, **24**(3): 299–31.

Part IV:

Transformations, Digitalization, Blockchain, FinTech

https://doi.org/10.1142/9781786349507_0015

Chapter 15

Blockchain Technology: Beyond Cryptocurrencies

Assen Slim[*,§], **Fernanda Arreola**[†,¶], **and Éric Magnin**[‡,‖]

**ESSCA School of Management, Paris, France and INALCO Paris, France*
†ISC Paris, Paris, France 92 916 Paris La Défense, France
‡University of Paris, Paris, France
§assen.slim@inalco.fr
¶farreola@iscparis.com
‖eric.magnin@u-paris.fr

15.1 Introduction

With an expected valorization of over 196 billion USD in 2020, cryptocurrencies are gaining significant prominence as vehicles of financial transactions. At the heart of these controversial currencies, there is a powerful state-of-the-art technology: Blockchain. Originally, Blockchain technology was created as part of the anarchist movement generated by the first cryptocurrency, Bitcoin.[1] Since then, this technology has been the source of inspiration for the creation of more than 1,500 cryptocurrencies.

[1]The Oxford Dictionary defines from 2006 a crypto anarchist as "a person who uses encryption when accessing a computer network in order to ensure confidentiality and protect oneself, in particular from government authorities".

Today, Blockchain technology goes far beyond the reach of cryptocurrencies and plays a central role in the production of new services within finance and insurance. Blockchain reduces intermediaries, transaction costs, and delays. Its potential attracts startups, large corporations, and public administrators. While some try to develop new commercial applications, others question its role in providing new kinds of services (as is the case with some governments).

There are at least six different evolutions for businesses that are likely to take place thanks to the power of Blockchain technology. (1) Blockchain will allow companies to think differently about their strategy and future development of competitive products. (2) It has the potential to reconfigure many industries and how they capture value. (3) Blockchain allows firms to solve inter-organizational issues and to facilitate the tracking of all contracts and transactions. (4) It is a vector of trust among firms. (5) Its adoption fosters a new way to build governance models.

The following chapter aims to further develop the second possibility that is open by Blockchain "the potential to reconfigure entire industries by way of adding new ways to create and capture value". To explain this, we first review the technical characteristics of Blockchain technology (other than cryptocurrencies). Then, we review the different potential applications that can be introduced thanks to blockchain: reduced transaction costs, incorruptible systems, the use of smart contracts, and automatic authentication, among others. The chapter also attempts to develop a new typology of business applications based on Blockchain. This typology follows the initial configuration proposed by Buterin (2013) ad that organized Blockchain use in financial, semi-financial, and other applications.

In this chapter, we respond to a specific gap in the literature dedicated to the subject. To date, the academic work is mostly concerned with the technical infrastructure necessary for developing cryptocurrency (Rodima-Taylor *et al.*, 2017), the monetary nature of cryptocurrencies (Lakomski-Laguerre and Desmedt, 2015), the interest of States to use them and emerging national regulations (De Filippi, 2004), or the role of cryptocurrencies as a new sociotechnical construct (De Filippi and Loveluck, 2016), (Rolland and Slim, 2017). Some other research has treated Blockchain on a more technological approach (Risius and Spohrer, 2017), (Meroni *et al.*, 2019), (Ruoti *et al.*, 2020), speaking about data and information controls (Cappiello *et al.*, 2019), of the rules necessary to treat information (Yeoh, 2017), (Ólnes *et al.*, 2017), (van Rijswijk *et al.*, 2019), and discussing the role of the capitalist economic institution in the deployment of the technology (Davidson *et al.*, 2018). Some rare examples have attempted a classification of applications based on Blockchain technology (Ribeiro, 2016), (Godebarge and Rossat, 2016), (Labazova *et al.*, 2019).

In summary, we dedicate this chapter to present the origins of the Blockchain and its principles of operation, and we showcase the diversity of applications in which it can be used.

15.2 The Characteristics of Blockchain Technology

15.2.1 *Origin of Blockchain technology*

In the 1980s, informal groups started gathering to find new ways to use cryptography within information technologies. After giving themselves the name "Cypherpunk",[2] these self-entitled groups of crypto-anarchists decided to use the technical capacity of cryptography (to date, reserved to governments) for the creation of new systems (Castor, 2017). This group aimed to conceive a decentralized IT protocol that could allow individual collaboration without the identification of the names and legal identities of the people exchanging information. In parallel, these groups developed a strong discourse against the central institution, starting by those run by the US Government, as they considered their power to rule the finance worldwide to be exorbitant. This is how, from their conception, the technologies that were conceived wished to render non-operative all institutions that had an Orwellian orientation (Chaum, 1985). In a direct reference to Marx, May called this a technical revolution that allows the exchange of anything (even drogues and illegal products) in perfect and fluid markets (May, 1992):

[2]Among the historical founders of these groups, we can quote David Chaum, John Gilmore, Timothy C. May and Eric Hughes.

> "An anonymous computerized market will even make possible abhorrent markets for assassinations and extortion".

For these groups, the cyberspace is conceived as the privileged zone for social interaction: in these zones, the "government is not destroyed, but it simply becomes redundant without any possible intervention" (Dai, 1998). The attention of the creators of this technology is therefore in the elaboration of a decentralized electronic coin. Several projects emerged from this conceptualization, giving the bases for what would become the architecture of Bitcoin: "Digicash" (Chaum, 1983), "b-money" (Dai, 1998), "Bit gold" (Szabo, 1998 and 2005).

The founding article explaining the concept of Bitcoin was published in 2008. In it, the "author", Satoshi Nakamoto,[3] discusses how he has been working on this conceptualization since 2007 (Nakamoto, 2008). Nakamoto announces his desire to find a solution to the problems derived from the digitalization of national and international currencies, which, to this date, require the intervention and mediation of certifiers and third-party institutions. These intermediaries exist to deal with emerging conflicts (the reversibility of transactions and the eventual creation of arbitrary currencies), but this mediation also causes an increase in transaction costs and in the frequency and intensity of monetary crises. To eliminate these third-party interventions, Nakamoto offers a collaborative, resilient, and secure Peer-to-Peer (P2P) architecture *via* the use of technology (identification by public keys, verification, and record-keeping of all payments *via* the use of computer science techniques). He proposes being capable of keeping track of all transactions within a community in a public and transparent environment secured by technology, calling this "Blockchain".

15.2.2 *The functioning of Blockchain technology*

The Bitcoin was conceived to "offer a new room for liberty" via a technical infrastructure (Nakamoto, 2008). This infrastructure was designed to be outside the reach of any central authority (De Filippi and Loveluck, 2016). As opposed to regular currency (fiat

[3]The mystery remains about the identity of the designer(s).

currencies held by banks), Bitcoin is a protocol within a P2P network that is itself-sufficient, which allows it to transfer secured data (the Bitcoins) without the need of an intermediary (a trusted centralized authority). This infrastructure is built upon three factors: double-key asymmetric cryptography, Blockchain, and an activity known as "mining".

The asymmetric key encryption (or double-key encryption) allows guaranteeing the right to stay anonymous, or more precisely to establish a "pseudonymity" for its users, making it impossible to falsify the identification of these pseudonyms as well as the identification of the amounts of bitcoin deposited in the electronic "wallets" of the users. After payment, the transmitter of bitcoins signs and authenticates his payment with his private key. Then the beneficiary of this payment receives the amounts sent over his wallet as long as this key is identified as the one associated with the emitter, allowing the decryption to transfer and authenticate the origin, without having to receive any specific information about the actors involved.

Blockchain corresponds to the historic memory of all transactions treated and validated by Bitcoin after its conception. It is "a ledger or, more simply, a chronological database of transactions recorded by a network of computers" (Peters and Panayi, 2016). This last characteristic is replicated within some computers within the system known as "full nodes". There is not one but thousands of reproductions of the Blockchain that are built and managed by many computers around the globe. The "full nodes" keep to date a live copy of the Blockchain, download and verify the validity of new blocks (the fact that they follow the rules), and finally they share new blocks with the network.

In Blockchain, we find also another concept called "light nodes" used by services or portfolios that, for practical reasons, cannot download the entirety of information gathered within the Blockchain. These nodes do not have a role in the verification of new blocks. The logic of light and full nodes dissuades from fraudulent activity as those who would like to "beat the system" would be forced to replicate the historical track record of all transactions and create systems that are even more developed than the existing "full nodes". This makes Blockchain a very secure technology with well-known validation criteria that is recognized by the community and that has required an accumulated amount of work for creation and protection.

A final relevant term is "mining". Mining is a system of Proof of Work (PoW) that relies on an SHA 256[4] algorithm that validates new transactions and adds them to the Blockchain. These transactions are validated in "blocks". These blocks are received by miners who, *via* the use of specialized software, validate that each transaction is legitimate and registered back into the Blockchain. The validation process consists of the resolution of several complex mathematical equations that are themselves dependent on an aleatory targeting system that is defined within the rules of the Blockchain. This aleatory feature guarantees that it is never the same miner that validates the transaction (Ribeiro, 2016). This "randomness" avoids a single miner from becoming more powerful than any other, which is one of the keys to the security of Blockchain.

Once the verification process or "Proof of Work" (PoW) is made by every miner, the solution to the "mathematical enigma" is recorded back in the Blockchain. This process, which takes ten minutes, allows users to avoid "double-spending" in using the same Bitcoins. Miners compete against one another, and their chances of validating a transaction will depend upon the computing power they have in place, relative to that of the other miners within the network. As restitution for their work, miners get every ten minutes a certain quantity of Bitcoin.

The negative side of the PoW is the fact that the calculation capacity necessary for validating a transaction is very energy-consuming, as it involves the "efforts" or "calculations" of all the different miners that compete to be the first to validate each block.[5] Each Bitcoin can be therefore seen as a "chain of digital signatures" (Nakamoto, 2008). And it is in this chain or protocol that relies on the credibility of a system that can assure a transparent currency where the quantities, growth levels, and distribution are known to everyone.

---

[4]The type of algorithm chosen is not the same for all cryptocurrencies (SHA 256, Scrypt, X13, SM3, CryptoNight-Lite, Ethash, Equihash, zk-SNARKs...). The algorithm defines both the difficulty of the computer calculations that miners' computers will have to solve, the speed of processing of new transactions in the Blockchain and the distribution of the new cryptocurrencies issued.

[5]It should be noted that from 2012, other much less energy-intensive validation methods have emerged, such as "Proof of Stake" (PoS) for example.

The technological infrastructure of Bitcoin, where an attacker would be forced to have more than 51% of the network to take control, is therefore efficient, safe, incorruptible, and inviolable. It allows the direct interaction of individuals without the need for calling a third-party for intervention. It excludes all forms of coercion. And the transaction costs are relatively low.

What does mining look like?

Mining requires three types of hardware. A processor (CPU), a graphic card (GPU), and the ASIC (application-specific integrated circuit). This hardware varies according to their hash speed (a mathematical algorithm that is used in cryptography), their versatility, their power (in watts), the noise they produce, and of course, their price.

The CPU, the most accessible tool for mining

The processor, or CPU, is the most accessible computing system available for mining. However, when compared with the GPU or the ASIC, its power is very limited, which explains why its use is only privileged when the encrypted information is not being mined by a large number of miners, or in cases in which algorithms are "CPU friendly". The "hashing" speed goes from 70 h/s for 54 W (Intel Pentium G4560) to 1500 h/s for 120 W (Intel Xeon E52686).

The GPU, mixing power, and versatility

The GPU is another tool for mining capable of analyzing all types of algorithms with a more powerful capacity than a CPU. There are two key manufacturers of GPUs: Nvidia and AMD. To optimize their processing power, GPUs are assembled in a rig that usually contains a power source (700 W to 1600 W), a motherboard (ex: ASRock H110 Pro BTC+; ASUS B250 Mining Expert), risers or adapters (ex: Riser X1), GPUs, and a ventilated or air-conditioned stand (see Fig. 15.1).

The ASIC: the most powerful, yet not versatile, choice

The Application-Specific Integrated Circuit (ASIC) holds a very high processing power. However, it is also a very specialized type of hardware that can only work with a very limited number of algorithms. The ASIC is usually composed of one or more chips

Fig. 15.1. Rigs of GPU (pixabay.com, photos free of use).

Fig. 15.2. ASIC Bitmain Antminer S9 (pixabay.com, photos free of use).

that are arranged on a card, joined by connectors (to allow it to connect to the internet), a power supply unit, many ventilators, and a container. The strengths of the ASIC technology are manifold: a very high speed of hashing (which increases the chances for a miner to be the first to validate a block) and a lower energy consumption. Its weaknesses, however, are also numerous. An ASIC can only mine a very limited number of algorithms, it can't be used for anything other than mining, it is very expensive, and new and more powerful ASICs frequently emerge on the market, which makes a return on investment more difficult. There are websites (like NiceHash) that allow miners to estimate the daily profitability of mining hardware and to determine the eventual gains or losses (Fig. 15.2).

To increase their profitability, miners have an incentive to join groups of miners that are known as "pools". These groups allow them to mine together and to share the gains.

Finally, there is a final option when it comes to mining, which consists of joining a cloud mining system. In this case, the miner pays other miners to rent out an unused part of their equipment. The renters receive, in return for their investment, the gains from the leased equipment. However, people choosing this option take the risk of paying rent in advance without being guaranteed that the equipment will work efficiently, or that it is not a scam.

15.2.3 *The different types of Blockchain*

After the creation of bitcoin, more than 1,500 cryptocurrencies have been created.[6] They are all based on specific Blockchain technologies as a way of differentiation (some are faster, while others are more traceable; some are cheaper to trade with, while others have tougher authentication protocols). Blockchains are said to be public because the entirety of its repository (historic of the transaction) is visible to everyone. A way of imagining public Blockchain is by thinking about a "big public book, anonymous, impossible to falsify, that everyone can consult and read" (Ribeiro, 2016). They are two main types of public Blockchain: the classical Blockchains and the "infrastructure" ones.

Classical Blockchains gather information than can be consulted by everyone. They work as safe data centers (Kolb *et al.*, 2020). For example, the Blockchain of Bitcoin has all the blocks that trace all the transactions in Bitcoins ever since the first emission of a "block genesis" by Satoshi Nakamoto in 2009. These blocks stock all the electronic signatures as well as other data including the purchases, the ownership of Bitcoins, the payments, etc.

The "infrastructure" Blockchains are capable of keeping and managing other types of information that are known as "Smart Contracts". The first Blockchain of this type, called Ethereum, was

[6]The Cryptoencyclopedia gives a complete list of registering cryptocurrencies. Retrieved from: https://www.cryptoencyclopedie.com/crypto-monnaies (23/05/2020).

conceived in 2013 by Vitalik Buterin, a Canadian developer of Russian origin. In his white paper (Buterin, 2013), he defines Smart Contracts as:

> "cryptographic 'boxes' that contain value and only unlock it if certain conditions are met".

It is necessary to avoid confusing smart contracts with regular contracts, as smart contracts are a set of predetermined rules that are inserted inside of a computing system to render it anonymous. Once the conditions or rules are fulfilled, the agreement is auto-executed. However, these contracts have, to this date, no legal validity. A smart contract is the technical application of a contract but not the contract itself.

The operation of a smart contract is based on the "if-then" principle (if the condition is verified, then the consequence is executed). Its originality resides in the fact that smart contracts are written using Blockchain and therefore they benefit from all the advantages of this technology (safety, timestamp, tamper-proof, reduced transaction costs, etc.). The application of a smart contract facilitates the writing of the contract, reduces judiciary interventions, avoids arbitrage or opportunism, and reduces ambiguity accruing from written or semantical confusion. Once the parameters are set, we can have certainty that smart contracts will be executed as planned, quickly and without the need for human intervention. Buterin saw three great opportunities for the implementation of Blockchain infrastructures (Buterin, 2013):

> "In general, there are three types of applications on top of Ethereum. The first category is financial applications, providing users with more powerful ways of managing and entering into contracts using their money. This includes sub-currencies, financial derivatives, hedging contracts, savings wallets, wills, and ultimately even some classes of full-scale employment contracts. The second category is semi-financial applications, where the money is involved but there is also a heavy non-monetary side to what is being done; a perfect example is self-enforcing bounties for solutions to computational problems. Finally, there are applications such as online voting and decentralized governance that are not financial at all".

The emergence of private Blockchains (Blockchains that contain information that is only visible by specific predetermined actors) and "consortium Blockchain" (a mix between public and private ones) are expected to help accelerate the diffusion of Blockchain technology to other economic domains.

Blockchains can be seen as technologies that are based on information that can be shared among participants of a network, for which the information is accessible to everyone and where the validation of transactions can be made by aleatory miners that operate in a network of nodes. Blockchain is also a complex ecosystem that relies on networks that distribute the work and allow the reduction of transaction costs and increased reliability of the system. Blockchain is also based on the resolution of complex mathematical problems that require the use of large calculation systems (computers) and that require the computation of a lot of energy since many validations, for the same transaction, can take place at the same time. But more importantly, Blockchain is a technology that can interest many domains other than currencies. Therefore, the question that is worth considering is the following. What are the radical changes that Blockchain can provide for the functioning of other economic and social activities?

15.3 The New Applications of Blockchain Technology

In this section, we will target three different aspects concerning the use of Blockchain. First, the factors that render Blockchain more attractive to businesses. Second, specific examples of novel applications to financial markets, and finally some examples of non-financial uses.

15.3.1 *Factors that render Blockchain attractive*

Seven factors make Blockchain attractive for business (Godebarge and Rossat, 2016): first, the impossibility of forging data; second, the cryptographic security; third, the lowering of transactions costs; fourth, data verification and authentication; fifth, the "community type" organization; sixth, the recording of data that is kept public; and finally, the rapidity of transactions. The authors develop these domains with specific examples for each.

The impossibility to forge data is a result of the PoW principle. According to this principle, the validation of a new block implies that this block can never be changed. The block keeps information that is traceable, reliable, and always accessible. We can imagine then that any type of document could be submitted to validation under this protocol (patents, tickets, notary documents, certificates, diplomas, etc.) and that we would be sure that there is no refutable doubt on when and where the data was created. This traceability would imply that inventors would not be obliged to submit their new inventions to public or private institutions (INPI, lawyers), as they would have irrefutable proof of the moment at which the work was produced.

The second area concerns safety, which allows actors to protect their identities as well as personal data. This safety is guaranteed by the private keys. From this point of view, applications of Blockchain for businesses would be way more advanced in securing private or personal information. For instance, when installing apps on our smartphones we accept to transmit our personal information to the developers of the apps and we also grant them access to a lot of personal information. However, the developers cannot guarantee that our information will never be stolen or fall into the wrong hands. In using Blockchain, users could hold total control over their data and information and be kept the sole owners of such. The access to their data would become transparent (users would know exactly who and for what purpose has accessed their information), and the owner of such data would hold the right to take or give permission to use it at any time.

The reduction of transaction costs, is, as simply explained by Nakamoto, due to the suppression of third-party certifications or validations. Because the number of intermediates is less, transaction costs are lower. This is a characteristic of the technology that can call the attention of the financial sector, but also of other sectors that need to rely on certification (imagine a Fairtrade coffee that was traceable and for which there was no need of having a certification organism attesting to the veracity of the information).

Data authentication, which is based on the principle of consensus and block validation, is also a very relevant source of value for businesses. Since this system is based on the “agreement” or “consensus” of members of a community to determine that something is “valid”, we can see this feature as a very good way of setting governance models. The Decentralized Autonomous Organizations (DAOs) are the most visible example of this type of organization, which follow rules that are contained in a consensus-driven system of shared data. DAOs are autonomous entities based on smart contracts that define the rules of governance. These rules are transparent and cannot be modified. These autonomous and decentralized organizations are "horizontal" and have a "high potential for disruption compared to the traditional vertical management rules inherited from the industrial revolution, where a small group of stockholders or investors takes decisions over a large pyramidal structure, with the hopes of making more profit" (Leloup and Mougayar, 2017). A good example is *The DAO* (created in 2016), an experience driven by the company Slock.it using Blockchain Ethereum. This initiative started with a funding round of 150 million dollars. A white paper established the right of participants to hold the right to claim back the funding at any time. All the governance rules are formalized, automated, and implemented through smart contracts (Jentzsch, 2016). The main objective of *The DAO* is to evaluate the investment projects that are submitted to it and to determine whether they should be funded or not. The risks of each funded project are spread among all the participants of *The DAO*. This means that the system can remain "secure" without having a "central" control. *The DAO* showed that the governance of organizations can be improved using Blockchain. This example suggests that new DAOs could be "an impossible to corrupt organization that belongs to its founders, those who financed their creation, where the rules are public and therefore there is no need to trust anyone since no one can change the code and it can be audited by all" (Tual, 2016). Some believe that it would be possible to reorganize efficiently public services by using DAOs (Atzori, 2017).

The community-based organization of Blockchain is also relevant to all activities that may require a vote. National elections, referendum, and others could be efficiently deployed in using Blockchain. Heavy and expensive systems could thus be replaced by others based on the Blockchain, easier to access, visible to everyone, and guaranteeing the anonymity of voters. More broadly, any digital peer-to-peer platform could be easily replaced by similar systems powered by Blockchain (Godebarge and Rossat, 2016).

The registration of information within Blockchain is a very trustworthy tool that can make it visible whenever there is an attempt to falsify or alter information. Therefore, activities that are based on the tracking of information over time can also be interested in

Blockchain applications. Some examples may include the food industry, medications, and even attempts to avoid firms' "greenwashing" (imagine being able to identify all the components of a system under a cradle-to-cradle perspective).

Finally, the speed of the transaction is an obvious tool that can help solve issues in situations that require digital validations but take too long to complete (international payments for example).

15.3.2 *The impact of Blockchain to financial markets*

It should be remembered that the role of the financial market is to put people with financing capacity in connection with companies or States in need of financing. Traditionally, we can distinguish between the regulated market (actors and the authorities that are authorized to create regulation) and the over-the-counter market (no protection of parties). Stocks, bonds, and financial derivatives instruments (such as futures contracts providing for future delivery of a commodity at a predetermined price) are usually traded on financial markets. The exchange of financial products is done in three steps: first the negotiation, then the clearing, and finally the payment/delivery. This implies several players such as the negotiators, the portfolio management firms, the investment service providers, the clearinghouses, the depository chambers, the central depositories, and the actors responsible for the product delivery. To assure that the transaction, once negotiated, takes place as expected, clearing and payment delivery systems are essential. The first one is possible thanks to clearinghouses. The latter take margins on transactions and require the actors to deposit an amount on a mutual guarantee fund. The second part is provided by a central depository whose role is to manage the financial securities and ensure their transfer when the settlement agent carries out the transfer of funds. This system can be interfaced (the titles and funds are not in the same place) or integrated.

Regarding this sector, what could be the benefits of Blockchain? Is this technology going to have a greater impact on the reduction of the time between transaction and settlement, the reduction of transaction costs, and the integration of clearing and settlement systems?

Engaging in financial transactions, investors would as usual contact brokers to buy or sell financial assets. The buying broker, acting for his client, and the selling broker would agree on a price and would put a smart contract on the Blockchain. The mining system would then automatically check the transaction. At the time of inclusion of the block hosting the transaction, the latter would be transferred to the clearinghouse, which would also check the transaction, before its transfer to the payment system that would automatically make the payment. Consequently, transactions could be carried out very quickly, in a few seconds against two or three days in the traditional system, hence reducing risks and costs.[7] This procedure could also link clearinghouses and payment-delivery agencies into an integrated system that could allow for more automation. Moreover, reporting tasks would be easier since they would be done directly within Blockchain. It would be even possible to avoid using physical contracts thanks to multi-signature wallets directly handled within Blockchain (Peters et Panayi, 2016). Finally, Wyman believes that Blockchain could result in transaction cost economies of about 15–20 billion a year (Wyman, 2016).

15.3.3 *The non-financial uses of Blockchain*

The non-financial applications of Blockchain are, in theory, limitless. They can consist of the financing of large investment projects (*Initial Coin Offering* or ICO), or simply by integrating Blockchain technology into new business models.

As opposed to an IPO (*Initial Public Offering*), which implies the launch of new stock in the trading market, the ICO is a "mechanism to raise external funding through the emission of tokens" (Momtaz, 2018). An ICO is a fund-raising exercise under the crowdfunding model, that is collected in cryptocurrencies. Concretely, a firm emits tokens that it sells as cryptocurrencies for launching a new project, and people (and firms) can buy these tokens. The ICO allows firms to overcome the very complex and difficult access to the venture capital system, which tends to only finance projects that are at a very early stage. Also, the tokens can be given many other uses including buying the product at the origin of the ICO, be resold as a financial

[7]HitFin, for example, proposes a private Blockchain able to deal with financial assets transactions and a bilateral clearing house. It expects a 17 seconds execution time.

title, or be reconverted into fiat currency. Platforms such as *Waves* in Russia or *Trade.io* in Hong Kong allow firms to get started in a few clicks. In 2019, USD 2.83 billion was raised in ICOs worldwide, after peaking at USD 13.54 billion in 2018 (Perreau, 2020). The ten largest ICOs to date: EOS (USD 4000 million), Telegram (1700), Bitfinex (1000), TaTaTu (575), Dragon Coin (320), HDAC (258), Filecoin (257), Tezos (233), Sirin Labs (157), and Bancor (153). The ICOs are more frequently used to finance the launch of decentralized applications. Nevertheless, there is no guarantee for investors, and some ICO can be real scams.

Therefore, there is a rapid evolution of the juridical and regulatory standards for launching ICOs. In France, the PACTE law (22 May 2019) has a section dedicated to ICOs in its article 26. The law stipulates that the French Financial Market Authority (AMF) could deliver a pre-approval to ICO projects that provide guarantees of protection to investors such as the provision of the funds raised. Moreover, the creators of tokens will have to be registered to operate in France and the ICOs will have minimum standards for the number of people necessary to validate the projects (at least 150 people). Finally, ICOs will be required to provide a white paper presenting the project's potential risks.

In synthesis, numerous domains have already adopted blockchain. Although our following list (and description) is not exhaustive, it sought to render visible the domains and activities for which Blockchain holds a promising future. These activities include digitalization, data exchange, data storing, control and certification, control of authorizations, Internet-reliant activities, activities on the domain of the Internet of Things (IoT), and collaborative activities.

When it comes to the digitalization of things, a simple case is the digitalization of documents that can be later sent and stored. For example, tickets purchased for shows could easily be stored in a Blockchain. This is the case of *Ticket 721*,[8] which develops this type of solution. The proof of the ticket's ownership they provide stays on the Blockchain forever. We could imagine that, in the future, candidates applying for a job could also request their schools (and some like HEC business schools are already testing this) proof of their studies which would discourage falsification or false representation.

[8] *Ticket721* website: https://ticket721.com/(consulted:21/05/2020).

When it comes to controlling activities, we can refer to all third-party organizations that are in the middle of certification processes. These companies could leverage on Blockchain to develop better services and processes and to hold reliable information on the different certifications given. Many companies in the construction and service sectors are already starting to deploy such solutions, as Blockchain-recorded certificates can allow a trustworthy and publicly available tracking of certified firms.

When it comes to authorizations and authentications, companies that require to confirm identities are already considering (or using) Blockchain. Imagine forgetting about a printed passport, or a student ID card, another type of key (even a virtual one) that could attest to the fact that you are who you say you are. The start-up *BlockStack*, offers to their customers a similar service, as their clients are given a Blockchain identity that enables them to validate their login information to different sites.[9]

In the case of the use of Blockchain for internet-oriented activities, the best example is the Internet of Things (IoT) and more specifically of connected objects. The ability to gather anonymous information about people (but yet reliable) could prove a very valuable source of information for collaborations between companies and governments to gather data on, for example, the health of iWatch users or the number of steps walked by citizens of different cities. The importance lies in the fact that the information owners would be respected by not being directly targeted or by having their details being sold on behalf of purely commercial interests.

When it comes to collaborative activities, we can very quickly expect the emergence of services that allow us to rent or use others' assets (cars, houses). Imagine a transparent system that allows you to see the real data of the use of a property (or car) to know that this asset can be used for the correct purposes (e.g. an Airbnb that respect the local city's laws or a car that has undergone all of its technical controls).

As shown, several emergent initiatives show the large variety of uses permitted by Blockchain. Other ideas are being developed in even more diverse industries such as online games, the sports industry, and others. The list is so long, that it would be impossible,

[9] *BlockStack* website: https://blockstack.org/ (consulted: 21/01/2020).

within the limits of the present chapter, to include all the potential applications.

15.4 Conclusion

Blockchain technology found its origins in the experience of cryptocurrencies. It allows us to organize the exchange of secured data inside of a distributed database. Its properties allow it to go beyond the horizon of cryptocurrencies and to find new applications in a large variety of areas. This technology is very disruptive and can be expected to accompany the revolution of many other sectors that rely on highly complex transactions. The development of Blockchain beyond cryptocurrencies and the eruption of new private and consortium Blockchain lead us, however, to ask ourselves relevant questions: what is the minimum size a network must have to guarantee the desired level of security? How can we standardize this technology to better conceive standards that regulate its functioning? How can these standards be known (and accepted) by the community? Who is responsible for creating (and safeguarding) these standards?

More than a technical revolution, blockchain could also become a vector for profound social change. The role of researchers, scholars, experts, and authorities is to be attentive to the evolution and potential applications of this technology.

Appendix A

Glossary

ASIC: The Application-Specific Integrated Circuit is an integrated circuit (IC) customized for a particular use (rather than for a general purpose). As a cryptocurrency mining hardware, it is used for one (or more) specific algorithm calculation.

Bitcoin: Cryptographic currency based on a peer-to-peer transactional system.

Block: The entirety of data stored on the blockchain.

Consortium Blockchain: A specific type of blockchain where the governance is assured by predefined nodes.

CPU: The Central Processing Unit can be linked to the computer brain.

CPU-friendly: Cryptocurrency or algorithm that promotes mining by CPU.

Cryptocurrency: An electronic currency that is exchanged in mode peer-to-peer via Blockchain.

Cryptography: The discipline that specializes in data protection. The technique used to guarantee the confidentiality of a message.

DAO: Decentralized Autonomous Organization, an organization using smart contracts from a blockchain as a way of assuring the governance of the participants.

Double spending: The act of paying twice the same asset.

Fiat: Money controlled by a State.

Fork: This is a subdivision of the blockchain of a cryptocurrency to change it.

GPU: The Graphics Processing Unit generally designates a graphics card.

Hash rate: Power/speed of computer hardware to mine a coin (algorithm).

ICO: Initial Coin Offering is a means of financing based on blockchain, widely used to finance new projects.

Miner: Node within a network that has the computational capability to add new blocks to the blockchain.

P2P (Peer to peer): Means of communication without a central body.

PoS (Proof of Stake): Mandatory mathematical resolution method that allows the inclusion of a new block by a miner. Its value is relative to the quantity of currency held by the minor with regards to other miners. PoS requires much less energy than PoW.

PoW (Proof of Work): Mandatory mathematical resolution method that allows the inclusion of a new block on the blockchain by a miner. Its value is relative to the computational power held by the miner regarding other miners.

Private Blockchain: A specific type of blockchain where the governance is assured by a single node.

Public Blockchain: A specific type of blockchain where the governance is assured by all nodes within the network.

Private Key: A key that is only held by the owner of a wallet, which allows him to identify himself for every transaction.

Public Key: Addressee of a wallet.

RIG: An assembly of several GPUs.

Satoshi Nakamoto: The pseudonym of the Bitcoin inventor whose real identity remains unknown.

Scam: Theft of cryptocurrencies. The most common examples in the world of cryptocurrencies are fundraising for a project (ICO) where the founders of the project disappear with the money raised.

Smart contract: A computer program that runs in the Blockchain infrastructure and that runs once the specific conditions have been fulfilled. It is tamper-proof and transparent thanks to the Blockchain.

Trusted third-party: An organization that authorizes the use of electronic signatures. This organization can receive transaction fees each time an authorization is requested.

Transaction: Operation of exchange that involves two or more actors. In the case of blockchain, a transaction can be defined as the addition of an object to a block.

Wallet: IT support used to store private keys and therefore to use cryptocurrencies.

Whitepaper: Document produced by the developers of a corner to present their project to the public and arouse their interest.

References

Atzori, M. (2017). Blockchain technology and decentralized governance: Is the state still necessary? *Journal of Governance and Regulation*, **6**(1): 45–62. DOI: 10.22495/jgr_v6_i1_p5.

Buterin, V. (2013). Ethereum White Paper: A next-generation smart contract & decentralized application platform. Retrieved from:

http://blockchainlab.com/pdf/Ethereum_white_paper-a_next_generation_smart_contract_and_decentralized_application_platform-vitalik-buterin.pdf.

Cappiello, C., Commuzzi, M., Daniel, F., and Meroni, G. (2019). *Data Quality Control in Blockchain Applications.* In Di Ciccio, C. *et al.* (Eds.), Chapter 12, "Business Process Management: Blockchain and Central and Eastern Europe Forum", Springer, pp. 166–181.

Castor, A. (2017). In santa barbara, an annual event brings together those closest to bitcoin's roots. *Forbes.* Retrieved from: https://www.forbes.com/sites/amycastor/2017/08/30/in-santa-barbara-an-annual-event-brings-together-those-central-to-bitcoins-roots/#7c6665437b60.

Chaum, D. (1983). Blind signatures for untraceable payments. *Advances in Cryptology Proceeding,* **82**(3): 199–203. Retrieved from: http://www.hit.bme.hu/~buttyan/courses/BMEVIHIM219/2009/Chaum.BlindSigForPayment.1982.PDF.

Chaum, D. (1985). Security without Identification Card Computers to make Big Brother Obsolete. *Communications of the ACM,* **28**(10): 1030–1044.

Dai, W. (1998). b-money. *Forbes.* Retrieved from: http://www.weidai.com/bmoney.txt.

Davidson, S., De Filippi, P., and Potts, J. (2018). Blockchains and the economic institutions of capitalism. *Journal of Institutional Economics,* **14**(4): 639–658.

De Filippi, P. (2014). Bitcoin: A regulatory nightmare to a libertarian dream. *Internet Policy Review,* **3**(2). https://policyreview.info/articles/analysis/bitcoin-regulatory-nightmare-libertarian-dream, DOI: 10.14763/2014.2.286.

De Filippi, P. and Loveluck, B. (2016). The invisible politics of Bitcoin: Governance crisis of decentralized infrastructure. *Internet Policy Review,* **5**(3). https://policyreview.info/articles/analysis/invisible-politics-bitcoin-governance-crisis-decentralised-infrastructure, DOI: 10.14763/2016.3.427.

Desmedt, L. and Lakomski-Laguerre, O. (2015). L'alternative monétaire Bitcoin: Une perspective institutionnaliste. *Revue de la régulation,* **18**(2). https://journals.openedition.org/regulation/11489#quotation, DOI: 10.4000/regulation.11489.

Godebarge, F. and Rossat, R. (2016). *Principes clés d'une application Blockchain,* EM Lyon, France.

Jentzsch. C. (2016). Decentralized autonomous organization to automate governance, Final draft. Retrieved from: https://archive.org/stream/DecentralizedAutonomousOrganizations/WhitePaper_djvu.txt.

Kolb, J., Abdelbaky, M., Katz, R., and Culler, D. (2020). Core concepts, challenges, and future directions in blockchain: A centralized Tutorial. *ACM Comput. Surv.*, **53**(1): 9:1–9:32. https://dl.acm.org/doi/pdf/10 1145/3366370 DOI: 10.1145/3366370.

Labazova, O., Ehling, T., and Sunyaev, A. (2019). From hype to reality: A taxonomy of blockchain applications. *Proceedings of the 52nd Hawaii International Conference on System Sciences.* DOI:10.24251/HICSS.2019.552.

Leloup, L. and Mougayar, W. (2017). *Blockchain: la révolution de la confiance*, (Eyrolles Paris, France).

May, T. (1992). The crypto anarchist manifesto. November. Retrieved from: https://www.activism.net/cypherpunk/crypto-anarchy.html.

Meroni, G., Plebani, P., and Vona, F. (2019). *Trusted Artifact-Driven Process Monitoring of Multi-party Business Processes with Blockchain*, In Di Ciccio, C. *et al.* (Eds.), Chapter 5, "Business Process Management: Blockchain and Central and Eastern Europe Forum", Springer, pp. 55–70.

Momtaz, P. (2020). Initial Coin Offering. *PLoS ONE*, **15**(5): 1–30. DOI: 10.2139/ssrn.3166709.

Nakamoto, S. (2008). Bitcoin: A Peer-to-Peer electronic cash system. Retrieved from: https://bitcoin.org/bitcoin.pdf.

Ólnes, S., Ubacht, J., and Janssen, M. (2017). Blockchain in Government: Benefits and implications of distributed ledger technology for information sharing. *Government Information Quarterly*, **34**(3): 355–364. DOI: 10.1016/j.giq.2017.09.007.

Perreau, C. (2020). ICO: définition, liste, la situation en France.... *Journal du Net*, mars. Retrieved from: https://www.journaldunet.com/economie/finance/1195462-ico-definition-liste-la-situation-en-france-decembre-2019/.

Peters, G. and Panayi, E. (2016). Understanding modern banking ledgers through blockchain technologies: Future of transaction processing and smart contracts on the internet of money, DOI: 10.2139/ssrn.2692487.

Ribeiro, A. (2016). La Blockchain et ses potentielles applications, *Université de Genève*, Retrieved from: https://archive-ouverte.unige.ch/unige:89 544.

Rijswijk van, L., Hermsen, F., and Arendsen, R. (2019). Exploring the future of taxation: A blockchain scenario study. *Journal of Internet Law*, **22**(9): 639–658.

Risius, M. and Spohrer K. (2017). A blockchain research framework. *Business & Information Systems Engineering*, **59**(6): 385–409.

Rodima-Taylor, D. and Grimes, W. (2017). *Cryptocurrencies and Digital Payments rails in networked global governance: perspective on inclusion and development*, In Campbell-Verduyn, M. (Eds.), Chapter 6, "Bitcoin and Beyond", Routledge, pp. 109–132.

Rolland, M. and Slim, A. (2017). Economie politique du Bitcoin: l'institutionnalisation d'une monnaie sans institutions, *Economie et Institutions*, **26**: 1–20. DOI: 10.4000/ei.6023.

Ruoti, S., Kaiser, B., Yerukhimovich, A., Clark, J., and Cunningham, R. (2020). Blockchain Technology: What Is It Good For? *Communication of the ACM*, **63**(1): 46–53. DOI: 10.1145/3369752.

Szabo, N. (1998). Secure property titles with owner authority. Retrieved from: http://www.fon.hum.uva.nl/rob/Courses/InformationInSpeech/CDROM/Literature/LOTwinterschool2006/szabo.best.vwh.net/securetitle.html.

Szabo, N. (2005). Bit Gold. Retrieved from: http://unenumerated.blogspot.com/2005/12/bit-gold.html.

Tual, S. (2016). Interview, In Yeretzian, A., Jeanneau, C., Stachtchenko, A., and Balva, C. (Eds.), Chapter 4, "La Blockchain décryptée", Netexplo, pp. 84–95.

Wyman, O. (2016). *The Fintech 2.0 Paper. Rebooting Financial Services*, Santander InnoVenture. 20 pages, https://www.finextra.com/finextra-downloads/newsdocs/the%20fintech%202%200%20paper.pdf.

Yeoh, P. (2017). Regulatory issues in blockchain technology. *Journal of Financial Regulation and Compliance*, **25**(2): 196–208. DOI: 10.1108/JFRC-08-2016-0068.

https://doi.org/10.1142/9781786349507_0016

Chapter 16

FinTech Development, Digital Infrastructure and Institutions in the SSA Zone

Teresa Schützeichel
School of the Economics and Business Sciences,
University of the Witwatersrand, Johannesburg, South Africa
terrykiboi@gmail.com

16.1 FinTech in Africa: Evolution of the Mobile Phone

The penetration of mobile phone technology in sub-Saharan Africa (SSA) has been phenomenal given the low levels of infrastructure investment. Very few technologies have penetrated the African continent as much as the mobile phone. According to the Global Systems for Mobile Communications Association (GSMA), mobile phone coverage in Africa was only at 10% of the total population as of 1999. This coverage was concentrated in North Africa (Algeria, Egypt, Libya, Morocco, and Tunisia) and in South Africa. Almost ten years later, in 2008, mobile phone coverage in Africa had reached 60% with a population of approximately 447 million people being able to get a signal. In comparison, the fixed line telephones had only reached 2.4 million connections on the continent (GSMA, 2017).

South Africa was the only SSA country with early mobile phone coverage. In 1995, there were approximately 600,000 mobile phones in use in SSA, the majority of which (circa 90%) were in South Africa. Almost fifteen years later the number of mobile phone units in use in SSA had leapfrogged, surpassing 300 million units. South Africa having led the way in terms of mobile phone adoption, rapidly reached saturation. Nigeria quickly followed, on the Western side of the continent. At the time, it also became the fastest growing economic market in SSA and soon had almost 75% mobile phone penetration.

The mobile phone technology in Africa has, over the last two decades, revolutionized the entire social fabric that connects individuals and communities. The ability of mobile phones to reduce communication costs especially with reference to rural Africa has set the technology on a trajectory to become a source of tangible social and economic benefits. Since people can send and receive information cheaply and quickly on various topics relating to economic, social, and political issues, it makes the mobile phone a force to reckon with. Its success lies in the fact that the investment infrastructure required as compared to fixed-line telecommunications options is much less and arguably cheaper.

Over time, the usage of the mobile phone has evolved from being simply a tool for passing on or receiving information. Its existence among a necessity-oriented continent has seen it metamorphosize into a financial services device. The reason for this was put very avidly by an interviewee for the handbook futures of Technology (Grosskurth, 2010) who stated that *"we in Africa demand much more from the mobile phone because of a lack of other options"*. In this regard, creativity has seen the mobile phone become a money transfer device, a savings and credit device, as well as a shopping wallet. In this chapter, we look at the case of Kenya in its mobile money revolution and what factors led to its success. We shall also briefly touch on the emerging issue of regulation technology and the strategies that regulators are considering for the Kenyan market.

This chapter proceeds as follows: Section 16.2 briefly outlines the mobile phone journey; Section 16.3 discusses M-PESA its success factors, how it evolved, its economic and social impacts, and its use in businesses; Section 16.4 gives a brief account of M-PESA in other countries including the challenges facing its adoption; Section 16.5 discusses consumer data protection; Section 16.6 looks at the evolution of RegTech and gives an example of the Regulatory Sandbox trial in Kenya as well as the different approaches to RegTech; Section 16.7

concludes the chapter as well as proposing areas for further research and ways of developing this chapter.

16.2 The Mobile Phone Journey in Kenya

In Kenya, the mobile phone first became available to the public in early 2000. Previously the mobile phone was an elite tool of communication and was possessed by very few. It was also a very expensive commodity and, unlike the sleek units now available, it was a huge device that could not fit in anyone's pocket. Prior to the beginning of the new millennium, possession of a mobile phone in Kenya required special consent from the ministry of telecommunications, authorized by the president. This protracted lengthy application for a mobile phone line has drastically changed over the years where the mobile phone is now ubiquitous as the country is reaching saturation level of penetration. A mobile phone line from the leading mobile telephone service provider Safaricom costs less than a dollar at $0,50. Its registration requires only one's identification document.

There are three major mobile network operators in Kenya regulated by the communications authority, Safaricom, Airtel, and Telkom Kenya. Safaricom was initially a subsidiary of Telkom Kenya when in 2000 the UK based Vodafone Group PLC acquired 40% stake and management responsibility. The government owned Telkom Kenya and later sold off 25% stake of their shareholding in Safaricom in 2008 to the public. It also has the largest market share in Kenya at 65% of mobile users in Kenya. The second largest is Bharti Airtel (commonly known as Airtel) controlling 21%, Telkom having 9%, and the other two smaller ones sharing the rest. Though Airtel was the first mover, Safaricom's market positioning managed to get it a larger subscriber market share. Its appeal to the Kenyan market was hinged on its ability to connect with the rural population and provide a sense of community ownership of the products and services provided.

Mobile phone adoption in East Africa took on two levels: the firm level and the individual level. Whereas firm-level mobile phone adoption was rapid, at the individual level it happened at a much slower pace. For firms, this was a natural transition given that the cost of landlines continued to increase while the service quality became poorer. To get a landline connection in Kenya, for instance, a firm had to wait approximately 100 days, with majority of firms also paying a bribe to facilitate this connection (read: facilitation fee). The average bribe reported then (2003) was, on average, USD 117 (Aker and Mbiti, 2010). The implicit and explicit costs of maintaining landline connection and services became too high for firms; thus the mass shift to mobile phones. For individuals, on the other hand, the number of users of mobile phones far exceeded the actual subscriptions due to the sharing factor. It was not uncommon for more than one household to share a handset, especially in rural areas. Subscription rates were therefore seemingly static in comparison to users (FSD Kenya, 2011, 2013) in the beginning. However, as handsets became cheaper, the subscription rate exponentially grew as each household and later each member of the household could afford to have their own mobile phone (FSD Kenya, 2011, 2013, 2016). Figure 16.1 shows the trend of mobile cellular subscription over the years.

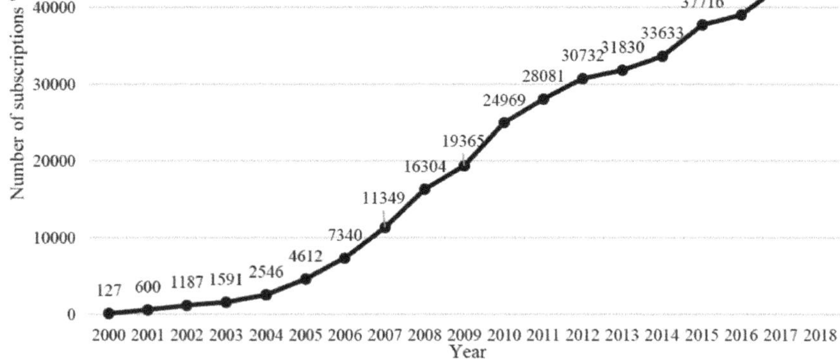

Fig. 16.1. Mobile phone penetration in Kenya 2000–2018.

Source: ITU Website (Country ICT Data 2000–2018).

16.3 Evolution of FinTech: The M-PESA Experiment and Its Success Factors

The literal translation of M-PESA is M for mobile and Pesa is the Swahili word for money. Safaricom introduced its money transfer platform in 2007 surrounded by a lot of skepticism. The banking sector, given its highly regulated nature, means that it is very conservative. As Chris Meyer[1] states "*the banking sector is the only industry where commitment to innovation is detrimental to a career*". This was certainly the case in Kenya when the proposal to test mobile money reached the Central Bank of Kenya (CBK). The quagmire was essentially fueled by the fact that neither the communications authority nor the central bank really had the mandate to regulate the product. This was because the platform was a telecommunications company offering a financial service — transfer of money. In a leap of faith, the then CBK governor agreed to a trial period where the DfID[2] together with Safaricom worked with a microfinance company, Faulu[3] Kenya, to pilot the use of the mobile phone to enable recipients of microcredit to make their repayments. On the one hand, this was very successful as the users did not need to travel from their homes in the slums or semi-urban areas to the Faulu Kenya offices to receive their credit and make loan repayments. On the other hand, it was

[1]Blog article discussing the three main reasons why FinTech is failing (Myers, 2017).

[2]Department for International Development of the United Kingdom worked with Vodafone the UK major shareholder of Safaricom.

[3]Faulu is a Swahili word meaning to succeed. This is a microfinance institution lending money to micro and small- scale entrepreneurs especially women to enable them to maintain and run their businesses on a day to day. Most of its customers repay a few dollars each week into the Faulu bank account through the peer group. The structure was such that the borrowers would form groups of about 20 people who would meet each week and give cash to the treasurer who would then take it to the bank accompanied naturally by "bodyguards", i.e. some group members. Safaricom's idea was to find customers with a real market need to use the service. Therefore their argument to Faulu was that the weekly deposit could be made less expensive, less time-consuming, and more secure (Hughes and Lonie, 2007). The "unsuccessful" part then became that the members did not need meet anymore each week. They would simply send the money to the treasurer who would in turn send it to the bank from their phones.

seen as 'unsuccessful' because inasmuch as the use of mobile money made transaction easier, users would not meet as often as before, contrary to the business interests of Faulu (Ngugi *et al.*, 2010).

During the pilot study, another interesting observation was made among the users of the mobile platform. Users started "saving" money received on the phone, using it as an overnight "safe box" (Ngugi *et al.*, 2010). It became apparent to users that unless there was a real need to withdraw the money, they need not do it. Users had started building trust in the system, reducing the skepticism that was there at the beginning. This gave Safaricom/Vodafone the push they needed to officially launch M-PESA on a larger scale. Using the "test and learn" approach to regulation, M-PESA was commercially launched in March of 2008. Early adopters were primarily working-class, male, urban-based individuals who would then send money back home to their spouses, the elderly, and young adults who were mainly rural based. The early users in turn helped integrate the rural-based population on to the mobile money transfer platform.

As a FinTech offering money transfer, M-PESA gained traction among the Kenyan population due to some critical factors. According to Ngugi *et al.* (2010), these factors were as follows:

1. Illiteracy among the unbanked rural population. This meant that the documentation required to be completed for one to gain access to a bank account was an impediment to majority of the population. Kenya at the time had a 60% illiteracy rate.
2. Bureaucracy and guarantee from an existing bank customer. Through the regulations of the CBK then on "Know your Customer" in an exercise to reduce information asymmetry, there was a large segment of the population that was naturally left out.
3. Amount of money required to open and maintain a bank account. As of 2007, the amount required to open a bank account was USD 105, and to maintain it was a monthly charge of USD 19. This was unattainable for approximately 70% of the population. According to the FSD Kenya national surveys on financial inclusion, majority of the respondents have constantly cited the lack of money to open and maintain a bank account as a reason for not having one (FSD Kenya, 2011, 2013, 2016).
4. The poor distribution of traditional banking services. Given the concentration of population in big towns and centres in Kenya, the

presence of financial services is also concentrated in these areas, with the rural areas left unserved. This gap for people to conduct financial transactions needed to be filled.

The issues described above showed that people needed a fast, cheap, simple, and reliable way to engage with financial services. M-PESA, in its simplicity, countered these barriers, enabling people to send and receive money as and when needed. The ease of registration for M-PESA, which requires only one's identification document (National ID or passport), a working mobile phone line, and no minimum balance, propelled it to success. Sending money from working professionals to their relatives at home was an uphill and sometimes expensive task. This was because it included service fees charged by the money transfer companies (e.g. Western Union), middlemen when relatives, friends, or bus drivers were used, and risk of theft. M-PESA eliminated these problems by reducing the cost of sending money, eliminating middlemen, and the use of technology made it safe, reliable, and fast.

In taking the test and learn approach to regulation, financial market regulators and supervisory institutions took a leap of faith as there was no set regulatory environment for digital financial services. This meant that the process to create the right government regulatory environment for the providers of mobile money would be in tandem. Although we focus here on M-PESA, due to its high market share, there exists also other players the main competitor, like Airtel money.

16.3.1 *Evolution of M-PESA in Kenya*

Although there is more than one mobile money service in Kenya, we focus here on M-PESA given the large size of its market share. The success of Safaricom's mobile money service was largely fueled by their "Bottom of the pyramid" approach in aiming at covering a large area of the population, which meant the poor in rural areas. The strategy in a nutshell was to captivate people's hearts and ride on the community spirit known as "Harambee". In this way, they made people feel like they owned the product. Figure 16.2 shows the strides made in the uptake of M-PESA by registered customers in a span of ten years. It started with the early adopters, i.e. male, working and

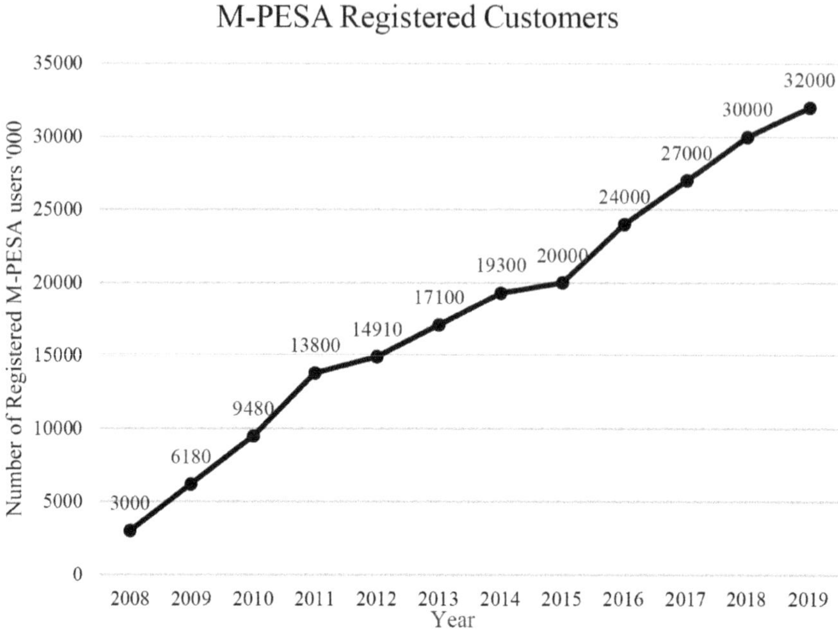

Fig. 16.2. M-PESA customer subscription since it was launched.

urban based, being able to send airtime credits to their relatives and family in rural areas. This demographic of women, the elderly, and young adults had been ignored by the mainstream banking sector. The concept succeeded based on three elements of the community strategy.

First, the use of Swahili language for the slogans and product taglines. Swahili is the second national/official language in Kenya that majority of Kenyans speak and understand without the perceived elitism associated with English. Sending of airtime credits was marketed using the term *Sambaza*, which in Swahili loosely translates to "to share". This enabled the users who were working and in urban areas to buy high-value airtime credits and share it with their relatives. Next came *okoa jahazi*, which means "to save the ship from sinking", and provided the possibility to get an "overdraft" on airtime credits which then get automatically repaid when one reloaded. From sharing credit, Safaricom realized that it was possible to scale up the M-PESA pilot and launch it nationwide. The slogan for the M-PESA service being launched in March 2008 was

Tuma Pesa Nyumbani which translates to "send money home". Marketing images of the elderly being able to receive money from their relatives in the city captivated many hearts.

Second, convenience associated with M-PESA. Safaricom teamed up with the basic utilities supply companies, i.e. for power and water, enabling people to make simple payments for utilities using their mobile phone.[4] The next step was making it possible for customers at the supermarket or local kiosk to pay for goods and services using their mobile phone. Initially, payments were made to the shopkeeper's mobile phone number. This has since evolved to include till numbers for businesses and paybill numbers for both companies and individuals.

Third, social good and community spirit. With the advent of "paybill numbers" on Safaricom's M-PESA, anyone in need, for example, of high medical bills, can raise funds without necessarily organizing a fundraising event. This can be done by the registration of a paybill number into which friends and relatives can send their contributions. This creates a happiness that transmits and shows a company that is not only interested in their profits but is also ingrained in the fabric of society. The tagline Safaricom currently has also evolved in this way to *Pamoja Twaweza*, which translates to "together we can". Figure 16.3 shows the simple interface of M-PESA on a phone.

16.3.2 *Blurring the boundaries: The fusion of telecom and financial services provision*

With the realization that people could store money on their phones if there was no need to withdraw it, the saving culture evolved. Majority of people, especially women, would previously save money under the mattress and would take their contribution to the Rotating Savings and Credit Association (ROSCA) commonly known as

[4]Their marketing image/advertisements using a family scene (mother and children) in the dark where she is cooking in the dark and child is trying to study with a kerosene lamp because the electricity is out playing on emotions. Her husband (and father) then sends her money which she uses to pay for electricity and in real time the power comes back on.

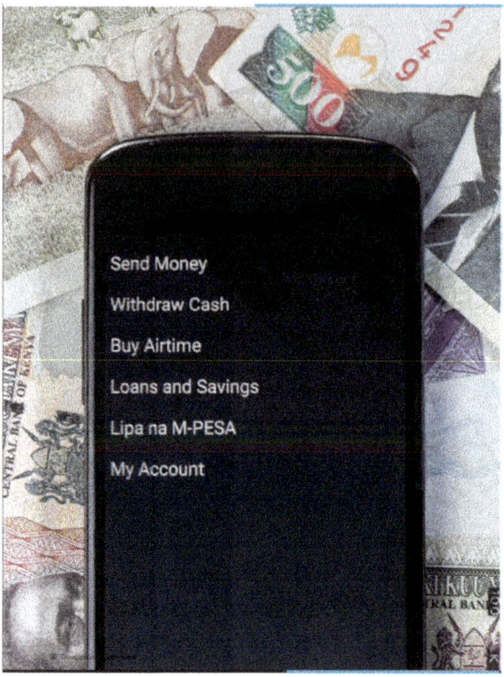

Fig. 16.3. M-PESA Interface on a user's mobile phone (GSMA, 2019b).

"merry-go-round"[5] at the end of the month. M-PESA provided a safer and more secure place for them to save their money, since under the mattress, it was constantly at risk of being stolen or repossessed by, at times, a drunken husband (Morawczynski, 2011). The use of M-PESA also enabled its users to make their contribution to the ROSCA. In this regard, the mobile phone through its simplicity, cheapness, and convenience transitioned continually from a simple communication device to money transfer to a savings platform.

---

[5]These are common, and they are officially known as Rotating Savings and Credit Associations (ROSCAs). Many a woman in Kenya have furnished their homes and taken their children to school using the help of their peers in these merry-go-rounds. The concept is simple: a group of peers come together and agree on a monthly contribution. Each month the total amount is given to one member and this pay-out rotates among all the members until each one had got then the cycle starts all over again.

On realizing the opportunity to integrate financial services, Safaricom in December 2012 rolled out M-Shwari,[6] a bank integrated model which allows M-PESA customers to borrow money based on their M-PESA history and save money on a mobile account that would in turn earn interest. There are other bank-led mobile integrated banking solutions, e.g. KCB M-PESA, but the uniqueness of M-Shwari is that it is **mobile-led,** which is the essence of this FinTech chapter. The users of this service can save, earn interest, and borrow money through their phone. They are not able to access funds through the custodian bank, Commercial bank of Africa (CBA), but rather only through the M-PESA platform. As at the end of 2017, M-Shwari loan-book stood at USD 2.27 million and savings were at USD 124 million (CBA, 2017) More recently, the platform has launched an overdraft service known as *Fuliza*, which means "to do something uninterrupted". This service enables individuals to continue carrying out a transaction even if they have run out of funds on their M-PESA account. It will be interesting to review how it develops and see how the risks of loan default both on M-Shwari and Fuliza will be tackled. This brief account of mobile money's evolution in Kenya strongly affirms the statement *"we in Africa demand much more of the mobile phone than other people who have other options"* made by one of the contributing authors in the handbook Futures of Technology in Africa (Grosskurth, 2010). Figure 16.4 shows the recently introduce "My Safaricom" app, which provides an inviting interface for M-PESA transactions.

The evolution of mobile money meant that the Telecom sector needed to become liberalized, ending the monopoly of Telkom Kenya. Upon entry of the first two main mobile network operators, Airtel and Safaricom, there was a need to introduce fair competition regulation. Upon the introduction of money transfer services, the CBK and the communications authority together with the government needed to figure out the right balance of regulation in the changed environment to encourage innovation but at the same time maintain a stability

[6]This is a paperless banking service offered through M-PESA which enables its users make savings deposits and get micro-credit (loans). This service is housed by the Commercial Bank of Africa which is the trustee bank for Safaricom's M-PESA operations. Users access the service purely through the mobile phone and need not go to the bank branch.

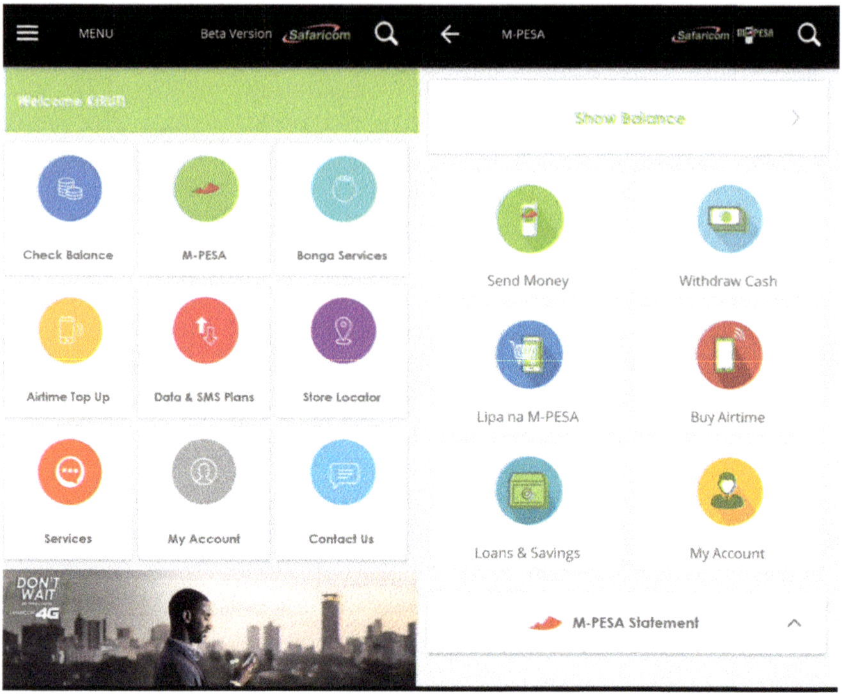

Fig. 16.4. My Safaricom App with M-PESA Menu open on the right (Itimu, 2017).

in the financial system. As government regulators first groped in the dark on regulation, the past 20 years have shown that they have almost got it right.

16.3.3 *Economic impact of M-PESA*

By enabling people to send money to one another to make payments for goods and services and transfer funds from their bank accounts and vice versa, M-PESA has revolutionized households' economic well-being. This simple service that has allowed its users to circumvent and/or sidestep the inefficient banking system has naturally strengthened Safaricom's bottom line, making it the most profitable company in East Africa and the highest taxpayer in Kenya (Safaricom, 2019; Wilson, 2019). Safaricom in this regard has managed not only to make substantial financial gains, continuously generating profit, but has also created a social and environmental impact necessary for sustainability.

Using a true value assessment methodology conducted by KPMG, Safaricom in 2019 reported a 6.3% contribution to the total gross domestic product (GDP) of Kenya. This translates to an absolute value of Ksh. 20.1 billion (USD 201 million). In addition to this, Safaricom's commitment to the improvement of Kenya's socio-economic status is evidenced by its "true value" assessment. This assessment is a monetization of their ability to sustain financial earnings and pay taxes and sustain jobs directly and indirectly, capital expenditure, as well as sustenance of the environment. In monetary terms, this value was estimated at 9.6 times of the financial profit for the financial year ending 31 March 2019 (KPMG, 2019; Safaricom, 2019).

Focusing on the social value that M-PESA has created, the absolute amount in the 2018/19 financial year stood at Kshs. 213.5 billion (USD 21.35 million). This value was driven by a growth in the number of customers, agents, and merchants.[7] For M-PESA users, the greatest benefit lies in their increased ability to manage and save money at lower transaction costs, less theft as well as the wellbeing that comes with access to goods, services, and opportunities and increased safety and security. This view reiterates evidence from a longitudinal study by (Suri and Jack, 2016) that M-PESA has managed to lift 2% of Kenyan households (194,000 households) out of extreme poverty. The positive impacts were more pronounced for female-headed households where women had the opportunity to change from a purely agriculturally based livelihoods to setting up and running businesses. This in turn increased their earnings, and with a behavioral backdrop of resilience and saving M-PESA provided the missing link to complete the chain.

16.3.4 *M-PESA from P2P to C2B and B2B*

The success of M-PESA P2P transfers led gradually to the use of the platform to make payments for goods and services. It became

[7]M-PESA merchants are a type of agent linked to a bank e.g. Cooperative bank, Equity bank and are spread out to provide banking services in a kiosk type set up for M-PESA users.

commonplace for customers to pay directly to the seller using the mobile phone owing mainly to its convenience and elimination of theft risk. This is commonplace, especially for making small payments to shopkeepers and street vendors. In most cases, it also provides the small-scale sellers with a trend of money received as well as if payments have been made in installments, and so they are able to keep track of their debtors. Household users also make payments to their staff, i.e. house helps and nannies, watchmen, as well as providers of handywork services such as plumbers, carpenters, and gardeners. In this case, the employer can have a paperless trail of payments made and their staff have a safe storage for their monthly earnings or weekly wages.

On realizing the potential that M-PESA had in making Kenya a cash lite economy, Safaricom saw this as its opportunity to make mobile money work in micro transactions. Its former and late CEO Bob Collymore stated,

> We want the mama mboga[8] to tell you that it is okay to pay for your sukuma[9] via M-PESA or for the kibanda[10] guy to say it is okay for our customers to pay for a plate of food via M-PESA. In the end, we want M-PESA to be celebrated not because it is a clever product; but because it is a product that is giving practical solutions to everyday problems.

To this end, June 2013 saw Safaricom launch "*Lipa na M-PESA*"[11] loosely translated to Pay with M-PESA'. This service provides businesses with an easy and convenient way to receive cashless payments from their customers. This service has two components: "Paybill" and "Buy Goods". The former is often used remotely where the customer has a formal relationship with an organization, and they have an account number that serves to identify the user. This is the e-commerce payment platform for M-PESA. For example, one uses the paybill option to make payments for utilities, e.g. to

---

[8]Mama mboga refers to the roadside food vendors often selling fruits and vegetables of whom most are women.

[9]Kale-like vegetable eaten as a staple in Kenya.

[10]Kibanda is Swahili for roadside food kiosk where majority of people who work in the city and especially in the industrial areas.

[11]See: https://www.safaricom.co.ke/personal/m-pesa/lipa-na-m-pesa/what-is-lipa-na-m-pesa.

pay the electricity or water bill. The customer keys in the business number or the paybill number then enters their account number and then makes the payment of the required amount.

The "buy goods and services" option is mainly used for retail transactions and is meant for immediate purchase of goods and services. These payments are made on site and are immediately confirmed by the seller. There is thus no formal relationship existing between the customer and the organization and one does not require an account number. This is service used for making payments for purchases in the supermarket or at the fueling station or paying for food at a restaurant.

These M-PESA payment solutions have enabled both simple single transactions and bulk payments with the added advantages of convenience, security, time saving, and real-time payments. The Paybill service specifically allows organizations to collect money on a regular basis from their customers through M-PESA. The funds collected by the organization can be used to further make payments to one's creditors, to pay salaries, or to pay for other services of the business. When small-scale entrepreneurs need a loan, the collections on Lipa na M-PESA is often used as a gauge for liquidity. In addition to this, there grows mutual trust between traders. Beck's 2015 study discussed a bi-directional causality between the use of M-PESA as opposed to cash when dealing with suppliers and access to trade credit. He found that the use of mobile money and trade credit complement each other. In addition to the benefit of avoiding the risk of theft in using cash for the trade credit borrower, the use of mobile money broadens the use of trade credit through its lower costs and ultimately increases the firms' production (Beck, 2015).

16.4 Mobile Money in East Africa and Around the World

Since the overwhelming success of M-PESA in Kenya, mobile money platforms have been launched in various countries around the world. In sub-Saharan Africa where access to financial services through bank accounts is limited, mobile money is playing an especially important role (GSMA, 2017, 2019; Safaricom, 2019). In considering the

UN sustainable development goals, M-PESA is enabling financial inclusion to un-/underserved rural communities and playing a key role in poverty reduction.[12] With governments realizing the substantial and positive impact mobile money can have on their economies as well as their societies, case in point M-PESA, more have emulated Kenya's enabling policies. The positive story in Kenya over the past decade and a half has proven that an enabling regulatory environment is a key cog that turns the mobile money wheel.

I outline briefly the introduction, subsequent adoption, and impact of M-PESA in Tanzania, the second country for Vodacom to launch M-PESA and then discuss the other SSA countries where Vodacom has a presence and has introduced M-PESA. In addition to this, I look at two other countries where their financial regulators have closed the door on the telecom, entangling it in bureaucracy and making it impossible to operate.

Tanzania was the second country in East Africa where Vodacom launched Vodafone's revolutionary mobile money transfer platform M-PESA. It was introduced in April 2008, a year after its launch in Kenya based on the successful adoption and uptake it had received in Kenya. With a similarly successful trajectory expected, 14 months later the story was quite different with only a small fraction of registered users (280,000 compared to 2.7 million users in Kenya in the same timeline) (IFC, 2010). Though similar to Kenya in a number of ways — more than 50% of the population did not have access to any kind of financial services, high rural population, medium levels of literacy as well as a conducive regulatory environment — why was it difficult to replicate the implementation with similar results?

The answer: a copy and paste implementation strategy based on poor market research.[13] Vodacom, in expecting the Tanzanian market to mimic Kenya, ignored some critically different factors of cultural practices, financial literacy, crime rates, and mobile phone penetration due to geographic dispersion. In contrast to Kenya, the

---

[12]See article by a Staff Reporter of the Mail & Guardian: https://mg.co.za/article/2018-06-01-00-m-pesa-ushers-in-a-new-wave-of-banking-infrastructure-in-africa/; (Suri and Jack, 2016), (White, 2012).

[13]See M-Money Channel Distribution Case Tanzania — Vodacom Tanzania (IFC, 2010).

culture of money remittance was already present and M-PESA only came to make it faster, cheaper, and less prone to theft. In Tanzania, sending money home was not as big a deal, and with the lower levels of crime and theft, sending money using a bus at a commission was functioning well.

The levels of financial literacy are impeded in Tanzania in comparison to Kenya due to a relatively better dispersion of bank branches. In addition, Kenyans had a higher rate of semi-formal as well as informal financial services usage as compared to Tanzania, where more than 50% of the population were not privy even to informal savings schemes. Safaricom also took the time to educate their customer base on the product, spending a lot of financial resources on training and matching product to need. Furthermore, it modelled its marketing campaigns to the grassroot population, enabling it to stay etched in the minds and hearts of the large poor populace.[14]

Fast forward ten years on after correcting their introductory mistakes and re-modelling their implementation strategy, Vodacom in Tanzania boasts the largest telecommunications market share at 32% and mobile money market share of 40%. They have more than 7 million registered M-PESA users with an agent spread of more than 106,000 mobile money agents across the country (Vodacom PLC, 2019). In addition to pure money transfer, M-PESA users have become more savvy, requiring more from the platform. To this end, Vodacom introduced the "Lipa Kwa M-PESA" service which provides a payment service for goods and services, like Kenya's Lipa na M-PESA. The platform has continued to further develop increasing its product offering to include provision of savings and loans through "M-Pawa".

The most recent of the developments in Vodacom's product value add for customers was the partnering with World Remit[15] for more convenient international money transfer through the M-PESA platform (World Remit, 2020). This is a substantial move as according to the World Bank, remittances from SSA migrants stood at USD 46 billion as at the end of 2018. This is an interesting development

[14]See ad campaign here: https://www.youtube.com/watch?v=nEZ30K5dBWU.
[15]World Remit is the leading online money transfer platform.

for Tanzania's M-PESA, and it is worth following to see how much remittances are made through it by the end of its first year.

Other SSA markets: M-PESA has been slowly introduced into the SSA markets where Vodacom operates since 2013. These markets are Mozambique (May 2013), Lesotho (June 2013), the Democratic Republic of Congo (DRC) (2013), Egypt (July 2013), and Ghana (September 2015). Except for Ghana and Egypt where the platform is known as "Vodafone Cash", the name M-PESA has been retained. The business case for M-PESA in these countries is evident given the numbers in terms of potential users and the rural nature of much of the population meaning lack of access to formal financial services. Thus, a solution for the financial inclusion agenda as well as a chance for the mobile money platform to give these economies a fighting chance at increased economic and social development.

However, M-PESA in these markets is still used primarily to send and receive money and buy airtime. Payments for goods and services is also still done on the person to person level. With few possibilities to make payments for utilities such as water, electricity, television — DSTV. The payments systems for goods and services enjoyed in Kenya (Lipa na M-PESA) and more recently in Tanzania (Lipa Kwa M-PESA) is being fronted with increased use of M-PESA, especially by small business owners, and the wave is coming.

It will be interesting to see how governments as well as Vodacom in these countries continue to figure out the opportunities that their populations present for them. The case of M-PESA presents a real chance for several economies in SSA to make a developmental leapfrog in terms of financial inclusion for households as well as enabling enterprise growth by providing small loans to businesses. The case for business growth is clearly shown in the collaboration with financial institutions to provide small to medium-size loans using the business's M-PESA track record as a liquidity gauge.

16.4.1 *Challenges affecting M-PESA adoption*

Based on some markets where M-PESA has failed in SSA, the challenges can be divided into two types: The first is understanding of the people's culture and meeting them at their needs — this understanding, or its lack thereof, dictates either success in the long run despite initial mistakes as in Tanzania or complete failure as is the case in South Africa. Paradoxically, South Africa is the home of Vodacom, but several failed starts caused the initiative to be scrapped in 2016. The main underlying reason is the simple fact that a large proportion of South Africans (75%) were banked whereas in Kenya majority were not (less than 30% had access to a formal savings account[16]). In South Africa, there was no desperate financial access need to be met.

The second issue lies with the regulatory environment or political will. For example, in Nigeria, mobile money lacks support despite the similarity between Kenya and Nigeria, both having bank-led regulatory environments. In its initial stages, mobile money needs to be initiated and driven by the telecommunication company. This was the game changer in Kenya, which is not the case in Nigeria. Telecommunication companies have been relegated to simple infrastructure providers whereas the mobile money element is driven by the financial bodies. If there is to be any progress with Nigeria, they need to critically re-look at its regulatory environment to make it conducive.

The other country is Ethiopia. The recent attempt by Safaricom in August 2019 to penetrate the 100-million-people market and launch M-PESA was nipped in the bud. The Ethiopian Central Bank cut short government talks with Safaricom stating that only locally owned non-financial institutions would be allowed to offer mobile money services. With Ethiopia's fast-growing mobile phone services market, there is increased interest among global telecommunication firms. However, these firms need to partner with the government-owned monopolistic mobile service provider Ethio Telecom, which makes penetration near impossible (Ngugi, 2020).

Around the world: In India, due to poor understanding of the product and government interference, M-PESA has been shut down, with Vodacom being required to surrender its operating license. In Albania (Eastern Europe), M-PESA failed to achieve the critical mass required to profitably sustain the platform. This also saw Vodafone bring the curtains down on M-PESA. Given the unique character of the targeted consumer as well as their needs, it is highly unlikely

[16]See Finaccess survey conducted in 2009 (FSD Kenya, 2011).

that there will be spread of M-PESA in western Europe or the Americas. However, there is a likely introduction in the Arab world, and it is a market to watch as there may be unprecedented benefits of the mobile money platform (de Soyres *et al.*, 2018).

16.5 Consumer and Data Protection

The use of M-PESA over the past 12 years has changed the way individuals interact with the financial system. This has in turn brought about the need for consumer protection and thus regulatory technology. Given the fact that more than 60% of the population in Kenya relies on M-PESA, regulators need to make sure that the system is reliable and not detrimental to the individual. The 2019 GSMA report on mobile network operations in sub-Sahara Africa brings to light the amount of "mobile big data" that accumulates over time. In using mobile networks, a huge amount of data about people's calling and messaging behavior and their geographic location is generated. When aggregated and anonymized, this data can provide valuable and actionable information for a variety of good use cases. It can also fall into the wrong hands and be misused. In this regard, there is a need for governmental regulatory agencies to play watchdog over the telecommunications companies to ensure the protection of data collected as a result of mobile technology use.

The majority of the world's mobile big data use cases are in the commercial as well as research and development of new products and services. In addition to this, there are some pilot projects that have demonstrated that certain information from mobile big data can be used in addressing environmental, social, and governance challenges. In sub-Saharan Africa an example of mobile big data use for social good was in Ghana between 2014 and 2016 where the data was used to track and tackle malaria.[17] Although the application of mobile big

[17]See GSMA report: Mobile impact on economic growth and social progress (2019). On page 18 of the report it gives a summary of how mobile big data in Ghana was used to track and map the spread of malaria, and to this end enabled the world health organization (WHO) together with the USAID to distribute insecticide treated mosquito nets to the affected areas. This information encompassing call data records which unlike the tedious use of surveys across

data for socially good causes is still at a very early stage in SSA, the GSMA feel that the potential impact is significant. This is due to the rapid adoption of mobile technologies already evidenced in the past and the infrastructure gap that causes a lack of enough relevant data to support efficient solutions and actionable insights (GSMA, 2019).

16.6 Evolution of RegTech

Mobile technology connects more people globally than any other technology, more so in sub-Saharan Africa where mobile networks cover approximately 90% of the population. This bushfire spread and coverage of mobile networks makes the mobile platform a preferred choice for creating, distributing, and consuming digital content and services (GSMA, 2017).[18] This in turn creates opportunities for mobile-based innovation which attracts talent and investment in the SSA region resulting in a tech start up ecosystem. As at July 2016, there were 314 active tech hubs across Africa, see Fig. 16.5. The majority of these are in South Africa, Kenya, and Nigeria (GSMA, 2017). These tech start-ups leverage on the scalability of mobile technology and are thus able to deliver broad economic and social benefits to a wide populace across the SSA region.

Whereas digital convergence is of benefit to consumers and the society alike, it continues to create regulatory challenges. Rapid innovation with reference to technology and business models as well as the need to capitalize on economies of scale and scope is blurring the boundaries between previously distinct markets and regulatory regimes. Governments in this regard need to pursue policies that incentivize infrastructure investments in promoting the development of digital economies. Therefore, regulatory policies as well as regulatory institutions need to adapt to changing market conditions so as not to stifle innovation, which would in turn harm competition, slow innovation, and deprive consumers of the benefits of

Ghana, provides insights on people's mobility and access to basic social services. This information is then continually used by the Ghanaian health service together with other partners to efficiently and effectively distribute equipment, personnel and other resources to the required areas.

[18]GSMA report on the mobile economy of sub-Saharan Africa, 2017.

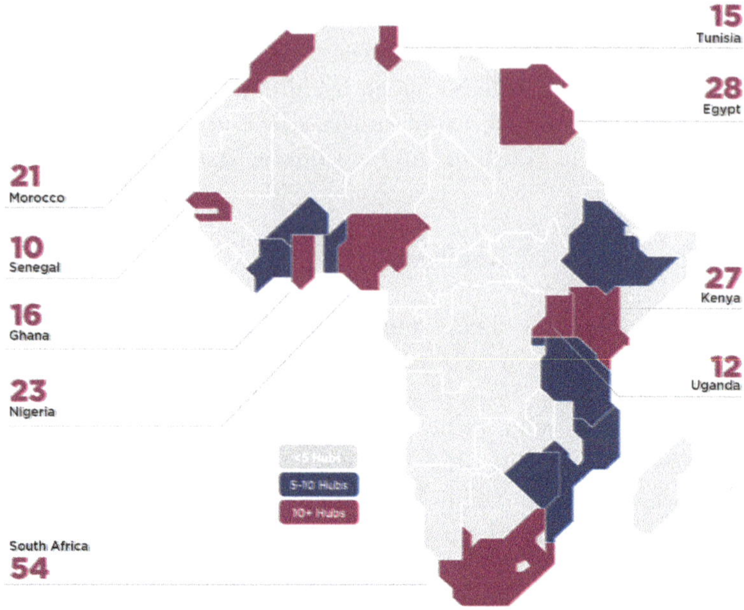

Fig. 16.5. Map of Tech hubs in Africa as at December 2017 (GSMA, 2017).

technological progress. Policymakers across the world and in SSA have started to recognize these challenges and are working to implement reform that will protect competition and consumers without stifling social and economic progress (GSMA, 2017). For this to happen, the following three key principle need to guide policymakers:

(a) Redesign of regulations and regulatory institutions around functionality as opposed to legacy technologies or industry sectors.
(b) Dynamism in regulation focusing on ex post implementation of rules as opposed to ex ante prescribed rules.
(c) More bottom-up as opposed to top-down regulation with re-evaluation of the goals to be accomplished.

With these in mind, governments and financial and technology regulatory authorities have set up "regulatory sandboxes".[19] For this

[19]The concept of a regulatory sandbox relates to a children's sandpit where they play with toys in the sand and using their imagination conceptualize and make different things and shapes and games in a controlled environment.

chapter, we are looking at regulatory sandboxes for FinTech start-ups which propose the use of technology to offer financial services. Since 2017, FinTechs in sandboxes have been allowed to test their products on consumers for a specific duration of time. The regulator in that time also has the space to define and test the rules that will guide the implementation of the innovations.

Regulatory sandboxes have been experimented with in high- and middle-income countries, where most of them did not have issues of financial inclusion. However, in emerging and developing economies, the question of financial inclusion is a prominent one. Therefore, as they begin to gain traction in developing countries their mandate has grown to include the promotion of financial inclusion. With mobile money in Kenya the regulators used a "test and learn" approach (Dias and Staschen, 2017) where after the product was launched regulators worked around the product and with Safaricom to develop a specific regulation which now clarifies the standards for mobile money providers in Kenya. Given that this may not be a sustainable way to approach the fast-growing number of FinTech solutions in Kenya, the Capital Markets Authority (CMA), as a financial markets' regulator, has come up with a FinTech regulatory sandbox to pilot the framework in Kenya.

16.6.1 *The Sandbox in Kenya*

Regulatory Sandboxes are not yet a widely spread and used phenomenon. They, however, provide a space especially in the financial inclusion area for positive change through innovation (Jenik and Lauer, 2017). Kenya belongs to the few countries[20] that have piloted regulatory sandboxes for their financial markets. In March 2019, the CMA got approval from its board for its Regulatory Sandbox Policy Guidelines Note,[21] which mandated it to begin receiving applications

---

[20]See (Jenik and Lauer, 2017) for a list of countries that have established or are in the process of establishing regulatory sandboxes.

[21]The Regulatory Sandbox Policy Guideline Note (PGN) is a guide to be used in the operational environment of a regulatory sandbox program and will in time inform future refinement of a Regulatory Sandbox Framework. See: https://www.cma.or.ke/index.php?option=com_phocadownload&view=category&id$=$54&Itemid$=$202.

from FinTech firms to its newly established sandbox. The firms are to conduct live tests of their innovative products, services, and solutions. The Sandbox is also intended to facilitate the regulator's understanding of emerging technologies, support the adoption of an evidence-based approach to regulation, as well as facilitate the deepening and broadening of the capital markets in Kenya (CMA, 2019).

The test period was set at 12 months and, upon successful completion and exit, the participants would have three options for consideration: the first if an existing license to operate in Kenya is applicable, it would then be granted; second, permission to operate in Kenya subject to compliance with set standards for a business whose operations fall outside of existing regulatory provisions; and third, denial of permission to operate in Kenya. Given that Sandboxes are not incubators, the firms that were eligible to apply for consideration needed to be incorporated in Kenya or, if foreign, already licensed by an equivalent capital markets regulator in their domicile country.

In July 2019, the CMA admitted three firms into the Regulatory Sandbox. The firms accepted were: (i) Innova Limited, approved to test its cloud-based data analytics platform designed for use by investors, fund managers, custodian banks, actuaries, pension administrators, and regulators; (ii) Pezesha Africa Limited, which will test an internet-based crowdfunding platform through which investors can provide loan facilities structured as loan notes (debentures) for SMEs; (iii) the third firm has chosen to remain anonymous, an option provided by the CMA restricting information to its test subjects. The Kenyan financial markets await the outcome expectantly after completion of the test period, which is around mid-2020. The sandbox concept, which allows live testing of technological applications to financial services under a less arduous regulatory regime, will hopefully be an encouraging experience for further applicants.

16.6.2 *RegTech solutions: Input approach vs pull approach*

Regulatory technology solutions are intended to aid regulators manage compliance and risk in digital finance using technology. According to (Dias and Staschen, 2018) RegTech together with

SupTech[22] are fundamental to improving the quality of data that supervisory and regulatory agencies need and use to make risk assessments as well as crucial supervisory, regulatory, and policy decisions. In addition, the use of RegTech would improve the quality of data that financial service providers report without imposing additional reporting burdens on the service providers. Over time, the use of data collection using technology could also reduce regulator's reporting costs. In a nutshell, there would be a migration from the use of manual reporting procedures by financial services providers and receipt of these manually filled-out templates by the regulator. There are two main approaches to automated reporting regarding data from financial services providers: the "input approach" and the "pull approach". Whereas each approach has its advantages as well as its drawbacks, both approaches are certainly superior to the use of manual reporting that has ,for a long time, been the norm. The use of either approach is highly dependent on country context.

In majority of the developed economies, there is a tendency toward the "input approach". The main reason for this is that financial inclusion is not a need as majority of their population is banked, i.e. there is no need for multiple players in financial services provision. Case in point is Austria, where the commercial banks together with Austria's central bank — Oesterreichische Nationalbank (OeNB) — came up with an initiative that would enable them to harmonize and integrate data. They formed a joint venture called AuRep (Austrian Reporting Services GmbH) which runs a common regulatory reporting platform which serves a central interface between the supervised banks and the OeNB.[23] In this system, granular data are gathered at the banks' systems and sent automatically to AuRep, forming a "basic cube". The data are then enhanced in the AuRep system into a series of datasets to be accessed by the OeNB as needed, such as "loan cube" or "deposit cube". The reduction in reporting costs against the initial investment required to build AuRep is yet to be seen, but it is expected in the long term. The system is currently

[22]Supervisory technology.

[23]See: https://www.reg.tech/en/our-solutions/banks-other-financial-institutions/regulatory-reporting-for-austrian-banks/.

running in its medium term and needs some time before we can see the financial savings. It has however reduced the time cost that was previously incurred through the manual supervisory authorities reporting.

Under the "pull approach", raw data are sourced by the regulator or supervisor directly from the financial service provider's (FSP) IT system. This is the case in markets with under-developed banking systems and where financial inclusion is still a goal to be attained. It is therefore not surprising to have majority of emerging market and developing economies using this approach (Dias and Staschen, 2017). With the trend and need for the diversification of financial services providers, non-bank financial service providers[24] are now included in the mandate of supervisory authorities. The challenge presented here is the ability of the supervisor to collect and analyze accurate, relevant, and timely information given the large and diverse set of FSPs with distinct risk profiles.

The National Bank of Rwanda (BNR) provides a case in point. The BNR partnered with a business intelligence and data analytics company, Sunoida,[25] to develop an electronic data warehouse (EDW) system. This system covers eight banks, three microfinance institutions, two money transfer operators, and one MNO. The EDW allows the BNR access to "pull" data from the FSPs' IT systems as opposed to having a compliance officer doing manual reporting. This eliminates errors and inconsistencies. The main concern with the pull approach is the possible legal implications of pulling data rather than receiving it. Second, the supervisor here is also responsible for transforming the raw data into standard formats and aggregating it to relevant indicators. Finally, privacy concerns arise where the regulator has access to all the data in the FSPs' IT system, some of which is sensitive and is not relevant for their supervisory mandate (Kamali and Randall, 2017). For now, we still have to wait and see how it all pans out. The choice of one approach over the other cannot at this point be made and probably will not be possible as they are both suited for their distinct markets.

[24]These include mobile network operators (MNOs), FinTech companies, financial cooperatives and microfinance institutions.

[25]See http://sunoida.com/ for information about the company.

16.7 Conclusions

The poor infrastructure in sub-Saharan Africa makes the exponential spread of mobile money an evolution that will change the face of financial inclusion in the region. Having experienced the transformative impact of M-PESA in Kenya regarding financial services, the space for further mobile applications has widened. The evidence from the Kenyan market shows the potential that is still available to raise the social and economic environmental standards of the population. The success factor is that these apps are developed from a needs point of view, i.e. with the customer in mind, which means that the transformative potential is quite high.

This in turn means that regulators and supervisory institutions have an important role to play in encouraging digital economic development. It calls, on the one hand, for an increased risk appetite on the part of the regulatory authority to allow FinTech start-ups to roll out and market test their innovative products and services. On the other hand, it requires the regulator to maintain a checks and balances system of rules that govern the function of the product or service as opposed to regulating the FinTech firm. Therefore, the regulatory sandbox approach is a welcome trial space to encourage the testing of innovative products by FinTech firms in a relatively relaxed environment. To weigh the benefits of regulatory sandboxes, we have to wait and see if they are a hit or miss in encouraging innovation, protecting competition, and providing the best products and services for consumers.

16.7.1 *Recommendations for further research*

To further develop this chapter, I propose continued research to determine the actual impact that M-PESA has had on Kenya's economy using a trend analysis of M-PESA contribution to GDP. Following Suri and Jack (2016) who have analyzed longitudinally the impact on household financial well-being, a firm-level longitudinal study should be considered to determine its contribution to business development in Kenya. Though M-PESA is a Kenyan phenomenon, there is no doubt that with the right strategic implementation it could prove successful in other regions. A comparative study on the progress Tanzania has made regarding the use of M-PESA should also be considered.

References

Aker, J. C. and Mbiti, I. M. (2010). Mobile phones and economic development in africa. *Journal of Economic Perspectives*, **24**(3): 207–232. https://doi.org/10.1257/jep.24.3.207.

Beck, T. (2015). *How mobile money is driving economic growth.* World Economic Forum. https://www.weforum.org/agenda/2015/09/how-mobile-money-is-driving-economic-growth/.

CBA (2017). *CBA and Safaricom celebrate ground breaking milestones as they mark the 5th Anniversary of M-Shwari.* CBA Group. https://cbagroup.com/newsroom/cba-and-safaricom-celebrate-ground-breaking-milestones-as-they-mark-the-5th-anniversary-of-m-shwari/.

CMA (2019). *Press Release — CMA Regulatory Sandbox.* Capital Markets Authority. https://www.cma.or.ke/index.php?option$=$com_content&view$=$article&id$=$561:press-release-cma-regulatory-sandbox&catid$=$10&Itemid$=$203.

de Soyres, F., Jelil, M. A., Cerruti, C., and Kiwara, L. (2018). *What Kenya's mobile money success could mean for the Arab world.* World Bank. https://www.worldbank.org/en/news/feature/2018/10/03/what-kenya-s-mobile-money-success-could-mean-for-the-arab-world.

Dias, D. and Staschen, S. (2017). Data collection by supervisors of digital financial services. *CGAP Working Papers*, 60.

Dias, D. and Staschen, S. (2018). RegTech and digital finance supervision: A leap into the future. *CGAP.* https://www.cgap.org/blog/regtech-and-digital-finance-supervision-leap-future.

FSD Kenya (2011). *Financial Inclusion in Kenya Survey results and analysis from FinAccess 2009.* FSD Kenya and the Central Bank of Kenya.

FSD Kenya (2013). *FinAccess National Survey 2013 Profiling developments in financial access and usage in Kenya* (p. 52). FSD Kenya and the Central Bank of Kenya. https://s3-eu-central-1.amazonaws.com/fsd-circle/wp-content/uploads/2015/08/30095841/13-10-31_FinAccess_2013_Report.pdf.

FSD Kenya (2016). *2016 FinAccess Household Survey* (No. 4; p. 36). FSD Kenya. https://s3-eu-central-1.amazonaws.com/fsd-circle/wp-content/uploads/2016/02/30093031/The-2016-FinAccess-household-survey-report4.pdf.

Grosskurth, J. (2010). *Futures of Technology in Africa: Vol. STT Publications.* Deltahage. https://stt.nl/stt/wp-content/uploads/2013/01/stt-toekomstverkenning-futures-of-technology-in-africa-2010.pdf.

GSMA (2017). *The Mobile Economy: Sub-Saharan Africa 2017* (p. 52). GSM Association. https://www.gsma.com/subsaharanafrica/wp-content/uploads/2018/11/2017-02-27-9e927fd6896724e7b26f33f61db5b9d5-1.pdf.

GSMA (2019a). *The Mobile Economy Sub-Saharan Africa 2019* (p. 40). GSM Association. https://www.gsmaintelligence.com/research/?file=36b5ca079193fa82332d09063d3595b5&download.

GSMA (2019b). *Mobile Money Enabled Cash Aid Delivery: Essential Considerations for Humanitarian Practitioners* (p. 23). GSMA. https://www.gsma.com/mobilefordevelopment/wp-content/uploads/2019/04/Essential_Considerations_for_Using_Mobile_Money.pdf.

Hughes, N. and Lonie, S. (2007). M-PESA: Mobile money for the "Unbanked" Turning cellphones into 24-Hour tellers in kenya. *Innovations: Technology, Governance, Globalization*, **2**(1–2): 63–81. https://doi.org/10.1162/itgg.2007.2.1-2.63.

IFC (2010). *M-Money Channel Distribution Case — Tanzania Vodacom Tanzania M-PESA* (p. 18) [Case Study]. International Finance Corporation.

Itimu, K. (2017). My Safaricom App For Android Gets Revamp, Adds MPESA Services. *Techweez*. https://techweez.com/2017/03/23/mysafaricom-revamp-adds-mpesa-services/.

Jenik, I. and Lauer, K. (2017). Regulatory Sandboxes and Financial Inclusion, CGAP Working Paper, 22.

Kamali, W. and Randall, D. (2017). *Leveraging "suptech" for financial inclusion in Rwanda* [Private Sector Development Blog]. World Bank Blogs. http://blogs.worldbank.org/psd/leveraging-suptech-financial-inclusion-rwanda.

KPMG (2019). *True Value Assessment Report — Safaricom* (Sustainability Report No. 5; True Value Case Study — Safaricom Ltd., p. 5). KPMG. https://www.safaricom.co.ke/sustainabilityreport_2019/our-business/the-true-value-we-have-created/.

Morawczynski, O. (2011). *Examining the Adoption, Usage and Outcomes of Mobile Money Services: The Case of M-PESA in Kenya*, 265.

Myers, C. (2017). 3 Reasons fintech is failing. *Forbes Media*. https://www.forbes.com/sites/chrismyers/2017/02/07/3-reasons-why-fintech-is-failing/.

Ngugi, B., Pelowski, M., and Ogembo, J. G. (2010). M-pesa: A case study of the critical early adopters' role in the rapid adoption of mobile money banking in Kenya. *The Electronic Journal of Information Systems in Developing Countries*, **43**(1): 1–16. https://doi.org/10.1002/j.1681-4835.2010.tb00307.x.

Ngugi, Brian (2020). Ethiopia closes door on M-Pesa. Business Daily Africa. https://www.businessdailyafrica.com/corporate/companies/Ethiopia-closes-door-on-M-pesa/4003102-5512542-l8x3ju/index.html.

Safaricom (2019). *Safaricom Annual Report and Financial Statements* (Annual Report No. 11; p. 210). Safaricom. https://www.safaricom.co.ke/images/Downloads/Safaricom_Annual_Report_2019.pdf.

Suri, T. and Jack, W. (2016). The long-run poverty and gender impacts of mobile money. *Science*, **354**(6317): 1288–1292. https://doi.org/10.1126/science.aah5309.

Vodacom PLC (2019). *Vodacom Tanzania Public Limited Company Annual Report 2019* (Annual Report No. 3; p. 140). Vodacom. https://vodacom.co.tz/en/annual_results/.

White, D. (2012). The social and economic impact of MPESA on the lives of women in the fishing industry on lake Victoria. *Independent Study Papers*, **2146**: 45.

Wilson, T. (2019). Safaricom bets future on mobile payments Mpesa. *The Financial Times*. https://www.ft.com/content/5eba36aa-6d7b-11e9-80c7-60ee53e6681d.

World Remit (2020). *Vodacom Tanzania and WorldRemit launch mobile money transfers to M-Pesa accounts in Tanzania*. WorldRemit. https://www.worldremit.com/en/news/vodacom-m-pesa-worldremit.

https://doi.org/10.1142/9781786349507_0017

Chapter 17

Fintech Development, Digital Infrastructure and Institutions in the MENA Zone

Youssra Ben Romdhane Loukil[*,‡], **Souhaila Kammoun**[†,§], **and Sahar Loukil**[*,¶]

[*]*University of Sfax, Tunisia*
[†]*IHEC, CODECI, University of Sfax, Tunisia*
[‡]*youssrabenromdhane776@hotmail.fr*
[§]*souhaila.kammoun@yahoo.fr*
[¶]*saharloukil@windowslive.com*

17.1 Introduction

In this connected global world, digital evolution is changing the structure of global competition, developing governments, and businesses and making a difference in people's lives (Rifkin, 2011 and Li *et al.*, 2015). Within this context, several bankers and traders have embarked on entrepreneurial adventures to rethink the model of finance through technological revolution. In a nutshell, new digital innovative technologies and financial innovation are reshaping the different areas of the financial services industry (Hazik and Hassnian, 2019). By deploying these technologies, financial innovations can lead to an increase in the productivity of services, which meets the expectations of consumers and therefore increases the country's investments (Triki and Faye, 2013). Among these technologies, Fintech is the most efficient that can be used by businesses and citizens.

Fintech combines two terms: finance and technology. According to Chiu *et al.* 2017; Prescott and Larose (2016), Tobias and Tommaso (2019); Yinqiao *et al.* (2017); Zavolokina *et al.* (2016), financial technology is a living, flexible, and dynamic body. This technology is defined as an innovative start-up that uses technology to project financial and banking services and economic solutions such as asset management and payment and remittances associated with computer technology (Guzy, 2016; Boot, 2017; Puschmann, 2017; Alt *et al.*, 2018; Kammoun *et al.*, 2019).

In recent years, financial innovation has gained substantial interest in academic research and practice. Several researchers have analyzed the role of Fintech in the development of countries, such as O'Connor *et al.* (2016), Nambisan and Majchrzak (2017), Hmann (2017), Autio *et al.* (2018), and Hazik and Hassnian (2019).

In this chapter, we do not intend to assess the relevance or the importance of the FinTech for the country and the financial industry, which is an indisputable fact. The study aims to identify the factors that influence Fintech growth in MENA countries, a problem that is underexplored in the literature, especially since the number of Fintech companies, in the MENA region, is increasing year-over-year generating remarkable profits. This new market can improve the economic performance of the countries in this zone. Despite the existence of obstacles to economic and financial development, the MENA zone has shown its weight in terms of digital revolution through technological innovations in general, and especially Fintech.

The overarching purpose of this chapter is to analyze the determinants of digital finance (Fintech) and the countries' economic development in the context of political uncertainty. The structure of the chapter is organized as follows. After the introductory section, we provide an overview of theoretical and empirical literature on the determinants of Fintech in MENA zone countries. Next, we present the dataset and methodology of the research. Finally, the study ends with the empirical findings, sets out the main conclusions, and provides some recommendations and practical implications.

17.2 Theoretical Framework

Fintech has attracted considerable interest in literature. Previous studies have focused more on the analysis of the impact of Fintechs on the economy (Foster *et al.*, 2017; Bahrini, 2019; Gupta *et al.*, 2019; Kammoun *et al.*, 2020; Loukil *et al.*, 2019; Ben Romdhane *et al.*, 2020) and in this chapter, the impact of factors related to economic and political stability on Fintechs is also analyzed.

Some empirical studies find that the adoption of financial technologies plays a crucial role in economic development through payment facilities, digital currencies, and improved customer relations (Ben Romdhane *et al.*, 2020); other studies point out that these technologies may have the potential to increase economic growth in emerging economies as well as in large economies. Within this context, Fintech appears as a platform for sustainable economic growth (Coyle, 2016; Watanabe *et al.*, 2018; Naveed *et al.*, 2018; Shin, 2019), and economic growth is strongly linked to financial inclusion (Kasekende, 2014; Guild, 2017; Chakraborty, 2018).

That being said, some empirical studies find that the use of technology services has negative effects on the economy over inflation. In this context, Kammoun *et al.* (2019) studied the impact of the Fintech on inflation in the MENA zone for 3 years (2011–2014–2017). These empirical results show that the approximate calculation of mobile money by debit card and digital payment has a positive effect on the rise in inflation. In the same vein, Suri (2017) and Alvarez and Lippi (2017) confirmed that credit cards caused inflation in the economic environment despite all these benefits. In contrast, Narayan and Sahminan (2018) argue that digitization plays an important role in reducing inflation, as it reduces costs and improves the quality of financial services. In contrast, the IMF (2018) noted that suspicion spreads into the phase of a technological revolution of innovation when the risks associated with money seem to be highest.

Despite ample empirical enquiry into the importance of Fintech from an economic perspective, few studies have examined the determinants of Fintech in a context of political, financial, and governmental uncertainty, a question that remains to be explored. To close this gap, this chapter investigates the role of economic and political conditions in fostering Fintech growth.

Within the scope and aim of this study, a synthesis of the main empirical results of some recent papers will serve as a backdrop to identify a range of factors used to show the benefits of Fintech in terms of a country's economic development. The estimated variables in the context of Fintech include freedom of investment, government efficiency, political uncertainty, inflation, and digital infrastructure.

But obviously, the results of empirical studies depend on the sampling (including the country observed, sample size, etc.), the period over which the study was observed, the type of data used, and the type of estimation model. In this empirical review, we take up each variable (each line in Table 17.1) and underline the results of empirical studies for each variable. The main variables and empirical findings are summarized in Table 17.1.

Table 17.1 provides an overview of how Fintechs has an impact on economic development and helps us to present the scope for our empirical research. Approaching the research question from another perspective, this review aims to provide insights into the factors that underlie and motivate the Fintech phenomenon, i.e. the factors that could advance Fintech growth in MENA region. The main reasons that motivate this empirical research are the following. First, the ultimate goal of our empirical study is to identify the main factors influencing and stimulating Fintech. Second, the MENA region is an area facing social movement and macroeconomic and political instability, and it would be noteworthy to see if instable macroeconomic and political conditions might foster financial innovation. In contrast, many people in the MENA region do not have access to financial services[1] such as credit, payments, insurance and pensions and thus suffer from lack of financial inclusion. And lastly, Fintech is nowadays an emerging field of innovation and entrepreneurship in the MENA[2] region, where the number of

[1]Less than 86% of adults in the region do not have a bank account, Democracy Index (2016), "Revenge of the 'deplorables'".

[2]According to the study by, Democracy Index (2016), Revenge of the "deplorables", most of the region's Fintech activity is concentrated in the United Arab Emirates, Lebanon, Jordan and Egypt, four countries that together host 73% of Fintech startups in the MENA region. The UAE is home to the largest sector of Fintech, with 29% of MENA's technological activities focusing on finance. Policymakers in the MENA region seem to be interested in financial technology, such as the implementation of the Financial Technology Accelerator at the Dubai International Financial Center (DIFC), which creates a more conducive environment for the development of technology solutions that encompass the financial services of the region, MEASA region (Middle East, Africa and South). In Egypt, the Central Bank has worked with other government institutions to facilitate mobile payments, which strengthens financial inclusion.

Table 17.1. A synthesis of recent empirical findings on the impact of Fintechs on economic development.

Variable	Empirical findings	Authors
Freedom of investment	Fintech supports private investment by leveraging existing mobile platforms to reduce the friction of fund intermediation between savers and investors. Institutional indicators.	Nepote-Cit *et al.* (2018) Claessens *et al.* (2018) Pejkovska (2018) Gomber *et al.* (2018)
	Rapid development and expansion of technology, investment activities, and traditional banking activities are evolving as new Fintech companies enter the market and increase the competitiveness of the industry.	Nicoletti (2017) Deloitte (2017) Rivzi *et al.* (2018)
	Fintech technology companies make investment and banking activities more transparent, accessible, and personalized.	Vasiljeva and Lukanovail (2016) Dorfleitner *et al.* (2017) Thompson (2017)
Government effectiveness	Corporations have suffered huge losses as a result of mismanagement and the existence of the constraints of seeking government assistance. These companies know that Fintech is very important to prevent bankruptcy and the country's economy.	Mitchell and McIntyre (2012) Pajarskas and Jociene (2014) Haan *et al.* (2015)
	Digital finance and financial inclusion offer several benefits to governments through reducing the cost of overall spending.	Frame *et al.* (2014) Davies *et al.* (2016)
	Fintech reduces poverty levels in developing and emerging economies.	Manyika *et al.* (2016) Gomber *et al.* (2017)

(*Continued*)

Table 17.1. (*Continued*)

Variable	Empirical findings	Authors
Political uncertainty	Political instability, security, and social peace have reduced the development of the offshoring sector.	World Bank (2018)
Inflation	The Fintechs play a very important role at the micro and macro levels and have a potential impact on inflation through mobile money. Some researchers confirmed that an increase in monetary velocity could spread inflation and destabilize the currency. This means that financial innovations, such as financial technologies, markets, and economic systems, are more exposed to systemic risk.	Efma and Oracle (2010) Kamukama and Tumwine (2012) Simpasa and Gurara (2012) Adam and Walker (2015) Wilson *et al.* (2015) Walker *et al.* (2016) Suri (2017) Lazzolino *et al.* (2017) Aron *et al.* (2015) Aron *et al.* (2017) Chui (2017) Narayan *et al.* (2018) Kammoun *et al.* (2020) Loukil *et al.* (2019) Ben Romdhane *et al.* (2020)
Digital infrastructure	Financial technologies are driving investment growth in emerging countries by improving the efficiency of capital markets infrastructure, including regulation and compensation, compared to other regions of the world. But, the new digital regulatory framework is not yet in place (digital code) to replace the current framework (telecommunications code), while the relocation incentive framework is implemented slowly in practice.	Regan (2017) Deloitte (2019)

Table 17.1. (*Continued*)

Variable	Empirical findings	Authors
	Concerns about Big Data, robots, and artificial intelligence are even more critical in the areas of Fintech finance and global finance, as they are systemic for both risks and benefits. Banks could also participate in a platform to automate payment tracking and optimize liquidity and risk management. Regulators will need to be convinced that the underlying technologies would be robust enough to reduce operational risk.	Adrian *et al.* (2019)

Fintech startups in the region doubled between 2013 and 2015, from 46 to 105. We discuss, in what follows, what are the determinant factors of Fintech as a driver of economic and social welfare (Thakor, 2019) in MENA region.

17.3 Data Description and Study Methodology

17.3.1 *Scope and aim of the study*

The underlying objectives of the study are to investigate the determinants factors of Fintech and to explain what could be done in order to move the sector forward for the development of the MENA region as well as to present a projection to decision-makers and to contribute to the literature by providing a new perspective to academicians and researchers. In this regard, we believe in that political and economic conditions, digital infrastructure, and institutions will contribute to fostering the Fintech industry in MENA region.

17.3.2 *Data and methodology*

We gather data from the World Bank's governance indicators to assess the quality of the Arab institutional framework government and data from the 2017 Global Findex data for ten MENA zone countries during 2011–2014–2017. We choose emerging countries especially Arab ones since they are considered as a Greenfield opportunity for the expansion of financial technologies. Our analysis focuses on key factors as digital infrastructure as the access to a banking account through a mobile phone and government-level indicators as government effectiveness, voice and accountability, corruption, and social and political stability. To approximate Fintech, we measure the amount of digital payment. In the regression, we attempt to control for other factors like investment freedom and inflation. The study uses the panel generalized least squares (GLS) technique and the multiple regression models for estimating the main determinants of Fintech, as follows:

$$\begin{aligned} FINTECH_{i,t} = {} & \beta_0 + \beta_1 DigitalInf_{i,t} + \beta_2 InstitutionnalIndicators_{i,t} \\ & + \beta_3 FreedomInv_{i,t} + \beta_4 Inflation_{i,t} + \varepsilon_{i,t} \end{aligned}$$

Where:

β_0 : is the intercept
β_1 : represents the coefficients of Digital Infrastructure
β_2 : represents the coefficients of Institutional indicators
β_3 : represents the coefficients of Investment Freedom
β_4 : represents the coefficients of Inflation
ε : represents error term

Table 17.2 reports the variables indications and measurements used in this research.

17.3.3 *Study findings and discussion*

17.3.3.1 *Impact of investment freedom on Fintech*

Regression results, overall, suggest that the investment freedom does positively and significantly at the 5% level affect Fintech. This result is in line with previous studies by Nepote-Cit *et al.* (2018), Mnuchin and Phillips (2018), Gomber *et al.* (2018), Walker (2016),

Table 17.2. Presentation of variables.

Variables vectors	Variables	Indication	Measurement
Digital Infrastructure	**Bank account access through mobile phone**	CHECK ACCOUNT	The percentage of respondents who report using a mobile phone or the internet to check their balance for a financial institution account in the past 12 months.
Institutional indicators	**Government effectiveness**	GOV. EFFECTIVNESS	Government Effectiveness captures perceptions of the quality of public services, the quality of the civil service, and the degree of its independence from political pressures, the quality of policy formulation and implementation, and the credibility of the government's commitment to such policies. Estimate gives the country's score on the aggregate indicator, in units of a standard normal distribution, i.e. ranging from approximately 2.5–2.5.
	Voice and accountability	VOICE	Voice and Accountability captures perceptions of the extent to which a country's citizens are able to participate in selecting their government, as well as freedom of expression, freedom of association, and a free media. Estimate gives the country's score on the aggregate indicator, in units of a standard normal distribution, i.e. ranging from approximately 2.5–2.5.
	Revolution	SOCIAL MOVEMENT	A dummy variable that captures the existence of a social revolution in a country.

(*Continued*)

Table 17.2. (*Continued*)

Variables vectors	Variables	Indication	Measurement
	Corruption	CORRUPTION	Control of Corruption captures perceptions of the extent to which public power is exercised for private gain, including both petty and grand forms of corruption, as well as "capture" of the state by elites and private interests. Estimate gives the country's score on the aggregate indicator, in units of a standard normal distribution, i.e. ranging from approximately 2.5–2.5.
	Political stability	POLITICAL STABILITY	Political Stability and Absence of Violence/Terrorism measures perceptions of the likelihood of political instability and/or politically motivated violence, including terrorism. Estimate gives the country's score on the aggregate indicator, in units of a standard normal distribution, i.e. ranging from approximately 2.5–2.5.
Control variables	**The freedom of invest-ment**	INVESTMENT FREEDOM	The business freedom component measures the extent to which the regulatory and infrastructure environments constrain the efficient operation of businesses. The quantitative score is derived from an array of factors that affect the ease of starting, operating, closing a business.
	Inflation	INFLATION	The percentage of annual inflation.

Nakaso (2016), and Diemers (2015). It implies that the development of Fintech depends on the degree of freedom to start a business, especially "start-ups" in the field of digitization. By the same logic, we find that digital infrastructure, approximated through mobile phone access to check financial institution account and balance in promoting the use of Fintech, promotes significantly Fintech at the 1% level. These results are expected and are consistent with the need for a favorable and sustainable environment for a county's digital development. So, to digitize their economies to be more competitive and make organizations more responsive and predictive of citizen needs transformation, MENA zone countries are engaging in digital transformation, BRI (2012) and CBSB (2017).[3]

17.3.3.2 *Impact of inflation on Fintech*

Our empirical results show that there is a positive relationship between Fintech and inflation. This supposes that they evolve in the same direction. To our knowledge, our study is the first to analyze the potential impact of inflation on Fintech through the increase of the monetary velocity.[4] According to the literature review, mobile money can affect inflation via saving and consumption. When mobile money increases the amount of cash and assets in the banking system, the money multiplier would increase. To achieve price stability, a central can act through its monetary policy, particularly in relation to the control of money supply and the setting of interest rates.[5] All previous studies were interested in the first sense of causality and

---

[3]See Fig. 17.1. Digital contribution to Middle East economy.

[4]The potential inflationary effects of mobile money have generally been framed by the Quantity Theory of Money (QTM). This is described by the relationship MV = PY, where M is the supply of money, V is the velocity of the circulation of money (the average number of transactions that a unit of money performs), P is the price level and Y is the volume of Saharan Transactions in an economy. (GSM Association report: The impact of mobile money on monetary and financial stability in Sub-Saharan Africa, 2019).

[5]This can be done via several methods, including: (i) Increasing/decreasing the amount of currency in circulation (e.g. printing money or creating electronic money); (ii) Varying the liquidity available for commercial banks to meet their reserve requirements; (iii) Changing short-term interest rates; and (iv) Conducting open market operations (i.e. buying and selling government securities).

Table 17.3. Panel regression analyze results (GLS regression).

Fintech	Coef.	Std. err.	Z	$P > \|z\|$	[95%] Conf.	Interval
Investment freedom	0.2147594**	0.0988776	2.17	0.03	0.0209629	0.4085558
Check account	0.8988075***	0.1497378	6	0	0.6053268	1.192288
Social movement	−10.52889**	4.781817	−2.2	0.028	−19.90108	−1.156704
Gov. effectiveness	20.06906***	7.170325	2.8	0.005	6.015477	34.12263
Voice	−7.835026*	3.057047	−2.56	0.01	−13.82673	−1.843324
Inflation	0.1625017	0.1087355	1.49	0.135	−0.050616	0.3756194
Political stability	2.146385	3.821968	0.56	0.574	−5.344535	9.637304
Corruption	−10.44971*	5.670797	−1.84	0.065	−21.56427	0.6648441
_cons	−22.35098*	12.54604	−1.78	0.075	−46.94076	2.238798
R^2	0.8053					
Wald chi^2 (P-value)	86.87(0.000)					

Note: $^{*}p < 0.1$, $^{**}p < 0.05$, $^{***}p < 0.01$.

support the Fintech's increasing effect on inflation (Walker, 2016; Narayan *et al.*, 2018; Chui, 2017; Kammoun, 2019; Loukil *et al.*, 2019 and Ben Romdhane *et al.*, 2020). The present research proves the second sense of causality. In fact, in a context of high inflation caused by velocity of circulation and volume transactions, the use of financial technologies flourishes and tends to increase. Indeed, in a context of high inflation due to the speed of trade and the volume of transactions, the use of financial technologies is booming and tending to increase.

The added value of our study combines the confirmation of previous studies and the participation in the reduction of the gap in the empirical literature by looking at the bidirectional effect between FinTech and inflation (see Table 17.3).

17.3.3.3 *Impact of institutional indicators on Fintech*

We next turn to institutional measures approximated by government-level indicators of corruption, government effectiveness, political stability, social movements, and voice and accountability. Empirical results show that in the context of social movement commonly known

Table 17.4. Democracy Index 2016, MENA Zone countries.

	Overall score	Overall rang	Regime type
Tunisia	6.4	69	Flawed democracy
Lebanon	4.9	102	Hybrid regime
Morocco	4.8	105	Hybrid regime
Palestine	4.5	110	Hybrid regime
Iraq	4.1	114	Hybrid regime
Jordan	4	117	Authoritarian
Kuwait	3.9	121	Authoritarian
Egypt	3.3	133	Authoritarian
Qatar	3.2	135	Authoritarian
Oman	3	141	Authoritarian
Bahrain	2.8	146	Authoritarian
Sudan	2.4	151	Authoritarian
Iran	2.3	154	Authoritarian
Libya	2.3	155	Authoritarian
Yemen	2.	156	Authoritarian
Saudi Arabia	1.9	159	Authoritarian
Syria	1.4	166	Authoritarian
United Arab Emirates	2.8	147	Authoritarian

Source: The Economist Intelligence Unit's Democracy Index 2016, Revenge of the "deplorables".

as social revolution in MENA zone countries during 2011–2014 and 2017 and resulting disruptions in the freedom of expression, the digital transformation has been restrained. We find that the two proxies for social unrest, VOICE and SOCIAL MOVEMENT, have, respectively, negative and significant impact at 10% and 5% on the development of Fintech. According to the democracy index 2016, except Tunisia, which ranks 69, the other countries rank higher than 102 since they have a Hybrid or Authoritarian regime. These ranks reflect social unrest resulting from the lack of democracy (see Table 17.4).

At first, this conclusion may seem unusual, but it could be easily apprehended since we deal with countries facing a big social movement resulting in a path of democratic transition for the first time in their histories. So, the freedom wave did not help when digital development and Fintech spread in terms of suitable context for new technologies adoption. As a moderating factor, we find that Fintech is expanded unless a government improves public services quality and is independent from political pressures through sound policy formulation and implementation. So, government effectiveness is crucial to lead to digitally enhanced lives for citizens. In this sense, authorities are requested to make serious efforts to promote innovation and push for the adoption of Fintech by the public sector to a higher level through the implementation of adequate governance structure. In fact, according to the McKinsey Middle East Digitization Index,[6] there is only 6% of the Middle East's population that lives under a digitized smart government. Figures 17.1 and 17.2 describe the state of digital development in MENA zone countries. Figure 17.1 shows that compared with the benchmarks share of digital contribution to GDP %, the MENA zone countries' contribution is weak, with only 1% and one unicorn. But, Fig. 17.2 shows that venture capital funding has room for improvement in the region, with 120 million USD nominal GDP compared to 2300 million USD in the United States and 640 million USD in the Asia Pacific.

Moreover, and as expected, we find that corruption has a negative and significant impact on Fintech. This result confirms the general rule of the need of healthy environment for the expansion of digital economy. In fact, in the MENA zone countries, suffering from the

Fig. 17.1. Digital contribution to Middle East economy.

[6]The McKinsey Middle East Digitization Index is the first effort to assess the level and impact of digitization in nine countries in the Middle East: Bahrain, Egypt, Jordan, Kuwait, Lebanon, Oman, Qatar, Saudi Arabia, Saudi Arabia and the United Arab Emirates United.

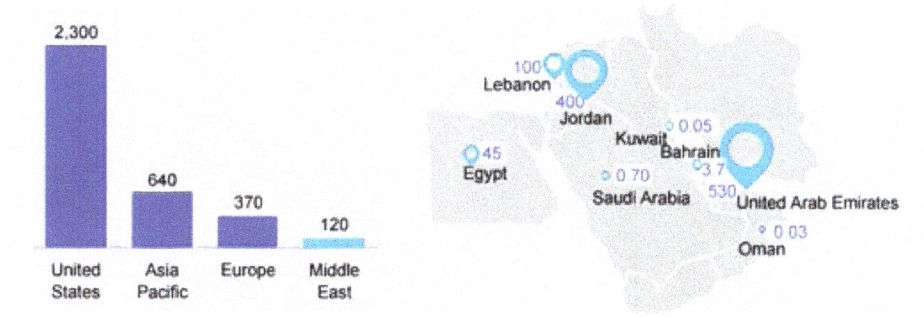

Fig. 17.2. Venture capital funding in digital, per million nominal GDP, USD. *Source*: Digital McKinsey (2016), Digital Middle East: Transforming the region into a leading digital economy.

lack of democracy and freedom of expression, corruption is more widespread (see Fig. 17.3).

According to The Economist Intelligence Unit's Democracy Index, for 2016 was, on the whole, another year of political stagnation in the Middle East and North Africa (MENA), with few countries making strides to foster democratic practices, and several sliding towards greater authoritarianism. Against such a context, Delia Ferreira Rubio[8] (2018) postulates that "*Corruption is much more likely to flourish where democratic foundations are weak and, as we have seen in many countries, where undemocratic and populist politicians can use it to their advantage*". The ranking of MENA zone countries under the corruptions index 2018,[9] which ranks 180 countries depending on their perceived levels of public sector corruption giving each a score from zero (highly corrupt) to 100 (very clean), shows that UAE and Qatar are less corrupted than the other

[7]https://www.transparency.org/cpi2018.

[8]Chair Transparency International.

[9]Since its inception in 1995, the Corruption Perceptions Index, Transparency International's flagship research product, has become the leading global indicator of public sector corruption. The index offers an annual snapshot of the relative degree of corruption by ranking countries and territories from all over the globe. In 2012, Transparency International revised the methodology used to construct the index to allow for comparison of scores from one year to the next. The 2018 CPI draws on 13 surveys and expert assessments to measure public sector corruption in 180 countries and territories, giving each a score from zero (highly corrupt) to 100 (very clean).

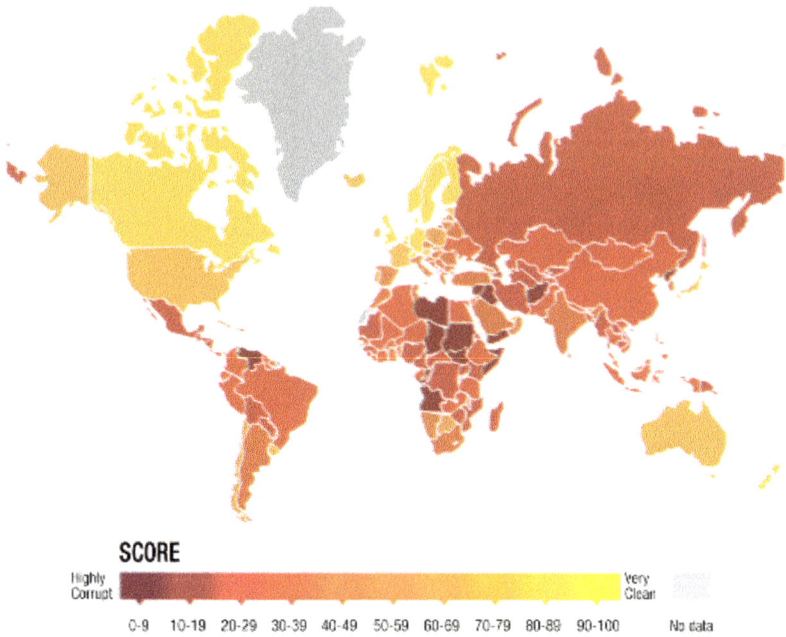

Fig. 17.3. Corruption index 2018.[7]
Source: Transparency International. Corruption Perceptions Index 2018: Statistically significant changes.

MENA zone countries while Libya, Yemen, and Syria rank at last (see Table 17.5).

These institutional indicators, such as the social movements and corruption, could explain the low digital technology adoption. In fact, a recent survey showed that among SMEs in MENA zone countries, just 18% in UAE, 15% in Saudi Arabia, and 7% in Egypt have an online presence. On the other hand, according to this survey, even more of customer journeys, channels, and internal processes and activities are getting digitized. Compared to 2005, cross-border flows was 150 times larger in 2015, as can be seen in the Fig. 17.4.

According to the McKinsey index, which combines 24 indicators to measure consumer, business, government, and ICT supply and innovation across every country, despite the ambitious aspirations of the governments to go digital, MENA zone countries are far behind the countries of reference (Norway, Singapore, South Korea, Sweden, and the United Kingdom). As exceptions, in terms

Table 17.5. The ranking of MENA zone countries under the corruptions index 2018.

	Country	Region	2018	2017	2016	2015
23	United Arab Emirates	Middle east and north Africa	70	71	66	70
33	Qatar	Middle east and north Africa	62	63	61	71
34	Israel	Middle east and north Africa	61	62	64	61
53	Oman	Middle east and north Africa	52	44	45	45
58	Jordan	Middle east and north Africa	49	48	48	53
58	Saudi Arabia	Middle east and north Africa	49	49	46	52
73	Morocco	Middle east and north Africa	43	40	37	36
73	Tunisie	Middle east and north Africa	43	42	41	38
78	Kuwait	Middle east and north Africa	41	39	41	49
99	Bahrain	Middle east and north Africa	36	36	43	51
105	Algeria	Middle east and north Africa	35	33	34	36
105	Egypt	Middle east and north Africa	35	32	34	36
138	Iran	Middle east and north Africa	28	30	29	27
138	Lebanon	Middle east and north Africa	28	28	28	28
168	Iraq	Middle east and north Africa	18	18	17	16
170	Libya	Middle east and north Africa	17	17	14	16
176	Yemen	Middle east and north Africa	14	16	14	18
178	Syria	Middle east and north Africa	13	14	13	18

Source: Corruption perception 2018 report.

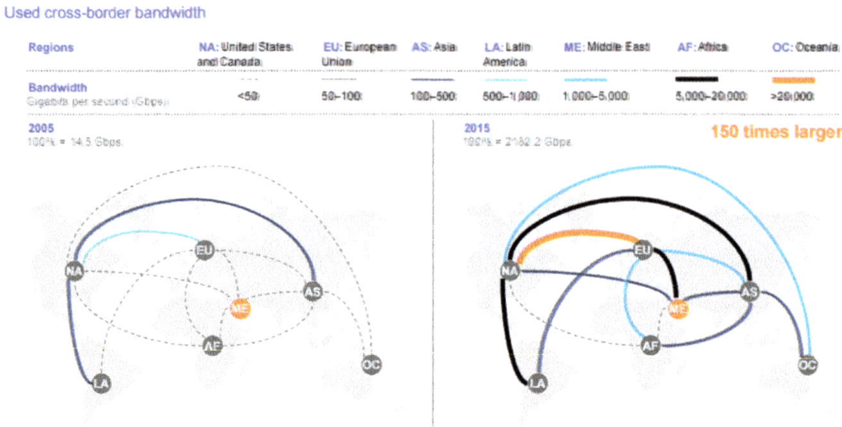

Fig. 17.4. Cross-border flows 2005–2015.
Source: Global Internet Geography, Tele-Geography, McKinsey Global Institute analysis.

of digital consumer adoption, Bahrain, Qatar, and the United Arab Emirates are among the top countries in the world, with more than 100 percent smartphone penetration and more than 70 percent social media adoption, even higher than in the United States, Benni *et al.* (2016).[10] In fact, UAE government leads the Middle East in digital adoption and is at the cutting edge of the digital world for several indicators.[11] But these indices hide a great deal of variation among countries.

We can conclude that successive waves of innovation in the MENA region and digital transformation provide massive opportunities to reshape current business structure and enhance customer's digital lives. But the Middle East is not moving forward enough to get closer to reach the full potential of digital technology (Table 17.6).

17.4 Conclusion

Digitization is not a passing tendency, it is a revolution on all levels, and especially in the world of financial transactions it is taking place

[10]https://www.mckinsey.com/featured-insights/middle-east-and-africa/digital-middle-east-transforming-the-region-into-a-leading-digital-economy.
[11]See The McKinsey Middle East Digitization report.

Table 17.6. Successive waves of innovation have shaped the worldwide digital economy.

Period	Indication	Assets/technologies	Business impact	People impact
1960s	Mainframes and databases	• Modem programming languages • Algorithmic advancement	• Business calculations, analyses • Database management systems	• Limited
End of the year's 1960s and early 1970s	Desktop and personal computing	• Desktops and PCs • Basic office software • Games and visual graphics	• Document processing • File storage	• Individuals with computers in larger firms • Gaming and document processing
End of the years 1970s and early 1980s	Business software	• Enterprise software	• Efficiency and automated business processes	• Creative destruction of jobs
End of the years 1980s and early 1990s	Internet and e-commerce	• Internet technologies • Personal computing	• B2B and B2C e-commerce • E-mail, chat	• Email, e-chatting, and VoIP[a] • E-commerce • Remote work via VPNs[b]
End of the years 1990s and early 2000s	Mobile broadband	• GPS • Wi-Fi, • 2G/3G • Laptops Mobile phones	• Remote work and 24/7 connectivity	• Connected anytime, anywhere

(Continued)

Table 17.6. *(Continued)*

Period	Indication	Assets/technologies	Business impact	People impact
End of the years 2000s and early 2010	Social media	• Social media • Smart phones and apps	• Big data • Predictive analytics • Internet of Things • Industry	• Data generation, content creation • Digital devices everywhere, consuming hours each day
Early 2010s and early 2020s	Big data and Internet of Things	• Smart devices and sensors • Real-time analytics	• Predictive algorithms, machine learning • Virtual reality glasses • Autonomous drones	• Data generation, content creation • Digital devices everywhere, consuming hours each day
Beyond 2020s	VR, 3 drones, robotics, artificial intelligence	• Predictive algorithms, machine learning • Virtual reality glasses • Autonomous drones	• Natural language processing • Advanced robotics • Drone surveillance	• Autonomous/assisted driving • First-person view (FPV) drone flights

Notes: [a]Voice over internet protocol.
[b]Virtual private networks.
Source: Author's recapitulative work from McKinsey Global Institute analysis.

right now and picking up speed every day. Fintech represents a significant change for the financial sector industry. Enthusiasm for the digital sector points to high growth potential in the near future, as consumers are clearly prepared and ready to quickly adopt new digital offerings. Several researches are available on the potential impact of Fintech on financial inclusion, economic development, and other institutional aggregates. But those studies focusing on the determinants of Fintech are limited. This gap needs to be closed through focused research on potential factors explaining Fintech's expansion. In terms of impact on economy, by 2020, the digital market is expected to add 95 billion USD every year to the Middle East's annual GDP. Our study is interested in MENA zone countries since they are considered as a Greenfield opportunity for the expansion of financial technologies. We use government-level data for ten 10 MENA zone countries during 2011–2014 and 2017. The multiple regression approach used digital infrastructure and institutional indicators and other control variables as explicative variables of Fintech development.

Empirical variables present a strong evidence for the crucial role of investment freedom and digital infrastructures for Fintech prosperity (Gomber *et al.*, 2018; Mnuchin and Phillips, 2018; Nepote-Cit *et al.*, 2018; Fortune, 2016; Nakaso, 2016; Walker, 2016; Diemers, 2015). So, digital transformation depends on a favorable context for "start-ups". Also, MENA zone countries are requested to more invest in digital infrastructure to digitize their economies, be more competitive, and make organizations more responsive to and predictive of citizen needs. We find that Fintech is expanded unless a government does improve public services quality and is independent from political pressures through sound policy formulation and implementation. On the other hand, we also find that digital transformation cannot expand in a context of social movement and resulting disruptions in freedom of expression. As expected, corruption also has a reducing effect on Fintech development. We should note that these empirical results still hide a great deal of variation among countries. Finally, we prove the second sense of causality between Fintech and inflation through the velocity of money explained by the increases in the amount of cash (saving and consumption) and assets in the banking system. In order to maintain price stability, via its monetary policy, the central bank can apply several measures and influence the money supply as an intermediate. Such politics would optimize the role of financial technologies in economies. Further studies should be implemented to present more details on Fintech's determinants in MENA zone countries and, more generally, emerging countries.

On the basis of this study, policymakers should improve their economies by developing their digital infrastructure, especially for businesses. However, the future of digitalization in the MENA region also requires addressing the various legal issues raised by new technologies in the market place, in order to protect customers and operators against risks and vulnerabilities. In this perspective, regulation could stimulate e-commerce, formalize payments, and ensure more digital payments.

References

Adam, C. S. and Walker, S. E. J. (2016). Mobile money and monetary policy in East African Countries. *Working paper*, 30 pages. University of Oxford.

Anjan V. Thakor (2019). Fintech and banking: What do we know? *Journal of Financial Intermediation*, **41**: 100833 https://doi.org/10.1016/j.jfi.2019.100833.

Alt, R., Martin, M., and Smits, T. (2018). FinTech and the transformation of the financial industry. *Electronic Markets*, **28**(3): 235–243.

Aron, J. and Sebudde, J. (2015). Inflation forecasting models for Uganda: Is mobile money relevant? *CSAE Working Paper Series*, Vol. 17, Centre for the Study of African Economies, University of Oxford.

Autio, E., Nambisan, S., Thomas, L. D. W., and Wright, M. (2018). Digital affordances, spatial affordances, and the genesis of entrepreneurial ecosystems. *Strategic Entrepreneurship Journal*, **12**(1): 72–95.

Aron, M., Rivadeneyra, F., and Sohal, S. (2017). Fintech: Is This Time Different? A framework for assessing risks and opportunities for Central Banks.*Bank of Canada Staff Discussion Paper*, 17–10, Bank of Canada.

Bahrini, R. and Qaffas, A. (2019). Impact of information and communication technology on economic growth: Evidence from developing countries. *Economies*, **7**(21). https://doi.org/10.3390/economies7010021.

Ben Romdhane, Y., Loukil, S., and Kammoun, S. (2020). Economic African development in the context of Fintech. Chapter 14 in *Employing Recent Technologies for Improved Digital Governance*, Ponnusamy, V., Rafique, Kh. and Zaman, N. (Eds.), pp. 273–289. IGI GLOBAL. doi: 10.4018/978-1-7998-1851-9.ch014.

Boot, A. W. A. (2017). The Future of Banking: From Scale & Scope Economies to Fintech. *European Economy — Banks, Regulation and The Real Sector*, **2**: 77–95.

Chiu, I. H. Y. (2017). The disruptive implications of fintech-policy. Themes for financial regulators. *Journal of Technology Law & Policy*, **21**(1). Available at SSRN: https://ssrn.com/abstract=2812667 or http://dx.doi.org/10.2139/ssrn.2812667.

Claessens, S., Frost, J., Turner, G., and Zhu, F. (2018). Les marchés du crédit Fintech à travers le monde: Taille, moteurs et enjeux de politique publique. *Quarterly Review*, Rapport trimestriel BRO.

Coyle, D. (2016). The political economy of national statistics. *Economics Discussion Paper Series* EDP-1603. Available at SSRN: https://ssrn.com/abstract=2850061.

Davies, S., Jackett, D., Kashyap, M., Nicolacakis, D., Qureshi, M., and Shipman, J. (2016). Customers in the spotlight: How FinTech is reshaping banking. *Global FinTech Survey*, PricewaterhouseCoopers.

Dorfleitner, G., Hornuf, L., Schmitt, M., and Weber, M. (2017). *FinTech in Germany*. Springer Nature.

Deloitte (2017). The connecting global fintech. Interim Hub Review, *Deloitte Report*.

Diemers, D., Lamaa, A., Salamat, J., and Steffens, T. (2015). Developing a fintech ecosystem in the GCC, *Strategy*, Available at http://www.strategyand.pwc.com/media/file/Developing-a-FinTech-ecosystem-in-the-GCC.pdf.

Dorfleitner, G., Hornuf. L., Schmitt, M., and Weber, M. (2017). *FinTech in Germany*. Springer Nature.

Efma and Oracle (2010). Are Banks ready for the Next Generation Customer? *Financial Services Software Limited*, 4–17. Available at: http://www.oracle.com/us/industries/financial-services/gen-y-survey-report-165297.

Foster, C., Graham, M., Mann, L., Waema, T., and Friederici, N. (2017). Digital control in value chains: Challenges of connectivity for east African firms. *Economic Geography*, **94**(1): 68–86.

Frame, W. S. and White. L. J. (2014). Technological change, financial innovation, and Diffusion in Banking. *NYU Working Paper*, 2451/33549.

Global Partnership for Financial Inclusion, (2011). The G20 principles for innovative financial inclusion: Bringing the principles to life. *GPFI report*.

Gomber, P., Kauffman, R., Parker, C., and Weber, B. (2018). On the fintech revolution: Interpreting the forces of innovation, disruption, and transformation in financial services. *Journal of Management Information Systems*, **35**(1): 220–265.

Gomber, P., Koch, J.-A., and Siering, M. (2017). Digital finance and FinTech: Current research and future research directions. *Journal of Business Economics*, **87**(5): 537–580.

Guild, J. (2017). Fintech and the future of finance. *Asian Journal of Public Affairs. Lee Kuan Yew School of Public Policy Research Paper*, 17–20. https://ssrn.com/abstract=3021684.

Gupta, R., Mejía, C., and Kajikawa, Y. (2019). Business, innovation and digital ecosystems landscape survey and knowledge cross sharing. *Technological Forecasting and Social Change*, **147**: 100–109.

Guzy, M. (2016). *FintechBook*. Wiley, Chichester, West Sussex.

Haan, J., Oosterloo, S., and Schoenmaker, D. (2015). *Financial markets and institutions: A European perspective*. Cambridge University: Third Edition Press, 978-1-107-02594-3.

Hazik, M. and Hassnian, A. (2019). *Blockchain, Fintech, and Islamic Finance: Building the Future in the New Islamic Digital Economy.* Paperback. De Gruyter Press.

Hmann, T. (2017). Fintech. Business & Information systems engineering. *The International Journal of wirtschaftsinformatik*, **59**(1): 69–76.

Kamukama, N. and Tumwine, S. (2012). Mobile money services: A liquidity threat to Uganda's commercial banks. *African Journal of Accounting, Economics, Finance and Banking*, **8**(8): 33–46

Kammoun, S., Loukil, S., and Ben Romdhane, Y. (2020). The impact of FinTech on economic performance and financial stability in MENA Zone. Chapter 13 in Naifar N. (Ed.), *Impact of Financial Technology (FinTech) on Islamic Finance and Financial Stability*, 253–277, IGI Global. doi:10.4018/978-1-7998-0039-2.ch013.

Kasekende, L. (2014). What role does financial inclusion play in the policy Agenda for inclusive growth in Sub-Saharan Africa? *Development*, **57**(3–4): 481–487. doi:10.1057/dev.2015.32.

Lazzolino, G. and Wasiken, N. (2017). The unbearable lightness of digital money. *Journal of Payments Strategy & Systems*, **9**(3): 229–241.

Loukil, S., Ben Romdhane, Y., Kammoun, S., and Ibenrissoul, A. (2019). Empirical determinants of fintech: Panel data analysis in the MENA Zone. *International Journal of Science and Engineering Invention*, **05**(05): 90–97. doi:10.23958/ijsei/vol05-i05/159.

Manyika, J., Lund, S., Singer, M., and White, O. (2016). *Digital Finance for All: Powering Inclusive Growth In Emerging Economies*. McKinsey Global Institute.

Mitchell, S. and Michael, M. (2012). Too big to fail? Size and risk in banking, *Academy of Banking Studies Journal*, **11**(2): 11–21.

Mnuchin, S. and Phillips, C. (2018). A financial system that creates economic opportunities Nonbank financials, Fintech, and Innovation, *Report to President Donald J. Trump Executive Order* 13772 on Core Principles for Regulating the United States Financial System.

Nambisan, S. and Majchrzak, A. (2017). Digital innovation management: Reinventing innovation management research in a digital world. *MIS Quarterly*, **41**(1): 223–238.

Narayan, P., Narayan, S., Rahman, R., and Setiawan, I . (2019). Bitcoin price growth and Indonesia's monetary system. *Emerging Markets Review*, **38**: 364–376.

Nepote-Cit, M., Ruberti, S., and Tran, V. (2018). Perspectives économiques régionales: Afrique subsaharienne. *International Monetary Fund*, HC800.A1 R445 ISBN: 978-1-48434-891-8.

Nicoletti, B. (2017). *The Future of Fintech: Integrating Finance and Technology in Financial Services*. Palgrave Studies in Financial Services Technology SBN 978-3-319-51415-4.

O'Connor, E., Allan, S., and Audretsch, B. (2016). Entrepreneurial ecosystems. *International Studies in Entrepreneurship book series*, ISEN, **38**.

Pajarskas, V. and Jociene, A. (2014). Subprime mortgage crisis in the united states in 2007–2008: Causes and consequences. *Ekonomika*, **94**(1).

Pejkovska, M. (2018). Potential negative effects of Fintech on the financial services sector examples from the European Union, India and the United States of America. *Thesis in Applied Sciences Bachelor of Business Administration*, 56. https://www.theseus.fi/bitstream/handle/10024/148416/Maja_Pejkovska_Theseus.pdf?sequence=1&isAllowed=y.

Prescott, N. and Larose, C. (2016). *FinTech Companies Face Big Privacy Challenges in 2016*. Available at: http://www.oracle.com/us/industries/financial-services/gen-y-survey-report-165297.

Puschmann, T. (2017). Business and information systems engineering. *The International Journal of wirtschaftsinformatik*, **59**(1): 69–76.

Regan, M. (2017). Capital markets, infrastructure investment and growth in the Asia Pacific Region. *International Journal of Financial Studies*, **5**(1): 1–28.

Rizvi, S. K. A, Naqviand, B., and Tanveer, F. (2018). Is Pakistan Ready to Embrace Fintech Innovation? *The Lahore Journal of Economics*, **23**(2): 151–182.

Rifkin, J. (2011). *The Third Industrial Revolution: How Lateral Power is Transforming Energy, the Economy, and the World*. New York, NY: Palgrave Macmillan, p. 304 ISBN 13-9780230115217.

Suri, T. (2017). Mobile money. *Annual Review of Economics*, **9**: 497–520. https://doi.org/10.1146/annurev-economics-063016-103638.

Thompson, S. B. (2017). Can financial technology innovate bene?t distribution in payments for ecosystem services and REDD? *Ecological Economics*, **139**(8): 150–157.

Tobias, A. and Tommaso, M. G. (2019). The rise of digital money. *International Monetary Fund*, Washington, D.C.

Triki, T. and Faye, I. (2013). Financial inclusion in Africa: An overview. African Development Bank, 148. ISBN: 978-9938-882-19-3.

Vasiljeva, T. and Lukanova, K. (2016). Commercial banks and fintech companies in the digital transformation: Challenges for the future. Journal of Business Management, (11): 25–33, Business Source Ultimate, EBSCOhost. Journal of Business Management, 11, ISSN 1691-5348.

Walker. (2016). Customers 2020: The future of B-to-B customer experience. Retrieved from https://www.walkerinfo.com/Portals/0/Documents/Knowledge,%20Center/Featured%20Reports/WALKER-Customers2020.pdf.

Watanabe, C., Moriya, K., Tou, Y., and Neittaanmäki, P. (2018a). Consequences of the digital economy: Transformation of the growth concept. *International Journal of Managing Information Technology*, **10**(2): 21–39. doi:10.5121/ijmit.2018.10202.

Wilson, M. N., Iravo, M., Tirimba, O. I., and Ombui, K. (2015). Effects of information technology on performance of logistics firms in Nairobi County. *International Journal of Scientific and Research Publications*, **5**(4).

World Bank (2018). *Global financial development report.* Washington D.C.

Yinqiao, L., Renée, S., and Laurens, S. (2017). The impact of FinTech start-ups on incumbent retail banks' share prices, *Financial Innovation*, Springer, Heidelberg, **3**(26): 1–16.

Zavolokina, L., Dolata, L., and Schwabe, G. (2016). The FinTech phenomenon: Antecedents of financial innovation perceived by the popular press. *Financial Innovation*, **2**(1), Springer, DOI 10.1186/s40854-016-0036-7.

https://doi.org/10.1142/9781786349507_0018

Chapter 18

Banks vs FinTech in the French Market

Firas Batnini[*,‡] **and Florian Bercaut**[†,§]

[*]ESSCA School of Management, Department of Finance, 55 Quai Alphonse le Gallo, 92513 Boulogne-Billancourt, France

[†]ESTIMEO, 28 rue du Chemin Vert 75011, Paris, France

[‡]firas.batnini@essca.fr

[§]florian.bercault@estimeo.com

18.1 Introduction

Fintech is growing around the world at an exponential rate, but in a multifaceted manner. Differences in national regulations or infrastructure can influence the growth of these innovative financial startups. In some developing countries, the massive investment in online trading companies called "Bigtech" has allowed rapid development of Fintechs. China is a good illustration of this. Large technology companies such as Alibaba and Tencent have concentrated their investments in financial services in recent years. In developed countries, confidence in the historic banking system is greater than in countries with weak banking. Despite a good level of infrastructure and internet usage in developed countries, payment security remains a priority, and investments in Fintech are very high. Finance is a highly regulated market and the banking market is well consolidated. Banking institutions, with their solid infrastructures and financial resources, are among the largest market capitalizations in Europe and the United States. The entry of new competitors has become very difficult without mergers and acquisitions or disruptive innovation. However, the 2008 financial crisis has weakened banks' grip on their customers. The latter having less and less confidence in the traditional banking system, especially the new "millennial" generation, which tends to use new payment methods such as mobile applications. The development of e-commerce continues to drive customers to adopt new online payment technologies, as shown by the payment solutions of Amazon or PayPal. To help them grow, some countries have set up "sandboxes", such as the United Kingdom, which allows Fintechs to test their services for a limited period of time with a specific number of customers, without necessarily complying with the financial regulations in force, to allow them some time to improve their services before reaching the full market.

Nowadays, the question that researchers most often ask is: "Fintech: is it a disruptive innovation?". There is no clear answer, as we are still at the beginning of the wave. However, the word disruptive can be precisely defined in order to be transposed to the Fintech industry. From the Latin etymology of the verb to break, the word disruption was popularized in the early 1990s by French advertiser Jean-Marie Dru. The word disruption can be compared to the word rupture. In his book "Disruption" published in 1997, Jean-Marie Dru defines disruption as "a dynamic methodology oriented towards creation", which seeks to break conventions and redesign the market via a new vision leading to new products or services. Dissimilar from incremental innovations, disruption is characterized by breakthrough innovations that open up new markets initially without direct competition. For an innovation to be disruptive, therefore, it must bring new technology and develop it with a new approach to the market and usages, in a way that large companies in the sector cannot adapt quickly to. In order to keep up with the disruptive wave, they must either restructure or go bankrupt. One example is the disruption of international phone calls. Telecom operators ruled this market for several years without agreeing to lower prices, until the day they saw the arrival of new competitors such as Skype or WhatsApp who used Voice over IP technology, and taking advantage of the arrival of 4G, who saw their market shares explode at the expense of the incumbents, who suffered a significant drop of their international call revenues (except in some countries where mobile operators prohibit their customers from using its applications). Fintech is now transforming the financial sector, particularly banking. As this chapter shows, the Fintech trend did not surprise the historic banks, which all have chosen to innovate throughout their history, as illustrated by the development of online banking, in-house Fintechs, and their collaboration and investment in Fintechs. If Fintech disrupts the financial sector, leading the historical leaders to take a decisive leap forward, the question remains of their ability to take the lead in the banking market in the future. Fintech's growth has often been driven by market opportunities or regulation restriction, and is targeting specific vertical banking business lines, such as payments, international transfers, or peer-to-peer (P2P) borrowing. Fintechs took advantage of a kind of passivity of banks, which have not tried to innovate to much in line with the mainstream and changing regulations, without worrying about new competition.

Why should this innovation profit new players, while the historic banks, despite significant resources, have not been able to take part? Innovation alone is not enough to justify the emergence of Fintech, but the costs of banking operations have not changed for quite some time despite significant economies of scale. Bankers have used this financial windfall to enrich their shareholders at their customers' expense. Philippon (2015) found that intermediation costs in the USA are 2% and have not changed for almost 130 years. Bazot (2018) confirmed these results in a similar study on the main European markets (UK, Germany, and France). The rapid growth of Fintech is largely due to new technologies, such as machine learning, artificial intelligence, big data, and Blockchain, which have simplified the analysis of client behavior; the algorithmic approach has allowed better management of complex tasks such as credit analysis. Furthermore, the development of infrastructures, such as high-speed internet and the increased use of 4G, necessary for neo-banks which allow consumers to manage their money via their mobile phones, has facilitated Fintech's growth. The remuneration of Fintechs, which often rely on a freemium business model based on the use of geolocation data as well as those from their clients' web browsers, is not enough to guarantee their survival. These fast-technological innovations don't allow banks to react quickly with their "legacy". Conversely, Fintechs rely on their flexibility and capacity to respond immediately to customer usage and behavioral changes. However, will the hypergrowth of Fintechs allow us to shake up banking giants? Fintech is a global trend, particularly in North America, which has been joined by Asia, while Europe is lagging behind, particularly France, which is known and recognized for its financial excellence through its traditional banks. Fintech has nibbled away some of its business lines, after which came a derogation to the banking monopoly through crowdlending and frontal competition with neo-banks. This brings us to our thesis: It is interesting to look at how far French Fintech is disrupting the world of traditional banks. Will Fintechs be able to disrupt banks and how will they react to this new wave of innovation?

18.2 Literature Review

According to Frame *et al.* (2019) Fintech is the outcome of the technology development and implementation in financial services. The relationship between financial services and technology was discussed by Berger (2003) who analyzed customer satisfaction and the impact of IT on productivity.

Fintech's peer-to-peer lending business has seen its growth accelerate over the past few years. They have created a new business plan different from banks. They act as a financial intermediary between investors and lenders. Their advantage lies in their ability to speed up the borrowing process, facilitate access to credit, and reducing borrowing costs. To innovate, the Fintechs have adapted very quickly to new technologies such as big data, cloud computing, or artificial intelligence to reduce the time needed to handle applications. The reports by Welltrado (2018) have shown that operating costs of credit are 2.7% for P2P lending platforms, which is the case of the Fintech Lending Club (the largest P2P lending Fintech in the United States), while it is 7% for a bank. This is due to the lack of regulation of Fintechs, which allows them to simplify the screening process, whereas banks are required to comply with regulations which have become increasingly demanding since the financial crisis of 2008, forcing banks to engage more capital. De Roure *et al.* (2019) in their studies found different results. They have analyzed the risk-adjusted interest rate, which shows that the real cost of bank lending is lower than the cost of P2P lending. Their findings are confirmed by Philippon (2015), who proved that technological innovation had no significant impact on the costs of financial intermediation. Furthermore, several studies have found that the most important contribution of P2P is not decreasing costs but reducing the processing time. Fuster *et al.* (2018) have confirmed the positive effect of technological innovation on treatment times.

Today, the P2P system is not perfect, and these Fintech are facing much criticism. Salisbury (2016) blamed the selection method of P2P lending files that have been highlighted by Moody's and Fitch studies that reproach them for relaxing credit conditions to increase transaction volumes, while increasing the risk and probability of non-reimbursement.

The study by Bartlett *et al.* (2018) reveals that the role of Fintechs is more important than might be expected. They highlighted the importance of Fintechs' social justice mission. Indeed, the arrival of Fintechs on the loan market has allowed several African-American and Hispanic borrowers to access mortgages with more equitable interest rates.

According to Gordon and McCarthy (2016), the cost of an SME credit application at a bank is the same when the amount is comprised between $100,000 and $1,000,000. However, today more than 60% of SME credit applications are less than $100,000, and therefore less profitable for the bank. While digitalization of these services can be an effective solution to the problem, it means that the bank must either develop its own technology or outsource operations that are not economically profitable yet.

Kumar (2016) has shown that mergers and acquisitions in recent years have led to a consolidation of banking markets, driving several banks to incorporate integrate different systems into an archaic and very complex IT system. Despite considerable financial resources and a portfolio of customers counted in the millions, banks are facing difficulties in developing their business model. According to Loderer *et al.* (2016), mature companies face more problems to be innovative compared to younger structures, as they have to overcome several administrative constraints before reaching their goals. For structures employing thousands of people, the smallest attempt to modify or upgrade is subject to multi-level approvals, which lengthens the time needed to complete new projects and increases the gap between the banks and Fintech companies, which have very few employees and a relatively new structure that is easy to adapt, giving them very useful agility and adaptability in the introduction of new technologies.

DeAngelo and Stulz (2015) found that banks are subject to capital requirements in order to minimize their default risk and protect customer deposits, which may increase the costs borne by banks. They are forced to ask for collateral on any credit application; if the customer cannot meet this request, her/her credit will not be approved. P2P Fintechs profited from this loophole by offering several unsecured credit lines. They are willing to take more risk to attract new customers. Hau *et al.* (2018) pointed out that Ant Financial, Alibaba's Fintech, provides credit to SMEs using its platforms based on real-time sales and customer ratings. If the company's score is above a specified cut-off point, it is awarded a line of credit, and if the score falls below the cut-off point, the credit will be stopped. This method offers advantages of being fast and low-cost, but provides no indication about the risk of non-payment borne by the SME, unacceptable for a bank.

Boot and Thakor (2000) found that, in order to protect themselves and compete with the Fintechs, banks focused their investments on customer relations by using new technologies to reduce the gap with Fintechs. Goetz (2018) concluded that the arrival of Fintechs and the pressure they have put on banks is precipitating transformation. Banks are working to become more efficient by improving the quality of their assets and provide better stability to the banking market.

The Fintechs' role is important for the financial sector's modernization, which is evolving toward more flexibility and transparency. The regulator must protect consumers; according to Dhar (2016), consumers who have not yet used Fintechs do not trust the algorithms and robot advisors who are going to scan their needs and propose an appropriate investment strategy. Regulation can be a handicap for young structures which do not have sufficient resources to set up a compliance service. Today, regulatory authorities such as Basel are working to introduce new rules with which Fintechs must comply to lessen the risk of fraud or system failure. Darolles' study (2016) concluded that regulation is necessary, but in order to allow Fintechs to grow, fair competition between all financial players must be established, based on each one's resources.

According to Mansilla-Fernandez (2017), unlike that in developing countries, investment in Europe in Fintech is greater. Investment is rising in those countries where the banking sector is highly competitive; moreover, electronic payment is highly correlated with the number of customers in possession of a bank account. Investments in Fintech increase, especially in the countries where the cost of borrowing is particularly high or in low-income countries such as in Africa.

Fintechs focus on specific niches or vertical business lines and are always on the lookout for customers, a situation which allows banks to react quickly to counter-attack, or sign partnerships with newcomers. Stulz (2019) found that most of the pressure is coming from Bigtech, which has a lot of financial resources and access to a mass of data, allowing them to carry out in-depth analysis of their customers' needs, and through their Fintechs they may challenge banks by offering a number of simple and useful services to their clients.

18.3 Fintechs Tackle Banking Sector with New Technology

To improve customer relations, Fintechs are going to leverage new technologies to automatize tasks and speed up the decision-making process and reduce the required investments in both infrastructure and transaction security. The market has been booming since 2014, driven by new technology and new banking regulations that have restricted banks' freedom of movement.

18.3.1 *Innovative technologies in the financial sector*

Fintech is an abbreviation for "financial technology", representing the combination of finance with technology. Fintech is defined as the use of disruptive technology to disrupt the financial business. As part of their developments, Fintechs will create new processes, products, and services to meet customer expectations, with faster and cheaper services. They are challenging the role of traditional financial players as the only intermediaries.

18.3.1.1 *From robotization to algorithms thanks to data production*

Artificial intelligence is now the reference technology in fraud detection. Fintechs use AI to improve their payment, lending, and insurance services. The use of AI in the financial services sector is growing, notably in helping to expand transaction volume with less workforce involvement. Fintechs often combine AI with Machine Learning (ML) to predict the future needs of their clients and to provide the latter with services matching their frequently changing requirements. The success of the combination of Artificial Intelligence and Machine Learning is due to each one's ability to handle very large quantities of data in real time. Banks lose billions of dollars every year due to identity fraud, and regulations require more and more guarantees to combat money laundering. To minimize the risk of fraud and comply with the Technology for Regulatory Requirement (KYC), Fintechs have introduced facial recognition interfaces using AI to speed up account opening processes and reduce staff costs with minimal risk. The use of AI and ML is not limited to customer needs analysis or fraud detection; today, Fintechs use the technology to forecast behavioral analytics, and data-driven marketing, which helps them to increase their turnover by detecting the needs and reimbursement capacities of their customers whose only intention is a car loan or first home mortgage.

However, we must be vigilant about the results obtained by these new technologies, as AI and Machine Learning are learning-based technologies, and provide predictive data based on historical behavior. If the economic situation grows, forecasts will be positive and they will be unable to anticipate a crisis, which may have very serious consequences. Technology is constantly evolving, and there is more and more discussion about Natural Language Processing (NLP), a machine learning model that can handle data in human language. For example, Bank of America offers its clients an NLP called Erica to support them in managing financial investments. To accelerate the data processing time, AI use is recommended in a cloud environment.

18.3.1.2 *Large-scale cloud storage and data processing*

To create financial services, companies must be able to handle big databases to keep track of the transactions made by their customers, which necessitates very large and expensive servers. However, with the rise of Cloud technology and the possibility of renting powerful servers at a very affordable price, the world of fintech has been completely transformed. The cloud has become essential for Fintech.

It is a system of data storage and access stored on a private or public server offering the benefit of large amounts of storage indispensable for big data analysis. The system's advantage is clearly a large amount of storage space, essential for Big Data analysis. At the same time, it eliminates investment expenses and reduces the personnel costs required for network management. The Private Cloud gives access to a network of servers dedicated to a single organization. This solution has been adopted by companies who want to keep control of their data. Banks have always refused to adopt the public cloud and prefer to have their own networks despite the heavy investment budget. To avoid cyberattacks and reduce the risk of fraud, some banks ask their supplier to build them a tailor-made offer, such as Bank of America did following the signing of a collaboration contract with IBM in November 2019. Pressure from Fintech has pushed some banks to take the plunge: they have started to use the public cloud by renting servers jointly with other companies, but access to data remains private. Today, the cloud market is monopolized by three Bigtech giants, Amazon Web Services, Microsoft Azure, and Google Cloud, which also offer data analysis services to their customers.

18.3.1.3 *Blockchain*

Today, Blockchain allows Fintech users within the industry to distribute and copy data through different channels without the risk of fraud or manipulation. Any attempt to change the information modifies the blocks and is quickly changed. Initially developed in collaboration with cryptocurrency by creating an independent digital currency (Bitcoin), Blockchain helps to track all financial transactions. Thanks to cryptography, security is reinforced, and transfers of money are accelerated. The first challenge for Fintechs is to obtain the trust of customers, who are concerned by the security of the system. However, a secure network is very expensive, and only banks have enough resources to guarantee their customers and regulators flawless security. This is where Blockchain comes in, it allows for the security of the system deployed at a more affordable price. Fintechs have a competitive advantage compared to banks that cannot switch to Blockchain easily. The cost of the implementation of Blockchain will be expensive, but the administration and the maintenance of the system will be much simpler. All Fintechs that use Blockchain have made significant savings due to lower data collection, lower auditing transactions costs, and less security expenditures required by the computer network. For example, in back-office operations, Blockchain provides control over cleary and settlement operations, even though Blockchain is more useful as a protection against the risks of cyberattacks, an extremely expensive incident for banks.

Blockchain is a decentralized, distributed, and public solution. The money placed in the banks is stored centrally, while Blockchain stores the data on decentralized servers; so, during a data transaction, the intervention of multiple intermediaries is eliminated. The infrastructure is distributed, allowing sharing information with several partners (banks or Fintech) with guaranteed transaction security. Banks have begun to use this technology despite the reluctance of regulatory authorities who refuse to decentralize client data. Today, Blockchain goes beyond the field of finance and can be used in other industries. However, it is important to note that banks most often use private systems — where they maintain control — rather than public ones.

18.3.2 *Fintech's business lines*

Fintechs work to improve the customer experience by meeting their needs and offering products and services adapted to the evolving market, resulting in the creation of new products. Fintechs, with funding and support from venture capital funds, can innovate and take the time to analyze customer behavior, whereas for various departments of a bank that operate on a just-in-time basis and on an annual budget, it is difficult to work over such long time frames. Fintech has not finished expanding its area of influence: payments, loans, Insurtech, and Regtech are among the flagship businesses in this fast-growing sector that we are going to develop.

18.3.2.1 *Payment or how to guarantee healthy competition*

Driven by new technologies and the democratization of smartphones, Fintech began by investigating solutions for payment and money transfers between individuals. The first service developed by Fintechs was mobile wallets and payments, thanks to the boom in mobile banking apps. With more and more mobile customers and round-the-clock consumption, banks need to respond instantly to their customers' requests, and adapt their services to evolving E-commerce hubs. Fintechs can facilitate money transfers between people with easy-to-use solutions that are often cheaper or even free of charge. They also have democratized foreign exchange operations, a sector where banks have been reluctant to change their policies with non-transparent fees and difficult to predict. Fintechs have abolished foreign exchange fees and commissions, such as in the case of London's Fintech Revolut. For example, in France, Lydia has managed to surpass two million regular users and has become a must-have application that allows people to transfer money for free and quickly. All you need is a phone number to transfer money between friends and family. The customer saves time and no longer needs to go to the bank to make a transfer that requires an account number.

The development of open banking, enabling all financial institutions to connect to store data through the use of Application Programming Interfaces (APIs), has become a major source of innovation. Data collectors offer customers an application that can centralize information from multiple bank accounts with a simple customer interface and the opportunity to schedule and receive real-time alerts. Data collectors require the customer's login and password to connect to their bank account. Today, its technologies raise new concerns about the security and integrity of data obtained by multiple aggregators. Regulators are addressing this issue and finding solutions to ensure the confidentiality and protection of consumers.

18.3.2.2 *Crowdlending or how to get around the banking monopoly*

Peer-to-peer lending gained in attraction after the 2008 financial crisis in the United States and Europe. Buchak *et al.* (2018) found that Fintech lenders tripled their market share in mortgage lending between 2007 and 2015. Despite strong growth in Fintech lending, however, their market share remains small. Bank lending in the United States represented $13,116 trillion in December 2018 while P2P lending is estimated at $150 to $490 trillion in 2020. The 2008 financial crisis occurred as a result of a huge investment in banks, exceeding the volume of transactions authorized, and bypassing the rules they chose to guarantee transactions, booking part of their activities off-balance sheet. Nonetheless, with the burst of the real estate bubble in the United States, the entire system collapsed, saved *in extremis* by government intervention that injected billions to support the same banks that caused the crisis and thus save the world economy from disaster. Since then, regulations have become stricter for banks and require more capital in exchange for the operations carried out to guarantee the stability of the financial market and limit any impact of a financial crisis on the economy.

In peer-to-peer lending, Fintechs act as financial intermediaries without committing their own capital. In case of default, only the investor will lose money, though the reputation of the P2P, and thus its rankings, will suffer. Most of their clients are hedge funds, venture capital interests, or banks, none of which tolerate any selection errors. In terms of payments, Fintechs are the most developed, but in terms of profitability the lending sector is the most lucrative. P2P remuneration is made in three steps: the borrower pays loan origination fees in addition to 1–6% fees and possible late repayment fees. Once the deal is finished, if the borrower repays the loan completely, investors pay the Fintech a bonus.

In addition to payment operations, the Bigtechs are interested in Fintech lending. The Chinese Fintech Ant Financial is moving towards SMEs, working with the Alibaba platform and offering them automated credit lines. The activation of this credit does not depend on a score calculated based on a complex model as required by the regulatory authorities for banks, but on the basis of the SMEs' traffic through the platform and their score as given by customers'; repayment is made by withdrawing funds from the revenues generated on the platform.

According to many experts, the credit market is intended to be fully automated. The use of Machine Learning and AI will allow a quick assessment of repayment capacity and default risk, without any human intervention. All the previous will lead a move toward lower bank fees, beneficial to the clients and not to the banks' shareholders.

18.3.2.3 *Insurtech or how to attack yet another banking annuity*

A new market is opening for Fintechs. After the financial professions, they will rush into the insurance business, a highly competitive market involving insurance companies, banks, and brokers.

Unlike banking services, where risk-averse customers prefer stability, insurance policy price comparators encourage customers to change companies to reduce their premiums. In insurance, the notion of risk is very important, and estimating the likelihood of occurrence of the risk has an impact on premium costs. New technologies have proved very useful for assessing risk and reducing insurance premiums. Fintechs are now able to ask their clients to put a geolocation tracker on their car and thanks to AI, collect data on trips, speed, and time of use, all for a better assessment of the client's behavior and leading to customized risk modeling to adapt the insurance contract to the clients' real needs. Insurtech is mainly interested in automobile, home, and health insurance. Thanks to the technology, new insurance contracts are emerging, covering risks that seemed unthinkable to assess. Cost is not the only benefit of Insurtech: the firms have worked hard on the quality of their services and on customer satisfaction. Thanks to chatbots, they allow claimants to file a claim quickly at any time, without waiting, and then obtain compensation quickly.

18.3.2.4 *Compliance and risk management* (*Regtech*)

To continue to grow, Fintechs must comply with banking regulations. Therefore, they are using more and more Regtech, or start-ups trying to assist companies in the financial sector to comply with regulations. Regtech use technology as a means of tracking regulatory developments, in particular the Anti-Money-Laundering and Know-Your-Customer protocols to combat fraud. Thanks to Regtech, Fintechs can outsource compliance management in an efficient and cost-effective manner. To achieve these goals, they use artificial intelligence, cloud computing, and machine learning technologies for automating the monitoring of all operations and reducing compliance departments' risk by protecting them from money laundering. To detect fraud, they carry out real-time monitoring of transactions and try to detect irregularities in digital payments, all of which are then forwarded to the compliance department which validates the transaction. Cloud computing plays an important role because it enables Regtech to log directly on to the source of the information and provide fast data transfer at low cost. However, venture capital funds have reduced their investment in Regtech significantly following the relaxation of the Dodd–Frank law on 22 May 2018, under pressure from banks; the latter considered the law to be top-binding, with no significant improvement in the security of the banking system, and only weakened small banks. It is interesting to note that Regtech solutions are used primarily by Fintechs and especially neo-banks, which are more likely to internalize innovative solutions. Conversely, banks are reluctant to consider Regtech as outsourced operators of major services.

18.4 Banks, Between Innovation and Regulation Constraints, Confronted to Fintech's Boom

Confronted with competition from Fintechs, traditional banks have increased their efforts to develop a better customer experience and put the customer at the center of their business strategies. Banks have many financial resources and a large portfolio of clients; however, their true capital is their client data, a real treasure that the Fintechs covet. They have customers' income, expenses, savings, and investment history data over several years, a substantial advantage compared to Fintechs that have just come on the market. Banks have developed strong brands and reputations that help them reassure their clients, including those who are risk-averse and cautious about innovation.

18.4.1 *Online banks' attempt at digitalization*

Over the last few years, banks have lagged behind the digital services offered to their customers. With a complex and expensive IT system, with several departments offering multiple services, changes have been difficult to achieve. Banks own their own IT infrastructure and employ thousands of IT staff to secure and maintain day-to-day operations. One of the reasons that banks are investing further in innovation is that they have not yet been able to implement new technologies into their daily operations. This is due to three factors: the risk of breakdowns; antiquated, overly complex IT systems that are several years old; and the need to support thousands of applications used by all their different customers around the world.

On the other hand, Fintechs are starting from scratch and possess an extremely flexible organization, allowing them to use the most up-to-date technology.

Banks do not offer end-to-end digital opening products, allowing customers to open an account online, because they are yet to set up a system for identification and automated account opening. To accomplish these goals, banks will have to improve customer experience, real-time data analysis, and automation to accelerate the time it takes to process customer transactions. In their compliance departments, some banks have been able to leverage this new technology to reduce operating expenses and reduce the costs generated by compliance. They produce governance documents required by regulators to check the risk models used in only a few minutes, whereas manually this operation can take a few weeks. The use of AI and ML has allowed for automatic detection of borrowers' default risks and improved the banks' anticipation power. Despite the clear contribution of Blockchain, regulatory authorities still have not given the green light to the banks for deployment due to the risk of fraud. Some banks are not favorable to the development of Blockchains, forcing them to migrate to a distributed environment and a decentralized system, which may end up in their losing complete control over their data. Other banks have moved forward and used Blockchains for the delivery and settlement of OTC contracts, in order to test the reliability of the technology and to convince the authorities of the system's efficiency. The banks' success depends on their ability to implement a new strategy based on innovation, but it also depends on how well these technologies (Machine Learning and Artificial Intelligence) are integrated into their IT architecture.

18.4.2 *Regulation as a restriction to institutional innovation*

After the financial crisis of 2008, Fintechs received an increasing number of customers who were not satisfied with banking services and who considered bank rates too high. The lack of confidence among customers represents a key driver for the development of Fintechs. At the same time, regulatory authorities have reduced banks' margins to ensure financial stability and consumer protection.

The United States voted the Dodd–Frank reform on July 21, 2010, and created the Consumer Financial Protection Bureau (CFBP), which was a new agency in charge of the protection of customers against credit card fraud, abuse of mortgages, and other financial products. They also adopted the Volcker rule, to prevent banks from handling some investment transactions that are considered speculative. Regulations have become stricter and the expense for banks has increased — for example, Citigroup now employs 30,000 people to manage compliance. Experts believe that these new rules have failed to regulate the financial sector, and only compromised the development of small banks.

However, the growth of Fintech remains a source of concern for the supervisory authorities who are trying to anticipate the future and avoid a new financial crisis. They have to prevent money laundering and criminal activities, and to achieve this, they have established several rules such as Know Your Customer (KYC), Anti-Money Laundering (AML) and the Bank Secrecy Act (BSA), applicable to all financial institutions, which have been regularly updated and adapted to the evolution of new technologies. In the case of non-compliance with regulations, the banks will have to pay heavy fines and may be subject to legal sanctions. The next step for regulators is for Fintechs to assess the risks of the financial services offered, to identify possible loopholes in the system, and, in cases of abuse, regulators will not hesitate to impose strict rules to protect customers against the threat of cybersecurity.

To counter the Fintech threat, the banks are asking the regulators to stop the fraudulent use of data collectors, who do not hesitate to collect all data available on their customers from the banks' digital platforms using screen scrapping, without sorting it. In the meantime, when new rules are voted, some banks, in order to block these aggregators, will often change the design of their websites to disrupt the function of Fintechs and undermine them. More and more consumer associations around the world are demanding the customers' right to retrieve all their banking data and transfer it to another financial institution. Since this threat has emerged, several banks have started to block access to their databases to account aggregators but are now faced with the European DPS2 law which prohibits this and aims to unlock bank data.

18.5 Banks and Fintechs in France: Cooperation, Competition, or Coopetition?

The data availability and computing power offered by clouds and AI contributes to the development of Fintechs. Despite very few resources, but due to simplified online procedures, Fintechs are beginning to target niches with a view to attracting the maximum number of customers. On some digital services, Fintechs have taken the lead over small or regional banks, unable to respond quickly to this revolution. They have a substantial advantage: thanks to new technologies, the Fintechs have been able to offer services adapted to customers' needs. Today, credit applications can be made over the internet or by phone, resulting in the whole process being accelerated, from application processing to validation. Despite a very large customer portfolio and know-how in credit analysis, customers still must book an appointment with their bank advisor and provide several documents to apply for credit and wait two to three weeks for an answer. The banking mobility plan in the 2017 Macron Law is designed to facilitate changing banks; if the customer has regular transfers and withdrawals, he will not have to reprogram them, since the transfer of all his operations from bank to bank will be done seamlessly.

Fintechs are always under the constant pressure of technological change. They have to constantly reinvent themselves in order to keep their customers. With the arrival of new competitors from other countries, it is sufficient for a ranking or a press article from their customers to change providers. This is what happens to French neo-banks who suffer from competition from N26 or Revolut, who developed their products in Germany or the United Kingdom and are now moving on to the French market.

18.5.1 *Fintechs in France*

Fintech adoption rates differ widely from one country to another. The first indicator is the Internet penetration rate in the country, the second is customer confidence in Fintechs and innovation, and the third is the amount of investment received, which depends on the interest of venture capital funds or investment banks in the business and the country.

The French adoption rate for Fintechs is one of the lowest in Europe. According to an IFOP survey conducted in France in 2019, among 1,000 people, only 21% of French people have an online bank account. Conversely, only 17% of people interviewed said that they use mobile phones as a means of payment thanks to NFC technology. The explanations for these very low figures are many, nearly 81% of people are suspicious about security vulnerabilities while 67% are afraid of over-consumption. When they are asked about their bank selection criteria, 93% highlight the simplicity of administering their account and 92% are looking for a strong customer relationship, followed by the desire to reduce financial fees. Fintechs have been able to adapt their services to customer expectations, making them simpler, faster, and, above all, more efficient.

The United Kingdom is the only European market that has been able to adapt quickly to this transformation, where digital payments increased by 13% from 134 billion USD in 2017 to 151 billion USD in 2019. In terms of growth, the French market is doing better with 17% growth in two years, but with half of the turnover; in 2017, digital payments represented only 74 billion dollars and 86 billion dollars in 2019. Today, the investment gap between the UK and France is very significant. In order to understand this gap, we have to analyze the crowdlending market in the UK, which went from 2.07 billion dollars in 2017 to 2.44 billion dollars in 2019, an increase of 17.5%. Whereas in France in 2019 the amount of crowdlending operations represented only $0.229 billion, i.e. 9.4% of the UK market.

The French market lags far behind the adoption rate of Fintechs, which explains the low amounts invested by VCs in French Fintech where lack of confidence for innovation among French consumers remains high. An important contrast exists between Fintech adoption rate and online banking in France; this gap can be explained by the strong growth of online banking supported by traditional banks which have invested a lot of money to improve their services and anticipate the Fintechs' growth. In order to gain time, some French banks have acquired online banks; there are eight major online banks, six of which are supported by traditional banks. The market is very competitive, which explains the weak development of Fintechs in France. Online banks are supported by traditional banks, which can offer all the products proposed by the parent bank. The Belgian market has the same structure as the French market because there is a

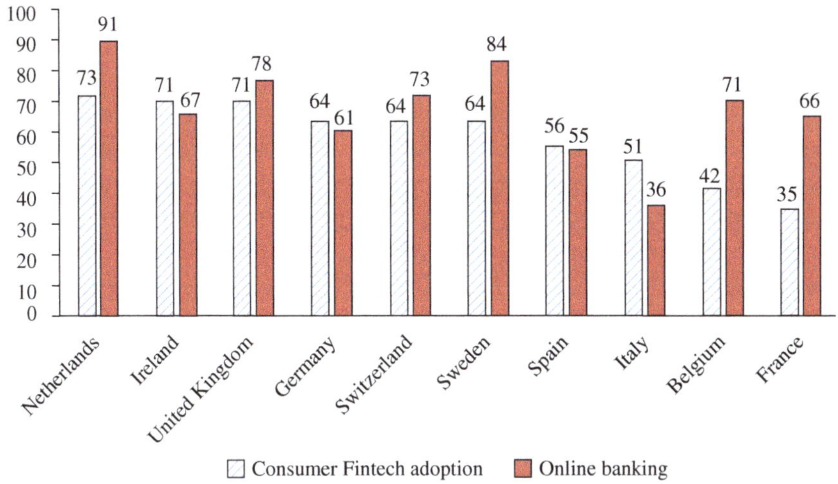

Fig. 18.1. Consumer Fintech adoption rates and Online banking penetration in select European countries in 2019 in percentage.
Notes: This graph shows Fintech's adoption rate ranked in descending order by country in Europe. The figure also shows the penetration rates of online banks which represent the percentage of people who already have an online account.
Sources: EY (Global Fintech Adoption) and Eurostat.

strong position of French banks that have implemented the same proactive policy (see Fig. 18.1).

18.5.2 *Reactions of French banks to the development of Fintechs*

Since the arrival of Fintechs, the conventional banking model has faced several challenges. The rapid adaptation of banks and their ability to change are crucial to their survival. Fintechs cannot be considered as competitors of banks, as they only target small segments of financial sector, namely certain business lines not covered by banks. To understand the threat to French banks, we need to analyze the evolution of Fintechs in China, which is the most developed and mature market in the world. The Fintech market started growing very early, taking advantage of the country's strong growth and a very high adoption rate. They benefited from the funding of Bigtech (BATX), who were able to create new financial services adapted to their E-commerce platforms and customer expectations. Alibaba, the largest E-commerce company in the country, created Ant Financial, the largest Fintech in the world, valued at more than 150 billion dollars. Its payment subsidiary Alipay, PayPal's main competitor, started its development on the Chinese market by establishing itself as the first payment platform. By collaborating with several Chinese banks and E-commerce platforms, Alipay continues to gain a foothold on other countries' markets by investing in foreign Fintechs. To avoid losing the battle before the fight, French banks have taken several initiatives with dedicated teams to create innovation incubators, invest in venture capital funds, perform targeted acquisitions, or sign commercial partnerships with different Fintechs. Thanks to a significant investment or a full acquisition in a Fintech, banks can often obtain representation on the Fintech's boards of directors and thus obtain total or partial control over it. Large banks often set up incubator and accelerator programs to obtain early financial participation in Fintech companies and specially to acquire innovation know-how.

18.5.2.1 *Collaboration between banks and Fintechs*

Banks cannot ignore this new competition and must move forward to cooperate with these new players. To secure their future, banks and Fintechs must recognize that their interests converge, because the services offered by Fintechs are very often complementary to banking services. Over the years, new collaborative models have developed, including assistance to Fintechs by traditional banks via incubators or accelerators. The survey conducted by Capgemini and EFMA (2017, 2018) among bank managers covered the strategies that they would most likely adopt to deal with the arrival of Fintechs; 91% of respondents preferred collaboration, including 71% who preferred to distribute the Fintechs' new products or services on their platforms, and 54% were ready to authorize Fintechs to distribute banking products on their platforms. Only 4% of respondents were willing to buy a Fintech due to the difficulty of determining the right purchase price, and 4% were willing to start up their own Fintechs.

When operating, Fintechs are forced to rent the banks' back-ends which, despite their age, can be expensive, in order to focus on the front-end and customer satisfaction. Fintechs know very well that one day or another they will be obliged to build their own back-end services to avoid the consequences of a risk of interruption in their collaboration with banks, who could deny them access to the latter's infrastructures. New technologies such as Blockchain represent the future of a fluid and efficient back-end system, but it is necessary to get all the players involved to sign up to this project before adopting it and obtaining the validation of the regulatory authorities. Peer-to-peer lending Fintechs present themselves as an alternative to banks, but the distinction between both players is difficult to draw because Fintechs have failed to bypass banks and create a parallel market — most deals are done in collaboration with traditional banks. The partnerships are two-way: the banks may give them client financing deals and then Fintechs will have to find appropriate investors, or the banks may invest in one of the proposed Fintech deals. This cooperation provides banks with more profit and cost-saving opportunities; concurrently, the main investors in P2P are banks. Many banks which have signed partnerships with Fintechs are beginning to be concerned about the constant development of these startups, and regret the fact that they have been serving as a launching pad for these Fintechs, which include companies whose value exceeds the large banks' market capitalization.

The French banks are not to be outdone, and they have realized that their future is linked with that of Fintech. Looking at the analysis of the JDN (2019), it can be seen that all French banks without exception have signed partnerships with French or foreign Fintechs. BNP Paribas, which is the leading French bank and the second-largest European bank, is very active and has signed 41 Fintech partnerships. It also supports several incubators and accelerators. It works with Plug and Play (American accelerator) within Station F (the largest incubator in Europe) to support Fintechs and help them to grow. It has developed its own WAI ("We Are Innovation") incubation spaces and entrepreneurship programs such as People's Lab and Innovation Booster. The same is true for all the major French banks with their own specificities. Banque "Caisse d'Epargne Rhône-Alpes" B612 incubator mainly hosts Fintech and Insurtech companies at an early stage of creation or acceleration, while Crédit Agricole has chosen to develop a generalist incubator throughout the country, the "Villages by CA". Finally, the Paris and

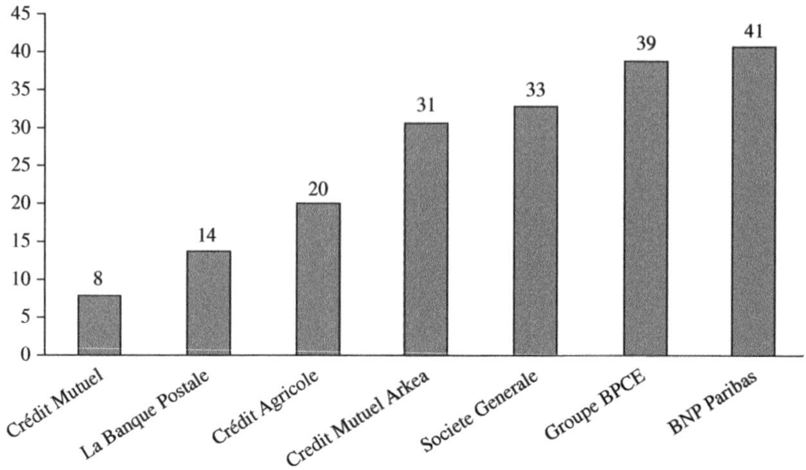

Fig. 18.2. Leading French banks by partnerships with Fintech companies 2019. *Notes*: This graph shows the results of a survey carried out by the *Journal Du Net* (JDN) in 2019 in order to measure the number of collaboration agreements between Bank and Fintech in France.

Co incubator dedicated to Fintech is sponsored by Société Générale and Crédit Municipal de Paris. The collaboration between banks and Fintech can create synergies and can be justified on sovereignty grounds, when banks want to face competition provided by Bigtechs such as the American GAFAM (Google, Apple, Facebook, Amazon, Microsoft) or the Chinese BATX (Baidu, Alibaba, Tencent, Xiaomi). The significant financial power acquired by them could enable the GAFAs to develop financial services for their customers, based on their new usages (see Fig. 18.2). These offers could be made alone or in partnership. Take, for example, Amazon's foray into SME lending and the new healthcare insurance company which it created with Berkshire Hathaway and JP Morgan.

18.5.2.2 *Bank's investment in Fintechs*

In terms of development, and despite innovative ideas and new technology, Fintechs, without funding, cannot reach their goal. In essence, this is due to the lack of profitability of their business model, since all revenues are dedicated to the development of digital infrastructures. The economic crisis triggered by the COVID-19 pandemic will have a significant impact on banks but especially on start-ups, because most investors are afraid of a long-term recession, even though the French government has excluded SMEs from government support to focus only on companies with high numbers of employees and whose activity is essential to the economy. The most important source of funding comes from venture capitalists, who have invested massively in France, but whose investments are still insufficient in Fintech. This situation has encouraged several Fintechs to become part of incubators created by banks in order to obtain enough funding for their development despite a loss of autonomy. In fact, within an incubator, Fintechs can be restricted if they wish to develop a service that may cannibalize the bank's services.

To explore venture capital and bank investments in Fintechs, we have collected data from the Dealroom database. For our sample we only selected European banks that have invested in more than 10 start-ups and we have selected 10 banks that had already invested in 148 Fintechs. In order to fully understand the role of banks in the development of Fintechs, it was important to see the total investment in Fintechs coming mainly from venture capitalists; the summary of the data obtained from Dealroom database is shown in graph 3. The analysis of this graph shows that French market lags far behind its neighbors, even being outperformed by the Swedish market in 2019. This is due to a very slow Fintech adoption rate in the French market. Despite government efforts to boost the development of start-ups, the competition with French banks is fierce and French Fintechs did not obtain similar regulation advantages as their British counterparts.

The French Fintech market does not enjoy the same attraction as the UK market or the German market, which since 2016 is attracting more and more investors. Among the world's largest banks, Goldman Sachs is the bank that has invested the most in Fintechs, with more than 120 investments worldwide. In Europe, only the British market (8 investments) and the German market (3 investments) have attracted their attention. No American bank has invested in the French Fintechs ecosystem. The competition in the Fintech market is played out between the American market and the Asian market. The only significant foreign investments in the French market concerns the Chinese group Tencent, which has financed two major Fintechs, thereby explaining the importance of the role of French banks.

Table 18.1. Fintech financing by the largest banks in Europe.

		Number of investments	Number of Fintech		Local Fintech	
Bank	**Country**	**No.**	**No.**	**%**	**No.**	**%**
BNP Paribas	France	101	23	23	8	35
Crédit Agricole	France	83	4	5	3	75
Societe Generale	France	30	13	43	4	31
Credit Mutuel	France	23	12	52	11	92
BPCE	France	17	12	71	4	33
Deutsche Bank	Germany	53	22	42	5	23
Commerzbank	Germany	29	23	79	8	35
Barclays	UK	65	24	37	7	29
HSBC	UK	49	13	27	2	15
Lloyds Banking	UK	10	2	20	2	100

Notes: From the Dealroom database, we have collected data regarding the funding of start-ups from the leading European banks. We have identified those investments that were intended to finance Fintechs, including those located in the same country as the investor banks.

The data in Table 18.1 show that French banks are very active in trying to compensate for a lack of international venture capital investment. French banks have taken this opportunity to support Fintech very early in their development to have a call option for integrating Fintech into the group in case of success. In our sample, French banks financed 64 Fintechs, German banks 45, and UK banks only 37. Considering these results, it is clear that bank investment is negatively correlated to the financing of venture capital in the country and that it is essential for the development of financial start-ups. French banks do not only finance local Fintechs but also invest abroad to diversify their portfolios and consolidate their positions internationally. Banks are not allowed to take significant risks, and their incubators cannot support multiple start-ups. In order to diversify risk, they have created corporate venture capital (CVC), which does not have the same objectives as venture capital that mainly try to make a profit. Corporate venture capital aims to finance young entrepreneurs who have promising ideas which, in case of success, may be attractive for the bank, especially in the case of a buy-out, since it will not have to pay 100% of the price. However, as the funds allocated to CVCs are limited, the fund manager must be sure before investing, and must often search for projects that already

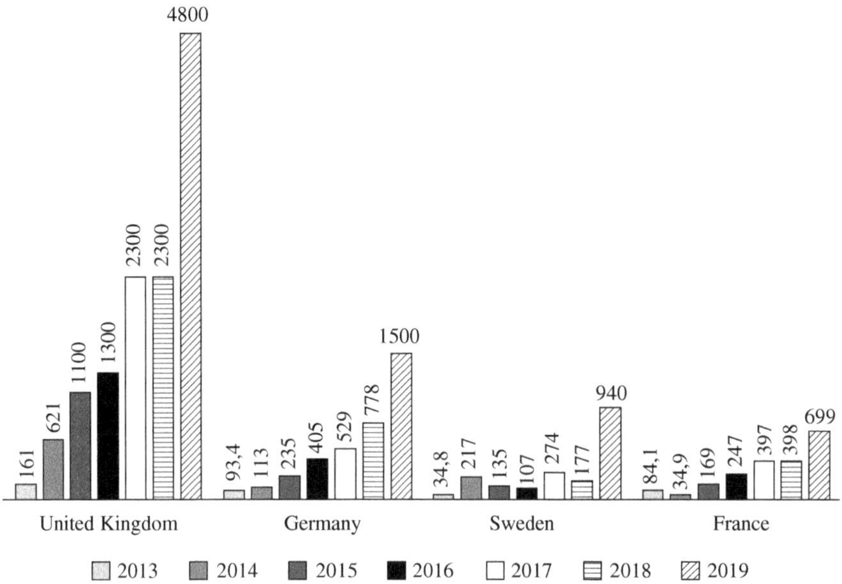

Fig. 18.3. Total Investments in Fintech in Europe in millions of Euros.
Notes: This graph shows the total amounts invested in fintech in Europe since 2013. We have selected the four most important countries.
Source: Dealroom.

have a significant client in the pipeline. The role of corporate venture capital goes beyond financing. It must monitor, give advice, help with recruitment, and develop a network to help the start-up grow quickly. Banks often avoid playing the role of CVC leader, as their only objective is to have a seat on the executive board in order to facilitate the buyout of the given Fintech in case of success. It's a win–win operation for both — if they succeed in helping each other, the Fintech will bring its technological skills and the bank its logistics know-how.

Compared to its British and German neighbors, France is lagging behind in capital investment (Fig. 18.3). The Fintech adoption rate in France is one of the lowest in Europe (Fig. 18.1), which is explained by investors' mistrust. Before deciding, venture capital funds, the main investors in Fintechs, must make sure that they can recoup their investment. They will analyze the probability of exit via acquisition or IPO, but the French financial market's lack of attractiveness reduces the chances for the latter and is one of the reasons behind the mistrust of VCs *vis-à-vis* the French market.

18.5.2.3 *Confrontation*

Many Fintechs can't survive on their own and need to collaborate with banks. Banks are preparing their reaction through the development of their own applications. For some services, Fintechs are always one step ahead, such as account aggregators, where customers can group several accounts together, something that banks cannot do.

With the arrival of Fintechs, several banks decided to develop their own digital services, and some have favored the creation of independent digital banks, which have their own entities, but depend on the parent company's products. To reach their goals, they have directed their customers toward digital products and online services. They started by suppressing all paper bank statements and offering some transactions performed online, such as transfers, free of charge. The data boom has made their processing quite expensive and somewhat difficult to process, but the arrival of the AI has made it much easier to analyze information in real time. To catch up, they replicated Fintechs and put into place more and more new technologies such as big data or machine learning to study their clients' behavior in order to offer them the best services. Today, to prevent the growth of neo-banks, the banks' strategy is more and more oriented towards integrating APIs and Openbanking. The banking system is progressively modernizing, but not fast enough. Their most important challenge is the upgrading of the IT system and the creation of an organizational structure which is better adapted to the market requirements. The banks' success depends on their efforts to implement a new strategy based on innovation, which in turn depends on how well their technologies (i.e. ML and AI) can be integrated into their IT architecture.

To catch up, some banks prefer to purchase Fintechs. In France, several examples can be cited, such as the acquisition of the account aggregator Linxo by Crédit Agricole, the acquisition of Compte Nickel (neo-bank) by BNP Paribas, KissKissBankBank (equity financing) by Banque Postale, and the German Fintech Fidar by BPCE. This solution is not liked by all banks due to the strong speculation around Fintech prices. Some banks would rather develop an internal platform which is cheaper but might come on the market too late. The acquisition of Fintechs could potentially cause some problems of zero-sum game integration with duplicate services between banks and Fintech.

Competition will be more difficult with neo-banks who offer their services to customers exclusively on mobile phones thanks to very well thought-out and easy-to-use applications that add new services, such as real-time account tracking, categorization of expenses according to criteria that can be modified by the customer, as well as management of credit card payment capacities. Banks offer other services that neo-banks do not yet have. Fintechs will have to obtain banking licenses from the regulatory authorities if they want to develop their own business-like banks, a drawn-out and difficult process that may give banks time to react.

18.6 Conclusion

In recent years, Fintechs have grown exponentially, following the financial crisis of 2008 which resulted in customers' mistrust of banks. For their development, Fintechs have used new technologies, which are easy to implement and affordable, as well as attracting investments from venture capital funds that seek to disrupt the banking sector. Fintechs have simplified access to information and have expanded the number of products and services offered to clients at a lower cost. They have also helped clients who had been excluded from the banking system to reconnect to the financial system. To win the war against the banks, Fintechs have focused on improving the customer experience by providing better, cheaper, and more transparent services.

Fintechs have not yet succeeded in creating disruptive innovation. It is difficult to compare them to the revolution in photography with the arrival of digital photos or the emergence of VOIP telephony for international communications, because these activities are not one of the economy's primary needs. The financial industry and the banking system represent pillars of the economy. In order to deal with economic crises, governments use banks first and enact monetary policies as a means of recovery. Once Fintechs are made to comply with the same rules and regulations imposed on banks, they will lose many of their advantages and will no longer be able to be as competitive as they are today.

The market for Fintechs is highly developed in the United States thanks to significant investments from venture capital and US investment banks, which have understood that Fintechs are going to be an important part of the banking landscape. In Europe, only the UK market has been able to stimulate the development of Fintechs thanks to flexible regulation and significant investments. The French market is very late in terms of Fintech development and has not been able to attract foreign investors; to back up this new ecosystem, French banks have been able to take this opportunity by building close relationships with new players and create accelerators or incubators to help Fintech start-ups grow. They have even hesitated in creating corporate venture capital to support the Fintechs' development financially. Simultaneously, all the banks have understood that the risk of inaction is more important than the risk of change. They have therefore developed their online services and started to use new technologies such as Artificial Intelligence, Machine Learning, or the Cloud to accelerate their processes and meet new customer expectations. Finally, the competition between banks and Fintech is not head-on, and the disruptive innovation proclaimed by the new players has yet to take place.

For the moment, competition from Fintechs has not yet affected banks' activity and does not represent a real threat for banking players who are well established in the landscape. Fintechs are still small players that tackle niche businesses; their business volumes remain very low despite double-digit growth rates in recent years, and their business model still not profitable. The banks will take the necessary time to innovate and take over the market shares recovered by Fintechs.

Banks should be wary of Bigtech that have E-commerce platforms and significant financial resources. The latter have put the customer at the center of their strategy and, with new technologies, have been able to quickly anticipate customer demands and offer better adapted solutions than those offered by banks. They have started to develop internationally by exporting their know-how in order to increase their market share. However, regulation remains a major obstacle in the development of Fintechs, as regulators are not ready to grant licenses to new players without guarantees regarding consumer protection and the stability of the financial system.

References

Bartlett, R., Morse, A., Stanton, R., and Wallace, N. (2018). Consumer lending discrimination in the era of FinTech. Unpublished working paper. *University of California, Berkeley.*

Bazot, G. (2018). Financial consumption and the cost of finance: measuring financial efficiency in Europe (1950–2007), *Journal of the European Economic Association*, **16**(1): 123–160.

Berger, A. (2003). The economic effects of technological progress: Evidence from the banking industry. *Journal of Money, Credit and Banking*, **35**: 141–176.

Boot, A. and Thakor, A. V. (2000). Can relationship banking survive competition? *Journal of Finance*, **55**: 679–713.

Buchak, G., Matvros, G., Piskorski, T., and Seru, A. (2018). Fintech, regulatory arbitrage and the rise of shadow banks. *Journal of Financial Economics*, **130**: 453–483.

Darolles, S. (2016). The rise of Fintechs and their regulation. *Financial Stability Review*, **20**: 85–92.

DeAngelo H. and Stulz, R. M. (2015). Liquid-claim production, risk management, and bank capital structure: Why high leverage is optimal for banks. *Journal of Financial Economics*, **116**: 219–236.

De Roure, C., Pelizzon, L., and Thakor, A. V. (2019). P2P Lenders Versus Banks: Cream Skimming or Bottom Fishing? *Working paper, Goethe University.*

Dhar, V. (2016). When to trust robots with decisions, and when not to. *Harvard Business Review.*

Dru, J. M. (1996). *Disruption: Overturning Conventions and Shaking Up the Marketplace*, Wiley.

Frame, Scott. W., Wall, L., and White, L. (2019). Technological change and financial innovation in banking: Some implications for Fintech. *Oxford Handbook of Banking*, 3rd edition, Oxford University Press.

Fuster, A., Plosser M., Schnabl, P., and Vickery, J. (2018). The role of technology in mortgage lending. *Federal Reserve Bank of New York Staff Reports*, 836.

Goetz, M. R. (2018). Competition and bank stability. *Journal of Financial Intermediation*, **35**: 57–69.

Gordon, K. M. and McCarthy, B. (2016). The state of small business lending: Innovation and technology and the implications for regulation. *Harvard Business School*, working paper, 17–42.

Hau, H., Huang, Y., Shan, H., and Sheng, Z. (2018). *FinTech credit and entrepreneurial growth.* Mimeo, University of Geneva.

Kumar, S. (2016). Relaunching innovation: Lessons from Silicon Valley, *Banking Perspective*, **4**(1): 19–23.

Loderer, C., Stulz, R. M., and Waelchi, U. (2016). Firm rigidities and the decline of growth opportunities. *Management Science*, **63**: 3000–3020.

Mansilla-Fernandez, J. M. (2017). *Numbers, European Economy: Banks, Regulation and the Real Sector*, **3**(2): 31–40.

Philippon, T. (2015). Has the US Finance Industry Become Less Efficient? On the theory and measurement of financial intermediation. *The American Economic Review*, **105**(4): 1408–1438.

Stulz, R. M. (2019). FinTech, BigTech, and the Future of Banks. *Journal of Applied Corporate Finance*, **31**(4): 86–97.

Salisbury, I. (2016). Lending Club's CEO Has Left and its Stock has Plunged. Should Lender Bail Out? *Time*. https://finance.yahoo.com/news/lending-club-ceo-left-stock-130040115.html.

Welltrado (2018). Global blockchain-backed loans marketplace ICO, *White Paper*.

https://doi.org/10.1142/9781786349507_0019

Chapter 19

Impact of Fintech on the Level of Competition in the EU Banking Sector*

Małgorzata Pawłowska[†] **and Aleksandra Staniszewska**
Collegium of Management and Finance, Warsaw School of Economics, Aleja Niepodległosci 162, 02-554 Warsaw
[†]*malgorzata.pawlowska@sgh.waw.pl*

19.1 Introduction

Nowadays, we are observing the ongoing revolution of the financial world. Entities creating new business models based on Fintech (including technology based on distributed ledger or artificial intelligence) have completely redefined the way consumers meet their financial needs (Blakstad & Allen, 2018; Nicoletti, 2017; Swain, 2019). In the era of a dynamically changing world, the younger generation of consumers is receptive and open to digitization, freely using innovative solutions within electronic channels that allow remote access to financial services (the internet, mobile devices). For the first time in history, bank clients do not have to visit a counter to conduct transactions and/or receive service. It has become possible for customers to proceed with their transfers, loans, and purchases of

*The chapter has benefited from valuable comments and discussions of participants in 4th Vietnam Symposium in Banking and Finance VSBF2019 Conference, Vietnam Hanoi.

investment products without the physical bank serving as an intermediary. Although digitalization is not a new factor to the financial markets (Dermine, 2016), the time required to pursue innovation has shortened. The financial markets have sped up with the pace of operations and flow of information (IMF, 2017). However, digital financial services became more convenient to not only younger generations but also traditional clients. Similarly, on the one hand, we observe that banks became bigger and bigger, which led to an increase the concentration of the EU banking sector (Laeven *et al.*, 2016; Pawłowska, 2016), and, on the other hand made space for new entrants into the financial services, including Fintech firms that could in turn affect the degree of concentration and contestability in financial services, with both potential benefits and risks for financial stability. Furthermore, the global financial crisis of 2008 has created interest in the issue of competition among banks — in both its assessment as well as its determinants. New technologies are one of the determinants. However, despite the growing number of studies on the development of the Fintech sector, there is still a lack of specific research on how the above changes affect competition levels and how to properly measure this phenomenon. Financial innovation may trigger widespread instability, which is why in academic research the balance between the costs and benefits of competition in the industry is still an open issue (Thakor, 2011).

The aim of this chapter is to investigate the impact of Fintech on the level of competition in the European Union (EU) banking sector. Additionally, the authors attempt to isolate the channels of the impact of new Fintech technologies on the level of competition in the financial market. Based on panel data analysis, we examined the following main hypothesis H0: *Despite the increase in concentration and the emergence of larger and larger banks, the development of new technologies does not cause a decrease in the level of competition in the EU banking sector.*

Three supporting hypotheses:

H1: *New technologies have a positive impact on the profitability of banks.*
H2: *Concentration negatively affects profitability.*
H3: *New technologies have a positive impact on competition between banks in the EU.*

The empirical results of measuring competition and Fintech factors in the EU banking sector presented in this chapter concern the period of 2013–2018. We have chosen this time frame due to the rapid emergence of Fintech solutions in the banking market. For competition measures, we used the Lerner Index. We have developed the regression model linking Fintech factors with the banking sector's traditional data. Fintech factors embraced development of electronic transfers, e-money, and the functionality of ATMs. Banking sector data includes the performance of banks in the European Union. The chapter is a further development of the research on competition in the banking sector provided by Navaretti, Calzolari and Pazzolo (2017) where the bottom line is that "*FinTechs enhance competition in financial markets, provide services that traditional financial institutions do less efficiently or do not do at all, and widen the pool of users of such services*" (Navaretti, Calzolari & Pazzolo, 2017, p. 9).

This chapter is organized as follows. The second part is a literature review concerning Fintech and the competition in the banking sector. The third part presents data and empirical models. The fourth part presents the results of the analysis based on the panel data. The summary provides an overview of the empirical results and the conclusions that we made.

19.2 Literature Review

19.2.1 *Fintech*

After the 2008 financial crisis, new technologies have become a leading factor in the transformation of the financial sector on a global scale (Blakstad & Allen, 2018; Jagtiani *et al.*, 2018; Nicoletti, 2017; Scardovi, 2017). The Merriam Webster Dictionary defines Fintech as "products and companies that employ newly developed digital and online technologies in the banking and financial services industries". Fintech is a sector that consists of companies that base activities (business models) on technologies and ICT solutions, creating services to meet the needs of financial services for clients in a more effective and friendly way. The sector includes supervised entities (e.g. banks, payment institutions, insurance companies, investment companies) and non-supervised entities (often start-ups using innovative tools or using innovative business models), even outside the financial sector. Another definition given by the Financial Stability Board (Bofondi & Gobbi, 2017) is that Fintech organizes activities in five broad categories: (i) payments, clearing and settlement; (ii) deposit, lending and capital raising; (iii) insurance; (iv) investment management; and (v) market support. These five classes cover virtually the entire spectrum of services provided by traditional financial institutions. New Fintech companies are threatening market shares and profit margins of the incumbents in virtually all business areas. A similar approach is taken by Bloomberg analysts (Robinson & Verhage, 2018) where Fintech is particularly present in the following six areas:

(i) peer-to-peer lenders such as Finding Circle, Lending Club, and Venmo. Before the technological revolution, banks and the traditional capital market dominated matching, borrowers with investors;
(ii) crowdfunding platforms such as Indiegogo and GoFundMe. These platforms help small entrepreneurs and social enterprises raise capital for activities, which previously was also reserved for small bank loans;
(iii) blockchain applications created to process transactions in cryptocurrencies. Before the cryptocurrency era, it was the regulated banking sector that provided security for the transactions. Blockchain is a free database that gives opportunity for other players besides banks to enter this market;
(iv) robot-advising like Giant Black Rock and Scalable Capital that use algorithms to adjust portfolios in line with clients' preferences. Before the Fintech revolution, portfolio advising was mostly reserved for licensed investment advisors in banks or investment fund companies. Fintech allows computers to step into the shoes of highly educated and well-paid investment advisors;
(v) mobile payments like PayPal and TransferWise let people transfer money around the world in any currencies from their phones or computers with much lower fees and shorter wait times than in banks;
(vi) traditional insurance companies are investing in insurance start-ups, which aim to shorten the time of life insurance purchases

from weeks into minutes. Insurance companies are also starting to use platforms to ensure fast and effective pay-outs of insurance in the case of insured events.

For the banking sector, Fintech opens new fields of competitiveness. It brings both positive and negative factors that may influence bank operations, especially in money transfers and credit. A positive factor may list chances to increase efficiencies and profit margins. As a negative factor, Fintech companies deprive banks from clients that seek cheaper and faster solutions for borrowing, transferring, and investment advisements. According to Vikram Pandit, a former Citigroup Inc. chief executive officer, technology may replace about 30% of banking jobs by 2023 (Pandit, 2017). Ernst and Young's 2018 Global Banking Outlook report states that the adoption of Fintech providers for money transfer and payment services rose from 18% in 2015 to 50% in 2017. This is why banks started to fight to maintain this market and enforced greater IT investments. Forty-two percent of banks expect rising technology budgets to have a very positive impact on IT, more so than any other banking function. Sixty-two percent of banks expect to become digitally mature or digital leaders by 2020 (Ernst and Young, 2018). Thirty-seven percent of banks, on average, expect to develop new technologies in-house. Broad research on the competitiveness in the Fintech credit and banking sector is presented by Claessens *et al.* (2018). One of the main findings is that the size of Fintech credit is negatively related to the competitiveness of its banking system and the stringency of its banking regulations. Another finding about Fintech and competitiveness in the banking sector was made by Thakor (2011). It was observed that more competitive financial systems (with lower entry barriers) developed greater incentives for innovation. More innovative financial systems are prone to financial crises. Taken together, these two findings implicate that greater competitiveness resulting from Fintech solutions jeopardizes the stability of financial markets.

Financial innovation triggers widespread instability, which is why in academic research the balance between the costs and benefits of competition in the industry is still an open issue (Thakor, 2011). Therefore, while the financial stability implications of Fintech have generally been judged to be small because of their relatively small size, this could change quickly with deeper involvement of the large technology providers. It is also possible that the fairly rapid move to open banking around the world could change the competitive dynamics in financial services (FSB, 2019).

However, together with growth of Fintech operations its impact on stability of banking sector will be increasing (e.g. Thakor, 2019; Leckow *et al.*, 2017; Frost, 2020). Types of barriers to entry in the banking market are changing. Regulations allow Fintech providers to join the market while some of the services are reserved for banks. As a rule, large closed networks reduce opportunities for competition. Theoretically, if the full range of services offered by banks is available for new parties, the competition will be forced to adopt new technologies, i.e. old financial institutions will have to adopt these to improve their service and reduce costs (He *et al.*, 2017). However, the key point in the discussion on Fintech impact on banking sector was made by Thakor (2019, p. 12). Despite the ongoing Fintech revolution and the increasing adoption of innovation, trust is the factor that distinguishes banks from other providers of financial services.

Furthermore, P2P lending mainly attracts unsecured borrowers. In the long term, banks prefer secured loans over unsecured products, which pushes borrowers without collateral out of the banking loan market (Besanko & Thakor, 1987). A wider range of lenders affects banking stability. Usually, more competition means lower margins, which leads to attraction with riskier assets (Besanko & Thakor, 1993). However, another argument (Boyd & De Nicolo, 2005) states that in a highly competitive market and low borrowing cost environment, the borrowers have low incentives to engage in riskier projects, thereby supporting the financial stability of banks. Probably, specific banking markets and particular institutions deal differently with growing competition from P2P lenders and Fintech pressure. Depending on size, capital, regulations, and moment of business cycle, banks benefit from or are at a disadvantage from the Fintech sector. Goetz (2018) presents research where lowering entry barriers on lending market increased competition and improved profitability and, therefore, stability and asset quality. Competition drives efficiency and stops from overlending. Rau (2020) proves that markets with high respect of law, low entry barriers, and high profitability of financial intermediaries offer higher volumes of alternative finance, especially P2P lending. Navaretti *et al.* (2017) shows that countries with low bank regulation measured with World Bank index have higher Fintech investments. Such a situation is also driven by the factor that regulations encourage new e-bank players to operate on such markets. For example, British Authorities (FCA) launch new license models for Fintech banks. Such regulations lead to reduction in the concertation and increase in the competition in the British banking sector. Claessens *et al.* (2018) found higher fintech credit volumes for those countries where specific licensing regulations attract new fintech players to enter the market.

The superior role of Fintech innovations is changing the financial sector into a more inclusive and efficient one that has positive impact on economic growth. Around 1.7 bn adults report lack of access to bank accounts (World Bank, 2018). For developing countries without infrastructure and broad bank chains, Fintech solutions on smartphones give opportunities for safe and reliable economic cooperation between distant parties. Fintech also solves the problem of expensive transfers cross-border for families engaged in work in different jurisdictions. Frost (2020, p. 6) suggest that "Fintech is growing where the current financial system is not meeting the demand for financial services". Digital innovations have a much shorter life cycle than other type of innovations. In fact, what was innovative last year becomes the new standard after 12 months. Only well-capitalized institutions can take the challenge in such battle. For small banks, becoming a Fintech leader is out of reach. Instead, innovative financial services providers enter the market rapidly (Dapp, 2014). Fintech adoption proceeds rapidly on the markets where banking sectors are concentrated and relatively uncompetitive. In such a high margin environment, banks reach higher margin and hence are more profitable (Frost, 2020, p. 7). As a result, the entrance of new Fintech players increases efficiency, lowers cost of financial services, and increases competition.

19.2.2 *Competition in the banking sector*

There are two major schools of thought in the methodology of assessing competition among banks: the structural approach and the non-structural approach (Bikker & Spierdijk, 2017; Vieves, 2016). The structural approach is based on the more conventional views of the relationship between competition and market structure. This approach embraces the structure-conduct-performance paradigm (SCP) and the efficiency hypothesis, as well as a number of formal approaches. The two most common non-formal structural approaches measure the impact of concentration on competition. The SCP paradigm (relating structure and conduct to performance) would suggest that more concentrated markets tend to be more collusive. The efficiency hypothesis, developed by Demsetz (1973), offers a competing explanation of the relationship between market structure and performance. This theory states that if banks enjoy a higher degree of efficiency than competitors, they can increase shareholder value or will gain market share by reducing prices. Both in the SCP and ESH models, measures of the concentration level (i.e. CR_K[1] and Herfindahl-Hirschman indexes — HHI[2]) are used to measure competition between banks (Bikker, 2004, p. 63). The result (performance) in the interactive SCP model, which is a response to market structure and technology, shows whether it is possible for new companies to enter the market. Fintech can also be considered as an opportunity to enter the market through new distribution channels (Fig. 19.1).

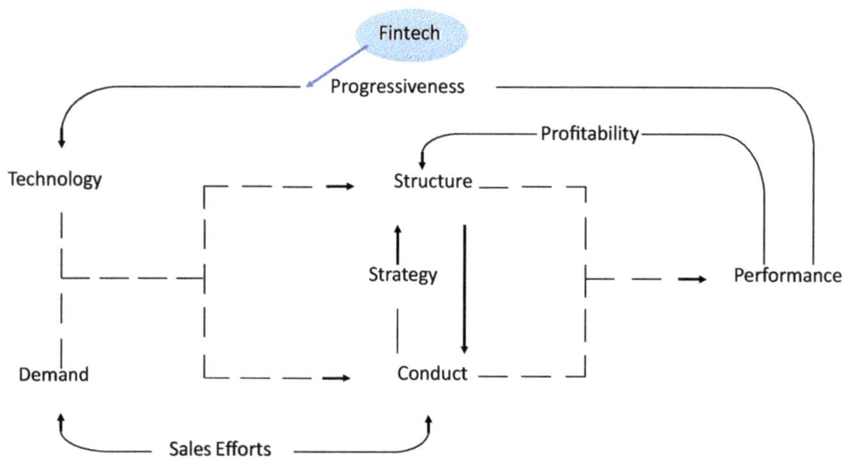

Fig. 19.1. SCP model with Fintech.
Source: Own elaboration based on Martin (1989), p. 19.

[1]The share of the five largest credit institutions in total assets (CR5).

[2]Herfindahl-Hirschman Index is defined as the sum of the squares of the market share of assets of individual banks (HHI).

In reaction to the theoretical and empirical deficiencies of structural models, non-structural models of competitive behaviour have been developed based on the new analytical theory of competition (New Empirical Industrial Organization — NEIO). According to NEIO, the intensity of competition should be assessed taking into account both the degree of concentration and the scope of entry into a given branch, defined by dynamic entry barriers. Therefore, applying exclusively the structural measures of concentration to gauge the level of competition has been abandoned. Finally, most of the measures of competition (i.e. Lerner Index proposed by Lernet, 1934, proposed by Boone, 2008) allow measuring the level of competition in the market for all banking products, while the level of competition in individual market segments may be varied. A significant issue regarding the banking sector, widely described in the literature, is the relationship between the consolidation of the banking system and competition. However, the general relationship indicates that a greater market share determines greater market power and less competition is not obvious. Many authors note that the intensity of competition may be different for markets with the same level of concentration. Referring to empirical analyses of the relationship between concentration growth and competition, many papers state that in the banking sectors of developed economies there are no clear links between increases in the system concentration and the level of its competition (Claessens & Laeven, 2004). However, while analyzing the volatility of CR5 concentration indicators in the EU banking sector, one may observe that for the periods 2004–2018 these indicators show an increasing trend. The increase in concentration ratios was fueled mainly by mergers and acquisitions carried out by large banks (Fig. 19.2).

It should be noted that empirical studies on the direction of changes in the level of competition over time in the EU generally have shown increased competition before the crisis despite increased concentration in the banking sectors of Europe (see, e.g. Clerides *et al.*, 2013; Weill, 2013; Bikker and Leuvensteijn, 2014). Furthermore, it should be noted that the competitors for banks in the credit market are not only banks. Competitors also consist of brokerage houses, companies (buyers of trade credit), real estate developers, and Fintech sector companies providing credit services. However, it should be noted that we distinguish two types of Fintech companies here: banks using Fintech technologies and companies included in the Fintech sector (including start-ups) that offer credit products without being banks.

It is worth highlighting that the presented measures of the level of competition after the financial crisis point to different directions of competition development. The market opens very rapidly for new and old players. Ernst and Young (2019) estimate global consumer adoption of Fintech services at 64%. On average, 75% customers use Fintech payment services. The leading markets are China, India, and South Africa. The extreme growth of these numbers appeared between 2015–2019. Fintech firms put competitive pressure on traditional banks, which is why banks are starting to increase investments in new technologies. Based on the press releases of Banco Santander, JP Morgan, Bank of America, and Wells Fargo, only these four banks planned to invest over USD $50 billion in digital development (Santander, 2019; Shevlin, 2019). Competition from newly established banks is also growing. Digital banks like Volt Bank, Xinja Bank, and Monzo obtained a full Authorized Deposit-Taking Institution license (APRA, 2019a; APRA 2019b; FCA website). According to the Monzo online press release, the digital Monzo concept gained over three million customers, which is one out of every 20 adults in the UK.

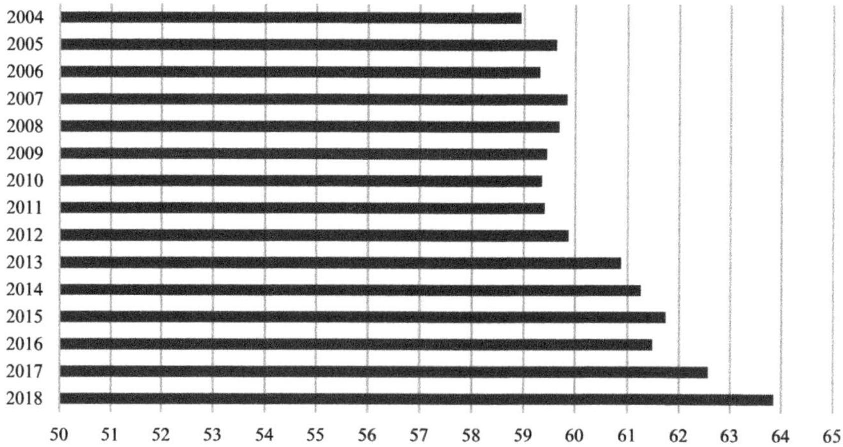

Fig. 19.2. CR5 in EU banking sector (average %) for the periods 2004–2018. *Source*: ECB and own calculation.

It should be noted that the financial crisis brought about a number of regulatory measures in the entire EU (CRD IV).[3] In addition, a directive was implemented in the banking sector for retail banks to standardize the payment services market according to the Payment Services Directive (PSD2).[4] For investment banks and asset managers, the Markets in Financial Instruments Directive (MiFID2)[5] was implemented, which is the basis of an EU regulation aimed at improving the competitiveness of EU financial markets and protecting investors by creating a single market for investment services and activities, in addition to ensuring a high level of harmonization.

19.3 Data and Models Specification

In order to estimate the impact of Fintech on the performance of the banking sector in EU countries, we take annual country-level data. The (unbalanced) panel covers the period 2013–2018 and shows that after reviewing the data for errors, we are left with 420 observations. There are two types of variables in the model (inside and outside of the banking sector). The variables from inside the banking sector come from payment statistics and electronic banking data from the European Central Bank. The variables from outside the banking sector concern Fintech credit and the KBW Nasdaq Financial Technology Index (KFTX).[6] Fintech credit is defined as all credit activity facilitated by electronic (online) platforms that are not operated by

---

[3]Directive 2013/36/EU of the European Parliament and of the Council of 26 June 2013 on the conditions for the admission of credit institutions to operations and prudential supervision of credit institutions and investment firms, amending Directive 2002/87/EC and repealing Directives 2006/48/EC and 2006/49/EC and Regulation (EU) No. 575/2013 of the European Parliament and of the Council of 26 June 2013 on prudential requirements for credit institutions and investment firms, amending Regulation (EU) No. 648/2012.

[4]Directive (EU) 2015/2366 of the European Parliament and of the Council of 25 November 2015 on payment services in the internal market (Payment Services Directive 2).

[5]Markets in Financial Instruments Directive II, Directive 2014/65/EU of the European Parliament and of the Council of 15 May 2014 on markets in financial instruments and amending Directive 2002/92/EC and Directive 2011/61/EU.

[6]The KFTX Nasdaq Financial Technology Index is designed to track the performance of financial technology companies that are publicly traded in the US Since financial technology companies are not easily categorized into a single

commercial banks. This approach is consistent with that taken in CGFS-FSB (2017). Fintech credit data comes from Claessens *et al.* (2018). Annual country-level data and macroeconomic data are collected from the Eurostat, the World Bank, and Payment Statistics from Statistical Data Warehouse ECB.[7]

In order to verify our hypothesis, we estimated two models: the first model examines the impact of financial new technology (Fintech) and concertation measures on profitability of banks and the second model examines the impact of financial new technology (Fintech) on competition. In order to verify the impact of Fintech technology on competition, we conducted a panel data multivariate cross-country regression analysis for a sample of 28 EU economies, based on the following baseline specification:

$$Y_{c,t} = \gamma_c + \mu_t + \beta_1 GDP_{c,t} + \beta_2 X_{c,t} + \alpha_2 MS_{c,t} + \alpha_3 Fintech_{c,t} + \varepsilon_{c,t} \quad (1)$$

where $Y_{c,t}$ is the profitability of banks in country c in year t, which denotes the return on assets ratio $ROA_{c,t}$ and also the return on equity (ROE) to determine the robustness.

As *independent variables* we define the following:

- $GDP_{c,t}$ is a country GDP growth;
- $MS_{c,t}$ is *market structure* indicator;
- $X_{c,t}$ is a vector of control variables that captures the bank performance;
- $Fintech$ is a vector of variables that capture the new technology.

As $X_{c,t}$ is a vector of control variables that capture bank performance, we consider the following:

---

industry group, index eligibility is not limited to securities within a particular industry classification. Securities eligible for index inclusion leverage technology to deliver financial products and services. Their distribution is nearly exclusively electronic, with limited to no "bricks and mortar", and their revenue mix is predominantly fee-based. The Index began on July 18, 2016, at a base value of 1000. Earlier listings are based on back-tests conducted by the stock exchange.

[7]Data available online at https://sdw.ecb.europa.eu/reports.do?node$=$10000 0760.

- the *Tier1* ratio (core-capital to risk-weighted assets, $Tier1_{ct}$) is an indicator of a bank's risk behaviour (the higher the capital ratio, the greater the risk aversion);
- the size is a log of total assets of banking sector (Total_assets_{ct}) for country$c$ in year.

As *market structure* indicators, we consider the following:

- the concentration of the banking sector, which was defined as a share of the five largest credit institutions in total assets for country$c$ in year ($CR5_{ct}$);
- the Herfindahl-Hirschman Index for assets (the sum of the squares of the market share of individual banks) for country c in year t (HHI_{ct}).

As *Fintech* used for this panel analysis from outside the banking sector, we consider the following:

- KFTX index ($KFTX_{c,t}$);
- Fintech credit[8] for country c in year t.

As Fintech variables from inside the banking sector come from Payment Statistics from ECB,[9] we consider the following:

- ATMs located in the reported country[10] for country$c$ in year t ($ATM_{c,t}$);
- credit transfers initiated electronically[11] for country$c$ in year t ($eCredit_{c,t}$);

[8]Due to large lack of data, this variable turned out to be insignificant in this research.

[9]Data in national currency is recalculated into euro using daily ECB reference exchange rate applicable to each transaction, or, if this is not possible, the average ECB reference exchange rate for the period for all transactions.

[10]This variable embraces ATMs both with a cash withdrawal function and with a credit transfer function.

[11]This variable covers payment service that allows the payer to instruct the institution holding its account to transfer funds to the beneficiary. It is a payment order or a sequence of payment orders made for the purpose of placing funds at the disposal of the beneficiary.

- value of card payments with cards issued Payment Service Providers[12] in bln EUR for countryc in year t ($Card_{c,t}$);
- all terminals provided by Payment Service Providers[13] for country c in year t ($Poster_{c,t}$).

As Fintech variables from inside the banking sector come from Eurostat,[14] we consider the following:

- individuals using the Internet for internet banking for country c in year t ($Indiv\_u\_Internet_{c,t}$).[15]

In the second model, all explanatory variables are defined in the same way as in the first model except the dependent/explained variable $Y_{c,t}$. In the second model $Y_{c,t}$. is defined as the competition between banks.

As competition we consider the following:

- the Lerner Index ($Lerner_{ct}$) for country c in year t. [16]

Table 19A.1 of the statistical Appendix presents summary statistics of key selected variables. Tables 19A.2–19A.3 of the statistical Appendix present the results of pooled OLS panel regression (Ordinary Last Squares) using two models. In Table 19A.2, a positive and significant coefficient α_3 is found for the first model for the following variables: ATMs located in the reported country (columns [1,2]), KFTX index (columns [1,2,4]) and individuals using the Internet (columns [1,2,3]). It means that *New technologies* had a positive and significant influence on the profitability of EU banks. In Table 19A.3, a positive and significant coefficient α_3 is found for the second

[12] This variable covers all payments made with cards issued in reporting country regardless of the cardholder's residency or the location of the payment.

[13] This variable covers all terminals provided by resident PSPs located in reporting country and terminals located in the reporting country irrespective of whether or not the provider is resident in the country.

[14] Available online on https://data.worldbank.org/indicator/IT.NET.USER.ZS on 20 March 2020.

[15] Individuals aged 16 to 74 using the internet for internet banking within the last 3 months before the survey (%). Internet banking includes electronic transactions with a bank for payment or for looking up account information.

[16] Data was collected from the World Bank.

model for the following variables: ATMs located in the reported country (column [1]) and KFTX index (columns [2]). It means that *New technologies* had a positive and significant influence on the impact on competition between banks in the EU. For two models, negative and significant coefficient α_2 is found. It means that concentration — measured in terms of the share of the five largest banks' total assets (CR5) and in terms of the Herfindahl-Hirschman Index — had a negative and significant influence on the performance of EU banks.

The first model allowed for positive verification of supporting hypotheses H1 and H2. The second model allowed for the verification of the hypotheses H2 and H3. The above supporting hypotheses allowed us to verify the main hypothesis that despite the increase in concentration and the emergence of larger and larger banks, the development of new technologies does not cause a decrease in the level of competition in the EU banking sector. Furthermore, the result of two models would be very important for macroprudential policy. First, on characteristic of fintech borrowers and incentives for choosing fintech credit over banking lending. Second, on lending standards in Fintech platforms. Combining the results of these two investigations would shed light on competitive edge of Fintech providers over traditional banking services.

19.4 Conclusion

The level of competition in the banking sector is influenced by a variety of factors. Internal factors are supervision regulations and the presence of national and foreign capital. External factors come with globalization, which brings solutions that are not limited to particular jurisdictions. Market activity in times of turbulent socio-economic reality is becoming a big challenge for mature enterprises. The development of new technologies is both an opportunity for the chance to expand, reduce the cost of doing business, and develop new market niches. Companies with an established position must constantly learn to function in new realities. Banks experience great pressure from innovative Fintech solutions. Banks have to compete with well-known local or international players from the same sectors, and also with "no borders" and "sky is the limit" IT ideas. For regulated and traditionally run enterprises, such a game is unprecedently difficult. Does it mean that banks will fail in this IT revolution?

Taking into account that public trust is associated with banking markets, there will always be a place for supervised, regulated banks. However, fields of service and levels of profit margins will probably turn to Fintech inventors.

This chapter attempted to determine the impact of Fintech sector development on the level of competition in the EU banking sector. To this end, an attempt was made to isolate the channels of the impact of new Fintech technologies on the level of competition in the market. On the one hand, the consolidation of the banking sector leads to increased concentration and decreased competition. On the other hand, the Fintech sector stimulates the increase of competition not only in the banking market but also in the entire financial sector. It should be noted that the impact of the Fintech sector is not easy to estimate due to the limitations of the measures of competition and the lack of comparable data. Our findings align with those of Navaretti *et al.* (2017). Based on panel data analysis, we find that despite the ongoing consolidation of the European banking sector, the Fintech revolution sparks competition in the market. The greatest constraint of the research was the choice, collection, and unification of the data set. Though most of the data comes from the European Central Bank and Payment Statistics, there are still lots of blackouts in the records. This confirms that the procedure of data monitoring in this area is still underdeveloped in many EU countries.

However, currently Fintech sector faces overwhelming pressure from rising costs of capital. Most of the companies from this sector are in the initial or developing stage of growth. As most of them require outside financing, the cost of capital is crucial for their growth perspective. On the one hand, coronavirus lockdowns and vanishing liquidity on the capital markets increase the cost of capital and reduce access to financing. On the other hand, brick banks and other financial institutions are forced to rely on Fintech solutions more than before the coronavirus era. Taking into account that in such unpredictable conditions Fintech offers solutions for distant communication, evaluation in healthcare, and finance, some of the Fintech companies might develop much faster than others. For example, in UK, Covid Credit is an emerging, quick tool evaluating bank account holders to check if they are entitled for compensation due to Coronavirus lockdowns (Fintech Futures, 2020). Evaluations are based on open banking, Fintech solutions, and steps taken by governments to stop spreading the virus.

The next step in the research should be to identify in detail the channels of the Fintech sector's impact on the level of competition, while allowing for an empirical measurement of this phenomenon. Therefore, the current article should be treated as a foundation for further empirical work. Allowing for proper measurement of the phenomenon perhaps requires the construction of new measures.

Appendix

Table 19A.1. Summary statistics of the main variables in the model of EU banking sector.

VARIABLES	Obs	Mean	Std. Dev.	MIN	MAX
Total assets	110	12.82669	1.852798	10.0031	16.315
CR5	140	62.02853	18.18167	26.18	97.28
HHI	140	0.13645	0.1567264	0.0245	1.3
ROA	112	0.6116071	0.7828621	−2.55	3.04
ROE	112	7.148288	8.340306	−29.28	24.07
Lerner	119	0.3031092	0.271226	−1.75	0.71
Tier1	113	17.39655	4.179684	10.89	35.21
GDP	112	2.975	2.781292	−1.4	25.1
KFTX	136	1128.053	231.6382	849	1434
ATM	134	162.6296	237.0836	2.07	867.67
Poster	118	4823.063	6557.318	0	31711.74
eCredit	123	89139.57	275248.3	196.4	1546847
Card	130	699.8477	1721.944	2.4	12470.4
Indiv_u_Internet	131	51.22901	23.34542	4	90

Source: Own calculations on the basis of ECB, World Bank, Eurostat data. This table provides summary statistics (mean and standard deviation (Std. Dev.) for all variables in the model. Data are observed yearly from 2013–2018.

Table 19A.2. Empirical results for the *first model* (ROA).

VARIABLES	(1) ROA	(2) ROA	(3) ROA	(4) ROA
Total assets	-0.32^{***}	-0.32^{***}	-0.31^{***}	-0.23^{**}
	(0.0885)	(0.0755)	(0.0807)	(0.1075)
KFTX	0.001^{*}	0.001^{**}	0.001	0.001^{**}
	(0.0003)	(0.0003)	(0.0003)	(0.0003)
ATM	0.001^{*}	0.001^{**}	0.001	—
	(0.0006)	(0.0005)	(0.0007)	—
CR5	-0.01^{*}	-0.01^{**}	—	−0.01
	(0.0057)	(0.0048)	—	(0.0076)
Tier1	0.02	0.02	0.03	0.02
	(0.0224)	(0.0201)	(0.0216)	(0.0237)
Indiv_u_Internet	0.02^{***}	0.02^{***}	0.02^{***}	—
	(0.0049)	(0.0042)	(0.0043)	—
Card	0.001	—	—	0.001^{***}
	(0.0001)	—	—	(0.0002)
GDP	0.02	0.03	0.05	−0.00
	(0.0247)	(0.0237)	(0.0449)	(0.0507)
HHI	—	—	-3.45^{**}	—
	—	—	(1.4636)	—
Poster	—	—	0.001	0.001
	—	—	(0.0000)	(0.0000)
eCredit	—	—	—	-0.001^{***}
	—	—	—	(0.0000)
Constant	3.23^{**}	3.25^{***}	2.65^{**}	3.05^{*}
	(1.3650)	(1.1781)	(1.1666)	(1.7818)
Observations	98	98	91	86
Number of id	25	25	25	24

Source: Own calculations. Standard errors in parentheses, $^{***}p < 0.01$, $^{**}p < 0.05$, $^{*}p < 0.1$.

Table 19A.3. Empirical results for the *second model* (Lerner).

VARIABLES	(1) Lerner	(2) Lerner	(3) Lerner	(4) Lerner
Total assets	-0.17^{***}	-0.13^{***}	-0.14^{***}	-0.13^{***}
	(0.0274)	(0.0321)	(0.0302)	(0.0247)
KFTX	0.001	-0.001^{*}	−0.001	−0.001
	(0.0001)	(0.0001)	(0.0001)	(0.0001)
ATM	0.001^{***}	0.001	−0.001	—
	(0.0004)	(0.0002)	(0.0003)	—
CR5	-0.01^{***}	-0.01^{***}	—	-0.01^{***}
	(0.0019)	(0.0023)	—	(0.0021)
Tier1	-0.02^{*}	-0.03^{***}	-0.03^{***}	-0.03^{**}
	(0.0106)	(0.0121)	(0.0111)	(0.0118)
Indiv_u_Internet	0.001	−0.001	−0.001	—
	(0.0016)	(0.0016)	(0.0015)	—
Card	-0.00^{***}	—	—	0.00
	(0.0001)	—	—	(0.0008)
GDP	0.02	0.03	0.02	0.03
	(0.0191)	(0.0230)	(0.0220)	(0.0200)
HHI	—	—	-3.80^{***}	—
	—	—	(0.7938)	—
Poster	—	—	0.001	0.001
	—	—	(0.0000)	(0.0000)
eCredit	—	—	—	−0.001
	—	—	—	(0.0000)
Constant	3.16^{***}	3.35^{***}	3.05^{***}	3.11^{***}
	(0.4014)	(0.5015)	(0.4290)	(0.4642)
Observations	98	98	91	86
Number of id	25	25	25	24

Source: Own calculations. Standard errors in parentheses, $^{***}p < 0.01$, $^{**}p < 0.05$, $^{*}p < 0.1$.

References

Australian Prudential Regulation Authority (APRA) (2019a). *APRA grants new authorised deposit-taking institution license to volt bank*, media release, 22 January, https://www.apra.gov.au/news-and-publications/apra-grants-new-authorised-deposit-taking-institution-licence-to-volt-bank, accessed 20 May 2020.

Australian Prudential Regulation Authority (APRA) (2019b). APRA grants new authorised deposit-taking institution license to Xinja Bank, media release, 9 September, accessed 20 May 2020.

Besanko, D. and Thakor, A. V. (1987). Collateral and rationing: Sorting equilibria in mono-polistic and competitive credit markets. *International Economic Review* **28**(3): 671–689.

Besanko, D. and Thakor, A. V. (1993). Relationship banking, deposit insurance and bank portfolio choice. In: Vives, X. and Mayer, C. (Eds.), *Capital Markets and Financial Intermediation*. Cambridge University Press, pp. 292–318.

Bikker, J. A. and Leuvensteijn, M. (2014). *A new measure of competition in the financial industry*. Routledge, London.

Bikker, J. A. (2004). *Competition and efficiency in a unified European banking market*. Books. Edward Elgar, Cheltenham.

Blakstad, S. and Allen, R. (2018). *Fintech Revolution*, Jeremy Williams.

Bofondi, M. and Gobbi, G. (2017). The big promise of FinTech. *European Economy — Banks, Regulation and the Real Sector, 2*, https://www.google.com/url?sa=t&rct=j&q=&esrc=s&source=web&cd=1&cad=rja&uact=8&ved=2ahUKEwi25_KW1_HmAhXLxaYKHZujDUQQFjAAegQIARAC&url=http%3A%2F%2Feuropean-economy.eu%2Fwp-content%2Fuploads%2F2018%2F01%2FEE_2.2017-2.pdf&usg=AOvVaw0-JoPn8cR3rwnd7X-Xcz0Y, accessed 20 May 2020.

Boone, J. (2008). A new way to measure competition. *Economic Journal*, **118**: 1245–1261.

Boyd, J. and Nicolol, G. D. (2005). The theory of bank risk taking and competition revisited. *Journal of Finance*, **60**(3): 1329–1343.

Clerides, S., Delis, M. D., and Kokas, S. (2013). *A new data set on bank competition* (No. 08-2013). University of Cyprus Working Papers in Economics.

Claessens, P. and Laeven, L. (2004). What drives bank competition? Same international evidence. *Journal of Money, Credit, and Banking*, **36**(3): 564–583.

Claessens, S., Frost, J., Turner, G., and Zhu, F. (2018). Fintech credit markets around the world: size, drivers and policy issues. *BIS Quarterly Review*, **23**(September): 29–49.

Dapp, T. (2014). Fintech — The digital (r)evolution in the financial sector Algorithm-based banking with the human touch. *Deutsche Bank Research*, 11 November. Available online: https://www.dbresearch.com/PROD/RPS_EN-PROD/Fintech_%E2%80%93_The_digital_%28r%29evolution_in_the_financia/RPS_EN_DOC_VIEW.calias?rwnode=PROD0000000000435629&ProdCollection=PROD0000000000451941, accessed 20 May 2020.

Demsetz, H. (1973). Industry structure, market rivalry, and public policy. *Journal of Law and Economics*, **16**: 1–9.

Dermine, J. (2016). Digital banking and market disruption: A sense of déjà vu? *Financial Stability Review*, Bank of France, 20, April.

Ernst and Young (2018). Global Banking Outlook 2018. https://www.google.com/url?sa=t&rct=j&q=&esrc=s&source=web&cd=1&cad=rja&uact=8&ved=2ahUKEwiM0dSRz-bkAhX2xcQBHfojDpwQFjAAegQIARAC&url=https%3A%2F%2Fwww.ey.com%2FPublication%2FvwLUAssets%2Fey-global-banking-outlook-2018%2F%24File%2Fey-global-banking-outlook-2018.pdf&usg=AOvVaw1nIO_0jJfeWheibhdOrZHc, accessed 20 May 2020.

Ernst and Young (2019). Fintech Adoption Index 2019. https://www.google.com/url?sa=t&rct=j&q=&esrc=s&source=web&cd=1&ved=2ahUKEwiJ0b2mzebkAhUnz6YKHaxcBwkQFjAAegQIBBAC&url=https%3A%2F%2Fassets.ey.com%2Fcontent%2Fdam%2Fey-sites%2Fey-com%2Fen_gl%2Ftopics%2Fbanking-and-capital-markets%2Fey-global-fintech-adoption-index.pdf&usg=AOvVaw1IUFvCGWApYJMFXm3H4iUG, accessed 6 January 2020.

European Central Bank (2019). Payment Statistics, Full report. https://sdw.ecb.europa.eu/reports.do?node=1000004051, accessed 20 May 2020.

Eurostat, Individuals using the internet for internet banking, https://ec.europa.eu/eurostat/tgm/table.do?tab=table&plugin=1&language=en&pcode=tin00099, accessed 20 May 2020.

Financial Conduct Authority (FCA), The Financial Services Register. https://register.fca.org.uk/ShPo_FirmDetailsPage?id=001b000002syvKiAAI, accessed 20 May 2020.

Financial Stability Board (FSB) (2017). Financial stability implications for FinTech. Supervisory and regulatory issues that merit authorities' attention, http://www.fsb.org/wp-content/uploads/R270617.pdf, accessed 6 January 2020.

Financial Stability Board (FSB) (2019). FinTech and market structure in financial services: Market developments and potential financial stability implications, https://www.fsb.org/wp-content/uploads/P140219.pdf, accessed 20 May 2020.

Fintech Futures (2020). Podcast Episode 2 |COVID-19: Is cash still king, https://www.fintechfutures.com/2020/04/what-the-fintech-episode-2-covid-19-is-cash-still-king/ 20 march 2020.

Frost, J. (2020). The economic forces driving fintech adoption across countries. *BIS* Working Papers, No. 838, February.

Goetz, M. R. (2018). Competition and bank stability. *Journal of Financial Intermediation*, **35**: 57–69.

He, D., Leckow, R., Haksar, V., Mancini-Griffoli, T., Jenkinson, N., Kashima, M., and Tourpe, H. F. (2017). Financial Services: Initial Considerations. *IMF Staff Discussion*, June, 17–5, https://www.imf.org/en/Publications/Staff-Discussion-Notes, (2017/06), 16. Available online https://www.imf.org/en/Publications/Staff-Discussion-Notes/Issues/2017/06/16/Fintech-and-Financial-Services-Initial-Considerations-44985, accessed 20 March 2020.

Jagtiani, J. and Lemieux, C. (2018). Do fintech lenders penetrate areas that are underserved by traditional banks. *Federal Reserve Bank of Philadelphia, Working Papers*, March, 18–13.

Lerner, A. (1934). The concept of monopoly and the measurement of monopoly power. *Review of Economic Studies*, **1**(3): 157–175.

Laeven, L., Ratnovski, L., and Tong, H. (2016). Bank size, capital, and systemic risk: Some international evidence. *Journal of Banking & Finance*, **69**: 25–34.

Martin, S. (1989). *Industrial economics, economic analysis and public policy.* New York: Collier Macmillan Publishers London.

Merriam Webster Dictionary, Fintech definition. https://www.merriam-webster.com/dictionary/fintech, accessed 20 May 2020.

Navaretti, G., Calzolari, G., and Pazzolo, A. (2017). Fi ntech and banking. Friends or foes? *European Economy. Banks, Regulation, and the Real Sector, 2*, https://www.google.com/url?sa=t&rct=j&q=&esrc=s&source=web&cd=1&cad=rja&uact=8&ved=2ahUKEwi25_KW1_HmAhXLxaYKHZujDUQQFjAAegQIARAC&url=http%3A%2F%2Feuropean-economy.eu%2Fwp-content%2Fuploads%2F2018%2F01%2FEE_2.2017-2.pdf&usg=AOvVaw0-JoPn8cR3rwnd7X-Xcz0Y, accessed 20 May 2020.

Nicoletti, B. (2017). *The future of FinTech: Integrating finance and technology in financial services.* Palgrave Macmillan.

Pandit, V. (2017). Bloomberg TV interview, 17 October, https://www.bloomberg.com/news/articles/2017-09-13/ex-citi-ceo-pandit-says-30-of-bank-jobs-at-risk-from-technology, accessed 20 May 2020.

Pawłowska, M. (2016). Does the size and market structure of the banking sector have an effect on the financial stability of the European Union? *The Journal of Economic Asymmetries*, **4**: 112–127.
Rau, P. R. (2020). Law, Trust, and the Development of Crowdfunding, available at SSRN: https://ssrn.com/abstract=2989056 or http://dx.doi.org/10.2139/ssrn.2989056, July 1.
Robinson, E. and Verhage, J. (2018). Quicktake Fintech, *Bloomberg Portal*, 26 November, https://www.bloomberg.com/quicktake/financial-technology-companies-disrupt-comfy-banks-quicktake, accessed 6 January 2020.
Santander (2019). Banco Santander accelerates digital transformation and platform strategy to drive growth and higher returns, Press Release 3 April 2019, https://www.santander.com/en/press-room/press-releases/banco-santander-accelerates-digital-transformation-and-platform-strategy-to-drive-growth-and-higher-returns, accessed 20 May 2020.
Shevlin, R. (2019). How much do banks spend on technology? *Forbes*, 1 April https://www.forbes.com/sites/ronshevlin/2019/04/01/how-much-do-banks-spend-on-technology-hint-chase-spends-more-than-all-credit-unions-combined/{#}f182c1e683a0, accessed 20 May 2020.
Scardovi, C. (2017). *Digital transformation in financial services.* Springer, London.
Thakor, A. V. (2011). Incentives to innovate and financial crises. *Journal of Financial Economics*, **103**(1): 130–148.
Thakor, A. V. (2019). Fintech and Banking. *SSRN Electronic Journal*, January, DOI:10.2139/ssm.3332550.
Vieves, X. (2016). *Competition and stability in banking: The role of regulation and competition policy*, Princeton University Press.
Weill, L. (2013). Bank competition in the EU: How has it evolved? *Journal of International Financial Markets*, **26**: 100–112.
World Bank (2018). The Global Findex Database 2017. April.

Legal Acts

Directive 2013/36/EU of the European Parliament and of the Council of 26 June 2013 on access to the activity of credit institutions and the prudential supervision of credit institutions and investment firms, amending Directive 2002/87/EC and repealing

Directives 2006/48/EC and 2006/49/EC as well as Regulation (EU) No 575/2013 of the European Parliament and of the Council of 26 June 2013 on prudential requirements for credit institutions and investment firms and amending Regulation (EU) No 648/2012.

Directive (EU) 2015/2366 of the European Parliament and of the Council of 25 November 2015 on payment services in the internal market (Payment Services Directive 2).

Directive 2014/65/EU of the European Parliament and of the Council of 15 May 2014 on markets in financial instruments and amending Directive 2002/92/EC and Directive 2011/61/EU.

https://doi.org/10.1142/9781786349507_bmatter

Index

A

Abu Dhabi Stock Market, 172
accelerators, 527
accountability, 4, 9, 11, 19, 21
accounting, 259
accounting standards, 352
actual impact, 477
adjusted returns, 233
adjustment cost, 33, 37
adverse (stressed, event or crisis), 173
adverse market circumstances, 174
Agency theory, 363
Airtel, 453
airtime credits, 458
Al Janabi model, 164, 166, 169
algorithmic approach, 509
algorithmic programming, 167
algorithms, 512
alternative assets, 136–138
annual volatility, 173
annualized volatilities, 174
Application Programming Interfaces (APIs), 517, 532
AR(1) processes, 41
Arab countries, 171
artificial intelligence (AI), 165, 184, 509–510, 513–514, 518–519, 521, 523, 532, 534
asset allocation, 164, 179, 183
asset prices, 73, 165
Asset Pricing Model, 131
assets price fluctuation, 62
association, 273
asymmetry, 261, 275
Auray, 29, 42
austerity, 27–28, 47
Ausschuss für Finanzstabilität (Financial Stability Committee), 15
Autoridad Macroprudencial Consejo de Estabilidad Financiera, 15
automated reporting, 475

B

Bahrain, 172
balance sheet, 134
Banca d'Italia, 15
Banco de España, 15
Banco de Portugal, 15
Bank for International Settlements (BIS), 5, 9, 20
Bank of England/Financial Policy Committee, 15
Bank of Greece, 15
Banka Slovenije, 16
bankers, 38
banking, 331
banking services, 482
banking system, 462
banks substantially, 336

Basel Committee of Banking Supervision (BCBS), 5
Basel II, 42, 162, 171
Basel III, 162, 171
BBD's index, 61
beat markets, 125
behavioral finance, 129
beneficial, 54
benefits, 145, 147, 150–151
beta distribution, 39
beta sensitivity coefficient, 173
big data, 165, 184, 509–510, 515, 532
Bigtech, 507, 513, 515, 518, 525
Bitcoin, 427, 430–433, 435, 444, 446
Blockchain, 425, 427–432, 435–444, 446, 509, 515, 521, 527
board, 385, 386–390, 392–395, 397–411
bond markets, 125
borrow, 37
borrowing, 509
borrowing banks, 29, 32, 35
borrowing banks borrow from savings banks, 29
borrowing banks make loans to domestic entrepreneurs, 30
bottom of the pyramid, 457
bottom-up regulation, 472
boundary limits, 170
bribe, 90, 103, 105–107, 110–113, 454
bribe frequency, 104, 112–113
bribe payment, 111
Bulgarian National Bank, 15
Bundesanstalt für Finanzdienstleistungsaufsicht (Financial Supervisory Authority), 15
business cycle, 39
business development, 477
business models, 350
Buterin, Vitalik, 428, 436
buy goods, 464
buy goods and services, 459, 462–463, 465, 467–468

C

cannot cope, 54
capital requirements, 5, 10, 14, 35
Capital Requirements Directive (CRD), 13
Capital Requirements Regulation (CRR), 13
capital-income, 54
capital-income tax, 44, 50
CAPM model, 131
carbon emissions, 131
cashless payments, 464
causal, 263
causality, 268
CDS, 190
CDS market, 207–209
central bank, 9, 16
Central Bank of Cyprus, 15
Central Bank of Ireland, 15
Central Bank of Kenya (CBK), 455–456, 461
Central Bank of Malta, 15
central interface, 475
Ceská národní banka, 15
channels, 255, 260
climate-friendly financial products, 335
closed-form parametric approach, 182
closed-form parametric method, 183
closed-form parametric methodology, 182
closed-form parametric process, 166
closeout horizons, 177
closeout period, 168–169, 177–181
cloud, 523, 534
cloud computing, 510, 519
cloud technology, 514
Cobb–Douglas, 38
coefficients, 273
cognitive constraints, 5–7
coherent measure of risk, 163
cointegration, 147
collectibles, 135–138, 149–150, 152–153

collective action problems, 8
collectors, 136–137, 143, 148–149, 152
Comité du risque systémique (Systemic Risk Committee), 16
Comitetul National pentru Supravegherea Macroprudentială (National Committee for Macroprudential Oversight), 15
commercial banks, 163
commercial interests, 7
Commission de Surveillance du Secteur Financier (Financial Supervisory Authority), 16
committee structure, 11
committees, 388, 399–405, 407–408, 410–411
communicating, 259, 261
competition among banks, 538, 543
competitive, 275
complex mathematical algorithms, 183
compliance, 88, 90, 92–94, 98–100, 102, 114
compulsory, 257
computation algorithms, 184
computational processes, 183
computational techniques, 161, 166, 184
concentration, 538, 544–545, 549, 551
conditional multivariate volatility, 200
conditional variance, 60
conditional volatility, 166
confidence, 59, 72
confidence interval, 162, 172
consolidation, 350
consortium Blockchain, 436, 444
consumer protection, 470
consumption tax, 44
contagion, 138, 147
contemporary risk management, 176
continuum of monopolistically competitive BBs, 35
contract, 257
control of trading risk, 164
control over appropriate instruments for achieving their objectives, 14
conventional emerging market funds, 215
conventional funds, 215, 217, 221
core, 41, 47
core ESG metrics, 345
corporate, 343
corporate conscience, 228
corporate disclosure, 352
Corporate Financial Performance, 337
corporate governance, 286, 293, 295–296, 308, 333, 339, 341, 386–388, 397–398, 402, 407–408
corporate investment, 71
Corporate Social Performance, 337
corporate social responsibility (CSR), 253, 285–286, 288, 290–302, 304, 305, 307, 309–312, 361, 363, 367
corporate social responsibility (CSR) rating, 237
corporate venture capital (CVC), 530, 531, 534
correlation, 192, 272
correlation factors, 162, 167, 178–179, 183
correlation matrices, 167–168
correlation parameters, 178, 180–181
corruptions index, 495
Corsetti, 39
cost, 260
counter-cyclical, 39
countercyclical capital buffer, 13
country boycotts, 228
Covid Credit, 552
credible equilibrium value, 129
credit crunch, 183
credit default, 125
creditors, 32
crisis market volatilities, 174
crisis-market outlooks, 183
critical mass, 469
crowdlending, 510, 524
cryptocurrencies, 427–428, 432, 435, 441, 444, 446, 515
cryptography, 429, 431, 433, 515
CSR committees, 287, 305–306, 310, 312

CSR performance, 287, 296, 305–308, 312
CSR-ESG investment, 338
CSR-ESG performance, 338–339
CSRC, 305–310
CSRD, 253
cultural understanding, 468
currency unions, 10
cyberattacks, 516
cyclical patterns, 42

D

daily and annual volatility, 173
daily volatility, 173–174
daily volume, 169
DAO, 438–439, 445
data, 264
data analytics, 184
DCC correlation, 205
DCC models, 189–192, 197, 199–200
DCC-copula-LVaR, 165
debt to GDP, 39
debt-to-GDP ratio, 29
debtor, 35
decentralized, 516, 521
default, 36
default risk, 27
demand, 47
demand function, 35
demographic characteristics, 387, 403
De Nederlandsche Bank, 16
denial of permission, 474
dependence measure, 167
depresses consumption, 47
derivative securities, 168
designated authority, 13
Det Systemiske Risikoråd (Systemic Risk Council), 15
development, 255
development of Fintech, 491
developmental leapfrog, 468
Dib, 29
different, 42
difficult to replicate, 466
digital consumer adoption, 498
digital content, 471
digital currency, 515
digital economic development, 477
digital economies, 471
digital finance, 482, 485
digital financial services, 457
digital infrastructure, 487–488, 502
digital payments, 488, 502, 519, 524
digital platforms, 522
digital services, 523, 532
digital transformation, 491, 493
digitalization, 511
Digitization Index, 494
directional, 268
directions, 275
disclosure, 253, 262
discretionary, 258, 261
disinvestment, 231
disrupt, 510, 522, 533
disruptive innovation, 508
distribution, 269
distributional consequences, 7
distributional effects, 5–7
diversity, 287–288, 293–300, 302–305, 308, 310, 312, 385, 388–390, 393–399, 401, 404–406, 408–410
Doha Stock Market, 172
Domini 400 Social Index, 229
Dubai Financial Market, 172
Dubai Financial Market (DFM) General Index, 179
dynamic conditional correlation, 164, 189–190, 192, 198, 201, 204, 207, 209
dynamism in regulation, 472

E

e-commerce, 508, 517, 526, 534
early adopters, 456–457
ease of registration, 457
economic, 331, 342
economic benefits, 471
economic capital, 163
economic development, 483, 501
economic performance, 332

economic sustainability, 337
effects, 44
efficiency, 125, 127
electronic data warehouse, 476
electronic payment, 513
emerging economies, 485
emerging financial markets, 162
emerging markets, 164–165, 168, 182, 184
emerging technologies, 474
emission, 256–267
empirical, 263
employee, 265
energy transition, 131
entrepreneurs, 37–38
environmental, 253, 332, 334, 341
environmental and social, 330
environmental and social disclosure, 351
environmental performance, 331–332, 343
environmental screening, 235
EPU, 58
equation, 268
equity portfolios, 162, 165
equity premium, 76
equity trading portfolios, 164–165, 180, 183
equity trading unit, 183
Erhvervsministeren (Minister for Industry, Business and Financial Affairs), 15
ESG, 241–243, 264, 333, 367, 369, 371–374
ESG compliance, 340
ESG criteria, 352
ESG development, 130
ESG goals, 329
ESG indexes, 352
ESG investing, 351
ESG investment, 332
ESG performance, 327, 329
ESG practices, 351
ESG principles, 337
ESG ratings, 327–328, 333, 343
ESG risks, 130
ESG scores, 238–239, 344
ESG screens, 237
ESG strategy, 336
ESG–corporate financial performance relation, 338
estimates, 273
Eesti Pank, 15
ETF or passive funds, 133
Ethereum, 435–436, 439
ethical, 101
ethical issues, 334
ethics, 87, 88, 90–99, 110, 114
EU banking sector, 538–539, 551–552
EU Council, 17
Euro Area, 28, 41
EURO crises, 18
Euro money markets, 127
European, 264
European Banking Authority (EBA), 17
European Central Bank (ECB), 4–5, 17
European Commission, 17
European law/Directives, 4
European Parliament, 17
European Systemic Risk Board (ESRB), 5, 17, 20–21
Eurozone, 4, 20, 21
ex ante probability of default, 39
excess returns, 228
expected returns, 166, 170
expert systems, 165, 184
extreme events, 163
extreme poverty, 463

F

factors in pricing, 130
fail overnight, 132
fat-tails, 176
feedback loops, 133
financial and operational constraints, 164
financial crisis, 539, 546–547
financial engineering, 165, 184
financial inclusion, 456, 466, 468, 475–477, 483, 501

financial industry, 123
financial innovation, 481, 538, 541
financial institutions, 162, 540, 542, 552
financial intermediaries, 518
financial intermediary, 510
financial markets, 59, 137, 142–143, 147, 153, 474
financial markets' co-movements, 78
financial performance, 286, 288–289, 292, 308–311, 340, 361–362
financial savings, 476
financial services, 455, 457, 461, 465–467, 475–477, 481, 538
financial services device, 452
financial services industry, 166, 184
financial stability, 3, 11
Financial Stability Advisory Council, 15
Financial Stability Board (FSB), 4, 540
Financieel Stabiliteitscomité (Financial Stability Committee), 16
financial stress, 6
Financial System Oversight Committee (FSOC), 11
financial technology, 165, 184, 486, 488, 513
financial tensions, 28
financial trading portfolios, 161–162
financial turmoil, 161, 165
financial well-being, 477
Finanssivalvonta (Finnish Financial Supervisory Authority), 15
Finanšu un kapitāla tirgus komisija (Financial and Capital Market Commission), 15
Finansinspektionen (Financial Supervisory Authority), 15
Finanzmarktstabilitätsgremium (Financial Market Stability Board), 16
Finanzmarktaufsichtsbehörde (Austrian Financial Market Authority), 16
FinTech, 165, 184, 456, 461, 474, 477, 481, 507, 510, 513–514, 516–517, 519–527, 529–534, 537–545, 547–549, 551–552
fintech borrowers, 551
Fintech companies, 482
Fintech credit, 541, 543, 547, 551
Fintech growth, 482, 484
Fintech industry, 487
FinTech start-ups, 477
Fintech's expansion, 501
firm risk, 361, 363–368, 370
first falls then rises, 47
first reduces the wage, 47
fiscal policy, 22
fixed line telephones, 451
flight to quality, 79
forecasters disagreement, 61
foreign exchange rate, 166, 181
formal financial services, 468
formal savings account, 469
fraction of deposits, 34
fraud detection, 513
frictions, 126
FTSE, 346
Fuliza, 461
fund assets, 217
fundamental values, 129
funding ratios, 14

G

Gaussian structure, 131
GCC countries, 172, 181
GCC markets, 161
GCC region, 171
GCC stock markets, 172, 180, 183
global financial crisis, 3
global financial meltdown, 161
global financial stability, 166, 184
good, 272
governance, 258
governance arrangements, 4, 9, 19–20
governance structure, 18
government interference, 469
government spending, 38

government's balance sheet, 28
government-owned, 469
Granger, 268
green bonds, 221
Greenfield opportunity, 501
GRI, 260
growth stocks, 229
Gulf Cooperation Council (GCC), 171

H

harmful effects on financial markets, 70
harmonize and integrate data, 475
Haut Conseil de Stabilité Financière (High Council for Financial Stability), 15
heterogeneous monopolistically competitive banks, 30
high-frequency trading, 131
holding (closeout) period, 168
holding period, 168
Hrvatska narodna banka, 15
human, 265–266

I

ICO, 441–442, 445–446
identical, 37
idiosyncratic, 267
illiquid asset, 165, 184
illiquid market conditions, 168
illiquid market settings, 174
illiquid multiple assets, 164, 166
illiquid securities, 168
illiquidity, 183
illiquidity of trading assets, 182
impact, 343
inaction bias, 5, 12
incentives, 274
incentivize infrastructure investments, 471
incubators, 527
indebtedness, 44
independence, 9, 12, 19, 21
index, 259, 266
indicators, 265
industry, 331
inflation, 483, 491
informal savings schemes, 467
information, 258
information access, 10
information efficiency, 128
infrastructure providers, 469
innovation, 385–389, 392–400, 403–405, 409–411, 461, 510–511
innovative start-up, 482
input approach, 475
institutional arrangements, 8
institutional memory, 6
insurance, 518
Insurtech, 519
interaction, 263
interbank, 27–28
interbank borrowing, 36
interdependence, 28
intermediaries, 134
internal risk models, 162, 165
International Monetary Fund (IMF), 5, 9, 20–21
international money transfer, 467
International Organization of Securities Commissions (IOSCO), 5
international spillover of uncertainty, 71
international transfers, 509
internet, 507
Internet of Things (IoT), 184
investment, 37
investment choices, 58
investment freedom, 488
investments, 342
investor's portfolios, 74
investors, 131–132, 136–137, 143, 145, 147–149, 152, 260
investors' expectations, 71, 73
irrationally, 129
ISS E&S, 348

J

Jarque–Bera (JB) test, 174–175

K

Kendall's tau, 167
Kiyotaki, 29
Knight, Frank, 57
Knightian uncertainty, 57
Komitet Stabilności Finansowej (Financial Stability Committee), 16
Kurtosis, 174–175, 269
Kuwait, 172

L

landline connection, 454
large exposure limits, 14
large-cap, 230
large-cap stocks, 229
later increases, 47
Latvijas Banka, 15
laws, 256
leapfrogged, 452
least efficient austerity, 53
legal implications, 476
legitimacy, 257
legitimacy theory, 362, 367, 375
Leontief technology, 35
leverage, 37
leverage ratio, 35
license to operate, 474
Lietuvos bankas, 15
linear, 70
Lipa Kwa M-PESA, 467
Lipa na M-PESA, 464–465
liquid, 125
liquidation (closeout) period, 161
liquidation days , 169
liquidation factor, 171
liquidation horizon, 162, 169, 181
liquidation multiplier, 164
liquidation period, 171
liquidity, 125–127
Liquidity Adjusted Value-at-Risk (LVaR), 166
liquidity buffers, 14
liquidity gauge, 468
liquidity modeling algorithm, 183
liquidity modeling technique, 183
liquidity models, 183
liquidity of assets, 128
liquidity risk, 128, 161, 164–165
liquidity risk management, 165
liquidity risk management models, 164
liquidity risk modeling, 168
liquidity trading risk, 161, 164, 182
Liquidity-Adjusted Value at Risk (LVaR), 165, 168–170, 174, 176–179, 181–182, 184
liquidity-adjusted VaR, 165, 184
live tests, 474
loans, 35
local BBs, 37
locally owned, 469
long-only, 165
long-only equity trading positions, 180
long-only trading positions, 183
LVaR limit setting, 176
LVaR limits, 176, 178–179
LVaR modeling algorithms, 182
LVaR optimization algorithm, 170
LVaR technique, 166
LVaR threshold limit, 180–183
LVaR trading limits, 164

M

M-Shwari, 461
Machine Learning (ML), 161, 184, 509, 514, 518–519, 532, 534
macro-prudential policy, 9
macroprudential authorities, 4
macroprudential measures, 3
macroprudential policy, 3–9, 18, 20–21
Magyar Nemzeti Bank, 15
management, 262
manual reporting, 475–476
mark-to-market, 166
market and liquidity risk exposures, 171
market liquidity risk, 182
market participants, 124, 134

market prices, 169
market risk, 163, 167, 181–182
market risk assessment process, 167
market risk management, 166
market share, 453, 457, 467, 544–545
market structure, 543–544
market value, 128
maximize, 37
maximum risk limits, 172
Mean-Variance (MV) method, 170
measure, 53
measurement, 263
measures, 27
MENA region, 487
merry-go-round, 459
meta-analysis, 233, 239
meta-study, 232
methodologies, 327
microprudential, 5, 10
microprudential supervision, 12
miners, 432–435, 437, 445
Minister Finansów (Minister of Finance), 16
Ministry of Finance, 16
ML, 521
mobile applications, 508
mobile banking apps, 516
mobile big data, 470
mobile money, 455–457, 461, 464–467, 469–470, 477, 483
mobile network operations, 453, 470
mobile phone, 451–455, 459–460, 464, 466
mobile phone adoption, 452–453
mobile phone coverage, 451
mobile phone technology, 451–452, 470–471
mobile platforms, 485
mobile-based innovation, 471
modeling algorithms, 168, 182
modeling techniques, 169, 182
modern finance, 123, 124
monetary policy, 3, 5–6, 10, 74, 501
money remittance, 467
money transfer, 452, 455–457, 460–461, 466, 467, 476
monitoring cost, 33
monopolistically competitive, 33
monthly newspapers search, 61
MSCI, 346
multi-asset dependence measures, 170
multi-assets portfolio, 171
multiple risk factors, 166
multiple trading assets, 180–181
multiple-asset, 162, 167, 169, 180
multiple-asset returns, 183
multiple-asset securities, 163
multiple-assets portfolio, 171, 183
multiplier, 183
Muscat Stock Market, 172
mutual fund industry, 214
mutual fund sector development, 227
Mutual Funds Industry, 213
mutual funds
  Allocation (or balanced), 222–222, 227
  Bond, 214, 221, 222, 227
  Equity, 214–215, 221–223
  Money market, 222
  Other, 222
  Performance, 227, 231–232, 235
  Property, 222
  SRI (socially responsible investing), 214–215, 217, 222–222, 227–232, 235–240, 242–243
  SRI assets, 213, 227
  SRI conventional, 214–215, 217, 221–222, 227, 231, 235–236, 238, 243

N

Nakamoto, Satoshi, 430, 432, 435, 438, 446
Nationale Bank van België/Banque Nationale de Belgique, 15
Národná banka Slovenska, 15
necessity-oriented continent, 452
neo-banks, 509, 520, 523, 532–533
net transmitter, 74

news, 129, 260
news-based uncertainty index, 61
non-bank intermediation, 22
non-normal distributions, 167
non-normality, 173, 176
non-observable nature, 58
nonfinancial, 258
non-financial criteria, 232
nonlinear, 70, 167
nonsubadditive, 164
normal (regular) market, 173
normal distributions of returns, 176
normal market condition, 174
normality assumption, 174
normalize ratings, 350

O

objective function, 170, 176
objective risk-function, 170
observations, 264
Odbor za finančno stabilnost (Financial Stability Board), 16
OECD, 375
okoa jahazi, 458
OLS, 268
Oman, 172
online banking, 509, 524
online payment technologies, 508
open banking, 517
operational and financial boundary limits, 170
operational and financial constraints, 170, 177
optimization, 178–183
optimization algorithms, 164–166, 170, 176
optimization case studies, 178–179
optimization dynamics, 177
optimization problem, 36
optimization procedure, 165
optimization process, 176–177
optimization technique, 177
optimum LVaR threshold limits, 183
organizations, 262
ownership, 265

P

Pamoja Twaweza, 459
panic sentiment, 79
paperless trail, 464
path dependencies, 5–6
pay-roll tax, 44, 47
paybill, 464–465
paybill number, 459, 465
payment security, 507
payment solutions, 465
payments, 509
payments for utilities, 468
Pearson's correlation coefficients, 167
peer-to-peer (P2P), 509, 430–431, 445, 509, 512, 527
peer-to-peer (P2P) lending, 510–511, 517–518, 527, 542
penalty, 36
perfection, 126
performance, 254, 288, 297–298, 304, 329, 342
performance indicators, 345
performance measures, 330
performers, 262
performing sustainable banking management, 332
periphery, 34, 41, 44, 47
permission to operate, 474
political, 260
political instability, 486
political news, 62
political stability, 492
political uncertainty, 483
portfolio choice and diversification, 165
portfolio diversification, 135, 143, 145, 147, 149–151
portfolio management, 163–164, 170
portfolio optimization, 170
portfolio risk, 162
portfolio selection, 165
portfolio theory, 124
portfolios, 134
potential effects, 27
potential impact, 471

potential users, 468
poverty reduction, 466
practitioners, 124
predictions, 273
pressures, 261
priced, 125
Priciples for Responsible Investment (PRI), 238, 240–241
prior-year returns, 231
privacy, 476
private cloud, 515
private information, 128
private interest, 7, 12
proactive, 254
probability distribution, 132, 176
probability of sovereign default, 39
production first increases then falls, 50
profit-maximizing SBs, 33
profitability, 336
proprietary trading, 181
proxies, 60
public cloud, 515
public disclosure requirements, 14
public information, 128
public interest, 6
pull approach, 476
pure and perfect, 125
purely financial information, 130
pushes up, 53

Q

Qatar, 172

R

random walk situation, 131
rating agencies, 345
rational, 125, 129
rational behavior, 123, 129
real estate valuation, 130
real option effect, 58
real-world trading case study, 171
rebalancing portfolios allocation, 75
redesign of regulations, 472
reduces, 44
reduces the demand of investment, 50
RegTech, 166, 184, 452, 474–475, 519–520
regular market outlooks, 180–181
regular market settings, 177–178
regulation, 87, 90, 94, 96, 98–102, 105–107, 109, 112, 114, 256, 510
regulators, 6
regulatory agencies, 470
regulatory authority, 477
regulatory challenges, 184
regulatory environment, 466, 469
regulatory mandate, 455
Regulatory Sandbox, 452, 472, 477
regulatory technology, 166, 184, 470, 474
relationship, 254, 268
reporting, 254, 257, 262
reporting processes, 161, 166, 184
RepRisk, 347
reputational risk, 363, 366, 373–375
resources, 256
responsibility, 343
responsible, 342
responsible investment, 215, 227
returns, 135, 138, 141–146, 148–153
rise, 44, 47, 50
rise in consumption tax and pay-roll tax, 54
rise of investment, 47
risk, 57, 130, 132, 258, 267
risk appetite, 182
risk assessment, 162
risk aversion, 71
risk computation algorithms, 183
risk computational techniques, 184
risk exposure, 161
risk factors, 172
risk limits, 176
risk management, 124, 162, 165, 167, 172, 176–177, 179, 182–184, 362
risk management regulations, 171
risk management unit, 183
risk modeling algorithms, 164
risk premium, 75
risk processes, 162

risk reporting process, 165, 184
risk–return tradeoffs, 170
risk-adjusted returns, 230–231
risk-budgeting, 172, 176
risk-capital, 163
robot advisors, 512
robust algorithm, 183
robust illiquidity risk factor, 183
robust modeling algorithm, 183
robust modeling technique, 162, 165, 184
robust optimization algorithms, 169
robust optimization techniques, 168
Rotating Savings and Credit Association (ROSCA), 459–460
rural Africa, 452
rural areas, 454, 457
rural nature, 468
R&D, 267

S

Safaricom, 453, 455–456, 458–459, 461–464, 467, 469
sample, 264
Saudi Arabia, 172
save money, 461, 463
saving banks receive deposits, 30
saving culture, 459
saving money, 456
savings and borrowing banks, 30
savings banks, 29, 32
savings banks collect deposits, 29
savings platform, 460
SBF120, 368, 372
scenario analysis, 162, 182
score, 265
screen, 228–229, 235
screening, 327
SDG, 334
self-interest capture, 12
send money, 462
sending money, 457
sending money home, 467
Sensefolio, 348
series, 268
severe market conditions, 179
shareholders value creation, 339
Shariah compliance screening, 340
sharing factor, 454
Sharpe ratio, 132
shocks, 129
short term, 47
short-sales, 165, 167, 178–179, 183
short-selling, 179, 183
Shuaa Arab Index, 172, 174
Shuaa Capital, 172
Shuaa GCC Index, 172, 174
shunned companies, 233
sides, 273
signaling theory, 361–362, 364–365
similar results, 466
sin stocks, 228, 234
size, 267
skewness, 174–175, 269
small-cap, 230
small-cap bias, 228–229
small-cap index, 228
small-scale entrepreneurs, 465
small-scale sellers, 464
smart contracts, 428, 436, 439, 441, 445–446
smart financial functions, 165, 184
social, 253, 272, 331, 334, 342–343
social and economic environmental, 477
social and environmental impact, 463
social aspects, 130
social benefits, 471
social fabric, 452, 459
social good, 470
social impacts, 332
Social Investment Forum, 229
social movements, 492
social performance, 332, 342
social responsibility, 340
social screening, 235
social value, 463
socially conscious, 214
socially responsible, 227
socially responsible behaviors, 341

Socially Responsible Investing (SRI), 213, 215, 221, 227–229, 232–233, 235, 236, 238–245, 330
Socially responsible investment (SRI), 242
socially responsible projects, 341
society, 272
socio-economic, 463
sovereign, 28
sovereign CDS, 190, 199, 207
sovereign default risk, 29
sovereign risk, 27
special consent, 453
spending, 39
SRI alternative funds, 222
SRI and conventional mutual, 215
SRI champion firms, 229
SRI characteristics, 229
SRI fund characteristics, 235
SRI fund flows, 231
SRI fund managers, 230, 234
SRI fund returns, 232
SRI investment, 234, 238–239
SRI investment flows, 232
SRI investors, 231–232, 234, 235, 237, 243–244
SRI mutual funds, 239
SRI portfolios, 229
SRI stocks, 239
stability, 87–90, 94–96, 98, 100–102, 104–105
stabilize, 39
stakeholder, 7, 255–256
stakeholder theory, 7, 255, 361–363, 366
standard deviation, 166
standardization, 350
statistics, 269
stochastic properties, 173
stock market indices, 181
stock market volatility, 62
stock markets, 174
stock markets indices, 174
stock prices, 62
stock prices/returns decline, 70
stock returns, 62
strategy, 259
strengths, 266
stress-testing, 162, 165, 176, 182–184
Stressed (Event) Market Outlooks, 177–179
stressed market conditions, 173
stressed market settings, 178–179
stressed markets outlooks, 162
stressed or event market outlooks, 180–181
sub-prime credit crunch, 165, 184
sub-prime financial crunch, 173
subscription rate, 454
successful completion, 474
successful trajectory, 466
supervisors, 123
supervisory authorities, 16
supervisory mandate, 476
supervisory regimes, 3
SupTech, 475
sustainability, 328, 342, 345
sustainability finance, 335
sustainability ratings, 344
sustainable, 255
sustainable business practices, 334
sustainable environment, 491
sustainalytics, 347
Swahili language, 458
systematic risk, 173–174
systematic risk factor, 173

T

tax expiration, 61
taxes on households, 38
TCFD, 241
TCFD implementation, 240
tech start-up ecosystem, 471
technical standards, 8
technological revolution, 481
Telkom Kenya, 453, 461
test and learn approach, 456–457
their risk, 133
theories, 275
theory, 260

third-party, 430, 433, 438, 446
through debt, 38
till numbers, 459
time inconsistencies, 5, 7
time-varying, 192
time-varying correlation, 189
top-down regulation, 472
total volume, 171
trading, 126
trading assets, 163, 166, 183
trading days, 174, 180
trading multiple assets, 162
trading participants, 126
trading portfolios, 168
trading risk management, 165, 181–182, 184
trading risk managers, 182
trading units, 177
trading volumes, 164, 169
traditional banking services, 456
transaction costs, 463
transaction price, 168
transmission channel, 74
transmitted, 47
transparency, 9, 19, 21
Tuma Pesa Nyumbani, 459

U

UAE dirham, 181
ubiquitous, 453
unbanked rural population, 456
uncertainty, 57
uncertainty averse, 77
under-developed banking systems, 476
unethical, 87
unethics, 105
United Arab Emirates, 172
unwanted biases, 134
US SIF, 240
US-EPU, 73
utilities payments, 459, 464

V

Value at Risk (VaR), 162–164, 167
Value at Risk (VaR) simulation models, 162
value creation, 353
VaR analysis, 163
VaR models, 163
VaR risk factors, 166
variables, 267, 269
venture capital (VCs), 516, 518, 523–524, 526, 529–531, 533
virtuous, 269
VIX, 60
Vodafone, 456
volatility, 133, 135, 137–138, 145, 147–148
volatility increase, 71
volume trading limit, 177
voluntary, 254–255, 257
voter groups, 7

W

wage, 47
wallet, 431, 436, 441, 446
withdrawal rate, 231

Y

yield in the long run, 53

www.ingramcontent.com/pod-product-compliance
Ingram Content Group UK Ltd.
Pitfield, Milton Keynes, MK11 3LW, UK
UKHW022107170926
8624IPUK00024B/175

9 781786 349491